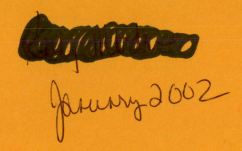

January 2002

PSYCHOLOGICAL CONSULTATION

and

COLLABORATION IN SCHOOL AND COMMUNITY SETTINGS

3rd Edition

A. Michael Dougherty

Brooks/Cole
Thomson Learning™

Australia • Canada • Denmark • Japan • Mexico • New Zealand • Philippines • Puerto Rico
Singapore • South Africa • Spain • United Kingdom • United States

Counseling Editor: Eileen Murphy
Assistant Editor: Julie Martinez
Editorial Assistant: Annie Berterretche
Marketing Managers: Jennie Burger/Caroline Concilla
Project Editor: Matt Stevens
Print Buyer: April Reynolds
Permissions Editor: Susan Walters

Production Service and
Copy Editor: Heidi Marschner
Compositor: Pre-Press Company, Inc.
Cover Designer: Margarite Reynolds
Cover Image: © PhotoDisc
Printer/Binder: R. R. Donnelley & Sons, Crawfordsville

Library of Congress
Cataloging-in-Publication Data
 Psychological consultation and
 collaboration in school and community
 settings / A. Michael Dougherty.—3rd ed.
   p. cm.
  Includes bibliographical references and index.
  ISBN 0-534-35555-2 (casebound)
  1. Psychological consultation. I. Dougherty, A.
Michael, 1945- Consultation. II. Title.
BF637.C56D68   2000
158'.3'023—dc21   99-28748

Wadsworth/Thomson Learning
10 Davis Drive
Belmont, CA 94002-3098
USA
www.wadsworth.com

International Headquarters
Thomson Learning
290 Harbor Drive, 2nd Floor
Stamford, CT 06902-7477
USA

UK/Europe/Middle East
Thomson Learning
Berkshire House
168-173 High Holborn
London WC1V 7AA
United Kingdom

Asia
Thomson Learning
60 Albert Street #15-01
Albert Complex
Singapore 189969

Canada
Nelson/Thomson Learning
1120 Birchmount Road
Scarborough, Ontario M1K 5G4
Canada

 This book is printed on acid-free recycled paper.

Preface

Psychological Consultation and Collaboration in School and Community Settings is written for graduate and undergraduate students in the helping professions. Students in counseling, psychology, social work, human resource development, and other helping-profession training programs will find this book helpful as they seek to acquire the knowledge and skill bases that lead to the effective practice of consultation and collaboration. This book can be used either as the primary text in consultation and collaboration courses or as a supplemental text in courses in the helping professions. Many instructors have found the text useful in introductory and "roles and settings" courses in counseling psychology, school counseling, school psychology, student development, mental health and community counseling, social work, and human resource development. Moreover, practicing consultants and collaborators can find in this book a wealth of practical and theoretical information to help guide their practice.

In this text, I use *human service professional* as a general term that encompasses counselors, psychologists, social workers, human resource development specialists, and members of other helping professions. At the same time, I have tried to respect the terminology used by the professions covered in this text.

PURPOSE

This book provides a thorough overview of what students and practicing human service professionals must know about the practice and theory of consultation and collaboration. It presents a generic model for application, surveys the various approaches to consultation and collaboration, discusses their organizational context, and reviews the many ethical and professional issues human service professionals face in delivering these services.

I have found that students learning about consultation and collaboration appreciate a practical model for delivering these services before they study specific approaches. As a result, I have provided a generic model of consultation and collaboration at the beginning of the text before discussing specific models. Students will also find a variety of case studies helpful in learning how to actually deliver consultation and collaboration services. Further, many professors note that the greatest challenge in teaching consultation and collaboration is to make them practical; therefore, I have included the numerous case studies to bring their concepts to life.

Finally, students say they benefit more from learning about consultation and collaboration when they are involved personally. As a result, I have structured the book so students can develop a personal model of consultation and collaboration. Each chapter begins and ends with questions that stimulate and encourage the reader to reflect on the material in that chapter. In the case studies, students are asked to make decisions about a particular consultant's or collaborator's behavior. Finally, each chapter ends with a few recommendations for effective practice.

ABOUT THE THIRD EDITION

In this edition, I have updated the material and refined the discussion of the topics. I have also included many new topics and more extensive coverage than in the second edition. The primary change is the inclusion of a significant amount of material on the service of collaboration. I have also provided in-depth coverage of how cultural diversity and technology affect consultation and collaboration. The most broad-based changes are an increased focus on school-based consultation and an increase in the number of case studies presented. I have revised Chapter 12, which focuses on school-based consultation and collaboration with administrators, teachers, and parents. Chapters 3–10 each still contain a detailed case study on school consultation or community consultation; I have added a brief commentary on each of these case

studies. These revisions create a balance that will appeal to instructors training students for practice in school settings.

I have updated the introductory chapter and have added a substantial coverage of collaboration. Chapter 2 has been significantly updated as well. Additions to Chapters 3–6 include discussions of the implications of cultural diversity on a particular stage of consultation and collaboration. Chapter 3 provides more extensive coverage of the social influence process, as well as a case study that illustrates each phase of the entry stage. Chapter 5 contains new material on treatment integrity and treatment acceptability. Although the remaining chapters on the generic consultation model contain fewer changes, they include significant updates and additional case studies. In particular, Chapter 7 contains new material on "Web-Consulting" and cultural diversity.

I have also substantially revised Chapter 8. For this edition, I have added coverage of time constraints, involvement of consultees, and pointers for how to determine whether to choose consultation or collaboration as the service of choice. A section entitled "Implications for Consultants and Collaborators" is included for each theory of organization, as well as for the topics of organization change and organizational culture. Chapter 9 has additional material on Schein's models for organizational consultation. Chapter 10 includes a discussion of Caplan's most recent work on mental health consultation. Chapter 11 updates Bergan and Kratochwill's model for behavior consultation. Chapter 12 has been significantly revised and updated in general. In Chapter 13, I have retained a shortened version of the case study of Acme Human Services Center because it illustrates how the approaches covered in the text are applied to a noneducational setting. In addition, I have included a transcript of a school consultation case and a school collaboration case, along with a reflective analysis of each. I hope that these additions will help the text become even more practical for the reader.

OVERVIEW

What will you discover as you read this book? *Psychological Consultation and Collaboration in School and Community Settings* is divided into three parts. Part I sets the stage for understanding what consultation and collaboration are and how they are practiced. Chapter 1 is an orientation to the practice of consultation and collaboration: it contains an introduction, a definition of consultation and collaboration, a brief historical overview, and a glossary of key terms used throughout the text. Chapter 2 includes a discussion of the characteristics of effective consultants and collaborators and of the roles in which they engage; it also reviews the current status of research in consultation and collaboration.

Part II describes in detail the ins and outs of the consultation and collaboration processes using a model that involves four stages: entry, diagnosis, implementation, and disengagement. Chapter 3 is about the entry stage—that is, how the consultation or collaboration process starts. Chapter 4 discusses diagnosis—how the consultant or collaborator can help determine the problem to be solved. Chapter 5 describes the implementation stage—how the parties involved attempt to solve the problem. Chapter 6 examines the ending of the consultation or collaboration process, including the difficulty consultants and collaborators face in assessing success and how they can say goodbye in a personal yet professional manner. Chapter 7 focuses on the ethical, legal, and professional issues consultants and collaborators encounter in their prac-

tices, such as dual relationships, issues related to diversity, and confidentiality. Chapter 8 deals with the pragmatic issues of working within an organization. (I have included this chapter because nearly all consultation or collaboration takes place within some type of organization.)

Part III surveys organizational, mental health, behavioral, and school-based consultation and their implications for collaboration. Chapter 9 discusses organizational consultation, including four specialized applications: education/training, program, doctor/patient, and process. Chapter 10 reviews mental health consultation; because of the traditional popularity of Caplan's (1970, 1993) model, I have made it the central focus of the chapter. I also review his recent writings on the nature of collaboration as a service for mental health providers. Chapter 11 explores how consultation uses behavioral technology both to benefit clients and organizations and also as an aid in training human service professionals and others. Chapter 12 covers school-based consultation and collaboration, including how these services can be provided to administrators, teachers, and parents. Chapter 13 presents case study applications to give a better sense of the nut and bolts of consultation and collaboration.

HOW TO USE THIS TEXT

This text can be used in several ways. Some instructors might want students who are training for work in schools to read Chapter 12 first and students who are training for work in community settings to read Chapter 13 first. This would give each student a sense of how consultation and collaboration are practiced in his or her field. Other instructors might want to begin with Chapter 7 to instill an understanding of the complexity and seriousness of the decisions made in the process of providing consultation or collaboration. Still others might want to start with the generic model and cover the specific approaches later, or vice versa. I have designed this book so that the material can be covered in the most logical order regardless of how a particular course is taught.

In addition, this text can be used in conjunction with *Psychological Consultation and Collaboration: A Casebook*, Third Edition, also published by Brooks/Cole-Wadsworth Publishing Company. The casebook contains several cases that describe real-life examples of consultation and collaboration and illustrate various approaches.

An instructor's manual is also available. It contains a variety of materials, including test questions, suggested class activities, and recommendations for teaching. I have taught courses in consultation and collaboration for over 20 years, and I believe this instructor's manual will be helpful in determining methods of teaching concepts and skills of consultation and collaboration.

ACKNOWLEDGMENTS

I would like to thank the many graduate students in counseling, psychology, and human resource development at Western Carolina University who contributed indirectly yet significantly to the development of this text. Their feedback on the consultation and collaboration course I teach was an invaluable asset in determining the final form this text would take. I also wish to thank the following graduate students, who have assisted me in various ways: Jenny Feid and Holly Harris.

I would also like to acknowledge my reviewers, including James Benshoff, University of North Carolina, Greensboro; James R. Bitter, East Tennessee State University; Rolla Lewis, Portland State University; Richard Schmuck, University of Oregon, Eugene; Charlotte Speltz, Winona State University; Carolyn Stone, University of North Florida; and Kenneth Wegner, Boston College. These individuals furnished me with a wealth of helpful ideas and many valuable comments.

Special thanks go to Robbie Pittman of Western Carolina University, who reviewed the material on evaluation in Chapters 5 and 6, and to Gerald Corey of California State University at Fullerton and Mary Deck of Western Carolina University for their suggestions concerning the organization of the text and the instructor's manual.

To my wife and life partner, Leslie, my deepest appreciation for her love, support, and understanding during the preparation of this text and for helping me remember that work is always there and love is not always as accessible. To my children, Ashley and Matthew, thanks for helping me remember how to play.

Finally, to the talented people at Brooks/ Cole and Wadsworth, I extend my gratitude for being able to work with a first-class group of professionals. It was a true pleasure to work with Jennie Burger, Marie DuBois, Susan Horovitz, Laurie Jackson, Heidi Marschner, Julie Martinez, Tessa McGlasson, Eileen Murphy, Roy Neuhaus, Robert Racine, Matt Stevens, Claire Verduin, Susan Walters, Jennifer Wilkinson, and others who helped make this book a reality.

Dedicated with love to my parents, Arthur and Cecilia;
and to my family, Leslie, Matt, and Ashley

To the Student

Consultation and collaboration are "head, heart, and hands" processes. You come to understand them, then you become a strong advocate for them, then you do them with a passion. The often-used metaphor of the bicycle rider sheds light on what it takes to be an effective consultant and collaborator. The front wheel provides direction, the back wheel provides the force, and the rider guides the bike to its destination. The rear wheel represents your technical skills (what you do when you consult or collaborate), the front wheel represents your skill with people (how you consult or collaborate), and the rider represents your personhood (who you are). When all three elements are in sync, it becomes more probable that you will succeed in your consulting and collaborating endeavors. This book will help you become an even better "bicycle rider."

You might want to take special note of the questions at the beginning of each chapter. They are designed to stimulate thought about each chapter's main points as you read. In addi-

tion, the questions at the end of each chapter will assist you in applying what you have learned through your reading. I hope you will take the time to reflect on these questions after you have completed each chapter. Each chapter concludes with a few suggestions for effective practice, which will help you determine how to use the chapter's material in your practice of consultation and collaboration.

In addition, supplementary readings are suggested at the end of each chapter. I have chosen these readings carefully and encourage you to read those that interest you. You will note that there are a variety of case studies throughout the text. The focus of some cases will not be in your professional training area. Nonetheless, the analysis of these cases can be quite beneficial to you, because it is the process of the analysis and not the cases themselves that is critical.

I also suggest that you look over Chapters 7, 8, and 13 after you read Chapters 1 and 2. Chapter 7 discusses ethical, professional, and legal issues. Even a cursory glance at this chapter will show you the importance of consultation and collaboration as professional activities.

Chapter 8 covers a variety of issues related to working in an organizational context. By skimming through this chapter, you can appreciate the complexity of organizations and, consequently, of consultation and collaboration within them.

Chapter 13 presents the case of Acme Human Services Center and illustrates how various consultation approaches can be applied to that case. This chapter also includes a case study transcript of both a consultation session and a collaboration session. By looking through this chapter, you can get a feel for the nuts and bolts of real-life consultation and collaboration. Once you have obtained a perspective on how consultants actually consult and how collaborators actually collaborate, you can more readily see the critical importance of such procedures as creating relationships with the people with whom you are going to work.

This is a book about consultation and collaboration: what they are, how they are effectively practiced, and the forms they can take. I sincerely hope that after reading this book you will be motivated and empowered to perform consultation and collaboration confidently and effectively.

Contents

The Case of Chris: Collaboration

Chris Gonzolez is the head counselor at a large urban secondary school that has a severe substance-abuse problem among its student body. The counseling department of the school has a well-defined procedure for referring substance-abuse cases to community resources. Chris has been studying several drug-prevention programs but is uncertain about which one would be best for the school. Chris contacts Leslie, who is a substance-abuse counselor at the community mental health center, and invites her to collaborate with him. Leslie is quite familiar with a number of substance-abuse programs for schools. Chris and Leslie agree to collaborate and meet for three two-hour sessions over a three-week period. During the first meeting they explore the school's substance-abuse problem in detail, and Leslie observes the overall operation of the school. In the second meeting, Leslie provides Chris information on possible substance-abuse programs with which Chris was not familiar. Chris helps Leslie understand the unique characteristics of the school and how they would affect any program. In the final meeting, Leslie and Chris problem solve and decide which program would be best for the school.

These examples are typical of the many opportunities for consulting and collaborating available to human service professionals. Indeed, consultation has become an increasingly powerful force in the helping professions and collaboration is increasing in its importance. A tremendous social demand for this kind of professional service has developed. Within two decades consultation has moved from an "emerging role" (Kurpius, 1978, p. 335) to an accepted role of human service professionals. Consultation has become a "specialized professional process" (Kurpius, 1986, p. 58) in the work settings of almost all human service professionals. In essence, consultation has emerged as a secondary service provided by people in the helping professions to assist a variety of professionals (such as teachers). Collaboration, as a direct service, has emerged as an alternative to consultation, particularly in settings where both the would-be consultant and consultee are employed in the same setting.

Consultation continues to be a cornerstone activity for mental health professionals (Sheridan, Kratochwill, & Bergan, 1996). Whereas social workers used to be only the recipients of consultation, they now have provided consultation services to a variety of constituencies for over two decades (Waltman, 1989). The 1980s saw a significant rise in the number of counselors providing services to organizations and their personnel (Wubbolding, 1990; Maher, 1993). Serious social issues like the AIDS epidemic have led many psychologists to take on community involvement through education/training consultation (Douce, 1993; House & Walker, 1993) as well as by providing mental health consultation services to primary care physicians (Pace, Chaney, Mullins, & Olson, 1995). School counselors spend at least 12 percent of their time performing consultation (Partin, 1993) and an undetermined amount taking part in collaboration activities. In some studies, elementary school counselors report spending more time consulting than in any other activity (Hardesty & Dillard, 1994). School psychologists, though consulting more than ever before, indicate a desire to do even more (Graden, 1989; Zins & Erchul, 1995; Reschly & Wilson, 1995), spending upwards to 25 percent of their time on consultation (Roberts & Rust, 1994). Recent reviews of the role of school psychologists indicate increased attention to collaboration as a service (Zins & Erchul, 1995). Human resource development specialists as well as members of other helping professions are frequently being called on to consult with employee assistance programs (Backer, 1988; Levine, 1985). Student development specialists are increasingly being asked to provide consultation in postsecondary educational settings (Conyne, Rapin, & Rand, 1997; Kressel, Bailey, & Forman, 1999; Newman & Fuqua, 1984). Mental health professionals frequently seek consultation primarily for the purpose of assisting their clients with a secondary goal of avoiding possible lawsuits based on malpractice. The onset of managed care and limited counseling sessions has led to the increased need for consultation among mental health counselors, psychologists, and social workers. Managed care has also given impetus to interagency collaboration. Community consultants are called upon to assist in a variety of programs, such as programs designed to prevent elder abuse (Wolf & Pillemar, 1994). Community psychologists have been expanding their application of consultation (Zins, 1998). Clearly, consultation and collaboration have increased in popularity as a role for human service professionals.

What kinds of things might you do as a human service consultant or collaborator? Consider the following list, which notes some broad examples:

- Provide requested information.
- Provide requested training.
- Provide solutions to a given problem.
- Conduct a diagnosis of a problem.
- Provide recommendations about actions to be taken.
- Build consensus among selected members of an organization.
- Improve organizational effectiveness.
- Improve the effectiveness of individuals in their work.

Part 1 introduces you to the worlds of consultation and collaboration, provides a frame of reference for their practice, and focuses on the skills and attitudes needed.

1

Introduction and Overview

Consultation is practiced by most human service professionals in a variety of settings for a variety of reasons. Consider the following examples:

- A psychologist helps a therapist deal with problems she is having with one or more clients in her caseload.

- A counselor works with a schoolteacher to improve classroom management techniques.

- A counseling psychologist consults with a nursing home director about recreation programs for patients suffering from Alzheimer's disease.

- A family therapist trains school counselors in family systems theory.

- A professor of human services assists a job corps center staff in becoming culturally skilled professionals.

- A human resource development specialist helps her organization survey employee satisfaction.

- A psychologist diagnoses the reasons for high turnover in a social services agency.

- A counselor assists the staff of a counseling center in identifying its major work concerns and in making plans to solve them.

- A mental health worker assists a Head Start program in evaluating its parent-training program.

- A social worker assists a group of rural human service agencies to build a network for responding to common issues.

- A community mental health worker trains a group of other mental health professionals in developing outreach and client advocacy strategies for assisting ethnic minorities.

These examples illustrate how consultants in the human service professions provide a variety of services under the rubric of *consultation*.

Human service professionals also collaborate. In its most generic form, collaboration involves a process in which two or more parties work together to assist another party or program toward some desired outcome (Allen, 1994). Consider these examples:

- A community counselor serves on an interagency team designed to help a family at risk.
- A school psychologist serves as part of a site-based management team in an urban school.
- A human resource management specialist serves as a member of a self-directed work team that is a permanent structure in a health care setting.
- A school counselor and teacher collaborate to assist a student, with the counselor providing counseling services to the student and the teacher changing the way she instructs the student in the classroom.
- Two mental health professionals in the same agency team up to help a client suffering from AIDS, each working with a different aspect of the case.

These examples illustrate how human service professionals can provide assistance to others (as well as receive assistance) through collaboration.

This chapter introduces the concepts of consultation and collaboration, defines them, shows how they differ from one other and from other services performed by human service professionals, and provides a glossary of key terms used throughout the book.

Here are five questions to consider as you read this chapter:

1. What do consultants and collaborators actually do when they provide services?
2. What are the differences among consultation and collaboration?
3. How would you define consultation and collaboration?
4. In what ways are the prototypical roles of healer and technological advisor compatible?
5. What are the implications of the phrase "There is no one best way to consult or collaborate"?

INTRODUCTION

Human service professionals provide consultation to, or collaborate with, individuals, groups, and organizations, usually in one of three organizational settings (MacLennan, 1986). One setting is within some type of human service agency, whose mission in part is to provide consultation/collaboration services to the community—for example, a community mental health center. A second setting is a private firm or independent practitioner offering consultation/collaboration services to the community—for instance, a psychologist in private practice offering stress management training to the employees of a job corps center. In the third setting consultants work "in house" and consult and collaborate within the organization that employs them—for example, a school counselor consulting with a teacher about a student's behavior.

When human service professionals consult, their primary purpose is to help others work more effectively to fulfill their professional responsibilities to an individual, group, organization, or community. The typical focus in human services consultation is changing behavior in some way, whether it is the behavior of a client or the behavior of program participants. Whereas the consultee maintains responsibility for managing the problem and carrying out any intervention procedures, the consultant maintains the ethical responsibility of making appropriate recommendations and overseeing the professional well-being of the consultee (Knoff, 1988). Collaboration differs from this process in that all parties involved have responsibility for some part of the outcome and reciprocally consult with one another.

Human service professionals generally consult or collaborate with other human service professionals, other professionals (such as teachers), and parents. There is a preventative aspect to all consultation and collaboration in that one of the goals is to prevent the problem at hand from becoming more severe and another is to prevent additional problems from arising (Zins & Erchul, 1995). As we will find out, this latter goal is often pursued by attempting to assist change at the systemic level (e.g., an entire school or organization). By focusing on systems, human services professionals can often determine the conditions inherent within the organization that contribute to the development and maintenance of problems within individuals (Zins & Erchul, 1995).

To consult and collaborate effectively you need to develop an understanding of how these services are practiced. A general framework for understanding and practicing consultation and collaboration will help you develop a cognitive map and a sense of direction for performing consultation. A familiarity with the types of consultation—usually categorized as organizational, mental health, and behavioral—will provide you with models that have

some applicability in particular situations (Mazade, 1985). Collaboration has evolved as a derivative of these models. There are several approaches to each of these types of consultation and collaboration.

Achieving these steps provides you with the basic rudiments from which you can develop a personal model of consultation and collaboration. You will consult and collaborate most effectively when you have integrated your knowledge with your unique personality. For example, I am a very social person; I need people around me. One way I use this trait in my own personal model of consulting and collaborating is by appreciating the importance of relationships in these contexts.

I make six very basic assumptions in this book. First, I assume that consultation and collaboration are very similar in terms of the skills needed and the processes engaged in. Throughout this text, what I write about consultation basically holds for collaboration. The main point to remember is that in collaboration, as opposed to consultation, the mental health professional assists in the intervention and also receives and gives consultation to other collaborators. In order to enhance the readability of the text I will frequently use the term *consultation* instead of phrases like *consultation and collaboration*. When it is necessary to differentiate consultation from collaboration, I do this explicitly in the text.

The second assumption is that *how* a consultant or collaborator performs is as important as *what* he or she does. This is very important because the perceptions of these processes by the parties involved are critical in determining their success. For example, as a consultant I might know what I need to do to help a particular consultee, but, if I don't know how to do it in a way that he or she sees as helpful, then the consultation is less likely to be successful. Of importance is how the working relationship is established. By consulting and collaborating under the supervision of well-trained professionals, you will understand *how* you consult and collaborate and the impact your behavior has on the effectiveness of these processes.

The third assumption is that consultation and collaboration are human relationships. Consultants and collaborators work *with* people. The personal sides of these services become as important as their professional sides. Human service professionals need to identify and clarify their values about both life and the professional services they offer so that they do not fall into the trap of inadvertently imposing those values when providing these services. Such an imposition can restrict the professional growth of the persons with whom they are working. In addition, a lack of self-knowledge about values can place blinders on a professional and lead to mistakes during the course of consultation and collaboration. However, when consultation and collaboration are viewed as human relationships, the respect, dignity, and welfare of the parties involved become paramount. Effective professionals excel by behaving in ways that demonstrate respect for their consultees and fellow collaborators and protect their welfare.

The fourth assumption is that human services professionals need training in these services. Many people consult and collaborate without ever having any proper training; they have learned to provide these services through a series of consulting and collaborating experiences alone. Only by chance do they develop a frame of reference for approaching consultation and collaboration opportunities. Flying by the seat of one's pants is dangerous in the de-

livery of any professional service because the professional (and sometimes the personal) aspects of other people's lives are involved. Consequently, human service professionals need to be well grounded in models and interventions related to consultation and collaboration. This knowledge creates an objective frame of reference for delivering professional services. Further, only such knowledgeable and skillful professionals lend credibility to consultation and collaboration as legitimate roles for human service professionals.

The fifth assumption is that there is no one best way to consult or collaborate. Relative to other functions that human service professionals deliver—such as counseling, psychotherapy, and teaching—consultation (and even more so collaboration) are not well researched. In addition, consultation and collaboration tend to occur within organizations, which adds a tremendous amount of complexity to their process and makes them difficult to evaluate. I tend to agree with the view that how one consults or collaborates depends on the context (Kurpius & Fuqua, 1993b; O'Neill & Trickett, 1982); that is, how one goes about the process effectively depends on the large number of factors that make up the situation that led to the request for service. Consequently, the best resources available to human service professionals are the limited amount of empirical research, a few adequately developed models, their own knowledge about people and organizations, an ethical and professional attitude, and the skills related to consulting and collaborating.

Maintaining an open mind about the various approaches to consultation and collaboration is important. Some readers are turned off by the term *behavioral* because it reminds them of horror stories about the misuses of behavior modification. Others are prejudiced against the term *mental health* because they automatically identify it with "shrinking someone's head" or using psychotherapy. Some readers may not like the term *organization* because it leads them to think of a bureaucratic structure in which rules and regulations are more highly valued than the people within it. However, since being effective in consultation and collaboration depends upon the context in which the services occur, an effective human services professional develops a broad repertoire of skills and a large knowledge base from which to provide service. Then, depending on the situation, the professional is able to use the most pertinent knowledge and appropriate skills available.

The sixth assumption relates to whether consultation and collaboration each are a science, an art, or a craft. I believe that what McKeachie (1986) noted about teaching applies equally to consultation and collaboration: It is more than a science, more than an art, more than a craft. It is all of these, along with commitment—commitment to oneself, commitment to the people with whom one is working, and commitment to the challenging endeavor of getting ideas and concepts out of the human services professional's mind and into the minds of others.

CONSULTATION DEFINED

What is consultation? This simple question does not have a simple answer. Basically, consultation is a type of service performed by counselors, psychologists, and human resource workers in which they assist another person who has responsibility for a case or program. However, defining the term *consultation* is as difficult as defining such terms as *counseling* and *psychotherapy*, and there is no widespread agree-

ment on the definition of consultation (Bergan & Kratochwill, 1990; Kurpius & Fuqua, 1993a; Mannino & Shore, 1986). In fact, the continued ambiguous use of this term makes quality research on the subject difficult (Gresham & Kendall, 1987). Some authors (for example, Schmidt & Osborne, 1981) argue that consultation and counseling are basically the same process. They are in the minority, however. The term *consultation* has been used to mean a variety of things and to encompass a variety of functions that provide it with its own identity (West & Idol, 1987).

Consultation tends to be defined in terms of the role and function of the consultant (Kurpius & Robinson, 1978). However, this method de-emphasizes the *process* of consultation. A variety of generic definitions of consultation have been suggested (for example, Gallessich, 1982; Parsons, 1996). These definitions generally agree about the role of consultation, but they differ on such issues as whether the consultee must be a human service professional or whether the consultant must be from outside the system in which consultation is occurring.

General agreement does exist on several aspects of consultation that can be used in formulating an acceptable definition. Most authors consider that the goal of all consultation is to solve problems. What constitutes a problem can, of course, vary significantly. An organization could seek a consultant to assist in such problems as alleviating poor staff morale or determining how best to evaluate the effects of a substance-abuse program. The term *problem* does not necessarily imply that something is *wrong*. It may simply refer to a situation that needs attention. That is, consultants not only assist consultees in developing solutions to defined problems (such as assisting an administrator in working out the glitches in a program),

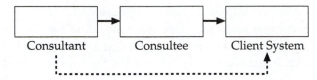

FIGURE 1.1
Relationships of the parties in consultation

they also empower consultees by assisting them in recognizing their needs and tapping the resources necessary to meet those needs (such as through strategic planning) (Witt & Martens, 1988). Consultants help consultees view the problem as part of a larger system to understand how it has developed, is maintained, and may be solved (Kurpius & Fuqua, 1993b). Hence, consultation can occur in a very broad range of problem-solving situations. In this sense, consultation is a unique activity (Kurpius, 1987).

A second commonly accepted aspect of consultation is its tripartite nature (Mannino & Shore, 1986); that is, it involves three parties: a *consultant*, a *consultee*, and a *client system*. The consultant delivers direct service to a consultee, who delivers direct service to a client system. The client system receives indirect service from the consultant through an intermediary (the consultee). Thus, the consultant provides assistance to the consultee that can positively affect the consultee's work with the client system. Figure 1.1 shows the relationships among the parties involved in consultation. The solid lines represent direct service; the broken line represents indirect service.

The reader should not assume from Figure 1.1 that the relationship among the consultant, consultee, and client system is a linear one. There are times when the consultant may want access to the client system (for example, for assessment, testing, or observation) (Kurpius & Fuqua, 1993b). Further, the consultant has an ethical and moral obligation to ensure that interventions designed to assist the client system

are appropriately carried through (Kurpius & Fuqua, 1993b). Having contact with the client system when necessary meets this obligation. Figure 1.2 shows one way of viewing the relationships among the parties in consultation with these ideas in mind.

In human service consultation, the consultant is often a human service professional, such as a counselor, psychologist, social worker, or human resource development specialist. The consultee is often another human service professional, or is another professional with some caretaking role (for example, a work supervisor, administrator, or teacher), or is a parent. There can be one or more consultees involved in consultation, and the client system can consist of one person, a group, an organization, or an entire community.

A third aspect of consultation on which there is substantial agreement is its goal of improving both the client system and the consultee (Zins, 1993). The term *improve* can, of course, mean many things, and hence a large number of approaches to consultation and a great many interventions become available to consultants. Thus, for example, a consultant might help a consultee, not only to work more effectively with a given moderately depressed client, but also to improve the consultee's ability to work with similar clients in the future.

Agreement on these aspects of consultation leads to a general and widely accepted definition: *consultation is a process in which a human service professional assists a consultee with a work-related (or caretaking-related) problem with a client*

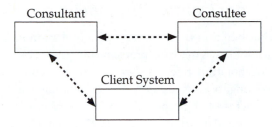

FIGURE 1.2
The triadic relationships in consultation

system, with the goal of helping both the consultee and the client system in some specified way.

The *content* of consultation deals with what is discussed, and the process refers to the problem-solving process and the nature of the interaction between consultant and consultee (Kurpius & Fuqua, 1993a; Meyers & Yelich, 1989).

COMMON CHARACTERISTICS

OF CONSULTATION

Can consultation be identified by certain common characteristics? A survey of the literature on the nature of consultation (for example, Gallessich, 1982; Gutkin & Curtis, 1982; Mannino & Shore, 1986; Mazade, 1985; Tindal, Shinn, & Rodden-Nord, 1990; West & Idol, 1987) suggests it can. In addition to the three aspects just discussed, some general agreement exists on the following characteristics of consultation:

- Either the consultee or the client system may be given priority over the other at a given time, depending on the consultation approach that is taken.
- The consultant provides indirect service to the client system by providing direct service to the consultee.
- Consultants can be either separate from or part of the system in which consultation is to occur; that is, external consultants or internal consultants.

- Participation in consultation is voluntary for all parties involved.
- Consultees are free to do whatever they wish with the consultant's suggestions and recommendations. They are under no obligation to follow the consultant's recommendations. The need for monitoring or being on call when the consultee implements the consultant's recommendations is necessary to ensure treatment integrity, which is the appropriate implementation of the recommendation by the consultee.
- The relationship between the consultee and consultant is one of peers, of two equals. Although the consultation relationship is equal in terms of the power of the consultant and consultee, it is unequal in terms of need; that is, the consultee needs help with a problem and the consultant does not (at least as far as the consultation relationship is concerned). The primary reason for consultation occurring is that the consultee expects the expertise of the consultant to be of some value with the situation at hand.
- The consultation relationship is temporary. Depending on the type, consultation may range from a single session to weekly sessions for more than a year. Whatever its length, however, the relationship is always

temporary (the consultant does not replace the consultee).

- Consultation deals exclusively with the consultee's work-related or caretaking-related problems. By definition, it never deals with the personal concerns of the consultee.

- The consultant can take on a variety of roles in consultation, depending on the nature of the problem, the skills of the consultee, the purpose and desired outcomes of consultation, and the skills of the consultant.

- Consultation tends to be collaborative in nature; that is, consultants and consultees work together to complement each other in solving the problems defined in consultation. The consultant brings expertise to bear on the problem and engages the expertise of the consultee to solve the problem (Brown, 1993; Henning-Stout, 1993). One cardinal exception is in carrying out the agreed-upon consultation plan. The consultee carries out the plan with the consultant remaining on call for further assistance. Another exception is when consultees have the skills but not the time to do a given task. For example, a consultee might ask a consultant to lead a workshop on substance-abuse counseling for the consultee's organization, even though the consultee is skilled in that task.

- Consultation usually occurs in an organizational context. Three key variables within an organization can influence the success of consultation: the people involved in consultation, how the process of consultation unfolds, and how change procedures are implemented.

COLLABORATION DEFINED

Collaboration is very similar to consultation in that it follows the same problem-solving process. Collaboration refers to "two or more people working together, using systematic planning and problem-solving procedures, to achieve desired outcomes" (Curtis & Stollar, 1995, p. 53). Collaboration is a role in which the helper accepts responsibility for the mental health aspects of a case (Erchul & Schulte, 1993). For example, a school counselor might work with a student on decreasing verbal aggression while consulting with the teacher about decreasing the student's verbal aggression in the teacher's classroom. Figure 1.3 illustrates the relationships of the parties involved in consultation.

Collaboration permits people with diverse expertise to combine efforts to accomplish the goal of helping a client, program, or organization. In collaboration each participant "alternately plays the consultant/expert and the consultee/recipient role in a forum where solution finding is jointly and equally shared among people with different knowledge and experience" (Thousand, Villa, Paolucci-Whitcomb, & Nevin, 1996). Collaboration improves upon the solutions the parties may have come up with independently. It involves shared ownership of problem definition and solutions, shared knowledge and expertise, and increased willingness to work together again (Thousand et al., 1996).

It is important to remember that a distinguishing difference between consultation and collaboration is that, in consultation, the consultee retains responsibility for the outcome, is considered to be the determiner of the suitability of possible interventions, and is responsible for adequate implementation of the intervention (i.e., ensuring treatment integrity) (Zins & Erchul, 1995). The basic trick of consultation is for the consultant to exert interpersonal influ-

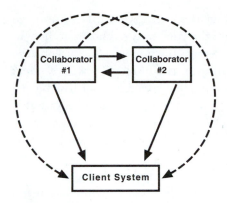

FIGURE 1.3
The relationships of the parties in collaboration

ence while maintaining a cooperative relationship (Zins & Erchul, 1995). In collaboration this is true for all collaborators.

In collaboration, the parties involved share the power in the decision-making process (Macmann et al., 1996). Decisions are made by the people involved, which allows for multiple views to be put forward. For example, in a school setting, a teacher's perspective is involved as well as that of the school counselor and school psychologist. Further, the teacher influences their behavior through his or her input. All team members are considered to have unique expertise and are expected to apply that expertise in helping the client system.

Collaboration as an option for service delivery has been around since the early 1970s and has been steadily growing in popularity ever since (Johnson & Pugach, 1996). It emerged as way to help consultees take on a greater sense of ownership in the problem-solving process, most particularly, the carrying out of interventions (Johnson & Pugach, 1996). In this way, both parties reciprocally influence one another in all aspects of the case, engage in joint problem solving, and have responsibility for some aspects of the case related to its outcome. Collaboration remains basically a one-on-one or small group process that em-

phasizes teams. It has recently evolved another aspect in which all members of the organization work "together and support each other on a set of multidimensional collegial interactions" to enhance the organization's effectiveness (Johnson & Pugach, 1996, p. 197).

Collaboration can occur in a variety of settings. For example, in schools, collaboration can occur during screening for special education services, development of individualized education plans (IEP), periodic review of students, and also with problem-solving intervention teams, and site based management teams (Shaw & Swerdik, 1995).

Collaboration often occurs in groups called teams, which are established whenever there is a collective effort to accomplish a goal such as helping the client system (Isgar & Isgar, 1993). Teams in which collaboration is the primary activity include task forces, work groups, and multidisciplinary teams.

Like consultation, the context or setting of collaboration can shape its nature. There are typically two contexts in which collaboration can occur: intraagency and interagency. For example, in intraagency collaboration, people from the same school setting work together to help some children and their families in increasing the children's academic achievement.

In interagency collaboration, a group from two or more agencies attempts to help a child make a successful transition from a juvenile evaluation center to a public school setting. Interagency collaboration is particularly common in early childhood settings. Collaboration in both these contexts presents its own unique challenges. In intraagency collaboration the major challenge is for the parties-at-interest to find the time to actually meet and implement the nuts and bolts of the collaborative process. In interagency collaboration, the major challenge is one of coordination of the efforts of two or more organizations to a common end. As Friend and Cook (1996) note, the policies and rules that guide the various organizations may entail considerable variance. Consequently, defining the parameters of collaboration can sometimes be difficult.

When the consultant and prospective consultees are employed in the same setting, it is difficult to meet some of the fundamental assumptions underlying consultation. For example, maintaining confidentiality at necessary levels can be challenging, the voluntary nature of consultation becomes questionable, and it is often difficult to relieve the consultant of *any* responsibility for the outcome of consultation (Caplan & Caplan, 1993; Zins & Erchul, 1995). Considering some of the difficulties a school counselor or school psychologist might face in attempting to provide consultation services in a school, some authors (e.g., Caplan & Caplan, 1993) have suggested that collaboration is the intervention of choice when the mental health professional is internal to the organization.

In collaboration, the school-based professional has equal responsibility for the overall outcome and primary responsibility for the mental health outcome of the case. In addition, the collaborating partners do not have the freedom to reject any aspect of the assistance to be provided to the client system. They must go along with the consensus reached as to how to proceed. Perhaps the best way to conceptualize collaboration is as consultation with a direct service component added. School-based mental health professionals need to be aware that they should be open to reciprocal consultation; that is, they too may take on the consultee role as necessary.

The following three brief and simple examples illustrate the scope of consultation and collaboration:

Case Example 1: Consulting with Juvenile Court Counselors

A juvenile court counselor group asks you to conduct a two-day workshop on approaches for counseling adjudicated maladjusted and nonmaladjusted youth. First you conduct a needs assessment. What do the consultees know, and what can they do? What do they need to know and do when it comes to working with adjudicated youth? You then design a workshop based on your findings, conduct the workshop, evaluate it, and follow up.

Case Example 2: Collaborating with a Teacher

Mary Smith, a teacher, and you agree to try to assist a student who Mary says is "incorrigible" and whom you view as lacking proper social skills with adults. You and Mary meet and establish a relationship. Mary describes what the student does that makes her label him as "incorrigible" and how often these negative behaviors occur. You give your opinions about the student's behavior. With that data in hand, you and Mary determine the acceptable level of the negative behaviors to be sought as well as the level of new desirable behaviors. Together you then develop a program that has Mary implementing some token economy procedures with the student in the classroom while you provide counseling services to the student. You help her with the token economy procedures and she assists with information that is helpful in counseling the student. At a later date, you both evaluate the effectiveness of the collaborative experience.

Case Example 3: Consulting with Another Human Service Professional

George is a community counselor providing therapy to a family who has a dying child, a new situation for him. George asks you for some suggestions in helping the family deal directly with the impending death of the child since this is causing severe problems within the family. You interview the family without performing any therapy and provide George with specific written recommendations for him to assist the family in dealing with this issue. You follow up and help George assess the progress he has made with the family.

CONSULTATION AND COLLABORATION COMPARED WITH OTHER HUMAN SERVICE ACTIVITIES

Consultation and collaboration can be compared with the four other common human service functions—counseling and psychotherapy, supervision, teaching, and mediation—as a way of making the concept of consultation clearer. Such comparisons were popularized by Caplan (1970).

Consultation and collaboration are different from *counseling and psychotherapy* in two fairly obvious ways. First, counseling and psychotherapy are dyadic in nature (they involve two parties: the therapist and the client) whereas consultation and collaboration are triadic. Second, counseling and psychotherapy deal with the personal problems of the client, whereas consultation/collaboration deal with work-related or caretaking-related concerns only. This is not to say that the effects of resolving a work-related problem cannot be therapeutic to the consultee or fellow collaborators. Still, consultants and collaborators, even if they are trained therapists, never provide counseling or psychotherapy to consultees or fellow collaborators, even if the work-related or caretaking-related problem being solved is determined to be due to a personal problem of the other professional or caregiver. In such cases, the human services professional brings up his or her concerns and then refers the other party for assistance. There is some evidence that consultants tend to be more controlling of the consultation relationship than counselors are of the counseling relationship (Henning-Stout & Conoley, 1987). A final point to remember is that when the consultant or collaborator is trained in counseling and psychotherapy, it is quite easy to inadvertently turn the consultation or collaboration session into a therapy session.

Another human service function that is different from consultation and collaboration is *supervision*. Supervision can be defined as "an intensive hierarchical, interpersonally focused relationship involving a supervisor who oversees the development of a supervisee's professional knowledge, skill, confidence, objectivity, and interpersonal interactions . . . for the purpose of facilitating or improving competence" (Knoff, 1988, p. 241). Supervision tends to be performed in dyads and implies an ongoing relationship, whereas consultation and collaboration are usually temporary, tripartite relationships. More significantly, supervision implies the power of one person over another. If I am your supervisor, I have the power to perform ongoing evaluations of your effectiveness on the job. These evaluations will be used in personnel decisions that affect you in many ways at work and thus create inequity in the relationship. Therefore, consultants or collaborators do not become supervisors of the people to whom they provide these services.

Teaching is also different from consultation and collaboration. Traditional teaching involves a predetermined, detailed lesson plan, whereas events in consultation and collaboration often dictate more spontaneous behavior by the parties involved. Further, teaching is an unequal relationship in which teachers have power over students and evaluate them, traditionally by some grading process. Human services professionals may assess consultee or fellow collaborator learning, but in a manner different from that used by teachers. A consultant or collaborator may, however, take on a teaching role on occasion. For example, a mental health collaborator might teach a fellow collaborator how to perform a behavioral counseling technique with a client, or an organizational consultant might teach a consultee the basics of survey design. Later in this text you will read about education/training consultation; it is one of the most commonly requested approaches to consultation.

Mediation is different from consultation and collaboration, although many consultants and collaborators use mediation techniques in group or organizational work. Mediation is a form of conflict resolution (Fisher & Brown, 1988; Fisher & Ury, 1981) in which the mediator takes on the role of third-party neutral. Mediation is similar to consultation and collaboration in that it has a problem-solving orientation, is tripartite

in nature, uses collaboration extensively, and involves a peer relationship among the parties. Mediation is different from consultation and collaboration in that it necessarily deals with conflict, never uses a teaching role, and does not allow room for suggestions or recommendations by the third-party neutral.

HISTORICAL OVERVIEW

Like any other human service function, the roots of consultation go back to ancient times, when two prototypical roles of consultation emerged: the healer and the technological advisor (Gallessich, 1982). The healer had the power to improve well-being, and the technological advisor could tell someone how to fix something or how to proceed to the next step in solving a problem. As human knowledge expanded, so too did the need for people who could help solve problems and provide technical expertise.

As consultation developed into a tool of human service professionals, the familiar medical consultation provided a model. If a physician noticed something about a patient that might require the attention of a specialist, he or she consulted with the specialist. Frequently, that meant turning the patient over to the specialist (consultant). The physician who originally handled the case frequently did not treat the patient again. Hence, in the original form of consultation, the consultant saw and treated the patient.

Such was the state of consultation around the turn of the 20th century. Then it became increasingly apparent to medical professionals that the referring personnel could benefit from participating in treating the patient further. This change in perspective fostered the emergence in the human service professions of consultation as we now know it. Additional forces that contributed to the emergence of human service consultation were the growth of the organization development movement and the community mental health movement (Brown, Kurpius, & Morris, 1988). These forces viewed the consultee as an active participant in the consultation process and viewed consultation as a developmental, preventative force that would continue to balance direct and indirect service activities. This shift led to the idea of consultant as trainer, that is, a professional party who would give away the skills of helping. The basic essence of consultation, as it emerged as a service delivery, was to enhance the methodological repertoires of consultees (Johnson & Pugach, 1996). The consultant was the expert who accomplished this task in a series of transactions with the consultee. Consultation became a primary activity for workers in the schools such as counselors and psychologists. The community counselor's role as a consultant has been less well established (Keys, Bemak, Carpenter, & King-Sear, 1998).

Consultation today, common in such human service professions as psychology, counseling, social work, and human resource development, has developed into three broad types: organizational, mental health, and behavioral. I will cover the historical development of each of these types in later chapters.

At the outset of the new millenium, the changing nature of organizations such as schools, has changed the amount of emphasis placed on the expert role (e.g., a counselor helping a teacher improve classroom management skills) to a more collaborative approach (e.g., a counselor and teacher working simultaneously on goals related to improved classroom behavior) (Bradley, 1994). Collaboration as a

distinct service emerged in education as a response to legislation involving the education of students identified as eligible for special education services. There has been a parallel increase in interest in collaboration as a mode of service delivery in profit and nonprofit organizations (Sherwood, 1993). For example in the mental health arena, collaboration emerged as an alternative to traditional consultation, primarily for internal consultants. In fact, the increase in having providers and recipients of consultation employed in the same organization made it increasingly difficult for some of the assumptions of consultation to be met and thereby gave impetus to the popularity of collaboration.

Finally, the increased complexity of organizations has demanded a more system-level approach to problem solving. The literature concerning consultation and collaboration has reflected increased interest in providing these services at the systems level. It is now common for consultants and collaborators to work on organization-wide issues and deal with problems that affect the entire organization (Johnson & Pugach, 1996). For example, counselors and psychologists are involved as consultants and collaborators in dealing with system-level issues such as those related to school reform. Consequently, today's human services professional needs to have the skills to consult and collaborate, not only at the individual level, but also at the systems level.

GLOSSARY OF KEY TERMS
USED IN THE BOOK

Because consultation is neither well defined nor has adequately developed its own identity, many of the terms used in the consultation literature are vague and confusing. Therefore, the glossary that follows contains some key terms used throughout this book. It is very important that you familiarize yourself with these terms to avoid confusion as you continue reading.

advocacy: a role consultants take on when they believe a certain course of action should be taken.

advocacy consultation: an expansion of the role of advocacy to a method of consultation entirely devoted to furthering some course of action.

behavioral consultation: one of the three major types of consultation; it attempts to assist consultees and their client systems through a systematic, problem-solving approach based on behavioral technology.

client: in some approaches to mental health and behavioral consultation, the person with whom the consultee is having a work-related or caretaking-related problem; in this instance the client constitutes the client system (see below). One of the goals of consultation is to improve the functioning of the client.

client system: the person, group, organization, or community with whom the consultee is having a work-related or caretaking-related problem. One of the goals of consultation is to improve the functioning of the client system.

collaborative consultation: the method of relating most consultants use when working with their consultees; it allows both parties to pool their strengths and resources in their efforts (however, the consultee typically carries out the plan developed in consultation). Any model of consultation can be implemented collaboratively.

collaboration: a service provided by a professional in which there is a shared responsibility for the outcome of the problem-solving process, including participation in interventions. Collaboration often occurs in teams of professionals and stakeholders working toward the same ends. Collaboration is characterized by mutual, reciprocal consultation among the parties involved.

consultant: a person, typically a human service professional, who delivers direct service to another person (consultee) who has a work-related or caretaking-related problem with a person, group, organization, or community (client system).

consultation: a type of helping relationship in which a human service professional (consultant) delivers assistance to another person (consultee) so as to solve a work-related or caretaking-related problem the consultee has with a client system.

consultee: the person, often a human service professional or a caretaker (for example, a parent, teacher, or supervisor), to whom the consultant provides assistance with a work-related or caretaking-related problem. One of the goals of consultation is to improve the current and future functioning of the consultee.

diagnosis: the second of the four stages of the consultation process. In this stage the problem to be solved in consultation is defined. Thus, in its simplest form, diagnosis is the equivalent of problem identification. In its more complex form, it is an ongoing process in which the target problem is continually redefined and worked on by gathering, analyzing, interpreting, and discussing data.

direct service: the assistance a consultant provides a consultee or that a consultee provides a client system. When consultants work with consultees they are providing direct service to them. When consultees work with client systems, they are providing direct service to them. This term is frequently contrasted with indirect service.

disengagement: the last of the four stages in the consultation process; it involves the winding down of consultation, including evaluation of the consultation, postconsultation planning, reduced contact, follow-up, and termination.

entry: the first of the four stages of the consultation process; it involves exploring the presenting problem, formulating a contract, and physically and psychologically entering the system in which consultation is to occur.

generic model of consultation: a model of consultation that contains those characteristics common to the various types of consultation and the approaches to these types. It is what distinguishes consultation as a unique helping relationship.

human service organization: a broad term describing an organization that provides some form of contact with clients and aims to improve the well-being of those clients and, therefore, of society. Counseling centers, mental health centers, Head Start programs, homes for the mentally retarded, and social services departments are all examples of human service agencies.

implementation: the third of the four stages of the consultation process; it is the stage in which action is taken on the problem. It begins with formulating and choosing a problem-solving plan and includes implementing and evaluating that plan.

indirect service: that type of service provided to the client system by the consul-

tant. The consultant affects the well-being of the client system by helping the consultee help the client system more effectively. It is one of the characteristics of consultation that differentiates it from other helping relationships.

mental health consultation: one of the three major types of consultation; it attempts to focus on the psychological well-being of all the parties involved in consultation. Its ultimate goal is to create a more mentally healthy society.

organization: a group of people put together for a common purpose. Almost all consultation, regardless of the type, occurs within some type of organization. It is one of the factors that influence the processes and outcomes of consultation.

organization contact person: that person in the organization in which consultation is being considered who initially contacts (or is contacted by) the consultant. This person is often a midlevel administrator who may or may not become a consultee. This person usually paves the way for the consultant's entry into the organization.

organizational consultation: one of the three major types of consultation; its primary goal is the enhancement of an organization's effectiveness. The organization itself is the client system, and the members of the organization involved in consultation are the consultees. Consultants frequently work together in teams when performing organizational consultation.

outreach: extending or making known available services to a target population.

parties-at-interest (stakeholders): those people (who usually belong to the organization in which consultation is occurring) who are not directly involved in consultation but are affected by the consultation process in some way. Parties-at-interest typically include contact persons and administrators. If the consultant belongs to an organization (for example, a mental health center), then those members of the consultant's organization indirectly affected by the consultation are also parties-at-interest.

tripartite: composed of three parts. With respect to consultation, it refers to the three parties involved: consultant, consultee, and client system.

work-related problem: the kind of problem considered to be suitable for the primary focus in consultation. In the case of consultation with people such as parents, the term *caretaking-related problem* is sometimes used instead. This term is often contrasted with *personal problems*, which are not directly dealt with in consultation.

SUGGESTIONS FOR EFFECTIVE PRACTICE

- Develop a working definition of consultation and collaboration with which you feel comfortable.

- Become very familiar with the characteristics of both consultation and collaboration so that you can do both well and differentiate between the two when necessary.

- Make a point to differentiate consultation and collaboration from the other professional services you will be providing.

QUESTIONS FOR REFLECTION

1. How do the roles of consultant, consultee, and client differ from one another?

2. What is the basic difference between indirect and direct service that consultants and collaborators provide?

3. In what ways can consultation and collaboration be called problem-solving processes?

4. Why is it important for consultants and collaborators to have a personal theory of these two services?

5. In what ways are consultation and collaboration similar? Different?

6. Many consultants are technological experts with little training in consultation theory and practice. What are some of the potential problems that such consultants can encounter when performing their work?

7. How can consultation and collaboration have the goal of improving the consultee or fellow collaborator and the client system at the same time?

8. Because consultants, by definition, work with consultees who have work-related problems, how can the consultation relationship be that of equals?

9. How would you as a collaborator determine which roles to take on during collaboration?

10. How is consultation similar to counseling and psychotherapy, to teaching, to mediating, and to supervising? How is it different?

SUGGESTED SUPPLEMENTARY READINGS

Started in 1990, the *Journal of Educational and Psychological Consultation* is put out by the Association for Educational and Psychological Consultants and published quarterly by Lawrence Erlbaum Associates. This journal serves as a forum for the exchange of ideas, theories, and research among professionals in the human services and education.

Consulting Psychology Journal: Practice and Research. This quarterly is the official journal of Division 13, Consulting Psychology, of the American Psychological Association. It presents various ideas related to the practice of consultation. In recent years, the journal has tended to emphasize organizational consultation.

"Consultation 1: Conceptual, Structural, and Operational Definitions" (Special issue). (1993a). *Journal of Counseling and Development, 71,* 596–708. This special issue is an update of the special issue of the *Personnel and Guidance Journal* entitled "Consultation I: Definitions, Models, Programs" which was published in 1978. This update, edited by Kurpius and Fuqua, is divided into five sections: Section 1 addresses conceptual and operational foundations of consultation; Section 2, assessment and organizational diagnosis: Section 3, organizational culture; Section 4, consultation in different settings; Section 5, research in consultation. This journal issue and the one described next represent the current thinking in consultation.

"Consultation II: Prevention, Preparation, and Key Issues" (Special issue). (1993b). *Journal of Counseling and Development, 72,* 115–223. This special issue is an update of the special issue of the *Personnel and Guidance Journal* entitled "Consultation II: Dimensions, Training, Bibliography," which was published in 1978. The new update, edited by Kurpius and Fuqua, is divided into three sections: Section 1 addresses primary prevention consultation; Section 2, professional preparation of consultants; Section 3, trends and topical issues such as ethical, legal, and multicultural issues. This issue is a fine complement to "Consultation I" and presents cutting-edge thinking in the area of consultation.

SUGGESTED WEB SITES

http:www.counseling.org/ctonline. This site presents *Counseling Today* online. You can explore this site for references to consultation.

http:www.counseling.org/eNews. This site is by subscription only; it is free and is sent to subscriber's e-mail accounts every two weeks.

http:www.counseling.org/journals. Abstracts from many journals of the American Counseling Association are available here.

http://members.apa.org/. If you join the American Psychological Association (APA), you can enjoy the convenience of searching APA journals, a database of abstracts, and general information. The search engine allows easy retrieval of information related to consultation and collaboration.

2

Consultants, Consultees, and Collaborators

If you were looking for a consultant or collaborator to work with people in your human service organization, what type of person would you hire? What kinds of professional skills would be needed in such a person, and how would you be able to tell if the consultant/collaborator truly possessed those skills? What roles would you want this person to take during his or her activities? What would be the most critical factor for you in determining whether or not to hire this prospective helper?

This chapter provides some answers to these questions—it discusses the characteristics that effective consultants and collaborators possess, the skills critical to successful consultation and collaboration, and the various roles that professionals take on when providing these services. In addition, we will examine two other important areas: the position (internal or external) of the consultant/collaborator to the or-

ganization in which service is to occur and the current status of research on consultation.

As you read this chapter, consider the following questions:

1. How are the personal characteristics of consultants and collaborators likely to influence the delivery of their services?

2. What skills seem necessary for consultants and collaborators, regardless of the role they assume in delivering their services?

3. Do any of the roles of consultants and collaborators tend to contradict one another?

4. In what ways should consultants and collaborators be multiculturally skilled?

5. To what degree can the research related to these services guide your practice?

As I have noted in Chapter 1, you can assume in this and the following chapters that the discussion of a given topic applies equally to consultation and collaboration unless I make a distinction. I avoid using the terms *consultation* and *collaboration* together to enhance the readability of this text.

INTRODUCTION

Consider the following two cases:

Case Example 1: An Ineffective Consultant

Dale Jones, a counselor, and Jackie Cheng, a social worker, work together in a community mental health center. Jackie approaches Dale for consultation regarding a migrant family that is part of Jackie's caseload. It seems that the family is having difficulty adjusting to the community, which consists primarily of retirees who have their summer homes there. When Jackie asks Dale for help in facilitating the family's adjustment, Dale makes light of the request by noting that by late fall both the retirees and the migrant family will be long gone.

Case Example 2: An Effective Consultant

Terri Brodski, a psychologist, and Jamie Stewart, a social worker, work together in a community mental health center. Jamie approaches Terri for consultation regarding a migrant family that is part of Jamie's caseload. It seems that the family is having difficulty adjusting to the community, which consists primarily of retirees who have their summer homes there. When Jamie approaches Terri about the family's problems, Terri asks her to present her concerns about the family in detail, and she listens to and clarifies Jamie's concerns. When Jamie shares discouragement about the possibilities of helping the fam-

ily, Terri offers encouragement and support, and asks how Jamie's work with the family ties into their agency's role and mission. Finally, they establish a verbal contract between them and agree to meet twice more about how Jamie can work more effectively with the family.

First, Terri observes Jamie working with the family. During the next consultation session, they exchange their impressions about the family, divide the family's adjustment problem into three smaller, more specific problems, and set goals to solve them. Terri then leads Jamie through a brainstorming session during which possible interventions are generated. Once they agree on an intervention for each problem, Terri assists Jamie in formulating their ideas into a feasible plan, which Jamie agrees to carry out.

During their final consultation session one month later, Terri and Jamie formally evaluate the degree to which each problem was solved and the effectiveness of the consultation process itself (that is, how well they worked together). They plan additional follow-up strategies for Jamie to use in later contacts with the family and agree that, within 30 days, Terri will make a follow-up call to Jamie concerning the family's progress. Then they say their goodbyes.

Terri clearly spent much more time and used more skills with Jamie than Dale did with Jackie. Terri displayed many of the characteristics of effective consultants. She used interpersonal skills when offering support and encouragement to Jamie. When Terri listened to and clarified Jamie's concerns, she used effective communication skills. She used several problem-solving skills with Jamie to identify ways to help the migrant family. Terri showed the skills of being a multiculturally sensitive consultant when she asked Jamie to share in detail her views of the family's problems. Terri also showed skill in working with organizations when she asked how Jamie's work with the family tied into the agency's role and mission, and she displayed ethical and professional behavior skills by spending the time and effort needed to help Jamie. As you can see from these two cases, there are characteristics and skills that differentiate effective consultants from ineffective ones. Let's examine these characteristics next.

CHARACTERISTICS OF EFFECTIVE CONSULTANTS AND COLLABORATORS

Because consultation and collaboration are demanding, the requirements to perform them successfully are also demanding (Kelley, 1981). Some research suggests that the best consultants seem to be guided by the need to make a difference in the lives of others (Bianco-Mathis & Veazey, 1996). But, beyond an internal drive, effective consultants must possess the following:

- a personal and professional growth orientation
- knowledge of consultation or collaboration and human behavior
- consultation or collaboration skills

A *personal growth orientation* involves the willingness of a consultant to grow and change as a person. Because consultation usually involves problem solving, which requires change on the part of the consultee, consultants need to be willing to model that change. A personal growth orientation does not necessarily mean that consultants must experience personal growth counseling or therapy, although such experiences can be quite beneficial. Rather, the concept of personal growth orientation entails

any aspect of a consultant's life in which he or she endeavors to "stretch." For example, one consultant might decide to accomplish the feat of hiking to every waterfall in a national park within a certain time frame; another consultant might volunteer 10 hours a week of free consultation services to a church group; whereas another consultant might participate in a personal growth group to improve his or her interpersonal effectiveness. In short, personal growth orientation is an attitude toward life that helps consultants become more effective human beings by periodically "stretching" themselves in some way.

A *professional growth orientation* refers to consultants' participation in activities that enhance the effectiveness of their consultation practices. Consultants often participate in workshops, training programs, academic courses, and supervised practice so as to remain current in their fields. In addition, many consultants seek additional training and knowledge to expand the parameters of their consultation practices. For example, one consultant, a university professor by training, might take a series of management and organizational behavior courses and so expand her consultation services to include human service agencies.

Thus, a personal and professional growth orientation helps consultants to practice what they preach more effectively. By experiencing growth in their own lives, consultants are better able to empathize with consultees about the barriers to growth that consultees normally experience and to be more authentic role models for those with whom they work.

Effective consultants, of course, also possess *knowledge of consultation* and a basic *knowledge of human behavior* (Levinson, 1985). Even though it seems obvious that consultants need to be knowledgeable about consultation, the fact remains that many practicing consultants have had no formal training in consultation other than any on-the-job training they may have received. This lack of any systematic means for acquiring knowledge about consultation creates issues concerning the professional limitations of consultants and the ways they assess their effectiveness. Regardless of how they acquire their knowledge, effective consultants know the ins and outs of consultation; that is, they possess a generic model of consultation and are knowledgeable about the various types of consultation. Such knowledge provides them with a sense of meaningfulness and adds direction to their practices.

Effective consultants must also possess knowledge about human behavior—including both individual and group behavior—for consultation is first and foremost a human relationship. Because consultants spend much of their time working with individual consultees, they need to know the basics of personality theory, normal and abnormal behavior, interpersonal relationships, and human communication. Knowledge of these topics is essential for maximizing the effectiveness with which each stage of consultation is accomplished. Further, a basic knowledge of group dynamics and organizational theory and behavior is quickly becoming a necessity for almost all consultants because most consultation occurs in and is affected by an organizational setting. Therefore, consultants need a working knowledge of organizations to maximize the effectiveness of their interventions.

Even when consultants have a growth orientation and are knowledgeable, if they are to be effective, they need to possess *skills in consulting*. Consultants must be able to *do* as well as *know*. Effective consultants have a broad repertoire of consultation skills that range from basic communication skills to sophisticated problem-solving intervention skills.

SKILLS NECESSARY FOR CONSULTATION AND COLLABORATION

Many skills are required of effective consultants and collaborators. Many authors point out the importance of competent interpersonal and communication skills (for example, Conoley & Conoley, 1992; Dustin & Ehly, 1984; Kurpius & Rozecki, 1993; Dougherty, Henderson, & Lindsey, 1997; Parsons & Meyers, 1984; Hyatt & Tingstrom, 1993). Competence in problem-solving skills is also essential (Kurpius & Robinson, 1978; Maris, 1985; Schindler-Rainman, 1985). Skills in working with organizations are increasingly needed (Egan, 1985; Schein, 1987, 1988). Because consultants, and collaborators even more so, are increasingly being called on to work with groups of consultees, skills in group work are a must. Skills in working with culturally diverse populations are increasingly important (American Association for Counseling and Development [AACD], 1991; Flanagan & Miranda, 1995; Ivey, Ivey, & Simek-Morgan, 1993; Lee & Richardson, 1991). Finally, well-developed ethical and professional behavior skills are essential to competency (Corey, Corey, & Callanan, 1998; Gallessich, 1982). The limited empirical research on the importance of the skill areas also supports the hypothesis that they are related to consultation success (see Knoff, McKenna, & Riser, 1991; Knoff, Sullivan, & Liu, 1995; Randolph & D'Ilio, 1990). For example, Knoff et al. (1995) found that there were two primary skill areas when prospective consultees were queried regarding consultant effectiveness: consultant knowledge, process, and application skills and consultant interpersonal and problem-solving skills. It is very likely that the same holds for collaboration.

Interpersonal and Communication Attitudes

Consultation is a human relationship that involves extensive communication. Interpersonal and communication skills, which are related to creating and maintaining effective human relationships, are essential for a consultant. Further, the attitudes from which these skills flow are as important as the skills themselves (see Adams & Spencer, 1986; Kurpius & Rozecki, 1993).

The desirable underpinnings for these skills are unconditional regard, empathy, and genuineness (Rogers, 1961). These attitudes form the core conditions on which an effective consultation relationship can be built. Without these attitudes in the consultant, the development of rapport with the consultee may take longer to achieve or may not occur at all. These attitudes exist on a continuum; their presence in a person is not an all-or-nothing thing. However, to the degree that consultants possess these attitudes, the conditions for successful consultation will be established (Kurpius & Rozecki, 1993).

Unconditional regard (often referred to as *acceptance*) refers to the willingness of the consultant to respect and accept the consultee as a human being who is worthwhile, has dignity, and can be liked or cared for by the consultant, in spite of the consultee's imperfec-

tions. Regard is often manifested by the consultant as nonjudgmental and nonpossessive behavior toward the consultee.

Empathy refers to the consultant's ability to understand—to tune in to and accurately perceive the consultee's experience without losing his or her objectivity. It is a posture of putting oneself in another person's shoes. Empathy helps in establishing rapport, trust, open communication, and a common ground from which consultation can proceed.

Genuineness is demonstrated when consultants feel free to be themselves in the consultation relationship—when they need not hide behind roles, become defensive, or play games with the consultee (Kurpius & Rozecki, 1993). As Bellman (1990) notes: "My goal is to establish a consultant role for myself that is really me and then to . . . 'be myself.' Being a consultant is more comfortable than playing one" (p. 18). Perhaps one of the greatest contributions of genuineness to successful consultation is the modeling effect it can have for the consultee. When consultees view consultants as genuine, they too can become more genuine (Block, 1981; Ross, 1993).

Other attitudes related to effective interpersonal and communication skills are a positive outlook about oneself and others, a willingness to take risks, a commitment to creativity (Hamilton, 1988; Schindler-Rainman, 1985), and a desire to be trustworthy (French & Bell, 1990).

In summary, although your skills are critical to your success as a consultant, your perspective may be just as important (Bellman, 1990). These attitudes and the behavioral characteristics that reflect them are linked to professional skills and knowledge in such a way that they affect how a consultee perceives a consultant's helpfulness (Bardon, 1986).

Interpersonal Skills

The interpersonal skills of creating, maintaining, and terminating relationships refer to our ability to get along with other human beings. Because consultation is a helping relationship, consultants need relatively high levels of these skills. The creation and maintenance of consultation relationships require the following major interpersonal skills:

- putting the consultee at ease (for example, making small talk)

- setting expectations about the relationship (for example, contracting behaviors)

- creating an environment conducive to collaboration (for example, determining early on what the consultee can and cannot do)

- creating an environment conducive to change (for example, talking implicitly and explicitly about how consultation is related to change)

- creating an appropriate consultant's image in the eyes of the consultee (for example, explaining early on who the consultant is and what he or she can do for the consultee)

- developing a social influence base built on prestige, trustworthiness, and similarity (for example, making explicit use of expertise, benign intent, and similarities to the consultee)

- being comfortable with oneself as consultant (for example, exuding confidence)

- noting and responding, not only to consultee verbalizations, but also to emotions and nonverbal behaviors (for example, reflecting a therapist's anxiety about working with a client who has AIDS)

- using appropriate humor (for example, being willing to laugh at oneself)

Interpersonal skills assist consultants in developing and sustaining strong relationships with their consultees. The strength and outcome of the consultation relationship are often directly related to consultee motivation, a commitment to change, and a positive attitude toward consultation (see West & Idol, 1987; Thousand et al., 1996). Consultant interpersonal skills are integral to working effectively in cross-cultural consultation (Gibbs, 1980). I agree with Kurpius and Rozecki (1993) who say that "if the consultant does not have a mastery of the art of communication and an understanding of the intricacies of interpersonal interaction, the consultation process will most often appear lifeless and unlikely to be of long-lasting help" (p. 143).

Communication Skills

The communication process between consultant and consultee can be construed as being central to the process of consultation (Daniels & DeWine, 1990; Thousand et al., 1996). Everything consultants do when they consult involves a system of language constructs (Daniels & DeWine, 1990, p. 304), that is, a system of symbols used to make sense of life events and experiences. Communication skills refer to people's ability to send and receive meaningful messages. Such skills tend to be more specific than relationship skills. As we know from our experiences with others, communicating is sometimes quite difficult. Consultants need to use a broad repertoire of communication skills to increase the probability of a successful outcome to consultation. There is some research that highlights the importance of communication in consultation (Erchul,

1993b; Dougherty, Henderson, Tack, et al., 1997; Safran, 1991).

There are many "basic" communication skills. Among the more important ones for consultants are:

- nonverbal attending (for example, keeping an open body posture)
- listening (for example, actively discerning a consultee's intended meaning)
- expressing empathy (for example, understanding the consultee's experience and accurately communicating that understanding back to the consultee)
- questioning (for example, asking consultees to expand on or be more specific)
- clarifying or paraphrasing (for example, putting consultees' expressions into the consultant's own words to demonstrate understanding or to help consultees understand themselves better)
- summarizing (for example, putting together the main points of discussion in order to determine the next step in the consultation process)
- providing feedback (for example, providing consultees with information about themselves for the purposes of examination and change)
- giving information (for example, informing the consultee of the possible ways a given client might be effectively helped)
- "speaking the same language" (for example, choosing plain language that avoids jargon)

Communication skills such as these are related to a successful consultation outcome in that they allow the consultant and consultee to ex-

change meaningful and accurate information, which facilitates more effective problem solving and aids relationship maintenance throughout the consultation process. Through the use of effective communication skills, the consultant is able to view the situation and the consultee from a variety of perspectives and enhance the possibilities of a successful outcome to consultation (Kurpius & Rozecki, 1993). In fact, communication and interpersonal skills build the foundation for the success all of the stages of consultation.

Problem-Solving Skills

Because consultation is by nature a problem-solving activity, consultants need to be highly skilled in problem solving (Kelley, 1981). There is some empirical evidence that problem-solving skills are essential even in the presence of effective interpersonal and communication skills (Curtis & Stollar, 1995). Some of the many problem-solving skills available to consultants are:

- setting the stage for problem solving (for example, defining consultation as a problem-solving activity)
- defining the problem (that is, isolating "what is to be fixed" during consultation);
- examining the conditions surrounding the problem (for example, noting antecedents and consequences)
- gathering, analyzing, and interpreting data pertinent to the problem (for example, surveying organizational personnel and providing feedback on the results)
- identifying any facilitating and restraining forces (that is, determining which forces are working for and against a given plan)

- designing interventions for a particular situation (for example, identifying consultee strengths that increase the likelihood of successful plan implementation)

- evaluating problem-solving attempts (that is, determining the degree to which a selected intervention worked)

- determining who will do what, how, and when during the problem-solving process (that is, arranging the responsibilities involved in carrying out the plan)

- predicting the ramifications and implications of solving the problem (that is, examining how change can affect other parts of the system)

Consultants use problem-solving skills such as these to assist their consultees in solving work-related problems. Many consultants attempt to facilitate the development of more sophisticated problem-solving skills in their consultees. The critical implications of these skills for successful consultation will become apparent in later chapters (Chapters 4 and 5) that discuss specific problem-solving skills.

Skills in Working with Organizations

As the cases presented at the beginning of this chapter indicate, almost all consultation occurs within some organizational context. Because of this, consultants need to have some basic skills—specific behaviors—in working with an organization as a whole. When successfully demonstrated, these skills increase the likelihood of a successful outcome of consultation. Without these skills, consultants and the consultation process itself can become victims of those organizational forces that have negative effects. Some of the more important skills consultants need when they work with organizations are:

- becoming accepted by the members of the organization in which consultation is to occur (for example, creating working relationships with prospective consultees)

- using organizational analysis (for example, determining who talks to whom under what conditions)

- providing feedback (for example, giving the consultee objective information about some aspect of the organization's functioning)

- gathering information (for example, using surveys to determine the attitudes of the organization's members)

- using a repertoire of organization-wide interventions (for example, providing a stress management program)

- determining the climate of an organization (that is, its working atmosphere)

- determining the culture of the organization (that is, its norms, standards, and values)

- using program planning (for example, assisting consultees in executing effective programs)

- determining how to utilize human resources within the organization (for example, assisting consultees in improving managerial styles)

As the list suggests, human service consultants need not have all the skills required to give the organization with which they consult everything it needs. However, such consultants do need selected skills that allow them to operate at an optimal level within the organization and assist with selected organization-wide changes. The importance of a repertoire of skills for working with organizations will become even more apparent in Chapter 8, which provides an orientation to organizations and how they function.

Group Skills

Because they are increasingly being called on to work with groups of consultees, effective consultants need to be skilled in working with a variety of groups. Several of the types of consultation you will be reading about later—such as education/training consultation, program consultation, process consultation, and behavioral system consultation—frequently demand the use of group work on the part of consultants. Further, group skills are particularly critical for collaborators because most collaboration occurs in teams. Some of the many group skills needed include:

- focusing and maintaining attention on task and work issues (for example, gently reminding the group when it gets off task)

- managing conflict within a group of consultees (for example, using mediation skills in assisting two conflicting group members)

- managing agendas of meetings (for example, helping group members determine what items should be on an agenda and how those items are to be dealt with)

- providing feedback to group members (for example, confronting members, avoidance of important issues)

- facilitating concrete and specific communication among group members (for

example, reflecting the true meaning of vague generalities)

- linking the comments of one group member to pertinent comments from others (for example, tying in a consultee's statement about one of her clients to another consultee's remark about one of his clients)

- facilitating the development of the group process (for example, knowing when to move from the getting acquainted stage to the working stage)

- using group management skills (for example, knowing how to terminate a group session)

- sensing and using group dynamics to help consultee groups meet their goals (for example, calling attention to the emotional current running through the group).

Increasingly consultants and collaborators are interacting in group modalities, thus amplifying the importance of group-related skills (Thousand et al., 1996)

Skills in Dealing with Cultural Diversity

One of the major challenges human service professionals encounter is discerning the complex role cultural diversity takes on in their work (Corey et al., 1998; Flanagan & Miranda, 1995; Jackson & Hayes, 1993; Plummer, 1998). As early as 1970, Caplan (1970) pointed out how cultural variables could adversely affect communication in consultation. Indeed the culture of the parties involved in consultation may well affect the efficacy of the mode of consultation being used (see Hayes & Prakasam, 1989, and Brown, 1997). There is no doubt that consultants need to take cultural differences into account (Wubbolding, 1991b). For example, by the year 2000 between 25 percent and 40 percent of students will be culturally or linguistically diverse (Harris, 1991). Consultants will increasingly be asked to consult with and about culturally diverse people and with organizations owned, managed, or populated by culturally diverse people (Jackson & Hayes, 1993). Competencies in becoming multiculturally skilled as a consultant include those related to beliefs and attitudes, knowledge and skills (Corey, 1996).

Multicultural competence is basic to effective consultation. As Corey et al. (1998) note, one of the major issues facing human service professionals is ". . . understanding the complex role that cultural diversity plays in their work" (p. 318). When consultants work from a multicultural perspective, they attempt to understand and deal with the sociocultural forces affecting the helping relationship (Gibbs, 1980). There are a significant number of multicultural competencies that have been established for human service professionals by Arredondo and her colleagues (1996). Consultants should bear in mind that all consultation is multicultural if the concept of culture is broadened to include diversity indicators such as gender and age (Das, 1995). Understanding your own cultural framework provides a context for understanding different cultural contexts (APA, 1993)

Being multiculturally skilled is essential for consultants and involves interpersonal, communication, problem-solving, ethical, and professional behavior skills such as the following:

- applying a knowledge and understanding of multicultural perspectives when performing consultation

- neither under- or overemphasizing cultural variables in consultation

- understanding how unique life experiences have influenced culturally diverse people

- integrating a knowledge of cultural diversity into effective practice

- not making value judgments about consultees (or client systems) who are culturally different

- challenging any stereotypic beliefs about culturally diverse groups

- viewing cultural differences as issues to meet, not as impediments

- using methods consistent with the life experiences and values of different minority groups

- possessing specific knowledge about the particular minority group served in consultation

- ensuring that definition of problems and development of goals take place within a cultural context

We are all limited by our cultural and ethnic experiences (Hays, 1996; Parsons, 1996; Corey et al., 1998). Further, consultation models tend to be deficient in the areas related to cultural diversity (Jackson & Hayes, 1993) and gender issues (Henning-Stout, 1994). Nonetheless, by increasing the level of our skills in working with those from different cultures and addressing the complexities of culture and gender as they relate to consultation, we can move toward effective consultation practice. For an excellent resource on competencies related to cultural diversity, see Arredondo et al. (1996). For an excellent resource for working with people from different cultures, see Lee (1995).

Ethical and Professional Behavior Skills

To be successful, consultants need to behave ethically and professionally. The necessary skills are often associated with internal feelings or beliefs that are explicitly demonstrated in consultants' behavior. Throughout their careers, all consultants encounter professional situations that require a set of skills based on sound ethical judgment. For example, what would you do if, as a consultant, you were "over your head" in trying to help a consultee work with a difficult client? Some of the myriad important skills that can help consultants act in an ethical and professional manner are:

- acting with integrity (for example, maintaining confidentiality)

- adhering to an ethical code (that is, adhering to accepted guidelines for professional behavior)

- engaging in consultation only within one's professional limits (that is, declining consultations for which one is not qualified)

- maintaining personal and professional growth (for example, engaging in professional development activities)

- having the intent to help (for example, being as thorough as possible)

- effectively coping with the stress of consulting (for example, using stress management skills)

- avoiding manipulation of others (for example, maintaining basic respect for others)

- using effective writing skills (for example, writing high-quality reports)

- using power for legitimate purposes only (that is, using one's skills to influence others appropriately)

Acting in an ethical, professional manner creates positive perceptions among the consultant's coworkers and contacts. Such perceptions contribute to the successful outcome of consultation because consultees are able to attribute to the consultant the social influence necessary for maximum effectiveness during consultation. Chapter 7 deals extensively with the ethical and professional behavior of consultants.

Possessing all these skills seems a tall order. The extent of a consultant's skills is best understood if they are seen as part of a continuum; no consultant either lacks or completely possesses each skill. And although it is important to note that effective consultants are not expert in all of these skills, they possess most of these skills to a moderate or higher degree. Developing the skills to be even more effective is a process that continues for the entire career of every consultant.

ROLES CONSULTANTS AND COLLABORATORS ASSUME

The Nature of Consultant Roles

Consultants can wear many hats. They use the skills described in the preceding sections in a variety of consultation roles or functions performed at any given time during the consultation relationship. Just as consultation is not easily defined, neither are the roles in which consultants function.

Consultants can take on any number of roles during a particular consultation relationship. The nature of the roles is usually defined in the consultation contract, although some authors (for example, Argyris, 1976) suggest that the real role is more often determined by the consultant through trial and error. Effective consultants are able to determine which roles are necessary, define them to the satisfaction of all parties involved, and then perform those roles.

The primary role a consultant takes on depends on several factors, including his or her abilities and frame of reference, the consultee's expectations and skill levels, the nature of the problem that consultation is attempting to solve, the model of consultation used, and the environmental context in which consultation is occurring (Lippitt & Lippitt, 1986; Schindler-Rainman, 1985).

The Categorization of Roles

Most categorization schemes put consultation roles on some sort of continuum. The most popular categorization approach is that of Lippitt and Lippitt (1986), in which consultants' roles lie on a continuum ranging from directive to nondirective roles. In directive roles the consultant is something of a technical expert, whereas in nondirective roles consultants tend to facilitate the consultee's expertise. Another approach to consultants' roles, that of Margulies and Raia (1972), includes task roles (those related to expertise) at one end of a continuum and process roles (those related to facilitation) at the other. Matthews (1983) proposed a continuum of consulting roles ranging from standard (expert) consulting to process (facilitative) consulting. Brown, Pryzwansky, and Schulte. (1995) described a system that categorizes consulting roles according to both a task/process dimension and a consultant's degree of active involvement. One final categorization scheme is a grid model using as its two axes consultant responsibility for growth and consultant responsibility for results (Champion, Kiel, & McLendon, 1990).

Regardless of how consulting roles are categorized, the bottom line is that categorization schemes tend to reflect the consultant's degree of involvement in the consultation process relative to that of the consultee. They guide the consultant in determining who is responsible for what tasks and how the consultant should proceed in consultation. For most human service professionals, the directive-nondirective categorization scheme of Lippitt and Lippitt (1986) seems most appropriate; the terms are familiar to most human service professionals, and they provide a very helpful rule of thumb because they imply the amount of control the consultant should have over the consultation process. The following discussion of common consultation roles is grounded in the categorization scheme of Lippitt and Lippitt (1986), but it also reflects my thoughts and those of other authors (for example, Gallessich, 1982; Margulies & Raia, 1972; Matthews, 1983).

Common Consultation Roles

Consultants can engage in the consultation process in a broad range of roles that vary in terms of how much the consultant directs the activity occurring in consultation (Lippitt & Lippitt, 1986); that is, some roles are more directive than others. Next we'll consider six consultation roles: advocate, expert, trainer/educator, collaborator, fact finder, and process specialist.

Advocate   The most directive consulting role is that of advocate. At first glance you would think that advocacy would not be a typical role the consultant takes on. As an advocate the consultant attempts to persuade the consultee to do something the consultant deems highly desirable. For example, a consultant relying on her superior knowledge about data collection in organizations might advocate the use of several methods in addition to what the consultee thinks is necessary. However, there is a trend toward looking at the advocacy role more in terms of "protecting the rights of those who are unable to help themselves, and seek due process, aid, and treatment for those persons" (Kurpius & Lewis, 1988, p. 1). In this sense advocacy is often combined with outreach: the promotion of available services to selected populations.

Consultants can act as advocates in a variety of ways (Kurpius & Lewis, 1988): as process consultants assisting groups in working effectively or becoming self-advocates; as identifiers of target groups needing advocacy, finding necessary resources and facilitating the advocacy attempts; and as agents who attempt to prevent target groups from needing advocacy at a later time.

On the one hand, consultants have a professional obligation not to engage in inappropriate advocacy roles (Remley, 1988). Yet they should not avoid situations that dictate that they become advocates. Some authors (for example, Conoley & Conoley, 1992; Kurpius & Lewis, 1988) promote a very positive view of advocacy, even to the point of calling it a type of consultation in and of itself.

However, to get a feel for the possible turmoil in which an advocacy role might place a consultant, consider the following: A school counselor is an advocate for a student (client system) identified as a possible dropout. Some school personnel (consultees) feel strongly that because the student cannot be adequately educated in the system as it stands, the student is better off in some setting other than the school. The counselor agrees that the system cannot meet the student's needs but maintains that it should obtain the resources to do so. This advocacy position places the counselor in a lose-lose situation. By attempting to change the system to benefit the client, the consultant risks losing consultee support. If the consultant does not attempt to change the system, the client may drop out.

There are times, situations, and issues for which advocacy is the most appropriate role for a consultant. One common example of an appropriate advocacy role is when the consultant detects within an organization a discrepancy between the way an organization is supposed to treat its clients and the way it actually treats them. Consultants can avoid misusing the advocacy role by maintaining a high level of self-awareness about such matters as poverty, racism, and value-related issues (Conoley & Conoley, 1985) and by maintaining a collaborative relationship with the consultee.

Expert The most common role that consultants take on is that of expert or technical advisor (Gallessich, 1982). In this circumstance the consultee needs some knowledge, advice, or service that the consultant can provide on request. When consultants are retained as experts over a long period of time, it seems apparent that the consultees (or organizations) retaining the consultants know what they need from the consultants. However, this is often not the case (Schein, 1988).

Consultants who consult with agencies about their programs—perhaps they are asked to make a diagnosis of what is wrong with an agency's client system—typically act in the role of expert. Consultants also function as experts when they are asked to recommend solutions to previously defined problems. For example, a consultant might recommend a training program in stress management for the members of the counseling department at a large secondary school. As in any other consulting role, the consultant does not treat the client system directly.

Consultants who engage in the role of expert need to be aware of the possibility that they can create dependence on the part of their consultees (Lippitt & Lippitt, 1986). The consultee can get used to having the consultant do the work and can effectively give the problem away to the consultant.

Consultants engaging in the expert role need to be aware that under such circumstances their consultees may not improve their own problem-solving abilities, especially if the consultant does not take the time and energy to help them to do so.

Here is an example using the expert role: Mary's parents ask you for assistance with their daughter, who is 9 years old and has only one friend. The friend uses Mary's vulnerability and frequently has Mary give up her toys and part of her lunch at school. You observe Mary at school a couple of times and watch her interact with many of her peers. You then write a brief report with specific suggestions for the parents to follow.

Trainer/Educator Very closely related to the role of expert is that of trainer/educator. Whereas the role of "technological advisor" does not imply change in the professional functioning of consultees, the role of a trainer/educator does. Consultants can engage in both formal and informal training and/or educating. Some authors (for example, Conoley & Conoley, 1992) contend that formal education/training activities such as workshops are not truly consultation because of the amount of preplanning involved. Others (for example, Lippitt & Lippitt, 1986) see the trainer/educator role as a legitimate and distinct approach to consultation itself (see also West & Idol, 1987). Perhaps these differences in viewpoint result because education is compared with consultation as if it were a different human service. One way to reconcile these different perspectives is to take the view that whereas consultants frequently train and educate, both formally and informally, this role is only one of a great many in which they engage.

Consultants are often asked to act in the capacity of trainer/educator. The role of trainer implies that the consultant has both the expertise in certain skills and the ability to create the conditions under which consultees can acquire those skills. The role of educator implies that the consultant possesses a body of knowledge that consultees desire and has the ability to teach them that knowledge. Formal training and education sessions usually take the form of workshops and seminars. For example, a consultant might train a group of program leaders in a human service agency in methods of motivating subordinates. Informal training/educating usually occurs between the consultant and the consultee during some other aspect of the consultation relationship. Thus, a consultant might teach a consultee how to gather baseline data on certain client behaviors.

One advantage of the trainer/educator role is that the consultee receives skills and/or knowledge that can perhaps be used repeatedly in the future, and thus the consultee's professional development is enhanced in some specific way. However, it is possible to erroneously assume that the consultee will actually use the newly acquired skills and knowledge in some way. Unless the consultant incorporates into the training the context in which the skills and knowledge are most useful, there is a strong likelihood that they will not be adequately put into practice in the future.

Consider this example, which uses the trainer/educator role: You are a practicing school consultant in a middle school. Your principal asks you to conduct some in-service training for the school staff on "Motivating the Underachieving Middle School Child." You agree to conduct the workshop and follow through.

Collaborator Consultants generally take a collaborative approach to consultation in that the consultant and consultee pool their resources and work together on the task of creating a successful consultation experience. Whereas the expert role in consultation acknowledges the consultee's need for assistance, the collaborator role acknowledges the consultant's need for the consultee's assistance. The consultee is encouraged to express his or her own ideas and modify the consultant's contributions. When used to describe consultants, *collaborator* refers to that role in which the consultant engages the consultee in a joint endeavor to accomplish a particular task at a particular time. The concept of complementarity is important in the collaborator role. Consultants do not perform for consultees tasks that the consultees could perform for themselves; they contribute expertise that consultees need to accomplish those tasks. Collaboration is frequently needed in identifying alternative solutions to a problem, in determining the positive and negative forces operating on various alternatives, and in making decisions about how to approach a given problem. You should note that collaboration, as a *role* for a consultant, is distinct from the *service* of collaboration. As I have noted earlier, in the service of collaboration, each collaborator takes responsibility for some aspect of the case.

In one example of a collaborative role, a consultant and a consultee might compare their observations of a client and come to a mutually agreed-upon diagnosis of the client's problem. In another case they might mutually agree on how much and what kinds of data need to be gathered about the consultee's organization.

Among the relatively few risks involved in engaging in the collaborator role is that consultants may not realize that they are affected by consultees' behavior. Perhaps the most common mistake human service professionals make as collaborators is to overestimate their consultees' abilities and consult in such a way that consultees' knowledge and skill inputs hinder effective consultation. To avoid this pitfall, consultants need some assessment of consultees' problem-solving abilities before assuming the collaborator role.

Conditions to enhance consultees' professional development are built into the role of collaborator. By participating in collaborative consultation, consultees' problem-solving skills are enriched for the future. In addition, their confidence is likely to increase because they feel a sense of contribution to the consultation process. Some limited empirical evidence suggests that consultees prefer a collaborative approach by consultants (Babcock & Pryzwansky, 1983).

The following example uses the collaborator role: You are a consultant working in a community mental health center with a colleague who has difficulty with a client. Together, you and the colleague pool your resources and contribute your respective strengths and abilities to resolve the difficulty.

Fact Finder The role of fact finder is one every consultant takes on frequently. In its simplest form it merely involves obtaining information. In the typical fact-finding role, the consultant gathers information, analyzes it, and feeds it back to the consultee (Lippitt & Lippitt, 1986). The consultant often takes on the fact-finding role to collect information necessary in clarifying or diagnosing a problem. Methods for gathering information include reading records, interviewing, observing, and surveying. (We will discuss several ways to gather information in Chapter 4.) Consultants can gather information on a consultee's client or on an entire organization. Fact finding can range from a simple, quickly accomplished task to a very complex, time-consuming one. A school psychologist (consultant) might administer an individual intelligence test to a student (client system) who is being seen by a school counselor (consultee) and report the findings back to the counselor. In another example, a consultant might design and send out a survey to an organization's members to determine the level of morale within the organization.

One question the consultant should ask before beginning fact-finding activities is, Why am I (and not the consultee) gathering this information? If the answers relate to lack of consultee expertise, political sensitivities, time constraints, or the consultant's need to learn more about the environment in which the problem is occurring, then the role of fact finder is a legitimate one. If the answer is because it's the consultant's job, not that of the consultee, to gather the facts, then the consultant should reexamine whether or not that role is appropriate.

Consider this example of a fact-finding role: You are consulting to determine why the personnel at a human service agency are exhibiting poor morale. You spend a great deal of time in the agency observing and interviewing personnel concerning the quality of

work life. You put the data together and interpret it for the head of the agency.

Process Specialist   The least directive role of the consultant is that of process specialist. When consultants take on the role of process expert, they focus more on the *how* than on the *what*. Instead of asking, What's going on? the process specialist asks, How are things going? When a problem is being solved, the consultant as process specialist does not examine the content but rather the problem-solving process itself. The focus is not so much on the nature of the problem-solving steps but on how those steps are accomplished. One approach to consultation with organizations, called process consultation, has as its major goal the enhancement of the consultee's understanding of the process events that affect everyday behavior (Schein, 1987, 1988). Two process roles seem to be emerging: the *process observer* role and the *process facilitator* role (Kormanski & Eschbach, 1997). In the process observer role, the consultant provides periodic feedback concerning the group's process, models problem-solving processes, assists the group in dealing with communication issues, and facilitates the group process. There has been some discussion that process consultation, although primarily a group consultation model, can be used with individual consultees and focus on the consultant-consultee interaction as a source of data. The point is, the process specialist works in such a manner that the consultee becomes a better and more independent problem solver in the future. We will discuss process consultation again in Chapter 9.

In one example of a process specialist role, a consultant might sit in on a school's faculty meeting and, at the end, ask the faculty questions to assist them in analyzing their interpersonal behavior relative to what was accomplished in the meeting. In this example the consultant merely puts into exploratory questions what he or she observed. In another case, a consultant might help an administrator learn how to have more effective meetings by using agendas. In this instance the consultant assists the consultee in making an intervention designed to give people more time to participate in meetings.

Because consultants typically focus on structure and content, they are often uncomfortable in the process specialist role. And because the role of process specialist frequently requires the consultant to work with more than one consultee, group process skills are necessary. One common mistake consultants make in the process specialist role is to assume they have permission to bring up interpersonal issues (Schein, 1988). Consultees should first ask if feedback is wanted or raise questions concerning interpersonal issues.

The following example illustrates the process specialist role: You are a consultant called on to help a team of middle-school teachers work "more effectively." You sit in on the group's meetings several times, get a sense for the group's "process," that is, how they do what they do, and then invite the group to examine their own functioning in a nondefensive manner.

Other Roles Other roles have also been suggested for consultants, including professional dissenter (Golembiewski, 1990), political strategist (Margulies, 1988), conceptual therapist (Raia, 1988), confidant (Greiner, 1988), cultural spokesperson (Lundberg, 1988), and raiser of expectations for increased productivity (Eden, 1990). However, these roles have not been as well defined as those already mentioned. Consequently, consultants will need to assess the

pros and cons of taking on any of these roles as they examine the organization in which they are consulting.

Clearly, consultants need to be able to move easily among the various roles described in this section or at least know their limitations to the degree that they can make referrals when appropriate (Schein, 1990c).

INTERNAL AND EXTERNAL CONSULTANTS

Consultants may or may not belong to the system in which consultation is to occur. An *internal consultant* is part of the organization in which consultation is occurring. An *external consultant* consults within an organization on a temporary basis. The entire consultation process remains the same regardless of the locus of the consultant.

Some authors (for example, Alpert & Silverstein, 1985; Brown et al., 1995) recommend that the concepts of internal and external consulting be viewed as ends of a continuum rather than as discrete entities. For example, an itinerant elementary school counselor may serve three different schools. Depending on one's viewpoint, the consultant can be seen as internal or external. A staff member at the school system's central office may note that, because the school counselor is employed by the system that runs the three schools and because everyone involved in the consultation also belongs to the school system, the counselor functions as an internal consultant. But consider another point of view: because the counselor is at a given school only infrequently, he or she is not really a part of that school. Thus, to most of the school's staff—those at the school every workday—the counselor is seen as an outsider, an external consultant. Therefore, whether the consultant is internal or external is determined to some degree by the perceptions of the members of the organization served by the consultation. Still other authors (for example, Bell & Nadler, 1985) suggest that the internal-external distinction receives too much attention since a consultant is always external to the problem to be resolved whether or not he or she is external or internal to the organization itself.

Is it more effective to be either an internal or an external consultant? The sparse empirical research on this matter reveals little. One study (Dekom, 1969), conducted decades ago, supports the contention that internal consultants can be effective. Case, Vandenberg, and Meredith (1990), in investigating managerial consultants, found that the value orientations of internal consultants are less likely than those of external consultants to reflect humanistic and democratic concerns, that external consultants were more likely to suggest structural changes in organizations than their internal counterparts, and that internal consultants were more likely to conduct more rigorous program evaluations than were external consultants. In extrapolating from this limited finding, there is one possible message for internal human service consultants: Don't get so caught up in the system that you lose your objectivity about the necessity for change.

It seems reasonable to suggest that effective consultants are effective whether or not they are permanently attached to the system receiving consultation. This contention is further supported by the fact that internal consultants are taking on many of the functions historically reserved for external consultants (Kelley, 1981). External consultants do, however, seem to be characterized by marginality; that is, they are only marginally admitted into the organization. They are likely to be objective, neutral, and comfortable with conflict, ambiguity, and stress (Goodstein, 1978; Tobias, 1990).

Many organizations with internal consultants hire external consultants with the expectation that the two work as a team (Kelley, 1981). Such a team approach can blend the objectivity, expertise, and "newness" of the external consultant with the knowledge of the organization, expertise, and continuity provided by the internal consultant.

There has been an interesting twist in the literature on internal consultants. In the past decade, there has been a movement to suggest that collaboration is preferred to consultation when delivered by professionals who are internal to the system. Because mental health or human resource specialists are considered experts in their area, they can provide and receive assistance from their fellow collaborators while also directly serving the client system. A driving force for this shift in thinking is that in organizations such as schools there is a very limited amount of time to assist clients and multiple treatment options can help compensate for this potential barrier to success.

CONSULTATION RESEARCH

As a practicing consultant you will want to verify that your practice is legitimate. One way to verify this is through examining the empirical foundations of consultation (Henning-Stout, 1993). Research in consultation is still in its infancy and is therefore not very sophisticated. Valid research findings can give direction to effective practice, but invalid findings can mislead the practitioner's attempts to determine appropriate consulting procedures. There is no easy way out of this dilemma. Since the current status of consultation research is both interesting and disappointing, it seems appropriate to warn consultants to read the literature very critically and with a healthy dose of skepticism.

Research on consultation usually involves one or more of the following areas: what consultants do (that is, consultant practice), the interaction between consultant and consultee (that is, consultation process), and the effectiveness of interventions (Froehle & Rominger, 1993).

Armenakis and Burdg (1988) note four types of consultation research, numbered in terms of increasing sophistication. First, there are experience-based writings (for example, case studies), typically written by the consultant, that describe a given consultation experience. Second, there is quasi-scientific research in which there is not adequate control over the variable being assessed, as distinguished from the third type, scientific research, which requires adequate control over the experimental conditions. The fourth type of research is meta-analysis, which attempts to tie together the results of several studies.

What do the results of the various types of research suggest about consultation? Meade, Hamilton, and Yeun (1982) pointed out long ago the difficulties surrounding research in consultation. In summarizing the research to date, these authors suggested that outcome studies found consultation to be effective (although they questioned the methodological soundness of most studies), that process studies were so limited that very few conclusions could be made, and that research on consultant characteristics was methodologically so poor that the whole area of research should be reconceptualized. They recommended that fu-

ture research use time-series designs in outcome studies, that consultation process studies utilize the case study method, and that multiple measures be used. They concluded:

> The state of research in consultation is that it is confused and inadequate; the paradox is that out of this muddle emerges a body of evidence suggesting that there is an enterprise (consultation) which is meaningful (effective) and which deserves greater clarification and elaboration (research). (p. 49)

Such was the state of consultation in 1982. After reviewing later research in organizational consultation, Armenakis and Burdg (1988) concluded that (1) the very limited scientific research on consultation creates a condition in which meta-analysis is not possible at this time; (2) organizational politics should be included as a research topic in consultation; (3) there is a need for more research on consultation success criteria; and (4) more research is needed on how consultation strategies are selected.

Schein (1993) suggests that consultants adopt a clinical research paradigm in conducting research on organizational consultation, which deals with very complex phenomena that are not assessable by traditional research paradigms. The essence of clinical research is that "someone in the organization has requested some form of help and that the researcher comes into the situation in response to the needs of the client, not his or her own need to gather data" (Schein, 1993, p. 703). So it is the organization's needs that provide the necessary condition for data to be available (Schein, 1993). Clinical researchers make hypotheses based on their experiences in the organization and test them by making interventions. They make use of their training in hypothesis formulation and observation, thus creating valid and useful clinical data.

In spite of the limitations just described, Golembiewski and Sun (1989), while acknowledging the limited scope of research efforts, still suggest after a critical review of the research literature that consultation efforts in the areas of organization development and quality of work life seem well worth their costs.

Duncan and Pryzwansky (1988) drew eight conclusions regarding research in human service consultation:

- Consultation research is still in its infancy.

- Reviews of research on consultation have been positive about its promise.

- Research in consultation typically has shown methodological flaws.

- As appreciation for the complexity of consultation has grown, so too has the sophistication of the research designs used to investigate it.

- Associated with this appreciation for consultation's complexity, there has been an actual decline in the number of doctoral dissertations investigating consultation.

- Schools are the most popular settings for consultation research.

- There is a disproportionate amount of research on process variables.

- Outcome variables should be included in all research.

In reviewing the research on school consultation, which appears to be more or less representative of research in other areas of human service consultation, Gresham and Kendall (1987) note that a lack of precision in defining consultation has led to a lack of precise research. They also note that most research is descriptive and has not considered environmental variables. The authors summarize the research in consultation in the following manner:

> Most consultation research can be described as limited in scope, univariate in nature, nonexperimental, devoid of a strong theoretical base, and unsophisticated in terms of research design and statistical treatment of data....Taken as a whole, the consultation literature can be characterized as a black box in which variables are poorly defined, poorly measured, and poorly controlled. (pp. 313–314)

Some of the more important things these authors describe that we know about consultation include the following:

- Most outcome research is conducted on behavioral consultation (see Bergan & Kratochwill, 1990).

- The empirical research support base is strongest for behavioral consultation.

- Dependent variables tend to include the frequency of consultation use by consultees and changes in clients, consultees, or both as a result of consultation.

- Long-term follow-up is typically a part of outcomes research.

- In process research, problem identification is the best predictor of problem solutions.

- Perceived communication skills of consultants by consultees is related to perceptions of consultant effectiveness.

- Consultees dislike jargon.

In a later review, Gibson and Chard (1994) evaluated 1,643 consultation outcomes using metanalysis. These authors concluded that consultation is at least moderately effective.

How can research in consultation continue to evolve? According to Froehle and Rominger (1993), five topics will need attention: (1) agreeing on a definition of consultation, (2) encouraging methodological diversity in consultation research, (3) addressing multi- and cross-cultural issues in consultation research, (4) enhancing the connection between research and practice, and (5) training consultants in research (pp. 694–695). Pryzwansky and Noblit (1990) suggest that case study approaches can be valuable assets in developing a knowledge base for consultation.

Dixon and Dixon (1993) add that consultation research can be improved through expanding the measures used to evaluate it and by defining its "boundary" conditions. They suggest that consultation outcome research should measure changes in the consultant and the consultee; in the interactions between the consultant, consultee, and client system; and in the system in which consultation is occurring. They further suggest that the boundaries of consultation be restricted to "an egalitarian relationship between consultant and consultee where . . . the focus is on a problem of a third party client, which . . . results in improvement in the client and in the abilities of the consultee" (p. 701). Gutkin (1993) notes that consultation research needs to move from defining the broad boundaries of consultation services to "qualitatively more refined and sophisticated levels of research . . . that will move us closer to answering questions such as what forms of consultation are most effective with which types of consultees having what kind of clients

with which sort of problems under what sets of circumstances" (p. 241).

Gresham and Noell (1993) add that future consultation research should address "socially significant goals, . . . using socially acceptable intervention methods that produce socially important, reliable, and cost-beneficial changes in behavior" (p. 269).

Kratochwill, Elliot, and Busse (1995) have suggested that future research in consultation needs to ensure stricter data presentation and collection procedures. These authors have also recommended that future research expand the use of effect sizes to allow for single-case and within-study meta-analyses (p. 116), thus allowing for an examination of connections between training and treatment outcomes.

Sheridan, Welch, and Orme (1996) reviewed consultation outcome research in educational settings from 1985–1995. They found that three-fourths of studies reported positive outcomes and that behavioral consultation research studies were most prevalent. The authors point out advances in methodological aspects of research such as design and multiple measures. Sheridan, Kratochwill, and Bergan (1996) found empirical support for change in both client system and consultee behaviors. These same authors investigated the research on consultation processes and determined that successful behavioral consultation was characterized by variables that included a cooperative attitude, clearly defined roles, and active involvement by all parties.

Such is the state of consultation research today. There are an increasing number of attempts to conduct valid research on consultation in both the human service and management consultation areas. Yet the research is very limited (Fuchs, Fuchs, Dulan, Roberts, & Fernstrom, 1992). For example, there is little if any research related to cross-cultural consultation (Duncan, 1995). Empirical research, however difficult it is to conduct, must be performed. As Gresham and Lopez (1996) note, "questions asked in consultation research often are not educationally relevant, treatment procedures used sometimes are either unrealistic or unacceptable in the daily practice of consultation, the target behaviors selected may not be the most relevant or important, and the results of consultation research frequently do not represent educationally or clinically important changes. In short, much of the consultation research appears to lack social validity" (p. 204). Again, consultants at this time should be hesitant and cautious about readily making any type of generalizations from most of the research in consultation. On the other hand, a summative view of the research, however limited, suggests that consultation has efficacy even if consultation practice has far outpaced the body of research on consultation (Dunson, Hughes, & Jackson, 1994).

SUMMARY

The characteristics of effective consultants result from their desire to grow personally and professionally, to acquire knowledge in consultation and human behavior, and to enhance their consulting skills. Consultants need interpersonal and communication skills that flow from a genuine attitude based on respect, as well as problem-solving skills, skills in working with groups and organizations, skills in dealing with cultural diversity, and skills in maintaining ethical and professional behavior.

Consultants take on a variety of roles during any given consultation, ranging from nondirective ones, such as process specialist, to directive ones, such as advocate. The role a consultant takes is a result of his or her abilities, the consultee's needs, and the nature of the problem.

The research on consultation is sparse. Although there is general support for the fact that consultation is an effective human service function, there is little specific guidance for practitioners. Research in the field needs to be read with a healthy skepticism.

SUGGESTIONS FOR

EFFECTIVE PRACTICE

- Make a commitment to try to consistently grow personally and professionally, increasingly learn about the knowledge of human behavior and consultation, and develop the skills of consultation.

- Practice the various roles that consultants and collaborators take on so that you can become comfortable with them.

- Develop each of the skills areas identified for effective consultants and collaborators.

- Become familiar with the empirical and qualitative research on consultation and collaboration as means to guide your practice.

QUESTIONS FOR REFLECTION

1. Which criteria indicate that you have an adequate personal and professional growth orientation as a consultant?

2. The basic attitudes from which a consultant's interpersonal and communication skills flow are critical to effective consulting practice. Why?

3. Why are interpersonal skills as important for the consultant as communication skills?

4. What are the most essential problem-solving skills for a consultant to possess? Why?

5. With which of the consultant roles discussed in this chapter do you feel most comfortable? Why?

6. Why are the skills in working with cultural diversity so critical?

7. What are the basic differences in consultant and consultee behavior when a consultant changes from a directive to a nondirective role?

8. What are the factors that determine the role a consultant will take on?

9. If you were a consultant starting a relationship with a consultee, what consultee characteristics would you consider especially crucial for successful consultation?

10. If the research results on consultation are so sketchy, how can consultants use them to enhance their effectiveness?

SUGGESTED SUPPLEMENTARY READINGS

Lippitt, G., and Lippitt, R. (1986). *The consulting process in action* (2nd ed.). La Jolla, CA: University Associates. Chapter 3, "Multiple Roles of the Consultant" presents a comprehensive approach to categorizing the many roles that consultants can take on. This article is a classic about consultation roles. The authors discuss each role and then speculate on the factors that influence when a given role will be taken on. Chapter 7, "The Consultant's Skills, Competencies, and Development," reflects a survey performed by the authors concerning the necessary components of an effective consultant. Skills, competencies, and attitudes are listed with sound rationales for their selection. These two chapters present a concise overview of the roles consultants can take on and the skills and attitudes necessary to fulfill them effectively.

Gresham, E. M., and Kendall, G. K. (1987). School consultation research: Methodological critique and future research directions. *School Psychology Review*, *16*, 303–316. Although this article deals with research issues in school consultation, a thorough reading of it will help you to appreciate the difficulties in conducting truly experimental research in consultation in any setting.

PART II

A Generic Model of Consultation and Collaboration

THE STAGES OF CONSULTATION AND COLLABORATION

Now that you have an idea of what consultation and collaboration are, what professionals do when they provide these services, and the skills they need, let's examine a generic model of consultation/collaboration. This model provides a framework for performing these services. It represents what counselors, psychologists, social workers and human resource specialists need to know to effectively consult and collaborate. As you can see in Figure II.1, consultation and collaboration follow a problem-solving format consisting of four stages: a relationship-building process, the definition of the problem, an implementation and evaluation of some plan, and a termination stage. Due to the relatively few empirical studies performed on the processes of consultation and collaboration, there are few cut-and-dried guidelines for effective practice. Therefore, you will find that putting the generic model to use is more an art than a science. Further you will note that, in every aspect of the problem-solving endeavor, the way consultees and fellow collaborators perceive your communication is every bit as important as what you actually say. Let me remind you that I will not use the phrase *consultation and collaboration* continuously throughout this and subsequent chapters; if there are differences between the two services at any of the stages, I will use the individual terms to differentiate.

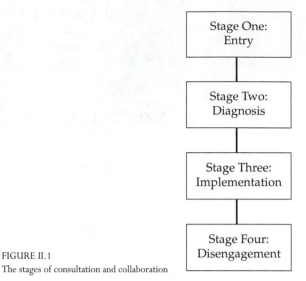

FIGURE II.1

The stages of consultation and collaboration

Stage One of the generic model represents the starting up of the consultation process. It is called *entry* because the consultant enters the organization and/or enters into relationships with consultees. In this stage, relationships are built, the parameters of the problem are examined, and a contract is agreed upon and made with consultees within the organization. This stage lays the foundation on which the remainder of the consultation rests.

Stage Two of this model is concerned with shedding light on the problem that was broadly examined during entry. In this stage, the problem is understood more clearly and deeply. The consultant and consultee set goals based on this understanding and begin to think of ways to meet those goals. The term *diagnosis* is used (as opposed to *problem definition*) because it implies an ongoing process.

Stage Three involves taking action to solve the problem: a plan is formulated, implemented, and evaluated. This stage is called *implementation* to reflect its primary focus on action and its secondary emphasis on planning.

Stage Four winds down the process; it is the period of disengagement. Consultation is evaluated and consultant involvement is reduced. Goodbyes are said and leave is taken. The term *disengagement* implies that the process of consultation goes through a gradual reduction in activity and is used instead of *termination*, which implies a more abrupt ending to the process.

Each of the four stages in the consultation process consists of four phases. I have chosen the term *phase* because it implies process, whereas terms like *step* imply more static events and fail to acknowledge that consultation is a very human endeavor that goes through its own life cycle. In a way, what McAuliffe (1993) said about career quests holds true for the process of consultation: it is "not random aimless activity for its own sake, but like the motion of a river, passing through many landscapes, its contents and shape changing along the way, while maintaining its essential identity" (p. 14).

There is nothing magical in having four phases for each stage; they merely result from the way I choose to view the consultation process. Other authors characterize the process differently (see Lippitt & Lippitt, 1986; Kurpius & Robinson, 1978; Stum, 1982; Sullivan, 1991). The important thing to remember at this point is that consultation can be divided into certain stages and phases. The stages (and the phases within them) frequently can overlap, depending on what happens during consultation. For example, while a consultant and consultee are in the process of implementing a plan, a different aspect of the problem might emerge that would require returning to the diagnosis stage. Further, some experts consider the implementation stage to occur continuously; that is, each of the consultant's actions during the entire consultation process is viewed as an implementation. You should note that it is normal, in real-life consultation and collaboration, for there to be movement back and forth between the various phases and stages (Curtis & Stollar, 1995). This generic model describes the consultation process in a general enough manner to include most of the models we will be examining later on in this text and provides a set of guidelines and behaviors to follow irrespective of the particular model you implement.

THE PHASES OF THE ENTRY STAGE

Stage One, entry, consists of the following phases:

- exploring organizational needs
- contracting
- physically entering the system
- psychologically entering the system

Exploring organizational needs refers to the process in which the consultant, consultee, and perhaps other parties-at-interest discuss the concerns that brought them together and then determine whether consultation should proceed. *Contracting* refers to the process of formalizing the agreement that consultation should take place. Expectations for all parties involved are stated in the contract, as are fees for services to be rendered and deadlines to be met. When a consultant *physically enters the system*, relationships are built, a work site obtained, the organization studied, and contact with the consultee begun. *Psychologically entering the system* entails the ongoing process in which the consultant gains acceptance as a temporary member of the organization. This phase actually lasts the duration of the consultation process, and it is a task that requires continual attention if consultation is to be fully successful.

THE PHASES OF THE DIAGNOSIS STAGE

Once the entry is accomplished, the consultation process proceeds to the diagnosis stage, which consists of the following phases:

- gathering information
- defining the problem
- setting goals
- generating possible interventions

When *gathering information*, the consultant and consultee also attempt to increase the chances of understanding the problem by isolating factors that are precipitating it. Data can be gathered through a variety of means, including surveys, interviews, observations, and examination of records. When *defining the problem*, the consultant and consultee analyze and interpret the data that have been gathered. It is especially important for the consultant and consultee to remain objective during this phase. A biased interpretation of the data can lead to an erroneous definition of the problem. Once the problem has been defined to the satisfaction of the parties involved, *setting goals* to overcome the problem occurs. The consultant has the responsibility to make sure that any goal that is set meets the criteria of being an effective goal. Once goals have been set, the consultant and consultee move on to *generating possible interventions* that could resolve the problem.

THE PHASES OF THE IMPLEMENTATION STAGE

Once a list of possible strategies has been generated, the consultation process moves to Stage Three, implementation, which includes:

- choosing an intervention
- formulating a plan
- implementing the plan
- evaluating the plan

This stage begins with *choosing an intervention* or group of interventions—activities the consultant and consultee think have the best chance of effectively

solving the problem. Using these interventions, the consultant and consultee em-
bark on *formulating a plan* that incorporates these interventions. The pros and cons
of a variety of possible plans are carefully scrutinized until the best plan is chosen
and tailored to the unique requirements of the client and/or the organization. In
collaboration, each party involved is assigned to and responsible for carrying out a
part of the plan. The third phase is *implementing the plan*, and the consultant usually
monitors the plan's progress once it has been implemented. In collaboration, unlike consultation, the human service professional takes responsibility for the mental health aspects of the case and is hence part of the implementation process. In
collaboration, the parties involved carry out their pieces of the plan and provide
ongoing assistance to one another as necessary. The final phase is *evaluating the plan*
once implementation has been completed. Based on the results of the evaluation,
the consultation process moves either back to a previous phase of some stage (for
example, defining the problem) or on to the stage of disengagement.

THE PHASES OF THE DISENGAGEMENT STAGE

Stage Four, disengagement, consists of the following phases:

- evaluating the consultation process
- planning postconsultation matters
- reducing involvement and following up
- terminating

Evaluating the consultation process can range from assessing consultee satisfaction
with consultation to measuring the impact of a system-wide intervention on the
behavior of the members of an organization. Evaluation must be a planned event so
that consultant and consultee alike will know what will be evaluated, by whom,
how, and when. *Planning postconsultation matters* involves deciding how the effects of
consultation are going to be maintained by the consultee and/or the organization.
This phase is essential in increasing the probability that follow-through occurs after
the consultant's involvement ends. *Reducing involvement* is the phase in which the
consultant creates conditions of decreasing contact with the consultee. This is also
the time when more and more responsibility for the results of consultation is taken
on by the consultee. *Follow-up* is the process in which the consultant monitors this
transfer of responsibility so as to iron out any unforeseen problems. *Terminating* is
the formal ending of the consultation process. It has professional aspects (for example, collecting final fees) and a personal side (for example, saying goodbye). Effective
consultants successfully accomplish both the professional and personal sides of termination (Dougherty, Tack, Fullam, & Hammer, 1996).

PUTTING THE GENERIC MODEL
INTO PRACTICE

There are three important points to make about putting the generic model of consultation into practice. First, consultation is a dynamic, interactive process that uses the various stages as needed (Meyers & Yelich, 1989). Things rarely, if ever, go in a textbook fashion. Equal attention should be paid both to *what* you are doing and to *how* you are doing those things.

Second, it is very important to get supervised practice in consultation. By "trying on" the model and putting it into practice, you can get a sense of yourself as a consultant. The more experience you get, the higher the probability that you will increase your effectiveness as a consultant.

Third, the collective wisdom concerning consultation suggests that the generic model be implemented in a collaborative manner whenever possible. You should be aware, however, that there is very little empirical evidence to support this point of view. Therefore, your own experience in each consultation will assist you in determining what roles to take on. Some limited empirical evidence suggests that consultants should be at least minimally in charge of the consultation process (Witt, 1990a; Gutkin, 1996). Consultees tend to view some degree of consultant dominance in which they follow the consultant's leads as being positive (Erchul & Chewning, 1990). Erchul and Chewning (1990) intimate that consultants may be more in control of their consultation relationships than they realize and that this control is positively perceived by consultees as indicating consultant competency. You may want to examine with your consultees the degree of your directiveness and their reaction to it during your supervised practice. For example, you may want to gain feedback from consultees regarding your questioning style (Hughes & DeForest, 1993). In collaboration, you will often be viewed as the expert in a certain area relative to the goals of helping the client system. For example, a school counselor might be viewed as the most knowledgeable about a child's capacity for learning.

AN EXAMPLE

The following two case studies are designed to show how the consultation and collaboration processes generally work. Although oversimplified, they will provide concrete examples to which you can continue to refer as you read and study the next five chapters. They represent idealized cases—for consultation and collaboration, like other human service activities, rarely proceed so smoothly—but, nonetheless, they provide a rough outline of how the processes work.

CASE II.1   Consultation

Assume that you are a school counselor who is going to act as a consultant. Your consultee is a schoolteacher and the client is a student of the teacher. You meet with the teacher, who discusses the behavior of the student, particularly the fact that the student rarely turns in homework. You help the teacher explore the problem and at the same time build rapport with him. You both agree that working on the homework problem is mutually agreeable, so you contract to meet three or four times to work on that problem. You agree to observe the student in the teacher's classroom and continue to use effective communication skills and gain the teacher's acceptance of you as a person he can trust. At this point you have completed the entry stage.

You and the teacher now start to gather information on the student; together you examine the student's cumulative folder. The teacher keeps track of when homework is not turned in and the conditions surrounding that behavior. Based on the data, you note that the student does not turn in homework on Tuesdays and Fridays but

does on the other school days. An interview with the student's parents reveals that they both attend school on Monday and Thursday nights and that the child is left with a babysitter. Based on this information you and the teacher redefine the problem as lack of parental supervision on Monday and Thursday nights. You and the consultee set the goal of having the student turn in all homework every other Tuesday and Friday for the first month, and every Tuesday and Friday thereafter. When generating possible strategies you come up with several ideas, which include the loss of recess time when homework is not turned in and the use of a parent-child contract for getting the homework done. You have now completed the diagnosis stage; you are ready to begin the implementation stage.

Weighing the pros and cons of each intervention, you and the teacher determine that the parent-child contract is the best alternative. You then formulate a plan that consists of obtaining parental cooperation and assisting in the formulation of a parent-child contract for getting homework completed

on the nights the parents are not home. When the parents agree to the plan, you and the teacher assist them in carrying it out. Strategies for appropriately reinforcing both the child and parents are included. The parents carry out the plan effectively; based on your evaluation, the goal has been met. The third stage, implementation, has just been accomplished. Now you go on to the disengagement stage.

In this final stage, you have the teacher rate his satisfaction with your efforts to assist him during each of the previous three stages. You then lay the groundwork concerning the way he will carry on with the student after you cease consulting. You check in with the teacher every two weeks or so to see how things are going. A month or so after your last contact you follow up to make sure that the homework is still being turned in. Toward the end of the next grading period you again check in about the student's performance. Because everything is proceeding well, you and the teacher agree to terminate consultation.

THE CRITICAL NATURE OF INTERPERSONAL COMMUNICATION IN THE GENERIC MODEL

As you implement the generic model you will soon discover the critical importance of effective interpersonal communication. You'll find that high levels of interpersonal communication skills are prerequisite to effective practice in consultation and collaboration. By being skillful in the ability to send and receive messages and develop relationships, consultants are more likely to engage in successful consultation practice (Dougherty, 1996–97). For example, the exchange of

CASE II.2   Collaboration

Assume that you are a school counselor who is going to act as a collaborator. Your fellow collaborator is a schoolteacher and the client is a student of the teacher. You meet with the teacher, who discusses the behavior of the student, particularly the fact that the student rarely turns in homework. You help the teacher explore the problem and at the same time build rapport with him. You both agree that working on the homework problem is mutually agreeable, so you contract to meet three or four times to work on that problem. You agree to observe the student in the teacher's classroom and continue to use effective communication skills and gain the teacher's acceptance of you as a person he can trust. At this point you have completed the entry stage.

You and the teacher now start to gather information on the student; together you examine the student's cumulative folder. The teacher keeps track of when homework is not turned in and the conditions surrounding that behavior. Based on the data, you both note that the student does not turn in homework on Tuesdays and Fridays but does on the other school days. An interview with the student's parents reveals

that they both attend school on Monday and Thursday nights and that the child is left with a babysitter. Based on this information you and the teacher redefine the problem as lack of parental supervision on Monday and Thursday nights. You and the teacher set the goal of having the student turn in all homework every other Tuesday and Friday for the first month, and every Tuesday and Friday thereafter. When generating possible strategies you come up with several ideas, which include the loss of recess time when homework is not turned in and the use of a parent-child contract for getting the homework done. You have now completed the diagnosis stage; you are ready to begin the implementation stage.

Weighing the pros and cons of each intervention, you and the teacher determine that the parent-child contract is the best alternative. You then formulate a plan that consists of obtaining parental cooperation and assisting in the formulation of a parent-child contract for getting homework completed on the nights the parents are not home. When the parents agree to the plan, you and the teacher assist them in carrying it out. Strategies for appropri-

ately reinforcing both the child and parents are included. You agree to counsel the child concerning the issues related to the child's lack of academic performance when the child is not under parental supervision. The parents carry out the plan effectively; based on your evaluation, the goal has been met. In evaluating your work with the student, you determine that the goals have been met. The third stage implementation, has just been accomplished. Now you go on to the disengagement stage.

In this final stage, you and the teacher rate your satisfaction with your respective efforts to assist one another. You then lay the groundwork concerning the way each of you will carry on with the student after you cease the collaboration process. You check in with each other every two weeks or so to see how things are going. A month or so after your last contact you follow up to make sure that the homework is still being turned in. Toward the end of the next grading period you again check in about the student's performance. Because everything is proceeding well, you and the teacher agree to terminate.

accurate and meaningful information with consultees can facilitate more effective problem solving and aid in the maintenance of cross–cultural relationships. You will also want to be aware of timing issues related to use of various interpersonal interventions. For example, some empirical research suggests that confrontation is better used in the latter stages of the consultation process (Dougherty, Henderson, Tack, et al., 1997; Dougherty, Henderson, & Lindsey, 1997). The team aspects inherent in most collaboration activities also dictate effective and skillful communication.

PERSONALIZING THE CONSULTATION AND
COLLABORATION PROCESS

Discussing consultation and collaboration in terms of stages and phases leaves out the human side of the process. As a consultant or collaborator, you are your best intervention (Bellman, 1990). That is, who you are as a person can affect the outcome of consultation or collaboration as much as what you do when you engage in these services. To include this human side, let's personalize the process of consultation and collaboration by showing the ways that you can "be there" for the people with whom you are working. I developed this idea after reading Gerard Egan's book *The Skilled Helper* (1998). Egan describes his counseling model as a series of steps for "being with" clients. Here is how you can be there for the people with whom you're working throughout the phases of the consultation process:

1. Listen well at the outset and take the time to build rapport.
2. Assist in formulating a contract that will make explicit the expectations you have for each other.
3. Start the consultation/collaboration process on the consultee's or collaborator's turf as soon as possible.
4. Proactively attempt to gain acceptance, not only by the consultee or fellow collaborator, but also by the organization in which the service is being provided.
5. Do your best to determine what information should be gathered on the problem and how best to do it.
6. Attempt to be unbiased as you assist in analyzing and interpreting the gathered data.
7. Ensure that the goals you and the consultee or collaborator set are effective goals that have a good probability of being successfully accomplished.
8. Be as creative and sharp as you can be when it comes to generating possible interventions.
9. Assist in examining the pros and cons of each possible intervention you and the consultee or collaborator consider.
10. Collaborate in putting together the best possible plan and considering the available resources.
11. Be available, as a consultant, to monitor the progress that is being made and as a collaborator to fulfill your part of the plan.
12. Provide assistance and encouragement in evaluating the plan.

13. Ask for evaluations of yourself and your services.

14. Assist in planning what needs to be done regarding the consultation or collaboration after you have left the scene.

15. Avoid dependence by the consultee or fellow collaborator through a gradual reduction in your involvement and foster their independence through intermittent follow-ups.

16. Say goodbye professionally and personally and let go of the relationship when that is in everyone's best interest.

My main goal in this part of the book is to provide you with an understanding for how to go about the general process of conducting consultation and collaboration. In the following chapters, I also provide a brief assessment of the state of research where appropriate. I should caution you that the research on consultation stages is quite limited, most often involves organizational or behavioral consultation, and, like other research in consultation, is difficult to assess. The research concerning collaboration is almost nonexistent and much of it is embedded in the research on consultation. As you read the next several chapters, I also hope that you will gain an appreciation of the complexity of the ethical, professional, and legal issues that surround the consultation/collaboration process. A final goal is for you to become aware of some of the pragmatic issues involved in consulting such as the influence of the organization in which consultation occurs.

3

Entry Stage

Just like a good novel, the consultation process should have a beginning, a middle, and an end. Frequently referred to as *start-up activities*, the entry stage can consist of one telephone call or several exploratory meetings. Throughout this stage the consultant and the organization contact person try to determine how advantageous consultation can be. The consultant should bear in mind that the success of the consultation depends in part on how well these start-up activities are accomplished (Brown & Kurpius, 1985). It is important to note that consultants will also have to "enter" every relationship they form with consultees.

The purpose of this chapter is to explain this beginning, or entry, stage of the consultation process. Entry, as both a distinct stage of consultation and a process in which the consultant begins to create relationships within the consultee organization, is complex and consists of four phases: exploring organizational needs, contracting, physically entering the organization's system, and psychologically entering the system. Here are five questions to consider as you read this chapter:

1. In what ways is the entry stage a complex process?

2. Why is the entry stage both a critical and delicate stage of consultation?

3. How directive should a consultant be in guiding the course of consultation during the entry stage?

4. There is more to a contract than what is written on the paper. What are the implications of the preceding statement for consultants?

5. How can a consultant psychologically enter the consultation system effectively and efficiently?

INTRODUCTION

To get a feel for the entry stage, consider the following situation:

Case Example

You are a professor of human services at a state university. A former student, now director of advising at a nearby community college, telephones and wants to come and talk with you about enhancing the quality of advising services at the community college. You set up an appointment, which will take place in your office.

During the appointment you assist the advising director in exploring the advising office's specific needs in regard to enhancing the quality of advising. You ask the director to make up a wish list to stimulate preliminary exploration. You ask what is going well and what is not going so well. You ask about the organizational environment in which advising occurs, and you ask for the advisors' views on the process of advising, its rewards, the level of administrative support for advising, and the advising director.

Based on this information, you agree to conduct two sessions with all the advisors. The first session is a workshop on effective advising, the second a troubleshooting meeting with the advisors to help them feel more heard by the parties involved in coordinating advising services. You and the advising director sign a contract to that effect.

The week before the workshop, you visit the community college and all of the work-

shop participants. You are supportive and ask them what things they would like to talk about. Next you arrange for the room at the community college in which the workshop is to occur. Then, when you open the first session, you ask the participants what they want and what they do not want out of the workshop.

Entry is the general process by which the consultant enters the system in which consultation is to occur. Glidewell (1959), in a now classic article, defines entry by an external consultant as the attachment of a consultant to an existing social system through the creation of temporary membership in an organization for a person who is to help that system. This temporary membership is accomplished by creating relationships that assist in determining which functions a consultant should provide to best help the organization accomplish its ends. Internal consultants (those permanently employed by the organization in which they consult) also have to enter, in that each consultation situation is new to them. Figure 3.1 shows the four phases of the entry stage of consultation.

PHASE ONE: EXPLORING ORGANIZATIONAL NEEDS

Consultation typically begins when a representative of an organization contacts a consultant for the purpose of *exploring* the possibilities of initiating a consulting relationship. It is not unusual for an organization to contact a consultant without knowing the precise or even the appropriate reason why consultation is needed. In fact, the toughest aspect of entry is making a quick and accurate assessment of what is troubling the organization. Some authors (Conoley

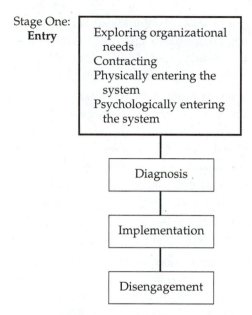

Stage One:
Entry

Exploring organizational
  needs
Contracting
Physically entering the
  system
Psychologically entering
  the system

Diagnosis

Implementation

Disengagement

FIGURE 3.1
The phases of the entry stage

& Conoley, 1992; Goodstein, 1978) note that rarely does an organization use refined techniques to determine its need for a consultant, and frequently the organization has misidentified its problem. Therefore, consultants should be cautious about moving too quickly into planning action during the beginning of the entry process.

Whether or not there is a firm grasp on what is needed in consultation, an organization usually contacts a consultant because it perceives it has a concern that cannot be solved within the organization or because there is an unfilled gap within the organization (Schein, 1988). In contrast, the process can also begin when a consultant contacts an organization and attempts to sell consultation services related to the typical concerns of organizations.

Before actual physical and psychological entry into the organization occurs, the consultant must deal with certain preentry issues (Cherniss, 1976, 1993), for example, whether the consultant appears to be the right person to

help the organization and determining the things to focus on during consultation. Other issues include dealing with disagreements, for example, on the nature of the problem as well as issues related to whose interests are being served and the ramifications of that choice (Cherniss, 1993). The process of considering these issues usually begins with an exploratory meeting referred to as the *first contact*.

First contact may be initiated by either party and usually involves the organization's contact person, perhaps some parties-at-interest (stakeholders), and the consultant. Ideally those involved should be knowledgeable about consultants and favorable toward their use (Schein, 1988).

The initial meeting for exploring organizational needs can occur either at the organization or in a neutral setting such as a restaurant (Gallessich, 1982). The advantage for meeting at the organization is that it allows the consultant on-site observations of the organization and the ways its personnel interact. There, the serious nature of the consultation relationship is reinforced because the meeting is not in a social setting. The advantages of meeting in a neutral site are that it gives the organization's contact personnel more of a sense of control and provides an informal setting that minimizes pressures to commit to a contract for consultation services.

Determining whether Consultation Should Take Place

The primary decision to be made during the preliminary exploration of organizational needs is whether or not consultation should be undertaken. There are six issues that relate to this decision:

- the degree of congruence between the consultant and the consultee system (Gallessich, 1982; Matthews, 1983) (for example, as regards value systems)
- the amount of resources the organization is willing to commit toward change (Lippitt & Lippitt, 1986) (for example, the amount of administrative sanctioning for consultees' participation)
- the appropriateness of the consultee's or the organization's characteristics (Mann, 1983; Matthews, 1983; Pipes, 1981) (for example, the amount of flexibility within the organization with regard to the changes consultation may involve)
- the ways in which the organization perceives the need for change (Mann, 1983) (for example, the degree to which prospective consultees see consultation as important in meeting the organization's goals)
- mutual understanding of the expectations for consultation (Cherniss, 1976, 1993)

(for example, the consultant and consultees being able to agree on how consultation should proceed and on desirable outcomes for all parties involved)

- agreement on who constitutes the consultee system, the client system, and parties-at-interest (Matthews, 1983; Golembiewski, 1993c) (for example, the consultant agrees to consult only with the crisis intervention team in a mental health center regarding approaches in counseling their clients)

Four questions shared by the consultant and the organization's contact person help to determine whether or not consultation is necessary and worthwhile: Why am I here? Who are you? What is likely to happen? What will be the result? (Bell & Nadler, 1985). The degree to which the four questions are answered to the satisfaction of both the consultant and the contact person eventually determines the success of the preliminary exploration of the organization's needs (Bell & Nadler, 1985).

The answers to these questions constitute the *task of familiarization*, during which consultants learn the ins and outs of the organization—for example, its history, mission, philosophy, and procedures (Caplan & Caplan, 1993; Jarvis & Nelson, 1967). Another part of this task is determining what the organization has done so far to solve its perceived problems, to what degree these activities were successful, and what factors prevented them from being more successful (Mann, 1983).

Why Am I Here?

The question Why am I here? is important to contact person and consultant alike. From the contact person's perspective, this question concerns perceived need. From the consultant's perspective, the question involves assisting the consultee in defining an appropriate problem or concern and assessing whether the consultant is the right person for the job.

Who Are You?

The question Who are you? concerns defining the roles taken on by the consultant, contact person, and others involved in consultation (Bell & Nadler, 1985). Answering this question entails identifying the roles and responsibilities of the consultant and the contact person (Cooper & Hodges, 1983). By discussing views, attitudes, and perceptions pertinent to organizational needs, values, and working styles, the consultant and contact person can determine the "goodness of fit" (Glidewell, 1959) between the perceived needs and the consultant's abilities pertinent to those needs. In determining their respective roles, both consultant and contact person need to remember that they represent their respective organizations as well as themselves (Caplan & Caplan, 1993; Caplan, Caplan, & Erchul, 1994).

What Is Likely to Happen?

The third question, What is likely to happen? really asks about means and ends: What is the goal of consultation? How will the goal be accomplished?

What Will Be the Result?

The fourth question is What will be the result? From the consultant's perspective, this concerns how the impact of consultation will be assessed and evaluated. From the contact person's perspective, the answer depends on how much change the consultation requires.

What Can Go Wrong

The initial exploration of the organization's needs can go awry due to inadequacies in both the consultant's and the contact person's behavior. What Ford (1979) noted long ago still holds today: a consultant can jeopardize the consultation relationship during the entry phase in several ways:

- fail to identify the real problem
- promise too much
- fail to specify consultant roles adequately
- fail to recognize a lack of competence with respect to the identified problem
- fail to adapt to the organization's particular problems and concerns

By bearing these potential pitfalls in mind and by monitoring their own behavior accordingly, consultants can frequently save the consultation process from difficulties.

Consultees can also prevent entry from proceeding smoothly. The following are some of the many things a consultee or contact person can do during the entry phase to jeopardize the consultation relationship:

- fail to screen a prospective consultant properly
- neglect to clarify how the consultant intends to operate within the system
- fail to clarify specific expectations of the consultant's role and behavior
- fail to identify the organization's problem accurately
- fail to explain to the consultant how the organization's resource limitations might affect the potential consultation experience

Consultants must be aware of these potential pitfalls as they assist the organization's contact person in exploring the organization's needs. Perhaps the best way to prevent such pitfalls is by allotting sufficient time to develop a mutual understanding, which leads to open communication and discussions that are as specific and detailed as possible. Effective questioning by the consultant is particularly important in avoiding these pitfalls.

A Brief Example of Exploring Organizational Needs   A mental health consultant is approached by the members of a religious organization to help them develop a program for enhancing the self-esteem of its youth group members. The consultant meets with three members of the organization's governing board and the youth group leader. Together the group explores the possibilities of what such a program might look like, the history of the program's idea, and the consultant's comparable experience. The consultant is satisfied that she can assist, and the consultees believe that she can be of assistance. The resources necessary for program development are available, and everyone agrees on what is expected from the parties involved. The consultant agrees to draw up and submit a proposal and contract to the board.

In summary, preliminary exploration of the organization's needs includes deciding who the consultees and client system will be, determining the consultant's role in the consultation process, and defining the organization's responsibility with regard to expectations about the consultant (Weisbord, 1984). Once this has been adequately accomplished and it is determined that consultation should occur, the information gathered in this phase can be used in contracting.

PHASE TWO: CONTRACTING

With a decision that consultation is to take place, the consultant and the consultee or contact person begin to discuss and negotiate the terms of consultation (Gallessich, 1982). This activity begins the phase of *contracting*. A good contract not only provides mutual understanding of the consultation process and clarifies roles and responsibilities, but it can also provide legal protection for consultants (Remley, 1993).

The Nature of Contracts

Every relationship is based on expectations, which, in the context of the consultation relationship, are usually made explicit in formal contracts (Blake & Mouton, 1983; Kolb & Frohman, 1970). The term *contract* has a variety of meanings when used in the delivery of human services. A contract in consultation is between the consultant and the organization and is typically an oral or written agreement that defines the parameters and character of the consultation relationship (Conoley & Conoley, 1992; French & Bell, 1990; Maas & Mann-Feder, 1994). In consultation relationships, the contract is an agreement "spelling out the expectations and obligations of each party, the frequency of meetings, the scheduling of appointments and access to personnel in the consultee system, the data to be collected, the provisions for review and modification of the program, and the amount and manner of payment of any fees involved" (Mann, 1983, p. 108). The contract reflects and clarifies the shared understanding between consultant and organization in three critical areas: what each expects from the relationship; how much time each will invest, as well as when and at what cost; and which ground rules the parties involved will follow (Weisbord, 1985, p. 306). When adequately worded, a contract provides a general guide for the consultation process, clarifies the roles and expectations of the parties involved, and provides a form of self-protection for both the consultant and the organization (Blake & Mouton, 1983; Caplan, Caplan, & Erchul, 1994; Kelley, 1981).

The contract can be oral, an exchange of letters, or a formal document. In collaboration, contracting is often informal, with the parties involved agreeing to take responsibility for the aspects of the case related to their area of expertise. The consultant should bear in mind, however, that a detailed written contract has the advantages of framing participants' roles and providing a focus for evaluating consultation services. In fact, Kirby (1985) suggests that any oral contract be followed up with a letter that states what has been agreed upon. Whatever form a contract takes, its particulars must be clear. Some authors (for example, Wilcoxon, 1990) recommend a formal, written contract at all times as a legal safeguard for the consultant.

The specificity of a contract depends upon how precisely the problem has been defined. A contract can be quite explicit, as in an agreement between labor and management, or it can be broad, as in a marriage contract (Blake & Mouton, 1983). To the degree that the contract is structured and specific, the consultant's role will be relatively constant. To the degree that the contract is general and unstructured, the consultant's role may vary (Lippitt & Lippitt, 1986). Since the matter of specificity can be an issue, it must be agreed upon when the contract is being drawn up (Alpert, 1982b). It is in the consultant's best interest to make the contract as specific as possible (Caplan, Caplan, & Erchul, 1994).

The stage of change in which the consultee's problem exists can be an important factor in developing the contract. There are typically four stages of change during which the consultee may seek help (Kurpius, Fuqua, & Rozecki, 1993): the *development* stage, as a problem begins; the *maintenance* stage, once a problem is established; the *declining* stage, when an existing problem begins to get worse; and the *crisis* stage, when the consultee is in dire need of immediate assistance. The consultant, through the use of judicious questioning, can determine the existing stage of change and create an appropriate contract (Kurpius, Fuqua, & Rozecki, 1993).

A contract has both formal and psychological aspects (Schein, 1988). The formal aspect of a contract covers such things as services to be rendered, type and amount of payment, and the length of consultation (Bell & Nadler, 1985). The psychological aspect of a contract refers to what each party hopes to gain from the relationship. The "psychological contract" is based on interpersonal trust, which cannot be put in writing, and it reflects a collaborative effort between the consultant and the organization's contact person concerning what each expects from the consultation process (Boss, 1985, 1993).

The Formal Aspects of a Contract

The formal aspects of contracting refer to the types of contracts used and their elements. There are several types of contracts that can be used in consultation. Consultants should be willing to help the contact person choose the type of contract that the nature of the consultation dictates. For an excellent discussion of contract types, consult Matthews (1983). Whatever type of contract is used, its development should be a joint venture by all parties involved in the consultation (Armenakis, Burdg, & Metzger, 1989).

Elements of a Contract

To develop and maintain a good working relationship between the consultant and the organization, certain key issues pertinent to the consultation should be covered in the contract (Matthews, 1983). A well-defined contract will minimize the possibilities of role conflicts, dual role relationships, and resistance—all of which can contaminate the consultation relationship. All consultation contracts should cover the following elements (Gallessich, 1982, pp. 272–273):

- general goals of consultation
- tentative time frame
- consultant's responsibilities (including services to be provided, methods to be used, time to be committed to the agency, evaluation of the degree to which goals are achieved)
- agency's responsibilities (such as nature and extent of staff contributions to consultation, fees to be paid to consultant [including expenses])
- consultant's boundaries (including the contact person to whom the consultant is to be responsible; people to whom the consultant is to have access [and those who are out of bounds]; consultant's access to departments, meetings, and documents; conditions for bringing in other consultants or trainees; and confidentiality rules regarding all information)
- arrangements for periodic review and evaluation of the consultant's work; explication of freedom of either party to terminate the contract if consultation progress is unsatisfactory

Figure 3.2 is a sample contract between a school system and a mental health consultant who is going to consult with school counselors and psychologists concerning ways of helping teachers manage stress effectively. This sample represents a relatively informal, simple contract that contains only those elements pertinent to the nature of the consultation.

The Psychological Aspects of a Contract

Contracting has psychological as well as formal aspects. The psychological aspect reflects a partnership in which the consultee's investment in the consultant's abilities is balanced by the consultant's investment in the opportunity to consult provided by the consultee (Bellman, 1990). The psychological aspects of a contract refer to the set of expectations that govern the consultation relationship (Boss, 1985, 1993). These expectations are not always directly communicated, agreed upon, or written down; however, they are more crucial to the consultation's success than a legal contract, and once broken they are difficult to repair (Kelley, 1981). The psychological contract is very important in collaboration because each of the parties involved has some responsibility for directly helping the client system. Therefore, early in the relationship it is imperative that the consultant assess and shape any expectations deliberately or unwittingly withheld by the organization's contact person (Schein, 1988). In effect, the consultant must determine what psychological and business needs are to be met through consultation. The psychological contract needs to be based on mutual honesty, realism, and interpersonal sensitivity (Boss, 1993). The following

Beach Town School System
Beach Town, USA

Contract

This is a contract between the Beach Town School System, herein called the party of the first part, and Jan Clovis, herein referred to as the party of the second part. This contract is entered into on the sixth day of February 2000 as follows:

The party of the second part agrees to serve as a consultant between March 6 and April 3, 2000, by providing education and training concerning stress management techniques for teachers to the counselors and psychologists employed by the party of the first part. Specifically, the party of the second part agrees to serve as a workshop leader and trainer for five days (each day from 9 A.M. to 4 P.M.): March 6, 13, 20, 27, and April 3 in the Beach Town School System workshop "Teaching Teachers Effective Stress Management Techniques." The party of the second part further agrees to conduct evaluations of the workshop participants' learning relative to the goals of the workshop and, with the permission of the participants, to share those evaluations with the contact person designated by the party of the first part. The party of the second part agrees to use Bernie Thompson, staff development director of the Beach Town School System, as the contact person for all matters pertaining to this consultation, including the possible use of additional consultants or the addition of other consultees as participants in the workshop.

The party of the first part agrees to pay the party of the second part a total of one thousand five hundred dollars ($1,500) plus expenses for travel and materials upon completion of the consultation services. The party of the second part also agrees to provide materials (including audiovisuals) as long as the request for such is made by February 15, 2000.

This contract is subject to renegotiation at any time and either party is free to terminate it if either determines the consultation progress to be unsatisfactory.

For the Beach Town School System

_____

Party of the Second Part

_____

Signature _____

Address _____

Social Security Number _____

Date _____

FIGURE 3.2   A sample contract

examples illustrate how psychological contracts can be broken:

Case Example 1 A consultant hired by a human service agency to assist in program development expected an office but was not provided one. The consultant's resulting resentment made it more difficult to focus objectively on the tasks to be accomplished.

Case Example 2 An organization's contact person wanted to be reached by the consultant each time he or she visited the organization. The contact person neither expressed this wish nor put it into the formal contract. When the consultant innocently restricted communication with the contact person, the contact person felt rejected and covertly began efforts to sabotage the consultant's activities.

The following is a summary of a case study reported by Reed, Greer, McKay, and Knight (1990) that further illustrates the importance of the psychological aspects of the contract. The authors report that they conducted a consultancy of nine meetings over a six-month period for the staff of a school for troubled students with the purpose of reducing staff stress levels. Prior attempts to reduce such stress were not successful, so the consultants were called in by the school administrators. However, the staff expected the consultants to provide consultation regarding difficulties they were having with individual students. The authors point out that although the administrators' expectations were covered, the nature of the consultation could have been better clarified for the staff. Consequently, a psychological contract was formed with the administration but not with the staff. The authors point out the need to ensure that all consultees are aware of and agree to the nature of the consultation process.

To avoid unfortunate occurrences like those just described, consultants should be clear about what is expected from both the organization and themselves. By explaining their roles to contact persons and consultees, consultants can build trust with key members of the organization (Schein, 1988). Consultants should explain what behaviors will occur and the rationale for them. Thus, a consultant who will observe the inner workings of an organization should clearly state that such observations will be made for the purpose of understanding organizational dynamics, not for gathering personal data about individuals.

In summary, if the consultant has effectively completed the preliminary exploration of an organization's needs, then the psychological aspects of contracting need less attention because mutual expectations have already been verbally expressed and agreed upon. The consultant's primary concern with regard to the psychological aspects of contracting is in involving the organization's contact person in mutual development of the formal contract. To the degree that this involvement happens, the ground rules for the consultation process and mutual cooperation on future issues and problems will be established (Boss, 1985). Such involvement of the contact person, of course, requires the investment of more time at the outset of the entry stage (Boss, 1985). Consultants will want to remember that as consultation proceeds, there may well be the need for renegotiating the contract (Caplan, 1993). Although it was written long ago, an excellent case study on developing a contract was written by Carner (1982).

A Brief Example of Contracting The head of a group home for abused adolescents currently has five male and five female clients. The head is concerned about physical contact between clients and staff and contacts you to consult about this matter. After an initial exploration of the organization's needs, you and the head develop a contract that will guide your consultation. You first agree to interview each of the three staff members and the head independently and then observe them discussing this issue in the next two staff meetings. You agree that all information you gather will be held confidential, set a fee, and put the contract in writing to be signed by both parties.

PHASE THREE: PHYSICALLY
ENTERING THE SYSTEM

Once a contract has been formalized, the consultant is ready to physically enter the system. *Physically entering the system* begins when the consultant first comes into contact with the members of the organization (Gallessich, 1982) and, where appropriate, creates consultant-consultee relationships. Physical entry is different from psychological entry, which is the ongoing process by which the consultant achieves increasing acceptance by the members of the organization.

A very important feature of physically entering the system is the consultant's work site within the organization. Should the consultant be assigned a private office or meet in designated meeting rooms or the offices of other staff members? The reality of organizational life is that having one's own office is a sign of status and prestige. By providing the consultant with a temporary office, the organization makes a symbolic statement of strong support for the consultant, one that sanctions and demonstrates the administration's willingness to allocate the organizational resources needed to support the consultation process. Because

collaborators are frequently internal to the organization in which collaboration is occurring, they have often accomplished the task of physical entry prior to the collaboration process.

Having an office and always being in it are two different things. When beginning the physical entry process, consultants should move about the work areas to begin building relationships with members of the organization. Consultees often feel most comfortable when the consultant is willing to meet them on their own turf. Thus, as soon as possible after entering the system, consultants should seek out everyone connected with the consultation. A specified time schedule that makes the consultant's comings and goings predictable is very useful in successfully accomplishing physical entry.

The consultant should proceed in a deliberate, cautious manner. Organizations are slow to change, and the consultant would do well to realize that appropriate physical entry will enhance the organizational members' acceptance so crucial to successful psychological entry. The consultant should adapt to the organization's schedules and thereby minimize any interruptions in the workday.

The consultant should remind the organization's contact person to inform the parties-at-interest of the consultant's upcoming entry into the organization. The members affected by consultation should be informed of the consultant's role and function, why that particular consultant was hired, what is to be accomplished within what time frame, and who is to be involved (Boss, 1985). Further, the work setting in which consultation services are to be delivered should be common knowledge (Schein, 1988). Such advance notification prepares the people involved for the consultant's entry. Finally, an open discussion concerning confidentiality and its limits is important, because it informs both administrators and consultees of what they can reveal to the consultant, and it can avoid problems later on (Conoley & Conoley, 1992).

A Brief Example of Physically Entering the System   Reread the preceding brief example of contracting and assume you are the consultant in that example. Since the length of your consultancy is brief (three weeks or so), you realize that you do not need an office at the home. Yet you will need a place to conduct interviews with the staff and suggest to the head that you use one of the staff offices so that you will not become overly identified with the administration of the home. You then ask the head to discuss your coming at least a week in advance. At your first visit, you mingle with the staff and clients and try to get a feel for the atmosphere that permeates the group home.

PHASE FOUR: PSYCHOLOGICALLY ENTERING THE SYSTEM

In actual practice, physical and psychological entry cannot be separated. *Psychological entry* refers to the gradual acceptance of the consultant by members of the organization in which consultation is being performed. Effective accomplishment of the first three phases of entry can enhance the consultant's acceptance by the organization. Because collaborators are frequently internal to an organization, they frequently have attained psychological entry.

In gaining psychological acceptance in an organization, the consultant should consider the two levels of operation in any organization. The process level concerns how an organization does what it does (Mann, 1978), that is, how it makes major decisions. The second level

involves the personal interactions among its members (Mann, 1978), for example, how peers are encouraged to support each other on the job to build the organization's morale.

Consultants who achieve psychological entry relatively quickly can be said to be "working smart." Because they realize that organizations attempt to maintain a state of equilibrium and stability (Parsons, 1996), such consultants create the conditions in which only minimal stress is placed on the organizational personnel involved in the consultation. They follow existing rules, regulations, and communication channels, and they ask to be judged on their deeds rather than on what they say.

When consultants try too hard to be like their own stereotype of an organization's members, adverse effects can occur. For example, Deitz and Reese (1986) provide examples of how a mental health consultant tried to take on the jargon used by the members of the law enforcement agency in which he was consulting. Rather than being seen as "family" by the officers, the consultant was seen as an oddball who would never be trustworthy or deserving of respect. Clearly, psychological entry can be made more difficult if the consultant works too hard and overidentifies with consultees.

The consultant's acceptance by the organization can be enhanced by keeping matters pertinent to consultation as simple as possible (Parsons & Meyers, 1984). The consultant should describe consultation interventions in concrete and specific terms, and changes in the organization's structure that result from consultation should be minimized. Further, the consultant will want to ensure that consultees perceive that the consultant is able, at the outset of consultation, to translate assistance to meet the needs of the consultee. To effectively psychologically enter the consultant must be perceived by the consultee as appreciating the consultee's role demands and stressors (Kelly, 1993).

Interpersonal Influence in Consultation

Social/interpersonal Influence Psychological acceptance can be accomplished through the use of social influence or the popular and broader term *interpersonal influence*. There has been increased attention paid to this area in recent years, due in part to the fact that consultants in any setting spend most of their time working with other adults even when the clients targeted for assistance are children (Gutkin, 1997). As related to consultation, social influence theory states that the people affected by consultation are more open to influence to the degree that they view the consultant as being attractive, trustworthy, and competent (Strong, 1968). Increasingly, consultation in the human service professions has been recognized as an interpersonal influence process (O'Keefe & Medway, 1997). For example, a consultant uses interpersonal influence such as persuasion when directing the focus of the consultation process onto the problem-solving process and away from mere chitchat. Interpersonal influence should not be mistaken for controlling or manipulation, but rather is a tool to assist in problem solving and dealing with the relational aspects of consultation (O'Keefe & Medway, 1997). For example, interpersonal influence may help minimize resistance and may, in fact, help consultees believe they have the self-efficacy to implement the plan they are discussing with the consultant.

Consultants are seen as attractive when the people with whom they work perceive similarities between themselves and the consultant. Consultants should take the personality of their consultees into consideration to enhance the quality of their psychological entry. They can also increase their attractiveness by identifying with and manifesting as many of the organization's values as are congruent with their own. To this end, consultants can accept and abide by the organization's routines (Gallessich, 1982), use the terminology common within it (Gallessich, 1982), and abide by its dress codes (Steele, 1975).

Consultants are perceived as trustworthy when they demonstrate understanding, appropriate use of power, respect for confidentiality, and credibility. Consultants can create trustworthiness (Egan, 1990) by avoiding behaviors that imply ulterior motives, using the power of social influence carefully, promoting the best interest of the consultee or the organization, and being realistic but optimistic about the ability of the consultee or organization to handle the demands of consultation. Trustworthiness can also be gained by refusing to take sides, by avoiding issues not in the contract, and by staying away from off-limit areas in the organization (Gallessich, 1982).

Expertness is the perceived possession of specialized knowledge or skills to solve a problem (Short, Moore, & Williams, 1991). One method of enhancing perceived expertness is to cite one's experiences relative to the situation at hand.

One of the most valuable tools consultants have for obtaining acceptance is the effective use of questioning. During entry it is better if consultants ask good questions about the system (to obtain some understanding of how organization's members perceive consultation) than if they rattle off what they already know about the consultee or the organization (Caplan & Caplan, 1993).

Consultants will not want to gain social influence at the expense of the consultee's need for self-responsibility (Egan, 1994). Consultants can become too accepted within the system. Those who become too accepted risk losing their objectivity and having members of the system blindly accept what they say (Caplan & Caplan, 1993; Egan, 1994). On the other hand, if consultees feel pushed to accept the consultant's point of view, they might well become resistant. Thus, consultants should strive to obtain enough social influence to make the necessary impact while facilitating the consultee's reflectivity on the consultant's input. Ultimately, consultants' social influence may be as critical as their having skills and knowledge in determining the effectiveness of consultation (Erchul & Raven, 1997; Short et al., 1991; Martens, Kelly, & Disken, 1996).

Models of Interpersonal Influence Consultation involves either direct or indirect attempts to influence change in consultees. Hence, below I explore two models related to attitude change, the Elaboration Likelihood Model (ELM) and French and Raven's bases of social power model, and discuss their significance with regard to working with consultees. You should note that an underlying assumption of this discussion is that any attempt to influence or change a consultee will be accomplished in an ethical and professional manner.

The ELM (Petty, Heesaker, & Hughes, 1997) offers a method to make sense of the antecedents and consequences of attitude change. Central to ELM is the idea that "attitude change can result from relatively thoughtful (central route) or nonthoughtful (peripheral route) processes" (Petty et al., 1997, p. 107). Thoughtful processes include examining the underlying assumptions of the consultant's information. Nonthoughtful processes rely on the idea that the information makes the consultee pleased or the consultee simply acquiesces to consultant expertise (i.e., consultant-knows-best type of thinking). Nonthoughtful processes do not challenge the consultee to put any kind of rigor into thinking about what the consultant is saying. As you might guess, thoughtful attitude change is more likely to be permanent than that which is nonthoughtful.

The essence of this model is that consultants have a better chance of interpersonally influencing consultees when consultees have the motivation and the ability to think about the benefits of the data provided by the consultant and its underlying assumptions. On the other hand, if consultees are less involved, it is highly unlikely that they will change their attitudes and behavior in a way deemed desirable by the consultant. In other words, change is more likely when the consultee has internalized and accepted the consultant's message and is not simply being compliant at the time of the recommendation.

Ways to motivate consultees to consider information reflectively include making the information personally relevant to the consultee, restricting the focus to areas for which the consultee is accountable, ensuring that the consultee has an adequate amount of information, avoiding being forceful in delivering information, taking measures to be viewed as a credible source of information, and keeping a positive emotional atmosphere in the relationship. Ways to make sure that the consultee has the ability to think about the merits of the information include minimizing distractions when information is being considered, providing adequate time for processing the information, avoiding technical language, using written follow-ups to consultation sessions, and avoiding trying to consult during chance encounters.

In addition to motivating and facilitating consultee thought, it is important to create the conditions that will help the consultee think and feel favorably about the consultant's recommendations. Two ways to accomplish this are to make the recommendations from the consultee's perspective (i.e., self-schemas) and to recommend an intervention that is congruent with the consultee's thinking about the problem. For example, a consultee with a humanistic bent has the client's problem explained from a humanistic perspective by the consultant.

As noted in Erchul and Raven (1997), French and Raven (1959) developed a typology that contains six bases of power that can be used for social influence. These bases, accompanied by examples, include:

- coercion—a consultee is fearful of confrontation by the consultant ("If I don't follow through with the plan, I will get confronted.")

- reward—a consultee views praise from the consultant as rewarding ("It feels good to be validated by the consultant.")

- legitimate—a consultee views the consultant's attempt to help as appropriate to the consultant's role ("It's right for the consultant to try to help me with this, it's part of the job.")

- expert—the consultant is viewed as being more expert in the consultee's opinion ("I should follow this recommendation. After all, the consultant knows more than I do.")

- referent—the consultant is viewed by the consultee as being similar ("Since we are all in this together, the least I can do is my part.")

- informational—the methods of persuasion by the consultant are viewed by the consultee as relevant ("I think I can really use these ideas to help my client.")

As you can note each of the bases of power can be of use to consultants in their attempts to help their consultees. In addition, these bases of power can be used by all parties involved in collaboration, where the influence is more reciprocal than in consultation. Whatever the basis of power that is used in social influence, the method by which the power is exerted is critical to the success of the influence (Erchul & Raven, 1997). Consultants and collaborators will want to reflect upon available power bases and their mode of implementing in order to have maximum influence on their consultees.

A Brief Example of Psychologically Entering the System As a consultant you are preparing to conduct a workshop for teachers in an elementary school on indicators of child abuse. Before you conduct the workshop, you visit several of the teachers' rooms, introduce yourself, start to learn names, and begin building relationships. In your conversations you note that you were once a schoolteacher and a school counselor. You mention how serious the topic is and that hopefully a child or two can be saved from being victimized as a result of the workshop. You are friendly, professional, and yet genuine.

MULTICULTURAL ASPECTS
RELATED TO ENTRY

People of differing cultural backgrounds can differ in the way they approach the consultation relationship (Gibbs, 1980). For example, an African American consultee may be primarily concerned about the interpersonal orientation of a white consultant, whereas a white consultee may be more interested in determining whether or not the consultant is able to be of assistance (i.e., instrumentally competent) (Gibbs, 1980). Clearly, consultants and collaborators will want to be knowledgeable about culturally different groups and take that knowledge into consideration as they accomplish the entry stage. For example, consultants will want to bear in mind that the amount of information communicated by words versus by context varies among cultures (Flanagan & Miranda,1995).

Some consultees or collaborators from differing cultural backgrounds may view the consultant as the expert. Consequently, consultants will have to determine whether they wish to enter the relationship in this context or aim for a more nonhierarchical, collaborative relationship

How consultants use their communication and interpersonal skills during consultation will to a large extent determine the success of consultation (Jackson & Hayes, 1993). One method consultants and collaborators can use to determine their suitability to work with consultees or fellow collaborators is to determine their level of comfort in dealing with any cultural or ethnic issues related to the problem being dealt with (Jackson & Hayes, 1993). Awareness of cultural differences and how they might impact the consultative relationship should be considered before contracting. Some clues for how effective a consultant is being with a culturally different person can be gotten from the entry stage because demonstrated cultural awareness during entry is most likely positively related to positive outcomes (Duncan, 1995).

Culturally different consultees may perceive consultants in terms of interpersonal orientation (the ability to positively socially influence others) and instrumental orientation (the ability to be perceived as competent) (Gibbs, 1980).

Consultants should be aware that it is likely that minority consultees will make a commitment to the consultation process based upon their perception of the consultant's ability to relate and the consultant's familiarity with the meanings of specific nonverbal behaviors across cultures (Flanagan & Miranda, 1995).

A FINAL NOTE ON ENTRY

Part of your work as a consultant may involve the work-related concerns of individual consultees. For example, you might consult with counselors in a community human service agency about their clients, with teachers concerning students about whom they have concerns, or with parents about issues regarding raising children. If you are going to be working with individual consultees within an organization, you will have to "enter" with each one, that is, explore their perceived needs that led to their requests for consultation.

You will have to develop a suitable contract with your consultees or fellow collaborators, be willing meet them on their own turf, and psychologically enter through building a good working relationship with them. In fact, some empirical evidence suggests that how well you can establish relationships with consultees is related to consultation success (Weissenburger, Fine, & Poggio, 1982; Hughes & DeForest, 1993). There is also strong support for the importance of a strong relationship from writers in the area of consultation theory such as Caplan and Caplan (1993). On the other hand, you have the potential to strongly affect consultees in their thinking (Granda, 1992)—you must successfully complete the entry stage not only with the organization, but with each consultee as well.

The limited research on entry with individual consultees suggests that the consultant's knowledge is not as important to consultees as are the relationship-building activities of the consultant (Martens, Lewandowski, & Houk, 1989). There is additional attention being paid to the consultees' cognitive responses to the help they are receiving (Uhlemann, Lee, & Martin, 1994). In other words consultees' perceptions about what is happening in the consultation relationship can be as important as what is actually happening. Therefore, as a practicing consultant you may well put a high priority on establishing solid working relationships with your consultees. In doing so, consultants will want to be aware that consultees may want a balance of directiveness and collaboration (Buysse, Schulte, Pierce, & Terry, 1994) and prefer some leadeship from the consultant in determining the content of consultation (Gutkin, 1996).

RESISTANCE TO CONSULTATION

No matter how many precautions consultants take to ease their physical and psychological entry into the system, some resistance to consultation is typical. Although such resistance is normal, this lack of cooperation with the process can present significant challenges to your consultation activities. *Resistance* is the failure of a consultee or organization to participate constructively in the consultation process (Wickstrom & Witt, 1993). Although resistance can occur during any phase of the process, it is most frequently encountered during the entry stage. Overcoming resistance involves accurately diagnosing its source. A common mistake made by

consultants is to assume that resistance is due to a negative attitude on the part of the consultee (Kratochwill, Elliott, & Busse, 1995; O'Keefe & Medway, 1997; Watson & Robinson, 1996).

Organizational Resistance

When consultants enter organizations ready to initiate change, they frequently encounter a healthy resistance to such change. This is an important survival mechanism that protects the organization from outside threats. However, all organizations must adapt to change, and resistance can impede the progress of this adaptation.

There are four sources of organizational resistance to consultation (Parsons & Meyers, 1984): the desire to keep things the way they are, the view of the consultant as an outsider, the rejection of anything new as nonnormative (a "we just don't do things that way around here" attitude), and the desire to protect one's own turf or vested interest. Resistance is common even in those organizations that want to change and that support consultation with appropriate degrees of money, time, and effort. In fact, the very title *consultant* can be threatening because it implies change. Because the organization's perception of the consultant's role early on in the consultation process is often unclear, resistance can be preempted by providing a clear picture at the outset of what the consultant is to accomplish.

Nontraditional views of organizational resistance assume that resistance is present only to the degree that organizations are conceptualized in terms of power and conflict (Merron, 1993). In these cases, what is labeled *resistance* is regarded as simply the expression of alternative views of organizational events and a consultant's focusing on what is *wrong* in the organization.

Consultee Resistance

Whereas relatively little has been written about organizational resistance to consultation, a great deal has been written about consultee resistance (Campbell, 1993; Dougherty, Dougherty, & Purcell, 1991; Erchul & Conoley, 1991; Hughes, 1983; Hughes & Falk, 1981; Meyers & Yelich, 1989; Randolph & Graun, 1988; Tingstrom, Little, & Stewart, 1990). In any helping relationship, resistance is both unavoidable and potentially helpful (Otani, 1989). Consultants must manage resistance to maximize a positive consultation outcome.

From a behavioral viewpoint, resistance can arise from the consultee's aversion to the consultation outcome. Consultees may believe that the benefits of consultation are not worth the costs (for example, it will take too much of their time) or that consultation will result in some form of punishment (for example, criticism by one's supervisor) (Piersel & Gutkin, 1983). Therefore, to minimize resistance the consultant should ensure that the cost of participating in consultation is at least matched by the benefits.

Cognitive dissonance theory can be used to analyze sources of consultee resistance (Hughes, 1983). Dissonance occurs when a person has concepts that are not in accord with each other or are illogical. For example, being a consultee and not liking it are dissonant concepts, and there is a strong likelihood that consultee resistance will ensue. Dissonance is minimized when a consultee buys into the consultation process. Ways to involve a consultee include keeping consultation a voluntary and peer relationship, showing how consultation can help but making no "guarantees," and making sure that the consultee has to put forth some effort in the consultation process (Hughes, 1983). By involving the consultee in these ways, the consultant creates a relationship in which the consultee is more likely to cooperate.

Hughes and Falk (1981) examined resistance to consultation from the perspective of reactance theory, which suggests that when you perceive that a freedom of yours is taken away, you will try to restore it (Brehm, 1966; Hughes & Falk, 1981). One implication for consultants is to avoid the overuse of persuasion and recommendations and instead provide consultees with choices whenever possible during consultation. In this way consultees are most likely not to experience any infringement of their freedom.

Dougherty et al. (1991) suggest that resistance can be due to a consultee's misconception concerning the nature of consultation, some dysfunction in the consultation relationship, fear related to the discomfort of disclosing need, or cognitive distortions that cause misunderstandings and lead to increased resistance.

Dealing Effectively with Resistance

There are several things consultants can do to minimize resistance:

- Create a strong relationship to build trust and alleviate fear.
- Collaborate whenever possible.
- Create the conditions for consultation to have a satisfying outcome and be worth the effort.
- Allow the consultee as many choices as possible.
- Throughout the process, point out how consultation might be helpful.

CASE 3.1   Entry for School Consultants

Maurice is a school-based consultant in a large, urban elementary school and frequently consults with many staff members, including the school's four administrators. The administrators ask Maurice to assist them in developing a dropout prevention program. Although Maurice is internal to the school, he realizes that he is external to the problem and must go through the entry stage very carefully.

In a first meeting with the administrators, Maurice and the group explore the possibilities of his being a consultant for the program. Maurice wants to make sure that he can be of assistance as well as ensure that the administrators see him as someone who can be of help. Together the group explores the underlying values concerning counseling that will guide the development of the program, how the program will be staffed, the kinds of resources that will be provided, and the flexibility available for fine-tuning the program. Maurice asks the administrators why they are interested in the program in the first place and what

they think it will do for the school. He then interacts with the group concerning what they view his role to be in helping develop the program and, correspondingly, their own roles. Finally, the group discusses the limits of Maurice's involvement given his other duties in the school.

Based on this exploration, all agree that Maurice should be a consultant for the program's development. Maurice suggests that a formal, written contract, although internal to the school, will help the parties involved stay on track with the project. He agrees to develop a contract for approval and submits one that describes the general goals related to the program's development, what roles he and the administrators will take on, a time frame, and a brief evaluation design for assessing the quality of the work accomplished through consultation.

In a brief meeting Maurice and the administrators review and agree to the contract, as well as make sure everyone involved has the same set of expectations. To enhance physical and

psychological entry, Maurice suggests a location for program development meetings, makes sure that he follows protocol in gaining access to the administrators, and acknowledges the fact that just because he is a consultant to the group does not make him an administrator or more important than any other staff member at the school.

Commentary

This case illustrates the importance of the maxim: You always have to enter. Even though Maurice was an internal consultant, he recognized that he was external to the problem and the consequent importance of appropriately entering. Notice that Maurice clarified his role very carefully and put things in writing. Even though he was functioning as an internal consultant, Maurice did not fall into to the trap of making the consultation process so casual that it would be difficult to keep it on task and remain in a problem-solving mode.

- Distribute the workload in consultation so that the consultee is doing his or her share.

- Give the consultee as much freedom as possible in all aspects of the process.

- Be clear about the nature of consultation from the outset.

- Challenge any cognitive distortions with specific disputing examples.

- Be as clear and specific as possible about what is expected of the consultee.

- Use examples to illustrate points.

- Try to minimize the new things a consultee has to learn.

- Link interventions to the consultee's explanation of the causes of the problem.

- Ensure that the consultee has the skills necessary to carry out the interventions.

CASE 3.2   Entry for Community Consultants

Marie, a mental health consultant operating out of a mental health satellite center, is contacted by Kristine, the director of a human resource development department of a local municipal government, to engage in some "train the trainer" consultation. She is interested in having her human resource development staff trained in consultation skills.

During their first contact, Marie thoroughly explores what Kristine would like to accomplish in the training, shares her own related professional experiences as well as her values regarding consultation in general and training in particular, and asks Kristine about her views of training and consultants. They discuss the human resource development department, its staff and mission, and how it is perceived by the rest of the organization. They also discuss the practical use of the consultation training to the department's staff and the resources that the department is willing to put into training. At the end of their discussion, both Marie and Kristine are positive about the prospect of working together. Before

she agrees to become a consultant, Marie asks if she could have a brief meeting with the human resource development department's five staff members to inform them about the proposed consultation.

Marie meets with the staff for a one-hour period, during which she gets to know the members in a leisurely fashion, briefly describes the proposed training and her own related professional experiences, and allows time for questions and discussion. At the end of the meeting, there is a consensus among group members that they are favorable about the training.

Marie contacts Kristine soon thereafter and clarifies the few issues that were raised in the meeting with the staff. Kristine mentions that the local municipal government has a form contract that is to be used by all departments when they hire consultants and that there was some flexibility in it for writing in items specific to a given consultation. Marie and Kristine agree to add a statement about the consultant's roles and the responsibilities of the director of the department.

Stopping by the human resource development office the day before the training sessions are to start, Marie makes a point of interacting with each of the participants and, with a couple of the participants, looks over the room in which the training is to be conducted. She provides a schedule for the training to the staff members as well as a couple of handouts on consulting ideas for human resource development specialists.

Commentary

It is of particular importance, as this case illustrates, for consultants to enter with each consultee as they enter the system. Marie wisely held a brief meeting with the consultees prior to beginning her training sessions with them. Notice how she also made personal contact with each of them on the day before the training. By taking the time to create relationships with consultees, consultants not only build trust and minimize resistance but they quickly move the consultation relationship to a partnership that allows for effective collaboration.

Perhaps the best method of dealing with resistance is to prevent its occurrence in the first place through understanding and involvement (Kelley, 1981). Understanding refers to the consultant's ability to comprehend and appreciate the consultee's views of events. Involvement refers to consultant's use of collaboration to prevent consultees from feeling overpowered. Understanding and involvement can reduce resistance because they focus on listening and learning—the consultant becomes a student and learns about the skills and perceptions of the consultee.

A Brief Example of Resistance to Consultation As you are consulting with a mental health practitioner about a client, you increasingly note that the consultee is avoiding direct eye contact with you as he is discussing his client. As you reflect on the consultation relationship, you note that you and the consultee are locked into a "yes, but . . ." kind of interaction in which you are making suggestions regarding the case and he is explaining how none of them could possibly work with this client. You acknowledge the issue by noting that you are getting frustrated with what is going on and that you imagine the consultee is too. You suggest both starting anew by focusing in on what the consultee wanted to have happen in the case and how both of you can collaborate to achieve it.

SUMMARY

The entry process in consultation is a critical stage. When successfully completed, it increases the probability that the entire consultation process will turn out successfully. The success of the entry process relies heavily on the consultant's skills and how well these skills are used to accomplish the tasks of the entry stage. The most critical skills in the entry stage relate to exploring problems, contracting, relating, and communicating. By effectively accomplishing the stage of entry, consultants not only set the stage for successful consultation; they also minimize the resistance that organizations and individual consultees can demonstrate.

Consultants should avoid the temptation to go quickly through the entry stage to get on with problem-solving activities. By effectively exploring the organization's needs, the consultant can help it determine its priorities for consultation. A well-designed contract makes the expectations of everyone involved explicit and prevents misunderstandings regarding consultation later in the process. Effective physical entry makes consultants less intrusive as they join in the organization's activities. By taking the time necessary for building relationships and gaining acceptance, consultants can become insiders and accomplish the difficult phase of psychological entry.

The research on the entry stage is quite limited. There is some evidence that consultees prefer a blend of facility and expertise in consultants and that the readiness for and a consultee's ability to change are more likely to lead to a successful consultation experience than will factors like consultee interest in the subject of the consultation (Armenakis & Burdg, 1988).

SUGGESTIONS FOR

EFFECTIVE PRACTICE

- Remember the maxim You always have to enter.

- A contract is one of the best ways of documenting expectations.

- Consider resistance to be a normal part of the consultation and collaboration process.

- Make a deliberate effort to psychologically enter the system and create a relationship with *each* consultee even if you are internal to the setting in which consultation and collaboration occur.

QUESTIONS FOR REFLECTION

1. What effects can resistance have on the consultant's performance?

2. Why is it important for the consultant to obtain sanctions for performing consultation from the organization's upper echelon?

3. Recall a situation in which an outsider entered your classroom. What were your immediate reactions? Relate your feelings to how members of an organization must feel when they encounter a consultant for the first time.

4. What characteristics would you look for in an organization or a consultee before you would agree to consultation?

5. Under what circumstances can resistance in consultation be seen as normal?

6. How can the power attributed to the consultant due to expertise or trustworthiness be useful in ameliorating resistance?

7. What are the key points consultants should consider in assessing their performance during the entry phase?

8. How would you as a consultant go about accomplishing psychological entry? That is, how would you go about the task of building relationships with and gaining acceptance by staff with whom you had no previous contact?

9. How would you go about the task of physically entering into consultation with an organization?

10. Under what circumstances do you think consultants should use formal contracts?

SUGGESTED SUPPLEMENTARY READINGS

If you are interested in reading in more depth and detail about the entry stage of consultation, here are some useful selected readings:

Marks, E. S. (1995). *Entry strategies for school consultation*. New York: Guilford. This text is dedicated to the nuts and bolts of helping consultants open the doors to effective consultation. The author emphasizes entry in school consultation, but consultants and collaborators in any setting will find useful information.

Glidewell, J. C. (1959). "The entry problem in consultation." *Journal of Social Issues*, *15(2)*, 51–59. This article is a classic and well worth reading. Glidewell was one of the first authors to promote the idea of the consultant as a person who temporarily attaches to a social system; he does an excellent job of pointing out that the process of entry can be accelerated or retarded by the perceptions of the members of the organization in which consultation is to occur.

Cherniss, C. (1993). Preentry issues revisited. In R. T. Golembiewski (Ed.), *Handbook of organizational consultation* (pp. 113–118). New York: Marcel Dekker, Inc. This is an excellent review of preentry issues. Two particular aspects of this article are dealing with conflict during preentry and choosing a primary focus.

4

Diagnosis Stage

The nature of the diagnosis stage depends on the type of consultation being performed. But just as some kind of diagnosis, either formal or informal, is made in counseling and psychotherapy (Hohenshil, 1996), so too is one made in consultation or collaboration. A mental health consultant working with a therapist may assist in diagnosing a client's problem and in prescribing a treatment plan. A behavioral consultant may examine the antecedents and consequences of students' selected classroom conduct and assist a teacher in implementing behavioral strategies to change that conduct. An organizational consultant may help an organization improve its efficiency by focusing on an individual, a group, a subsystem, or the organization as a whole. The process of diagnosis remains the same for all consultation, although the types of data gathered will depend on the type of consultation being performed.

The preceding chapter discussed the entry process, in which the consultant engages in a preliminary exploration of organizational needs, formulates a contract, and physically and psychologically enters the system. The stage following entry is called the diagnosis stage and has four phases: gathering information (which answers the question What information do we need to find out where we are?), defining the problem (which answers the question Where are we?), setting goals (which answers the question Where do we want to be?), and generating possible interventions (which answers the question What are some things to do that might help us get there?).

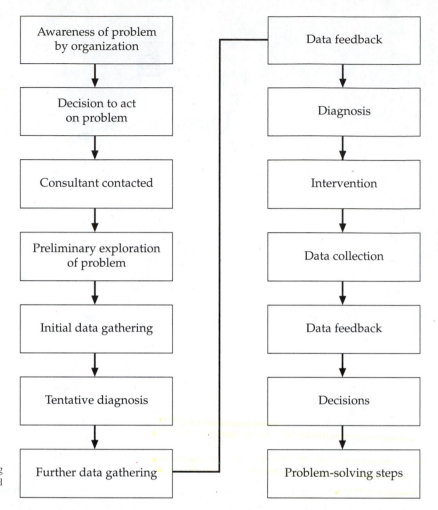

FIGURE 4.1
The interrelationships among
diagnosis, data gathering, and
intervention (French, 1972)

Figure 4.1 shows how diagnosis, data gathering, and intervention relate to one another. The consultant's relationship with the consultee is critical to the successful completion of this stage. Unless the consultant is able to obtain accurate, pertinent information and assist consultees in translating this data into a list of functional and viable alternative interventions, then it is likely that the wrong problem will be solved.

As you read this chapter, consider these questions:

1. How does a consultant determine where to collect information within the organization?

2. How does a consultant determine who should gather the data needed to define the problem?

3. What factors should be considered in setting goals?

4. How can a consultant assist a consultee in developing a set of possible interventions?

5. In what ways is diagnosis an ongoing event?

INTRODUCTION

Assume for the moment that you are the consultant described in the following example:

A Case of Diagnosis

You are a human service professional in private practice with a caseload of clients, and you perform consultation with other therapists and human service organizations. The director of a county social service agency requests that you assist in resolving some of the agency's problems. You have successfully completed the entry stage, and therefore you have a rough idea of what the agency's problems are, have contracted with it, have gotten to know the staff, and are set up in the office of a part-time staff member. The director is concerned about the morale within the agency: people work behind closed doors, put-downs of clients are frequently heard, backlogs of paperwork are large, and little camaraderie is apparent.

When consulting with the director, you agree to design and conduct a survey about what it is like to work in the agency. You agree to interview a random number of the staff about their personal views of their professional work site, and, based on the results of this information, you assist the director in determining what's the matter. You divide the problem into three smaller problems: morale, high case-

loads, and little administrative support and encouragement. You then assist the director in setting some goals to ameliorate these problems. You break these down further into more specific subgoals (for example, more oral and written praise and support from the director for jobs well done). Once goals have been set, you and the director come up with a variety of intervention alternatives for meeting the set goals.

As this example illustrates, consultants are sometimes asked to assist in determining the nature of a problem prior to making some form of intervention. Thus, this stage of consultation—in which the consultant performs this assessment in the roles of information seeker and detective—is called the *diagnosis stage*.

Diagnosis is the identification of the forces underlying or precipitating the current way things are in a given situation. From another perspective, diagnosis is the ". . . meaning or interpretation that is derived from assessment information when it is interpreted through the use of a diagnostic classification system" (Hohenshil, 1996, p. 65). Diagnosis may pertain broadly to the present state of a system, including the many positive forces giving rise to desirable outcomes, or may be narrower in the sense of focusing on the dysfunctional forces that are producing undesirable outcomes, or may focus on changes in the state of the system over time (French, Bell, & Zawacki, 1978, pp. 115–116).

A critical part of diagnosis is determining that part of the organization in which the problem is located. How the consultant approaches the diagnostic stage depends on the purpose of consultation, the complexity of the problem, and the time available (Argyris, 1970). For example, Tichy (1983) lists three types of organizational diagnoses based on complexity:

- radar scan diagnosis (which involves a quick examination of the organization to locate problem areas)
- symptom-focused diagnosis (in which information is examined relative to known problem areas)
- in-depth diagnosis (which involves a systematic, detailed organizational analysis)

Another important aspect of the diagnosis stage involves determining who constitutes the client system—an individual, a group, a subsystem, or the entire organization—for the nature of the client system affects diagnosis. As the client system increases in size, the complexity of the diagnostic stage usually increases as well: The more complex the diagnostic stage, the greater the need to use several methods to collect data from a larger group of people.

Every consultant brings to and uses in the diagnostic process at least three theories (French et al., 1978). The first, descriptive and analytical in nature, is the theory by which the consultant attempts to understand the ins and outs of organizational events and behaviors. In this view, for example, behaviors might be considered rather more critical than attitudes in understanding events. A second theory, one of change, consists of the consultant's views of how events influence one another and change. For example, one view of this theory might state that structure, not people, determines change. Finally, consultants have a diagnostic theory, which consists of a set of notions to determine what is dysfunctional or wrong. One example might be the viewpoint that a problem must be a long-standing one in order to be severe.

Assessment refers to the kind of information used in diagnosis (Hohenshil, 1996). The kind of information used for diagnosis depends on a given consultation model's view of what must be examined to find out what is wrong. Three major areas or domains that consultants may examine in their diagnoses are consultee characteristics, client system characteristics, and environmental characteristics (Brown et al., 1995). Consultants' theories of description-analysis, change, and dysfunction significantly affect which domains are examined and how a diagnosis is made. By being aware of their own theories, consultants can use them to accomplish accurate, effective diagnoses and avoid being unwittingly victimized by them during the diagnostic stage.

The diagnosis stage, like the entry stage, is very complex. It involves the four interrelated phases depicted in Figure 4.2: gathering information, defining the problem, setting goals, and generating possible interventions.

PHASE ONE: GATHERING INFORMATION

The Nature of Information Acquisition

An accurate diagnosis requires accurate information. The terms *data* and *information* are used interchangeably in this discussion. Although data gathering never ceases during the consultation process, there is a formal time for the process of gathering information.

The first step is to conceptualize the problem. Some idea of the problem is obtained during the preliminary exploration of organizational needs. The results of the preliminary exploration are, in part, determined by the model of consultation to be used, for each model has its own view of human behavior, of what is necessary for change, and of what constitutes the client

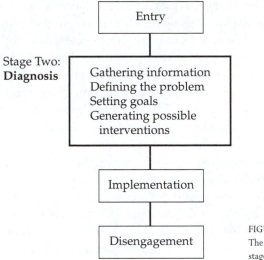

Stage Two:
Diagnosis

Entry

Gathering information
Defining the problem
Setting goals
Generating possible
   interventions

Implementation

Disengagement

FIGURE 4.2
The phases of the diagnosis
stage

system. These factors in turn will determine the types of methods used to gather data.

Still, the consultant must assign some parameters to the task of consultation before diagnosis can begin (Goodstein, 1978). It may be best to start with problems as they are perceived by the consultee (Huse, 1975); such action demonstrates the consultant's collaborative attitude.

Like good detectives, consultants must gather and analyze data to understand what is going on; then they can use that understanding in assisting the consultee system to determine what changes it wants to make (Steele, 1975). Depending on the model of consultation in use, the consultant can draw from several data sources: genetic data, current descriptive data, process data, interpretive data, consultee-client system relationship data, and client system behavior data (Beer, 1980; Bergan & Kratochwill, 1990; Caplan & Caplan, 1993).

- Genetic data: This type of data includes easily accessible, common information

(for example, an organization's role and mission statement) and historical information (for example, reports and memos). (Example: A consultant might read the role and mission statement of a human service agency and decide to determine the degree to which the agency's members are aware of it.)

- Current descriptive data: As its name implies, this type of information describes an organization as it currently exists. The organization's physical layout and its command and salary structures are all descriptive information. (Example: A human service agency asks for a consultant's help with its internal communication problems. The consultant examines the agency's organizational structure as a prelude to determining how superiors and subordinates within the agency communicate with one another.)

- Process data: Process data involve the organization's methods, including how decisions are made and how meetings are conducted. (Example: A consultant acts as an observer at a crisis intervention team's staff meeting to determine who talks to whom about what.)

- Interpretive data: This kind of information tends to be subjective and have emotional aspects to it. Interpretive data include members' attitudes, beliefs, and perceptions about the organization, its means of functioning, and the ways members relate to one another. (Example: A consultant gathers information about how school counselors perceive the support given them by the teachers in their school.)

- Consultee-client system relationship data: The dynamics between the consultee and the client system constitute this type of data, including the nature of interpersonal relationships, their direction, and how communication takes place. (Example: A consultant watches a videotape of a consultee providing therapy to a client to help the consultee work more effectively with the client.)

- Client system behavior data: This type of information includes characteristics of the client system, such as level of intelligence, nature of the problem, levels of coping, the frequency of adaptive and maladaptive behaviors, and related environmental conditions. (Example: A school psychologist consulting with a school counselor administers an individual intelligence test to the counselor's client so as to suggest some effective helping strategies the counselor can use with that client.)

A great number of data sources are available to consultants, depending on the nature of

consultation. For example, consultants working with consultees whose client system is an organization may want to examine genetic data (for example, forms for writing up client reports from past years), current descriptive data (for example, current forms for writing up client reports), process data (for example, how the decision to use a given form for writing client reports was made), or interpretive data (for example, the results of a survey, that reveal how staff feel about the current form used to write up client reports). Consultants working with consultees who have individual clients tend to rely on consultee-client system relationship data (for example, the theoretical approach the consultee is taking with the client) and client system behavior data (for example, the nature of the client's behaviors with which the consultee is having difficulty). Whatever the type of data being gathered, it must be precise and meaningful (Newman & Fuqua, 1984). Imprecise data can intensify existing problems due to misdirected interventions. Data should also be selective, relevant, and understandable (Golembiewski, 1993a).

Scanning

Using the presenting problem as a starting point, it is a good idea for the consultant to scan the context in which the problem is thought to occur. *Scanning* is the process of looking at the big picture, including information about events and relationships within the organization's internal and external environment (Gallessich, 1982). Scanning prevents a premature focus on the problem's more obvious major elements to the exclusion of other factors that may be more germane to the problem (Steele, 1975). Scanning procedures can provide data for determining the validity of the problem, for identifying forces supporting or inhibiting effective change, and for detecting problems that are deeper than the ones identified in the preliminary exploration (Gallessich, 1982). In addition, scanning can prevent an a priori determination of the problem's nature and can counteract the consultant's professional and personal biases.

Hypothetically, a consultant could scan the entire domain: consultee, client system, and environment; in practice, scanning must be cost effective. Therefore, consultants typically use their theories of description analysis, change, and dysfunction to scan these systems. To avoid biases, the consultant describes these theories and the results of scanning to the consultee, who can then add additional perspectives to the analysis of the diagnosis stage. Once the entire context of the problem has been scanned and the results of the scanning interpreted, the consultant and consultee are ready to focus on more specific data.

Methods for Gathering Information

The information used in consultation is obtained by either unobtrusive or obtrusive data-gathering devices. Unobtrusive devices would disclose historical data (for example, memos), external data (for example, interviews with former clients of the organization), and observational data (for example, observing a meeting in action) (Bell & Nadler, 1985). Unobtrusive measures are not likely to interrupt the organization's normal flow of everyday activities or to be seen as threatening by the organization's members. Obtrusive data-gathering activities include those that in some way ask for a reaction from the members of the organization. Examples of this type of data gathering include questionnaires, surveys, and interviews with an organization's personnel. Because these activities directly assess the organization through its

members and may imply impending changes within the organization, they can be threatening and elicit resistance. Regardless of the method of data gathering used, the consultant can minimize resistance by ensuring that all appropriate personnel are informed of the data's anticipated uses.

Data can be soft such as subordinates' impressions of the organization's leadership, or hard, such as statistical data on the number of clients who perceive that the organization has helped them in some way (Gallessich, 1982). A general rule for data gathering is to move from less to more structured methods (Parsons & Meyers, 1984). For example, concerning the morale of an entire organization, it is best to gather general information first, such as a survey of a selected sample about the level of morale, and more specific information later, such as views concerning specific causes of the quality of morale. Instruments and procedures used to gather data should, whenever possible, be designed to take into consideration the uniqueness of the consultation situation.

The methods used for gathering information in consultation depend on the nature of the client system and the perceived problem. A consultant working with a consultee who is a therapist experiencing difficulty with a case requires different information than would a consultant working with an organization suffering from poor morale. Nonetheless, the most common information-gathering methods used in consultation include examining documents and records; giving questionnaires, surveys, and interviews; and observation (Lippitt, Langseth, & Mossop, 1985).

Documents and Records Consultants and consultees sometimes erroneously assume that they have to collect all of the data needed to make a diagnosis (Nadler, 1977). All organizations generate a wealth of information and keep some form of records, including numerical data and written communications. Use of records is often considered unobtrusive because their examination does not interrupt the organization's normal flow of work. Records are frequently referred to as secondary data because the information in them has already been collected.

The consultation party who is responsible for data collection searches these documents without the aid of any structure or procedure (Nadler, 1977). A variety of documents supply the consultant with data for use in making a diagnosis (Gallessich, 1982, p. 234): job descriptions, agency policies and manuals of operating procedures, historical records, annual reports, budgets, audits, personnel statistics, orientation procedures, promotion policies, program descriptions, grant proposals, client demographic profiles, surveys of client use of services, public information brochures, logs and appointment calendars, and case records.

By comparing an organization's current and past records and documents, the consultant may be able to identify trends and forces influencing the organization (Brubaker, 1978) and can determine who corresponds in writing with whom, how critical information is disseminated throughout the agency, and so forth. Reviewing relevant documents is a data-gathering technique that is frequently underused by consultants.

Examining records as an information-gathering technique has several strengths, including the use of existing information, cost efficiency, the wealth of relevant material, and the data's credibility with members of the organization (Fuqua & Newman, 1983). In addition, records are typically free from response bias and are nonreactive.

The use of documents as an information-gathering device also has weaknesses, among which are potential inaccuracy and incompleteness, limited availability, difficulties in data analysis, and the possibility of increasing resistance among consultees and the organization as a whole (Fuqua & Newman, 1983). Nadler (1977) corroborates these weaknesses by noting that records frequently have little relation to reality and that pertinent information is often difficult to retrieve. In addition, the consultant must frequently rely on the consultee's assistance in determining the validity of existing data and in identifying which data might be diagnostically useful.

Questionnaires and Surveys Questionnaires and surveys are actually self-administered interviews that allow for simultaneous collection of information from several sources (Parsons & Meyers, 1984). There is a tremendous body of literature on conducting and interpreting questionnaires (Egan, 1985). The three types of questionnaires are the standardized, the modified, and the custom made.

Standardized questionnaires are available either commercially or in research journals. Their validity and reliability have been demonstrated in the research literature. *Modified* questionnaires are usually standardized questionnaires that have been adapted in some way to meet specific needs of the data-gathering process. For example, a school counselor might adapt a questionnaire used in a mental health center for use in a school setting. When a questionnaire is *custom made*, it is developed by the consultant and consultee for a specific purpose. Custom-made questionnaires require a substantial amount of time to construct and often lack high levels of validity and reliability. The type of questionnaire or survey a consultant chooses depends on the precise nature of the information needed to make an adequate diagnosis (Goodstein, 1978).

Most questionnaires and surveys use fixed responses (Nadler, 1977) for respondents' information about their attitudes, perceptions, or points of view. A current trend toward incorporating some open-ended responses in questionnaires allows respondents to personalize their responses. However, these are difficult to summarize and interpret (Burges, 1976).

There are several advantages of using surveys and questionnaires as data-gathering techniques. They allow sampling of large numbers of people simultaneously, are cost effective, and can be used for a variety of purposes. Responses can be quickly and easily collated and statistically analyzed. Questionnaires and surveys are probably the most powerful data-gathering tools for yielding maximum information in the most efficient manner (Greiner & Metzger, 1983). They can be used to gather data for defining a problem, to provide clues about which data-gathering techniques (for example, interviews) should be used subsequently, or in conjunction with interviews of a sample of the respondents (Nadler, 1977).

Questionnaires and surveys also have disadvantages. They are nonempathic—the instrument does not interact with the respondent in a personal way—which can cause indifference toward the questionnaire on the part of the respondent. They lack adaptability; that is, they are prestructured. If some questions are inappropriate for some respondents, nothing can be done about it. They can also be difficult to interpret; different respondents may interpret the same question differently. Further, surveys and questionnaires can suffer from response bias, in which the respondent answers all items in a set way rather than each item on its own merit. Fordyce and Weil (1978) criticize questionnaires because they can produce canned results and because consultants frequently use them when direct human communication, such as

interviews, is more appropriate. For a detailed discussion of the use of questionnaires in data collection, consult Goode and Hatt (1972).

Interviews One of the best ways to understand a client system or an organization is to ask the people in them what they think and feel. Such a technique, the interview, is another commonly used form of data gathering (Gallessich, 1982). Even though interviews are used in all phases of the diagnostic stage (Parsons & Meyers, 1984), the nature of the interviewing process will depend on the type of model from which the consultant operates, the issues the interviews are to explore (Goodstein, 1978), and the consultant's earlier observations (Schein, 1988). Effective interviewing demands that the consultant be sufficiently skilled to note the interviewee's nonverbal and verbal behavior during the interview. Depending on how the interview is conducted, the consultant can uncover both positive and negative opinions and attitudes on a large number of relevant topics (Fordyce & Weil, 1978).

The interviewing process can be formal or informal, as can its setting, which can affect the type of information shared by the interviewee (Steele, 1975). Both groups and individuals can be interviewed, though interviewees are less likely to distort data in a group interview and also are less likely to share their true views and feelings (Greiner & Metzger, 1983). The process by which interviews take place is usually determined by such factors as cost and the data-gathering potential of the interviewing style.

Different types of interviews produce different types of responses from different people (Egan, 1985). There are three common types of interviews: unstructured, structured and open ended, and structured and fixed response (Nadler, 1977). *Unstructured* interviews are typically characterized by a minimal direction of their content by the interviewer (consultant). *Structured and open-ended* interviews consist of a set of preselected questions that the consultant asks the interviewee. *Structured and fixed-response* interviews provide both predetermined questions and responses from which to choose.

Interviews have several advantages (Nadler, 1977). They are adaptive—the interviewing process can be modified depending on the course of the interview. For example, if an interviewee provides an ambiguous response, the consultant can ask for clarification or an example of what the interviewee means. Interviews can be a source of detailed information on several topics and can provide rich sources of data about problems and their causes. Further, interviews allow the consultant to express empathy and understanding to the interviewee, and as a result, the interview process can be used to build rapport with some members of the organization.

Interviews also have their disadvantages. They are one of the most costly forms of data gathering in terms of both time and expense (Neilsen, 1984). The interviewee's responses can be affected by the consultant's biases to the degree that these biases dictate the types of questions asked. Interviewee bias can also affect the data obtained because the consultant can record not only the interviewee's perceptions but also observations of the consultee's behavior. Consequently, the results of interviews should be carefully validated. Two additional potential disadvantages of interviews are the inaccessibility of interviewees and the perceived threat that what interviewees say could somehow later be used against them. The reasons for interviewing and the uses made of the interview data should be made known to all parties-at-interest prior to the onset of the interviewing process (Fordyce & Weil, 1978).

Observation   Data can be collected through observation—the deliberate viewing of events. This most obvious way to collect information puts the consultant in direct contact with the people, activities, and/or environment about which information is being collected (Nadler, 1977). Consultants must make choices about what, when, and how much to observe; such choices lend observations structure that can range from a strictly defined to a general framework. The consultant's basic question regarding observation is, How can the observation be structured so that meaningful and useful data can be collected? (Nadler, 1977, p. 133). The three types of observation—structured, semistructured, and unstructured—differ in the degree to which observers watch and record the observations.

Structured observations typically use procedures or instruments that specify what type of behavior is to be observed and how it is to be recorded. *Semistructured* observations have relatively unstructured observations but highly structured recording. *Unstructured* observations have no strict guidelines for what is to be observed, what is to be recorded, or how recording should take place. Figure 4.3 illustrates a form used in a structured observation.

Observation has several advantages. It provides data on behavior rather than on reports of behavior and can note behaviors unrecognized by organization members or the client system. It can also be one of the more objective data-gathering methods. Observational data have strong face validity; that is, such data have concrete referents to back them up, whereas interviews and questionnaire data can be accused of being overly subjective. Further, this type of data is also current, whereas questionnaires generally sample respondents' past perceptions. Finally, observation, like interviewing,

**Form to Report Functional Relations
over Several Days and Time Periods**

Day, Date, & Time (Class Period): _____

Location (Classroom): _____

Teasing

Defined as negative comments to others about something they have done, how they look, or a threat.

Setting Events/Antecedents

    Activity when teasing occurred: _____

    Others nearby: _____

    Activity before present activity: _____

    Any other events before that seemed relevant: _____

Consequences

    Actions of teacher: _____

    Actions of peers: _____

    Any other consequences: _____

Nonteasing

Peer-directed comments that are positive or neutral. Comments about external activities or events (e.g., sports, class), compliments, statements of fact (e.g., about the assignment) not about the peer.

Setting Events/Antecedents

    Activity when nonteasing occurred: _____

    Others nearby: _____

    Activity before present activity: _____

    Any other events before that seemed relevant: _____

Consequences

    Actions of teacher: _____

    Actions of peers: _____

    Other: _____

SOURCE: From Kazdin, A. E. (1995). *Behavior modification in applied settings* (5th ed.). Pacific Grove, CA: Brooks/Cole. By permission of publisher.

FIGURE 4.3   Observations for Functional Assessment

is adaptive: The consultant can adjust what is to be observed as the situation demands.

Observation is not without its liabilities as a data-collection method (Nadler, 1977). Like interviewing, observation is expensive. The coding and interpretation that must be applied to observational data is subject to observer bias, and the less structured the observation, the more likely observer bias will enter into the process. As is the case with questionnaires, sampling is also an issue in observation. Observations require sampling with regard to people, time, space, and activities, and such intensive sampling can be costly in time and money. Finally, observation has the potential liability of observer effect. *Observer effect* is the impact observers have on the behavior of those being observed. For example, counselors being observed by a consultant may be more empathic than usual with clients simply because they are under observation.

In summary, each data-collection method has its advantages and disadvantages. Consultants should consider using multiple and valid data-gathering methods as a way of both overcoming the liabilities of a given method and eliminating inaccurate or distorted data. Consultants should ensure that the information gathered is as valid and accurate as possible and have an agreement with the consultee as to how to integrate the data from multiple sources (Macmann et al., 1996).

A Brief Example of Gathering Information   A counseling psychologist has contracted to assist a preschool program in determining how parents view its strengths and weaknesses. As the psychologist meets with the program director to develop a plan, they decide to gather survey and interview data from a random sample of half the parents (one-fourth of the se-

lected group will be interviewed, the other three-quarters will be surveyed). The consultant agrees to develop a structured interview and develop a survey that is compatible with the interview. The consultee suggests that the consultant be responsible for conducting the interviews while the consultee takes care of getting the surveys sent out and the results collated.

PHASE TWO: DEFINING THE PROBLEM

After the data has been collected, it must be analyzed. The importance of defining the problem cannot be overemphasized (Gutkin & Curtis, 1982; Osterweil, 1987). This phase is quite critical because the task to be accomplished is defined and thus affects the rest of the consultation process (Pryzwansky, 1989) and has been linked to eventual success in consultation (Bergan & Tombari, 1976).

To define a problem the consultant and the consultee should have a systematic, deliberate, and predetermined plan for analyzing the data (Nadler, 1977). In addition, cultural sensitivity needs to be shown and technician-like diagnostic procedures avoided (Smart & Smart, 1997). When involved in the details of gathering information, it is easy to forget that the purpose of the collecting is to shed light on the problem (Heppner, Kivlighan, & Wampold, 1992). Thus, the consultant and consultee should consider working together as a team to analyze a situation and choose the proper strategies that are likely to lead to the accomplishment of desired goals (Armstrong & Wheatley, 1990). In addition, there is some evidence to suggest that consultants who openly model the problem-solving process as they go through it create a road map that enhances consultee understanding and use of the process (Cleven & Gutkin, 1988; Zins, 1993). Such modeling can prevent bias in determining how much of the problem is internal to the client system (for example, traits) and how much is external (for example, environments) (Martin, 1983).

Data analysis is made up of a conceptual model and a technical component (Nadler, 1977). The conceptual component—the diagnostic perspective described earlier—should have been agreed upon by the consultant and the consultee before data are gathered, as should the techniques for analysis. Analysis of the data may suggest new hypotheses concerning the problem that require collection of additional data and subsequent analysis.

As the consultant and consultee examine the data, a more complex conceptualization of the problem often occurs. There is some evidence that defining the problem is not as easy as the literature suggests (Conoley, Conoley, & Gumm, 1992). Thus, consultants will want to take into account the problem-solving approach used by their consultee in examining the data (Medway, 1989; Pryzwansky, 1989). Further, how the consultee conceptualizes the problem might well influence the consultant's conceptualization.

During the significant amount of time spent on analyzing and interpreting data, the consultant and consultee determine how a broad range of factors affects the problem (Brown et al., 1995): how it develops over time, how past events are causing the present problem, or how future expectations are related. A clear, specific problem statement with corresponding objectives is crucial in assuring that the correct problem is attacked.

It is important that the problem statement be in language that is acceptable to the consultee (Dustin & Ehly, 1984). To this end, Oster-

weil (1987) suggests generating several alternative definitions of the problem from which the consultant and consultee can choose using three criteria:

- reasonability—the degree to which the definition seems logical to both consultant and consultee

- workability—the degree to which the definition seems practical and leads to new directions of action

- motivation—the degree to which the consultee will be willing to take action on the defined problem.

A Brief Example of Defining the Problem A school administrator asks a school counselor for assistance in determining which programs the school's counseling department should implement. The counselor interviews a select group of administrators, teachers, parents, and students about the types of programs suitable for counseling department sponsorship. Based on these interviews the department uses four surveys designed for and sent to a random sample of each group: administrators, parents, teachers, and students.

The counselor and administrator agree to conceptualize the data analysis based on the common themes that emerge from each of the four surveys. In addition, they agree to look for any program suggestions that are unique to any given set of responders. They ask themselves the following questions: Is there a consensus among the groups concerning the programs the counseling department should sponsor? What program suggestions are unique to each group? What are the implications of this information for planning programs?

Survey items are tallied and their relative ranks determined for each of the four groups.

A given program would be seriously considered if it is ranked in the top four in importance by two or more groups. The remainder of the data, though not given priority for the development of a particular program, is to be taken into account as the counseling department reviews its entire set of activities.

In general, defining the problem requires the consultant and consultee to interpret the analyzed data according to some mutually accepted conceptual scheme and determine the data's meanings and limitations (Lorsch & Lawrence, 1972). These efforts ideally result in both an appropriately defined problem and a cognitive map for the consultee's future use (Lorsch & Lawrence, 1972). Once the problem has been defined to the mutual satisfaction of consultant and consultee, the consultant facilitates a commitment from the consultee to act on it (Redmon, Cullari, & Farris, 1985).

PHASE THREE: SETTING GOALS

Setting goals is an important phase in the diagnostic stage. Consultants need to be experts in goal setting because it is likely that their consultees will not be (Egan, 1985). Goal setting focuses on which actions will effectively solve or ameliorate the identified problem or problems (Egan & Cowan, 1979).

The Process of Setting Goals

Goal setting is the central point of the diagnostic process (Egan, 1994). Empirical research (for example, Latham & Lee, 1986; Locke & Latham, 1984) supports the notion that, when properly performed, goal setting has positive benefits. Because choosing goals establishes what specific ends are to be accomplished, goal setting should not be rushed (Egan & Cowan,

1979), because inappropriate or poorly refined goals may be chosen.

Goal setting, then, is a process of shaping, a movement toward concreteness and specificity from a broader, more general perspective (Egan, 1985). If the problem is complex, the goal of resolving the problem will likely be complex, too (Egan, 1985).

The first step in goal setting is to "discover new goal possibilities" (Egan & Cowan, 1979, p. 143) related to the problem. To accomplish this end, Egan and Cowan (1979) suggest the creative strategies of divergent thinking, brainstorming, scenario writing, and fantasy.

Once goal possibilities have been determined, the consultant and consultee engage in the following goal-setting steps (Locke & Latham, 1984):

1. Specify the task or objective.
2. Specify how the task or objective will be measured.
3. Specify the target or standard to be reached.
4. Specify the time span involved.
5. Prioritize possible goals.
6. Rate goals with respect to difficulty and importance.
7. Determine coordination requirements.

Based on these goal-setting steps, the consultant and consultee choose the most appropriate goal, which is then evaluated and adjusted in light of the characteristics of effective goals.

Characteristics of Effective Goals

A *goal* is a specific outcome that is sought to solve or improve a problem; a *complex goal* is one that can be divided into subgoals (Egan,

1985). In the context of consultation, success is a complex goal that can be broken down into subgoals: success in each phase of each stage of consultation.

For the goal-setting process to be successful, goals should be written in clear, specific, behavioral terms (Egan & Cowan, 1979). Such specificity facilitates selecting appropriate interventions to solve the problem and evaluating those interventions. Specific goals allow the consultant and consultee to regulate and evaluate the effectiveness of interventions designed to meet those goals (Latham & Lee, 1986). If, for example, a consultant and a consultee determine that the goal is improved morale, it would be insufficient until they specified what they meant by *morale* and *improved*.

Effective goals are verifiable in some way, preferably by measurement. Consultants and consultees must determine what should be measured, how it should be measured, and when measurement should take place. Accomplishment of goals can be verified either quantitatively or qualitatively. Measures of quantity include volume and rate, whereas measures of quality include accuracy and novelty (Egan, 1985). Cost-effectiveness—whether the expense in meeting a goal was worth the benefits derived from accomplishing it—also should be taken into consideration in goal setting. Worthwhile goals are those that are meaningful to the people involved in achieving them; they are considered to be worth the effort required to accomplish them.

Three factors determine whether a goal is realistic: resources, control, and obstacles (Egan, 1985). The consultant and the consultee must determine the adequacy of available resources for accomplishing the goal. Thus, a mental health consultant whose consultee is a teacher may have to determine whether the school has the resources needed to help the teacher's

emotionally disturbed student (client). The consultant should ensure that the consultee has some control over whether or not the goal is met, and the consultant and consultee must determine if the goal is adequate.

Obstacles to the accomplishment of any goal must be expected. Thus, for example, even though a consultant and consultee may have chosen as a goal the accomplishment of a treatment plan for the consultee's client, the client may not be willing to attend the number of counseling sessions required for effective implementation of the plan. The consultant and consultee should try to anticipate and neutralize any obstacles to the successful accomplishment of a goal.

Goals reflect the values of the people attempting to accomplish them, and they should conform to the values of the consultant, consultee, client system, and the organization (Egan, 1985). Consultants may occasionally need to help consultees clarify their values so as to set effective goals. Further, consultants may also need to reflect on their own values so that they do not inadvertently impose them on their consultees during this phase of the diagnostic process.

The consultant and consultee should determine who else needs to be informed about goals. Clear communication about goals to parties-at-interest is essential to receiving the cooperation crucial to the accomplishment of the goals, especially when the accomplished goals will affect many of the organization's members.

A Brief Example of Setting Goals A social worker is consulting with the principal of a rural school on how to involve community agencies with the school more. In setting goals to accomplish this, the consultant engages the administrator in both brainstorming and scenario writing. They brainstorm on the types of organizations that could become more involved with the school and write scenarios depicting the nature of the involvement for each agency. Based on examining goal possibilities, the consultant and consultee determine that they will contact seven agencies within the next two months and sell them on the idea of becoming more involved with the school. Together they assess the feasibility of the goal, and the social worker agrees to coordinate attempts to accomplish the goal.

PHASE FOUR: GENERATING POSSIBLE INTERVENTIONS

Once the consultant and consultee have chosen an acceptable goal, they are ready to enter the last phase of the diagnosis stage—generating possible interventions to accomplish the goal.

Like goal setting, generating possible interventions is a critical step in the diagnostic stage. Whereas the goal suggests what the consultant and consultee want to accomplish, interventions are things they can do to accomplish that goal. An *intervention* is a force that attempts to modify some outcome. In consultation, interventions are the actions or activities that, when put together in a systematic manner, make up a plan to achieve a goal.

It would be a mistake for the consultant to assume that because consultees know what goals they want to accomplish, they also know all of the ways to go about accomplishing them. By discussing alternative interventions, consultants can ascertain both the consultee's knowledge of various types of interventions and what the consultee has tried so far to solve the problem. Developing a broad array of interventions to choose from is related to consul-

tee willingness to implement the selected intervention (Gresham & Lopez, 1996).

Consultants can assist their consultees in generating possible interventions by using prompts (stimuli or reminders) that stimulate the consultee's creativity. These prompts include (Egan, 1998):

- *people* who might assist the consultee in achieving goals, such as resource people or role models (for example, a program evaluator for a newly implemented program)

- *places* that might be more appropriate for implementing a plan (for example, an off-campus location for a faculty retreat)

- *things* that may lead to an easier way of accomplishing a goal (for example, computer technology for a proposed corporate reorganization)

- *organizations* that could sponsor or assist the consultee in some way (for example, a private charitable foundation to provide funding for a pilot program)

- *prepackaged programs* whose goals are similar to the consultee's (for example, a stress management program for teachers at a school)

- *consultee resources* that can be used to a large degree to generate possible interventions, particularly when the consultee is going to carry out the intervention that is ultimately selected (for example, the consultee being the counselor for a client about whom a goal has been set)

Brainstorming is a powerful strategy that consultants can use to help consultees generate a list of possible interventions (Pfeiffer & Jones, 1974; Summers & White, 1980). Such a technique assists the consultant and consultee to go beyond the usual consideration of only one or two alternatives in choosing an intervention. Whenever a consultee's work-related problem has some unknown factors and some uncertainty about the best way to solve it, it is appropriate to take the time necessary to generate and analyze a list of alternative interventions (Carlisle, 1982). By following the rules of brainstorming, consultants can increase the probability that consultees will generate an adequate list of possible interventions. The rules of brainstorming include the following (Pfeiffer & Jones, 1974):

- Do not evaluate strategies as they are being generated.

- Generate as many interventions as possible.

- Creativity and novelty are at a premium when generating a list of possible interventions.

Once the consultee understands the ground rules, the consultant and consultee brainstorm for an agreed-upon period (for example, five minutes). The consultant and consultee should write down or tape-record interventions as they come to mind. After the brainstorming period, the consultant and consultee reconsider and clarify each item to complete this list of possible interventions.

If the consultee is unfamiliar with the brainstorming process, the consultant should provide some practice sessions first. For example, the consultant and consultee could brainstorm ways people could stay dry after being caught out in the rain. Brainstorming does not replace the sound professional judgment of either the consultant or the consultee. Rather, it is simply a technique to enhance the quantity and quality of inputs into the decision-making process. Consultants should be aware that brainstorming is very demanding intellectually, because one must consider the future, examine complex situations, recall previous experiences, and use creativity.

A Brief Example of Generating Possible Solutions A consulting school psychologist and a high school counselor agree that their goal is to alleviate the test anxiety of an international student. To bring to mind possible interventions, the school psychologist asks the school counselor questions, including the following:

"Who do you think can assist you in your work with this student?"

"What do you think is the best setting for working with the student?"

"What things such as CD-ROMs and booklets might be available for you to use?"

"Are any organizations that work with international students available to be of help?"

"Do you know of any companies who have prepackaged programs for test anxiety or for helping international students get acclimatized to American schools?"

"What professional abilities do you have that you can use directly with the student?"

MULTICULTURAL ASPECTS

RELATED TO DIAGNOSIS

Multicultural influences can impact the diagnosis stage (Jackson & Hayes, 1993). For example, a consultee's or fellow collaborator's view of the methods used for data gathering may be influenced by cultural variables such as

---

CASE 4.1   Diagnosis for School Consultants

Geri is a school-based consultant who is working with a teacher concerning a child who has difficulty remaining in his classroom seat. During the diagnosis stage, Geri and the teacher decide that Geri should observe the child in the classroom on at least three different occasions and conduct an informal interview with him. During the observation, Geri is to observe the social conditions that surround the child's getting out of his seat as well as the antecedents and consequences of this behavior. In the interview, Geri is to inform the child that the teacher is concerned about his behavior. The teacher has asked Geri to talk to him about it and about his feelings toward the class, the teacher, his studies, and his own behavior.

Geri conducts the observations, interviews the child, and then meets again with the teacher. Together they determine that the child's behavior is most likely due to the attention he receives from his buddies for disturbing the class. Geri and the teacher discuss what is reasonable behavior for the child; the goal is for the child to decrease his inappropriate out-of-seat behavior by 50 percent the first month and 75 percent the second month. They decide on a second goal—for the child to increase the frequency of socially acceptable classroom behaviors by 25 percent over a 3-month period. Geri and the teacher begin to brainstorm possible interventions, but don't evaluate any of the items at this time. They come up with interventions such as a change in the child's seat, a teacher contract with the child, a teacher face-to-face talk with the child, a parent conference that includes the child, a student assistant program, and a realignment of the entire structure of the classroom.

Commentary

Diagnosing the problem is a very important element in the consultation process. It is very easy for consultants and consultees to pay lip service to diagnostic procedures in organizations such as schools when there are numerous time constraints. Look at it this way, would you prefer the physicians you see to perform cursory examinations (that is, data-gathering procedures) on you? Certainly, you wouldn't because they might well be missing significant information related to your well-being. So too in consultation, it is better to ensure that you and the consultee have adequate data so that you have a higher probability of accurately defining the problem.

---

context. Consultees or fellow collaborators from high context cultures may prefer interviewing or observational methods whereas those from low context cultures may prefer methods such as reading documents or conducting surveys.

Consultees of different cultural backgrounds may prefer a fluid definition of the problem while others prefer a concrete and detailed process of defining the problem. There can be cultural differences related to perceptions of what goals need to be set. Whereas, for example, one collaborator may view a whole family as the focal point of the goals, another collaborator may believe a particular member of the family should be the focus. Cultural differences can play a part in determining what kinds of interventions are generated. Consultees or fellow collaborators influenced by high cultural context may want to avoid interventions that that they see as time bound, perceive to be overly structured, or view as exclusively dealing with authority figures. Further, the cultural aspects of the client system are a variable in determining the types of interventions that might be successful (Flanagan & Miranda, 1995).

SUMMARY

Diagnosis is a critical stage in consultation. Indeed, if the wrong problem is defined, then the wrong problem is solved. During this stage, the consultant and consultee collaborate in gather-

---

CASE 4.2   Diagnosis for Community Consultants[1]

Martin, a community consultant, was asked by a local hospital to assist in the development of a community AIDS prevention program. Martin's consultees are a community health practitioner, a hospital-community relations coordinator, and a physician with a strong interest in the prospective program.

At one of their first meetings, Martin brought up the idea that a lot of information needed to be gathered to get a focus on how the program might look. He noted that it would be valuable to determine the success of several existing AIDS and HIV education programs. The group reached a consensus that it would be foolish to try developing a program without proper study.

Their first task was to find out about as many of the existing programs as possible. Through Martin's facilitation, the group would review the literature, make calls to existing programs, and visit a few programs that were close to the community. The physician agreed to call several programs, Martin and the hospital-community relations coordinator agreed to review the literature at a local university library, and the entire group agreed to make site visits to three existing programs.

As they reviewed all of the gathered information, one theme became

quite evident: Many AIDS and HIV education programs were unsuccessful due to poor planning and lack of community involvement. Martin then helped the group define the problem in terms of the question What is the best type of AIDS prevention program for this community? Once the problem was defined, Martin and the group developed and prioritized a set of goals. In developing the goals by writing a scenario of what a quality program might look like, they realized that a quality program might be beyond the scope of the hospital's resources.

The prioritized goals were: start a publicity campaign to promote the need for an AIDS/HIV education program, develop a task force to promote and plan the program, develop targets for the programs within the community, and develop short- and long-term plans that demonstrate sensitivity to the social and cultural contexts of AIDS/HIV. The following are some of the series of possible interventions they felt would help in meeting their goals: involve possible target group members in the development of the program; ask target group members to be part of the task force; include culturally relevant content and media in publicizing the need for the program;

use community recognition to reward members who assist in the development of the program; and maintain the use of Martin as a consultant for developing short- and long-term plans.

Commentary

External scanning can be one of the most effective diagnostic procedures consultants, consultees, and collaborators employ. In your work as a consultant or collaborator, scanning will prevent you from working in a vacuum and from reinventing the wheel. The use of goal setting by writing desired scenarios can be an interesting process for the consultant and consultee to engage in. Such scenarios provide a rich narrative that is often lacking from traditional goal setting statements. Putting goals in priority order enables the consultant and consultee to remain aware of the most important tasks at hand while providing them with a map to guide their efforts. Clearly, diagnosis involves more than figuring out what's the matter.

[1] The idea for this case study came from the articles in the section entitled, "Special Feature: AIDS and HIV," *Journal of Counseling and Development,* 71(3): 1993, 259–309.

---

ing information by various means, in defining a problem from that information, in setting a goal to resolve the problem, and then in generating some possible interventions to accomplish the goal. Diagnosis should not be rushed; consultants should encourage their consultees to remain patient and avoid the tendency to define the problem hastily.

This stage of consultation requires that the consultant and consultee gather the appropriate information necessary for defining the problem. To do this effectively, the consultant and consultee need to know both what information they seek and the methods by which they are going to gather it. Because each method of data gathering has its advantages and disadvantages, the consultant and consultee must carefully weigh the pros and cons of each. Further, they need to analyze the data using some valid method that is consistent with the goal of consultation. Both quantitative and qualitative methods can be used in defining the problem.

Once the problem has been defined to the satisfaction of the parties involved, goal setting is initiated. Goal setting, like all phases of diagnosis, should be collaborative to enhance the likelihood that the consultee will obtain an effective set of diagnostic skills for future use.

Upon the completion of goal setting, the consultant and consultee generate a list of possible interventions. This is one of the more creative phases of diagnosis, and it is also one of the most difficult because consultees may experience conflict and uncertainty about having so many possible courses of action, especially if the majority of them appear to be equally effective in reaching a desired goal (Ashford & Cummings, 1983). Therefore, the consultant may need to assist the consultee in selecting some of the better alternatives. There is some evidence that such direction by the consultant is not a detriment to the consultation process (Houk & Lewandowski, 1996). Ultimately, the major goal of the consultant during this phase is to assist the consultee in developing an adequate number of possible interventions.

The research on diagnosis is sparse. There is some evidence about the frequency with which diagnostic models are used, but none on the relative effectiveness of different approaches to diagnosis. The research on providing consultees with feedback regarding the result of the data-gathering stage indicates that feedback is necessary and desired by consultees; as well, the response to such feedback is affected by how it is presented (Armenakis & Burdg, 1988).

There is some evidence that enhancing the problem-solving techniques of consultees improves consultee performance during consultation (Zins, 1993). To this end, Zins (1993) suggests that consultees be trained directly in problem-solving and intervention techniques, that consultants provide overt modeling of the problem-solving process for consultees, and that potential consultees receive direct training in problem solving prior to receiving consultation services as part of preservice training.

SUGGESTIONS FOR EFFECTIVE PRACTICE

- Remember that diagnosis can be an ongoing process and that numerous aspects of the problem may change as time goes on.
- Define the problem and related goals as specifically as you can.
- Use scanning as a tool to give direction to your choice of interventions.
- Involve consultees and fellow collaborators as much as possible in the data-gathering process.
- Avoid the temptation to bypass the phase of generating possible interventions.

QUESTIONS FOR REFLECTION

1. What do you envision as the most difficult phase of diagnosis for you to function in? Why?

2. Which 10 skills are most needed by consultants to increase the chances that the diagnosis stage will be successful?

3. Consider your answer to the previous question: in which of these skills do you think most of your consultees will be deficient? Why?

4. What is the most practical way to scan a presenting problem? How would you determine what to scan?

5. How can you best teach consultees to enhance their skills in diagnosis?

6. Which methods of gathering information would you be most likely to use? Why?

7. Once the data have been collected, how does a consultant go about assisting a consultee in defining a problem?

8. Of the characteristics of effective goals mentioned in this chapter, which do you think are the most difficult to meet?

9. How would you assist a consultee in generating a list of several possible interventions?

10. You have now read about the entry and diagnosis stages of consultation. In what ways does the diagnosis stage build on a successfully completed entry stage?

SUGGESTED SUPPLEMENTARY READINGS

Egan, G. (1985). *Change agent skills in helping and human service settings.* Pacific Grove, CA: Brooks/Cole. Although somewhat dated, this is an excellent text that takes a systems approach to change agentry. Chapter 6, entitled "Clear and Realistic Goals," provides broad coverage of the topic of goal setting. I strongly recommend this chapter. Another excellent chapter is Chapter 3 on data gathering.

Hohenshil, T. H. (1996). Editorial: Role of assessment and diagnosis in counseling. *Journal of Counseling and Development, 75,* 64–67. This article presents a concise and valuable perspective on the role of assessment and diagnosis. Although it focuses on a counseling context, you will find a wealth of information to employ in consultation and collaboration.

Nadler, D. A. (1977). *Feedback and organization development: Using data-based methods.* Reading, MA: Addison-Wesley. This book is the classic text on using data as a tool for change in organizations. It provides coverage of the use of records, questionnaires, interviews, and observation in data gathering. It contains a wealth of information, including two chapters on feedback.

5

Implementation Stage

Consultants and collaborators need to assist their consultees and fellow collaborators in taking some action to solve the problem identified in the diagnosis stage. This "action stage" of consultation is implementation. The consultant often functions as a resource person and trainer during this stage. The various models of consultation (Chapters 9–11) conceptualize the implementation process differently and use different types of interventions. An organizational consultant might spend a lot of time determining the level of the organization at which to intervene and then selecting an intervention appropriate to that level. A mental health consultant might carefully determine whether the problem in consultation is due to the consultee or to the client before identifying possible interventions. A behavioral consultant might determine which types of reinforcement are most effective with a given client and then choose an intervention that includes those types of reinforcements. Regardless of the model of consultation in use, however, the process of implementation remains the same.

This chapter covers the implementation stage of consultation, which is composed of four phases: choosing an intervention, formulating a plan, implementing the plan, and evaluating the plan.

As you read through this chapter, here are some questions to consider:

1. How does a consultant assist a consultee in choosing the most appropriate interventions from among those generated at the end of the diagnosis stage?

2. What are the pros and cons of the various types of interventions?

3. How do the consultant and consultee tailor the chosen plan to the organization in which it is to be implemented?

4. What is the consultant's role in implementing the plan?

5. How can the consultant and consultee determine the degree to which the plan was successful?

INTRODUCTION

Consider for a moment the following:

A Case of Implementation

A staff development coordinator in a human service organization has been working with a consultant on some of the organization's concerns about improving the quality of its work environment. The coordinator's immediate superior calls the coordinator in and asks what progress has been made with the consultant. The coordinator indicates that the problem has been identified, explored, and analyzed. Further, several prospective interventions have been identified. The supervisor then asks what the next steps will be. The staff development coordinator replies that a plan will be formulated and the logistics of implementing it worked out. The plan will then be put into action and evaluated. The supervisor then asks for a time frame within which all of this will occur.

This sequence of events is quite common in consultation. Many times people within the organization in which consultation is occurring have relatively little idea about how complex and time consuming effective consultation is. The staff development coordinator was in essence telling the supervisor that consultation had progressed to the implementation stage. She and the consultant had devised and were ready to choose among several possible in-

terventions, formulate a plan, tailor it to the organization's needs, put it into action, and then evaluate the degree to which it worked. Clearly, good planning is essential to successful consultation, yet it is very easy to neglect. Because every plan has its advantages, disadvantages, and possible glitches, there is no one best plan, but rather one that has the highest probability of succeeding.

Figure 5.1 illustrates the phases of the implementation stage. In choosing an intervention, the consultant and consultee answer the question What are we going to do? In formulating a plan, they answer the question How are we going to do it? They actively try to solve the problem in the phase of implementing the plan, and in evaluating the plan they ask How did we do?

As was the case in the entry and diagnosis stages, the implementation stage is critical in the consultation process: imagine the difficulties that would be encountered if an inappropriate plan were chosen for a given problem. The consultant and consultee would come up with the wrong solution for the right problem. Or if a proper plan were chosen but the wrong interventions were used, the consultant and consultee might have the right solution put together in the wrong way.

In the implementation stage the client or client system is now ready for some form of direct assistance from the consultee or indirect service from the consultant. The consultant must make sure that the consultee formulates an appropriate plan and correctly implements it; evaluating the plan is one of the consultant's highest priorities. Consider a situation in which the right plan, the right strategies, and correct implementation are combined, but the consultant and consultee have failed to design an appropriate evaluation of the plan. In this

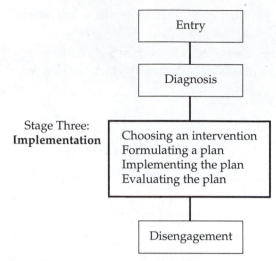

Stage Three:
Implementation

FIGURE 5.1
The phases of the implementation stage

situation, the consultant and consultee have no way of accurately determining the degree to which the plan actually worked.

The consultant may need to train the consultee in the interventions implemented during this stage; for example, a mental health consultant might need to train the consultee, a school counselor, in a specific procedure for desensitizing a child with school phobia. As in other stages in the consultation process, consultants take a collaborative approach whenever possible and avoid doing anything for consultees that they can do for themselves. In addition, the consultant typically relies on the consultee for information about the culture of the consultee's organization and the exact role of the consultee relative to the client system (Erchul & Schulte, 1993).

The implementation stage is important to the consultee because it represents some action on the problem that prompted the request for assistance in the first place. In this stage, the consultee either makes some intervention with a client system or benefits directly from some intervention by the consultant, who assumes that the experience will give the consultee useful skills for handling similar work-related concerns in the future.

PHASE ONE: CHOOSING

AN INTERVENTION

Since consultees may have a large number of interventions available to them, they may experience conflict because all of the interventions look good. Therefore, the first phase of the implementation stage involves selecting one or more interventions that have a high probability of being successful. One way to accomplish this is to make sure that all of the interventions being considered have research to back their efficacy (Lentz, Allen, & Erhardt, 1996). In addition, consultants should remember that knowing about a wide range of potential interventions is not enough. As Elliot and Busse (1993) note: consultants must also ". . . be sensitive to the skills and perceptions of their consultees and be able to clearly communicate treatment procedures so that they are implemented with integrity" (p. 194).

One effective procedure the consultant can use in helping a consultee choose among possible interventions is decision counseling (Janis & Mann, 1977). Although developed for use in counseling and psychotherapy over two decades ago, this procedure is useful for ensuring that the consultee goes through the process of choosing an intervention in an appropriate manner. The process of *decision consultation*, which is based on effective decision making, consists of eight questions consultants can ask consultees. The following questions are adaptations of those developed by Janis and Mann (1977, p. 371):

- To what degree has the consultee developed a wide range of alternative interventions?

- To what degree has the consultee considered the objectives and related values of the possible interventions?

- To what degree has the consultee weighed the potential negative consequences, risks, and potential payoffs of each intervention?

- To what degree has the consultee searched for new information relative to each intervention?

- To what degree has the consultee processed the consultant's comments about potential positive and negative factors related to the interventions?

- To what degree has the consultee made a final determination of the interventions' potential positive and negative consequences, as well as the driving and

inhibiting forces that affect their implementation?

- To what degree does the consultee have the capacity to successfully execute the chosen intervention?

- Which interventions have been set aside for use in contingency plans?

By engaging the consultee in the pursuit of answers to these questions, the consultant can help the consultee make a reasonably effective choice of interventions and can ascertain not only the degree to which the implementation appears satisfactory to the consultee, but also whether any adaptation of the intervention by the consultee will negatively affect its impact. The use of this process helps to ensure that the intervention selected is logically related to the information gathered and is congruent with the reasons the problem is believed to exist (Macmann et al., 1996). In addition, the process involved in this kind of assistance can rub off on the consultee, who can then be more effective in choosing interventions for similar problems in the future.

By engaging in decision consultation, the consultant can increase the probability that the consultee will follow through with the agreed-upon intervention. Consultants should note that consultees do not always follow through on the intervention they commit to (Conoley & Gutkin, 1986). Whether consultees will accept an intervention appears to be a function of their perception of the fit between the problem and the intervention, their beliefs about the intervention (for example, humaneness), the level of difficulty in implementing it (Noble & Dickinson, 1988; Erchul & Chewning, 1990), and the quality of the consultant-consultee relationship (Conoley, Conoley, Ivey, & Scheel, 1991). Therefore, the consultant should address these considerations when developing a rationale for an intervention. Being able to explain a wide variety of interventions from several different perspectives is a very desirable skill for consultants (Conoley et al., 1991), and it helps to avoid considering a limited number of interventions due to bias or favored interventions (Barnett & Lentz, 1993). Decision consultation also helps facilitate the use of more idiosyncratic, innovative, research-oriented interventions (Barnett & Lentz, 1993)

Consultants should be aware of potential obstacles to the successful completion of this phase. First, the consultee and consultant must process a tremendous amount of information in selecting the intervention (Wheeler & Janis, 1980). Second, it is difficult to predict realistically the specific outcomes of various interventions due to the possibility of unforeseen events and potential human error (Wheeler & Janis, 1980). Therefore, the consultant should consider having the consultee keep a consistent, detailed set of notes concerning alternative interventions (to facilitate discussion about the possible impacts of given interventions). The process of supporting the intervention should also be taken into consideration. In other words, the technical components need to be blended together with an ecological understanding of the problem setting (Lentz et al., 1996). There are some additional guidelines that can assist consultants and consultees in choosing an adequate intervention (Zins & Erchul, 1995):

- Try to use positive interventions first.

- Avoid complex and intrusive interventions.

- If the consultee is to learn a new skill, incorporate it into daily routines as much as possible.

- Promote interventions that require the least amount of time.

Types of Interventions

You are hungry, so you decide to go to a restaurant that offers a smorgasbord. As you walk through the smorgasbord, you have a difficult time selecting from among the offerings because they all look so good. You decide to choose one item that is representative of each of the four food groups. So you choose one meat, one dairy product, one cereal product, and one green vegetable—and then you proceed to enjoy your meal.

You have, in effect, just classified all of your possible food choices into four categories and then chosen from each of them. By categorizing your options, you made your decision about what to eat much easier.

Indeed, consultants and consultees have a smorgasbord of interventions available to them. Therefore, consultants typically categorize all the possible interventions that might be put together in a plan, which expedites the decision-making process.

In dealing with a problem situation, an intervention can be a single task, a series of related tasks, or a series of unrelated tasks organized around a common theme (French et al., 1978). One or more interventions can be put together systematically into a plan that is tailored to the unique problem that has been identified.

Effective consultants have a large number of interventions in their repertoire to most effectively assist their consultees. Such expertise allows the consultant flexibility in combining programs to meet the goals of consultation. Do you know about the carpenter who could only use a hammer? He saw every problem as a nail to be hit.

Consultants who do not have knowledge of and skill in many types of interventions tend to conceptualize solutions in terms of what they know how to do instead of what is really needed.

A useful device for obtaining a broad perspective on interventions is a classification system (Kurpius, 1985). According to French and Bell (1990), interventions can be classified into the following categories:

- families of interventions (for example, education/training activities)

- types of interventions (for example, theory intervention)

- mode of interventions (for example, problem solving)

- task versus process interventions (for example, problem solving versus team building)

- target group of the intervention (for example, the individual)

- underlying causal mechanisms of the intervention that lead to change (for example, increased communication and interaction)

- depth of intervention (for example, anonymous questionnaire versus personal interview)

A categorization of interventions based on target groups is a convenient one and is used in the following discussion. The target group is usually the client system. A classification scheme developed by French and Bell (1990) includes the following targets: individuals, dyads/triads, teams and groups, intergroup relations, and the total organization. Though developed for interventions in organizational consultation, this scheme can easily make up a generic classification system useful to all consultants.

Individual Interventions

Because individual interventions can also be designed to assist the organization as a whole by improving the functioning of selected individual members (Kurpius, 1986), individual interventions can apply in a variety of consultation settings (Fuqua & Newman, 1985). The previous chapter discussed ways to determine when individual interventions are appropriate. Fuqua and Newman (1985) suggest that consultants commonly use two general types of individual interventions: consultee-focused intervention and educational/training intervention. In effect, all individual consultation interventions attempt to assist the consultee by alleviating a lack of knowledge, skill, confidence, or objectivity.

Consultee-focused interventions are used when the consultee is experiencing a work-related problem due to a lack of objectivity or confidence (Caplan & Caplan, 1993) or a lack of skill in problem solving and decision making (Fuqua & Newman, 1985). Educational/ training methods are used when the consultee has a knowledge or skills deficit in a given area (Fuqua & Newman, 1985) or desires self-improvement in a given area (Parsons & Meyers, 1984).

Consultee–Centered Case Consultation
This intervention is one approach to the mental health consultation model and is given in-depth coverage in Chapter 10. This approach suggests that the problem in consultation resides in the consultee (for example, some personal matter), rather than in the client, and blocks any progress with the client (Caplan & Caplan, 1993). By using indirect procedures, the consultant helps the consultee regain an objective view of the case, at which point the consultee-client helping relationship should proceed effectively.

Problem-Solving/Decision-Making Education/Training Because consultation is a problem-solving endeavor, consultees need at least marginal problem-solving skills if they are to generalize newly learned consultation skills to future work-related situations. Hence, consultants frequently must educate or train their consultees to approach work-related problems systematically through the enhancement of problem-solving and decision-making skills (Fuqua & Newman, 1985). For example, a human resource development specialist might assist a group of administrators in a community agency program deal with problems in the agency's strategic planning process.

Stress Management Stress management interventions basically focus either on helping people manage stressors more effectively or on reducing the occurrence of stressors in the first place (Ivancevich, Matteson, Freedman, & Phillips, 1990). Interventions can involve reducing the stress involved in a situation (such as undergoing a job performance review), helping people modify their appraisal of potentially stressful situations (such as noting that the annual job performance review is not "the end of the world"), and helping individuals cope more effectively with stressful situations (Ivancevich et al., 1990). For example, in *stress inoculation training* (Meichenbaum, 1977, 1985), the consultee is taught to recognize debilitating self-talk about the work situation and replace it with coping self-talk. Through this process, consultants can help their consultees change their internal dialogue and create a more positive frame of reference concerning work.

Stress inoculation training is analogous to the way vaccine inoculations build a person's medical defenses. Through exposure to mild doses of stressful situations and by rehearsing positive responses to them, consultees learn how to build more effective coping defenses to use with work-related concerns. Too frequently, consultees see stressful situations as all-or-nothing demands (for example, totally cure the client or no progress has occurred); through stress inoculation training, consultees learn to take a stressful situation and break it down into four phases: preparing for a stressor, confronting and handling a stressor, coping with feelings of being overwhelmed, and reinforcing self-statements (Meichenbaum, 1977).

Coaching and Counseling Coaching and counseling activities are interventions that help consultees define learning goals, become aware of how others perceive their behavior, and learn new behaviors that might help in achieving defined goals (French & Bell, 1990). The consultant makes these interventions only after the consultee has "owned" a work-related concern and is ready to improve his or her work-related performance (Schein, 1988). For example, a consultee might want to improve his or her listening skills at the work site. The consultant gathers feedback on the consultee from a variety of sources and, after presenting the feedback, engages the consultee in a joint exploration of alternatives (French & Bell, 1990).

In the role of coach, a consultant assists consultees in deciding what they want to learn, helps them to learn those behaviors, and is instrumental in evaluating the degree to which such behaviors meet desired goals. Resnick and King (1985) have developed an interesting variation of coaching and counseling called *shadow consultation*. In shadow consultation, the consultant makes observations of the consultee's behavior during the workday and provides assistance based on them.

Life- and Career-Planning Activities Life- and career-planning activities are structured interventions that help consultees examine courses of action in attempting to achieve their life and career goals (French & Bell, 1990). Because career planning is part of life planning, both are generally performed concurrently. Aimed at the individual's development, these activities usually take place in one-day to one-week workshops and frequently include clarification of life goals, acceptance of the life cycle, recognition of one's strengths and limitations, and how to contribute to the next generation (Lippitt, 1982b).

Dyadic and Triadic Interventions

Sometimes consultants are called on to make interventions that are most effective with groups of two (dyads) or groups of three (triads). Interventions aimed at these small groups are limited but popular due to frequent use of dyadic and triadic work groups in human service organizations. Some of the types of interventions that are useful with individuals can be used to increase effectiveness of dyads and triads. Further, many of the interventions typically aimed at large groups, such as team building, are appropriate for use with these small groups.

Third-Party Peacemaking Conflict, common in most organizations, usually stems from parties' different perspectives on the same events. A strong cultural bias of avoidance in dealing with conflict exists in human service organizations (Carlisle, 1982). Differences between two consultees can be effectively dealt with in a variety of ways, including third-party peacemaking (Golembiewski & Rauschenberg, 1993), an intervention unique to dyads and triads, which is used to resolve interpersonal conflict.

The consultant guides a process in which two parties directly confront one another and use conflict resolution techniques (Fisher & Ury, 1981; French & Bell, 1990). The term *third party* refers to the consultant, who presumably is skilled and objective in terms of the conflict's resolution or management. The consultant is interested in improving the conditions and the manner in which the conflicting parties manage the conflict (Prein, 1987).

Interventions for Groups and Teams

Organizations make extensive use of teams and groups (French & Bell, 1990), and consultants frequently are called on to make interventions to enhance the effectiveness of an intact group or team. Interventions with groups or teams can be one of the most powerful of consultant interventions (Kurpius, 1985). The most common group or team intervention is the education/training approach, which is covered extensively in Chapter 9. Other interventions are described here.

Team Building A team is a group of individuals working together in a coordinated effort. Team building is the process by which a team's individuals attempt to improve the group's functioning through analyzing and evaluating their interactions (Lippitt, 1982a). The term *team building* came about because selected interventions lead to increases in team cohesiveness and effectiveness. Note that the consultant is not a member of the team with which he or she is working (French & Bell, 1990).

During team building the consultant acts as a facilitator and a collaborator (Wigtil & Kelsey, 1978). The consultant can assist the team in determining how it should proceed, developing short- and long-term goals, creating teamwork, strengthening interpersonal relationships, and designing and using instruments to assess team performance and progress

(Lippitt, 1982a). Special attention is paid to how the team's various members use power. For an excellent discussion of team building, see Vogt (1989).

Nominal Group Technique The nominal group technique (NGT) (Delbecq, Van de Ven, & Gufstafson, 1975) is a group problem-solving process designed specifically for engendering the members' involvement and creativity. The NGT is based on two assumptions: that all group members need only the proper encouragement to induce them to express their ideas, and that the exchange of ideas and group decision making contribute to greater acceptance of decisions by the individuals involved.

The NGT is a structured problem-solving meeting with a "one-person-one-vote" orientation; superiors and subordinates all have equal status in the NGT. The technique yields a large quantity of high-quality, specific ideas and encourages independent thinking by participants. The process is highly motivating, and participants experience the satisfaction of task accomplishment as well as the social reinforcement of having worked effectively together (Delbecq et al., 1975). The consultant acts as a facilitator of the problem-solving process, as well as a taskmaster who ensures that the steps of the NGT process are completed (Sandland & Dougherty, 1985).

Quality Circles Quality circles are small problem-solving groups (Kurpius, 1985) whose members are typically from the same work area. The groups meet for one to two hours per week to discuss concerns, investigate the sources of those concerns, make recommendations, and take authorized corrective action. The sharing of information is essential in quality circles (Kovach, 1998). Their objective is to improve work quality, productivity, and motivation (Dewar, 1980).

The consultant's primary role with regard to quality circles is educating and training potential members and administrators in the ways quality circles work. Consultants may want to recommend that quality circle participants are highly rewarded because of the stress of participation (Jennings, 1988). The quality circle concept has expanded to include quality improvement teams. The primary difference is that quality circles tend to focus on one task or issue whereas quality improvement teams tend to be more permanent and focus on issues related to quality as those issues emerge.

Work Teams Work teams are "small groups of interdependent individuals who share responsibility for outcomes for their organizations" (Sundstrom, DeMeuse, & Futrell, 1990, p. 120). Consultants can make use of work teams in meeting the goals of consultation, usually by taking on the role of facilitating an environment in which the team can function effectively (Conyne et al., 1997; Kovach, 1998). There are four basic applications of work groups: advice and involvement, production and service, projects and development, and action and negotiation.

Teams whose purpose is advice and involvement typically have a short group life, are not extensively linked to other units in the organization, and provide proposals and recommendations (Sundstrom et al., 1990). For example, a consultant facilitates a group of therapists in determining ways to provide more timely services to clients while at the same time cutting down the length of time allocated to staffings.

Production and service groups are teams that may have a brief or extended group life, relate their work to what other units in the organization are doing, typically repeat their process, and provide coordinated services (Sundstrom et al., 1990). Consultants assist groups such as these by using group dynamics principles and processes to enhance communication and productivity (Conyne et al., 1997). For example, a school counselor works with an individualized education program (IEP) team to provide the best service to a student with behavior disorders.

Teams that handle projects and development usually have a brief group life, are made up of individuals from a variety of specialties, and generally produce a report as their output. For example, a consultant assists a community task force charged with developing an AIDS awareness program.

Action and negotiation teams often engage in the same brief event many times, have specialists as members of the team, and coordinate their actions with other parties-at-interest (Sundstrom et al., 1990). For example, a group of consultants provides training in mediation skills for a group of school counselors and psychologists.

Focus groups Focus groups are both an intervention and a qualitative research technique (Kormanski & Eschbach, 1997). They usually consist of 7–10 members who are chosen due to their relationship to the topic to be discussed. Although the consultant selects the topics that will be focused on, the objective is to determine the consultees' perspectives on these topics. The reactions of the consultees guide the direction the focus group takes. Focus groups allow consultants to observe group process. They also act as source of rich data about selected topics and provide a detailed data bank from which to draw conclusions. Focus groups

have the advantage of having high face validity but the disadvantage of producing data that is difficult to analyze (Marshall & Rossman, 1995). Focus groups can be used for a variety of purposes such as determining workers' beliefs about diversity management in their work settings (Russell-Chapin & Stoner, 1995).

Interventions for Use between Groups

Human service organizations are made up of several groups that interact with and affect one another. One group frequently experiences tension or conflict with one or more other groups within the same organization. Consultants can assist groups to relate more effectively by using strategies designed to alleviate group conflict. Two or more interdependent groups are put together as a single unit and engage in joint activities (French & Bell, 1990).

The two major types of intergroup interventions—team building and organizational mirroring—work because the group interactions are structured to maintain control (French & Bell, 1990). All information is shared between groups: there are no secrets and the consultant engenders a spirit of constructive problem solving (French & Bell, 1990).

Intergroup Team Building Intergroup team-building activities attempt to improve the communication and cooperation between two groups, reduce inappropriate group competition, and develop recognition of group interdependence (French & Bell, 1990; Kurpius, 1985). The accomplishment of these tasks can lead to more harmonious functioning within and between the groups.

Organizational Mirroring When the increased effectiveness of three or more groups is desired, organizational mirroring is frequently used (French & Bell, 1990). In this technique, one group, called the host group, receives feedback from other groups about the ways it is perceived; the technique's goal is to change the host group. To keep the number of participants manageable, representatives of each of the groups (rather than the entire membership of each group) are involved (Fordyce & Weil, 1971). As in intergroup team building, the consultant acts as the process's facilitator, enforcer of norms, and coordinator. As an example, a consultant might lead while a group of school counselors (host team) receives feedback from select groups of administrators and staff on their perceptions of the counseling department's programs. For an interesting variation on organizational mirroring, see Gemmill and Wynkoop (1990) and Gemmill and Costello (1990).

Dispute Systems Design Dispute systems design is essentially conflict management training that minimizes costs and maximizes benefits (Brett, Goldberg, & Ury, 1990). It most commonly focuses on mutual interests rather than rights or power. Consultants using this intervention provide the parties in conflict with the necessary negotiation skills, incentives, and resources (Brett et al., 1990). Consequently, consultants often take on the role of trainers, motivators, and resource persons. As an example, a school counselor might use this intervention in managing a dispute between a school principal and the representatives of a student group over student rights in the school. The counselor would train the parties involved in negotiation tactics, provide the necessary information for managing the dispute, and act as an advocate for an interest-based, rather than a rights- or power-based, solution.

Interventions for the Entire Organization

Interventions that attempt to enhance an entire organization's effectiveness are called organizational interventions. Many interventions used primarily at the organizational level also can be used as intergroup and team interventions. Consultants who intervene at the organizational level must be experts in organizational theory and dynamics, in addition to having the basic skills required of all consultants. The most common organizational interventions include process consultation, survey feedback/action research, collateral organization, and strategic planning.

Survey Feedback/Action Research Survey feedback/action research owes much of its development to the social psychologist Kurt Lewin (1945, 1951). It is an intervention designed to systematically collect data about some system (through surveys and/or interviews), analyze the data, and feed results back to appropriate personnel in workshop settings (Ivancevich, Szilagyi, & Wallace, 1977). The problem is diagnosed and action steps planned during the workshop meetings (French & Bell, 1990). One underlying assumption of this approach is that whatever discrepancies are noted from interpreting the data will create the motivation to change things (Goodstein, 1978). Another underlying assumption is that ongoing feedback is necessary to keep the organization on course in terms of its role and mission. Survey feedback/action research takes on a cyclical approach: research, data collection, feedback, planning, action, and evaluation (Frohman, Sashkin, & Kavanagh, 1978); depending on the outcome of evaluation, the process may be repeated.

Collateral Organization One common organizational intervention consultants can recommend is the collateral organization—a small unit within the existing organization. It is very much like a task force except that it is permitted to work outside the existing norms of the larger organization. This license to create its own norms allows the collateral organization the freedom necessary to attack "ill-structured" problems (Zand, 1978, p. 293) that are difficult for the larger organization to solve. This intervention is used with high-priority, system-wide problems that involve people from more than one section of the organization. The consultant acts as a resource person to administrators and to the members of the collateral organization itself. However, the consultant does not meet formally with the collateral group except on an as-needed basis.

Strategic Planning Strategic planning is a futuristic and visionary intervention process that helps organizations deal better with the future (Fuqua & Kurpius, 1993; Kormanski & Eschbach, 1997). It emphasizes process over product, separates vision from the steps to accomplish that vision, sees change as a positive force, involves as many people in the organization as possible, is long term by nature, and takes into consideration the needs and security of the people involved in the planning (Fuqua & Kurpius, 1993). The main roles of the consultant are to make sure everyone involved understands the process and to guide the consultees in determining where they want the organization to go and how they are going to get there, as well as in developing specific action and monitoring plans.

Because choosing an intervention varies somewhat in consultation and collaboration,

below I provide an example of choosing an intervention in each using the same scenario.

A Brief Example of Choosing an Intervention in Consultation Ellen, the head of a community agency serving developmentally disabled adults, has been consulting with Lisa, a mental health worker specializing in consulting to management. Ellen is feeling all of the pressures associated with being placed in charge of an important program. The diagnosis has pointed to Ellen's deficiency in management training. Lisa and Ellen discuss the large array of interventions that could be made in this situation, and select several interventions that seem likely to be successful. Lisa leads Ellen through the decision consultation by asking her eight questions related to her concern about lack of management skills. Based on outcomes to these questions and a determination of Ellen's beliefs about the possible interventions, Lisa and Ellen choose a general intervention, shadow consultation, in which Lisa will follow Ellen at work for three days and then provide feedback on possible management skills Ellen may want to pursue as part of her professional development plan.

A Brief Example of Choosing an Intervention in Collaboration Ellen, the head of a community agency serving developmentally disabled adults, has been collaborating with Lisa, a mental health worker in the agency specializing in consulting to management. Ellen is feeling all of the pressures associated with being placed in charge of an important program. Lisa is concerned that she needs to be more effective in her work of providing more effective services to the management of the agency. The diagnosis has pointed to Ellen's deficiency in management training and Lisa's lack of a systematic plan for assisting management. Lisa and Ellen discuss the large array of interventions that could be made in this situation and select several interventions that seem likely to be successful. Together, Lisa and Ellen engage in decision consultation by asking and answering the eight questions related to their concerns. Based on outcomes to these questions and a determination of their beliefs about the possible interventions, Lisa and Ellen choose a general intervention, shadow consultation, in which Lisa will follow Ellen at work for three days and then provide feedback on possible management skills Ellen may want to pursue as part of her professional development plan. They also choose a focus group approach through which Lisa will determine more effective approaches for her providing her services. Ellen, who has expertise in conducting focus groups, agrees to help monitor Lisa's progress.

PHASE TWO: FORMULATING

A PLAN

Once the consultant and consultee have been able to decide on one or more interventions that have a high probability of helping meet the goal that has been developed, they begin formulating a plan. A *plan* refers to a detailed step-by-step method for doing something and is formulated beforehand. For our purposes, formulating a plan refers to joining the pieces of the interventions into a sequence and generating appropriate time lines (Egan, 1998). It is critical in this planning phase that the consultant emphasize the collaborative nature of consultation to ensure that the consultee has a ready-made commitment to the plan (Parsons & Meyers, 1984; Erchul & Chewning, 1990). It

is usually best for the consultant and consultee to formulate a few possible plans and then choose the plan that appears to have the highest probability of succeeding.

Good plans shape successful consultation outcomes. When formulating a plan, the consultant and consultee should consider the what (objectives), the where (locale of the implementation), the when (time frame), the how (methods, procedures, sequence), and the who (who is responsible for which elements [Bittel, 1972]). In doing so, the consultant and consultee can plan more effectively.

Plan formulation is a complex activity that requires time to accomplish adequately. The consultant and consultee first determine the plan's objectives, choose its procedures, and establish the time frame in which it is to be carried out. Next, they assign responsibility for carrying out each part of the plan. Each step is scrutinized again and adjusted as necessary. Finally, they assess the plan in terms of its feasibility, cost effectiveness, and capability of succeeding.

Consultants and consultees should adhere to several principles of formulating plans (Egan, 1985). Plans should be clearly linked to the established goals; a connection must exist between what the consultant and consultee want to accomplish and how they are going to accomplish it. A variety of plans to accomplish set goals should be constructed and examined. Brainstorming is a helpful procedure for generating a variety of plans. Plans should be evaluated in terms of the criteria of effectiveness, efficiency, and ability to meet human needs. Steps in plans should be viewed as subgoals and measures taken to see that the subgoals meet the criteria of effective goals. Plans should have reasonable time frames for completion and be sufficiently detailed. Finally, plans should be examined in terms of their feasibility as contingency plans.

Once plans have been formulated, the consultant and consultee choose a plan. One common way of choosing the best plan is *force-field analysis*, a method of determining the driving and restraining forces affecting the accomplishment of a goal (Lewin, 1951). Restraining forces inhibit movement toward a plan's successful implementation and driving forces support the plan's successful outcome. Force-field analysis helps consultees gain perspective on possible plans' pitfalls and strong points, and such awareness allows consultees to adapt plans to the specific settings in which clients are being served.

In using force-field analysis, the consultant has the consultee review each plan that has been generated. For each plan, the major restraining and driving forces, identified by brainstorming, are listed (Parsons & Meyers, 1984) and examined in detail. Depending on the plan, one or more restraining and driving forces over which the consultee has some control are identified for modification. The consultee and consultant then brainstorm ways to minimize the selected restraining forces and maximize the selected driving forces for each of the plans. They look at the relative weights of the restraining and driving forces, and those plans whose restraining forces outweigh their driving forces are discarded. From the remaining plans, one plan and a backup contingency plan are chosen. Specific adaptations of the plan to the unique needs of the client or client system are worked out.

In addition to using techniques such as force-field analysis, the consultant and consultee can work together to create a checklist to avoid the following pitfalls, which frequently contribute to the failure of plans (Ehly, 1993; Kurpius, 1985):

- trying to accomplish too much
- formulating too large a plan
- overanalyzing the plan, which causes disinterest and resistance
- underanalyzing the plan and failing to anticipate pertinent problems
- failing to consider the plan's system-wide impact
- inadequately defining the plan's desired outcomes
- failing to consider the human-side factors

As a final safeguard the consultant and consultee may want to "walk through" the process one time to see who is affected in what ways by the plan. This technique is often referred to as anticipatory rehearsal (Lippitt & Lippitt, 1986, p. 21).

In summary, to choose a plan, the consultant helps the consultee consider each plan's comprehensiveness and positive and negative consequences, as well as the adequacy of the consultee's information about each plan. The consultant checks out the acceptability of the treatment by helping the consultee make a judgment of the appropriateness and likely effectiveness of the selected intervention (Dunson et al., 1994). High treatment acceptability indicates a high level of willingness to proceed with the intervention in the situation at hand making it more likely that the consultee will both stick with the intervention and implement it appropriately. Further, the consultant helps the consultee integrate the consultant's input regarding the plans and makes a final check of each plan's potential positive and negative consequences. The plan builds upon the natural interaction between the consultee and the client system and the realities of the environment in which the plan is to be carried out (Lentz et al., 1996). Finally, the consultant assesses the consultee's capacity to carry out plans and develop contingencies successfully.

A Brief Example of Plan Formulation in Consultation A school counselor is consulting with a school principal about the most appropriate type of in-school suspension program. They develop three possible plans for operating the program: a punitive approach, a "time-out" approach, and a counseling approach. The pros and cons of each approach are weighed, and the consultant makes sure that the administrator possesses adequate knowledge of and the basis for each plan. The consultant's input into the various plans is clarified and a force-field analysis is applied to each. Together they decide that the in-school suspension plan with a counseling focus is the best plan; the "time-out" approach is chosen as a contingency.

A Brief Example of Plan Formulation in Collaboration A school counselor and a school principal are collaborating about the most appropriate type of in-school suspension program. They develop three possible plans for operating the program: a punitive approach, a "time-out" approach, and a counseling approach. The pros and cons of each approach are weighed, and the school counselor makes sure that the administrator possesses adequate knowledge of and the basis for each plan. The administrator ensures that the school counselor is aware of how to deal with the organizational dynamics of program implementation. A force-field analysis is applied to each possibility. Together they decide that the in-school suspension plan with a counseling focus is the best plan; the "time-out" approach is chosen as a contingency.

They agree to implement the program by each taking on a variety of the responsibilities.

PHASE THREE: IMPLEMENTING THE PLAN

Now that the consultee and consultant or collaborators have narrowed the possibilities and formulated a plan, they are ready for action. The plan designed in the previous phase is now put into operation, and the focus of consultation turns to making sure that the plan is followed in such a way that it achieves the desired results. Unfortunately, this phase of consultation has received little research attention (Gresham & Kendall, 1987).

Although putting a plan into action seems quite straightforward on the surface, it is actually a very complex process. For example, the consultant and consultee should engage in role analysis (Golembiewski, 1993b) to ascertain who is responsible for the tasks involved, while recognizing that each brings unique skills to the problem-solving process (Lentz et al., 1996). And because it is rare that one or more unforeseen circumstances do not arise when the plan is put into effect, the consultant and the consultee should be flexible in adjusting the plan in light of unanticipated events (Bittel, 1972). The consultant should reassure the consultee that events sometimes get in the way of the plan's implementation and that most often this is due to factors in the complex real-life environment in which all interventions must eventually be made.

The consultant can increase the probability of successful plan implementation by providing tactical assistance. *Tactics* is "the art of adapting a plan (program) to the immediate situation"

(Egan, 1985, p. 132), possibly on short notice. For this reason, consultants should consider maintaining contact with consultees during the implementation phase.

Consultant availability can be a critical factor in the success of an intervention, because of the reliance on the consultee (who may not be as well trained as the consultant) to carry out the intervention. By monitoring the consultee's implementation of the intervention, the consultant is, in effect, providing a quality control mechanism to the process (Caplan et al., 1994). Careful monitoring by the consultant will help to ensure that the consultee has or acquires the skills necessary for reflective implementation. It will also provide the contact necessary to prohibit consultees who think they have the necessary skills from implementing a procedure which, in actuality, they lack the ability to implement (Caplan et al., 1994).

Because the consultant and consultee made plans jointly, it is reasonable to assume that the consultee may welcome contact with the consultant during implementation (Conoley & Conoley, 1992). Such contact can be in the form of technical assistance (for example, plan revision) or emotional and cognitive support (for example, encouraging the consultee to take risks). For example, the consultant may engage in the functional outcome analysis (FOA) in order to evaluate and/or monitor interventions (Noell & Gresham, 1993). In collaboration, of course, both parties are responsible for some aspect of the implementation of the plan. As a result, they will provide the necessary support to one another during the implementation.

Some consultants monitor the consultee's intervention efforts through a series of brief interviews and/or observations of the consultee during the implementation process (Bergan & Kratochwill, 1990). Such contact allows consultants to gather data from the consultee concerning the effectiveness of the intervention; this data can range from a description of the consultee's and client's behavior during the intervention to measurements of changes in the client. A note of caution: during the implementation phase the consultant must exercise care to prevent excessive dependency in some consultees who may inadvertently rely too heavily on the consultant's expertise (Lippitt & Lippitt, 1986). For example, a school counselor consulting with a teacher might judiciously use questions to stimulate the teacher to take more responsibility for implementing the plan. In collaboration, the monitoring is typically accomplished through team meeting in which team members report on their progress and receive input from the others.

Treatment Integrity

Choosing a proper intervention and formulating an effective plan do not guarantee successful implementation. Consultees may not carry out a carefully designed plan. An improperly implemented intervention can damage the consultation process. Treatment integrity refers to the degree to which the intervention is implemented as intended (Lentz et al., 1996). One reason for the lack of implementing interventions as designed is the cost incurred by the consultees during the phase of implementation (Noell & Gresham, 1993). There are two types of costs in implementing interventions: objective (for example, time) and subjective (for example, inconvenience). So too, there are two types of benefits: objective (for example, a change in the client system's behavior) and subjective (for example, a sense of accomplishment). Interventions that are complex and time consuming are particularly at-risk. Assessing intervention costs allows consultants to help consultees determine the conditions under which interventions are implemented and maintained with minimal adverse by-products so that the benefits outweigh the costs (Gresham & Noell, 1993).

One method of assessing the cost-benefit ratio for interventions is *functional outcome analysis* (FOA) (Gresham & Noell, 1993). In short, FOA determines the amount of effort required to accomplish a desired outcome. In other words FOA answers the question How much does it cost to get the desired change in the client system?

Social validity, an aspect of treatment integrity, refers to the notion that the parties involved agree to the value of the intervention (Lentz et al., 1996). It involves the social significance of goals, the social acceptability of the procedures, and the social importance of effects (Gresham & Lopez, 1996). Consultees are more likely to follow through on an intervention if they see the goals of consultation as socially significant and worth the cost of meeting them.

Treatment acceptability refers to the concept that the parties involved believe that the intervention is in line with their value systems and their perceptions of what it takes to help the client system. If consultees view the intervention and the plan to implement it as acceptable, then they are more likely to be willing to self-monitor or be monitored by the consultant (Erhardt, Barnett, Lentz, Stollar, & Reifin, 1996). Not all interventions developed by the consultant and consultee are viewed as equally acceptable. Acceptable interventions usually have the following characteristics: simple, time effective, free of jargon, dealing with a severe

situation, and something that the consultee is knowledgeable about (Gresham & Lopez, 1996).

Social importance refers to the consultees' view that the intended changes are important to long-term functioning of the client system. Consultees are more likely to follow through with plans when they view the intervention as making significant differences in the life of the client system.

A Brief Example of Implementing the Plan in Consultation Mary, a school consultant, is assisting Louise, a third-grade teacher, in helping a student diagnosed as having test-taking anxiety. The plan they have devised together involves a cognitive behavioral approach that focuses on the child's "self-talk." The teacher instructs the child in a variation of stress inoculation training. As the child is applying this strategy during an exam, he starts saying aloud the coping phrases that were to be said silently to himself. Mary, who had been monitoring Louise's implementation of the plan, assists Louise in revising the procedures for instructing the child in stress inoculation training procedures. At the same time Mary is quite cautious in avoiding the creation of any dependency on her by Louise.

A Brief Example of Implementing the Plan in Collaboration Mary, a school counselor, and Louise, a third-grade teacher, are collaborating together to help a student diagnosed as having test-taking anxiety. The plan they have devised together involves a cognitive behavioral approach that focuses on the child's "self-talk." The teacher instructs the child in a variation of stress inoculation training. As the child is applying this strategy during an exam, he starts saying aloud the coping phrases that were to be said silently to himself. Mary provides individual counseling to the child in terms of stress management procedures the child can use. Mary, who had been monitoring Louise's implementation of the plan, assists Louise in revising the procedures for instructing the child in stress inoculation training procedures. At the same time Louise assists Mary in understanding the various strategies that might help Mary's work with this particular child.

PHASE FOUR: EVALUATING

THE PLAN

After the plan has been implemented, it must also be evaluated. Evaluating the plan is a part of a larger evaluation effort that assesses the effectiveness of the entire consultation process. As it relates to the plan implementation, *evaluation* refers to the collection of data/information about the implementation to determine its effectiveness in meeting the specified goals. Both the plan itself and how it was carried out need to be evaluated (Macmann et al., 1996). If the evaluation suggests that the plan has been successfully implemented to an appropriate degree, the consultation proceeds to the disengagement phase. If the analysis finds that the plan was not successfully implemented to the degree sought, then the consultation relationship will revert back to a previous phase such as defining the problem and proceed from there.

Evaluation of the plan within consultation frequently involves two processes: implementation evaluation and outcome evaluation. First, implementation evaluation determines whether the implementation occurred as originally planned, what problems were encountered in the implementation, and how these problems affected the outcomes. You will re-

member in the discussion of the third phase of this stage—the actual implementation of the plan—that we discussed such items as tactics and unforeseen glitches that might occur. Implementation evaluation reviews these items in case the consultant and the consultee choose to develop alternative plans and strategies.

Second, outcome evaluation determines whether, and the degree to which, the goals of the plan have been achieved. Questions to answer include: To what degree was the plan successfully implemented? What are the next steps that need to be taken? and How can the glitches that occurred be eliminated? If the plan did not meet its goals, the evaluation may shed some light on reasons why. In this case, the consultant and consultee can revisit the problem and determine the subsequent phases that need to be repeated in the problem-solving process.

Evaluation of the plan is frequently considered to be out of the realm of expertise of the typical consultant and consultee (Parsons & Meyers, 1984). However, consultants are increasingly being held accountable for the quality of their services. They must at least be able to evaluate their own interventions (Gallessich, 1982), and they should also assist in evaluating their consultees' plans. Unfortunately, there are an inadequate number of well-researched methods to measure the costs and benefits, either objective or subjective, of interventions (Barnett & Lentz, 1993).

Outcomes can be measured in terms of what happened to the client or client system as a result of some plan. The consultant and consultee have a variety of instruments and techniques available for this purpose, but basically there are three ways to evaluate a plan's outcome: individualized goal attainment measures, standardized outcome assessment devices, and consumer satisfaction surveys.

Individualized goal attainment measures are "techniques whereby the efficacy of services is measured according to criteria that have been specifically tailored to the needs, capacities, and aspirations of the person(s) receiving services" (Anderson, Frieden, & Murphy, 1977, p. 293). One example is concrete goal setting used with goal-oriented progress notes. Ideally the consultant and consultee have already performed concrete goal setting during the diagnosis stage of consultation. Plan evaluation then becomes a simple procedure of determining the degree to which each goal was accomplished. For example, if the plan called for the client to reduce the number of cigarettes smoked from 40 to 6 a day, then it is relatively easy to monitor the degree to which this goal is being met.

Measurement of individualized goal attainment is often accomplished through goal attainment scaling (Kratochwill, Elliott, & Busse, 1995). In this technique, the dimensions representing desired changes in client behavior are scaled (for example, from 1 = minimally attained to 5 = totally attained), expected levels of attainment are set, and scores are determined at the end of the plan's implementation.

Standardized outcome assessment devices measure the accomplishment of goals through some norm- or criterion-referenced device. Checklists and ratings scales are typically used in consultation. For example, if a consultee assessed a client's career maturity on a standardized instrument and later retested the client on the same measure, the client's progress toward the goal of increased career maturity could be ascertained by the differences between the scores.

Consumer satisfaction surveys attempt to assess the opinions and attitudes of the client or client system regarding the services and effects of the plan provided to them (Anderson et al., 1977). These data, typically gathered through an interview or questionnaire, are quite subjective and of questionable validity if used as the only indicator of the plan's success.

For a more in-depth and step-by-step discussion of evaluation methods in consultation, see the section entitled "Evaluating the Consultation Process" in Chapter 6.

A Brief Example of Evaluating the Plan

Yvonne, a community projects consultant, is working with Ashley, the head of an Upward Bound program, concerning the implementation of personal counseling to the program's teenage participants. Their efforts over several sessions have given birth to and implemented a personal counseling program. They are now at the stage of evaluating its success. Because they conducted ongoing evaluations of the program, Yvonne and Ashley have a sense of its success. The goal attainment measures they developed for each of the program's 20 participants show that the average participant benefited from the program to a level of 4.1 on a 5-point scale. On a standardized problem checklist, the students also reported fewer concerns after counseling. Student opinion surveys showed that they preferred group counseling over individual counseling, although the latter was also of benefit.

MULTICULTURAL ASPECTS RELATED TO IMPLEMENTATION

Cultural differences can influence the perception of how interventions are selected and implemented. For example, interventions focusing on the use of groups may be preferred and the time required for implementing an interven-

---

CASE 5.1   Implementation for School Consultants

Barbara, a human service professional working in a large urban secondary school, is consulting with Shirley, who is the school's chief administrator. Both have spent time in the business world prior to entering education and are familiar with "total quality management" programs. Shirley is very interested in implementing quality management concepts throughout the school. At this point in the consultation, they are ready to choose from several goals and a long list of possible interventions to get the program into place.

To obtain the support of the entire staff, Barbara and Shirley have thought of numerous ways to help them freely buy into learning and utilizing total quality management concepts. Ideas ranged from having the district superintendent make an announcement that the school would implement the program to having a series of departmental meetings led by heads in which teachers as well as staff from other departments could freely discuss the proposal.

To develop school-wide ownership of the program, Barbara and Shirley tested each intervention using decision consultation questions to assess how the intervention would fit the environment of the school, the kinds of resources and personnel necessary to do an adequate implementation, and the glitches that might occur if the intervention was put into place.

They decided that a grassroots approach to getting the program accepted is probably the best plan since the school district had a history of imposing new programs on schools without their input. Thus, how they attempted to get the program accepted was the most important step. First they decided that Shirley would hold a school-wide faculty meeting to present the program as a possibility along with her personal recommendation as chief administrator. However, she would also make it clear that she was not going to force the program on the school. She would discuss her rationale for wanting the program, what it would do for the school, and also what it would cost in terms of staff behavior. Department heads would then be taken on a one-day retreat during which the the program would be discussed and debated. The heads would then use regularly scheduled departmental meetings to discuss and debate

the program with staff. Shirley would hold another regular faculty meeting dedicated to the total quality management idea and have open discussions about it.

Shirley put the plan into action and frequently used Barbara as a resource. She bounced ideas off of Barbara concerning ways to approach certain resistant department heads. After the plan was implemented, Shirley conducted an anonymous survey of the staff's views of the program and how they had been approached about it. The survey's results were very positive, and Barbara and Shirley took the next step toward implementing the program.

Commentary

Decision consultation is an excellent method for selecting an intervention given the context in which it is to be implemented. This case shows, through decision consultation, how the history of prior program implementation in the school affected what intervention was selected and how that intervention was implemented. Note also the importance of consultants "staying online" while the consultee is implementing the intervention.

---

tion may not be highly valued by some cultural groups. There is some evidence that cultural variables may not play an important part in the level of intervention acceptability (Naumann, Gutkin, & Sandoval, 1996). Nonetheless, the cultural views and expectations of the parties involved should be considered when selecting an intervention (Jackson & Hayes, 1993).

When a plan is being formulated, differences in opinion about the importance or necessity of a time frame for the plan's implementation can exist. In addition, people with some cultural backgrounds will prefer collaboration to consultation based on their views of interdependence. In cases such as these, even collaborators will want to make sure that the team

CASE 5.2   Implementation for Community Consultants

Roy is a mental health consultant who has been working with Robbie, a counselor for a residential summer program for academically gifted students at a small state university. Robbie is working on his master's degree in counseling at the university. During their second session, Roy and Robbie have gotten to the point of generating several possible interventions for helping Zachary, one of the program's students.

Zachary has been having a series of interpersonal conflicts with many of the other academically gifted students in the program. It appears that he offends his peers by playing the game "Who's Most Gifted?" During their third session, Roy helps Robbie select an intervention to help Zachary. Through use of decision consultation, they choose individual counseling with Zachary as the best approach. Robbie has the counseling skills, and he and Zachary have a good working relationship already established. Robbie's beliefs about individual counseling seem congruent with making it the method used, and Zachary's needs for some skills in dealing with his peers would be accomplished by this method. Robbie realizes that Zachary would probably benefit most from being in a counseling group with his peers but strongly believes that Zachary is not ready to be in such a group. Robbie

designates the group as a possible contingency plan in case the individual counseling relationship falls through.

In formulating a plan, Roy and Robbie decide that both supportive and behavioral approaches are needed to help Zachary. A supportive approach would help him to not feel singled out or considered sick in some way, while the behavioral approach could help him quickly learn some interpersonal skills to enjoy and benefit from the summer program. Roy and Robbie determine that the best way to evaluate the success of counseling will be the self-report of Zachary as well as Robbie's observations of Zachary and his peers during the next three weeks of the program. In deciding to be tactful yet honest with Zachary, Robbie invites him to become involved in counseling. Robbie hopes to get Zachary excited about their project in which Zachary can design his own methods for relating more effectively to his peers.

As they conduct a brief force-field analysis on the plan, the only loose end that emerges is the possible rejection of Zachary by his peers in spite of any constructive changes he might make. Roy helps Robbie choose an initial target group of Zachary's peers for him to try his new skills with first. The target group will be students with whom Zachary has had no known conflicts.

After success with these students, Robbie could help Zachary target those students with whom he has had some difficulties.

Robbie then implements the plan with Zachary. Robbie consults with Roy over the next two weeks about behavioral rehearsal procedures and methods of giving specific feedback. As the summer program ended, Robbie notices Zachary being more positive about his peers and less in need of being the best at everything. Zachary's peers seem to make less of a big deal about Zachary to the degree that Zachary made less of a big deal about himself. They accept him as one of them.

Commentary

The development of a contingency plan is an important part of the planning process. Without a contingency plan, consultees are left in a "sink or swim" predicament if the primary plan falls through. Force-field analysis teases out possible glitches in a plan and enables the consultant and consultee to better align the plan with its goals. Force-field analysis procedures enabled Robbie and Roy to refine their plan to accommodate Zachary's situation. Notice also the importance of Robbie's staying in touch with Roy during Roy's work with Zachary in terms of behavioral rehearsal.

doesn't attempt to divvy out the responsibility for various aspects to individuals, but rather they will want to keep more of a team approach to implementation.

In terms of evaluation of the plan, input from consultees or fellow collaborators is critical so that the perspectives of different cultures are considered. People from high context cultures, for example, may approach evaluation of the plan in a quite different manner, relying more on a constructivist model. For example, efficiency, a must in a plan in a traditional low context culture, may not be of particular interest to a person from a high context culture. Similarly, whether or not the plan was executed in a timely fashion may not be nearly as relevant as the social impact the plan will have. Even the preferred model of evaluation itself may be framed in a social consensus, constructivist model rather than the traditional positivist, empirical model so frequently employed in consultation and collaboration.

SUMMARY

The implementation stage of consultation consists of choosing an intervention, formulating a plan, implementing the plan, and evaluating it. In this stage, the consultant provides the consultee with practical assistance to meet the goals set to help the client or client system.

A vast number of interventions are available for use in plans. Interventions can be categorized in a variety of ways, but classification by target level is the most common. Although interventions usually focus on improving the efficiency of the consultees' workplace by increasing the effectiveness of the targeted level, they may be effective at more than one level. As a consultant, your role in interventions can range from that of facilitator to that of trainer/educator. Make sure that you have the expertise in a variety of interventions and keep abreast of the burgeoning number of interventions available to you.

Once the appropriate intervention or interventions are chosen, consultants help consultees formulate and choose an appropriate plan. During plan implementation, the consultant provides the consultee with tactical assistance and also monitors his or her procedures.

After the plan has been implemented, evaluation is performed to assess the degree to which it was effective in realizing its goals. Then the consultant and consultee determine whether consultation should continue. If the plan is considered to have worked satisfactorily, consultation moves to its next stage—disengagement. As in entry and diagnosis, the research on the implementation stage is quite limited. Research on developing a plan suggests that consultees who feel that they can have a positive impact regarding plan implementation are more willing to take responsibility for the planning process, as opposed to those who feel their efforts may have no impact (Armenakis & Burdg, 1988). Research on the implementation stage in organizational consultation suggests that getting a change institutionalized as a result of implementation is related to several factors including commitment of the individuals involved and continued sanctioning by high-level administrators (Armenakis & Burdg, 1988).

A final note on implementation: Some authorities (for example, Schein, 1990a) suggest that it is the attitudes of the consultant and consultee, in addition to the implementations themselves, that help to make specific interventions effective.

SUGGESTIONS FOR
EFFECTIVE PRACTICE

- Ensure that consultees and fellow collaborators have the skills and an acceptant attitude toward the interventions being considered.
- Have a plan that is the result of the input of all stakeholders.

- Have a monitoring mechanism in place that will examine the progress the plan is making.

- Avoid the temptation to disregard evaluation of the plan.

QUESTIONS FOR REFLECTION

1. What is unique about the consultant's behavior during the implementation stage?

2. How would you as a consultant help a consultee choose an appropriate intervention?

3. Look over the interventions discussed in this chapter. How many of them could be used at more than one level?

4. `Which of the interventions for individuals have the most danger of turning from consultation into counseling/psychotherapy? Why?

5. Which of the interventions described in this chapter could be most effectively implemented by a group of consultants rather than by one alone? Why?

6. What are some ways in which consultants can learn new interventions?

7. Under what circumstances would you monitor a consultee's implementation of a plan?

8. What kinds of tactical assistance might most consultees require during plan implementation?

9. What are the basic differences between plan evaluation and evaluation of the process of consultation?

10. What should the consultant and consultee do if the evaluation of the plan indicates

that little success in meeting the plan's goal was achieved?

SUGGESTED SUPPLEMENTARY READINGS

French, W. L., and Bell, C. H., Jr. (1990). *Organization development: Behavior science interventions for organization improvement* (4th ed.). Englewood Cliffs, NJ: Prentice-Hall. This book provides an interesting and practical overview of various interventions available to consultants. Of particular interest is the authors' discussion of the various ways in which interventions can be categorized. This book has become more-or-less a classic for those who work as organizational consultants. Still, this book has a tremendous amount of information that consultants in any setting will find invaluable.

Lentz, Jr., F. E., Allen, S. J., & Erhardt, K. E. (1996). The conceptual elements of strong interventions in school settings. *School Psychology Quarterly, 11(2)*, 118–136. This article provides a wealth of information on developing powerful interventions. Although written from a school perspective, consultants and collaborators in any setting will find excellent ideas. Of particular interest is a section entitled "Principles guiding development of strong interventions."

Kurpius, D. J. (1985). Consultation interventions: Successes, failures, and proposals. *Counseling Psychologist, 13(3)*, 368–389. This article has two basic merits: first, an updated summary of various intervention strategies available to consultants, including those aimed at individuals groups, and organizations; second, an emphasis on the point that all interventions, regardless of their level of implementation, occur in some context, typically an organizational one. The author notes that interventions often fail because this organizational context is not properly taken into considera-tion. After reading this article you will be familiar with a broad range of possible consultant interventions and have some awareness of the time it takes to determine which intervention to choose in a given consultation problem.

6

Disengagement Stage

If the entry stage is characterized by the question Hello, what can I do for you? then the disengagement stage is characterized by the question What do we need to take care of before I say goodbye? In effect, the disengagement stage winds down what was started up in the entry stage. Disengagement refers to the ending of the consultation or collaboration relationship.

The purpose of this chapter is to discuss and explore the disengagement stage, during which the consultant and consultee evaluate the consultation process, make plans for integrating the effects of consultation into the system after the consultant leaves, go through a period of reduced contact, make provisions for follow-up, and terminate the consultation process itself. Figure 6.1 illustrates the phases of disengagement. The process of taking leave includes say-

ing goodbye to the consultee system and the people within it. Effective consultants consider both the human and the professional aspects of terminating the consultation process. As you read this chapter, you should bear in mind that very little of the consultation/collaboration literature related to stages has focused on the disengagement stage (Dougherty et al., 1996).

As you are reading the chapter, here are some questions to consider:

1. When does the process of disengagement really begin?

2. What issues need to be taken into consideration during postconsultation planning?

3. What are the basic differences between evaluating the process of consultation and evaluating the plan in the implementation stage?

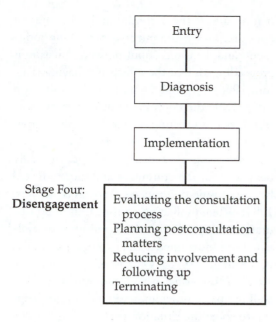

FIGURE 6.1

The phases of the disengagement stage

4. How would you arrange for follow-up with a consultee organization?

5. What effect does the length of time the consultant has spent with the consultee or organization have on what the consultant should do during the disengagement stage?

INTRODUCTION

Once the consultant and consultee have evaluated the plan, they must decide whether to continue or discontinue consultation. The length and complexity of the consultation or collaboration process can complicate this decision (Dougherty et al., 1996) The decision to continue most often results from an evaluation that indicates the goal was not met satisfactorily (Brack, Jones, Smith, White, & Brack, 1993). The consultant and consultee usually return to the end of the diagnostic stage and generate other possible interventions; occasionally, they may need to redefine the problem. In some other cases, continued consultation may be needed because the consultee or organization has an additional work-related concern about which consultation is desired. In these cases, the consultation process typically reverts to the entry phase of exploring organizational needs.

Consider the following situation: You are a consultant who for two years has been working with a human service organization for an average of four hours a week. You have worked with several individual consultees, have done a lot of team building and organizational-level interventions, and have had your own office space and clerical assistance.

Leaving would not be as simple as packing your briefcase and walking out the door. What would you need to accomplish before you left? To whom would you say goodbye? How would you help the system plan to maintain the benefits of consultation after you have gone? How would you evaluate the process of consultation? What arrangements for follow-up would you make?

Consider the following scenario in which disengagement is poorly done:

A Case of a Botched Disengagement

You have worked very closely with a certain consultee who has assisted as your coleader in many of the interventions you have made. Without any warning you announce to him that after two years of working together, today is your last day on the job and you wish him the best of luck in the future. He leaves the room upset and slams the door. As you track him down and discuss the situation, you find out that he has grown close to you over the two years and now resents being treated so impersonally; your decision to tell him that you were leaving for good at the end of the day caused the resentment. He feels that some weeks before you should have said when you were going to leave.

Consultants and collaborators can minimize problems during disengagement by accurately timing its initiation, by developing proper postconsultation/collaboration planning, by properly reducing involvement, and by following up and planning a formal time to terminate (Dougherty et al., 1996).

PHASE ONE: EVALUATING THE CONSULTATION PROCESS

The Role of Evaluation

As it relates to consultation, evaluation might be defined as the systematic collection of infor-mation about the activities and outcomes of consultation for the purpose of making judg-ments and decisions about how consultation is proceeding and/or the effects it is having (Patton, 1986). A properly performed evaluation can provide the consultant with a quality control device, a learning device, legal protection, and a marketing tool (Kelley, 1981).

Evaluation is constructive and mutually beneficial for the consultant and those affected by the consultation process (Parsons & Meyers, 1984). When evaluating consultation or collaboration, the parties involved will want to evaluate both instrumental and expressive elements (Chowanec, 1993; O'Driscoll & Eubanks, 1992). *Instrumental performance* refers to how well the party providing assistance did in helping to solve the situation presented. *Expressive performance* refers to the people-side of the relationship and deals with the level of comfortability of the parties involved. The bottom line is this: to enhance their performance consultants should consider evaluating not only what they did, but the way their behavior was perceived by the consultee.

Because the evaluation process is not always easy to perform, it is not unusual for consultants to consult others about how to evaluate both their services and the consultation process itself (Gallessich, 1982). Still, consultants and consultees should realize that they do not need to be experts in evaluation or research to adequately perform the practical evaluations required in consultation. Whereas merely going through the motions of evaluation is professionally inexcusable, a simple yet credible evaluation can be very informative (Caplan & Caplan, 1993). Consultants need to be aware that at the opposite extreme, they can spend so much of their time evaluating the consultation process that its human side can get lost in the volume of information collected and interpreted.

Pertinent evaluation information should be provided to the consultant, the consultee, administrators of the organization in which consultation has occurred, and (in some cases) the client. The consultant should take measures to see that the results of evaluation are not used in the following covert and inappropriate ways: for protection of an ineffective consultee or program, to avoid decision making, as a public relations tool, or for getting rid of an effective but unpopular consultee or program.

Consultants and consultees need two primary skills to perform evaluation effectively: the ability to identify the consequences of their actions, and the ability to compare results to some standard. Although these skills were identified in the context of counseling clients on skills they need to change their behavior effectively (Egan, 1998), they are certainly needed by the consultant and consultee as well.

Deciding who should conduct the consultation evaluation is difficult, and perhaps the best rule of thumb is: it depends. The consultant and consultee will usually make this decision during the contracting stage. In some cases the consultant helps the consultee gather and make sense of the data; in other cases the consultee gathers the data, and the consultant assists in its interpretation; in still other instances someone other than the consultee (for example, the organization's contact person) conducts some aspects of the evaluation. Some organizations even have special departments to evaluate services like consultation. So long as the people who perform the evaluation are qualified to do so and have no conflict of interest, it probably does not matter who conducts given aspects of it. Regardless of who performs it, consultants are responsible for arranging an

evaluation of their services, and they should also conduct a separate self-evaluation. Frequently, consultation is evaluated only at the end of the process, but evaluation is an *ongoing* process that should be performed throughout the consultation process.

Three steps are common to all evaluation processes: formation of criteria, assessment of attainment of the criteria, and utilization of results. *Formation of criteria* refers to the creation or designation of the criteria (frequently goals) that will be used to assess those aspects of consultation under evaluation (Anderson et al., 1977). Decades ago, Lippitt (1969) noted that developing evaluation criteria is one of the most difficult problems facing consultants. Systematically assessing the degree to which criteria have been met involves determining what, how, and by whom information is to be gathered, as well as how it is to be analyzed. Utilization of results involves disseminating the results to appropriate parties, often for some form of decision making (Anderson et al., 1977). For example, an organization might use the results of consultee satisfaction surveys to decide whether or not to retain a particular consultant.

Consultation is typically evaluated by examining pertinent data gathered from observations, questionnaires, surveys, interviews, and the organization's documents. The use of a multimethod approach to evaluation, which provides more than one perspective on the results obtained, may add information valuable in interpreting the data and can reduce response bias. The use of devices for gathering data is discussed in Chapter 4.

When evaluating consultation, it is appropriate to gather data from the client system, the consultee, the consultant, and other parties-at-interest. To make evaluation manageable, the consultant and consultee should determine during the formation of the contract which kinds of evaluative information should be gathered from which parties.

Consultants may want to evaluate three general consultation topics: the plan that was carried out in the implementation stage, the overall effects of consultation and the consultant's behaviors, and the efficacy of certain stages and phases along the way. The decision concerning which topics to evaluate depends on the type of evaluation, the nature of the problem, and the level at which consultation occurs. For example, an organizational consultant might be interested in evaluating the impact of consultation on total organizational effectiveness, participants' attitudes toward the change process itself, or the efficacy of a specific intervention (Beer, 1980). It is very important that the consultant, consultee, and (if necessary) other parties-at-interest plan what is to be evaluated, how evaluation is to occur, and who is going to perform it and when. Such planning prevents evaluation procedures from becoming overwhelming.

The following questions provide a starting point for identifying the many things that can be evaluated at the end of consultation:

- To what degree has behavior in the client or client system changed in the desired direction?

- To what degree was the consultant able to enter the system psychologically?

- In what ways has the organization changed as a result of consultation?

- To what degree have the goals established in the contract been met?

- To what degree have established timetables been met?

- How successfully has a given intervention been carried out?

- How effectively has the consultant established an effective working relationship with the consultee?

- To what degree has consultation been worth the cost in time, effort, and money?

Some authors (for example, Goodstein, 1978; Parsons & Meyers, 1984) note specific items that can in some way be evaluated:

- consultee preference for given models of consultation

- initial planning of the consultation process

- quantity and quality of consultee reports about the work-related problem

- progress made relative to each consultation stage

- organizational variables that affect the consultant process

- consultant behaviors at each consultation stage

- consultee behaviors throughout the consultation process

- client behaviors throughout the consultation process

- consultee satisfaction with consultation

- the degree to which goals are being attained

- adequacy of each consultation contact

- interpersonal behaviors of the consultant and consultee

- institutionalization of change

An examination of these questions and items indicates three criteria that are used in evaluating consultation: behavior change, cost effectiveness, and attitudes/opinions about consultation (Swartz & Lippitt, 1975). Changes in behavior are looked for in the client or client system (Dickinson & Adcox, 1984), but consultees can also be examined for such changes. For example, an evaluator could look for a reduction in the number of physically aggressive behaviors by a student (client) or an increase in the number of open-ended questions a consultee asks a client.

Cost effectiveness is a judgment call: Were the costs in the terms of time and resources needed for consultation worth the returns? Thus, the administrator of a human service agency might calculate how much time and resources it took to have a consultant reorganize the agency and compare those costs with the perceived benefits of the consultation. Attitudes and opinions about benefits of the consultation can range from indexes of consultee satisfaction with the consultant to views about the overall success of the consultation.

Consultants should make sure that they in some way receive an evaluation of their services, for this is frequently left out of the consultation evaluation process (Lundberg, 1985). Such feedback is essential in spite of the fact that it is ethical for the consultant *not* to perform evaluation if the organization cannot afford it or is unable to otherwise provide the necessary resources (Matuszek, 1981). Consultation evaluation can be viewed throughout the consultation process, or it can be considered once it has run its course. Just as the consultant is continually entering the system, continually diagnosing, and continually intervening, so too should he or she be continually evaluating. The evaluation performed along the way by the consultant and consultee is referred to as *formative evaluation* (Scriven, 1967). The

process of consultation is evaluated without respect to the ultimate product. For example, a consultant and a consultee might use formative evaluation to investigate the degree of success of the diagnosis stage.

When the consultant and consultee evaluate the effects of the consultation process at its conclusion, such an evaluation is referred to as a *summative evaluation* (Scriven, 1967). Its role is to determine the effects of consultation outcomes; it sums things up at the end of the process and evaluates the product. For example, the consultant and consultee might decide to assess a training program's effect on the participants' morale.

Formative Evaluation

One of the best ways to conduct formative evaluation in consultation is to perform evaluations at the end of each phase. Such evaluations will assist the consultant and consultee in determining whether to stick to the current course of consultation or to modify the process. Evaluation can be formal (such as using written surveys or performing observations on some combination of consultant, consultee, and client behaviors) or informal (such as a discussion between the consultant and consultee or other parties-at-interest concerning how a given phase has progressed).

Human service professionals are familiar with and traditionally positive toward the use of surveys. Thus, consultants may want to develop questionnaires and surveys related to each of the phases of the consultation process. One good source for questionnaire and survey examples is Parsons and Meyers (1984); sample evaluation questions for the phases of each stage of the consultation process are provided later in this chapter. These questions can be helpful in developing a frame of reference, whether evaluation is conducted by surveys, observations, interviews, or the examination of records.

Formative Evaluation across the Consultation Process   Certain useful questions can be asked in the various stages of consultation; the answers obtained are helpful in evaluating each stage to make decisions concerning the progress and subsequent direction of consultation. The following questions are adapted from an evaluation form developed by Parsons and Meyers (1984):

- How many contacts have been made with the consultee?

- What is the average length of the contacts?

- What is the average length of time between contacts?

- What progress has been made so far?

- What issues have come up that still need to be handled?

- Who needs to be apprised of what has been done so far?

- What does the consultee think about what has happened to date?

- To what degree is the consultee satisfied about what has happened?

- What does the consultee think about the consultant's style?

- What details need to be worked out?

- What does the consultant think about what has happened so far?

- To what degree is the consultant satisfied with what has happened?

- What are the consultant's impressions of the consultee?

- Are there any changes needed in the way consultation is being conducted?

Among the innovative ways to conduct a formative evaluation is to use a metaphor in providing feedback to the consultant (Lundberg, 1985). The appropriate parties describe the consultant in terms of some metaphor (for example, "a perpetual-motion machine cranking out unceasing good ideas"). The metaphors are shared with the consultant in a group setting. Open discussion ensues and themes related to consultant effectiveness and ineffectiveness are elicited and explored. The consultant then summarizes the feedback and plans subsequent actions in the consultation process.

As noted earlier, it is useful for consultants to evaluate their effectiveness at the end of each phase of the consultation process. In the following section, I provide questions that may be asked during each phase of the entry stage. Consultants can convert these questions into surveys or checklists, use them for directing observations, or develop them as a basis for interviewing: Figure 6.2 is an example of a survey for use in the formative evaluation of the exploration of organizational needs, whereas Figure 6.3 is a sample checklist for evaluating the contracting phase of the entry stage. The following example of formative evaluation of the entry process can easily be extended to each of the other stages; the consultant simply evaluates each phase of the current stage before moving on to the next stage.

Formative Evaluation of the Entry Stage
In the entry stage, the consultation process progressed through the phases of exploring organizational needs, contracting, physically entering the system, and psychologically entering the system. The consultant and consultee can

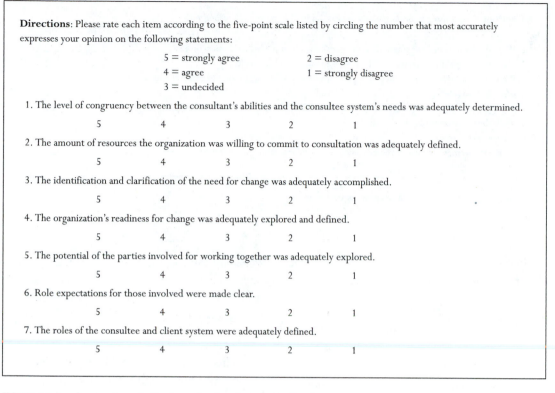

Directions: Please rate each item according to the five-point scale listed by circling the number that most accurately expresses your opinion on the following statements:

> 5 = strongly agree   2 = disagree
> 4 = agree   1 = strongly disagree
> 3 = undecided

1. The level of congruency between the consultant's abilities and the consultee system's needs was adequately determined.

> 5   4   3   2   1

2. The amount of resources the organization was willing to commit to consultation was adequately defined.

> 5   4   3   2   1

3. The identification and clarification of the need for change was adequately accomplished.

> 5   4   3   2   1

4. The organization's readiness for change was adequately explored and defined.

> 5   4   3   2   1

5. The potential of the parties involved for working together was adequately explored.

> 5   4   3   2   1

6. Role expectations for those involved were made clear.

> 5   4   3   2   1

7. The roles of the consultee and client system were adequately defined.

> 5   4   3   2   1

FIGURE 6.2 Sample survey for evaluating the exploration of organizational needs

evaluate each of these phases as a guide for conducting subsequent consultation phases.

Exploring Organizational Needs Some questions used in formative evaluation during this phase include:

- To what degree was the level of congruence between the consultant's abilities and consultee system's needs determined?

- Was the amount of resources the organization was willing to commit to consultation adequately defined?

- To what extent was the identification and clarification of the need for change accomplished?

- How well was the organization's readiness for change explored and defined?

- How well was the potential for working together explored by the parties involved?

- To what degree were role expectations made clear?

- How well were the roles of consultee and client defined?

Directions: Please place a check mark on the line under the appropriate response.

	YES	NO
1. Were the professional expectations of the parties involved spelled out in the contract?	____	____
2. Were the personal expectations of the parties involved made explicit?	____	____
3. Were the conditions under which each party involved would invest time and other resources adequately defined?	____	____
4. Were ground rules under which the parties involved would operate specified clearly?	____	____
5. Were the boundaries of consultation defined?	____	____
6. Was the nature of the contract reviewed with all appropriate parties?	____	____
7. Were arrangements made for the periodic review and evaluation of consultation?	____	____

FIGURE 6.3 Sample checklist for evaluating the contracting phase

Contracting The questions that can be asked about contracting are more specific than those for the previous phase:

- How effectively were the professional expectations of the parties involved spelled out in the contract?

- To what degree were the personal expectations of the parties involved made explicit?

- Were the amount of time and other resources each party would invest, the times they would invest them, and the costs of those investments adequately defined?

- How precisely specified were the ground rules under which the parties involved would operate?

- How well were the boundaries of consultation defined?

- To what degree was the nature of the contract reviewed with the appropriate parties?

- Were arrangements made for the periodic review and evaluation of consultation?

Physically Entering the System Evaluation of the physical entry into consultation is relatively straightforward. Some questions useful in evaluating this phase include:

- Is the selected work site conducive to effective consultation? Is the selected work site strategically located?

- Is the consultant appropriately balancing the amount of time spent at the work site with the time spent moving throughout the organization? To what degree does the consultant adapt the schedule for consultation activities to the regular schedule of the organization?

- To what degree have the parties affected by consultation been informed about the nature of consultation, its purpose, and its time frame?

Psychologically Entering the System Even though psychological entry cannot be divorced from physical entry, its aspects can be evaluated by the judicious selection of questions. Some questions that can be used in evaluating this phase include:

- To what degree has consultation placed minimal stress on the parties involved?

- To what degree has consultation placed minimal stress on the organization's structure and processes?

- To what degree has the consultant developed social influence within the organization?

- How effectively has the consultant obtained some sanction for consultation from the organization's top-level administrators?

- How effectively has the consultant built strong professional relationships with all parties affected by consultation?

In summary, evaluation of the entry stage—as with any of the other stages—is best applied to each of its phases. The consultant and consultee must agree on the most appropriate methods of evaluation and must limit the number of events that will be evaluated.

A Brief Example of Formative Evaluation in the Consultation Process Monica, a mental health consultant, has been consulting with Wendell, the director of a community council on aging program, on a "Reminiscences on Life" program series the council has been holding once a month in the community services center in a small rural town. The program was designed to bring seniors of the community together to recall wholesome reminiscences of their life experiences and share them with youth volunteers who were being trained by the council on aging to work with the elderly. Monica and Wendell came up with

an evaluation scheme for evaluating the program prior to its inception. After five program sessions, they evaluated the program by means of a survey with the 12 seniors participating in the program, the program's two other staff members besides the director, and the 24 youth to whom the seniors had been sharing their reminiscences. After they conducted the evaluation, Monica and Wendell decide to "evaluate the evaluation." They determined that perhaps they should have spent more time on interviewing the participants and less time on surveying. Although the program's staff members had no complaints about the evaluation, some of the seniors had trouble seeing and said they couldn't read the survey very well. Several of the youth said it was hard to take the survey seriously and that they found it to be an unwanted demand on their time. As Monica and Wendell examined the results, they determined that a structured interview approach to evaluating the program would lend the most valid data. The seniors would appreciate the time given to them by a program member one-on-one, and the youth would be offered not only time to speak about how they felt, but also some coupons for free pizza. Monica and Wendell concluded that although the evaluation plan was appropriately linked to the goals of the program, the data-gathering methods were not adequately chosen or implemented. In addition, more methods of data collection like a combination of interviews, observation, and surveys were in order.

Summative Evaluation

Summative evaluation refers to the evaluation of outcomes or products (Scriven, 1967); indeed, it is often referred to as *product evaluation*.

Consultants and consultees use summative evaluation to determine if the objectives of consultation were met. In some circumstances consultants can benefit from consulting with experts in evaluation concerning the design of summative evaluation procedures.

An exhaustive treatment of the many possible designs used in summative evaluation is beyond the scope of this book. Excellent resources already available to consultants and consultees can provide guidance in designing evaluations of the consultation process; they include *Research Design in Counseling* (Heppner et al., 1992), *Single Case Experimental Designs* (Barlow & Hersen, 1984), and *The Scientist Practitioner* (Barlow, Hayes, & Nelson, 1984). I will, however, present a brief overview of some of the ways to perform summative evaluation in the following sections.

The Pre-Post Method The pre-post method attempts to assess changes that result from consultation by measuring variables related to desired changes before and after the consultation process. For example, a consultant might measure an organization's morale before and after an intervention designed to improve it. The advantages of this method are that it is relatively simple and requires a minimum of time to perform.

The pre-post method is particularly valuable when the variables being measured are specific and observable (Swartz & Lippitt, 1975). Because there is no control group, however, this method is of limited value. Changes that were sought and achieved may not be directly attributable to consultation because of other factors—such as changes in the organization—and life experiences may just as well explain the results (Dougherty & Taylor, 1983).

Still, this method is a step above nonstandardized observation and anecdotal accounts in that it provides more useful information and more conclusive evidence.

The Group Comparison Method The group comparison method adds clout to the evaluation by including a comparison or control group, which strengthens the evaluation's validity; a group that received consultation services is compared with a group that did not receive such services. This method allows the consultant and consultee to be more confident that any changes found in the measurement are specifically attributable to consultation itself and not to extraneous variables. For example, a consultant might train half of an agency's crisis intervention team in cognitive therapy strategies for crisis situations. The other half of the team, which would receive no training, would be used as a control group. The performance of both groups is assessed and compared on selected criteria.

Sometimes consultants use a no-contact control group or an attention-only control group. In using a *no-contact control group*, the only contact with the group occurs during the assessment of the dependent variables (measures of the factors to be changed by consultation). In an *attention-only control group*, the assessment of the dependent variables is made and the group is informed of the nature of consultation services without receiving these services directly. Attention-only control groups are useful in that they eliminate the possibility that the attention paid to the consultees and/or clients, not consultation itself, led to differences in the dependent variables. Several potential problems can be associated with the group comparison method of evaluation: management of the control groups, developmental complexity of the experimental design, and required statistical knowledge beyond the expertise of consultant and consultee.

The group comparison method is particularly useful in a follow-up assessment using the same measurements taken in posttesting. It is the method of choice when comparative performance data are particularly desirable (Swartz & Lippitt, 1975). Because of the complexity of the group comparison method, it is a desirable, but relatively infrequently used, method of consultation evaluation.

Time-Series Method   The time-series method involves establishing a series of measures on one or more given variables over time (Barlow et al., 1984). The primary difference between this method and the group comparison and pre-post methods is that the time-series method uses more frequent assessments of designated variables. The effects of intervention are then assessed in terms of measured behaviors' variability, their level of occurrence, and possible trends (Barlow et al., 1984). Thus, pertinent information can be gathered on a measurement's changes over time (Barlow & Hersen, 1984). This method may or may not use a control group. As an example, a consultant and consultee might make a series of observations on how an imagery program affects a client's eating behavior at breakfast, lunch, and dinner.

Multiple baseline designs are one example of the time-series method. Multiple baselining reduces the effects of random influences on behavior change by replicating the change obtained in one period with that in subsequent periods; each subsequent period serves as a control for the earlier period (Barlow et al., 1984). Time-series methods are most effective

when it is likely that a large number of variables are affecting the outcome of consultation.

Case Study Method   The classic definition of a case study is "a report of an intensive analytical and diagnostic intervention on an individual or other social unit, in which attention is focused on factors contributing to the development of personality patterns and/or behavior patterns" (Shertzer & Linden, 1979, p. 460). Case studies have ". . . a unique strength in providing a format to understand the dynamics of a situation, linking context, processes, and outcomes" (Pryzwansky & Noblit, 1990, p. 297). They are often conducted under naturalistic conditions (Bergan & Kratochwill, 1990). The case study method can be used to monitor and/or analyze the effects of consultation on the consultee and/or the client system (Pryzwansky & Noblit, 1990); for example, a consultant might conduct a case study on the effects of quality circles on job satisfaction in a community service agency. Although it is descriptive in nature, the case study method does not excuse the consultant and consultee from identifying specific and behaviorally defined goals at the outset of consultation (Bergan & Kratochwill, 1990). It does, however, permit application of consultation evaluation to an individual consultee and/or client with a minimum of statistical work even though they require detailed data collection (Pryzwansky & Noblit, 1990).

The case study can provide insight into previously unsuspected relationships affecting consultation (Ary, Jacobs, & Razavieh, 1985). The case study is, however, very susceptible to bias and use of this method requires careful judgments about the efficacy of consultation. Because of its uncontrolled nature, consultants and consultees can have only limited confidence about the cause of any observed effects (Barlow et al., 1984). To the degree that a case study is comprehensive, it can be quite time consuming. Case studies are often viewed as a lower-level evaluation tool, but they can be used to evaluate consultation adequately (Barlow et al., 1984; Barlow & Hersen, 1984).

Self-Report Assessment Method The self-report assessment method is frequently used at the end of the consultation process to evaluate the effects of consultation. This method makes use of such instruments as rating scales, surveys, checklists, and questionnaires, which can be developed by the consultant and consultee or are available in some standardized form. When using assessment and evaluation instruments for any purpose, the consultant will want to bear several important points in mind (Cooper & O'Conner, 1993): first, develop a specific connection between the goals of consultation and the instruments chosen; second, consider using a combination of assessment instruments that reflect hard, soft, and qualitative methods; third, use repeated measures (as encouraged); and fourth, inform consultees of the limitations of any instruments used, which is an ethical obligation.

In summative evaluation, self-assessment can be used in all of the previously mentioned methods, including a postconsultation assessment measure. The method tends to lack rigor in terms of experimental design and can easily provide inaccurate results if the precision of the instruments used is inadequate. However, this is a very common method of evaluating consultation, and its use has been enhanced by significant improvements in the development of questionnaires and surveys (for example,

Birnbrauer, 1987; Oher, 1993). The self-report method is particularly appropriate for evaluating consultation in terms of consultee satisfaction, consultant satisfaction, and perceived consultant effectiveness.

In summary, the evaluation of consultation effects moves the consultant into the realm of experimental design, which may require more sophistication in this area and statistics than the consultant and consultee possess. Under such circumstances they must either seek outside assistance or develop a suitable evaluation method that is within their levels of expertise. Because of the time, effort, and expense that outcome evaluation can require, the evaluation plan used must be cost effective. The consultant must ensure that evaluation results are described completely and accurately and are disseminated to the appropriate parties, such as the consultee, organization contact person, administrators, and other appropriate parties–at–interest.

A Brief Example of Summative Evaluation in the Consultation Process Bonnie has been consulting with Dorothy concerning a "Back on Your Feet and on Your Own" program at a local shelter for battered women. Half of the women in the shelter have agreed to be trained in a program designed to help them reestablish themselves as independently functioning members of the community. The other half were promised the same training provided that the evaluation of the training was positive. After three months, the group comparison method was used in the evaluation. Differences were found between the experimental group and the control group on several measures ranging from personality inventories and interviews to survey results and the impressions of the experimental group's counselors regarding the effectiveness of the training. Results of the evaluation suggested that the training might well benefit the women. The control group was immediately provided with the training.

PHASE TWO: PLANNING POSTCONSULTATION/ POSTCOLLABORATION MATTERS

The consultant can increase the chances that the results of consultation will be maintained after his or her departure by using effective postconsultation planning. Plans for this purpose rely heavily on the resources available to the consultee and the organization. In collaboration, this phase involves all of the collaborators "getting on the same page" with regard to what activities, if any, they will be engaging in after the collaborators stop formally meeting about the client system.

The consultant and consultee can effectively plan postconsultation procedures by following many of the procedures used in the formulating a plan phase of the implementation stage of consultation. You may want to review the planning process in Chapter 5, including determining objectives, establishing procedures, defining steps, assigning responsibilities, and testing for feasibility, cost effectiveness, and capabilities. A classic technique called force-field analysis (Lewin, 1951) is a useful technique in assessing the forces that may aid or impede the accomplishment of plans. With the proper planning, then, the consultant can help the consultee and organi-

zation effectively follow through on the results of consultation.

A Brief Example of Planning Postconsultation Matters   A marriage and family therapist has been consulting with a counseling psychologist who is working with a couple on enhancing their relationship. The family therapist has assisted the consultee in using therapeutic metaphors with the couple. Consultation has proceeded effectively. Together the consultant and consultee formulate a plan for how the consultee will proceed with the couple after consultation has ended. Part of the plan to enhance their emotional intimacy involves helping them write their own metaphors.

PHASE THREE: REDUCING INVOLVEMENT AND FOLLOWING UP

Once postconsultation plans have been formulated to the satisfaction of the parties involved, the consultant initiates a period of reduced involvement and enacts follow-up procedures.

Reducing Involvement

Reduced involvement refers to the gradual reduction in the consultant's contact with the consultee and the organization, which effectively prevents abrupt termination. The consultee and other appropriate parties begin to pick up the slack left by the consultant's declining involvement. In collaboration, reducing involvement refers to the gradual reduction of contact of the collaborators with one another.

One method proved effective in reducing involvement is called *fading*, a lessening of contact and involvement with the consultee and the organization. For example, if a consultant has been meeting with a consultee on a weekly basis, contact might be faded to once every two weeks, then to once every three weeks, and so on. Similarly, the consultant's visits to the organization are reduced over time. As the consultant is fading contact, his or her roles are gradually taken over by the consultee. The reduced involvement reinforces independence in the consultee and the organization.

Some authors (for example, Bell & Nadler, 1985) advocate that the consultant be available on an as-needed basis while the consultee and the organization try to manage the changes brought about by consultation. However reduced involvement is accomplished, it should be negotiated (Schein, 1988), for then it is clear to everyone involved that reduced involvement does not mean no involvement (Schein, 1988).

A Brief Example of Reducing Involvement and Following Up   A school counselor has been meeting weekly with a teacher regarding some classroom management problems the teacher has been having. As a result of consultation the teacher has made great strides in eliciting appropriate behavior from the students. The consultant has helped the teacher plan how the class will be managed for the entire term and how data on the students' behavior will be collected. To reduce the consultant's involvement, the consultant and consultee set two final meetings at three-week intervals before terminating the consultation.

Following Up

Planning follow-up procedures can reduce the stress that comes with winding down consultation. Follow-up refers to the process of periodically determining how well the results of consultation are being maintained over time and how well the consultee and organization are performing postconsultation efforts. Follow-up provides the consultee and organization with a regular "check up" (Kelley, 1981, p. 218). Follow-up is important because it provides some indication of consultant availability, an opportunity to salvage plans that have not been effectively carried out, some assistance while promoting independence on the part of the consultee and the organization, and some prevention of future problems (Kelley, 1981). There has been some criticism that follow-up is generally not well done (Zins & Erchul, 1995). When properly accomplished, reduced involvement and follow-up fill a gap between postconsultation planning and termination.

A Brief Example of Follow-Up   A human resource development specialist has been training volunteers who work with incarcerates in a rehabilitation program. Three months after the training has concluded, the specialist calls the program director to check on how the volunteers are doing according to a format agreed on during postconsultation planning.

PHASE FOUR: TERMINATING

Like human relationships, consultation requires closure; termination provides that closure in a formal, ritualistic manner. Termination formally ends a process and ideally leads to a sense of satisfaction with whatever has been accomplished and a mutual sense of esteem for the parties involved (Bell & Nadler, 1985). It also provides an appropriate time for celebrating whatever successes have been achieved. However, the termination process has received relatively little attention in the consultation literature (Dougherty et al., 1996; Gilmore, 1993).

Termination is a critical element in the consultation process. If performed properly, it can lead to subsequent requests for consultation (Dougherty et al., 1996). If performed inappropriately, it can result in dissatisfaction of the consultee and the organization. Inappropriate termination can affect the manner in which postconsultation planning and subsequent consultation experiences are perceived. Inappropriate termination procedures include a unilateral decision (by either the consultant or consultee) to terminate, abrupt termination, indefinite retention of consultation (no formal end point), and unnecessary extension of the consultation process by any of the parties involved.

Abrupt termination is a shock and can be a distraction (Bell & Nadler, 1985). Conversely, unnecessary extension of consultation is a particular danger to consultants in private practice and to consultants internal to the organization who feel they must always have something to do. As the termination process is begun, consultants should maintain awareness of their need to be needed and avoid engendering dependence (Bell & Nadler, 1985). A lingering consultation prevents the human side of termination from receiving adequate consideration.

A meeting that concludes postconsultation planning is an excellent time to deal with any unresolved issues before the consultant or collaborator's formal departure, and such a ritual can set the termination process in motion. A formal review of the consultant's final report is one proven method of effectively accomplishing termination (Bell & Nadler, 1985; Gilmore, 1993). Here participants can discuss the progress made in consultation relative to the contract and stated goals of the consultation, and at this time a clearly defined point of termination can be set. This definite ending point can prevent unnecessary dependence on the part of the consultee or the organization (Parsons & Meyers, 1984). Finally, discussing future possibilities for consulting is another way of easing the stress of termination.

Two possible emotional issues can affect either consultants or consultees at termination time: dependence and depression (Kelley, 1981). No one wants a good and wholesome relationship to end; when the parties involved in such a relationship become aware of its imminent end, a sense of loss begins to develop. Consultants, consultees, and other parties will have grown accustomed to each other and may consequently have come to need each other more than is readily apparent; the possibility of mutual dependence exists. These phenomena can be minimized to the degree that the consultation process was properly implemented; in being aware of their potential and anticipating them, consultants can help the consultation process come to a personally and professionally satisfying conclusion. When consultants and consultees avoid these issues, the issues do not go away (Kelley, 1981). Rather, these unresolved feelings can lead to undesirable consequences such as anger among the parties involved or an unnecessary extension of the consultation process.

CASE 6.1   Disengagement for School Consultants

Rosie, a school-based human service consultant, has been working with Wilma, a fourth-grade teacher, about a boy named Leo in Wilma's class. Leo had become increasingly withdrawn over the first grading period of the academic year and Wilma had contacted Rosie for consultation. The two professionals evaluated the plan they had put into motion and determined that Leo's level of participation in class activities had increased dramatically thanks to an increase in group activities initiated by Wilma as well as the special attention she provided him.

As they wound down the consultation process, Rosie and Wilma reviewed their work together and shared their perceptions of the experience. Rosie engaged Wilma in a reflective discussion of each stage of consultation they went through. By use of selected questions, Rosie and Wilma concluded that although the majority of the process went quite smoothly, they had some difficulties in actually defining how Leo's withdrawing behavior manifested itself. They determined that Wilma saw Leo as more withdrawn than Rosie did and that these different

perceptions led to some difficulties in defining the problem. Wilma agreed that the quick manner with which Leo responded to her interventions suggested that perhaps she had misconstrued his behavior.

Rosie and Wilma reviewed the results of pre- and postconsultation measures, which included a behavior checklist and observational data they had both filled out on Leo periodically. Rosie discussed how she had analyzed the data statistically and cautioned Wilma about the limitations of the data. The two then focused their discussion on whether the results obtained with Leo were worth the cost of having Wilma work with him in the classroom rather than having him sent for individual and group counseling. Wilma admitted that at first she wanted Rosie to take Leo and "fix" him so that she wouldn't have to continually prod him to get involved in classroom life. She had to admit that she was pleasantly surprised with the quick progress that Leo had made.

Rosie and Wilma then changed the focus of their meeting to discuss the kinds of behaviors that Wilma would

engage in after consultation was completed to keep the gains Leo had made. They agreed that informal contacts with Leo as well as verbal reinforcement for social interactions should be continued on an intermittent level. Rosie agreed to check in with Wilma at two-week intervals for a month after which they would terminate their relationship. During the next academic year Wilma contacted Rosie again for assistance with two other students she was concerned about.

Commentary

Evaluation of the plan is essential to having the parties involved believe in the process. Notice the effort Rosie made to ensure that Wilma had a thorough understanding of the nature of Leo's behavior change. Notice further how this might well be linked to Wilma's seeking additional consultation with Rosie about different students the next school year. Part of disengagement is planning postconsultation procedures with the consultee. In this case Rosie and Wilma made plans to assist Leo in maintaining the progress he had made.

A Brief Example of Terminating   Sherill, a school-based consultant, has worked with several teachers for a period of four semesters on managing work-related stress. The stress management program was now being phased out, and it was time for Sherill to terminate the consultation relationships she formed. At the last meeting of the group, Sherill gave her work phone number to each participant and conducted a brief discussion in which each member responded to the question, "What have I learned from this experience?" Sherill then provided a light snack over which each group member sent every other member a "telegram."

CASE 6.2 Disengagement for Community Consultants

Hernando, a hospital social worker, has been an internal consultant to a long-term care team at a community hospital. The team consists of an activity therapist, a patient advocate, the charge nurse, the director of physical therapy, and a part-time social worker. The two-fold problem of staff and patient morale led to the consultation.

With its 55 beds typically filled, the long-term care program was continually experiencing severe stress, and the problem was considered to be significant. Hernando's reputation throughout the hospital led to his being asked to consult. For the past three months he had worked intensely with the team members, who in turn took the resulting ideas to their units for review and decision making.

Consultation had resulted in a complex plan of interventions that was evaluated and determined to be fairly successful. The primary changes for staff included flexible work scheduling and a stress management group. Improved caregiving to patients including getting them fed and taken to bathroom facilities within proper time frames. In addition, significant changes

to the activities program made it more appealing to the patients.

To begin winding down the consultation process, Hernando requested a special two-hour meeting with the team, during which he and the group evaluated the consultation process. Hernando asked the group for face-to-face as well as written feedback in the form of a consultee satisfaction survey he had developed for his work at the hospital. Hernando provided his observations of what had transpired and how effective he thought the process had been. The group discussed what had happened as a result of the consultation and how much these changes had cost—the group agreed that the changes had been somewhat painful. They noted that, at first, there was a tendency for the different work groups assigned to the program to feel severely understaffed and to believe that this was causing the problems.

Only after discussions with the different shifts—led by Hernando and the appropriate team member—did any kind of group ownership of the problems begin to emerge. Only then were goals set and implemented. The group of consultees and Hernando de-

cided that he should follow up with them during the next two months to work out any glitches. The team would continue to take responsibility for monitoring the impact of the recent changes. Six months after the beginning of the consultation, Hernando followed up with the team one last time. Since things were continuing to go smoothly and the morale of the staff and patients alike was improved, Hernando and the team officially terminated their intense yet successful relationship.

Commentary

Evaluating the consultation process is good business on the part of consultants. In this case Hernando, through a face-to-face evaluation process, allowed the consultees to express their deeper feelings about the consultation process and most likely created the conditions for the consultees to communicate more genuinely among themselves in the future. Follow-up procedures, such as those implemented by Hernando, demonstrate the consultant's commitment to the consultee as well as provide opportunities for refining any postconsultation planning.

The first part of the telegram read, "I encourage you to keep on . . ." The second part of the telegram read, "I encourage you to work on . . ." Members then shared what others had written to them. Sherill then thanked the group and the meeting was adjourned.

MULTICULTURAL ASPECTS RELATED TO DISENGAGEMENT

Multicultural influences can have a strong effect on the evaluation of the consultation process. For example, the cultural experiences of some consultees or collaborators may suggest that the evaluation be informed by general questions and would therefore bring into question the suitability of checklists or questionnaires. Just as in evaluating the consultation plan, consultants and collaborators should be cautious about assuming what kind of evaluation process is to be conducted. Cultural differences can relate to perceptions of what needs to be accomplished during postconsultation and postcollaboration planning. Whereas, for example, the consultant may judge the progress to date as time to begin withdrawing from the relationship, the consultee may have a perception that there needs to be increased collaborative activity.

The cultural experiences of the parties involved can influence follow-up. For example, some fellow collaborators may desire frequent follow-up contacts, not due to dependency, but to their view of social professional relationships.

The critical nature of termination becomes even more apparent when consultants and collaborators take cultural experiences into consideration. Depending on one's cultural experiences, the termination process may be considered as one that should be rather drawn out. For example, the rituals of some cultures suggest that consultants terminate with an approach that involves a series of brief meetings. To ignore cultural differences in disengagement is to risk jeopardizing the current relationship as well future consultations.

SUMMARY

Disengagement in the consultation process involves a sense of letting go on both professional and personal levels. Its four phases include evaluating the consultation process, planning postconsultation matters, reducing involvement and following up, and terminating. Disengagement, which should be differentiated from termination, should not be rushed; it should be a well-planned and well-executed procedure.

Evaluation of consultation is frequently done poorly and as a result does not provide any consultation participants a chance to examine how well they have done or how they have grown. Therefore, consultants should be ready to assist their consultees in evaluating consultation and should ensure that evaluation of their own services is part of the overall evaluation procedure.

In postconsultation planning the consultant asks the consultee, How are you going to follow through after I am gone? This planning process places increased responsibility on the consultee and the organization to make effective use of the products of consultation. Postconsultation planning is an appropriate time for consultees to express their concerns about the consultant's leaving and for the consultant to encourage them to realize that they have the abilities to follow through.

The egos and self-esteem of everyone involved in consultation are affected during reduced involvement. Being needed as a consultant is gratifying, and thus it is sometimes difficult to let others follow through on what the consultant has been instrumental in accomplishing. The consultant can more effectively reduce involvement by remembering that one goal of consultation is to help the consultee and the organization continue to function without the consultant. Consultants can take pride in being instrumental in enabling consultees to use the new skills they have learned.

During follow-up the consultant takes on a troubleshooting role in which help is provided to the consultee or organization on an as-needed basis. It is important to define what is meant by "as-needed" so that dependence is not fostered.

Termination is the formal ending of the consultation process. Saying goodbye is not always easy. Consequently, formal termination does not always occur or may be done in a stiff, artificial manner. By being perceived as fair, competent, human, and effective, consultants can take leave with an enhanced reputation, which can be intrinsically satisfying and earn them subsequent consultation opportunities.

SUGGESTIONS FOR EFFECTIVE PRACTICE

- Design all evaluation procedures prior to carrying out the plan.

- Remember that formative evaluation can be as valuable as summative evaluation.

- Use fading procedures for reducing involvement.

- Bear in mind that following-up procedures, although frequently neglected, help to sustain gains made by the consultee or fellow collaborators.

- Avoid abrupt terminations.

QUESTIONS FOR REFLECTION

1. How does the term *disengagement* differ from the term *termination?*

2. In what ways is disengagement a winding down of the consultation process?

3. For what purposes can evaluation of the effects of consultation be used?

4. As a consultant, when in the consultation process would you start to plan evaluation procedures?

5. How does a consultant proceed in determining what events to evaluate?

6. How would you handle evaluation of consultation if both you and your consultee lacked the expertise to perform sophisticated evaluation procedures?

7. What kinds of things should be accomplished in postconsultation planning?

8. What is the major difference between reduced involvement and follow-up?

9. How would you go about the process of psychologically terminating the consultation process?

10. What does the following statement mean: The consultant begins termination upon entry into the consultation process?

SUGGESTED SUPPLEMENTARY READINGS

Heppner, P. P., Kivlighan, D. M., Jr., and Wampold, B. E. (1992). *Research design in counseling.* Pacific Grove, CA: Brooks/Cole. This book provides invaluable evaluation information for consultants, whether or not they are trained as professional counselors. I recommend this as a handbook to help consultants determine how to evaluate the effects of consultation. Even though the book's focus is on research, its concepts are easily translatable into evaluation procedures. Chapter 14, "Process

Research," should be of high interest to consultants. I strongly recommend this book to consultants who believe their evaluation skills need a boost.

Dougherty, A. M., Tack, F. E., Fullam, C. B., & Hammer, L. A. (1996). Disengagement: A neglected aspect of the consultation process. *Journal of Educational and Psychological Consultation, 7,* 259–274. This article examines and summarizes the existing literature on disengagement in consultation. The authors describe the stage of disengagement, identify important stage-specific consultant skills and roles, examine relevant psychological dynamics, and suggest how to avoid pitfalls during this stage. The authors conclude with recommendations for further study.

Parsons, R. D., and Meyers, J. (1984). *Developing consultation skills.* San Francisco: Jossey-Bass. Chapter 11, "Evaluating the Process and Impact of Consultation," is an excellent resource for examples of questionnaires, surveys, and checklists that consultants can use in designing evaluations of consultation procedures. The authors provide an example of a formative evaluation checklist, a consultee satisfaction survey, a paper-and-pencil simulation to test the impact of training, and a program input checklist. These sample instruments are of great value in illustrating the kinds of consultation events that are evaluated and the methods by which evaluations are conducted.

7

Ethical, Professional,
and Legal Issues

T hroughout their careers, all consultants and collaborators encounter ethical, professional, and legal dilemmas about which they must make decisions. Decisions of this type require sound judgment. Frequently, the problems do not suggest clear and specific courses of action for the consultant to resolve them. This should not be surprising, for most consultation issues are complex (Snow & Gersick, 1986) and ethical dilemmas will be frequent (Parsons, 1996).

In this chapter, we will examine how ethical, professional, and legal issues may affect your consultation practice. We will also examine how consultants can make ethical decisions regarding them. There are few cut-and-dried answers when it comes to the ethics of consultation. Consultants frequently have to depend on their sound professional judgment when they make ethical decisions. For example, you will face issues related to the ambiguity about your responsibilities to the consultee organization (Trickett, 1992). However, studying the issues that consultants encounter will provide you with a better understanding of the importance of ethics and the complex and human side of consultation. Further, exposure to these ideas can help you develop the competencies and professional perspective necessary for effectively delivering your consultation services.

Here are some questions to consider as you read this chapter:

1. What professional and ethical obligations do consultants have beyond those to their consultees?

2. What are the basic legal issues that consultants encounter?

3. If consultation is just an emerging field and not yet a distinct profession, then how can there be a uniform code of ethics applicable to all consultants?

4. What are some professional and ethical issues related to consultant effectiveness?

5. How do multicultural issues affect the ethical practice of consultation?

INTRODUCTION

Consider the following scenario of an ethical dilemma:

Case Example

You are a consultant working with a group of consultees in a human service organization. The consultees are all section heads within the organization, and you are training them in becoming more effective decision makers. It was clear from the outset that you were in no way to report to the organization's administration your opinions about any of the section heads' decision-making abilities. It was further understood by all the parties involved that you were to maintain total confidentiality about all aspects of the consultation.

After two months of training, the chief administrator asks you to evaluate the decision-making skills of a particular section head so that a personnel decision can be made about her. The administrator assures you that the information will not go beyond your conversation with her and that no one will know that you ever said anything about the section head's decision-making skills. When you reiterate that confidentiality was guaranteed at the outset of the training, the administrator becomes angry, demands that you share the requested information, and threatens to terminate consultation immediately if you do not cooperate.

What would you do if you were the consultant in this case study? Would you be tempted to share the information secretly?

What are your ethical obligations to the section head? What are your ethical obligations to the organization in which consultation is occurring? What is your ethical obligation to your profession? As you can see from this scenario, consultants must develop ethical standards as part of their professional practice.

Although ethics has been a neglected topic in consultation in the past, it has been receiving more attention in recent years. For example, one journal dedicated to consultation, the *Journal of Educational and Psychological Consultation*, has added a new column entitled "Legal and Ethical Issues in Consultation" (Pruett, 1998). Several ethical, legal, and professional issues have arisen as consultation has become more widely practiced and as the number of people directly and indirectly affected by consultants' behavior has grown. Therefore, consultants need to become increasingly aware of the ethical and professional dilemmas they will encounter. For example, when consulting with organizations, human service consultants may encounter and have to make decisions about issues related to deception, coercion, risk to people, invasion of privacy, and the probability of the success of selected interventions (Tannenbaum, Greene, & Glickman, 1989). Very little has been written about specific ethical issues related to collaboration. At this time, practitioners are encouraged to apply the ethical decision-making processes covered elsewhere in this chapter to ethical dilemmas related to collaboration.

When grappling with difficult issues, consultants need some guidelines that can help them develop a sense of ethical responsibility. As human service professionals, consultants have an obligation to behave in such a way that they bring no harm to themselves, their consultees, the client system, the organizations involved, or society at large. Because consultation is by nature complex, the consultant is frequently caught in ethical dilemmas (Snow & Gersick, 1986). In addition, consulting is a powerful activity that involves changing the parties involved. Finally, what Anderson (1992) writes concerning counseling in general has specific implications for consultation: "The forces of public and professional accountability, consumerism, credentialism, and professionalism . . . are dictating a need for higher standards of practice" (p. 22).

Just as ethical issues are receiving more attention in consultation, so too are legal issues. Since consultants can be sued for malpractice or breach of contract and can encounter a variety of other legal difficulties, they need to learn about the laws affecting their practices and act in a manner that reflects that knowledge.

ETHICS AND

PROFESSIONAL ISSUES

As it pertains to consultation, *ethics* refers to standards of moral and professional conduct. *Morality*, on the other hand, deals with perceptions of right and wrong behavior and is based on judgments of behavior from a broad view such as religion or culture (Corey et al., 1998). Ethical conduct comes from putting together an awareness of an ethical code and its underlying principles (Bersoff, 1996).

Ethical issues in the mental health profession are regulated both by laws and professional codes (Corey et al., 1998). Ethics represent aspirational goals (Corey et al., 1998) that reflect the ideal standards of the profession and are enforced by the appropriate organization (Remley, 1996). Corey et al. (1998) distinguish between *mandatory ethics* and *aspirational ethics*.

Mandatory ethics refers to complying with minimal standards, a kind of "dos and don'ts" way of behaving. From this perspective, professionals basically look outside of themselves, such as to rules of an organization, for guidance in dealing with ethical dilemmas (Newman, Gray, & Fuqua, 1996). Although the concept of mandatory ethics is useful, the complexity of the consulting relationship does not easily lend itself to using mandatory ethics (Newman et al., 1996). Consider, for example, the complexity of issues related to confidentiality due to the triadic nature of consultation.

Aspirational ethics refers to "the attempt to accomplish the maximum in moral and ethical outcomes" (Newman et al., 1996, p. 231). The concept of aspirational ethics can help the professional aim for the highest standards of professional behavior and go beyond the "letter of the law" (Corey et al., 1998). Compared to mandatory ethics, aspirational ethics are more general. Examples of aspirational goals include integrity and social responsibility (Newman et al.,1996).

When a human service professional functions in the capacity of a consultant and follows broad, written ethical guidelines, such guidelines are typically referred to as an *ethics code*. An ethics code serves to discourage inappropriate practice and protects the recipients of the services being rendered. In a positive sense, ethics codes stress adherence to rigorous professional standards and promote exemplary behavior. Recent ethics codes, such as those of the American Counseling Association (ACA) and the APA have both a mandatory and an aspirational component (Corey et al., 1998). The standards of practice of the ethics code tend to deal with mandatory ethics while the codes of ethics typically deal with aspirational ethics (Corey et al., 1998).

Because codes of ethics tend to be general, they do not dictate specific courses of action. Further, the ethical codes of most human services professional groups contain very few, if any, guidelines specific to the practice of consultation. As a result, in your practice, you will often face ethical dilemmas with no specific guidance for action. There is as yet no code of ethics specific to consultants and one is needed. Each consultant can only apply the code of ethics of his or her profession and make the best possible professional decisions when applying the code to a particular situation (Corey et al., 1998). A naive consultee being served by a consultant who has no specific guidelines for behavior creates a high-risk situation in the consultation process (Robinson & Gross, 1985). One way to improve this situation is to develop more detailed case materials to serve as guides for making practical ethical decisions (Lowman, 1985).

Many consultants belong to various professional organizations. Most of these organizations—for example, the ACA, the APA, the American Society for Training and Development (ASTD), the National Board for Certified Counselors (NBCC), the National Association of Social Workers (NASW), and the National Organization for Human Services Education (NOHSE)—have developed some sort of code of ethics. Thus, many consultants enjoy the privilege of having (and have the responsibility of following) some general guidelines that apply to the professional behavior of any human service professional.

By belonging to one of these organizations, the human service professional agrees to adhere to that organization's code. Some organizations, such as the ACA, have specific statements about the ethical conduct of consulting

behavior. Other codes, such as that of the ASTD, make no explicit mention of consultation. The result is that there are some guidelines for acting as a professional in the general areas of competence (for example, not providing services for which one is not competent) and responsibility (for example, maintaining confidentiality) (Robinson & Gross, 1985). But there are few guidelines specific to consulting behavior, such as applying principles of confidentiality in an organizational setting. The basis for this problem is that consultation is a relatively new function for human service providers. Consequently, many ethical issues are just beginning to be addressed across the human service professions.

In conclusion, consultants can use the ethics codes of their organizations only as general guidelines. These guidelines cannot identify appropriate actions for all situations (Tannenbaum et al., 1989), and the final decision for what constitutes a correct course of action in a given situation rests with the professional (Corey et al., 1998). Further, there is an emerging issue that the ethics codes of many mental health organizations may be subject to cultural bias (Pedersen, 1997). As Pedersen (1997) notes, "not only do ethical guidelines need to be interpreted in each situation, but they must also be interpreted for and within each cultural context"(p. 230). Thus, developing personal methods for making ethical decisions is crucial for the consultant. The bottom line is that consultants, within the broad guidelines, need to make informed, sound, and responsible judgments (Corey et al., 1998).

What Corey et al. (1998) state about counseling also holds true for consultation: "Ethical issues . . . are often complex and multifaceted, and they defy simplistic solutions. There are many gray areas that require decision-making skills. The process entails not only learning information about ethical standards but also learning how to define and work through a variety of difficult situations" (p. 4). To assist human service professionals in making such judgments, I recommend the following steps, which have been assembled from a variety of sources by Corey et al. (1998, pp. 16–17):

1. Identify the problem or dilemma.

2. Identify the potential issues involved.

3. Review the relevant ethics codes.

4. Know the applicable laws and regulations.

5. Obtain consultation from trusted colleagues.

6. Consider possible and probable courses of action.

7. Enumerate the consequences of various decisions.

8. Decide on what seems to be the best course of action.

In addition to mastering and using an ethical decision-making process, consultants themselves can engage in peer consultation activities. Peer consultation is a process in which professional development activities and support are mutually provided by one or more professionals. For example, if I am experiencing difficulty with some of my consultation activities I might seek some consultation for the consultant. Peer consultation can occur in support group types of venues and by telephone or the Internet. Peer consultation activities can be valuable in assisting consultants to cope with ethical dilemmas, prevent legal entanglements, and enhance their professional competence.

What kinds of professional and ethical issues do consultants face in their practices? The following issues are all involved, and I will address them throughout this chapter: values, multicultural issues, competence, training, the consultant-consultee-client relationship, the rights of the consultees, group work, and interventions. I have also included a discussion of ethical issues relating to organizational consultation in this chapter because human service professionals are increasingly being called upon to deal with organizational problems and development.

Values and the Consultant

As in any helping relationship, values play an integral role in the consultation process. The consultant, the consultee, the members of the client system, and the parties-at-interest to consultation all have values formed by their life experiences, and each party involved in or affected by consultation is in turn influenced by each other's values. Consequently, the sheer number of people involved (usually three or more) suggests that conflict of values should be expected (Parsons, 1996). The trick is for the consultant to use values to enhance the consultation process without abusing power (Corey et al., 1998).

It would be naive for consultants to think that their own values do not influence the consultation process while thinking that those of the other parties do. Clearly, it is important for consultants to possess a reflective understanding of their values and how they influence the practice of consultation. In fact, the ethics codes of the ACA (AACD, 1995) and the NBCC (1997) note that self-awareness, including awareness of one's values, is important when consulting. Consequently, consultants will want to understand the role their own values take on in the creation and resolution of the ethical dilemmas they face in their practice.

A significant professional issue for consultants is the degree to which they let their values dictate their behavior in consultation. Consultants who impose their values on consultees or other parties-at-interest are on very shaky ethical ground because they are depriving others of their due freedom. There are, however, some sets of values that inform consultants' work. Community psychologists, for example, tend to value self-determination, and that value will affect the consultation process (Prilleltensky, Peirson, & Nelson, 1998). At the other extreme, when consultants are overly cautious about imposing their values on others involved in consultation, they risk rendering the consultation impotent. A middle ground appears to be one in which consultants are aware of their values, make a commitment not to impose them on others, and go about the consultation process as effectively as they can.

Value Conflicts In our culturally diverse society, the potential for value conflicts is high. When consultants' and consultees' values do conflict, effective progress in consultation can be blocked. The bottom-line for consultants is whether or not to refer the consultee to another consultant. Just as when value conflicts arise in other helping relationships such as counseling (Corey et al., 1998), there are no easy conflict resolution solutions in consultation. Consultants experiencing value conflicts should be honest with themselves in determining whether they can remain objective enough to work with those with whom they disagree.

When value conflicts do occur, they are probably best met head-on. The consultant can model effective conflict resolution skills for the consultee as they work through the conflict, and together they can determine whether and how consultation is still feasible.

There are three areas in which value conflict issues are likely to arise in consultation: worldviews (including cultural perspectives), views of organizations, and views of the client or client system. Consider the following examples of values conflicts:

Example 1: Differences in Worldviews Gene and Phil, both mental health professionals, are consulting regarding several clients in Phil's caseload. Gene's cultural background is different from Phil's. As consultation ensues, Gene is increasingly disturbed by Phil's apparent lack of concern about being prompt for their sessions. When Gene questions him on this, Phil notes that from his perspective, time is a convenience for humans to use and not an indicator of politeness. Phil relates that in his culture time just "happens" and is viewed more as a convenient way to track events rather than something that drives events. Gene's view is that time is very critical and important and that every act on the job must be completed in an efficient and timely fashion. To act otherwise is certainly unprofessional and possibly unethical. If you were Gene, how would you attempt to manage these different views so that effective consultation might take place? Should Gene refer Phil to another consultant? Do you think Gene is open to examining his view of life and accommodating differing views?

Example 2: Differences in Views of Organizations Bobbie is a mental health consultant assigned to work with the law enforcement professionals in a large urban police department. Bobbie has to negotiate constantly between the often conflicting values associated with mental health and law enforcement. When a high-ranking police officer used a consultation session to deal with ways to prevent bypassing the chain of command, Bobbie inadvertently made light of the situation and was puzzled when the police officer did not return for a second consultation session. Why do you think that one minor slip-up caused the officer not to return? In what ways do you think Bobbie could have prevented such a slip-up? What Bobbie didn't recognize was the taboo in law enforcement circles against bypassing the chain of command, whereas in a mental health setting, such behavior might be viewed as inappropriate and worthy of reprimand but is certainly not such a big deal. A perceived value difference concerning views of behavior probably caused the officer's absence. Because the officer did not perceive the consultant to be knowledgeable about or respectful of law enforcement values, he prematurely terminated consultation.

Example 3: Differences in Views of the Client System A consultant working with the administrator of a substance-abuse program in a human service agency finds that the administrator thinks of the program's clients as "welfare bums" who are "sponging off" society and the agency. The consultant, in contrast, views the clients as sick and in need of rehabilitation. How would you proceed if you were the consultant? How would you specifically deal with the value conflict in which you find yourself? Clearly, this situation has no easy answer.

In summary, because values are connected to every important decision made during the consultation process, consultants must be aware of their own values (Corey et al., 1998) and make a commitment not to impose them on consultees. The consultant's values can, how-

ever, be used to make appropriate decisions (Lippitt, 1983). The issue concerns how much consultants should allow their values to influence their behavior in consultation and when they should reveal their values (Snow & Gersick, 1986). When value conflicts emerge, the consultant should deal with them in a nondefensive, professional manner. Because value conflicts can occur relatively frequently in our diverse society, there has been increasing attention paid to them recently in the consultation literature. Interested readers may want to consult Jackson and Hayes (1993), Tobias (1993), Pedersen (1997), and Brown (1997).

Multicultural Issues

Multicultural issues are important elements in ethical and professional decision making. In fact, some authors (e.g., Tarver Behring & Ingraham, 1998) have called for making culture a central component in the field of consultation. Increasingly, our society is becoming culturally diverse. This diversity is reflected in the workplace (Steward, 1996; Plummer, 1998). As a result, as a consultant or collaborator, you will most likely have contact with people with varying cultural backgrounds. When working with consultees or fellow collaborators who are culturally different or with consultees or fellow collaborators whose clients are culturally different, you may well encounter many ethical dilemmas. Fortunately, most ethics codes underscore the helper's responsibility to take cultural contexts into consideration when delivering services. For example, the ethics codes of the ACA (1995), the APA (1995), and the NASW (1996) all cite respect for cultural diversity as essential to best practices. In their practice, consultants can place themselves in ethical jeopardy by ignoring diversity factors because such neglect can infringe upon rights of consultees with different worldviews and values.

The experiences of growing up in a different culture can create language patterns, learning styles, and ways of acting that differ from those of the majority culture. For example, speech in high-context cultures, such as Native American cultures, relies heavily on nonverbal aspects of communication, whereas low-context cultures like that of the majority culture rely more heavily on the use of words (Miranda, 1993). It is easy to imagine a person from a low-context cultural background wanting a person from a high-context cultural background to think, act, and speak more concretely and quickly. The implications for the development of ethical dilemmas in consultation and collaboration are obvious.

People from differing cultural, ethnic, or racial backgrounds can vary in a variety of ways including values, language patterns, and child rearing patterns (Thomas, Correa, & Morsink, 1995). Obviously, there can be differences within cultural groups regarding these same constructs which make generalization difficult (Tobias, 1993). As a result, specific cultural characteristics may assist professionals with information in dealing with consultees, fellow collaborators, and their clients to the degree those people possess those characteristics (Correa & Tulbert, 1993; Wubbolding, 1991b). Nonetheless, working effectively with people from differing cultural backgrounds requires knowledge of and respect for their cultural heritage and worldviews (Miranda, 1993; Henning-Stout, 1994; Tarver Behring & Ingraham, 1998).

To practice ethically, consultants need to demonstrate sensitivity to and respect for cultural differences when they provide their services whether to families, in schools, or in any other organization. If consultants or collaborators do not take such differences into account, they can inadvertently cause difficulties in the helping relationship or exploit others. When consultants or collaborators do not act with multicultural sensitivity, they often become frustrated in attempts to be of service, get locked into their "expert" role, and become more content oriented (as opposed to process oriented) (Dougherty, 1996–97). There is some likelihood that the effectiveness of their communication will suffer.

Consultants and collaborators have a professional and ethical obligation to be aware of the influence of their culture and gender on their work with people of different cultural identities. Consultants and collaborators should recognize that their models of service delivery and perhaps even their ethics codes are deficient in the areas related to ethnic, racial, and cultural diversity (Jackson & Hayes, 1993; Soo-Hoo, 1998; Pedersen, 1997; Weinrach & Thomas, 1998).

Clearly, multicultural influences need to be taken into account when providing consultative and collaborative services (Duncan & Pryzwansky, 1993; Goldstein, 1998). I believe what Axelson (1993) says about counselors is also true for consultants and collaborators: namely, they should possess an awareness and comprehension of their own cultural group and the cultural group of their consultees and fellow collaborators. Consultants need perceptual sensitivity toward their own personal values and beliefs as well as those of consultees and fellow collaborators, and they should have a comprehension of the impact of the experiences of the mainstream culture on the parties involved in the helping process.

The Case of Sidney Sidney is a Caucasian consultant who has a private consulting practice in a large urban area. Sidney is contacted by a minority neighborhood group because of his reputation for advocacy work. The neighborhood group is interested in forming a network that provides neighborhood members access to resources related to their personal and social welfare as well as enhancing their own sense of empowerment. Sidney agrees to provide consultation free of charge. As he begins work with the consultees from the neighborhood organization, he starts out by sharing the importance of advocacy. As he continues many members of the group believe him to be condescending. He even occasionally uses terms like "you people" and "you need to get on with it!" When one of the members approaches Sidney about his behavior, Sidney explodes and says: "I am helping you people and not even charging you! You're lucky I just don't stop the whole deal right now. Remember, I am an expert on advocacy for disenfranchised groups." How could Sidney's worldview have gotten him in this unfortunate predicament? What values was Sidney using that seemed to make the consultation go awry? Assuming that Sidney had good intentions, what might you suggest to him about the way he went about trying to help?

The Case of Chi Chi, a Hispanic counselor, is consulting with Michael, an African American psychologist, about one of Michael's cases. As Michael describes the case of an abused child, Chi immediately focuses in on the family unit for discussion and directs Michael to talk more in a "family therapy" mode. Chi is aware of his own strong views about how families influence the individual family members and how treatment should focus on the entire family and perhaps the extended family. When Michael refocuses the discussion on the child, Chi confronts what he believes to be Michael's resistance. Chi ends up persuading Michael to look at the problem from Chi's perspective. Do you see any possible ethical conflicts for Chi in this case? Can you identify any ways in which Chi could have acted differently in his consulting with Michael? Could cultural variables have played a part in the way both Chi and Michael conceptualized the case?

Consultant Competence

The issue of consultant competence has received much attention: the ethics codes of the major organizations in which many consultants have membership (for example, the ACA [1995], the APA [1995], and the ASTD [1992]) all make statements to the effect that members should deliver only those services and accept only those positions for which they are qualified. The ethics code of the NBCC (1997) explicitly makes this statement for consulting. These qualifications are usually determined by the consultant's training and experience.

The parameters of competence are maintaining high levels of professionalism, knowing one's professional limitations, knowing when to decline and refer, and avoiding consultation activities when personal concerns could affect professional performance (Corey et al., 1998; Lippitt & Lippitt, 1986).

Maintaining High Levels of Professionalism Consultants can do several things to maintain high levels of professional competence:

- Belong to and participate in professional organizations.

- Obtain the appropriate national and state credentials, certificates, and licenses for the profession in which they are trained.

- Participate in continuing education activities in general.

- Participate in continuing education activities (both didactic and experiential) that pertain to the consultation services they deliver or would like to deliver.

- Coconsult with more experienced colleagues.

- Consult under the supervision of a trusted colleague or a designated supervisor.

Underlying the maintenance of professionalism is consultants' desire to grow in their work. Consultants with such a growth orientation attempt to stretch themselves so that the depth and breadth of their knowledge and skills increase. This willingness to grow professionally also provides consultees a positive role model that stimulates their growth and desire to participate more fully in consultation.

The Case of Roger After Roger earned his doctorate in a human service profession, he proudly thought that he had "done it all." He became an active consultant and worked with many community groups on what he liked to call "family dynamics." Mary was one of Roger's consultees several years before. When she again became one of his consultees, Mary got the eerie feeling that she was hearing the very same thing she had heard from Roger almost 10 years earlier. New terms like *empowerment* were thrown in for some of the same old ideas. When Mary challenged Roger and asked him his views on family systems and codepen-

dency as they related to the topic being discussed in the consultation, Roger became flustered, noted quickly that there was probably no connection, and promptly changed the subject. Has Roger kept updated in his field? Do you feel he has behaved ethically or has a high level of professionalism?

Knowing One's Professional Limitations

Prior to entering a consultation relationship, consultants must assess whether their personal and professional competence is adequate for the task. Although it is easy to suggest ways of maintaining high levels of professionalism as a consultant, it is more difficult to suggest methods of knowing one's limitations. The ethical codes of the ACA (1995), the APA (1995), and the ASTD (1992) state that a knowledge of one's limitations and/or abilities is essential. Probably the most important thing that consultants can do in recognizing their limitations is to make a commitment to maintain high levels of objectivity and integrity while placing the needs of the consultee and the organization above their own (Lippitt & Lippitt, 1986). By asking themselves the following four questions in order, consultants can stay focused on their limitations:

1. What can I do, given this situation?
2. What is the right thing to do in this situation?
3. Do I have the ability to do the right thing?
4. What is the right thing to do that is in the best interests of the consultee and the organization?

By carefully pondering these questions, consultants are less likely to make errors in judgment with respect to their limitations.

There is no substitute for the combination of personal and professional self-awareness and the commitment to put forth one's best effort when consulting.

The Case of Shirley Shirley recently received her master's degree in one of the helping professions, which included taking a course in consultation. She received a phone call from a church group offering her a fee for providing a workshop on eating disorders. Although Shirley was not knowledgeable about eating disorders, she took the consultation. She studied the topic for a week and then presented a two-day workshop. How well do you think Shirley knows her professional limitations? Did she have the right to conduct a workshop just because the group asked her to? If you were Shirley's work supervisor, how would you handle the situation if you became aware of it?

Knowing When to Decline and Refer
When consultants realize they are "in over their heads" in terms of what is expected of them, they need to decline providing consultation services and make an appropriate referral. The story of the consultee walking up to a consultant and asking, "Are you an expert in X?" to which the consultant responds, "Sure, just give me an hour," comes true all too often. Several professional organizations' ethical codes state that services should be delivered only if it is anticipated that the provider can effectively manage the existing problem as well as any others that may arise.

A related issue involves the representation of oneself as a consultant. Consultants must state explicitly what they stand for, who they represent, and what they can and cannot do as consultants. This obligation to represent oneself honestly and accurately includes advertising. The ACA (1995), the APA (1995), and the ASTD (1992) all make explicit statements with regard to honest disclosure about oneself both in person and through advertising. In fact, the ethical code of the APA (1995) devotes more coverage to public statements than to any other ethical principle.

Closely tied to the issue of representing oneself honestly is the issue of remuneration. Consultants typically charge the "going fee" for a given type of consultation service with a given type of organization in a given geographic area. The ACA (1995) specifically states that its members must refuse any type of remuneration when consultation recipients are due those services through the member's organization. Consultants must consider for each potential consultation whether they are in a position to charge fees in the first place and, if so, how much.

How do consultants respond when they are asked to provide services for which they are not qualified? The answer lies in referral procedures. Consultants have the responsibility to determine at the outset of consultation (in exploring organizational needs) whether or not they can be of assistance. When consultants determine that they cannot be of assistance, they should consider making a referral to a qualified consultant; even if a referral is not possible, the provision of services should be declined anyway.

Consultants sometimes decline to offer their services when the time required for consultation is longer than they have available. Thus, it would be unethical for consultants to take on a two-year project when at the outset they know they would be available for only six months.

The Case of Jackie Jackie holds a doctorate in a helping profession and has been working with a mental health center for 10 years. She is actively seeking another professional position in another part of the country and is approached by a community group to consult with them in developing a two-year self-advocacy project for the homeless in the area. Although Jackie has a great deal of expertise and interest in this area, she refers the community group to another consultant because of the possibility that she might be relocating. This scenario reflects a common concern in our mobile society: The consultant may not be around to finish what he or she agreed to complete. In this case, Jackie certainly knew when to decline and refer.

When Personal Concerns Affect Professional Performance Consultants, of course, have the same kinds of personal concerns and problems as anyone else, and these can negatively affect their professional performance to the degree that consultation services are not adequate. In this case the consultant should consider stopping the services and making an appropriate referral. In fact, the APA code of ethics (1995) states that when members suffer from personal concerns that affect professional functioning, they should seek out consultation regarding whether or not to continue providing services. Therefore, consultants who are experiencing high levels of stress should be particularly aware of their ability to provide adequate professional services.

Consultants need to be aware of their personal needs throughout each phase of the consultation process and should take measures so that those needs do not replace the needs of the consultee (Corey et al., 1998; Robinson & Gross, 1985); such an awareness decreases the

probability that the consultant will behave unethically.

If an exception must be made with regard to consulting despite a lack of competence, Wallace and Hall (1996) suggest that this should be done only when certain conditions are present:

- if it can be clearly established that there is no other consultant in the area who is better qualified
- if the consultant possesses parallel training and experience for the consulting task
- if the consultant has adequate time to prepare for the consulting task
- if the consultant makes all these limitations clear to the employing agency
- if it is a crisis situation that requires immediate intervention

Training as an Ethical Issue

Training is actually an aspect of consultant competence. Consultants must make sure they have the adequate training to perform the services for which they contract. Consultation is not "watered-down" counseling/psychotherapy and its skills do not come naturally from being trained in these methods (Caplan, 1993, p. 44; Caplan, Caplan, & Erchul, 1994).

Although there are some guidelines for training, it is ultimately up to individual consultants to decide whether they have received sufficient training to deliver competent services in a given consultation situation. The development of ethical behavior in consultants might be enhanced if they were required to engage in supervised, controlled consultation experiences during training (Crego, 1985).

Because of the paucity of empirical research conducted on training in consultation, it is very difficult to state categorically how consultants can be adequately trained. The current state of affairs reflects a "shotgun" approach that provides widely divergent formal and informal training opportunities; the trend is toward training in a generic model (Gallessich, Long, & Jennings, 1986). The solution to current needs may lie in supervised training conducted by experienced consultants trained in supervision. But at this time there are relatively few guidelines for training consultants. Regardless of how they receive training, consultants are still ethically bound to determine whether they are adequately trained to provide services in each consultation situation as it arises.

The Consultant-Consultee-Client Relationship

The consultant-consultee-client relationship is very complex. What obligation, for example, does the consultant have to the consultee's client? What parameters of this relationship relate to the consultant and consultee? Can the consultant-consultee-client relationship be examined only in the context of the organization in which consultation is occurring?

In general, the consultant-consultee-client relationship can be examined in isolation or within an organizational context; both views shed light on ethical issues. When considered in isolation, ethical issues revolve around each party's obligations and how well these are fulfilled. In an organizational context, ethical issues go beyond the isolated relationship. For example, when confidentiality is to be maintained, where within the organization do we set its limits? Next we'll consider the ethical issues surrounding the complex consultant-consultee-client relationship in terms of work-related focus, dual relationships, and freedom of choice.

Work-Related Focus   The code of ethics of the ACA (1995) states that the focus of the consultation relationship, from the outset and throughout, should be on work-related problems and not on the parties involved. It can be inferred from this code that personal relationships with consultees and their clients is questionable ethical behavior. Further, this same code of ethics also implies that the consultation relationship should be contractual and based on well-defined, mutually agreed-upon expectations (for example, nature of the problem, goals of consultation, and desired results). This straightforward assumption must also be considered in light of the fact that the consultant and consultee represent their respective organizations (Snow & Gersick, 1986); either party may have obligations to others not directly involved in but directly affected by consultation. Attempting to sort out these obligations can be very difficult.

The Case of Sheila   Sheila is a talented school counselor with a knack for relating effectively to students and teachers alike. As part of her consultation role, Sheila's principal asked her to conduct a teacher support group to focus on work issues. Sheila agreed and as the support group developed, some members increasingly asked for help on personal domestic issues such as relationships with spouses and children and eating disorders. Sheila expressed her concerns that the group was getting too far away from its original intent and tried to refocus the group. Was Sheila right in refocusing the group? Might she have taken any other measures under referral to help the members meet their perceived needs? If you were Sheila, would you find it somewhat difficult not to let the group go where it wanted to go?

Dual Relationships Increasing attention has been paid to dual relationships in consultation (Dougherty, 1992b, 1997a, 1997b; Herlihy & Corey, 1997; Newman, 1993). The APA code of ethics (1995) suggests a thorough assessment of the potential for harm before engaging in such relationships. *Dual relationships* are those in which a professional has more than one role with another person. As an extreme example, a consultant experiencing sexual intimacy with a consultee has dual relationships—one professional, the other personal. Dual relationships can occur due to a shift in roles (Pearson & Piazza, 1997). For example, a consultant may be appointed to an administrative position in which a current consultee now also becomes a subordinate. Dual relationships frequently cause conflicts of interest as well as role conflicts.

Maintaining two professional roles in the consultation relationship can be particularly hazardous to consultants and their consultees. The two most common second roles in consultation relationships are counselor/psychotherapist and supervisor.

There is often a fine line between where consultation ends and counseling begins. Therefore, it is relatively easy for a consultant who is a trained counselor or therapist to move the consultation relationship into one that also provides counseling or therapy. When this occurs, the act of counseling contaminates the consultation relationship by focusing on personal problems and by de-emphasizing the work-related problems on which consultation was contracted. The use of counseling or psychotherapy in the consultation relationship, when it occurs, usually results once the consultant has determined that the basis for the work-related problem resides more in the consultee than in the client. Rather than providing direct counseling services to the consultee, consultants should refer the consultee for assistance.

Dual relationships also occur when supervision is somehow incorporated into the consultation relationship. It is relatively easy for the consultant who has had supervisory training and administrative experience to include supervisory activities in what should be an exclusively consultative relationship. Because supervision implies the use of evaluation, control, and power over someone, supervision violates the peer nature of the consultation relationship. Use of supervision in consultation allows the consultant to build an illegitimate power base, creates the potential for conflicts of interest, and violates the original consultation contract.

What are some of the potential problems that result from a dual role relationship? There are several reasons for caution when determining whether to engage in dual relationships (after Dougherty, 1997b):

- The complexity of the consultation process has led to difficulties in determining the boundaries of the consultant's role and consequent difficulties in discriminating between appropriate and inappropriate practice.

- The difficulties in defining consultation lead to difficulties in defining the roles of consultants.

- Multiple roles in relationships can cause conflicts of interest that can reduce the efficacy of consultation.

- Multiple roles can cause the consultee to have contradictory expectations.

- Trained counselors can zero in on affective concerns and personal problems.

Therefore, there is a natural danger for turning consultation into counseling.

- Consultees may have an obligation to their organizations not to use consultation for personal purposes (such as counseling).
- Publicity about a consultant engaging in dual role relationships could dissuade potential consultees from seeking consultation.

The bottom-line question consultants must ask themselves concerning dual relationships is, Do the potential conflicts outweigh the potential benefits of serving in both capacities? (Herlihy & Corey, 1997). As I have noted elsewhere (Dougherty, 1997b), human service consultants should be very cautious about engaging in dual professional relationships. If a mistake is to be made, it is better off to be conservative and engage in only one professional relationship.

It is my opinion that the benefits of serving in two professional roles in the consultation relationship are outweighed by the potential conflicts. Extreme caution should be used before engaging in supervision or counseling relationships with consultees (Knoff, 1988). I agree with the position of Kitchener and Harding (1990) that human service professionals "should never enter such relationships when the potential for harm is high unless there are strong offsetting, ethical benefits for the consumer and the risks are clearly discussed" (p. 153). Dual relationships in consultation should be avoided whenever possible. They simply make a very complex relationship even more complex.

The Case of Freddie Freddie, a social worker, is consulting with Norma, the director of a religious counseling center, about some problems she is having with some of the staff at the center. As Norma is discussing the problems, she brings up some very significant aspects of her private life that are affecting her relationships with the staff. Out of the blue, Norma asks Freddie for personal counseling as well as consultation. If Freddie agrees, is he involved in an inappropriate dual relationship? If he agrees to the dual role, how can Freddie assess whether the benefits outweigh the possible dangers? If you were Freddie, what would you do?

Freedom of Choice Providing consultees and their clients with freedom of choice is one of the major ethical obligations of consultants. Ethical issues related to freedom of choice concern assurances that the consultee is acting in the client's best interests. They also therefore concern the creation of dependence, the misuse of power, and inappropriate manipulation of consultees by consultants.

Consultees should always perceive that they have the freedom to do whatever they wish with consultants' recommendations. Such relieves the consultant from being responsible for the consultee's behavior, assuming that the consultee acts in a professionally responsible manner (Fanibanda, 1976). This requires consultants to take certain steps when they consider consultees' actions to be negative (Snow & Gersick, 1986). The first step is to point out the inappropriate behavior to the consultee. Beyond this, there is little consensus as to how the consultant should proceed (Snow & Gersick, 1986). The consultant may have the option of pointing out the consultee's behavior to the consultee's employer or may terminate the consultation relationship, thereby placing the consultee's behavior beyond the consultation relationship.

Consultees cannot have complete freedom of choice if they are dependent on their consultant. This issue is also addressed by the ACA (1995), whose code of ethics specifically states that the consultation relationship should be such that the consultee does not become dependent on the consultant and learns increased self-direction. It is the consultant's responsibility to make sure that dependence does not occur. Because the very purpose of consultation is to assist consultees and their organizations to function more effectively and autonomously, it is unethical for consultants to create and maintain dependence on the part of consultees (NBCC, 1997).

Closely related to the issue of dependence is that of power. The potential for an imbalanced power relationship is a common ethical issue for consultants (Corey et al., 1998). One of the most common abuses of power in the consultation relationship occurs when the consultant violates the peer nature of the relationship and pressures the consultee to get something accomplished. For example, a consultant might push a certain plan of action on the consultee. Consultants need to remember that, although the consultation relationship is equal in terms of status, it is unequal in terms of need. This inequality due to need raises issues related to how the consultant maintains the peer nature of the consultation relationship. The consultant is helping the consultee meet a need. If the consultant gets anything out of this process, it is simply as a by-product. Taking a collaborative stance toward consultation, whenever possible, helps to ensure that the misuse of power is minimized.

A second abuse of power involves misusing the relationship with the consulting organization's administrators to achieve something that should be accomplished through other chan-

nels (Glaser, 1981). For example, a consultant might ask an administrator to send through channels a memo concerning preferred action plans when it was agreed at the outset of consultation that consultees would develop action plans independent of the administration.

A third misuse of power occurs when a consultee is forced to participate in consultation; because such coercion violates the voluntary nature of consultation, it is unethical behavior. In addition, consultants must ensure that their consultees are not receiving undue pressure to participate from their administrators.

A fourth misuse of power relates to the advocacy role a consultant might take on for personal reasons (Brown, 1988). For example, a mental health consultant might exploit the director of a program for the homeless who prefers to go through proper channels by demanding immediate change in the program. In this case, the consultant's hidden agenda might be to gain a power position with the program's board of directors.

Consultees cannot have freedom of choice if they are being manipulated by consultants (Hughes, 1986; Newman, 1993). Therefore, from the outset consultants should discuss with their consultees the ways in which consultants will attempt to influence them. Consultants can maintain their consultees' freedom of choice by discussing their own values and by helping consultees to critically consider consultants' suggestions on their own merits (Hughes, 1986). This can also be accomplished by ensuring that there is agreement and understanding in terms of the goals of consultation (AACD, 1995). In summary, the consultant-consultee-client relationship presents many ethical issues. Clear expectations concerning the relationship, avoidance of dual relationships, and freedom of choice for all parties involved contribute to maintaining ethical behavior on the part of consultants.

The Case of Teresa   Teresa is an internal consultant in the human resource development department of a large psychiatric hospital. Part of her role is to consult with heads of other departments on topics such as "total quality management." Marcie, one of the hospital's department heads, was told by her supervisor that she had to get help in running her department from Teresa. Teresa is keenly aware that Marcie needs some assistance and at the same time has a negative attitude about consultation. If Teresa proceeds with consultation with Marcie, is Marcie's freedom of choice being violated? If you were Teresa, how would you handle this situation in an ethical manner?

Rights of Consultees

Closely related to the issues concerning the consultant-consultee-client relationship are those surrounding the rights of consultees, which include two major issues: confidentiality and informed consent. As it applies to consultation, confidentiality can be viewed as an ethical responsibility (Corey et al., 1998) of the consultant to protect the consultee and the consultee's clients from inappropriate disclosure of information shared within the consultation relationship. The ethics codes of the ACA (1995) and the ASTD (1992) implicitly deal with confidentiality as it relates to consultation, while that of the APA (1995) mentions it explicitly. Informed consent refers to sharing with the consultee information pertinent to consultation so that the consultee will know what is involved and will participate fully and effectively in the process. The codes of ethics of the ACA (1995), the APA (1995), and the

ASTD (1992) all mention informed consent, although not specifically regarding the practice of consultation.

Confidentiality   Confidentiality in consultation is both important and complex. Confidentiality is meant to protect privacy and promote trust (Taylor & Adelman, 1998). The consultant is obligated to develop guidelines that safeguard the confidentiality of parties involved in consultation as well as educate consultees about the nature and limits of confidentiality (Corey et al., 1998; Newman, 1993). These guidelines should be developed during the entry stage and put into the consultation contract. In fact, it is a good idea for the contract to state clearly how information gathered during consultation will be used (Stein, 1990). Guidelines should be structured to protect the consultee's oral and written communications and records (Robinson & Gross, 1985). It is a good idea to follow the practice noted in the APA (1995) ethics code of protecting the identity of parties involved in consultation and sharing only that information necessary to achieve the purposes of consultation. Two aspects of confidentiality that should be considered are the tripartite nature of consultation and the limits on confidentiality (Snow & Gersick, 1986).

Consultation is by definition tripartite, which implies that three parties (and possibly more) can have knowledge of information that is disclosed during consultation. The simplest example is a consultee sharing information about a client to a consultant. In a more complex example, an external agency might require a report from a consultant about some aspect of consultation. The potential for several parties to acquire information may create trust issues in consultation and makes confidentiality a primary ethical concern for consultants. The

consultant must create procedures for determining what information is to be shared with
whom, when, how, for what reasons, and what
the likely impact of sharing will be (Snow &
Gersick, 1986).

Consultants can increase their awareness of
the complexity of confidentiality by asking
themselves the following questions:

- What can I tell my own organization
  about what is said both in consultation
  and in the consultee organization?

- With whom can I share information in
  the consultee organization?

- What steps do I need to take to ensure
  the safety of computer-accessible
  information?

Posing and answering such complex questions at the outset of consultation, getting consensus on the answers, and publicizing this
consensus can prevent problems from occurring later on in the consultation process.

There is no such thing as total confidentiality. Confidentiality has limits and it is up to the
consultant to forge some agreement concerning those limits. This is particularly true with
the advent of interagency collaboration (Taylor
& Adelman, 1998). The limits of confidentiality
refer to those instances that would dictate that
confidentiality be set aside. The limits of confidentiality are commonly discussed in terms of
weighing individuals' rights against the needs
of society (Sheeley & Herlihy, 1986). It is usually assumed that consultants must get permission from their consultees or from members of
the organization affected by the consultation
before sharing information. But in cases where
permission is not granted, what do consultants
do when they have what they feel are good
reasons for revealing the information? Specifi-

cally, what should consultants do when they
determine that a consultee is mistreating a
client or that a program is counterproductive
for the client system? There are no clear-cut
answers in determining when confidentiality
should be set aside in consultation (Snow &
Gersick, 1986). I am of the opinion that confidentiality should be set aside when consultants
determine to the best of their ability that the
best interests of society are not being met, or
the client system is being violated in some way.
When setting aside confidentiality, the consultant determines and takes responsibility for
who is to be told, what they are to be told, and
in what manner.

The second way in which the limits of
confidentiality are discussed involves the concept of anonymity (Snow & Gersick, 1986).
When maintaining confidentiality, the consultant can share information only with the permission of the consultee or an appropriate
member of the organization. When maintaining anonymity, the consultant can share the information but must protect its source. The use
of anonymity has the advantage of facilitating a
flow of information, which can be critical to
the success of consultation that focuses on an
organization as a whole. Using anonymity can
be a very useful strategy for consultants: It prevents them from having "one helping hand tied
behind their backs" when they have information that could be helpful if it were shared but
are restrained from sharing by a lack of permission to do so.

The Case of Gus Gus, a mental health consultant with a large number of community service
agencies, is asked to consult for six months
with several of the staff in an area nursing
home concerning the use of reminiscences as a
tool for improving the quality of life of the eld-

erly. Midway through the consultation period, Gus is approached by the administrator of the nursing home. She relates that she is going to have to cut several of the staff in a downsizing move and would like Gus's opinion on whom to lay off. As a consultant, what ethical issue is facing Gus? Does the fact that the administrator hired Gus give her any rights with regard to her request?

Informed Consent Informed consent is very important in delineating the rights of consultees (Clayton & Bongar, 1994; Herlihy & Corey, 1997). To determine whether they want to be involved in consultation in the first pace, consultees need to be as fully informed as possible about the nature and goals of consultation, issues of confidentiality, their right to privacy, the voluntary nature of participation, and complete freedom in following or not following through on the consultant's recommendations (Hughes, 1986). Consultees have the right to know about how any information obtained from the consultation process will be used (Newman, 1993). The guidelines suggested by Corey et al. (1998) for counselors and therapists who work with clients seem quite appropriate for consultants and their consultees.

Informed consent should be considered an ongoing process and not a one-time event (Corey et al., 1998). This view of informed consent prevents the consultant from making the mistake of overloading the consultee with too much information at the outset of consultation, and it permits candid discussion of the most critical information about which the consultee needs to apprised.

Even though consultants should view informed consent as an ongoing process, they must still ask themselves what consultees need to know at the outset. Providing the consultee with a copy of the ethics code of the consultant's discipline can be a good starting point (Deitz & Reese, 1986). A good practice for answering this question is for consultants to place themselves in their consultees' shoes and ascertain what they would like to know at the outset of consultation. By empathizing with their consultees, consultants are in a better position to answer questions patiently and provide information. Instead of merely being a routine exercise, the sharing of information to obtain informed consent can be a rapport-building event for consultant and consultee.

The Case of Sid As part of his job as a staff development specialist in a community mental health center, Sid provides a group of consultees an instrument designed to assess their ability to work effectively on a team. Based on their performance on the instrument and other measures, the consultees will be assigned to autonomous work teams. As the training is winding up, several of the consultees' supervisors contact Sid regarding what he found out about the consultees' suitability as team members. If Sid shares what he knows, is he violating the consultees' right to informed consent? What is Sid's obligation to the center in this situation? Does the employing organization have any rights in this situation? How could this problem have been avoided in the first place?

The Consultant and the Group

Because of its cost effectiveness, an increasing amount of a consultant's practice is with a group of consultees or part or all of an organization. Because consultation with groups raises unique ethical and professional issues, it is given separate consideration here. If you are interested in consulting with groups, I strongly recommend that you refer to the *Ethical Guidelines for Group Counselors* (1989) and *Professional Standards for the Training of Group Workers* (1990) published by the ASGW.

Consulting with Groups with Caseloads
When a consultant considers working with the same group of consultees for an extended length of time, a basic issue that is raised is one of competence. To what degree is the consultant experienced and trained in group consultation? How aware is the consultant of group process and group dynamics? Because consulting with a group is much different from and more complex than working with an individual consultee, it is critical that consultants have some form of training in group consultation before embarking on such a venture.

A second issue that reemerges when consulting with a group is informed consent. To what degree have the consultees been made aware of the differences between individual and group consultation? Has participation been made voluntary? Have the consultees been made aware of what is expected of them within the group? As in individual consultation, informed consent should be an ongoing process.

A third issue that resurfaces in group consultation is confidentiality. Clearly, the consultant cannot guarantee confidentiality for anyone in the group except him- or herself. In fact, many consultees will subscribe to a code of ethics such as that of the ASGW (1989), which specifically mentions that group cases be discussed only for professional consultation and educational purposes. Even in these cases, group members should be informed of any limits to confidentiality regarding their cases. Because most consultees are also professionals, it is not unreasonable to expect them to live up

to their obligations with respect to confidentiality. Many authors (for example, Corey et al., 1998) suggest that group leaders encourage confidentiality by providing a written policy statement at the outset and/or casually but seriously mentioning confidentiality throughout the life of the group.

A final issue that reemerges is that of dependence. Consultees can become dependent within a group more easily than when they experience consultation as individuals, especially if the group is supportive and safe. The group can become a professional "family," and consultees can readily experience a sense of belonging and cohesiveness. Consultants can help reduce consultee dependence by moving especially cautiously into the disengagement stage and by placing special emphasis on consultees' independent functioning throughout the duration of consultation.

The Case of Lucy Lucy, a mental health practitioner who is consulting with a group of school counselors about their cases, is very concerned about confidentiality because the consultation is occurring at a variety of school sites. She prepares a statement about confidentiality, distributes it during the first meeting with the consultees, and mentions confidentiality intermittently throughout the course of the consultation relationship. In your opinion, has Lucy acted in an ethical manner? Is there anything else she could do to encourage confidentiality? What are the consultees' obligations regarding confidentiality in this situation?

Consulting with Training Groups Consultants are increasingly being retained to educate or train consultees. In their extensive treatment of the ethics of training groups, Pfeiffer and Jones (1977) list five basic issues of concern to consultants engaged in education or training: deception, co-optation, inappropriate techniques, inattention to application, and rehashing.

In this context, *deception* refers to the willful misleading of consultees as a part of an educational or training strategy. Consultants are obligated to correct any misconceptions that may result from such deception and duly inform consultees of the goals and objectives of training activities by some form of debriefing.

Co-optation involves forcing a consultee to do something he or she does not want to do by such means as excessive persuasion or group pressure. Such a practice of course violates informed consent and the right to privacy. Co-optation in any form is unethical and can be minimized by making the learning/training environment a safe one for all involved.

The use of *inappropriate techniques* frequently stems from the consultant's need to use some "pet" methodology, either due to a lack of understanding between consultant and consultees concerning what is to be accomplished or possibly due to poor planning by the consultant. A way to avoid this predicament in educational and training experiences is to take the norms of the consultee group into consideration during planning.

Inattention to the application of training occurs when measures to apply the lessons of the educational experience are not taken. The consultant is ethically bound to assist consultees in applying what they have learned. The work of such authors as Kirkpatrick (1975) and Birnbrauer (1987) provides guidance for consultants in determining consultees' reactions to educational or training experiences, what they learned from those experiences, new behaviors that resulted from their new knowledge, and the results of those behaviors in terms of the consultees' professional growth.

Consultants have an ethical obligation not to repeat or *rehash* the same educational/training experience with the same consultees. In addition, consultants should keep their education and training offerings current and full of vitality (Pfeiffer & Jones, 1977). Consultants involved in education and training should take their own professional growth as seriously as that of their consultees; indeed, the ASTD code of ethics (1992) explicitly states that members should keep informed of pertinent knowledge in their fields.

The Case of Selli Selli is known as a hotshot consultant who can entertain the most subdued groups of trainees. She has a well-polished "dog and pony show." Some of her consultees comment, "See Selli once and you know everything she knows!" Selli suggests to her organization contact person that she offer a series of 10 training sessions. When asked for a proposal with a list of objectives, Selli comments that she views such things as unnecessary. "After all," says Selli, "the show's the thing." What are your views about Selli's behavior? Could she possibly be guilty of rehashing the same thing in her session time and time again? Does she seem to allow for application of her training by her consultees?

Ethical Issues in Intervention

The ethical as well as the technical adequacy of interventions must be determined (Newman, 1993). Three important intervention areas that involve ethical issues are individual- versus systems-level interventions, use of assessment data, and the empirical validity of interventions (Newman, 1993).

When considering individual-level interventions, the consultant needs to determine that the intervention is not meant merely to accommodate the organization's needs. For example, it would be unethical for a consultant to recommend a certain developmental guidance program for use by teachers merely as a way to cut the number of school counselors in a school. If the consultant determines that the system is "sick," interventions at the individual level may also be ethically questionable because of their marginal effect on the problem.

The use of assessment data can present many ethical issues. Primary among these is the improper use of assessment devices so that freedom of choice and the principle of informed consent are violated (Newman, 1993). The potential for unethical behavior occurs often in personnel decisions. Consultants need to make sure that all parties-at-interest are properly informed about the use of any assessment instruments. Consultants should also bear in mind the impact of culture on assessment procedures and consider using multiple assessment and "indigenous consultants" (an appropriate representative of the client system's cultural group) in both assessment and intervention in cross-cultural consultation (Moseley-Howard, 1995).

Consultants must make every effort to see that their interventions have some desired effect. There has been very little attention paid to this in the consultation literature (Newman, 1993). The scale and scope of available interventions makes their selection, implementation, and evaluation very difficult. Consultants should be familiar with the empirical research as it relates to the efficacy of interventions and should attempt to make sound judgments when selecting interventions.

The Case of Ozzie Ozzie is hired as a consultant by a human service agency to help determine if the child and adolescent services sections could be combined as a cost-cutting measure. As Ozzie is gathering data, the director of the agency pushes the reorganization as the only recommendation she wants to hear. Ozzie determines that the reorganization is not an appropriate strategy because it would put an excessive burden on the personnel who serve the agency's clients. In his report, Ozzie suggests that reorganization is not a feasible alternative and makes other cost-cutting recommendations. Did Ozzie act in an ethical manner? What types of pressure do you believe he experienced when the director attempted to influence him? Did Ozzie attempt to recommend the best possible solution?

ETHICAL ISSUES IN ORGANIZATIONAL CONSULTATION

Human service specialists are increasingly being called upon to provide services at the organizational level. A school psychologist might, for example, assist a site-based management team in developing methods to prevent staff burnout. In another example, a community counselor might work with the board of directors of a church group in examining and revising the administrative structure of the church's operation in order to facilitate effective communication. Organizational consultation is one of the most complex types of consultation. Consequently, the ethical issues can also be highly complex. As you will read in later chapters, the goal of organizational consultation is to help the organization function more effectively in some specified way. Ethical issues can easily arise when this overarching goal is being pursued. If you review the case example at the beginning of this chapter, you will note how easily ethical dilemmas can arise during organizational consultation.

The nature of organizations can lead to a variety of ethical issues for consultants (Newman et al., 1996):

- Consultants have significant ethical responsibility to ensure the proper effects of interventions, and those effects can be difficult to determine at the organizational level.

- Consultants frequently rely exclusively on the subjective reports of consultees, although consultees can have biased and distorted views of the organization and its functioning.

- Conflicts of interest within the organization itself can complicate the goals of consultation.

- Differing views of the organization can make setting goals difficult.

- Voluntary participation on the parts of consultees can be difficult to ascertain.

Because of the complexity of organizational consultation, consultants may want to consider adopting *aspirational ethics* (Newman et al., 1996). Aspirational ethics is also called *virtue ethics* (Jordan & Meara, 1990). Virtue ethics attempts to integrate the character of the professional with his or her practice. Aspirational ethics is not based on the question What shall I do? but on the question Who shall I be? (Newman et al., 1996). The use of virtue ethics by consultants lays the foundation for moral considerations as part of the organizational consultation process. By taking this orientation, consultants will continually be examining their behavior in terms of whether it is the right course of action to take.

The Case of Bryan Bryan is a human resource development specialist in a community college. A trained counselor, Bryan has been asked to assist the academic affairs committee of the college to make recommendations for new programs to the college's president. As Bryan attempts to assist the group in making its decision, it becomes obvious that a lot of the committee members are allowing politics rather than the best interests of the college to guide their decision making. Bryan asks the group for some time to share his thoughts on the committee's processes to date. At a meeting he directly yet professionally shares his views that the committee may be having their own special interests in mind when determining the academic future of the college. Was Bryan, in your opinion, using aspirational ethics in this situation? Was he taking a big risk with the group? What would you have done in this situation?

CONSULTING OVER
THE INTERNET

As telecommunications and technology continue to impact our society, so too do they have the potential to affect how consultation is delivered. With the onset of e-mail, list servers, chat rooms, and file transfer protocols, consultants are able to develop a variety of methods for providing consultation. For example, a group of counselors can engage in peer consultation via e-mail or a chat group (Kruger & Struzziero, 1998). In another example, a mental health consultation may deal with a consultee about a case exclusively through e-mail. Although there is no data that demonstrates the amount of consultation that occurs over the Internet, as early as 1997, there were at least

275 counselors offering services over the Internet through their home pages (Sampson, Kolodinsky, & Greeno, 1997).

Extrapolating from the ideas of Sampson et al. (1997) on WebCounseling and applying them to consultation suggests the following consultation applications on the information highway: computer-based networking with consultees regarding cases, marketing of services via WWW home pages, delivery of consultation services over the Internet and through videoconferencing, data collection and assessment through the use of computer-assisted instruction, videoconferencing with more than one consultee at various remote sites, and the delivery of self-help materials and resources with the consultant being "on call" to assist as needed. As a side note, advances in technology have the potential to impact the way consultants use face-to-face meetings in unique ways. For example, face-to-face meetings may be used more for relationship building and less for the transmittal of information (Sampson et al., 1997). However, the impact of technology on consultation raises a variety of ethical issues.

Issues raised by the use of what I refer to as "WebConsulting" can be categorized as technology-related aspects of the basic issues already discussed in this chapter. These include obtaining permission to consult with members of an organization without physically entering the system and confidentiality. Examples of issues related to confidentiality include the privacy of material sent over the web, the use of encryption methods, how long transmission will be preserved, difficulties in verifying the identity of the parties involved, and appropriate procedures for releasing information with other electronic sources (NBCC, 1998). In a

related issue, consultants will want to remember that lack of attention to information security can violate consultee confidentiality (Sampson et al., 1997). Consultants need to ensure that the messages they receive and send electronically are protected as needed and that the consultee has access to privacy when sending information to the consultant.

Another issue revolves around location-specific factors. Consultants need to make sure they assess the impact of local variables as they attempt to assist consultees. For example, a mental health counselor should be aware of the limitations imposed on the counseling activities of school personnel prior to making recommendations regarding interventions.

Consultants should also be aware of how relationship development can be affected by technology. Trusting relationships tend to develop rich and more valid discourse than do those based on superficial acquaintance. Consultants will want to keep this in mind as they determine the depth of relationship necessary to accomplish the goals of consultation. A minimal consideration is contact with consultees over the phone or through videoconferencing.

Little has been written in the area of Web-Consulting. Some organizations such as the NBCC (1998) have adopted standards for Web-Counseling. Consultants can use standards such as these to assist them in dealing with related ethical issues that arise in their practice.

THE CONSULTANT AND THE LAW

Relatively little has been written on the legal issues that concern consultants. For example, a recent text on psychology and the law (Swenson, 1997) does not even list consultation in its index. Because consultation is still an emerging profession, relatively few guidelines on professional behavior exist to guide the courts when consultants encounter legal entanglements. Still, as human service professionals, consultants deliver their services in a sociolegal environment and should be aware of legal matters that affect them (Swenson, 1997; Woody & Associates, 1984). For example, school-based consultants need to be aware of the legal considerations of offering advice to school personnel about students (McCarthy & Sorenson, 1993). Some authors such as Calfee (1997) caution that lawsuits brought against human service professionals, although few, are on the rise.

Consultants will want to remember that mandatory law, if it applies to a given consultation situation, takes precedence over ethical or other concerns, and consultants who violate the law are subject to legal consequences (McCarthy & Sorenson, 1993). The importance of attention to legal issues in the helping professions is emphasized by the fact that the ACA and the APA have set up legal defense funds for members involved in certain types of litigation (Anderson, 1996). The bottom line is: when dealing with issues that may have legal ramifications, consultants may well want to consider seeking legal advice (Remley, 1996).

Malpractice

We'll now consider a legal issue of paramount importance to consultants: malpractice. Human service professionals are accountable for the quality of their services (Woody & Associates, 1984). Further, the reluctance to initiate lawsuits against human service professionals has been reduced (Woody, 1989). In malpractice, the service recipient is in some way damaged by improper services offered without good faith or through neglect or ignorance (Corey et al., 1998). Corey et al. (1998) note that "malpractice is the failure to render professional services or to exercise the degree of skill that is ordinarily expected of professionals in a similar situation" (p. 139). Consultants can be sued for performing the wrong services or for failing to provide the correct services. How can the right or wrong type of service be determined? Applying what generally happens to professional counselors (that is, professionals with no well-defined professional identity in the eyes of the law) (Anderson, 1996) in a similar situation leads to this conclusion: the court would attempt to determine whether a typical professional consultant would act in a way similar to the way the consultant in question acted. An answer in the affirmative would likely lead to no liability, whereas a negative answer could lead to liability (Anderson, 1996).

Tort lawsuits are the most common type involving malpractice (Swenson, 1997). To determine whether a consultant was guilty of malpractice, a court would seek answers to the following questions:

- Did the defendant (consultant) have a professional obligation to the plaintiff?

- Was that duty breached by the consultant?

- Is there a causal link between the breach and the damage to the plaintiff?

To answer these questions, the court would probably attempt to determine whether the consultant showed "requisite skill and care" (Anderson, 1996). However, because these terms are not yet adequately defined for consultants, courts tend to rely on already-established standards for related professions that perform consultation for defining standards for appropriate professional consulting behavior (Anderson, 1996).

Malpractice suits can occur in just about any area of consultation practice. A recent literature review of the causes of malpractice (Clayton & Bongar, 1994; Corey et al., 1998, pp. 141–145) cites the following behaviors that could cause legal entanglements for consultants:

- misrepresenting one's training and skills
- failing to respect integrity and privacy
- using improper diagnosis and assessment techniques
- using improper methods to collect fees
- making inappropriate public statements (libel and slander)
- failing to honor agreements (breach of contract)
- failing to keep adequate records
- failing to provide for informed consent
- providing poor advice

Of these torts, those based on lack of skill are the most prevalent (Swenson, 1997). In summary, consultants can be sued for malpractice whenever there is the likelihood that they have provided services either without the proper skill or without the proper care.

Avoiding Legal Entanglements

It is safe to assume that the vast majority of consultants want to avoid legal entanglements. How should they go about doing this? It is most important that consultants learn about any state laws that may have implications for their practices. Ignorance of the law is not an excuse if a consultant is called into court.

Consultants should provide proper services—only those services in which they are skilled—with care. The old adage "An ounce of prevention is worth a pound of cure" could not be more true when it comes to avoiding legal entanglements.

Consultants should consider joining a professional organization that has an ethics code and should adhere to that code's principles and standards. Such adherence facilitates delivering consultation services with the proper skill and care and assists the consultant in determining standards of professional conduct.

Consultants need a personal and professional growth orientation based on a healthy and honest self-awareness. Knowledge of one's limitations and abilities as a person and as a professional enhances a consultant's ability to make the correct decision concerning whether a given consultation service should be undertaken in the first place.

Consultants should do well each of the little things their profession demands of them:

- Use a written contract.
- Keep accurate records.
- Discuss fees at the outset of consultation.
- Discuss confidentiality and its limits as a matter of course at the outset of every consultation relationship.
- Make sure that any advertising or promotional activities provide current and accurate information.
- Seek consultation from a trusted colleague or a supervisor when in doubt about proper procedure.
- Foster open communication at all times.

CASE 7.1   Ethics for School Consultants

Terry is a consultant based in a junior high school, and she is consulting with a newly hired and inexperienced in-school human service professional, Burt. Burt is conducting a group for students who received more than three Fs on their latest report card and has asked Terry to consult with him regarding "helping these kids out." As Burt describes the group's progress, Terry notices that he has not informed the group of its purpose or made any attempt to promote confidentiality. She also notes that Burt talks to teachers readily about the members' behavior and puts several of the members down by calling them "air heads." At the same time, he exhibits a commitment to the members and to the success of the group.

It is apparent to Terry that Burt does not want feedback on his behavior but rather desires techniques for more effectively helping the students in the group. Terry feels very frustrated during two of her consultation sessions with Burt and perceives him as having a low level of self-awareness and being impervious to how others might perceive him. She has come to resent what she sees as a basic contradiction in Burt—namely, his enthusiasm to help students and the disrespectful way in which he talks about them outside of the group.

During a third session, as Burt keeps asking for techniques to achieve this or that, Terry becomes angry not only at Burt but at herself for being angry with Burt. In the middle of the session, she excuses herself for a couple of minutes to check on an appointment. While out of the room, she uses some stress management techniques on herself. Her internal dialogue is saying things like, "It's awful that he talks about kids that way and still thinks he's committed to help them." As she continues to process her feelings, Terry begins to manage her anger effectively and realizes what she wants to do.

On returning to the room and before Burt can start talking again, Terry tells him that she has something to discuss. She briefly shares her perception that the reason Burt is having trouble with his group may not be due only to the kids but perhaps also his own actions in and out of the group. Terry assures Burt that she believes in his commitment to the students, mentions the behavior that she is concerned with, and asks him if that is the image he wants to project to students, parents, and staff members. In a gentle yet straightforward way, Terry refers to the ACA code of ethics and some of the questions she has about Burt's conduct.

As Terry is talking, Burt shows surprise and becomes genuinely interested in what she is saying. He notes that his attitude may be because of his father's flippant attitude about life. He praises Terry for her sensitivity and perceptiveness and asks her to help him work on his attitudes and behavior, saying, "After all, if my personal life is messing up my professional life, I guess I'd better start there." Terry shares with Burt her appreciation for his willingness to look closely at himself and his interest in counseling. Because she is a school consultant, Terry points out that she feels very uncomfortable doing this and details how being both his counselor and his consultant might destroy their ability to work effectively together. She mentions to Burt the positive results of counseling she received from a local therapist and refers Burt to that counselor.

When Burt comes back for two more consultation sessions, the mood of the relationship is relaxed and yet very work oriented, with Burt speaking compassionately of one of the group member's difficulties.

Commentary

This case illustrates the importance of self-awareness on the part of consultants. If Terry had not possessed a strong sense of self-awareness and insight into herself, her anger might well have jeopardized her relationship with Burt. This case further demonstrates how easy it is for consultants to slip into possibly damaging dual relationships with their consultees. Given Terry's feelings of anger toward Burt combined with her strong willingness to help him, she might easily have trapped herself in a relationship that involved both consultation and counseling.

CASE 7.2   Ethics for Community Consultants

Cindy is the director of a prerelease center for incarcerates preparing for parole. Cindy and her five staff members all have master's degrees in one of the helping professions. The center runs a coeducational seven-week program for incarcerates who are eligible for parole no more than six months after the program's conclusion. Part of the center's role is to assess the suitability of the program participants for early parole.

The center staff have been experiencing difficulties in communicating with incarcerates who are known to suffer from substance abuse. At a needs assessment meeting, the staff concluded that they would like to hold a communication skills workshop that focused on working with substance abusers. As a result, Cindy contacts Sharon, a social worker in the community. Sharon has several years' experience in corrections and an excellent reputation for conducting workshops and making presentations. Cindy contracts with Sharon for a four-day workshop on "Communicating Effectively with the Substance-Abusing Incarcerate."

Sharon does an outstanding job in conducting the workshop. The staff are very open about their views and feelings about communication and how the center responds to known substance abusers. An evaluation of the workshop indicates that the staff felt very positive about the knowledge and skills they had gained from the workshop.

Two weeks later, Cindy calls Sharon to tell her that she is being promoted to a new position and that her immediate supervisor has asked her to choose an interim director from the staff of the center. Cindy also states that she values Sharon's opinion highly and that she realized how close Sharon got to each staff member during the workshop. Cindy asks Sharon to analyze each staff member, rank them, and name her top three choices for the interim director position. Sharon feels uneasy as she talks with Cindy. She puts off agreeing or rejecting Cindy's proposal by telling her she will respond before the week is over. As Sharon considers the reasons for her uneasiness, she realizes that Cindy's request is inappropriate. After all, Sharon was not hired to evaluate anyone but to conduct a workshop. Further, if she were to comply with Cindy's request, she would be depriving the staff members of their right to know about and consent to Sharon's imparting infor-mation (in this case, impressions) about them to their director. As Sharon reviews her professional organization's code of ethics, she realizes that her uneasiness was well founded. She calls Cindy and politely yet assertively denies her request.

Commentary

As you see from this case, Cindy put Sharon, perhaps inadvertently, in an ethical dilemma revolving around both informed consent of consultees and knowing one's limitations as a consultant. For Sharon to comply with Cindy's request for information about the workshop participants would clearly violate the consultees' right to informed consent. Further, when Cindy asked Sharon to analyze and rank the workshop members, Cindy was assuming that Sharon has expertise in staff evaluation procedures. Sharon did not, in fact, possess those skills and was put in the position of having to decline Cindy's request for an additional reason, namely, she did not possess the expertise to do what Cindy was asking regardless of whether the consultees had consented to being evaluated.

By taking such steps, consultants can dramatically reduce the likelihood of legal entanglement. Consultants who know what they are doing and why they are doing it have relatively little to fear, even though the boundaries of their professional behavior remain relatively indistinct in the eyes of the law.

SUMMARY

This chapter has presented an introduction to the closely related ethical, professional, and legal issues that pertain to consultation in the human service professions. The complexity of consultation increases the complexity of the ethical issues consultants face in their work. Consultants can maintain professional standards by being aware of issues involving values, competence, training, the consultation relationship, the rights of consultees and their clients, and consultation in groups. Pryzwansky (1993) notes that the future of ethical guidelines for consultation practice "depends primarily on the degree to which consultation is considered to be a profession rather than an indirect service intervention" (p. 344). Most legal issues that consultants encounter concern malpractice. Consultants can maintain a sense of ethical and professional responsibility and avoid legal entanglements by being committed to their own personal and professional growth. Finally, for consultants to be more confident in their ethical behavior, more specific ethics codes and more deliberate training of consultants in ethical decision making are needed.

SUGGESTIONS FOR

EFFECTIVE PRACTICE

- Strictly adhere to the ethical code of your profession.

- Seek out consultation from trusted colleagues when you are in doubt about how to proceed in consultation or collaboration.

- Avoid legal entanglements by documenting all procedures you employ and by rigorously adhering to your profession's ethical code.

QUESTIONS FOR REFLECTION

1. If ethical guidelines are by definition general in nature, how can consultants apply them in specific situations?

2. To what degree do you agree that ethics codes of most human service organizations are culturally biased? Explain your position.

3. As a consultant-in-training, how would you want to be trained in ethical decision making?

4. To what degree do consultants require specific training to consult in a given area?

5. What are the consultant's professional and ethical obligations to the consultee?

6. What are the consultant's professional and ethical obligations to the consultee's client?

7. In what ways are consultants most likely to violate the rights of their consultees during consultation?

8. How does a consultant go about developing a personal and professional growth orientation?

9. If you were a judge in a court of law and a consultant was being sued for malpractice, what information would you want to know to determine whether malpractice had occurred?

10. How can there ever be a code of ethics for consultants when there are so many different professional groups whose members perform consultation as one of their primary functions?

SUGGESTED SUPPLEMENTARY
READINGS

I hope you are interested in learning more about the ethical, professional, and legal issues that affect consultants. I strongly recommend the following readings for study and reflection:

Anderson, B. S. (1996). *The counselor and the law* (4th ed.). Alexandria, VA: ACA. Being aware of legal issues is essential for consultants. This text covers, from a legal perspective, a variety of topics ranging from the helping relationship to avoiding liability. The author views consultation with colleagues as significant in making decisions related to effective practices and in avoiding claims of malpractice.

Corey, G., Corey, M. S., and Callanan, P. (1998). *Issues and ethics in the helping professions* (5th ed.). Pacific Grove, CA: Brooks/Cole. This book provides a wealth of information for professionals and students in any of the human service professions. Ethics and issues specifically related to consultation are given adequate coverage, and the authors' ideas on several issues have relevance for consultants. Chapter 3,

"Values and the Helping Relationship," provides excellent information that consultants can extrapolate and apply to their practices. Chapter 4, "Client Rights and Counselor Responsibilities;" Chapter 5, "Confidentiality: Ethical and Legal Issues;" and Chapter 7, "Managing Boundaries and Multiple Relationships" all present important information that consultants can use in developing their own standards of conduct. The appendix of this text contains the current ethics codes of the major helping professions.

Swenson, L. C. (1997). *Psychology and law* (2nd ed.). Pacific Grove, CA: Brooks/Cole. This thorough text provides a broad coverage of a variety of legal issues practicing human service professionals encounter. Part 2 of the text, "Practice and Malpractice," provides four chapters from which practicing consultants can extrapolate and apply material to consultation situations. This text puts consultants into the world of legal realities, a world far different than that in which most of us practice. Swenson's point that satisfied consumers rarely sue is well taken.

8

The Pragmatic Issues of Working within an Organization

There are a variety of issues and forces that you will encounter in your practice of consultation and collaboration. All consultation occurs in some organizational context which contains complex forces that affect, for better or worse, the individuals who make up the organization (Cherniss, 1998). It is important for consultants to be familiar with the technical and social forces and structures that will impinge on the consultation environment (Hansen, Himes, & Meier, 1990; Kelly, 1993; Knoff, 1995; Talbott, 1988). These forces and structures include organization climate, the administration's view of consultation and collaboration, and the organization's authority, decision-making structure, and communication structures (Forman, 1995). This awareness is essential as consultants ". . . must be able to conceptualize problems and interventions from an organizational perspective and utilize information about organizational processes in their consultation activities with agencies and organizations" (Illback & Zins, 1993, p. 87).

Consultants are increasingly being called on to engage in organizational consultation and need to take into account the organizational context of consultation as well as consultation theory and practice so as to maximize the probability of being successful (Knoff et al., 1991; Knoff, 1995; Illback & Zins, 1993). Further, human service consultants must be versed in the nature of organizations and must be skilled in working with them. For example, Kelly (1993) notes that mental health consultants are subject to the forces of the environment in which they consult but that their training is basically in individual therapy. Organizational factors about which consultants may want to be knowledgeable include: recent changes in organizations and our society, the theory of organizations that consultants themselves hold, the nature of organizational change, dealing with organizational culture, involvement of stakeholders, the training of consultees, and time constraints.

This chapter provides the working knowledge of the pragmatic issues related to providing consultation in an organization. Because consultation is one way to help organizations change so that they can function more effectively, consultants need to know what organizations are; how they develop, grow stagnant, and change; and what the connection is between an organization's individuals and its ability to meet its goals and objectives. Knowledge of organizations also helps consultants better understand their consultees' position in an organizational context.

As you read this chapter, keep the following questions in mind:

1. How can you cope with the time constraints imposed upon you by the structure and culture of the organization for which you are consulting?

2. If organizations are so complex, how can a consultant or group of consultants accomplish real changes in them?

3. How are organizations like live organisms?

4. What factors are involved in organizational change?

5. How does organizational culture affect the behavior of individuals within the organization?

INTRODUCTION

Consider this situation:

Case Example

In your job as chief administrator of a large human service agency, you notice an excessive turnover rate in two of your organization's six departments. You have made several unsuccessful attempts to rectify the problem; you know what is wrong, but you don't know how to fix it. As a last resort, you decide to call in a consultant. In preparing for the first meeting with the consultant, what exactly would you tell him or her about your organization, the people in it, the problem, and the solutions you've tried? Where would you suggest the consultant begin to try to help?

If you were the consultant in this situation, what information would you want to know? What values and biases about "how to fix things" would you bring into the consultation setting? Which personnel would you want to interview? How would you go about solving the problem? How would you know whether or not consultation had been successful? The answers to these and many other important questions depend on how well you (the consultant) and the human service agency's administrator understand the nature of organizations.

Organizations of all kinds abound in our society: schools, businesses, human service agencies, and industries. People organize because they think it is the best way to reach their goals. To be effective in organizational consultation, consultants need to understand organizations themselves, as well as what prompts people to think and behave as they do within organizations.

An organization has the following: cooperation among many individuals, certain common goals, a division of labor, and a hierarchy of authority (Jerrell & Jerrell, 1981, pp. 134–135).

Organizations can be defined in terms of what they do, how they are set up, and what their goals are. Management is a specialty task in organizations that helps them meet those goals. How organizations are managed raises many values issues, and organizations are often criticized for their values and the ways they are run. For example, some human service organizations are criticized for valuing rules and regulations more than the clients they serve. An organization's values and behaviors become quite evident when it must face several, constantly changing issues. Regardless of the specific issues an organization faces at a given time, the basic issues remain constant: complexity, organizational size, and technology.

Organization development consultation attempts to explain the whats, hows, and whys of organizations and to help them increase their effectiveness. When a consultant goes into an organization, the first step is to develop a basic definition of the organization. The theoretical frame of reference with which the consultant enters the organization determines what the consultant sees. The consultant defines the organization by performing an assessment to clarify its basic nature. Consultants usually have training in one of the four components of organizations—environment, people, structure, and process—but also need a general perspective on organizations to be able to compare one with another.

Recent Changes in Society and Organizations

Some understanding of recent changes in society and organizations provides consultants a framework for being more effective in assisting the organizations with which they consult. At the advent of the new millenium, basic societal change has affected new workers: There has been a diminishing percentage of young people entering the work force; new workers are less skilled than those of previous generations; women continue to make up at least 60 percent of new workers; and over 33 percent of new workers come from minority groups (Offermann & Gowing, 1990). In the case of continuing workers, there exists a vast increase in the number of middle-aged workers, a bias against these workers because of their age, an increase in retirement issues, and a change in attitudes by workers toward more meaningful and involving work experiences (Offermann & Gowing, 1990). Issues in the workplace in the 1990s that have continued into the first decade of the millenium include those related to dependent care, substance abuse, AIDS, women at work, stress (e.g., violence in the workplace), and cultural diversity (Luke, 1993).

In addition to societal changes, organizations themselves are changing. Organizations, including human service organizations, have been going through several changes (Burke, 1993). The change from growth to consolidation has impacted organizations in every sector of society. Implications for consultants include dealing with issues related to downsizing, assisting with the management of "flatter" organizations, and helping to define the core competencies needed to effectively run the organization/agency.

Organizations have been experiencing change at an increasingly rapid pace. Implications for consultants include how to best gather and process information in order to react to ever-changing conditions. A further implication of rapid change is that consultants themselves must be willing to deal effectively with ambiguity and uncertainty.

Organizations have become more complex; the number of specialized people performing different tasks has increased. This increased complexity and diversification makes it much more difficult for an organization to have a common purpose and makes coordination difficult for management. Consequently, members do not know what others in the organization are doing: the left hand doesn't know what the right hand is doing. Organizations are also more complex due to increasingly rapid technological development (Turnage, 1990; Burke, 1993). As Burke (1993) notes: ". . . chaos is more likely to be our new form of stability" (p. 12).

The managers of organizations and agencies have moved from being unaware of organizational change concepts to being quite familiar with them. The challenge to consultants is to make sure that managers and others are capable of acting on their awareness of the meaning of terms such as *vision*, *organizational culture*, and so forth.

Organizations and agencies are becoming more concerned with ethics. Our society is becoming even more litigious, perhaps contributing indirectly to the concern over ethical behavior, and many human service organizations are taking a look at their core values as they relate to serving their client systems.

There is a greater competition among all types of organizations (Beer & Walton, 1990), including human service organizations. Organizations, therefore, will be looking for longer term consultation rather than touch-and-go advice, gearing consultation to long-term effects through help with immediate problems and providing specific (not general) help.

Because human service consultants frequently consult with human service agencies, it is important for them to be aware that in the past two decades such organizations have undergone alterations in one or more of the underlying foundations of culture, politics, ecology, economics, and technology. The following list of changes, noted by Gallessich (1982), have forced human service organizations to be more flexible, have a broader spectrum, and be adaptable, and they still hold true today:

- a shift from the government to the individual as the major support for human services

- a shift in public attitude from the idea that society causes many human service problems and therefore should have a part in ameliorating them

- a change in the role of clients, who have become more demanding and less compliant

- some regulation in licensure by professional organizations such as the ACA, the APA, and NASW, which can influence who can practice in certain human service agencies

- the introduction of computers and data-processing procedures that require retraining of many personnel and open up new methods of working with clients

- an overlap in services among agencies, which affects human service agencies' ability to serve client systems and causes some agencies to compete with and be counterproductive to the work of other agencies serving the same clients

■ an increased scrutiny by the mass media of the work of human service agencies as representatives of the public (such pressure can force an agency to perform too rigidly "by the rules")

Implications for Consultants Human service consultants will be increasingly called upon to assist organizations and their members manage and cope with such changes. Organizations are likely to want help in the following areas that impact organizational culture and climate: focusing more on the human side of management, resolving the human resource problems caused by mergers and acquisitions, and providing training in effective communication regarding the impact of change (Offermann & Gowing, 1990). Organizations are also likely to need consultants in the following areas related to maintaining organizational productivity: optimizing organizational structure, restructuring the nature of work toward increased use of team approaches, maximizing the use of technology, creating effective work environments, improving services and products (Offermann & Gowing, 1990), and offering motivation (Katzell & Thompson, 1990). The increase in technological developments in the workplace will add to problems of stress among management and staff, leading to increased use of consultants in stress management training capacities (Turnage, 1990). The increased competitiveness among organizations will require that consultants help managers become more effective in the following areas: taking the leadership in accomplishing needed changes through better use of the skills of empowering others, envisioning desired outcomes, providing resources, and modeling desired practices (Beer & Walton, 1990).

Because many of these organization needs are related to the human factor, human service consultants will find themselves increasingly involved in work with business and industry as well as the traditional areas of public and non-profit organizations. Education/training consultation will be in demand because so many of organizational needs relate to maximizing the talents of personnel (Goldstein & Gilliam, 1990). Further, personnel problems such as absenteeism, turnover, and lost productivity can be due to poor morale and, in turn, to management problems, since in many organizations, consultants can help managers improve their skills and clarity in laying out job assignments, roles, and expectations to staff (Armstrong & Wheatley, 1990).

Regardless of how they will be employed, consultants will need to be competent in the use of power, to blend structural changes with people changes, and to learn quickly yet thoroughly the nature of the organizations with which they are consulting (Beer & Walton, 1990; Illback & Zins, 1993).

THE INFLUENCE OF ORGANIZATIONAL THEORY

Consultants develop a broad perspective on the nature of organizational forces by considering each organization with which they work relative to some organizational theory. The consultant's organizational theory is the glue that holds together events into a meaningful form. Organizations' day-to-day functioning are guided by the particular theories of organization they adhere to. By being aware of such theories, human service consultants will understand the ways things are done in a particular organization and, as importantly, the way the forces that impact that organization are interpreted. Further, the theory on which an organization is based affects the way processes such as consultation are performed.

Historically speaking, *organizational theory* is the study of the structures and processes of organizations and the behavior of groups and individuals within them (Pugh, 1966). Because they attempt to explain these complex entities and how they are best designed, most theories must simplify organizations; how this is accomplished depends on which factors are considered relevant (Argyris, 1970). A comprehensive coverage of different organizational theories is beyond the scope of this text; interested readers can gain in-depth information from such books as *The Social Psychology of Organizations* (Katz & Kahn, 1990). The following overview of two organizational theories highlights the different perspectives from which organizations can be studied. I particularly believe that a view of the bureaucratic model and the systems model provide a contrast for consultants to consider as they analyze organizations.

Before the turn of the century, organizations were considered individual entities, such as church, government, and so forth. With the rise of capitalism in the late 19th century, organizations came to be viewed as a "class of collectivities" (Khandwalla, 1977). The classical model of organizations came into vogue near the beginning of the 20th century and was epitomized by Max Weber's model of bureaucracy (Mitchell, 1978). This model is considered a "machine" theory. *Machine theory* is a generic term that implies that each organization is built according to the blueprint derived from its purpose, just as each machine is built according to a set of specifications (Katz & Kahn, 1978).

The Bureaucratic Model

Weber designed the bureaucratic model as the ideal of organizational effectiveness. Its principles, which are "means to ends" in nature, emphasize the structure of the organization over the human element. Rules and regulations are important and provide order and continuity. Jobs are analyzed in terms of what is required to do them effectively, and the most highly qualified people are placed in them. Communication patterns are vertical rather than horizontal, with each unit under the direct control of a higher unit. Emphasis is placed on the written record, with all decisions, acts, and regulations written down (Mitchell, 1978).

According to this bureaucratic theory, organizations were meant to be efficient, effective, and equitable. However, the potentially counterproductive elements in this model can lead to red tape, rigidity, apathy, and resistance to change (Khandwalla, 1977).

Implications for Consultants Consultants encountering an organization emphasizing bureaucratic values will want to be sensitive to the lines of authority, the dedication to the written word, and the importance of rules and regulations. They should be on the lookout for apathy/morale issues, views of leadership among the organization members, concern over confidentiality, and the nature of the informal power structure.

The classical models of organizational theory, such as the bureaucratic model, emphasize specialization of tasks, standardized role performance, uniformity of function, and avoidance of duplication (Katz & Kahn, 1978). These models are inadequate in that they do not provide for interaction between the organization and its environment and thus deny the organization a means to change (Katz & Kahn, 1978).

Open Systems Organizational Theory

One of the most popular models of organizational theory is *systems theory*, which provides a broadly based perspective on organizations developed from attempts to understand biological events (Gallessich, 1982; Kurpius et al., 1993). Systems theory is integral to the consultation-related activities of community psychologists and is becoming increasingly popular with other human service professionals (Juras, Mackin, Curtis, & Foster-Fishman, 1998).

A *system* can be defined as "a set of interrelated elements or components" (Jerrell & Jerrell, 1981, p. 135). Kurpius (1985) defines a system as "an entity made up of interconnected parts, with recognizable relationships that are systematically arranged to serve a perceived purpose" (p. 369). In systems theory, *organizations* can be defined as "dynamic entities continually interacting with their environment, changing and adapting to develop congruence between people, process, structure, and external environment" (Beer, 1980, p. 15). According to systems theory, everything is interrelated and interdependent (Covey, 1991). When applied to organizations' and consultants' behavior in organizations, system theory suggests that events impact and are impacted by whatever transpires.

From the perspective of consultation, a system is ". . . an orderly combination of two or more individuals whose interaction is intended to produce a desired outcome (Curtis & Stollar, 1995, p. 52). There are two types of systems: closed and open. Closed systems are not affected by their environments: they have a finite amount of energy, and when that energy

is used up the system runs down. Open systems, in contrast, have permeable boundaries and can obtain energy from and send energy back to the environment (Katz & Kahn, 1978). Organizations can be viewed as open systems. As Jerrell and Jerrell (1981) note, "systems receive inputs from the environment and subject those inputs to a transformation process to produce outputs that are fed back into the environment" (p. 135). This phenomenon is called the input-throughput-output function of the system.

The systems view of organizations identifies four components (Kurpius, 1985; Kurpius, et al., 1993): a framework (pattern of activities), goals, methods and operations, and people.

The systems theory of organizations assumes that organizations are open systems; they are not isolated, closed entities, but instead are subject to internal and external influences (Lee, 1993; Curtis & Stollar, 1995). Systems theory considers the organization to be a totality, and it directly examines the interrelationships among an organization's subsystems and between the organization and its environment (Curtis & Stollar, 1995).

The most fundamental property of a system is the interdependence among its parts (Kurpius, 1985). The systems approach is helpful in conceptualizing the multidimensional parts of a system as an integrated whole (Argyris, 1964), and it assumes that an organization is more than the sum of its parts (Mitchell, 1978). Organizations (and the people within them) are seen as adaptive (Mitchell, 1978) and as social systems operating within larger environments (Katz & Kahn, 1978). Organizational behavior is seen as dynamic and cyclical; the primary cycle in human service organizations consists of intake, treatment, and output of the client system (Gallessich, 1982).

Characteristics of Systems When viewed as open systems, organizations have nine characteristics (Henning-Stout, 1993):

1. *Importation of energy.* No social structure is self-sufficient: the organization must draw new energy from other organizations, from the material environment, and from people such as consultants.

2. *The throughput.* Energy is transformed as it goes through the organization. In a human service organization, throughput can be service to clients, training of existing personnel, addition of new staff, and so forth.

3. *The output.* The organization exports some product into the environment, such as some new service to the client system.

4. *Systems are cycles of events.* Organizations have an input-throughput-output cycle; the output product supplied to the environment provides energy for repetition of the cycle.

5. *Negative entropy.* Entropy is the degradation process of all organisms toward death or disorganization. Organizations can arrest this entropy by importing more energy than they expend. This process of energy storage is called negative entropy.

6. *Information input, negative feedback, and the coding process.* Information input can give the organization signals about the environment and the organization's relationship to it. One type of information input is negative feedback, which allows the organization to stay on its chosen course or, if necessary, change course. The reception of inputs into the organization is selective; that is, the organization can attend to only so many inputs, and those inputs are the only ones among many that the organization tunes in. This selective mechanism is called coding, and the coding procedures of an organization are determined by its functions. (For example, if a mental health center learns that the community would fund a dropout prevention program, it might make plans to develop and implement such a program.)

7. *The steady state and dynamic homeostasis.* The importation of energy can maintain a constancy in the flow of energy such that an organization is characterized by a steady state. Dynamic homeostasis refers to the basic preservation of the system's character. In preserving its character, the organization must import more energy than it exports. In adapting to its environment, an organization moves toward assimilating the external resources considered necessary for survival. Hence, organizations attempt to grow both quantitatively and qualitatively over time.

8. *Differentiation.* Organizations move in the direction of differentiation and elaboration: roles within the organization become specialized and the number of such roles tends to increase. (For example, a mental health center might differentiate from a single team to a crisis-intervention team, a substance-abuse team, and any number of other specialized teams.)

9. *Equifinality.* The principle of equifinality proposes that organizations can reach the same end by different means: this is the "there's more than one way to skin a cat" principle. (For example, a single human service organization might use any of several methods to improve its public relations image.)

Subsystems within the Organization The subsystems of an organization are integrated by means of the norms, roles, and values present within the system (Katz & Kahn, 1978). Role behavior is sanctioned by norms that are justified by values. Five subsystems within organizations are built around the organization's norms, roles, and values (Katz & Kahn, 1978):

- the technological or production subsystem
- the support subsystem
- the maintenance subsystem
- the adaptive subsystem
- the managerial subsystem

The *technological subsystem* is concerned with the quantity and quality of the work accomplished within the organization (Katz & Kahn, 1978). For example, in a counseling center the direct delivery of services to the client system—the throughput—constitutes the technological subsystem. Organizations are often classified according to the type of product they provide, and the products of human service organizations are the clients they serve. (More precisely stated, the product of human service agencies is "better" people.) The technological subsystem is responsible for the input-through-put-output cycle.

The *support subsystem* is concerned with the procurement of inputs, the disposal of outputs, and the maintenance of an environment favorable to the organization (Katz & Kahn, 1978). For example, a university might seek funding (procurement of inputs) for a counseling program for learning-disabled college students. Upon termination of the program, a written report is submitted to the funding agency (disposal of outputs) and the program is widely publicized to attract students and strengthen its public image (maintenance of a favorable environment).

The *maintenance subsystem* is concerned with connecting people within the organization to their roles (Katz & Kahn, 1978). It is not concerned with the material being worked on (typically the client system in human service organizations), but rather with the equipment used to get the work done. In human service organizations, this concern relates to getting people who work for the organization into their proper roles: patterned human behavior. This subsystem integrates people into the system through recruitment, socialization, training, rewarding, and sanctioning, and it is concerned with input with respect to maintenance (for example, recruitment of personnel).

The *adaptive subsystem* helps an organization exist in a changing environment. It is specifically concerned with sensing and interpreting important changes in the external environment. Functions such as long-range planning, research and development, and market research are part of the adaptive subsystem.

The *managerial subsystem* controls, coordinates, and directs the other subsystems of the organization and adjusts the total system to its environment. There are two major types of managerial subsystems: regulatory mechanisms and the authority structure.

Regulatory mechanisms gather and interpret data about the organization's input-through-put-output cycle and give feedback to the system about its output in relation to its input (Katz & Kahn, 1978). In a human service organization, a follow-up study of clients' perceived benefits from the organization would be an example of a regulatory mechanism.

Organizations must have a defined and established decision-making framework called the *authority structure*. This structure describes the organization of the managerial system with regard to the positions at which decisions are made and the routes through which they are implemented (Katz & Kahn, 1978).

Implications for Consultants Because of the current popularity of the systems view, I have provided extensive coverage of the implications of this perspective. O'Neill and Trickett (1982, pp. 4–5) have pointed out six implications for consultants taking on a systems view of organizations:

- Consultation is an activity designed to intervene in the social context.

- An important source of knowledge is understanding the social context where consultation is occurring.

- Cultural and institutional diversity is a positively valued fact of life for the consultant.

- Consultation interventions should be matched to the organization within which consultation occurs.

- Priority should be given to predicting the side effects of consultation.

- Interventions should be designed in such a way that the organization's resources are managed and preserved.

In addition, just as each person is unique and special, so too is every system (Curtis & Stollar, 1995). Consultants need to take a fresh perspective each time they enter a new consultation setting. Further, because the effects of consultation can go far beyond those intended, consultants should ensure that communication flows smoothly and accurately throughout the subsystems of an organization. You no doubt have heard horror stories about organizations such as schools or mental health centers in which the staff in one area was totally unaware of what the staff in other areas was doing and planning even though they are affected by those decisions.

Other implications of systems theory for consultants include helping an organization maintain focus on its core mission, promoting the use of feedback as a self-regulating mechanism to expedite change, and assisting with the maintenance of internal and external boundaries so that work flow goes smoothly (Lee, 1993). The field of community psychology has added the additional element of the community as a part of the system in which organizations exist (Kloos et al., 1998). The community is viewed as both a possible target for consultation and collaboration as well as a force impacting the organization.

The goal of consultation using systems theory can be a change in the *microsystem* (i.e., the closest social elements of the defined client system), the *mesosystem* (i.e., the near but not immediate influences, such as the general influence of family and friend), and the *exosystem* (i.e., the most remote factors, such as ethical and legal procedures) (Kurpius, et al., 1993, pp. 416–417). Conceptualizing at these levels permits the consultant to design interventions at multiple levels. Effective consultants using systems theory will take into account the relationships between the problem at hand and systems variables. The interaction between the client system and the environmental context (i.e., the various systems levels) will be assessed in consultation.

The bottom line is that consultation based on systems theory has as its goal an increase in the level of problem-solving expertise of the system. While the immediate goal is to assist the system with a specified problem, the ultimate goal is to assist the system to be a more effective problem solver on its own. As a result of this perspective, the use of training in problem-solving activities for consultees is strongly encouraged.

Systems theory as it relates to consultation is not without its criticisms (Ridley & Mendoza, 1993). The theory offers little direction beyond abstract generalizations and does not use consultation-specific language. Although systems theory gives a broad view, it does not help the consultant with what to do once the view is in hand. Further, because systems theory deals mostly with subsystems, it has not developed a view of the system itself as part of a larger system (macrosystem). Consultation based on systems theory is at best "primitive" (Kurpius et al., 1993, p. 415).

Now that we have examined the bureaucratic and systems theories of organizations, it should be clear that when consultants enter an organization, they regard it and analyze it based on some theory of organizations. Whether you realize it or not, you have your own theory of organizations. The more you are aware of it, the more you will know what you are looking for and also what you are likely to overlook; you will also be in a better position to understand how your consultees view their organizations and the concomitant implications this has for your consultation.

Will you see the organization relative to the bureaucratic theory and assume that the members of the organization need to be controlled by certain highly regulated structures? Will you adopt the position of the systems theorists and look at the interdependencies and interrelationships among the organization's subsystems to understand the organization?

Whatever questions you ask, the variety of organizational theories available to consultants suggests that consultants should take a flexible view in analyzing organizations. The following lists present questions that consultants subscribing to various organizational theories might ask when analyzing an organization (adapted from a list developed by Khandwalla, 1977):

Questions for Analyzing a Bureaucratic Organization

- What are the structural strengths and weaknesses of the organization?
- What kind of bureaucracy is the organization?
- What factors made it assume this form?
- What anticipated and unexpected consequences has this form of bureaucracy had?

Questions for Analyzing a Systems Organization

- What are the organization's major subsystems?
- What are their properties?
- How do they interact?
- What are the properties of the organization as a whole?
- What kind of relationship does the organization have with its environment?
- How does the organization adjust to changes in its environment?
- Does it use multiple modes of adjustment?
- How do changes in the organization affect its various subsystems, and how do changes in any of its subsystems affect the organization as a whole?

ORGANIZATIONAL CHANGE

Consultants frequently help organizations change. The following discussions incorporate current thinking about effective organizations and the principles of organizational change.

Approaches to Change

Organizations change in response to pressure from internal or external forces. Most organizations, including schools, are not adept at making changes (Lee, 1993). Depending on how well an organization monitors its internal and external environments, change may be either well planned or forced on the organization through a crisis situation. The larger the organization, the more people, groups, and political constituencies are involved—and change must be planned with all of them in mind (Beer, 1980).

When an organization senses the need for change, it looks for new directions to proceed. Consultants (whether external or internal) who are freed from traditional organizational constraints can have a part in providing these new directions (Beer, 1980). From a philosophical perspective, there are three views of planned change: the empirical-rational approach, the normative-reeducative approach, and the power-coercive approach (Chin & Benne, 1985).

The *empirical-rational approach* assumes that people are rational by nature and will follow their rational self-interests once these are made known. Thus, any proposed changes are presumed to be congruent with the self-interests of the organization and its members. Because the organization and its members presumably are rational and motivated by self-interest, changes will be adopted only if they can be rationally justified and gains are evident (Chin &

Benne, 1985). In other words, according to this approach, changes in cognitions produce changes in behavior (Gallessich, 1982). This approach's credibility is based on scientific research and the process of educating people for change.

The *normative-reeducative approach* does not deny the role of rationality in change but points out that change is supported by sociocultural norms based on attitudes and values. Change involves a shift in those attitudes and values away from old patterns and a commitment to new patterns (Chin & Benne, 1985). This approach views people as social by nature; their shifts in emotion about something will bring about change. Further, change is not only intellectual; it also involves feelings and attitudes (Chin & Benne, 1985).

The *power-coercive approach* to change focuses on the ingredients of power and the ways it is used in bringing about change. This approach relies on the use of political, economic, and moral sanctions in the exercise of power; it assumes that externally based sanctions are necessary for change to occur.

Change can also be examined in terms of the source from which the impetus to change comes. These "power structures" are top-down, bottom-up, and shared (Greiner, 1967).

In the *top-down approach*, change is implemented on authority of the organization's leadership, which also defines the problem and determines the solution (Beer, 1980). That change is to occur can be communicated in the following ways:

- decree (for example, memorandum)
- introduction of technology (for example, personal computers)
- replacement (for example, changing key personnel)

- changes in structure (for example, reorganization of a subsystem)

Top-down changes are usually unilateral (Beer, 1980), are usually introduced rapidly, and involve only a few key, top-level administrators in the decision-making process.

The *bottom-up approach* to change is the opposite of the top-down approach. Because responsibility for change is delegated to members lower in the organization (Beer, 1980), administrators typically are not involved and know little about the changes (Beer, 1980). Bottom-up change can occur in the following contexts (Beer, 1980):

- training sessions (for example, team building)
- staff groups (for example, peer teaching and training in different managerial approaches)
- experimental units (for example, groups designed to take services to locations near the residences of the client systems' members)

In the bottom-up approach, leadership in the organization relinquishes significant amounts of power and authority (Beer, 1980). Bottom-up changes are usually slow and subject to the influences of special-interest groups.

The *shared approach* involves a continuous interaction among members of the organization's different levels, and a process of mutual influence ensues (Beer, 1980). The shared approach to change can involve the following (Beer, 1980):

- iterative communication (for example, a top-level administrator defines the problem and assigns staff to gather data and develop solutions. The process

is reviewed frequently by members throughout the organization.)

- decision-making task forces (for example, top leadership defines the problem and the parameters of the solution but has the task force generate solutions. Top leadership then makes the final selection of the most appropriate solution.)
- diagnostic and problem-solving task forces (for example, a group composed of individuals from all levels of the organization defines the problem and generates and implements a solution.)

Because they typically involve personnel from throughout the entire organization, shared approaches to change are usually slow, and, because so many people are involved, ownership of changes is usually strong (Lippitt, 1993).

The Nature of Organizational Change

Change in an organization involves realignment, adaptation, alteration, or modification to tasks, technology, structures, and components (Cooke, 1979). Change is a part of the daily routine of any organization; it can be precipitated by internal or external forces and can be planned or unplanned (Lippitt, 1969). If these forces are adequately monitored, then change can occur in a planned and systematic way. If these forces are not adequately monitored, crises ensue and the organization is forced to cope in a less orderly, less effective manner. Pressure to change can be strong and can demand great adaptability from an organization. Nonprofit organizations frequently have a more difficult time coping with and planning for change because they are not subject to the marketplace forces that act on for-profit organizations.

Organizations are subject to the following principles of change (Cooke, 1979):

- Change is likely to involve all facets of the organization.
- Forces both inside and outside the organization can generate pressure for change.
- The same forces that give rise to the need for change can also complicate the management of change in organizations.

As it relates to organizations, change has the following characteristics (Beckhard, 1979, pp. 19–20):

- It must be "owned" by the key people in the organization—usually people at several levels.
- It must be managed from the top.
- It must be system oriented: it must relate to the total organization or to significant parts or subsystems.
- It must have an extended timetable.
- It must be related to the organization's mission and goals. Organizational changes "for change's sake" or for improving internal conditions are not likely to be maintained. Efforts to achieve change must be responsive to organization-environmental interfaces; it is no longer practical to improve internal effectiveness without explicit attention to the relationship between an organization and its environment.
- It must be implemented through the organization's leaders; facilitators can help in planning, but implementation must be managed by the leadership.

Real organizational change will not take place and be maintained unless the following three conditions exist:

1. There must be a sufficiently high level of dissatisfaction with the status quo to mobilize energy toward some change.
2. Leaders must have some vision of the desired result of change.
3. Leaders must envision and communicate some practical first steps toward this desired result if energy to begin change is to be mobilized.

In addition to these basic principles and characteristics of organizational change, organizations can experience some complications related to change (Cooke, 1979). First, change may be difficult to achieve because immediate results cannot be seen. Second, for changes to be successful depends on their being deemed necessary by all members of the organization. Finally, initiating change can be particularly difficult in organizations with highly specified roles and centralized systems for authority and communications. However, if the uncertainty involved in change cannot be reduced with well-defined roles and clear lines of authority, members may become frustrated and abandon the effort to change.

Burke (1993) points out that attempts to change organizations should aim for change in the following areas in the presented order: behavior, attitudes, and values. Behavior change leads to change in attitudes which can, in turn, change culture.

Implications for Consultants Human service consultants in any setting generally consult with the purpose of achieving change in an organization or on the part of an individual or group of consultees within that organization. Clearly, to be most effective, consultants must be familiar with many models for conceptualizing organizational change and understand how change is viewed in the organization in which they are consulting (Fuqua & Kurpius, 1993). Consultants are well advised to buy into the method of change typically used by the organization prior to recommending or implementing their own views. Because change is such a sensitive issue for people, consultants should minimize the stress of change whether for an individual or an entire organization. They will also want to ensure that ideas for change are integrated into the organization, that changes are conducted by members of the organization with top-level sanctioning and involvement, and that change strategies are well planned and implemented. For example, consultants can use "learning diagnosis" (Beer & Spector, 1993), which involves organizational members in the diagnostic process and assists them in acquiring the "willingness, skills, and ability to discuss the undiscussable" (Beer & Spector, 1993, p. 644) while tailoring the diagnosis to the strategic tasks of the organization. Finally, consultants will need to develop an operational view of organizational effectiveness (Ridley & Mendoza, 1993), which can help the consultant and consultee develop a framework for effective change. By using such activities, consultants will better understand the change process within an organization and can thereby minimize resistance and enhance the probabilities that their efforts will be successful.

DEALING WITH ORGANIZATIONAL CULTURE

Although the term *organizational culture* is not well defined, the concept is important for consultants to be aware of in terms of designing and implementing successful strategies (Jenster & Bigler, 1989; Schein, 1990b). I have dedi-

cated extensive coverage to organizational culture because of its current popularity.

Culture can be defined as "a pattern of basic assumptions invented, discovered, or developed by a given group as it learns to cope with its problems of external adaptation and internal integration that has worked well enough to be considered valid and, therefore is to be taught to new members as the correct way to perceive, think, and feel in relation to those problems" (Schein, 1990b, p. 111). Manifestations of the organization's culture include climate, group norms, roles, systems, politics, and values. The culture is maintained by the socialization of members new to the organization. Successful organizations have the following cultural attributes: uniqueness in their philosophy, a focus by management on maintaining the philosophy, deliberate attempts to integrate the philosophy throughout the organization, and involvement by all staff in communicating and reinforcing an organization-wide view of events and decisions (Jenster & Bigler, 1989; Lundberg, 1993).

Consultants need to be aware of an organization's culture because it has a very strong impact on whether or not a given plan of action will be successful. For example, if school-based human services professionals are expected to have large caseloads, then there will be limited time available for consultation and collaboration (Bramlett & Murphy, 1998). Clearly, consultants need to have a sense of how an organization defines itself in terms of its culture. In addition, it has been suggested that different segments of an organization may define themselves in terms of culture differently than does the entire organization (Jenster & Bigler, 1989). For example, schoolteachers may have a different organizational culture than school administrators. Consider the situation in which you are a consultant asked to conduct in-service training for junior high school teachers on the characteristics of the middle school child. While the administrative unit sees this as an important step in moving the school toward a middle school concept, the teachers might see the training as another unnecessary imposition on valuable time and another set of expectations without any subsequent reward. You can readily see that the intervention of in-service training would not likely be successful without the consultant's understanding of how the two units within the school tend to view the use of the consultant's training.

What does a consultant look for when attempting to understand an organization's culture? According to Schein (1990b), culture manifests itself in terms of the interaction of artifacts, values, and basic underlying assumptions. *Artifacts* refer to relatively superficial things such as dress code, annual reports, role and mission statements, and the various interpersonal rituals people engage in. Consultants may intervene at this level by helping the organization reorganize the way people problem solve (for example, by setting up quality circles). *Values* refer to the espoused ways people think and feel in the organization. Consultants can intervene at this level by conducting team-building exercises among various subgroups within an organization (for example, between teachers and support personnel). *Basic underlying assumptions* refer to those views of the organization that are taken for granted and are unconscious. A basic implication for consultants is that interaction with members of the organization is essential to get to these assumptions. Another implication is that getting to the underlying assumptions of the organization can assist the consultant in suggesting the right type of interventions. Consultants can intervene at this

level through leading exploratory groups in which consultants raise focused questions and consultees volunteer to analyze their deep-seated views of the organization. Table 8.1 summarizes Schein's (1990b) ideas regarding the underlying dimensions of organizational culture and their underlying assumptions.

Implications for Consultants By having the skills to understand an organization's culture, consultants are better able to get a feel for an organization's history, current behavior, and future aspirations (Schein, 1990b; Lundberg, 1993), which will help him or her approach consultation and in particular select the best interventions.

By understanding an organization's culture, consultants are better able to manage the cultural forces that impact their consultation and to help an organization change in constructive ways. In addition, they and their consultees might well attain a better understanding of the behavior of the organization, which can be linked to effective change within the organization. Knowledge of culture is essential when consultants are asked to help clarify individual roles within the organization, restructure for accommodating change, develop the management function within the organization (Lewis, Lewis, & Souflee, 1991), address internal politics (Jones, 1986), and understand how contextual variables shape behavior within the organization (Kuh, 1993; Lundberg, 1993).

COMMITMENT BY STAKEHOLDERS

The importance of involving stakeholders in any kind of change is well documented. Stakeholders are those parties effected by the consultation activities in some ways. The identity of

Table 8.1   Some Underlying Dimensions of Organizational Culture

DIMENSION	QUESTIONS TO BE ANSWERED
The organization's relationship to its environment	Does the organization perceive itself to be dominant, submissive, harmonizing, searching out a niche?
The nature of human activity	Is the correct way for humans to behave to be dominant/proactive, harmonizing, or passive/fatalistic?
The nature of reality and truth	How do we define what is true and false, and how is truth ultimately determined in both the physical and the social world—by pragmatic test, reliance on wisdom, or social consensus?
The nature of time	What is our basic orientation in terms of past, present, and future, and what kinds of time units are most relevant for the conduct of daily affairs?
The nature of human nature	Are humans basically good, neutral, or evil, and is human nature perfectible or fixed?
The nature of human relationships	What is the "correct" way for people to relate to each other, to distribute power and affection? Is life competitive or cooperative? Is the best way to organize society on the basis of individualism or group mind? Is the best authority system autocratic/paternalistic or collegial/participative?
Homogeneity versus diversity	Is the group best off if it is highly diverse or highly homogeneous, and should individuals in a group be encouraged to innovate or conform?

SOURCE: From Schein, E. H. *Organizational Culture and Leadership: A Dynamic View*, Table 3, p. 86. Copyright 1985 by Jossey-Bass, Inc., Publishers.

these stakeholders is not always obvious (White & Loos, 1996). As early as 1970, Gerald Caplan (1970) advocated involvement of stakeholders in the consultation process. The changes often associated with consultation are time consuming and energy intensive. As a result, stakeholder involvement can be related to successful change and minimizing resistance to consultation interventions (Kress, Cimring, & Elias, 1998). To illustrate the importance of this point, consider the futility of trying to design a teacher support group without involving the teachers that the group is meant to assist. The bottom line is that stakeholders need to be involved in change efforts of a consultation from the outset and throughout the entire process (Curtis & Stollar, 1995; Adelman & Taylor, 1998; Cherniss, 1998). Consultants will also want to be aware of the political aspects of the organization in which consultation and collaboration is occurring (Bramlett & Murphy, 1998). In addition, school consultants will want to be aware of the barriers and incentives for community groups such as parent organizations to be involved in school activities and reform (Good et al., 1997).

Gatekeepers are those who are in authority who can sanction consultation activities. As you will note, the more the change efforts of consultation are focused at the organizational level, the more important sanctioning by gatekeepers becomes. Getting a commitment from gate-keepers and having them involved in the change process as necessary, can enhance the likelihood of a positive outcome in consultation (Robinson & Elias, 1993). Although at first glance, the involvement of gatekeepers seems straightforward, you will want to remember that gatekeepers exist not only in the formal, but also in the informal, power structures of most organizations.

TRAINING CONSULTEES

When you function as a consultant in an organization, you will want to enhance the problem-solving skills of real and potential consultees. Traditional yet effective methods of assisting in the acquisition of these skills consist of training, practice, and follow-up (Curtis & Stollar, 1995). Needless to say, the more that the members of an organization possess these skills, the more likely that effective change can occur within the organization (Shaw & Swerdick, 1995). The same holds for collaboration (Idol, 1998). A consultant or collaborator may start such an organizational change initiative by training, for example, a school improvement team. There are a variety of proven problem-solving methods available for use including the generic model provided in this text. Again, the consultants would be wise to plan such a skills acquisition program by involving gatekeepers and stakeholders from the outset.

TIME CONSTRAINTS

One of the biggest issues you will face in work as a consultant or collaborator is finding the time to perform it adequately (Hobbs & Colli-son, 1995; Bramlett & Murphy, 1998). Whether you work in a school, a clinic or agency, or a business and industry setting, you will be challenged to cope with time constraints. Part of the time constraint issue involves the mindset by many consultees that consultants are professionals to whom a problem is given to be fixed. In this mindset, consultees frequently see themselves functioning mainly as referral sources for the consultant. Some managers, for example, do not see their role as collaborating with the consultant and then implementing the recommendation, but rather view the consultant as one who can come up with a traditional training intervention that should fix the problem. Managers often think, "If employees are not motivated, then come up with a training application that will get them motivated and then implement it." Rarely, will the consultant hear: "Help me figure out what *I* can do to help motivate my employees."

Involving consultees in more collaborative approaches frequently entails educating them about the nature of consultation and training them in problem-solving procedures. Administrators and supervisors who sanction consultation as a desired activity in the organization also legitimatize the use of time for consultation purposes. In some organizations, the use of consultants is considered a professional growth activity that is rewarded during the annual review process.

An even more critical issue is the severe time constraints faced in most organizations. Increasingly organization members are being asked to do more with less. This makes time an even more precious commodity in organizations. As a result, school-based, as well as external, consultants will need to consult on the run (for example, discreetly in the hallway of a school) and keep initial attempts to establish consultation simple and time efficient (Bramlett & Murphy, 1998).

Methods to create time for effective consultation include scheduling meetings in advance as much as possible, doing as much data gathering as possible early on in the consultation process, and training prospective consultees in the problem-solving process prior to consultation. In schools, teachers can be given more time to be consultees by being given release time, having teacher aides assigned to them, and by using some team meeting times for consultation (Erchul & Martens, 1997). Another possible method of dealing with time constraints is to have an "entry presentation" at a faculty meeting that orients teachers to consultation and allows the consultant to began entry on a group basis (Zins & Curtis, 1984). Training consultees directly in selected interventions is another effective method of dealing with time constraints (Watson & Robinson, 1996).

Indirect ways for finding time to consult and collaborate include publicly articulating the rationale for consultation/collaboration, having leadership participate in these activities, defining staff roles to include consultation/collaboration, creating a schedule that allows time for these activities, providing occasional additional time for these activities during the work day, and providing incentives for engaging in these activities (Thousand et al., 1996).

Perhaps the best solution to dealing with time constraints is to have the consultation process unfold in a series of short meetings that meet the schedules of the parties involved. Rather than leaving important elements of the process out and using a bare bones approach, distributing the process out allows for a quality experience and increases the probabilities of a successful outcome.

WHETHER TO CHOOSE CONSULTATION OR COLLABORATION

You will frequently be faced with the decision to choose between consultation and collaboration as the service of choice in particular situations. Below I describe some guidelines to assist you in this choice process.

First, ask and answer the question, How does the organizational culture view each of these services in terms of preference? In some instances, it might well be that collaboration is regarded as the "new kid on the block" and therefore is not perceived to be as legitimate as consultation. On the other hand, for professionals who are internal to the organization in which services are to be provided, collaboration may be preferred because it presents many stakeholders with a piece of the action of implementation.

Second, ask yourself, How do I really feel about consultation and collaboration? Do I think consultation puts me too much in the expert role? Do I think collaboration forces me to give up too much power in the case? It is important for you to know where you stand on issues like these as they will affect your choice of services. Before you proceed with consultation you need to determine if the assumptions underlying consultation (e.g., confidentiality, the voluntary nature of the relationship, nonhierarchical status within the relationship) are met. If they are not met, collaboration may well be the method of choice.

CASE 8.1   Organizational Concepts for School Consultants

Sharon is a school-based consultant who has transferred to an elementary school after 15 years of working in a middle school. The central office of the school system has recently mandated that each school must develop a wellness program for its staff and students within the first nine weeks of school. Sharon's principal has assigned her the task of designing the program. Because Sharon is new to the school, she decides that she must carefully do her "homework" to design an effective program. It's an opportunity for her to learn about her new work environment and get a project done at the same time. Yet Sharon is disconcerted by the nagging question of why the principal would give a new staff person a project like this.

As Sharon began to familiarize herself with students, staff, and the physical plant of the school, she found out many interesting things. The school was run in a very businesslike manner. Sharon was expected to develop her proposal and send it directly to the principal without discussing it with anyone. She was to schedule a weekly 15-minute appointment with the principal in his office to update him on her progress. She found out that rules and regulations were of paramount importance to the principal. Staff had to sign in and out of school, and a high priority was put on keeping detailed records. Teachers appeared to be very friendly with one another and the

"informal power structure" of the school kept up the morale of teachers and staff alike. It was obvious to Sharon that there was a rather large communication gap between the faculty and administration. The principal was highly respected yet seen as overly concerned with the mechanics of running the school at the expense of its "human side." The students dreaded going to his office but typically liked their teachers.

Sharon felt the principal gave her the job because of her qualifications and because he didn't want to take time away from any teacher's instructional obligations. To the principal, the teachers' job was to teach. Ancillary personnel like Sharon were to do ancillary tasks.

Sharon was very used to the middle school concept. What she found out as she began developing her project shocked her; she would have to be careful not to let her own values about how the school should be run interfere with her project and her attitude toward the principal. Sharon sensed that the values of the teaching staff were basically those related to a humanistic view of education, whereas the administration valued "getting the job done." A deeper underlying assumption appeared to be "the administrators are the bosses, let them do their thing, but don't let them get in the way of our doing our thing." "Like two ships passing in the night and not noticing each other," thought Sharon.

The wellness program would mean some changes, which in this school meant in a somewhat autocratic "top-down" manner. She also noted that the informal power structure of the school supplemented the principal's authority and got things done in a less legalistic and more personal manner. In reflecting on how to proceed with developing her proposal, Sharon made a list of as many of the school's organizational characteristics as she could come up with and then looked at them in terms of force-field analysis.

Commentary

As experienced consultants will tell you, there is more to organizational change than appears on the surface. Wisely, Sharon took the time to analyze the organizational context in which her project was to take shape. She further had the insight to look at the development of her project in terms of both the formal and informal power structures in the school, thus increasing the chances of having a "politically correct" yet "user friendly" program. Notice her attempt to creatively use a force-field analysis of her school's characteristics to guide her planning. This case clearly illustrates the importance of consultants being aware of the organizational forces that impact their practice and the importance of taking these forces into consideration in their attempts to be of service.

CASE 8.2   Organizational Concepts for Community Consultants

Ward is a counseling psychologist asked by a hospital-based hospice program to provide consultation services to its staff. Because the program had been in existence only a few years and Ward had limited experiences with the hospice staff, he decided to proceed cautiously in developing his consultation for the staff. Part of his approach was to ensure that he first studied the organization in which he was going to consult before proceeding further.

He had been introduced at a staff meeting and the director of the program had taken Ward around the unit for a day introducing him to the staff members on an individual basis. Ward then spent three days orienting himself to the hospice program: he observed and interacted, paid attention to a variety of aspects of the program's culture, and noted that the staff dress code was less rigid than that of the rest of the hospital, that families were encouraged to visit their loved ones at any time and were warmly seen by the staff as participants in the care of their loved ones, and that there was a sense of camaraderie among the staff as being special people serving a higher need of society.

As Ward tried to determine the theoretical nature of the problems, he constantly kept in mind the influence of his lengthy experience in the military as a psychologist. With this perspective in mind, he noted that the hospice program was designed with a human relations approach. The people in the program held frequent team meetings, program decisions were made through consensus-seeking meetings, and the program director acted as a buffer against the strong bureaucratic element of the hospital at large. Staff stated and the patients concurred that teamwork was important and that interdependence was more valued than independence.

Although they were not espoused as values, the program seemed to work on the underlying principles that satisfied staff contribute more compassionately to patient welfare and that people and love were more important than rules and regulations. In interviewing staff, patients, and the patients' families, Ward determined that changes in the program were based often on a normative-reeducative basis and on a shared approach involving people from all levels of the program including patients' families. Based on what he had learned about the hospice program, Ward set about to develop a proposal that would outline a consultation program suitable for the type of "mini-organization" the hospice program seemed to be.

Commentary

Ward, as any perceptive external consultant would, took the time to analyze the organization in which he was going to work. Notice that Ward investigated the manifestations of the organization's culture by noting indicators such as employee dress and attitudes. Ward also attempted to grasp the "philosophy" of change in the hospice unit in order to make sure that he could minimize resistance to his consultative efforts. Finally notice how Ward attempted to design a program with the unique characteristics of the organization in mind.

Your own skill level will also influence your decision to use consultation or collaboration. On the one hand, consultation demands the ability to guide and control the problem-solving process while empowering the consultee. On the other hand, collaboration demands the ability to balance the reciprocal influence that the parties exert on each other in collaboration. As you gain experience in both consultation and collaboration you will become equally comfortable with both processes.

The level of skill of the prospective consultee or collaborator will influence your choice of services. If the other party is not skilled in what is most likely to be implemented and time for training is not feasible, then collaboration is in order. If time is not a factor or the other party is relatively highly skilled in terms of possible interventions, then consultation may well be in order.

The bottom line is that the choice between using consultation or collaboration is frequently a judgement call with either choice being an adequate one. As in determining whether to provide any other service, the nature of the problem, the context in which it occurs, and the skills of the parties involved interact together to influence your choice.

SUMMARY

Whether they are internal or external to organizations or in an educational or community setting, consultants will need a basic understanding of organizations to maximize their effectiveness as consultants.

How consultants view the broad range of organizational theories—from those that emphasize organizational structure to those that emphasize the human side of organizations—determines how they think organizational change should occur. Because the process of change within organizations is very complex, consultants can use a variety of approaches and many methods to assist organizations in the process. Consultants must study an organization's culture to understand it well enough to implement change effectively.

SUGGESTIONS FOR

EFFECTIVE PRACTICE

■ Consider the culture of the organization in which consultation or collaboration is occurring in deciding how to proceed.

■ Be able to clearly articulate your view of organizations as part of your professional development as a consultant.

■ Have a sense of organizational change procedures in the organization in which you are delivering services.

QUESTIONS FOR REFLECTION

1. Do you think that most members of a typical human service organization could explain how their organization really operates? Why or why not?

2. What is organizational theory?

3. Why is a firm understanding of organizational theory important for a consultant?

4. Why should a consultant have a "personal" theory of organizations that is carried into the consultation process?

5. How could a consultant teach members of an organization about their own organization?

6. What are the advantages for consultants of the systems model of organizational theory?

7. You are hired as a consultant to a human service organization. As you enter the organization for the first time, what types of things and activities would you look for? How would you find out more about these things and activities?

8. What are some of the ways that the adaptive subsystem of an organization can monitor its internal and external environments?

9. Which approach to change do you hold to most firmly: the rational-empirical, the normative-educative, or the power-coercive? Why?

10. Why is an understanding of organizational culture so essential in being an effective consultant?

SUGGESTED SUPPLEMENTARY

READINGS

Offermann, L. R., and Gowing, M. K. (1990). Organizations of the future. *American Psychologist, 45(2)*, 95–108. This excellent article reviews trends in American society and its organizations as we experience the start of the new millennium. I strongly recommend this article because it provides consultants with a current perspective for viewing organizations and the types of situations with which they are going to need assistance. The authors cite the implications for change in a cogent manner. It will be an easy step for you to apply what they discuss to your work as a consultant.

Schein, E. H. (1990b). Organizational culture. *American Psychologist, 45(2)*, 109–119. Schein is one of the leaders in organizational consultation. Although many of the examples in this article relate to business and industry, human service consultants will find a wealth of information related to organizational culture. Schein does an excellent job of providing both the theoretical and practical aspects of organizational culture as they relate to consultation.

PART III

Models of Consultation

Now that you have studied the process of consultation in general, we will consider some popular models. Because there are no detailed models of collaboration, I will restrict discussion of this service as it applies to the various models of consultation under discussion. Each model of consultation provides a conceptual definition for practice (Kratochwill & Bergan, 1990). All models of consultation can help consultees deal with a work-related concern through a problem-solving process. The ways problem solving is accomplished varies according to the model under consideration. In addition, most models can help consultees be more effective with similar or related problems in the future.

Some models of consultation are more structured than others, and the consultant may act in the role of technical expert, expert diagnostician, or expert facilitator. Although all models have a well-defined approach to solving problems, no model has developed a theoretical basis from research to prescribe how the consultant and consultee should interact with each other. In fact, some authors (for example, Gallessich, 1985) suggest that the practice of consultation is basically *atheoretical*. Three factors impede the development of adequate theories of consultation: the very attitude among consultants that consultation is an atheoretical process, the rapidity of change in consultation practices, and problems in performing research on consultation and its effects (Gallessich, 1985). To overcome these obstacles, Gallessich (1985) suggests that consultation models be categorized by value structure, which results in three models:

- a scientific-technological model (based primarily on the values of the scientific method)

- a human development model (based primarily on the values of human growth and development)
- a social/political model (based primarily on the values from the social/political aspect of the consultee's work)

In spite of such suggestions as these, most authors still rely on the more traditional way of characterizing consultation models—in terms of their derivatives. These models, which will be covered in this part of the book, include organizational, mental health, and behavioral consultation. The name associated with a given model of consultation serves to identify its primary focus.

Organizational consultation tends to consider the entire organization to be the client. *Mental health consultation* focuses on the implications of human service professionals' mental health–related programs and their work with clients. *Behavioral consultation* focuses on specific changes in clients, client systems, and/or consultees.

Traditionally, models of consultation differ with respect to five dimensions: conceptualization of the problem, goals, methods and assumptions, consultant roles, and professional values (Gallessich, 1982).

Organizational consultation conceptualizes the problem in terms of an organization's structure and processes and has the goal of modifying those structures and processes to ameliorate some problem through carefully designed interventions that affect the organization's system. The consultant takes on one or more of a variety of roles to assist consultees. Those values are advocated that enhance the organization's overall effectiveness by helping its members become more satisfied and productive. An increasing number of organizations outside of business and industry settings use organizational consultation.

There is no one "organizational consultation," but rather a series of approaches that consider the organization to be the client system. Program consultation and education/training consultation are included in the discussion of organizational consultation because of their similarities to other organizational approaches: Both can improve the effectiveness of the organization in which consultation occurs, even though their roots are not specific to organizational consultation.

Mental health consultation conceptualizes a problem in terms of mental health constructs. The goal of alleviating the mental health problem is accomplished by helping consultees work with their clients or with the mental health implications of their programs. The consultant acts either as facilitator or technical advisor in advocating the value of enhancing the mental health functioning of all involved in consultation. Mental health consultation focuses both on helping consultees help their clients and on helping consultees become more effective professionals. In the past, mental health consultation was strongly influenced by psychodynamic theory.

Behavioral consultation conceptualizes the problem in terms of reducing the difference between the current frequency of some problem behavior and the desired frequency of that behavior. This behavioral goal is accomplished through the use of interventions based on the principles of learning. The consultant acts as both expert and guide and advocates that behavior be changed in a precise, scientific manner. Behavioral consultation is based on social learning theory.

As the field of consultation has developed, the differences among these three major models have become increasingly less distinct. All consultation is organizational in that it occurs within an organization of some kind. All consultation concerns mental health by either directly or indirectly affecting the psychological well-being of the consultee and the client system. All consultation is behavioral because by its very nature it implies change: when consultees, clients, and client systems such as organizations respond positively to consultation, they change their behavior.

Indeed, there are probably more similarities than differences among these models. Organizational consultation, for example, is becoming increasingly aware of mental health issues. Empirical research on organizations suggests that satisfied personnel work more productively than do dissatisfied personnel (Katz & Kahn, 1978). Behavioral consultation increasingly focuses on how behavioral technology can be used to help organizations more effectively meet their missions.

The models that are commonly used in schools—Adlerian consultation and instructional consultation—are covered in Chapter 12. Adlerian case consultation is a form of mental health consultation. The Adlerian C-group consultation is a unique approach to education/training consultation that is often used with teachers and parents.

Four emerging theories of consultation include those based on Gestalt (Nevis, 1987), psychoanalytic (Kets de Vries & Associates, 1991), rational emotive therapy consultation (Lange & Greiger, 1993) and chaos theories (Peters, 1988) (see also Brack et al., 1993). Because the development of these theoretical approaches to consultation is in its infancy, they are not covered in this text.

As noted, some authors (for example, Dworkin & Dworkin, 1975; Gallessich, 1985) have suggested that consultation approaches be classified by their major goal or function rather than by model. However, most writers still categorize the models of consultation according to the primary focus of each. Hence, in the next few chapters we'll discuss the organizational, mental health, and behavioral models of consultation separately, all the while noting the rapidly disappearing differences among them. One caution: consultants should not become too reliant on models. Although models can help consultants guide their practice (Brack et al., 1993), models can also overly focus their attention on aspects of the model instead of the features of the consultation setting (O'Neill & Trickett, 1982). Further, practicing consultants, irrespective of what model they employ, will want to be aware that "consultation represents an ongoing process that is often mediated by factors such as interpersonal skills, relationship dynamics, problem severity, willingness of participants, competencies of consultees and clients, and many other issues" (Sheridan et al., 1996, p. viii).

9

Organizational Consultation

Given your basic familiarity with organizations and the ways they operate, we'll now examine how consultants operate within organizations. Why do consultants work in organizations? As Bellman (1990) notes, "in this imperfect world full of imperfect people, we try to get things done through large, imperfect organizations—organizations of our own creation" (p. 69). Consequently, the main goal of organizational consultation is improvement in the organization's effectiveness, and this can take many forms and utilize a multitude of methods. Many types of organizational consultation originated in business and industry settings, whereas the mental health movement influenced others.

In this chapter we'll consider the historical development of organizational consultation and define some important terms. Then we'll ex-

amine a few of its key concepts, drawing from the discussion of the preceding chapter. We'll consider three specific models of organizational consultation: purchase of expertise, doctor-patient, and process consultation (Schein, 1969, 1987). In discussing the expertise model, we'll focus on education/training and program approaches. In the doctor-patient model, diagnosis is emphasized. In the section on process consultation, Schein's model is explored.

For each of these approaches we'll examine the goals, roles, and functions of the consultant and the consultee's experience in consultation. We'll consider some applications of organizational consultation by discussing its techniques and procedures, and we'll note some contributions and criticisms of this kind of consultation.

Here are some questions to consider as you read this chapter:

1. Why is consulting with organizations more complex than consulting with individuals?

2. Who or what makes up the client system in organizational consultation?

3. How can a consultant evaluate the effects of organizational consultation when the process is so complex?

4. How should a consultant select from the multitude of available interventions?

5. What are the basic differences among the various approaches to organizational consultation?

INTRODUCTION

Consider the following example, which covers just one of several approaches to organizational consultation:

Case Example

You are a human service professional who is asked to consult with a rehabilitation center staff. The center, which serves as a counseling facility for incarcerates nearing eligibility for parole, is having staff conflicts that are adversely affecting the success of its programs. The center's head administrator asks you to sit in on three of the regularly scheduled weekly staff meetings and provide the staff feedback concerning how they might resolve their conflicts. As you observe the meetings, you take notes on such things as what and how things are said, as well as who talks to whom. You provide feedback to the staff at a special meeting and then help the group process that feedback. As a result, three areas of conflict are identified: some staff are perceived as being too hard on the clients, some staff are perceived as being too

soft on the clients, and the center has no evaluation system in place to determine whether it really helps its clients. You agree to spend an additional session with the staff to help them resolve their conflicts and to help a select group of staff develop procedures for evaluating the effectiveness of the center's services.

Organizations are groups of people put together for a particular purpose. Each of these complex entities has goals and objectives. When they have difficulty meeting their goals and objectives, organizations frequently seek the help of consultants. Indeed, consultants are used so frequently by business, industry, and human service organizations that we now call many approaches *organizational consultation*. Organizational consultation is based on the concept that an organization can be made to function more effectively through the efforts of one or more consultants who work with some (or possibly all) members of the organization. Thus, the organization itself or one of its parts becomes the client and the members are the consultees.

Increasingly, professionals who provide consultation (either internal or external) are being asked to assist with organization-wide concerns and issues. Consider a school counselor or school psychologist who assists a group consisting of seventh-grade teachers and parents to decrease the number of fighting incidents among a selected group of students. Or for example, a school counselor might be asked to develop an intervention assistance program to assist teachers to meet the academic and behavioral needs of their students (Curtis & Stollar, 1995). Managed care, downsizing, and expanding ecology have created a variety of opportunities for human service professionals to consult with organizations to assist them in coping with these phenomena (Sperry, 1996).

Organizational consultants can fulfill the following functions (Schein, 1987, p. 20):

- provide information that is not otherwise available

- analyze information with sophisticated tools not available to clients or their subordinates

- diagnose complex organizational and business problems

- train clients or their subordinates to use diagnostic models that help them make better decisions

- listen and give support, comfort, and counsel during troubled times

- help implement difficult or unpopular decisions

- reward and punish certain kinds of behaviors (by using status as an "outsider" as a special source of authority)

- transmit information either up the normal chain of command or laterally as needed

- make decisions and give directives on how to proceed if for some reason line management cannot do so; and take responsibility for decisions, allay anxiety that may attend the uncertainties of consultation, and in other ways provide the emotional strength to help others through difficult situations

Human service professionals, through their specialized training, are particularly suited to provide organizational consultation (Cosier & Dalton, 1993; Barak, 1994).

Historical Background

Organizational consultation first emerged in the 1890s in industrial settings. Consultants, experts who focused on manufacturing productivity, were called on to fix production problems (Heyel, 1973). In open systems terminology, the early organizational consultants dealt with the technological subsystem of the organization (Gallessich, 1982). At the outset of organizational consultation, consultants combined industrial engineering with time and motion studies and were often referred to as management engineers (Heyel, 1973).

During World War I, organizational consultants frequently were considered efficiency experts; they were concerned with functions such as input-output ratios and the relationships between humans and tools (Heyel, 1973). During the 1920s, organizational consultation expanded into other subsystems of industrial organizations, particularly management and maintenance.

The Great Depression created a crisis in which many businesses, industrial and nonindustrial alike, were forced to fight for survival. This financial crisis produced conditions conducive to a new consultant activity: helping "sick" organizations (Heyel, 1973). Although *sick* referred to finances during the Great Depression, the term has since come to refer to any aspect of an organization considered to be problematic.

With the advent of group dynamics research and the call to improve work conditions during the 1940s and 1950s, psychology entered business settings, and motivation and leadership studies became quite popular (Chapiro, 1981). Organizations became increasingly aware that technological efficiency could be dehumanizing and that improved conditions could lead to greater productivity (Aplin, 1978). Organizations, therefore, no longer needed to be sick to benefit from the assistance of a consultant; rather, healthy organizations could become more efficient and effective in meeting their goals by obtaining consultant services in motivation and leadership. Thus, consultants became increasingly involved in serving organizations in such matters as lines of authority, types of leadership, and the distribution of labor (Gallessich, 1982).

The national attention given to the concept of mental health and the emergence of mental health consultation (see Chapter 10) began to influence not only human service organizations, but business and industrial organizations as well. Greater emphasis was placed on the psychological well-being of the worker on the job. Organizational leaders began to realize that satisfied workers were crucial to effective and productive organizations. Coincident to the national emphasis on mental health was the emergence of organization development.

Organization development is the application of the behavioral sciences to an organization's internal workings to increase its efficiency and effectiveness (Huse, 1978). The organization development effort focuses "on the characteristics of the workplace as a whole, with the consultant attempting to use a variety of interventions that can integrate organizational and individual needs" (Lewis & Lewis, 1986, p. 202).

Organizational consultation developed under the influences of applied behavioral science and managerial science (Shultz, 1984): From behavioral science came laboratory training methods, the use of the survey research and feedback method, and autonomous work groups (Huse, 1978); from managerial science came quantitative analysis of business activities, particularly managerial decision making (Shultz, 1984).

The laboratory training methods are a series of experimental activities that focus on developing skills for more effective organizational functioning. Development occurs in a laboratory setting in which group members experiment with new behaviors and are given feedback. The new behaviors are then supposedly transferred to the work site (Rudestam, 1982).

In the survey research and feedback method, results of surveys about the organization are conveyed to the respondents to further pinpoint problem areas (Huse, 1978) and to generate discussion (Gallessich, 1982). Such discussions are intended to improve relationships among the participants and help solve identified problems.

The Tavistock Institute of London developed a psychoanalytic theory of groups that influenced organization development (Goodstein, 1978; Rice, 1969). Much of this institute's work focused on study groups formed to examine how participants dealt with issues of authority, leadership, and norms (Goodstein, 1978). Participants were to take their newly acquired knowledge and apply it in their own organizations, which frequently led to the development of autonomous work groups within organizational settings (Huse, 1978).

In 1969, Edgar Schein wrote a landmark text entitled *Process Consultation* (Schein, 1969). This text strongly influenced the human side of organizational consultation and gave great momentum to legitimizing organizational consultation in all types of organizations, including educational institutions. Schein emphasized focusing on process events such as leadership style and balancing individual needs and organizational goals (Kormanski & Eschbach, 1997).

Managerial science, which accompanied the development of management as a profession (Shultz, 1984), focuses on finances and quantitative analysis of all aspects of management. Unlike applied behavioral science, managerial science focuses almost exclusively on the tangible and the quantitative.

Organization development influenced another field called human resource development (HRD), which developed during World War II out of military and industrial organizations' need for competent personnel (Chalofsky & Lincoln, 1983). The philosophical framework of HRD is the development of human potential (Chalofsky & Lincoln, 1983).

Whereas organizational consultation focuses on the workplace as an entity, HRD focuses on the individuals within the organization. HRD consists of the learning experiences "that are organized, for a specified time, and designed to bring about the possibility of behavioral change" (Nadler, 1980, p. 5). HRD gained recognition when the ASTD emerged and promoted HRD nationally. HRD can take place in educational as well as business and human service settings (Maher, Cook, & Kruger, 1987).

A current trend in organizations is to provide counseling for employees on the work site through, for example, employee assistance programs. This trend has led many counselors in organizational settings to become increasingly involved in organizational consultation activities (Lewis & Lewis, 1986).

The emergence of organization development and HRD has given legitimacy to using either internal consultants (when present) or outside consultants (whenever internal ones are absent or unskilled in the area of service for which consultation is needed). The inclination to use organizational consultants in the private and public sectors has spread recently to the previously reluctant "third" sector of human service organizations (Goodstein, 1978).

ORGANIZATIONAL CONSULTATION DEFINED

In spite of the many attempts to define it, there is no agreement on a single definition of organizational consultation. What is clear is that there are many types of such consultation, and how it is performed depends on the theoretical orientation of the consultant, the nature of the organization, and the nature of the problem for which consultation is sought (Lewis & Lewis, 1986).

Organizational consultation can be defined in terms of what the consultant does. Accordingly, Sinha (1979) provides the following definition:

> An organizational consultant is a professional, internal or external to the client system, who applies behavioral science knowledge in an ongoing organization with the explicit objectives of managing change and increasing its effectiveness. He [or she] engages in a wide variety of activities, often called interventions, such as organizational diagnosis, team building, intergroup activities, survey feedback, training for managerial effectiveness, restructuring organization, role negotiation, sociotechnical system design, planning and goal setting, counseling and career planning, etc. The type and choice of interventions and relationship a consultant establishes with the client system often define the approach and style of consultants. (p. 8)

In addition, all organizational consultants have as their goal the enhancement of the human and organizational capabilities of the client system through a process of collaboration between consultant and consultee (Sinha, 1979).

A synthesis of many authors' views on organizational consultation might produce the following generic definition: organizational consultation is the process in which a professional, functioning either internally or externally to an organization, provides assistance of a technical, diagnostic/prescriptive, or facilitative nature to an individual or group from that organization to enhance the organization's ability to deal with change and maintain or enhance its effectiveness in some designated way.

Some confusion surrounds the terms *consultee* and *client system* in organizational consultation. Consultees are those people in the organization with whom the consultant works; frequently they are mid- to high-level managers or those who provide direct services to clients. In the organizational consultation literature, the term *client* often refers to the consultee, particularly when the discussion concerns those in the organization with whom the consultant is working. With respect to organizational consultation in this text, the term *consultees* refers to those with whom the consultant works directly; the *client system* is always the organization or some part of it.

KEY CONCEPTS IN ORGANIZATIONAL CONSULTATION

Most of the key concepts concerning organizational consultation were discussed in the preceding chapter. However, two are sufficiently important to highlight: the organiza-

tion as client, and the fact that process is as important as content.

The Organization as Client

The client system in organizational consultation is usually the organization or some part of it. In any case, the goal of organizational consultation is to enhance the overall effectiveness of the organization, making the organization the client system. This can be a hard concept to grasp because many consultants are used to viewing the client system as either an individual or a relatively small group.

The more complex the organization, the more complex the client system becomes. Organizations are systems made up of interactive and interdependent parts; consulting with one part of the organization can affect all of its parts. Organizations are made up of people, each of whom possesses a unique set of attitudes, values, beliefs, and behaviors. Individuals in an organization are affected not only by these attributes of their coworkers, but also by the social relationships that exist within the organization (Jerrell & Jerrell, 1981). When consultants provide services to one part of the organization, the potential impact on other parts must be considered.

Among the concepts important to understanding the complexity of the organization as client is the principle of *synergy*, which states that the whole of a set of products is greater than the sum of its parts. When buildings, offices, people, and machines are put together in a certain way, they become more than the sum of their parts (organizations). This concept makes understanding organizations even more complex. By viewing the entire organization as the client, consultants will understand the complexity of the potential ramifications of their interventions and avoid oversimplified consultation methods.

Process Is as Important as Content

An important underlying assumption of organizational consultation is that process is as important as content; that is, *how* something is done can be as important as *what* is done. Thus, how people communicate with one another in an organization is as important as what they communicate about, and how an organization goes about solving a problem is as important as the nature of that problem (Golembiewski, 1993e). If we think of the problem to be solved as the content, then the process can be thought of as the method by which the problem is defined and solved (Schein, 1978). There is even a specific kind of consultation, called process consultation, that focuses on the process of organizational behavior rather than on its content.

In organizations, process factors are distinguished from structural factors, such as departments and lines of authority. These structures coordinate and control tasks in an efficient and timely manner (Jerrell & Jerrell, 1981), but they are surrounded by process factors, such as informal relationships, traditions, and culture (Schein, 1987, 1988). Further, how people perceive a structure (for example, their job's role) determines how they relate to others within the organization and how they act in that role (Schein, 1988). Only when its members are smoothly interacting with one another can the organization be functioning effectively. Consultants often help organizations become aware of the interactions between process factors and their members to assist them in functioning at optimal levels (Schein, 1987; Golembiewski, 1993e).

Process and content are often subtly related: there can be a connection between an organization's problem and how the problem is being worked on. Schein (1978) illustrates this connection by telling about a group that chose as its "topic" leadership (content) while it was experiencing a leadership struggle (process) among several of its members. Consultants frequently have the difficult task of deciding whether or not to focus on the interaction between process and content.

Edgar Schein's Models of Consultation

Whereas traditional models of organizational consultation such as that of Blake and Mouton (1983) provide a broad conceptual framework for organizational consultation, more specific conceptualizations have been developed.

Schein (1988) has conceived three models of consultation: the purchase of expertise model, the doctor-patient model, and the process model. Both the purchase of expertise and doctor-patient models are versions of "expert" consultation (Schein, 1978). They focus on what needs to be done. In the *purchase of expertise model*, the consultee "purchases" a consultant who can provide expertise (knowledge or skill) to solve a previously determined problem. In the *doctor-patient model*, the consultee "purchases" the consultant's ability to both diagnose a problem and prescribe an appropriate set of solutions for it. The consultee retains control of defining the problem in the purchase of expertise model, but not in the doctor-patient model. In the purchase of expertise model, the consultee has already identified the solution (what the consultant does), whereas in the doctor-patient model neither the problem nor the solution is defined prior to consultation.

Table 9.1   Schein's Models Compared

	EXPERT	DOCTOR	PROCESS CONSULTANT
Defines problem	Consultee	Consultant	Consultee with consultant
Suggests an intervention	Consultant	Consultant	Consultee with consultant
Major responsibility for work in consultation	Consultant	Consultant	Consultee
Consultee learns more effective problem solving	No	No	Yes

The *process model* views consultation as a "set of activities on the part of the consultant which help the [consultee] to perceive, understand, and act upon process events which occur in the [consultee's] environment" (Schein, 1988, p. 11). It focuses on *how* problems are solved. In process consultation, the consultee "purchases" the consultant's ability to help the consultee focus on process (as opposed to content) events; this approach focuses on how problems are solved, rather than on the content of problems.

There are two versions of the process model: the catalyst version and facilitator version. The *catalyst* version of process consultation occurs when the consultant does not know the solution to some problem but can help the consultee formulate his or her own solution. The *facilitator* version occurs when the consultant may have ideas (content) about solutions but withholds them to help the consultee clear up his or her own dilemma by going through the problem-solving process. Effective consultants use the version of process consultation that is most appropriate to the circumstances (Schein, 1987).

There is some evidence that consultee readiness and the amount of time available for consultation relate to the choice of Schein's models (Stayer & Dillard, 1986). Consultees with low readiness and little time may want and be best suited for the purchase of expertise model. Consultees with high readiness and sufficient time might be more suitable for process consultation. Schein's models of consultation are compared with one another in Table 9.1, which is adapted from O'Connell (1990).

Schein's models form the basis of the following discussion of organization development consultation. First, education/training consultation and program consultation are discussed as examples of the purchase of expertise model. Next, the process of diagnosis is given special attention in the discussion of the doctor-patient model, and then the process model of consultation is considered last.

The Purchase of Expertise Model When consultees request help from consultants, they frequently are seeking some form of expertise, which can take the form of the knowledge or skill to fix a predetermined problem. Some combination of information, methods, tools, and support is provided to the consultee (Sullivan, 1991; Lawson, 1998). The essence of this model is that the consultee knows what the problem is, what needs to be done to solve it, and who can be of help (Schein, 1987, 1988). The consultee is in effect saying to the consultant, "Here's the problem; fix it." This model is by nature very content oriented. The consultant functions as a content expert (Schein, 1990c). For example, a consultant leads a workshop on communication skills for a group of teachers who feel they need to enhance their communication skills.

For the purchase of expertise model to be effective, four basic assumptions must be met (Schein, 1987, 1988). The consultee must have made a correct diagnosis of the problem, chosen the right consultant, correctly communicated the problem, and thought through and accepted the consequences of consultation. If the consultee has not made the correct diagnosis, the entire consultation will be invalid: the right consultant may have been chosen, but the wrong problem will be solved.

If it becomes apparent that consultation is solving the wrong problem, the consultant is under no obligation to assist the consultee in making a new diagnosis. It's the consultee's responsibility to ensure that the consultant has the skills and abilities to meet the consultee's needs and to correctly communicate the nature of the problem. By using effective communication skills such as clarifying responses, the consultant can assist the consultee in expressing the perceived problem in such a way that both parties agree about its exact nature. However, ultimately it is the consultee's responsibility to correctly communicate the problem.

Inherent in the purchase of expertise model is the assumption that the consultee has thought through the consequences of consultation. Things happen when consultation takes place; a change in one part of an organization often affects other parts. Sometimes consultees are not fully aware of the potential long- and short-term impact of consultation. For example, polishing the communication skills of mid-level managers might have the unwanted impact of

making them too assertive in trying to improve the entire organization. From the outset, effective consultants help the consultee think through the consequences a consultant's activities could have.

In summary, the purchase of expertise model is often appropriate when a problem has been well defined, such as when a consultant can provide specific information or training or when a glitch arises in a human service program. It works best when the consultee has ascertained the consultant's suitability for the job and has thoroughly thought through the consequences of consultation (Schein, 1978). Two of the most common forms of purchase of expertise consultation provided by human service consultants are education/training consultation and program consultation.

Education/Training Consultation The education/training approach is the most frequently used kind of purchase of expertise consultation. The use of consultants in education/training is often referred to as *staff development* or *professional development activities*. Recent changes in organizations (see Chapter 8) have dictated an increased need for education/training consultation (Goldstein & Gilliam, 1990). Consultants provide education/training services in any number of settings, and topics range from motivation techniques and classroom discipline to substance-abuse prevention and effective parenting. The reason for this type of consultation is the facilitation of change or improvement in an organization or one of its subsystems. Education/training consultation can occur in a group or on an individualized basis.

As its name suggests, this approach emphasizes the two most common roles of the consultant: educator and trainer (Gallessich, 1982). In this type of consultation, the consultant shares expert knowledge and/or skills by some education means, such as a lecture on motivation, or through some kind of on-the-job training, such as a workshop on techniques for motivating supervisors. Gallessich (1982) defines the education/training model as prearranged, organized services, in contrast to the impromptu educational and training activities that are incidental to most forms of consultation. This cost-effective model, an exemplar of the technological approach to consultation, is information-centered and emphasizes the dissemination of concepts, information, and skills rather than the formulation of a diagnosis (pp. 109–110).

Consultation Goals The primary goal of the education/training consultation is the increased effectiveness of the organization that results from the consultee's improved professional functioning in the area on which education and/or training focuses. The idea is that consultees will learn something new related to their job or, in the case of parents and guardians, something related to their caregiving responsibilities. When consultation is educative in nature, some form of information is being provided; when the consultant acts as trainer, however, the learning is usually experiential and focuses on "learning to learn" (Lippitt & Nadler, 1979).

Whether a consultant uses an educational or a training approach depends on whether the goal of consultation is to affect cognitive learning or to change attitudes and behaviors (Tobias, 1990). In an example affecting cognitive learning, a consultant might provide a junior high school faculty an in-service program on the differences between a junior high school and a middle school. In an experiential learning situation, a consultant might have mid-level managers practice different types of strategies to strengthen their leadership skills.

Education and training can also be combined in consultation. For example, a group of ministers might first be taught the characteristics of depression by a mental health consultant and then participate in supervised counseling sessions in which they attempt to detect these characteristics by role-playing. Whether the consultant emphasizes education, training, or both depends primarily on what the consultee perceives the problem and its solution to be.

Consultant Function and Roles The consultant in education/training consultation functions as an expert who possesses information or skills that the consultee needs and transmits that knowledge in one or more of the roles of advisor, educator, trainer (Gallessich, 1982), or technical expert. The consultant's function is to provide the information and/or the training that best matches a consultee's interests and needs (Conoley & Conoley, 1992).

In addition to assisting in needs assessment and in planning and implementing education/training interventions, the consultant also assists in the evaluation of consultation. Although many organizations have standard evaluation forms to help in this task, many consultants prefer to use their own forms, which can be specifically tailored to any particular evaluation. The purpose of evaluation is to determine whether consultees have learned the appropriate knowledge and/or skills required for the intervention in use.

The critical skills needed to function effectively as a consultant in education/training consultation include (Lippitt & Lippitt, 1986, p. 36):

- assessing the training needs related to the problem
- developing and stating measurable objectives for learning experiences

- understanding the learning and change process
- designing a learning experience
- planning and designing educational events
- going beyond traditional training and using heuristic laboratory methods
- using multiple learning stimuli, including multimedia presentations
- functioning as a group teacher or trainer
- helping others learn how to learn

Consultants should remember that they also have a commitment to the organization and should consider any organizational impact the education/training may have.

The Consultee's Experience in Consultation The major role of the consultee is to be a good learner. Consultees are expected to learn the knowledge or skills they are taught, adapt them if necessary, and use them on the job to contribute to the organization's overall effectiveness. Consultees accomplish these tasks by giving the consultant honest and accurate information during needs assessment, being cooperative and motivated learners during the education/training process, and attempting to implement their new knowledge on the job.

During the needs assessment, the consultee is interviewed (or fills out a survey form) to identify topics for education/training, to give opinions on the nature of the problems of concern during the consultation, and to provide some idea of his or her willingness to participate in the consultation.

Most consultants agree that if consultees must be coerced, however subtly, to participate, positive benefits will probably not accrue from consultation. If consultee participation is voluntary, cooperation and motivation can be enhanced during consultation by providing spe-

cial incentives for participating. Consultees can also be taught to understand that consultation is a process, to know how to initiate consultation, to understand that the timing of a request for consultation can affect both the process and the outcome, and to determine when to choose consultation from among the available services (Brown, Pryzwansky, & Schulte, 1991, pp. 240–241). Consultees can be encouraged to implement what they have learned by education/training methodologies that help them to personalize the material. It is one thing to listen to a lecture on management styles; it is another to be asked to consider how the different management styles match or contrast with a consultee's own style. Responding to consultees' perceived needs during the entire consultation process is an effective way to maximize the likelihood that consultees will follow through on consultation activities. However, as in all forms of consultation, it is ultimately up to consultees to decide whether or not they'll use the information and/or training received.

Application: Consultant Techniques and Procedure The education/training model consists of four steps: needs assessment, planning the education/training activities, performing them, and evaluation.

Either the consultant or the organization's contact person conducts the needs assessment, which identifies the content of education/training sessions and occasionally the problems that consultation can help ameliorate. Needs assessments help identify discrepancies between "what is" and "what is desired" (Cook, 1989). Through the use of interviews, needs assessment can obtain in-depth information and opinions. This method is comprehensive, but it is very expensive and time consuming. In other cases, needs are assessed through questionnaires, which are cost effective and provide informa-

Our organization has set aside the week of April 10 for staff development training. Your frank and candid responses to the following items will assist the training division in arranging for training and development activities that coincide with your needs. In the next few weeks we will collate your responses and put them into a questionnaire that will help us to formulate specific training needs and activities. Please answer the following questions carefully and return them to the training division by the end of this week. All responses will be kept anonymous. Thank you for your participation.

1. I would benefit from knowing more about the following recent trends in my field:
2. I would benefit from discussing the following current issues in my field:
3. I would like to know more about the following new skills areas that are currently receiving much attention in my field:
4. List the needs within your part of the organization that you think staff development should address.
5. List the needs within the entire organization that you think staff development should address.
6. Add any suggestions you think are relevant to the week of staff development.

FIGURE 9.1   A sample needs assessment form

tion that is relatively easy to collate. However, questionnaires frequently lack depth, and the framing of questions can affect the kinds of responses obtained. An example of a needs assessment form is provided in Figure 9.1.

Consultants should consider the nature of adult learners when *planning* activities (Cross, 1984; Knowles & Associates, 1984; Knox, 1986). Adults have learning behaviors that are influenced by past experience, current abilities and roles, and future aspirations (Knox, 1977). For example, although adult learners tend to be conservative in their educational outlook, they still enjoy innovative teaching methodologies. Many corporations and other organizations have applied modern concepts of adult learning in their education/training consultation.

The term *andragogy* refers to the art and science of helping adults learn (Knowles & Associates, 1984). There are several important points about andragogy that consultants should consider in their planning: adult learners are internally motivated, task oriented, and rich resources for one another (Knowles & Associates, 1984).

In *performing* the education/training, the consultant should attempt to use methods that are appropriate to the consultees' characteristics and the objectives of the consultation. Many education/training consultants use designs that incorporate methodologies (Gallessich, 1982; Garmston & Wellman, 1992) such as lectures, media and materials, structured laboratory experiences, small group discussions, behavioral role modeling, movement, and feedback. Further, the ways such methods are performed is critical to their success (Friend & Cook, 1996). For example, timing and the use of props and humor are important to successful education/training activities (James & Dougherty, 1985; Friend & Cook, 1996).

How consultees respond to the consultant at the outset of education/training also affects the ultimate success of the consultation. Therefore, regardless of the methods used, the consultant should make an attempt to create a good working climate (Conoley & Conoley, 1992), including:

- using moderate levels of self-disclosure at the outset

- being open about any concerns that relate to how the education/training is proceeding

- treating consultees with respect

- being open to consultee feedback
- learning consultees' names as quickly as possible
- being able to laugh at oneself when things go wrong

In addition, consultants using this type of consultation should consider the culture of the organization and permit participation by the consultees in all aspects of the education/training.

During *evaluation* of the education/training, consultants often use questionnaires and pre- and post-intervention measures of pertinent material. Evaluations of education/training interventions are becoming increasingly sophisticated (Gallessich, 1982), including feedback loops that allow continuous adaptation of procedures and methods for measuring the impact of education/training on the entire organization. There appears to be a trend from norm-referenced to criterion-referenced measures of learning in education/training evaluations (Gallessich, 1982). Chapters 5 and 6 of this text cover related points on evaluation in more detail and depth.

In summary, education/training is evaluated both formally and informally by participants who assess its usefulness, by consultants who assess "how it went," and by administrators who decide how the organization might be affected (Knowles & Associates, 1984).

Case Example of Education/Training Consultation A human service professor at a university was asked by the director of personnel services of a large school district to conduct some workshops for the district's school counselors and psychologists. When the consultant asked the director what kinds of workshops were desired, the director responded with,

"You know, some of that new counseling stuff." The consultant advocated the use of a needs assessment instrument to give prospective participants input about the nature of the workshops, and the director agreed to gather the information by using a form developed by the consultant.

The needs assessment revealed that the participants desired information and training for dealing with AIDS, teenage pregnancy, and date rape. The consultant planned the activities by developing behavioral objectives to be accomplished through a variety of methods. A balance was struck between providing information and skills training. The consultant also took the needs of adult learners into consideration during the planning process.

One workshop was held on each topic. Additional input from the participants was obtained at the beginning of the first workshop. Several methods were used during the workshops, and a good working climate was developed and maintained throughout the workshops. At the conclusion of each workshop, the participants evaluated the consultant, the workshop content, and the usefulness of the session. The consultant's views concerning the workshop and its effects on the participants were sent to the personnel services director in a written report.

Program Consultation Most human service organizations have programs that frequently require programmatic consultative services. Program consultation is a form of purchase of expertise consultation in which the organization in some way uses the consultant to help plan a new program or revise or deal with factors that affect an existing program. Program consultation is unique in that it is restricted to a specific program and its goals (Gallessich, 1982).

In program consultation, the organization "purchases" some kind of technical assistance. The organization perceives a need with respect to the program and hires a consultant to help fulfill that need. For example, a consultant might be hired to help design an evaluation assessing whether a program has met its goals; indeed, evaluation is the primary reason consultants are hired to assist with programs. Even though program consultation does not require any new skills on the part of the consultant, it clearly demonstrates how consultants can work with organizations to meet their goals (Gallessich, 1982; Hosie, 1994).

Program consultation is becoming increasingly popular due to human services and for-profit organizations' increased emphasis on programs, the increasingly complex technology related to programs, and the trend toward cost-effectiveness and accountability in organizations (Gallessich, 1982; Hosie, 1994). In addition, the professional standards of organizations in which consultants work demand that evaluation of programs be performed (Kratochwill, Mace, & Bissel, 1987). Outside consultants frequently use program consultation as a way to "get their feet in the door" of an organization and eventually perform other types of consultation. Many internal consultants are also called on to assist in program evaluation (Mason, De-Mers, & Middleton, 1984).

The primary goal of program consultation is to provide an organization technical assistance so that a given program is successful. Consultation services can be provided for any aspect of a program, including development and evaluation. Consultation is usually requested for some skill or knowledge that the organization neither possesses nor has time to use. Because program evaluation is the most frequently requested form of program consul-

tation, we'll focus now on how program evaluation consultation is performed. You should keep in mind that the program planning evaluation steps listed in Chapter 6 are not applicable here since the program already exists.

Consultation Goals Program evaluation is "a systematic set of data collection and analysis activities undertaken to determine the value of a program to aid management, program planning, staff training, public accountability, and promotion" (Hagedorn, Beck, Nuebert, & Werlin, 1976, p. 3). The goal of program evaluation is to improve current decision making in the program being evaluated and to help develop policy (Hosie, 1994). Thus, the effort, effectiveness, and adequacy of a program can be improved (Illback, Zins, Maher, & Greenberg, 1990). Organizations want to know if their programs are meeting their goals and objectives. When they are not sure how best to determine this, organizations frequently turn to program consultants who evaluate with a variety of methods and then transmit their findings to the organization so that program decisions can be made. For example, a consultant might assist in evaluating the effects of an employee assistance program in a large textile firm.

A secondary goal of evaluation in program consultation is increasing the consultee's ability to evaluate current and subsequent (similar) programs. If this goal is part of the consultation, the consultant might also function in the education/training consultation model described earlier in this chapter; in this case the consultant "gives away" the very skills that led to the need for a consultant in the first place. The integration of consultation and evaluation skills creates an approach that can be particularly useful in human service and educational settings (Mason et al., 1984).

Consultant Function and Roles In this model consultants act as experts in program development: they provide accurate, timely, and useful information to decision makers so that the program can be run more effectively. The consultant conducts exploratory meetings with consultees to determine the needs of program evaluation, develops a program evaluation design, obtains consultee feedback on the design, and redesigns the evaluation (Matuszek, 1981; Hosie, 1994). The consultant then carries out the evaluation by collecting and analyzing data and filing a report. The process of designing a program evaluation can be very time consuming; much of the consultant's time is spent in preparation and planning (Illback et al., 1990).

Consultee Experience in Consultation The consultee's primary role in this model is to provide the consultant with as much accurate information as possible, which is critical in the initial stages of program evaluation because the consultant needs as much information as possible to develop the appropriate design. Therefore the consultee must make a commitment to spend whatever time and effort are required to be interviewed or to react to the consultant's progress in formulating a suitable evaluation design. Ideally the organization's administrative structure will sanction the consultees' participation so that they feel free to cooperate.

Consultees should do everything possible to ensure that consultants can function independently, particularly when internal consultants are asked to do program consultation that focuses on evaluation. Consultees should inform consultants before the evaluation what they will do if the results are positive, neutral, or negative to the program. Further, consultees can help consultants by determining the type of final report that will be submitted: Will the report be sent directly to a top administrator? Should the report be written in non-technical language? Finally, consultees should inform consultants of any recent events within the organization that might affect the results of the evaluation.

Application: Consultant Techniques and Procedures Four steps in program consultation focus on evaluation: hold ongoing meetings with consultees to design the evaluation, collect data, evaluate it, and write a final report.

After program evaluation has been requested, the consultant completes the entry stage as in any other consultation situation. Once the consultant is given permission to consult, the parties to receive the consultant's findings should be determined. The consultant is then ready to develop the program evaluation design, which involves a series of meetings with the consultees, typically called the *program staff*. The participants try to identify what decisions are to be made, determine who the organization's important decision makers are, and discuss how the program evaluation will tie into the decisions to be made (Matuszek, 1981; Hosie, 1994).

The consultant meets with the consultees for as many meetings as necessary until both consultant and consultees are confident that all parties have an appropriate understanding of what is to occur and why. From all of this information, the consultant begins to put together an evaluation design that dictates the who, what, where, and when of the evaluation procedure.

Regardless of the model of evaluation the consultant uses, there are four evaluation standards to bear in mind: accuracy, utility, feasibility, and propriety (Matuszek, 1981). Accuracy standards relate to the methodological soundness of the evaluation. Utility standards relate to the concept that evaluation should have some practical application. Feasibility standards deal with whether the evaluation design is appropriate for the program in the first place. Propriety standards relate to any ethical or legal issues that are connected to the evaluation. Once the consultant has put together the program evaluation design, a final review is held with the consultees and parties-at-interest. Any needed modifications in the design are made at this time.

The consultant is now ready to carry out the design. Data are collected and analyzed according to the design plan. Program consultants anticipate problem areas in carrying out the evaluation and stay in contact with all parties involved during data collection and analysis (Hosie, 1994). After the data have been analyzed, the consultant writes and presents a formal report so that appropriate action can be taken. The consultant will frequently involve program staff in making use of the evaluation results (Illback et al., 1990). (For an interesting description of program consultation at the university level, see Dodson and Vaccaro [1988].)

Case Example of Program Consultation
Pat, a psychologist in private practice, is selected by a human service agency to help evaluate its Big Sister-Big Brother program, which has been in operation for three years. Although the agency thinks that the program is "doing okay," there appears to be a high turnover rate among its volunteers. Pat has had considerable experience with program evaluation and has worked with volunteer programs in the past.

He starts out by holding a meeting with the program's staff to design an evaluation. Four other meetings are held to make sure that the parties involved are in agreement about what is going on and that the evaluation is proceeding smoothly. Pat and the program staff then collect information on the volunteers and the children in the program, including how long volunteers tend to stay with the program. Methods are determined for assessing the program's impact on the children. Pat then analyzes the collected data and presents a report to the program staff. Among other things, the data show that volunteers last an average of nine months, receive little recognition or encouragement from the agency, and are not sure what is expected from them.

Pat recommends a training program for the volunteers, more personal contact with the volunteers by the program's staff, and some form of recognition for service as a volunteer. The program's impact on the children was deemed to be positive. Parents reported that volunteers gave their children additional, desirable adult role models and helped "keep the kids off the streets." The children liked the program because they "got to do a lot of extra things that were fun."

The Doctor-Patient Model Sometimes consultees know something is wrong but don't know what it is. When consultation is requested, the consultant is given the power to make a diagnosis and prescribe a solution. It is as if the consultee is saying, "I don't know what's wrong. Find out and tell me how I can fix it." In the doctor-patient model (Schein, 1987), another type of expert consultation, the consultee is "purchasing" the consultant's expertise in diagnosing and prescribing. Schein (1990c) points out that the consultant's role in the doctor-patient model differs from that in the purchase of expertise model because "it empowers the consultant to dig into the workings of the organization and to combine information gathering expertise with knowledge of organizations such that a deeper and consultee-relevant diagnosis can be reached" (p. 264).

For the doctor-patient model to be effective, the following assumptions must be met (Schein, 1987, 1988):

- The diagnostic process itself is seen as helpful and not disruptive.

- The consultee has correctly interpreted the organization's symptoms and has located the "sick" area.

- The person or group defined as "sick" will provide the information needed to make a valid diagnosis; that is, they will neither hide data nor exaggerate symptoms.

- The consultee understands and will correctly interpret the diagnosis provided by the consultant and will implement whatever prescription is offered.

- The consultee can remain effective after the consultant leaves.

The very act of calling a consultant to perform a diagnosis is an intervention, and the consultant should make sure that the consultee is aware of this. If the consultee is unaware that diagnosis is an intervention or does not explain the consultant's presence adequately, then the consultant's efforts can meet considerable resistance that can adversely affect the results of consultation.

Because organizations are very complex entities, faith that the consultee has correctly interpreted the symptoms and knows where the organization is "sick" is a very large assumption (Schein, 1987). Consultees can easily misconstrue and misjudge events on the job. In addition, consultees and consultants can easily get caught in a cycle of incorrect diagnoses due

to the consultee's desire for help and the consultant's desire to give it.

The doctor-patient model assumes that consultees and other members of the organization are straightforward and honest with the consultant about their perceptions of the organization's problems (Schein, 1987). The nature of this honesty is a function of the organizational climate: if the climate is one of mistrust, then the consultant is not likely to get the real story; if the climate is one of trust, the consultees and other organization members are likely to tell the consultant everything and may even exaggerate the problem. The consultant also needs to be cautious about creating dependence among consultees.

What will happen if the consultee doesn't like the consultant's diagnosis? Even if the diagnosis is accepted, what guarantees are there that the prescription is going to be implemented? It may not be accurate to assume that the consultee will accept diagnosis and prescription and remain effective after the consultant leaves—especially if the consultee did not learn any problem-solving skills during the consultation. If a similar problem arises for the consultee in the future, the consultant will have to be called in again.

Clearly, the relationship between the consultant and consultee is critical in the doctor-patient model of consultation. The consultant must be able to gain the trust of the consultee so that open communication can occur. If the consultee trusts the consultant, then real issues helpful to the diagnosis are more likely to emerge. In addition, if the consultant is able to create an effective relationship with the consultee and develop professional credibility, the prescription provided to the consultee also has more credibility.

In summary, the doctor-patient model works best when the consultee is willing to use a consultant, has observed and described the symptoms accurately, does not have the ability to perform the diagnosis and prescription, and is willing to follow through on the consultant's recommendations. A possible drawback of this model is that consultees might not enhance their problem-solving skills and may become dependent on the consultant (Schein, 1987). Consultants need to be aware that prescriptive advice is hard to follow, particularly if the consultee's skill level has not been assessed (Hanko, 1987). Because many ideas in the doctor-patient model, including diagnosis, are covered in Chapter 4, only a brief overview of this model is given now.

Consultation Goals The consultant's primary goal in the doctor-patient model is to define the organization's problem and to recommend realistic interventions to ameliorate that problem. Enhancing the consultee's diagnostic skills is not a goal in this model.

Consultant Functions and Roles The consultant functions as an expert who enters the system, interviews consultees and parties-at-interest, collects data, makes a diagnosis, and recommends a solution. The consultant may well be hired to implement the solution, in which case he or she would change to the purchase of expertise model. Whereas the latter model demands content expertise on the part of the consultant, the doctor-patient model demands expertise in diagnostic and prescriptive skills.

Consulting skills that are critical to the doctor-patient model include:

- diagnostic skills
- a broad repertoire of prescriptive skills
- an in-depth knowledge of organizational theory

- the ability to "read" organizations
- data collection skills
- data interpretation skills
- human relations skills

Consultee Experience in Consultation The main task of the consultee is to be a good "patient"—that is, to tell the consultant in as honest, objective, and accurate a way as possible the areas in which the organization has problems. The consultee should realize that the very act of using a consultant will affect the organization in some way. The consultee's tasks also include assisting the consultant in gathering additional data, ensuring that the consultant's diagnosis is fully and accurately understood, and advocating that the consultant's prescription be implemented.

Application: Consultant Techniques and Procedures In the doctor-patient model consultants enter the system as they would in any other consultation model. The major step in this model is to determine how best to go about making a diagnosis which is based on the situation, not the consultant's inclination to make diagnoses (Beer, 1980). Common problem areas in an organization include its purpose, structure, interpersonal relationships, leadership, informal devices it uses to build a sense of teamwork, and reward structure (Weisbord, 1976). The method used to diagnose the organization's problems should obtain information about how its people see the organization's internal processes (Beer, 1980). It is crucial for the consultant to ensure that people involved in the diagnosis feel free to express their true thoughts, opinions, and feelings.

After the data have been gathered, the consultant analyzes it and formulates a diagnosis.

The diagnosis defines problems in the organization in terms that the consultee can both understand and utilize (Argyris, 1970).

The consultant typically follows one of three paths after making the diagnosis (Schein, 1990c): the consultant shares the diagnosis with the consultee as the basis for collaborating on finding a solution, shares the diagnosis and ends the consultation relationship, or makes recommendations and then helps implement them. In the latter case, the consultant then moves from the doctor-patient model to the purchase of expertise model.

Usually the consultant determines what is best for the consultee to do about the problem (Goodstein, 1978). However, consultants cannot necessarily help consultees make a commitment to change; they can only prescribe some solutions that the organization is capable of carrying out and tailor them to the unique aspects of the organization. Generalized prescriptions are rarely successful because they fail to consider the uniqueness of each organization.

Case Example of Doctor-Patient Consultation A counselor in a community counseling center was asked to be an internal consultant to improve the center's effectiveness in delivering services to its clients. She was chosen because of her effective diagnostic skills, her solid working knowledge of organizations, and her trustworthiness. The consultant was given "free run" of the center and was charged with defining the center's problem areas and prescribing some ways to effectively manage them.

She began by informing all staff members of the nature of consultation. Interviews and surveys were used to gather data from the center's administration and staff and from former clients. Complete confidentiality was guaranteed to all involved. Information was sought on such factors as interpersonal relationships,

views of the center's organizational climate, and the center's role and mission. Based on the analysis of the data, the consultant concluded that there was little consensus concerning the center's overall role and mission, which led to a lack of understanding of how the center was run and what the staff and administration were supposed to do. In turn this lack of understanding led to inadequacies in the area of program development.

The consultant prescribed a review and subsequent modification of the center's role and mission statement. Further, she recommended development of a five-year strategic plan based on the modified role and mission statement and suggested that all employees be involved in each of these activities.

The Process Model Schein (1990c) points out that failure to involve the consultee in the diagnosis may lead him or her to misdiagnose the problems inadvertently. This led Schein (1987, 1988) to formulate his model of process consultation. The basic difference between this model and the purchase of expertise and doctor-patient models is that the consultant's expertise includes skills to involve the consultee in defining the problem, to form a team with the consultee, and to ensure that the consultation process focuses on the consultee's needs. The consultant's expertise lies in making the consultee a more effective problem solver in the future (Golembiewski, 1993e). Process consultation can be defined as guidance provided to some group by an individual "trained in group dynamics and organization development" (Kormanski & Eschbach, 1997, p. 137).

Sometimes a consultant is needed to supplement the consultee's problem-solving skills—the consultee knows something is wrong and wants to figure out what it is and what to do about it. Process consultation is what the consultant does to help the consultee identify, understand, and change the process events that occur within an organization (Schein, 1978, 1987). The focus of consultation is not on the content of the problem, but rather on the process by which problems are solved. The consultee "owns" the problem (and continues to own it throughout the consultation process) and "purchases" the consultant's expertise in handling process events.

Process consultation is based on the premise that often things in an organization can be changed only if the consultee is involved in diagnosing the problem and generating solutions. Because of the complexity of problems in organizations and the consultees' familiarity with them, consultees' input into the diagnosis is crucial. In addition, advice given by consultants can be counterproductive in that it can cause resistance, power struggles, and resentment (Schein, 1987). Because organizations continually undergo change, there will always be problems to be diagnosed and solved. Thus, it is important that consultees "learn how to learn" to solve problems (Golembiewski, 1993e).

The relationship between the consultant and the consultee is extremely important. The consultant must create an environment of trust and credibility and help the consultee feel safe enough to own the problem and work on it throughout the consultation process. Such tasks demand empathy, respect, and genuineness on the part of the consultant.

Process consultation works best when the following assumptions are met (Schein, 1987, pp. 32–33):

- The consultee is distressed somehow but does not know the source of the distress or what to do about it.
- The consultee does not know either what kind of assistance might be available or which consultant could provide the help needed.
- The nature of the problem is such that the consultee not only needs help in figuring out what is wrong but would benefit from participation in the diagnostic process.
- The consultee has "constructive intent," is motivated by goals and values that the consultant can accept, and has some capacity to enter into a helping relationship.
- The consultee is ultimately the only one who knows what form of intervention will work best in the situation.
- The consultee is capable of learning how to diagnose and solve his or her own organizational problems.

In a nutshell, process consultation assumes that consultees must acquire and maintain ownership of their problems, that they do not fully understand these problems, and that they can learn to design and manage change on their own (Ledford, 1990).

The process consultation model is most applicable when a consultee with some problem-solving ability is willing to learn how to work out solutions without seeking content assistance or giving the problem to the consultant for diagnosis. By focusing on the *how* rather than the *what* of problem solving, the consultant and consultee collaborate, enabling the consultee to solve current concerns and similar ones in the future. Schein (1990c) admits that the need for content experts will increase in the future but that their services will not be well utilized unless their efforts are combined with process consultation.

Consultation Goals The primary goal of process consultation is to help consultees gain insight into the everyday events occurring within the organization. It attempts to teach consultees to act on those events and become more adept at identifying and modifying them in ways that achieve their goals (Schein, 1987). If the consultant and consultee are successful, the ultimate goal of increasing the organization's overall effectiveness is also met.

Consultant Functions and Roles The primary roles played by the process consultant are facilitator and catalyst. The consultant collaborates with the consultee such that consultation becomes a joint effort (Goodstein, 1978). Rather than providing content expertise, the consultant facilitates consultees' process of self-discovery and self-exploration so that they are able to use their skills in identifying and addressing the problems at hand.

The consultant must be an expert in processes that occur at the individual, interpersonal, and intergroup levels; content expertise in the consultee's institution's area of perceived difficulty is not required. The consultant helps the consultee obtain insight into the everyday human activities in an organization (for example, who talks to whom about what), which are viewed as critical to the appropriate diagnosis of an organizational problem (Schein, 1988). The process consultant provides less structure and direct input than would a consultant operating in either the purchase of expertise or doctor-patient models. This lack of structure can be threatening to the consultee because of unpredictability inherent to process consultation (Ledford, 1990).

In addition to creating a climate conducive to consultee exploration and input, the process consultant assists in gathering data about the relationships within the organization and members' perceptions of organizational processes. The consultant then assists the consultee in making a diagnosis using these data,

and process-oriented interventions such as agenda setting and feedback are made by the consultant and/or the consultee. Finally, the consultant helps the consultee evaluate the consultation by looking for changes in values and interpersonal behaviors within the organization (Schein, 1988; Golembiewski, 1993e). The consultant's success is measured by how effectively consultees define and achieve their goals and whether the changes produced remain effective in the long run (Schmuck, 1976). Once the evaluation has been concluded, the consultant reduces involvement and terminates the consultation.

Consultee Experience in Consultation The consultee—a person within the organization and perhaps a manager—senses that something is not quite right in the organization, that things could be better, and that he or she wants them to improve. The consultee uses the consultant to translate vague feelings and perceptions into concrete actions to enhance the overall effectiveness of the organization (Bennis, Benne, Chin, & Corey, 1985).

The major role of the consultee in this model is that of an active collaborator and teammate (Murrell, 1993). The consultee is assumed to have some problem-solving skills and be knowledgeable about his or her organization. The consultee provides the content of the consultation and participates in the processes at issue as the consultee's process skills dictate. The consultee then discusses content issues and the nature of the perceived problems, sets goals, and attempts to make plans for action (Schmuck, 1976). The consultation process itself helps the consultee define diagnostic steps that lead to action plans or organizational change (Bennis et al., 1985). Process consultation can be more demanding and threatening to consultees than other types of consultation because its open-ended emphasis may lead to uncomfortable areas or issues (Ledford, 1990).

Application: Consultant Techniques and Procedures
The premise of process consultation is that organizations are merely networks of people. If these networks are not functioning effectively, there will be extreme difficulty in accomplishing the tasks of the organization (Schein, 1988). Process consultation attempts to enhance the overall functioning of the organization by helping the consultee change values and develop skills. In effect, the consultee's development is accomplished when the consultant models the desired values and skills. Through collaboration, the consultee begins to take more and more responsibility for the diagnosis and implementation of procedures. As the desired skills and values become more evident in the consultee's behavior, the consultant gradually disengages from consultation.

There are seven overlapping steps to process consultation (Schein, 1988):

1. making initial contact with the consultee organization

2. defining the relationship, formal contacting, and creating a psychological contract

3. selecting a setting and method of work

4. gathering data and making a diagnosis

5. intervening

6. reducing involvement

7. terminating

The process consultant spends a significant amount of time building relationships with consultees and assumes that, without trust, the consultee will not deal with the basic issues that are concerning the organization and therefore consultation will not likely be successful. In addition to developing trust, the consultant selects a work site close to "where the action is." By being able to observe the real work of the organization, he or she is able to ask the right kinds of questions to help consultees explore things such as organizational culture and values.

The process consultant favors the use of interventions that maximize opportunities for consultee-consultant interactions. Consequently, observation, informal interviews, and group discussions are used frequently by process consultants.

The process consultant considers data gathering to be a crucial process that should be conducted in a manner consistent with the consultee's values. Further, the process consultant believes that plans for gathering data should be general in nature because the only way to determine how to proceed is to use experiences resulting from initial data-gathering strategies.

As process consultation proceeds, the consultant can intervene in a variety of ways. Schein has categorized these in terms of their tactical goals—exploration, diagnosis, action alternatives, and confrontation—because the process consultant usually moves through these interventions in that order as the consultation process unfolds. The consultant uses exploratory questions to stimulate the consultee's thinking and to determine his or her views. Diagnostic interventions are used to involve the consultee in the diagnostic process, action alternatives help convince the consultee that something can be done about the situation, and confrontative interventions are used to test the consultee's motivation and willingness to act (Schein, 1987, 1988).

Regarding evaluation, the process consultant determines what outcomes might occur as a result of consultation and how they are to be measured. As its ultimate goal, process consultation attempts to improve organizational performance by changing values and interpersonal skills in key personnel.

Case Example of Process Consultation A group of teachers at a secondary school were unsatisfied with the general quality of communication between the staff and students and wanted to improve the communication efforts of the staff as a whole. They asked Gene, the school counselor, to sit in at their meetings and act as a "sounding board," which he agreed to do.

Time at the end of each meeting was allocated for Gene to give feedback to the group. He was also asked to help the group stay on task and get through the problem-solving process. During the consultation Gene provided feedback to the group on its problem-solving skills, challenged it to define its goals more precisely, and suggested that group members develop specific ways to evaluate their attempts to communicate better. All in all, he helped the group members become more effective problem solvers. Finally, Gene provided feedback on the group's ways of gathering information from students and the types of interventions it developed for improving communication. When everyone involved was satisfied with the way things were going, Gene reduced involvement with the group and attended only every third meeting.

COLLABORATION FROM AN ORGANIZATIONAL PERSPECTIVE

The aim of organizational collaboration is the same as organizational consultation: the enhanced functioning of the organization. Because of the tremendous increase in "in-house" human service professionals, such as human resource development specialists, organizations are uniquely poised to maximize the benefits of collaboration. Structures such as self-directed work teams, quality circles, and project management teams all lend themselves to having the human service professional function as a collaborator. In organizations where collaboration is relatively new, human service professionals can train members of the organization in problem-solving skills and team functioning. The human service professional can then participate as a collaborator and take responsibility for the outcome of some aspects of the project, as well as providing consultation to and receiving it from fellow collaborators.

Because of its collaborative nature, the process consultation model may be the easiest to adapt to collaboration. Human services professionals will need to adapt the purchase of expertise and doctor/patient models to include a method for empowering fellow collaborators to use their own expertise to a higher degree.

The emergence of the internal consultant role also has implications for collaboration in organizations (Caplan et al., 1994). Managers, for example, may find it more suitable to have some responsibility for some part of a plan, rather than be seen as a person trying to consult with a subordinate, thereby walking the thin line between supervision and consultation (Caplan et al., 1994).

SUMMARY, TRENDS, AND CONCLUSIONS

Summary

Organizational consultation encompasses many types of consultation performed by consultants, internal or external, to organizations and who function as technical experts, diagnosticians, or process experts. Regardless of the role, organi-

---

CASE 9.1   Organizational Consultation for School Consultants

Doris is a middle school consultant who was asked by the administration of her school to work with one of its interdisciplinary teams. The team consisted of a social studies teacher, a math teacher, a science teacher, and a language arts teacher.

The team leader had been complaining to the administration that certain team members consistently go "around" her rather than "through" her when communicating with the principal. This was in spite of the fact that the principal had reminded the other team members of proper protocol.

As Doris was determining how to approach the team, she realized that part of the problem was the principal's high level of approachability. The principal met with Doris and the team and asked them to work together on resolving the apparent problem the team was having. The principal mentioned that the team may want to use Doris for building some procedures for communicating outside of the team.

Doris started out by meeting with the team during its planning session. As she heard the intensity of the feelings among the team members, she decided that process consultation was in order. It was obvious to Doris that *how*

things were being said was just as important as *what* was being said.

Doris suggested (1) that the team knew it had a problem in internal and external communication (the team members, including the leader agreed), (2) that the members were in the best position to determine how to resolve these issues, and (3) that they engage in a collaborative effort that would help them solve not only their current concern but similar ones in the future. She and the team agreed to meet for three sessions during the next month.

In playing the roles of facilitator and catalyst, Doris raised questions for exploration and helped the team look closely at itself and its communication processes. She raised the issue of authority when it appeared that there were differences in whether the team leader was "in charge" or a "group spokesperson." The team felt awkward as it attempted to be humane yet honest. The teachers had worked together for over 10 years but only recently had been placed together as a team.

At the close of the third session when Doris asked the team to evaluate her, themselves, and the progress that had been made, the members

generally acknowledged that as an objective and facilitative person, she had been of great assistance in helping them help themselves. Though they had initially been defensive and looked for blame rather than taking responsibility for the problems they were experiencing, the members had come to agreement about the role of team leader, resolved their authority issue, and improved their communication in terms of concreteness and authenticity. Doris followed up in one last meeting a month later.

Commentary

Doris demonstrated some excellent skills in determining which approach to organizational consultation she might take. She noted the significant amount of emotion surrounding the team's functioning and accurately determined that process consultation, with its more interpersonal focus, was an appropriate method to start out with. She also astutely determined that if the goal was to get the team to collaborate more effectively, then the approach to consultation should be one, like process consultation, that places people in a position of collaborating to solve their problems.

---

zational consultation is predicated on the notion that an organization can increase its overall effectiveness through consultation. The organization itself, or one of its parts, is the client, and consultees are people in the organization with whom the consultant works.

Organizational consultation has its roots in the fields of industrial technology, manufacturing productivity, the applied behavioral sciences, and managerial science. Important work

in organizational consultation includes that of Blake and Mouton (1983), Schein (1987, 1988), and Lippitt and Lippitt (1986).

The basic assumptions of organizational consultation are that the process is as important as content; the behavior of individuals, groups, and organizations is cyclical in nature; and satisfied personnel make for effective organizations.

Organizations suffer because their personnel lack the knowledge, skills, or values to

CASE 9.2   Organizational Consultation for Community Consultants

The general manager of the local branch of AME Telephone Company contacted the local mental health agency for the purpose of developing and implementing a professional outplacement counseling program. The company was undergoing a downsizing mandated by its parent company. The general manager informed the director of the mental health agency that the parent company had made funds available for the purpose of counseling displaced workers. The manager noted that almost half of the unit's 56 workers were going to be laid off.

Maria, a community mental health consultant, was assigned to explore the possibilities of the agency working with the telephone company. Using the principles of program consultation, she spent a great deal of time with the manager discussing the nature of the telephone company, which was a typical bureaucracy, like many other telephone and utility companies she had worked with over the past 20 years. Everyone had their assigned duties and did them well. The general manager was aware of the bureaucratic structure and attempted to ensure adequate morale by having an upbeat newsletter and recognition of birthdays. He also used a personal touch by getting out and about the divisions of the company and he knew each employee by name.

After she had a feel for the organization and made some conclusions as to its nature, Maria informed the manager about some general principles of outplacement counseling and the possible structures that such a program

could take on. She noted the importance of the program on the morale of those employees remaining with the company, as well as the goodwill the program could develop with the departing employees. Maria and the manager discussed the positive impact that an outplacement program could have not only on the local unit but on the parent company's national reputation. Any outplacement program has three phases: preparing the company to make terminations, helping those employees who are terminated find new jobs, and assisting remaining employees to feel secure.

As Maria and the general manager roughed out an outline that Maria could develop into a program proposal, they concluded that the general manager himself should undergo some training in effective termination, determined that severance packages should be discussed with the employees being terminated prior to the offering of outplacement services, and discussed the nature of outplacement counseling services needed by the employees. Since the company was in a moderately rural area, many of the employees' families had lived in the area for generations. Hence, part of the counseling process would encourage employees to discuss their feelings concerning termination, myths and realities about finances, career counseling, and placement.

Maria and the manager discussed outplacement concepts that seemed particularly applicable to the employees being terminated at the telephone

company: job hunts within and outside the local community, "creating your own job" strategies, testing and assessment of a candidate's aptitudes and skills. Finally, they determined what the outplacement counseling program could do for the remaining company employees and addressed occupational wellness.

Based on their discussion, Maria developed a proposal for the program and submitted it to the mental health agency director and the telephone company general manager for approval. The program included a detailed blueprint for how the program was to be implemented and an extensive evaluation procedure that included input from all employees as well as placement success data.

Commentary

Maria did an excellent job of being thorough in her approach to program consultation. Instead of plugging in a canned program, she analyzed the organization and considered some of its unique aspects. Notice how she educated the general manger and made him part of the intervention. Maria also looked at the outplacement counseling program from the perspective of the entire company by including something for the remaining employees. Such systemic thinking enhances the probability of successful program implementation.

The idea for this case study came from an article by Siobhan McGowan (1993) entitled "Employees, Managers Work It Out after Layoffs" in *Guidepost*, *35(10)*, pp. 1, 10.

function at optimal levels of effectiveness. Organizational consultants, armed with a broad repertoire of techniques grounded in organizational theory, attempt to help consultees deal with the complexities of organizational life and enhance effectiveness.

Consulting with organizations is a little like feeding a hungry animal: in living its life, the organization uses up energy and becomes hungry. If it doesn't get some food (consultation) it cannot function optimally and will eventually starve to death.

Trends

The major trends in organizational consulting are linked to several societal factors: a rapid movement toward an information society; the ever-increasing pace of change in all aspects of life (Backer, 1985); the growing awareness that change requires systemic thinking; the realization that change can be successfully accomplished only through influence, not by force (Goodstein, 1985); and increasing diversity within organizations (Plummer, 1998). These factors have created the following general trends in organizational consulting: a continued reliance on computer hardware and software, a primary consideration of the effects of organizational culture and diversity on consultation efforts when selecting interventions, and the willingness and ability of organizational consultants to "wear many hats" when they provide services. For example, as diversity continues to increase in the work force, consultants will need to be increasingly sensitive to workplace diversity issues related to organizational infrastructure, job satisfaction, relationships among staff, and work productivity (Steward, 1996).

One trend in organizational consultation is the tendency to combine process consultation

with the purchase of expertise and doctor-patient models (Schein, 1990c). Schein (1990c) suggests that such combinations involve consultees at more significant levels in the consultation process and enhance the probability of success in consultation. By combining process consultation with other forms, the consultant ensures that the consultee is appropriately invested in the process, that the appropriate problems are being worked on, that the diagnosis is relevant and clear to pertinent parties, and that the solutions generated are appropriate for the organizational context and culture (Rockwood, 1993; Schein, 1990c).

One trend in education/training consultation has been the emergence of performance consultation (Robinson & Robinson, 1995). Performance consultation assumes that solutions proposed by education/training approaches often miss the mark because what are really needed are solutions that are based on *performance*. Performance consultation assumes that the focus should not be on skill acquisition because much of the research on training suggests that trainees do not follow through after the training. While the education/training approach focuses on training activities and experiences, performance consultation teaches the skills and knowledge related to specific job performance. In short, performance consultation makes the shift from what consultees need to learn to what they must do.

There has been increased involvement of organizational consultants in employee assistance programs (EAPs) (Myers, 1988). Consultants may assist managers in planning both remedial and preventative programs, consult with EAP staff regarding processes such as evaluation, orient supervisors to the various components of EAPs, and engage in general consulting tasks such as preparing publicity for EAP program components and orienting service providers (Myers, 1988). Organizational consultants have also increasingly become involved in nonprofit organizations, such as churches, to assist with a variety of issues such as attendance and levels of giving (Baard, 1994).

There is an increasing emphasis being placed on determining how and when to apply models of organizational consultation. Fuqua and Kurpius (1993) have developed seven principles for assisting consultants in determining how best to select from among consultation models.

1. Consultants should select models congruent with the perceived needs of consultees and the organization.

2. Consultants should clearly articulate to consultees which model is being used.

3. The major goal in model selection should be expanding consultees' conceptual framework.

4. The model should allow consultees to generalize from the enhanced conceptual framework after the consultant exits.

5. The most powerful implementations will involve development of the consultees.

6. There is more positive power in sharing the application of models with consultees.

7. The application of multiple models will more likely lead to consultation success than will applying a single model.

Finally, there is a trend toward creating standards for organizational consultation assessment and evaluation. Cooper and O'Connor (1993) have developed a conceptual framework for organizational consultation measures based on the focus of the intervention (that is, specific individual, group, or organizational processes) and the target of the assessment (that is, individual, group, or organizational processes). In addition, there is increasing emphasis on the fact that a combination of quantitative and qualitative assessment measures can be of great benefit to organizational consultants.

Conclusions

Because organizational consultation encompasses a variety of approaches, it is difficult to assess its major contributions. It has, however, clearly contributed to improving workplace conditions (for example, through process consultation) and helping organizations become more diverse and accountable (for example, through program consultation).

Organizational consultation has emphasized the idea that meeting human needs and increasing productivity are interconnected (Brown et al., 1991). The specialized types of consultation available in organizational consultation have increased (Gallessich, 1982). Organizational consultation's concept of the organization-as-client has helped organizations understand the importance of organizational culture; indeed, most organizations now realize that much individual behavior is strongly influenced by organizational culture (French & Bell, 1990). Organizational consultation has also demonstrated that working with groups of consultees can be a cost-effective way to meet workers' needs and increase organizational effectiveness.

The criticisms of organizational consultation are frequently those directed at organization development, including that it has not fulfilled its early promise to integrate or systematize its interventions. The following criticisms were adapted from a critique of organizational consultation by Gallessich (1982, pp. 221–222). Unfortunately, they are still true today.

- It is too preoccupied with interpersonal process to the detriment of problem-related factors such as budgeting and technology (French & Bell, 1990; Margulies & Raia, 1972).

- Its interventions are often "band-aids on an open wound" and hence are not effective in solving many organizational problems in the long run (Burke, 1980). (For example, there is an over-reliance on the use of workshops to solve identified concerns.)

- Its results are often "cosmetic" or only involve "fine-tuning" (Schein & Greiner, 1977).

- Its consultants sometimes perform "dirty work" or "spy" for managers and other administrators (Friedlander & Brown, 1974).

- Its consultants sometimes produce such grand designs that their interventions in effect are worse than the organization's problems were in the first place (Klein, 1969).

- Its consultants sometimes try to apply methods of business and industry when providing organizational consultation to human service agencies (Golembiewski, 1969; Caplan et al., 1994).

There are yet other criticisms of organizational consultation. Some organizational consultants rely on one or two pet interventions, particularly workshops (Huse, 1978), and some cannot always take into account administrators' deeply rooted assumptions about administration and personnel—assumptions that may differ from those held by the consultant. Hence, there is at the outset of consultation tremendous potential for resistance that may never be overcome.

Schein (1987, 1988) noted that the purchase of expertise and doctor-patient models are limited because they rely on basic assumptions that are rarely met in practice. Therefore, they are at best superficial and, at worst, counterproductive. Because organizational consultation is complex and organizations themselves are slow to change, organizational consultation is likely to last a long time and be quite expensive (French & Bell, 1990).

Organizational consultation frequently does not accurately take into account the external forces operating on the organization. Thus, performing consultation with an organization on Madison Avenue will require dealing with external forces quite different from those operating on an organization in the rural South. Organizational consultation is also criticized for not realizing its potential because researchers and practitioners have not developed better theories (Adlerfer, 1990).

These criticisms reflect more the imperfections of practicing organizational consultants than imperfections in the models and their principles. Accordingly, better training procedures for organizational consultants are as likely to produce improvements as would refinements in organizational consultation models.

SUGGESTIONS FOR

EFFECTIVE PRACTICE

- Be able to determine if you should be using the purchase of expertise, doctor/patient, or process model of consultation.

- Remember that your ultimate goal in organizational consultation is to assist the entire organization in some way.

- Use the dictum *How* you do what you do is as important as *what* you do.

QUESTIONS FOR REFLECTION

1. What historical forces led to the development of organizational consultation?

2. How can an organization be a client?

3. Differentiate among the purchase of expertise, doctor-patient, and process models of consultation.

4. Why are the purchase of expertise and doctor-patient models particularly limited?

5. Explain how both education/training and program consultation are examples of purchase of expertise consultation.

6. Why is program evaluation the most common function of the program consultant?

7. Process consultation aims for changes in values and skills of the consultees involved. How are these values and skills related to organizational effectiveness?

8. Is it really possible for a consultant to produce an accurate diagnosis of an organization's problem? Why or why not?

9. Why do so few consultees follow through on the prescriptions made by organizational consultants?

10. How can multicultural issues be dealt with at the organizational level?

SUGGESTED SUPPLEMENTARY READINGS

If you are interested in organizational consultation, you may want to read some of the following books:

Conyne, R. K., and O'Neil, J. M. (Eds.). (1992). *Organizational consultation: A casebook*. Newbury Park, CA: Russell Sage Foundation. This text presents five case studies of organizational consultation in a variety of settings. Each case study follows a specified format. Of particular interest is the last chapter, which analyzes and synthesizes the case studies. This book is an excellent resource for learning the practical, hands-on side of organizational consultation.

Schein, E. H. (1988). *Process consultation: Its role in organization development*. Volume 1 (2nd ed.). Reading, MA: Addison-Wesley. This classic text is a must for anyone interested in consulting with organizations. Schein discusses process consultation in detail and in relation to the purchase of expertise and doctor-patient models.

Schein, E. H. (1987). *Process consultation: Lessons for managers and consultants*. Volume 2. Reading, MA: Addison-Wesley. This is Schein's latest contribution to the field of process consultation. Filled with case studies, this text discusses advances in process consultation since Volume 1 was published. Of particular interest is Schein's discussion of new classifications of process consultation interventions. Its business and industry orientation should not diminish the wealth of applicable information in this book. Interested readers should note that this text was written for those who already possess a basic familiarity with process consultation.

10

Mental Health Consultation

Mental health consultation has provided the foundation for the development of consultation as service delivery approach (Henning-Stout, 1993). Mental health consultation is based on the idea that society's mental health can be promoted through the efforts of consultants who work with human service personnel (such as counselors) or with administrators of human service programs (such as the director of a factory's employee assistance program). The recipients of the consultant's efforts are the "primary agents in preventing mental disorders in a population" (Caplan, 1993, p. 41). If the consultant can enhance the effectiveness of the consultee, some emotional problems will be reduced, making referral to an expert unnecessary (Meyers, Brent, Faherty, & Modafferi, 1993). More precisely, mental health consultants assist their consultees with specific work-

related problems, such as a difficult case or glitches in a mental health–related program. An important goal of mental health consultation is not only to help consultees cope with their specific work-related problems, but also to improve their general level of functioning so that they can be even more effective in the future. As Caplan, Caplan, and Erchul (1994) note, writers in the field need to "underscore the importance of mental health consultation *in the service of primary prevention*" (p. 6).

Mental health consultation has been used in schools (Cohen & Osterweil, 1986; Osterweil & Plotnik, 1989), nursing homes (Meeks, 1996), hospices (Lindberg, 1996), religious settings (Malony, 1991), medical settings (Drotar, 1987; Quirk, Strosahl, Kreilkamp, & Erdberg, 1995), criminal justice agencies (Dodson-Chaneske, 1988), police hostage negotiation teams (Butler,

Leitenberg, & Fuselier, 1993), community residences for people with developmental disabilities (Hyman, 1993), employee assistance programs (Shosh, 1996), postsecondary education settings (Amada, 1993), youth shelters (Grigsby, 1992), the postwar theater (Garland, 1993), and a variety of other settings. It has been used for many purposes including assistance with cases, organizational change, and diversity training (Russell–Chapin & Stoner, 1995; Shosh, 1996). It is difficult to promote the mental health of society in a preventative way, but mental health consultation attempts to do just that. Consider the difficulty: how would you promote the unique mental health needs of each of the numerous subgroups in our culture?

In this chapter we'll consider the historical development of the mental health consultation model and examine Caplan's model (Caplan, 1970; Caplan & Caplan, 1993) of mental health consultation. This model is included both because of its historical and practical utility and because Caplan is considered to be the one person who put consultation on the human services landscape. Included are the approaches the model can take, their respective goals, the consultant's role, the consultee's experience in consultation, and the techniques and procedures used. We will examine a relatively new professional role called *mental health collaboration*. We will also consider the ecological perspective to mental health consultation. Finally, we will cover some contributions and criticisms of the model and cite some trends in mental health consultation that have led to modifications of Caplan's model.

As you read this chapter, consider the following questions:

1. What are some of the differences and similarities between mental health consulta-

tion and the generic model we've already examined?

2. What difference would it make if a mental health consultant's primary goal in working with a human service worker was to make him or her a better worker in general, rather than to help the client under discussion?

3. What are the basic differences between mental health collaboration and mental health consultation?

4. How would a consultant best determine the reasons that a human service worker or administrator is having difficulties with a work-related problem?

5. Are there really differences between work-related and personal problems? If so, what are they?

INTRODUCTION

Historical Background

Mental health consultation is a part of the community mental health concept that asserts that services should be available as needed within the community and should be integrated with other human services. As Conoley and Wright (1993) note: "Caplan's model of mental health consultation is the prototypic consultation approach. It has the longest history and is based on the most traditional psychological understandings of human behavior" (p. 178).

Mental health consultation began in the late 1940s with the passage of the federal Mental Health Act of 1946 (Yolles, 1970), which created the National Institute of Mental Health (NIMH) and provided states federal moneys for the purpose of supporting mental health services. Public acceptance for community-based mental health services increased in the 1950s; the idea that mental health services were limited to treating severely disturbed individuals in residential treatment centers waned. In 1963, Congress passed the Community Mental Health Centers Act, which provided federal funds for the construction of mental health facilities in local communities and called for consultation and education services to the community.

The concept of the prevention of mental illness became very important both because there was a large discrepancy between the need for services and the ability to meet those needs (Caplan & Caplan, 1993) and also because the efficacy of psychotherapy in treating mental illness was under criticism (Meyers, 1981). The ability of local mental health centers to provide preventative services thus became one of the criteria for being considered for these federal funds. Consultation services were seen as one type of preventative service to public and private human service professionals, who would become more effective as they attempted to meet the mental health needs of their clientele (Yolles, 1970). Consultation was to be a method for helping non–mental health professionals learn the mental health skills necessary to assist those people for whom they had professional responsibility (Watson & Robinson, 1996).

A trend that paralleled public and federal interest in preventative services was a shift in the conceptualization of consultation. Before 1950, consultation in agencies was considered to be an extension of clinical psychiatric consultation (Beisser & Green, 1972). In other words, consultation was viewed in terms of the medical consultation model: the psychiatrist examines the patient, makes a diagnosis, and prescribes treatment to the professional in charge. Two trends emerged around 1950 to change this view: professionals other than psychiatrists came to be viewed as legitimate consultants, and it became clear that problems in treating cases could be due, not only to a lack of knowledge or skills on the part of those in charge of treatment, but also to the consultee's personal concerns or to organizational factors present in the consultee's work site. A few articles incorporating these trends began to appear in the early 1950s, and evidence increased substantially in the mid-1950s.

Around this time Gerald Caplan arrived on the scene. A psychiatrist by training, Caplan's name has become synonymous with *mental health consultation*. In fact, mental health consultation is frequently referred to as the *Caplanian model*. He is often credited with "discovering" the usefulness of mental health consultation and describing its various forms (Mazade, 1983).

Caplan attempted to incorporate and apply the ideas of public health in his consultation model (Kelly, 1987). By improving a community's ability to create resources for the promotion of mental health, the prevalence of mental illness would be diminished. By having consultants work with consultees to serve their clients better, mental health would be promoted more widely than possible by a mental health practitioner working individually (Kelly, 1987). For example, if a mental health consultant helped a group of three teachers raise the self-esteem of the students in their classrooms, the consultant, by working directly with three people, would indirectly affect the lives of over 90 students in a relatively short time. Contrast this with the idea of having the practitioner work individually with all 90 students or even work in each of the three different classrooms, one at a time. Clearly, consultation could be a time-saving and efficient mode for promoting mental health.

Caplan's 1970 book, *The Theory and Practice of Mental Health Consultation*, reflects his experiences as a consultant and his research in consultation. Caplan relates that his interest in mental health consultation began around 1949, when he was a member of a team of psychiatrists, social workers, and psychologists at a child guidance center in Israel. Part of the team's duties was to attend to the mental health needs of over 16,000 immigrant children who were cared for in about 100 residential centers. Referrals to the team far outweighed its ability to provide direct services to the children.

The operation of the team under these circumstances led to five discoveries by Caplan. First, the caretakers seemed to have a very restrictive perception of possible management strategies. Second, many of them had very stereotypic perceptions of the children and their difficulties. Third, they were frequently quite upset, and their personal concerns affected their ability to be objective about the children with whom they were working. Fourth, their narrow perceptions, stereotypic attitudes, and personal issues could be ameliorated by particular consultant attitudes and interventions. Finally, the team could learn a substantial amount of relevant information about the children and caretakers by visiting the institution, rather than by bringing the caretakers and children to the team's central office.

Out of Caplan's experiences in Israel, the basic rudiments of his model began to take shape. Consultation could be viewed as working with another person to help a client. Consultation typically would take place on the consultee's turf, and the consultee's perceptions of the client would be the basis for consultation. The consultant would need to be especially observant of the consultee's perceptions and would look for possible distortions, stereotypes, and personal issues that might adversely affect working with the client. The consultant would be objective yet sympathetic and would focus on the client as a person with problems, not as a problem who happens to be a person. When the team members working with the children were treated in this way, they seemed to be able to return to their duties with renewed enthusiasm and a broader perspective on working with clients (Caplan et al., 1994).

After his experiences in Israel, Caplan continued to develop his model of consultation at Harvard's Schools of Public Health and Medicine, where he began to use the term *mental health consultation*. He formally developed the concept of the consultation as a collaborative relationship among equals. The idea that consultation need not occur in a crisis situation, but could also be used for preventative measures, also emerged as did techniques of group consultation. Through Caplan's efforts, mental health consultation became conceptualized as a "method whereby a small group of mental health specialists would guide and support . . . non–mental-health-specialist caregivers, such as doctors, nurses, teachers, clergymen, and welfare workers, in mastering the cognitive and emotional challenges of . . . their traditional duties" (Caplan, 1993, p. 45). Professionals in the human service professions were now able, through consultation, to work at a systems level. Caplan has continued updating his views over the years (Caplan, 1974, 1977) and has recently cowritten a revision of his first text, entitled *Mental Health Consultation and Collaboration* (Caplan & Caplan, 1993).

Mental health consultation has expanded over the years in spite of federal spending cutbacks. Most models remain adaptations of

Caplan's. There has been a move away from the psychodynamic orientation toward more eclectic approaches; that is, mental health consultants are free to conceptualize their consultees, clients, and the dynamics of the organizations in which they work from any number of perspectives and approaches. One of the more common perspectives is the ecological perspective covered later on in this chapter. In addition, mental health consultants now regularly consult with other mental professionals and parents as well as non–mental health professionals such as teachers. Learning to conduct mental health consultation can be a challenge. Some experts consider it more difficult to master than psychotherapy (Iscoe, 1993).

MENTAL HEALTH

CONSULTATION DEFINED

Consider this relatively simple form of mental health consultation:

Case Example

You are a social worker who consults with psychiatric nurses concerning approaches to counsel the relatives of Alzheimer's disease victims. One of your consultees is having difficulty with a family of a certain patient. As you listen to the consultee describe the case, you get the impression that the patient's "Jekyll and Hyde" personality is keeping the family off balance. You suggest that the nurse teach the family some self-talk strategies they can use when the patient is acting out. You refer the nurse to several sources of information on self-talk strategies and agree to provide the consultee a training session on these strategies.

This example erroneously suggests a relatively simple definition of mental health consultation. Various attempts have been made to define mental health consultation (for example, Hershenson & Power, 1987). The most consistently recognized definition of mental health consultation is Caplan's:

> a process of interaction between two professional persons—the consultant, who is a specialist, and the consultee, who invokes the consultant's help in regard to a current work problem with which he is having some difficulty and which he has decided is within the other's area of specialized competence. The work problem involves the management or treatment of one or more clients of the consultee, or the planning or implementation of a program to cater to such clients. (Caplan & Caplan, 1993, p. 1)

Subsequent attempts at defining mental health consultation (for example, Hodges & Cooper, 1983; Mannino, MacLennan, & Shore, 1975) have elaborated on the type of help the consultant provides while holding to the basic ideas in Caplan's definition. Notice this emphasis in the following definition by MacLennan, Quinn, and Schroeder (Bloom, 1984, p. 155):

> Mental health consultation is the provision of technical assistance by an expert to individual and agency caregivers related to the mental health dimension of their work. Such assistance is directed to specific work-related problems, is advisory in nature, and the consultant has no direct responsibility for its acceptance or implementation.

This definition suggests that the consultant will function as a technical expert who advises.

Hodges and Cooper (1983) have expanded on Caplan's definition by adding some of the specific role behaviors the consultant uses in helping consultees:

> Community mental health consultation can be defined as the process by which a mental health professional interacts with community-based professionals and other service providers (the consultees) to supply information, skill training, and individual-process change or system change in order to help the consultee or the system better serve the mental health needs of the people in the community. (pp. 19–20)

It is a method in which mental health professionals can become, in effect, public health practitioners by taking into account how external events impacted the internal processes of community resources such as teachers (Kelly, 1993). The consultant's knowledge of the psychology of the individual could be used in more systemic initiatives such as classroom management strategies.

In summary, mental health consultation is a process in which a mental health professional interacts with another professional and assists him or her with the mental health aspects of a work-related problem that concerns either a client or a program. The consultant uses knowledge and skills to assist the consultee with the specific concern and, in addition, attempts to improve the consultee's ability to function in the future. The consultee has the freedom to choose whether or not to apply the assistance provided in consultation and remains responsible for the client or the program. The bottom line is that the consultant serves to assist the consultee with the psychological elements of a current work-related or caregiving problem related to a specific client or program (Erchul & Schulte, 1993).

KEY CONCEPTS OF MENTAL HEALTH CONSULTATION

Basic Characteristics

From Caplan's point of view, mental health consultation has several basic characteristics, awareness of which is essential for understanding his view: (The following list is adapted from Caplan & Caplan, 1993, *Mental Health Consultation and Collaboration*, pp. 21–23. Copyright Jossey-Bass. Reprinted by permission of the publisher.)

1. Mental health consultation is a method used by two professionals in respect to a lay client or a program for such clients.

2. The consultee's work problem must be defined by him or her as being mental health related, such as a mental disorder or personality idiosyncrasy of the client, the need to promote mental health in the client, or interpersonal aspects of the work situation. The consultant must have expert knowledge in these areas.

3. The consultant has neither administrative responsibility for the consultee's work nor professional responsibility for the outcome of the client's case. She or he is under no compulsion to modify the consultee's conduct of the case.

4. The consultee is under no compulsion to accept the consultant's ideas or suggestions.

5. The basic relationship between the two is coordinate; there is no built-in hierarchy or authority-subordinate tension, which in our culture potentiates the influence of ideas. The consultees' freedom to accept or reject what the consultant says enables them to take quickly as their own any ideas that appeal to them in their current situation.

6. The coordinate relationship is fostered by the consultant's membership (typically) in another profession and his or her arrival into the consultee's institution from the outside.

7. The coordinate relationship is further supported by the fact that consultation is usually given as a short series of interviews—two or three on average, which take place intermittently in response to consultees' awareness of their current need for help with a work problem. The relationship in individual consultation is not maintained and dependence is not fostered by continuing contact. In group consultation there may be regular meetings, but dependence is reduced by peer support.

8. Consultation is expected to continue indefinitely, for consultees can be expected to encounter unusual work problems throughout their careers. Increasing competence and sophistication of consultees in their own profession improves the likelihood of their recognizing mental health complications and asking for consultation.

9. Consultants have no predetermined body of information that they intend to impart to a particular consultee. They respond only to the segment of the consultee's problems that the consultee exposes in the current work difficulty. The consultant does not seek to remedy other areas of inadequacy in the consultee but instead expects other issues to be raised in future consultation.

10. The twin goals of consultation are to help consultees improve their handling or understanding of the current work difficulty and through this to increase their capacity to master future problems of a similar type.

11. The aim of consultation is to improve consultees' job performance, not their sense of well-being. It is envisaged, however, that, because the two are linked, consultees' feelings of personal worth will probably be increased by successful consultation, as will their capacity to deal in a reality-based socially acceptable way with certain life difficulties. In other words, successful consultation may have the secondary effect of being therapeutic to consultees.

12. Consultation does not focus overtly on personal problems and feelings of consultees. It respects their privacy. The consultant does not allow discussion of personal and private material in the consultation interview. This does not mean that consultants disregard the feelings of the consultee. They are particularly sensitive to the feelings and to the disturbance of task functioning produced by personal problems. They deal with personal problems, however, in a special way, such as by discussing problems in the context in which they relate to the client's case and the work setting.

13. Consultation is usually one of the professional functions of a specialist—even if he is titled *consultant*. He should use the consultation method only when it is appropriate. At other times he should use different methods. Sometimes the demands of the situation will cause him to put aside his

consultation. For instance, if he gets information during a consultation interview that leads him to judge that the consultee's actions are seriously endangering the client (such as failing to prevent a suicide or to pursue treatment for a dangerous psychosis), he should set aside his consultant role and revert to the basic role of a psychiatrist, psychologist, or social worker. He will then give advice or take action that the consultee is not free to reject. This destroys the coordinate relationship and interrupts the consultation contact in favor of a higher goal. Such dramatic occasions are rare, but the possibility demonstrates the realistic limits of this method.

14. Finally, it is worth emphasizing that mental health consultation is a method of communication between a mental health specialist and other professionals. It does not denote a new profession, merely a special way in which existing professionals may operate.

These fourteen characteristics represent the basis for the practice of mental health consultation from Caplan's perspective. Although the consultant is the expert, the relationship is an equal one. The nature of the consultant-consultee relationship is crucial: the consultant assists with work-related problems only and does not deal directly with the consultee's personal concerns. The consultee's work problems may be viewed from a psychodynamic perspective, and the goal of consultation is to enhance the consultee's current and future ability to function professionally. The consultant does not take any supervisory authority over the consultee's actions and has no responsibility for the client/program (Caplan, 1993). Further, it is essential that the consultant take organizational influences into account when conducting consultation (Conoley & Wright, 1993).

Psychodynamic Orientation

The Caplan model uses a psychodynamic approach to consultation, for, as a trained psychiatrist, Caplan was heavily influenced by the work of Sigmund Freud. The Caplan model relies on an intrapsychic view of behavior change (Meyers, 1981); this psychodynamic orientation makes the Caplan model one of the most complex consultation models (Conoley & Conoley, 1992). A detailed discussion of the psychodynamic approach is beyond the scope of this book. Those interested in reviewing Freud and his modifiers should consult a good text on theories of counseling and psychotherapy, such as Corey's *Theory and Practice of Counseling and Psychotherapy* (1996). A brief review of psychodynamic perspective follows. The *psychodynamic approach* fosters the concept that our behavior is a product of unconscious motivation and that most of our personal issues result from early childhood experiences. These issues often lead to inner conflicts that affect our behavior and cause us problems. Because these inner conflicts are usually unconscious, we are often unaware of the causes of our behavior. True behavioral change must deal with these unresolved conflicts from the past; merely dealing with the behavioral manifestations of a person's problems only results in the emergence of another problem because the core problem has not been adequately addressed. This phenomenon is often referred to as symptom substitution.

Not every difficulty a consultee has with a case or program is due to inner conflict. A difficulty might stem from a lack of appropriate professional knowledge about some aspect of the case. But from Caplan's perspective, when the consultee's inner conflicts are causing problems with a case or program, they must in some way be addressed to ensure the consultee's adequate functioning with the current case and with similar cases in the future. Changing overt behaviors will only provide temporary change. Because the consultant does not provide psychotherapy to the consultee, the consultee's inner conflicts must be dealt with indirectly.

In his recent writings (e.g., Caplan et al., 1994), Caplan has stressed the importance of taking into consideration not just the psychodynamics of the individuals involved but also those operating in the organizations represented by the consultant and consultee in addition to those in the community itself. Hence Caplan's thought has evolved into one that takes into consideration the larger systems context of consultation.

Transfer of Effect

Transfer of effect refers to the concept that what is learned in one situation should be usable in similar, future situations, which is central to the Caplanian model (Meyers, 1981). Consultee-centered consultation improves the consultee's capacity to function effectively and to benefit current clients as well as similar ones in the future. By listening to the consultee's perceptions of the client or program and extrapolating the pertinent information concerning the consultee's difficulty, the consultant by indirect means can help the consultee be more objective. In addition, by retaining responsibility for the case or program, the consultee is set up for optimal learning and generalization to future cases (Erchul & Schulte, 1993).

Types of Consultation

The manner in which mental health consultation is conceptualized is a critical factor in terms of how it is practiced. The consultant should have a system to anticipate what is likely to happen in each consultation situation and to identify effective strategies with which to approach the consultation. To accomplish this end, Caplan (1970) devised a classification system with two major divisions. The first concerns whether the consultant *focuses on a case* (for example, a client at a halfway house) or *focuses on an administrative problem* dealing with a mental-health-related program (for example, helping a health science teacher implement a unit on substance abuse).

The second division concerns whether the consultant's primary goal is "giving a specialized opinion and recommendation for a solution" (Caplan, 1970, p. 32) (for example, observing a client and recommending a specific therapeutic technique) or "attempting to improve the problem-solving capacity of the consultees and leaving them to work out their own way of solving it" (Caplan, 1970, p. 32) (for example, helping a parole officer be more objective about a case with a parolee). The goal is thus to change either the *client* (or program) or the *consultee*.

These two divisions make up four types of consultation: *client-centered case consultation, consultee-centered case consultation, program-centered administrative consultation*, and *consultee-centered administrative consultation* (Caplan, 1970). This classification formed the early organization of consultation types, and most reconceptualizations of types are summaries of Caplan's work (Hodges & Cooper, 1983).

TABLE 10.1   Caplan and Caplan's Consultation Classification in Terms of Level, Target, and Goal

	CLIENT-CENTERED CASE	CONSULTEE-CENTERED CASE	PROGRAM-CENTERED ADMINISTRATIVE	CONSULTEE-CENTERED ADMINISTRATIVE
Level	Case	Case	Administrative	Administrative
Target	Client	Consultee	Program	Consultee
Goal	Behavioral change in client	Enhanced consultee performance in delivering services to clients	More effective delivery of program	Enhanced consultee performance in programming

Each of the four types of consultation has a different level of intervention, an identifiable target, and an identifiable goal (Bloom, 1984). Table 10.1 presents Caplan and Caplan's (1993) classification as defined by these three factors.

THE CONSULTATION PROCESS

Next we'll examine these four types of mental health consultation in terms of their goals, the consultant's function and role, the consultee's experience in consultation, and the use of consultation techniques and procedures. Because of its unique nature and its impact on the development of mental health consultation, consultee-centered case consultation is covered in more depth than are the other three types.

The Client-Centered Case Consultation Process

Consultation Goals   Client-centered case consultation is the most commonly used form of mental health consultation. It typifies what most human service professionals think of when they hear the word *consultation*. The consultant is viewed as an expert or specialist who

can diagnose and recommend an intervention. The consultee presents a case in which a client has mental health problems that are causing the consultee some difficulty. The primary goal of this type of consultation is to develop a plan to help the client. Secondarily, the consultee is better able to handle similar cases alone in the future as a result of contact with the consultant. However, only limited educational benefit to the consultee is expected from this type of consultation because the consultant spends very little time with the consultee.

Consultant Function and Roles   The consultant functions primarily as an expert in assessing the situation, diagnosing the client, and making recommendations for the consultee's use in the case. Specifically, the consultant builds a relationship with the consultee (in ways previously discussed); assesses the client's difficulty by gathering information from the client and other sources; assesses the consultee's strengths, weaknesses, and work setting by visiting the consultee at work; and files a written report, usually a letter or a case record, which should (if possible) be reviewed in a meeting with the consultee. In this way, the consultant can improve the consultee's functioning in similar cases in the future. It is the consultee's responsibility to use the written report and the conference with the consultant in dealing with the case. In other words, the consultee takes the consultant's report and develops and implements a plan of action. Finally, the consultant plans for a follow-up session with the consultee.

Consultee Experience in Consultation

Consultees in client-centered case consultation focus on providing the consultant with as much pertinent information and professional opinion as possible regarding the case, such as the consultee's role relative to the client system and any constraints that have been laid upon the consultee.

Even though the consultant is likely to observe, interview, or test the client, the consultant wants to know how the consultee views the case. The consultee, then, is not only a link between the consultant and client but also a professional collaborator who knows the client better than the consultant and knows best how to deal with the client within the consultee institution.

The consultee's primary responsibility is to adapt and carry out the consultant's recommendations, but the consultee is free to accept or reject any or all of them. The consultee may require the assistance of the consultant in implementing a given recommendation but must ask for such assistance. Finally, the consultee participates in a scheduled follow-up session with the consultant.

Application: Consultant Techniques and Procedures

It is not unusual for a written note to accompany a consultee's request for consultation, and it is best for the consultant to respond to the consultee with some form of personal contact so as to build a relationship, clarify what the consultee desires from the consultant, and obtain more information on the client.

In assessing the client, the consultant has two basic questions: Should the client be referred for specialized treatment? What can the consultee do to help the client in the consultee's work setting? These are answered by listening to the consultee (and perhaps the client and his or her significant others when applicable).

It is quite risky to provide client-centered case consultation in the consultant's office. Without assessing the consultee and the consultee's work setting, the consultant can rely only on the client's report about the consultee and the work setting. Because the consultant needs to know about the strengths and weaknesses of the consultee and the consultee institution to make effective and realistic recommendations, the consultant should visit and perform consultation in the consultee institution.

One of the consultant's major tasks in client-centered case consultation is writing a report for the consultee. This report, typically supplemented by a face-to-face meeting with the consultee to clarify the report and answer questions related to it, should be written in language appropriate to the consultee's institution, should be practical, and should avoid condescending terminology. The main body of the report should focus on how the client is or is not coping in major areas of life and include some recommendations as to how the consultee can facilitate improved client functioning in appropriate areas.

A Sample of a Consultant's Written Report The following is a portion of a consultant's report prepared by a counselor working with a teacher having difficulty with Dana, a third-grade student who steals from other children in the classroom:

The stealing behavior is most likely caused by Dana's need for security. The objects taken are usually food (for example, snacks) or school supplies (for example, pencils). The fact that Dana makes little attempt not to get caught perhaps suggests that there is the perception on her part of too little attention. Stealing objects thus helps Dana feel more secure and get attention.

I recommend that the teacher make a deliberate attempt to praise Dana throughout the school day for appropriate classroom behaviors. In addition, she could be assigned some classroom responsibilities (for example, erasing the board) and then be reinforced for acting responsibly. Dana's security might be increased if the teacher frequently communicated to her that she belongs in the classroom and that the teacher takes care of all children in the classroom. Such verbalizations can reduce insecurity.

Implementation of the consultant's recommendations is the consultee's prerogative because he or she has responsibility for the case. However, the consultant can help determine whether the consultee has the knowledge and skills required to perform the suggested interventions. Such a judgment is best achieved by having a history of sustained contact with the consultee so that an assessment of consultee strengths and weaknesses is possible before the formulation of recommendations.

Follow-up by the consultant is crucial: it provides the consultant a rough evaluation of the effects of consultation; it provides feedback on how the consultant's interventions affected the consultee in the case under discussion, which could be useful to the consultant in improving future interventions; and it conveys consultant interest to the consultee and improves their relationship so that the consultee may actively seek additional consultation about the current or some other case.

Case Example of Client-Centered Case Consultation Tracy is a resident psychologist consulting with Kim, an activity therapist, concerning a patient in a residential psychiatric hospital. The therapist reports that the patient, a 15-year-old, refuses to engage in any activity therapy. The client shows up on time but just sits and watches as the other patients engage in the therapy.

Tracy observes the patient in several hospital settings, including activity therapy, and interviews the patient's primary therapist concerning the case. She determines that the patient appears to have few friends at the hospital but is friendly and approachable. She also concludes that Kim has the ability and motivation to assist the patient to begin participation in activity therapy.

Tracy writes a brief report suggesting a "buddy system" for the patient. Kim would implement the program, in which one or two higher functioning patients could become friends with and accompany the patient to the activity therapy group, where they could perform the activities together. Tracy shares this recommendation in a final consultation session with Kim, who agrees to the recommendation, and takes steps to implement the program. Tracy follows up after two weeks to monitor the intervention.

The Consultee-Centered
Case Consultation Process

Consultation Goals The primary goal of consultee-centered case consultation is improvement of the consultee's ability to work effectively with a particular case as well as with similar cases in the future. "In consultee-centered case consultation the consultant's primary focus is upon elucidating and remedying the shortcomings in the consultee's professional functioning that are responsible for his difficulties with the case with which he is seeking help" (Caplan & Caplan, 1993, p. 101). In other words, this approach reestablishes professional objectivity in the consultee by getting rid of the "unusual ineffectiveness" (Conoley & Wright, 1993, p. 179) that is due to the consultee's "baggage" that he or she brought to the case. Improvement of the client is the secondary goal. As in client-centered case consultation, the case is the focus of discussion, although usually the consultant does not see the client because the goal is to help the consultee. The consultant helps the consultee by hearing his or her subjective view of the case.

Consultant Function and Roles In consultee-centered case consultation, the consultant plays the roles of detective, expert, and educator. In the role of detective, the consultant seeks out the consultee's cognitive and emotional problems through active listening and judicious questioning. The consultant discusses the case with the consultee in the role of an expert mental health professional. As an educator, the consultant provides the consultee the information and/or training needed to solve problems with this and similar cases in the future. Thus, the consultant builds a relationship with the consultee, assesses his or her problem with the case, and intervenes to alleviate the problem.

The consultant asks the consultee to discuss the case, and the remainder of the consultation relationship involves such discussions. The consultant, however, is more directive than in client-centered case consultation in that the consultee is asked to discuss selected aspects of the case, which provides the consultant information about the consultee's work difficulty. As the consultee discusses the case, the consultant categorizes the consultee's work difficulty as a lack of knowledge, skill, confidence, or professional objectivity. The consultant intervenes to resolve the consultee's particular work problem. The so-called "grist for the mill" in consultation comes from the consultee's "subjectively determined story" (Caplan & Caplan, 1993, p. 101), not from the real facts about the case.

Consultee Experience in Consultation In consultee-centered case consultation, the consultee's task is to enter into the consultation relationship and discuss a case that is causing difficulty. Under the consultant's guidance, the consultee elaborates on the particulars of the case. When the consultant makes interventions to assist the consultee, it is up to the consultee to implement those recommendations, which often include ways the consultee can improve professional functioning. The consultee maintains full responsibility for the case under discussion.

During the initial stages of consultation, the consultee may have a very narrow view of the case. Indeed, consultees often do not know why they are having difficulty with cases. In responding to the consultant's judicious questioning, the consultee's perceptions of the case are enriched and broadened so that the "cognitive grasp and emotional mastery" (Caplan & Caplan, 1993, p. 101) of the particulars of the case are increased.

Application: Consultation Techniques and Procedures There are four types of consultee-centered case consultation, one for each of the four reasons that consultees may have difficulty with cases: lack of knowledge, skill, self-confidence, and professional objectivity. Now we'll consider each of these four types of consultation, which can be performed individually or in groups.

Lack of Knowledge When the difficulty with a case is due to lack of knowledge, the consultee might not have sufficient understanding of the client's problem, some important client characteristics, or both. According to Caplan (1970), the consultee may lack either factual or theoretical knowledge needed to deal effectively with the case.

The consultant imparts the missing knowledge to the consultee in a manner conducive to the consultee's success in the case under discussion as well as for possible similar cases in the future. It is very important that the consultant provide this information without violating the coordinating nature of the relationship, a task best accomplished by capitalizing on the consultee's motivation to learn information relevant to the case at hand. The consultee's education results from applying the needed knowledge to the current case, which also maintains the desired consultant–consultee relationship.

Lack of Skill The consultee may well have the knowledge required to understand a case but lacks only the skill to intervene effectively. In this situation, the consultant should avoid the temptation to supervise the consultee's conduct of the case.

Procedurally, the consultant and the consultee conduct a joint appraisal of the case: they explore the problems, what the consultee has tried so far to help the client, and what the consultee could yet do to resolve the issue. Such a procedure broadens the consultee's perspective on the case, provides a broader context for perceiving subsequent similar cases, maintains the coordinate nature of the relationship, and preserves the consultee's self-esteem. The consultant determines the degree of the con-

sultee's skill deficit, describes what skills are needed to deal effectively with the case, and explores with the consultee the means to get the appropriate skills training within the consultee institution. If such training is not available within the consultee institution, the consultant can provide the training.

Lack of Self-Confidence Lack of self-confidence can cause confusion and uncertainty about how to handle a case. It can result from consultee inexperience (for example, being assigned a particular client problem for the first time or being a beginner on the job) or be a generalized trait within the consultee that manifests itself in reduced on-the-job functioning.

The goal of the consultant is to provide support and encouragement by fostering hope, confidence, and courage by affirming the consultee's strengths and capabilities. Reassurance, which damages the nonhierarchical nature of the relationship, should be avoided. The consultant's second goal is to help the consultee find a peer support group within the consultee institution.

Lack of Professional Objectivity The consultant considers lack of objectivity only after lack of knowledge and lack of skill are eliminated (Erchul, 1993a). Lack of objectivity is the most common problem among consultees who work in institutions that have a knowledgeable, skilled staff and a supervisory system. Hence, most consultee-centered case consultations are of this type. The consultee's lack of professional objectivity is a defective judgment—an inability to maintain an appropriate professional distance. The consultee's role functioning, perceptions, and judgments are impaired by subjective factors that make him or her unable to apply existing knowledge and skills to the case effectively.

By the time the consultee seeks out consultation, confusion, frustration, incompetence, and declining self-esteem are often evident and can cause a lack of professional poise. The coordinate nature of the consultant–consultee relationship is in greatest jeopardy in consultee-centered case consultation because the consultant appears to be in control of personal issues in the professional setting, whereas the consultee is not. Therefore, the consultant should *indirectly* help the consultee recapture professional objectivity by discussing the client, the consultant, or some fictitious client in a story or parable. The consultee's problem should not be dealt with directly. The consultee's confidence and poise must be maintained (Caplan, 1993).

Lack of objectivity in even the most knowledgeable and skilled consultees can result from five somewhat connected reasons: direct personal involvement, simple identification, transference, characterological distortions, and theme interference (Caplan & Caplan, 1993, p. 108).

When a consultee loses professional objectivity due to *direct personal involvement*, the relationship changes from a professional to a personal one. An obvious example is when a consultee falls in love with a client. Because of the emotional nature of personal relationships, objectivity is lost. Professionals should keep a certain distance from their clients to maintain objectivity, and personal involvement alters the balance of that relationship by causing the consultee to be either too close or too distant from the client. Consultees are frequently unaware of their personal involvement with their clients and do not realize they are fulfilling their own personal needs at the expense of those of the client.

Simple identification occurs when the consultee does not merely empathize with but instead identifies with the client (or some person in the client's life) and loses the sense of neutrality so essential to maintaining objectivity. The consultee identifies with some real charac-

teristic of the client (or person in the client's life), such as race, gender, or some behavior pattern the consultee considers idiosyncratic. For example, a consultee who is a minister might overidentify with a client who is also a minister. The client is then described in a positive, sympathetic manner, while others in the case are viewed in derogatory terms. The consultant can relatively easily identify simple identification because of the obvious similarities between the consultee and some person in the case.

A *transference* distortion occurs when the consultee transfers onto the client feelings and attitudes from key relationships in the past. Once the consultee's predetermined attitudes and feelings are imposed on the client and objectivity is lost, the consultee is unable to assess the client's real situation. For example, a consultee who has difficulty with authority figures due to her childhood relationship with her mother might have difficulty dealing with a client who is the head of a large company. The transference relationship tends to be repeated over time in similar cases.

Minor disturbances in consultees, often referred to as *characterological distortions* of perceptions and behavior, can cause consultees to lose their professional objectivity. Caplan defines these distortions as personality problems most people have that interfere with the effective delivery of human services to the client. To illustrate this point, Caplan (1970) tells of a teacher, with a tendency toward sexually acting out, who anxiously attributed to several of her students harmful sexual behaviors that a consultant later described as quite normal.

Caplan's concept of *theme interference* is a special type of transference reaction that causes consultees to lose their professional objectivity. Theme interference becomes apparent to a consultant when the consultee is "blocked" from progressing with a case for no explicable reason. For example, a consultee who has difficulty dealing with anger might impose this trait on the client, in effect saying, "Unless this client deals with his anger during our sessions together, no progress can be made in this case." For some reason, the consultee has identified with some aspect of the client's case.

According to Caplan and Caplan (1993), theme interference develops in the following manner: "A conflict related to actual life experiences or to fantasies in the consultee that have not been satisfactorily resolved is apt to persist in his preconscious or unconscious as an emotionally toned cognitive constellation which we call a 'theme'" (p. 122). The theme is a recurring symbol of an unresolved problem and has a preemptory quality (Rogawski, 1978). When suffering from theme interference, the consultee sees the case as being hopeless and makes several inappropriate problem-solving efforts (Erchul & Schulte, 1993). Themes generally repeat themselves, carry a negative emotional valence, and take the form of a syllogism. This syllogism has two statements that constitute a prejudicial stereotyped notion (Rogawski, 1978) and are perceived by the consultee to be linked in such a way that they are inseparable: an "initial category" followed by an "inevitable outcome."

The initial category is a statement that signifies the condition that was characteristic of the original unresolved problem in the consultee's life. In reality, the client may or may not fit the stereotype, but still the consultee applies the stereotype to the client. The stereotype is imposed when consultees form their impressions of the client; certain pieces of information are put together and the initial category is formed. Placing the client in the initial category leads to expectations that are typified in the inevitable outcome, which is a rigid assumption of an "inescapable failure" (Rogawski, 1978, p. 325).

When put together, the initial category and inevitable outcome take the following form: if A (initial category) happens to anyone, then B (inevitable outcome) must occur. One example might be, "If my client doesn't deal with his anger, we will never make any progress in therapy." In such cases the consultant must assume that the consultee has a problem in dealing with anger and that the client may or may not have the same problem.

The problem with theme interference is that, by losing objectivity, the consultee is unable to see that there are many possible outcomes to any problem and that several possible interventions are available to achieve those outcomes. This lack of objectivity causes inconsistent, sometimes panicky behavior in the consultee, and the subsequent lack of progress in the case reaffirms the belief in the inevitable outcome. Thus, a vicious cycle develops. There is, however, one source of consolation for the consultee: the inevitable outcome happens to the client, not the consultee. Theme interference tends to recur as long as the theme is manifest.

There are two basic methods the mental health consultant can use to relieve theme interference in consultees. These methods are subtle and designed to "alter the emotional theme underlying the lack of objectivity" (Henning-Stout, 1993, p. 21). First, the consultant helps the consultee reassess the cues in the client's case that led to placement in the incorrect category in the first place. Such a reevaluation helps the consultee see that the original perceptions were erroneous and return to professional objectivity because the inevitable outcome is no longer pertinent. Caplan and Caplan (1993) label this technique *un-*

linking (p. 125) because it unlinks the client from the consultee's theme.

Whereas unlinking attempts to invalidate the initial category, the second approach, called *theme interference reduction*, attempts to invalidate the inevitable outcome. The consultant invalidates the "If A, then B" syllogism by helping the consultee reexamine the evidence on which the inevitability of the outcome is based. The consultee is then able to view the previously inevitable outcome as merely one of an array of possible outcomes (and not necessarily a very likely one at that). The influence of the consultee's theme then begins to wane.

Theme interference reduction affects the consultee on both cognitive and affective levels. Theme interference reduction techniques neither exacerbate resistance nor cause a loss of face because the consultant accepts the consultee's view of the initial category: the consultant does not try to deal with the consultee's inner conflicts directly but rather through their discussion of the case. When properly carried out, theme interference reduction helps consultees by lowering their level of tension, raising their level of objectivity, weakening the theme, and reducing the likelihood that the theme will be displaced on subsequent cases.

Several techniques are effective in theme interference reduction, and all of them have the following steps occurring over a three- or four-week period: assessment of the theme, the consultant's intervention, and ending and follow-up (Caplan & Caplan, 1993). The expression of intense feelings by the consultee is permitted as long as the consultee expresses feelings about the case and does not believe that the feelings are about him- or herself (Caplan, 1993). Part of the consultant's job is to help the consultee feel safe while expressing emotionally sensitive material.

In assessing the theme, the consultant examines the consultee institution, the affective and cognitive reactions of the consultee to the case, indications of an initial category and inevitable outcome, and the possibility that there is more than one theme.

Once the existence of theme interference has been established, the consultant can make one or more of the following interventions (Caplan & Caplan, 1993):

- verbal focus on the client
- verbal focus on an alternative object— the parable
- nonverbal focus on the case
- nonverbal focus on the consultation relationship

A *verbal focus on the client* is the most commonly used technique in theme interference reduction. The consultant discusses with the consultee the evidence for the inevitable outcome by examining in significant detail the facts concerning the case, by which the so-called inevitable outcome is seen instead as one possible outcome among many others. The likelihood of the inevitable outcome's occurrence is explored specifically and in depth to ensure that the consultee does not consider the consultant to be prejudiced against that outcome. By such a thorough examination, the consultee realizes that the inevitable outcome is not even among the most likely outcomes. For example, when a consultee thinks a client must deal with the issue of avoidance of competition, a consultant might help the consultee consider several other therapeutic approaches to pursue with the client.

Parables are used when the consultant thinks it important to create greater distance between the consultee's growing awareness of the theme and its connection to the personal issues in his or her life. It must be remembered that consultation is not psychotherapy; the consultee's personal issues are not to be discussed, even though they may be affecting the case. Once the consultant identifies the initial category and the inevitable outcome and decides that the case under consideration is not a good vehicle to break the connection between the two, a verbal focus on an alternative object is often used.

In using a parable, the consultant artistically creates a believable story concerning the identified theme but uses a fictitious client in a fictitious case. The details of the current case are used as a springboard for creating the anecdote, but details are changed significantly so that only basic similarities to the client and consultee remain. Discussion of the fictitious case then results in the realization that the so-called inevitable outcome was only one of many possible outcomes and that the fictitious case did indeed have a different outcome. Thus, for example, when a consultee suggests that a client *must* agree to assertive training to overcome shyness, the consultant might relate a story about a fictitious client who overcame shyness by going through a cognitive behavioral form of counseling.

Because the consultee is likely to consider the consultant a role model, the ways the consultant responds nonverbally to the consultee's anxieties about the case can be a very powerful tool in theme interference reduction. When the consultant uses a *nonverbal focus on the case*, the consultant's nonverbal behavior demonstrates to the consultee in a relaxed state free of anxiety that the consultant is not really worried that the inevitable outcome must occur. This technique works only if the consultee perceives that the consultant has dealt with the case seri-

ously and thoroughly and has appreciated both the consultee's concern for urgent action and the client's situation. In a simple example, when a consultee nervously relates the specifics of a case, the consultant would maintain a calm demeanor.

A *nonverbal focus on the consultation relationship* is needed when the consultee transfers themes not onto a case but onto the consultant, particularly when the consultation relationship is well developed and contains emotional connections between the two parties. If the consultee transfers a theme by ascribing a certain role to the consultant and then plays the complementary role, the consultant needs to show the usual acceptance of the initial category and then invalidate the inevitable outcome through discussion of the case. However, the expectation of the inevitable outcome should be dealt with in a nonverbal manner, that is, by remaining calm, objective, and free from anxiety. By staying "cool, calm, and collected" both about the case and the transference occurring in the consultation relationship itself, the consultant is working on both planes simultaneously. For example, when a consultee suggests that the consultant should be as upset about the case as the consultee is, the consultant shows appreciation for his or her view but remains calm about what is happening in the consultation session.

In an adaptation of Caplan's theme interference reduction model, Sandoval (1996) suggests a constructivist model that has the consultant assist the consultee in thinking at a deeper level about the complexity of the issues related to the case.

Once theme interference reduction has taken place, the consultant proceeds to terminate the consultation relationship. The consultee will continue to work on the case with the realization that any successful outcome is due to the efforts of consultee and client. Because the theme has theoretically been reduced, the consultee is more likely to be successful with similar cases in the future. The consultant offers to provide assistance with future cases and suggests that the consultee report on the outcome of the current case at that time.

Case Example of Consultee-Centered Case Consultation A mental health consultant is working with a social worker whose caseload consists primarily of indigent families. The consultee brings up a case about the members of a particular family the consultee thinks are "just plain lazy" and are becoming more so because of the welfare they are receiving. The consultee notes that the middle class is the ultimate loser. The consultant listens carefully to the consultee's subjective view of the case, notes the consultee's defective judgment, and determines that the consultee's difficulty in working effectively with the family is due to theme interference.

The consultee views hard work and effort as vehicles for achievement. The theme interference takes the form of the syllogism: unless the family overcomes its laziness (initial category), family members will never amount to much (inevitable outcome). The consultant notes that the consultee appears to be fixated on the "laziness" of the family.

In attempts to reduce the theme interference, the consultant calls this case a tough one and suggests that three consultation sessions over a three-week period might help alleviate the problem. During the consultation sessions, the consultant listens and reacts calmly to the consultee's frustrations concerning the case. The consultant then describes two cases involving "lazy" families in which therapeutic benefits were attained, even though the families remained "lazy." As a result of these fictitious case examples, the consultee feels more comfortable about working on the case and begins to consider alternative approaches to it, such as training in child-rearing practices. The consultant agrees to follow up at a later date concerning the consultee's progress with the case.

The Program-Centered Administrative Consultation Process

Consultation Goals In program-centered administrative consultation, the consultant comes into an organization and consults with an administrator with regard to the mental health aspects of some program or the internal functioning of the organization. The consultant enters the organization, assesses and defines the problem, and makes a written report that includes a series of recommendations. It is up to the consultee to take the consultant's report and adapt and implement it within the organizational setting. Consider this example based on an article by Petti, Cornely, and McIntyre (1993): The mental health unit of a university medical center was asked to conduct an assessment of a mental health program for at-risk children and adolescents in a rural county. The scope of the consultation was to evaluate the services of the local mental health center to the county, examine independent service providers as supplements to the programs of the local mental health agency and recommend scope of services for at-risk children and adolescents. The consultation resulted in a five-year plan developed by the mental health center in conjunction with representatives from the county. A follow-up study after the implementation of the five-year plan indicated separate service units for children and adolescents and a successful mechanism for coordinating services by all mental health providers in the county.

The specific goals of this type of consultation depend on the nature of the consultation request and could include recommendations to deal with problems in program development, organizational planning, or program functioning. A secondary goal is that the consultee will learn to deal more effectively with similar program problems and issues in the future. Just as client-centered case consultation makes recommendations for working with a given client, administrative-centered program consultation makes recommendations for an administrative plan of action. As with client-centered consultation, a minimum of time is spent in direct contact with the consultee. The goals of program-centered administrative consultation are met in a relatively brief time, generally ranging from several hours to a few days. The consultant is seen as an expert who comes in, assesses the situation accurately, and writes knowledgeable recommendations.

Consultant Function and Roles The consultant needs sufficient data-collecting, action-planning, and communication skills to be able to make findings and present recommendations in a form understandable to the principal consultee and other members of the consultee institution. The consultant should be a content expert, that is, have a thorough knowledge of the problem area in which the program administrator (principal consultee) requests assistance. The consultant also should be knowledgeable and experienced in organizational theory and practice, program development, fiscal policy, administrative procedure, and personnel management.

It may be advantageous for an organization to hire a mental health consultant, rather than a generic management consultant of the purchase of expertise type discussed in Chapter 9, because he or she can assist more effectively with the mental health aspects of a program.

The consultant must be particularly careful to create effective relationships with staff members of the consultee institution because their help might be needed in gathering data. For example, the consultant may obtain significant amounts of information from individual and group interviews with staff including information about the internal and external forces working on the organization.

The consultant must consider two issues when performing program-centered administrative consultation. The first concerns being responsible for collecting and analyzing the data required to solve the problem and make recommendations. Therefore, the consultant must do more than merely help the organization's staff determine what data they want to collect since they may lack the knowledge, skill, and confidence necessary to make that determination. Because the consultant bears responsibility for the content of the assessment and the recommendations, the amount, type, and timing of data collection should ultimately be based on his or her expert knowledge and objectivity.

The second issue relates to the consultant's authority with the organization's staff members affected by the consultation. In program-centered administrative consultation, the consultee is the administrator who requested the consultant. This administrator, like any consultee, needs a coordinate relationship with the consultant and is free to accept or reject any or all of the consultant's report and recommendations. The consultant's relationship to the administrator's subordinates, however, is not coordinate. Therefore, in this type of consultation the sanctioning process should guarantee that the consultant's requests for information and cooperation will be honored by all involved.

Consultee Experience in Consultation

The consultee in program-centered administrative consultation is the program administrator who expedites the hiring of the consultant in the first place. (This may or may not be the person who initially contacts the consultant.) The administrator should be the principal consultee because of the power of that position to both sanction the consultation and ensure that the consultant's recommendations are carried out at the end of consultation.

The consultee's task is to meet with the consultant to discuss the main reasons the consultant is being hired, any strategies for clarifying the problem that involve some of the organization's staff, and the time frame for consultation, as well as to select methods of approving the consultant's activities throughout the organization.

Because the consultant needs considerable knowledge about the organization to determine which data to collect and to make realistic recommendations, the administrator should make available as much information as possible concerning the organization's nature and methods of operation. The administrator also produces a rank-ordered list of administrative problems about which the consultant's assistance is being requested.

During the consultation the consultee should have as much contact with the consultant as the consultant deems necessary and should complete two primary tasks: to provide the consultant an ongoing broad view of the organization and the interactive nature of its subsystems, and to react to the consultant's tentative findings so that he or she can modify the recommendations at key times during the consultation process.

After the consultant's report has been filed, the consultee is responsible for the degree to which the recommendations are accepted and implemented. Finally, during follow-up the consultee is expected to assist the consultant in assessing the impact of consultation.

Application: Consultant Techniques and Procedures

How does the consultant proceed in program-centered administrative consultation? In the beginning of consultation, needs are explored, the contract is negotiated, the administrator is identified as the principal consultee, and the approximate amount of time the consultant and the consultee will spend together is established.

In obtaining an overview of the problems and their ramifications, the consultant makes a rapid initial assessment of the consultee institution's structure and culture and the nature of its problems. At this stage, the consultant is interested in forming general impressions and hunches that will provide a procedural blueprint for the remainder of the consultation. This process of obtaining a general overview is frequently referred to as *scanning* (Gallessich, 1982, p. 315).

Once the principal problems are identified, the consultant must gather additional information to shed light on them and to formulate potential solutions. Data are gathered by conducting formal and informal interviews with both individuals and groups, by observing the behavior of the organization's members in their routine work patterns, and occasionally by using questionnaires.

Based on the information gathered, the consultant begins to develop interim recommendations, which are then provided to the principal consultee and other authorized parties-at-interest. The consultant incorporates the reactions received into progressively more detailed, complex, and sophisticated recommendations.

During assessment and the reformulation of interim recommendations, the consultant should maintain as much contact with the primary consultee as is feasible. Such contact provides the consultant with reactions from the organization's administration, maintains the consultee's interest in the consultation, and increases the likelihood that some of the consultant's skills will "rub off" on the consultee.

By progressively modifying the recommendations made to solve the problem, the consultant has used a collaborative approach. The final recommendations should have both a short-term and a long-term focus and should detail procedures required to implement the recommendations.

Because the consultant's report is typically distributed widely and throughout several levels in the consultee institution, it should be written in a formal style and should cover the issues and problems investigated well enough to be understandable to parties-at-interest who had no direct contact with the consultant. It is up to the principal consultee to determine which, if any, of the recommendations will be implemented.

Finally, the consultant should set up a follow-up schedule before terminating the consultation and should arrange to receive the results of the implementation of the recommendations.

Case Example of Program-Centered Administrative Consultation Marilyn, a mental health consultant, is working with an administrator, the head counselor, and the dropout prevention coordinator of a large urban secondary school. The focus of consultation is the school's dropout prevention program. The dropout rate for the school is one of the highest in the state and is still increasing in spite of the dropout prevention program, which has been in existence for three years. Marilyn has been asked to make recommendations to improve the program. Before the onset of consultation, Marilyn made a thorough study of the dropout prevention programs in the state.

She spent one day in the school to get a feel for a typical school day and during the next week conducted in-depth interviews with the administrator, the head counselor, and the dropout prevention coordinator about their perceptions of the program. A few "high-rise" students and some teachers were also interviewed. The results of these interviews led Marilyn to conclude that the program was viewed as a stigma or as "mickey mouse" by virtually everyone except the school's principal and the program coordinator. The program coordinator was viewed as being inadequately trained for the job, as having a "cake" job, and as not being sensitive enough to the needs of the students in the program.

Based on these findings, the consultant made some interim recommendations for changing the program's image and for getting the coordinator additional training. These recommendations were shared with the appropriate staff members and were modified according to their input. The following is part of the consultant's final written report:

> Problem 1.1. The image of the
> dropout prevention program is poor
> among students and many staff members. The interviews conducted by the
> consultant suggest that most students
> view the dropout prevention program
> as "not a cool place to be." Students in
> general perceive students associated

with the program as rejects. The school counselors see the program as a "dumping ground" for students who are having a difficult time adjusting to school. The teachers tend to think of the program as one more "non-academic" activity at school. The administration and dropout prevention coordinator see the program as being adequate.

The following suggestion is made: The administration of the school should appoint a Dropout Prevention Program Advisory Committee with representatives from the administration, the program, students, the counseling department, and teachers. The dropout prevention coordinator would present the committee an annual plan for working with potential dropouts as well as methods of promoting the program's image throughout the school. Special attention needs to be paid to student views of the program.

The consultant followed up three months later and found that the school was actively engaged in carrying out these recommendations. The dropout prevention coordinator was enrolled on a part-time basis in a master's degree program in counseling.

The Consultee-Centered Administrative Consultation Process

Consultation Goals Consultee-centered administrative consultation is the most complicated, interesting, and demanding type of consultation. The consultant is hired to work with an organization's administrative-level personnel to help solve problems in personnel management or the implementation of organizational policy. The goal is to enhance the professional competency of an administrative staff (Erchul & Schulte, 1993). The consultant gathers information from within the organization to identify its problems and help consultees overcome them. The consultant can work with an individual although most often there is more than one consultee.

The primary goal of consultee-centered administrative consultation is an increased level of consultees' professional functioning with regard to program development and organization so they help the institution accomplish its mission in the future—this form of consultation is educative in nature (Mendoza, 1993). A secondary goal is producing positive program change.

Consultant Function and Roles In consultee-centered administrative consultation, the consultant may work with one or more administrators referred to as *principal consultees*. The consultation is expected to be long-term, ranging from a few months to more than a year. Depending on the size of the consultee institution and the nature of the requested consultation, more than one consultant may be used. The consultant needs the same skills required for program-centered administrative consultation, including expertise in group consultation and specialized knowledge of social systems, administrative procedures, and organizational theory. In particular, the consultant must be able to understand how these skills relate to individuals and subgroups within the consultee institution, as well as to how the institution relates to the broader community. A final skill needed is the ability to scan the entire organization and make quick judgments about portions of the organization to examine in more depth.

Upon determining who the consultees are, the consultant enters the organization, performs relationship-building activities, studies the social system of the institution, plans an intervention, intervenes at the individual, group, or organization level, and then evaluates and follows up.

The consultant is more or less "free to roam" through the organization and assists in defining problems and gathering data. Consultants present ideas to consultees and encourage them to discuss and act on them.

Recent trends in consultee-centered administrative consultation suggest that consultants should focus on trying to achieve lasting organizational change (Caplan et al., 1994). This can be accomplished by attempting to reduce stressors in the organization, by assisting in developing programs that deal with crises that may arise, and by creating mechanisms such as EAPs that permit individuals to seek psychological assistance on an easily accessible basis.

Consultee Experience in Consultation

The principal consultee in this type of consultation is the administrator who hired the consultant. This administrator has the job of helping the consultant decide whether additional forms of consultation are required, whether there are to be other consultees, and how they are to be involved in the consultation process. As in consultation of any kind, the principal consultee negotiates the contract, assists in getting sanctions from the top administrator, and provides the consultant logistical support for studying the organization's social structure.

The consultee must determine the extent of contact with the consultant and arrange meetings at which the consultant can present findings to all consultees involved. It is important that consultees know from the start that the consultant will discuss the findings with them for their consideration and input. Al-

though the primary focus of consultation is on organizational problems, an important goal is for consultees to use the consultant's input to further develop their own skills. As in all consultation, the consultees take the consultant's contributions and do with them as they see fit.

Application: Consultant Techniques and Procedures

The beginnings of consultation are the same as in the other types of mental health consultation and more or less follow the entry procedures discussed in Chapter 3. The consultant in consultee-centered administrative consultation, however, has two unique problems at the onset of consultation. The first is determining who, in addition to the administrator, will be consultees. The administrators may want the consultant to have contact with subordinates so that they can inform the consultant about the organization. The consultant would then use this information while consulting with the administrator. However, the administrator may want the consultant to consult with the subordinates concerning issues and problems within the organization. Whichever is the case, it is very important for the consultant to be sure that everyone involved is aware of the nature of the consultant's role.

The second problem is to ensure both that members of the consultee institution understand that the consultant is an agent of change who can move freely within the organization and that the threat they perceive in the consultant's position of power is minimized. Members of the organization may suspect that the consultant is a spy for the administrator, an agent who will use psychological influence to get them to do what the administrator wants, or an outsider who wants to mold the institution into some preconceived form. This perceived threat can be minimized by building proper relationships, including maintaining coordinate relationships, communicating openly, and proceeding cautiously when introducing interventions.

As the consultant studies the organization's social system, problems and issues are identified and then presented to the consultees concerned. The consultant's intervention is a neutral one that is restricted to "increasing the range and depth of their [consultees] understanding of the issues and to augmenting their emotional capacity to use such knowledge productively. It is then up to them to work out solutions in the light of their own personal and role-related choices" (Caplan & Caplan, 1993, p. 272). The most effective way for the consultant to remain neutral is to keep in mind the consultation processes of collecting information, making a consultation plan, and intervening to implement the plan.

Data collection has more constraints in consultee-centered administrative consultation than it does in program-centered consultation. First, staff participation in data collection is voluntary, even though it is administratively authorized. Second, because the people from whom the consultant is collecting data are potential consultees, relationship building must be accomplished as well. Third, although consultants have the freedom to collect data about any aspect of the organization, they would do well to focus on issues that are both important to the staff and related to changes the staff would like to make.

In planning the intervention, the consultant should avoid the temptation to intervene too quickly and should review the findings, set some goals, and determine how these goals are to be met. Each intervention has a time limit, should be related to a problem the consultee thinks is important, and targets an individual, a group, or an organization.

As in all types of consultation, the consultant schedules a follow-up session in which to evaluate. If the consultation is ongoing, the consultant is then free to move on to another problem.

Case Example of Consultee-Centered Administrative Consultation A community counselor was consulting with the staff of a community mental health center that was working with an increasing number of clients with special problems, including AIDS. A former staff member had, in fact, recently contracted the disease. The staff seemed familiar with the controversies surrounding AIDS, but were ill at ease about such problems because of denial of the disease by some patients.

The consultant decided to use a consultee-centered approach but did not focus directly on the AIDS issue until some consultees brought it up. Once the subject was broached, the consultant attempted to extend the consultees' knowledge of denial in some AIDS patients.

The consultant met with the group of consultees for four sessions to discuss coping with client denial and shared information on the feelings helpers often have when working with chronically ill patients. After the four sessions, the consultant evaluated the consultation process with the principal consultee and arranged for a follow-up in six months.

Modifications of the Caplanian Model

Caplan and Caplan have recently updated the ideas expressed in *The Theory and Practice of Mental Health Consultation* in a new text entitled *Mental Health Consultation and Collaboration* (1993). The vast majority of Caplan's original ideas remain the same, though several have been expanded.

In addition to developing the concept of collaboration as an alternative to consultation, Caplan and Caplan have modified the earlier model in some relatively minor ways. For example, they more strongly support consultation with groups of consultees so that members can assist one another. The support that group members can provide one another allows the consultant to maintain a peer relationship with the consultees.

The consultant roles—mediator and conciliator—have been advocated by Caplan and Caplan for use in specific situations such as helping divorcing parents safeguard their children's rights and form a collaborative relationship for dealing with the children as parents.

Some of Caplan and Caplan's techniques such as theme interference reduction have received criticism for being manipulative in nature. For example, Henning-Stout (1993) recommends referral to other mental health professionals in case of loss of professional objectivity. However, Caplan and Caplan (1993) argue that the intention of the consultant is what determines whether or not the manipulation is unethical and that the consultant and the manipulator both try to note the other person's weaknesses—the manipulator to undermine the person, the consultant to help the consultee overcome those weaknesses. Thus, they conclude that if the consultee knew about the benign nature of the consultant's manipulations, he or she would judge the manipulation as positive. Further, Caplan and Caplan suggest that when consultees seek consultation, they are giving tacit or explicit consent for any interventions, including benign manipulation. These authors also conclude that not every consultee is suitable for consultee-centered consultation and that, in such cases, consultants should move to a client-centered method that excludes any manipulation. They also note that many of the principles and basic techniques of mental health consultation are quite appropriate for use by consultants outside of the mental health field.

The Ecological Perspective

New models of mental health consultation are increasingly examining the human-environment interface, which has led to greater emphasis on systems, behavior modification, and human ecology (Mannino et al., 1975; Smith et al., 1997). Termed the *ecological approach*, this view emphasizes that behavior is a function of the interaction of the characteristics of the environment and those of the individual (Conoley & Haynes, 1992; Kloos et al., 1998). This trend implies less emphasis on case-oriented models and more on those concerned with ecology and events (Klein, 1983; Thomas, Gatz, & Luczak, 1997). Hence, mental health consultants are increasingly moving into the area of organizational consultation.

The ecosystem, the interacting systems related to the individual and their environment, provides the context for understanding human behavior. The ecological perspective provides consultants with ways of making changes within a given system, helps individuals contribute significantly, and helps people adapt to the setting in which something is expected of them.

The ecological perspective suggests that a strong consultation relationship and shifts in consultee attitudes are insufficient to effect change (Kelly, 1983). Rather, the resources in the organization must be taken into account. In such models, the consultant becomes part of the community's system and changes the ecological interactions to produce a milieu that promotes mental health (Klein, 1983).

Prevention is a key goal of the ecological perspective (Trickett, 1986). The setting constitutes the client system in this perspective and is usually either an organization or the community at large. Interventions are "aimed at developing long-term adaptive processes for the betterment of the setting and its members" (Trickett, 1986, p. 189). Interventions and strategies for any model of consultation can be used when appropriate. Consultation is successful when the organization or community is able to locate and develop its own resources, which are then linked to external resources (Kelly, 1987). Each setting is viewed as having its own unique physical and social characteristics. In its own way, the ecological perspective has several of the characteristics of the doctor-patient model discussed in Chapter 9, namely, an emphasis on diagnosis and the attempt to tailor intervention to the setting. The ecological perspective is radically different from the doctor-patient model in that it has a preventative orientation, a strong emphasis on the consultant-consultee relationship, a strong focus on ecological variables, a consideration of the way an organization is conceptualized, and a focus on collaboration throughout the consultation. Two guiding principles for the consultant include: the client system is a part of a functioning social system and disturbances are not things inside the individual but are discordances in the system. The term *discordance* refers to the differences between the individual's abilities and the demands of the environment (Conoley & Haynes, 1992).

Proponents of the ecological perspective (Brown, 1988; Tindal et al., 1990) suggest that a great deal of mental health consultation fails to consider the environmental context within which it takes place. For example, whereas consultants typically realize that consulting in a

school is vastly different from consulting in a hospital's human resource development program, they rarely consider that one school differs vastly from another (Kelly, 1987). Consider a second example in which a consultant helps a therapist cure a client, but the client returns because he or she is unable to fit into the community. As O'Conner and Lubin (1984) note, "Mental health is in the hands of the community, not the therapist" (p. 187).

In contrast, to think ecologically is to consider how people, settings, and events can become resources for positive developments in individuals and total organizations, as well as how these resources can be managed and conserved (Trickett, Kelly, & Vincent, 1984). This model assumes that consultee power is needed to effect true change—for example, in reducing the constraints due to social structure and processes within an organization (Kelly, 1987). The ecological model is based on principles that emphasize the interactions between individuals and their environments.

There are three premises of the ecological perspective that guide the consultant (Kelly, 1987, p. 3):

- Each social setting has a finite number of resources to maintain and develop itself.

- An adaptive environment has members who have a variety of competencies.

- The purpose of a preventative intervention is to activate and develop resources.

The role of the consultant is to identify the social resources of the setting and help members help one another (Kelly, 1987). This is accomplished in part by the consultant being as aware of the setting and its external environment as the individuals in that setting. Such mutual assistance helps the organization or community adapt, cope, and become empowered (Kelly, 1987). In short, the ecological perspective provides consultation that nurtures the opportunity to acquire competencies for self-development in the presence of social support (Kelly, 1987, p. 4).

There are several principles that guide the behavior of the parties involved in consultation from an ecological perspective (Kelly, 1987). I have selected five of these to provide an overview of this approach.

1. People, settings, and events are resources for the development of the consultation, which takes into account the fact that these features are present in all social settings and make up the raw material from which change occurs. Thus, consultants scan the entire social organization for resources to develop preventative actions within the everyday life of the organization (Kelly, 1987). For example, a consultant notes that the teachers' lounge in a school may be an excellent setting for teachers to discuss innovative ideas.

2. The ecological paradigm advocates the conservation and management of resources, which taps the vast social energy within the individuals in a given setting so that they become resources for each other. Thus, the consultant assesses the resources within an organization with an eye toward developing those that are used extensively while saving those that are overused (Kelly, 1987). For example, a consultant determines how sensitive topics can be discussed with impunity in a human service agency.

3. The positive qualities of people, settings, and events in every organization can be activated to empower the membership. Activating qualities such as enthusiasm, infor-

mal settings such as "the coffee room," and events such as birthday celebrations should be encouraged. Thus, consultants identify and employ such qualities as personal initiative, social settings, and informal events as growth opportunities for the organization. For example, a consultant organizes a series of "brown bag" luncheon meetings whose topics emerge from the informal interactions of the participants.

4. The dominant means of growth and change are coping (how members of the organization deal with stress) and adaptation (how they undergo changes in "fitting into" the organization) (Kelly, 1987). Thus, consultants maximize the qualities of coping and adapting, for example, by sponsoring a series of wellness activities such as stress management or exercise programs.

5. Consultation is a flexible improvisational process with no set way of proceeding. Thus, consultants may want to maximize networking within the setting to identify resources and strategies (Kelly, 1987).

In conclusion, the ecological perspective involves all members of the setting in preventative measures by identifying its strengths and weaknesses. With a systems view, the resources are then developed so that the setting is self-enhancing. The goal is the creation of an effective social setting in which all members contribute to its maintenance and growth by serving as resources for each other. As you might have surmised, this approach to consultation is very demanding and can be quite time consuming. The ecological perspective is just that—a perspective. It does not attempt to be a model of consultation. Therefore, it is up to consultants to interpret the principles of this perspective as guidelines for effective practice. The ecological approach, although valuable, has yet to reach its promise as a way to aid communities and community groups (Trickett, 1993).

Case Example of the Ecological Approach to Consultation A community psychologist was consulting with a family service center concerned about its work environment. By coming from an ecological perspective, the consultant had a lot of leeway in how she might proceed. Realizing that each family service center is a unique setting, the consultant investigated how the people at the center interfaced with their work setting.

She reviewed the history of the center, observed the people in their work environment, and conducted interviews to determine how newly hired people were oriented and how employees were acknowledged during the everyday course of events. The consultant provided a survey that assessed the workers' views of their real and ideal work settings. In noting discrepancies between the real and the ideal, she found that employees had issues with the degree of autonomy they felt, the amount of work-related stress they experienced, and the quality of communication with supervisors. Areas of strength included reward for productivity, acknowledgment for effort, and opportunities for professional development.

Based on her findings, the consultant and staff engaged in a variety of interventions to enhance the center's quality of life. First, they capitalized on informal elements of the center. People were encouraged to take breaks together, flexible work scheduling was introduced, and a staff volleyball team was formed. Quality circle problem-solving groups with participation at all levels of the center were created. Finally, a community advisory group for the center was created and an internal network was formed to smooth the flow of communication. These empowering interventions were designed to prevent the center from experiencing major problems.

The consultant's final report noted that assisting the center from an ecological perspective would have been much more difficult if the director had not been supportive of change. Further, it appeared that the center staff were now involved in daily operation of the center to a degree that they could be self-supporting.

COLLABORATION FROM A MENTAL HEALTH PERSPECTIVE

As you are aware, Caplan developed his model of consultation in the context of an external consultant who becomes a temporary member of the consultee organization. As increasing numbers of mental health professionals such as school psychologists and school counselors were hired in the schools and started providing consultation services, there were some strong effects on Caplan's original consultation model. These effects included the idea that it would be more difficult for the consultee to reject the consultant's recommendations; that the level of expertise of the consultant would make a nonhierarchical relationship impossible; and that an in-house mental health expert would, under normal circumstances, be expected to participate in the intervention and thereby would be responsible to some degree for the outcomes of the case (Caplan et al., 1994). As a result, Caplan and Caplan have expanded the concept of *collaboration* into a process complementary to, but different from, consultation.

Collaboration does not take away from consultation but adds to it (Erchul, 1993a). The difference is this: in collaboration, the mental health practitioner determines which cases to discuss, takes responsibility for the mental health outcomes of the case, and typically (but not always) joins in the treatment of the client and seeks changes in the host organization that will benefit the clients; in consultation, the consultee chooses which case to discuss, remains responsible for the outcomes of the case and makes any interventions, and does not seek changes in the host institution unless asked to do so.

Caplan (1993) makes the distinction between collaboration and consultation in this way: "The essential difference between *collaboration* and *consultation*, as I use the terms, is this: In *collaboration*, the mental health specialist joins the caregiving team inside the community institution, such as a school system or a general hospital, and accepts responsibility for the mental health outcome of its cases. The specialist may fulfill his or her mission by ensuring that the other team members deal effectively with the clients, in line with his or her assessment of their needs, or else he or she may undertake to implement part or all of the diagnostic and remedial plan him- or herself" (p. 46). As you can see, in collaboration, the collaborating specialist takes primary responsibility for the mental health outcome of the case or program and equal responsibility for the overall outcome of the case or program (Caplan et al., 1994).

The major implication of Caplan and Caplan's recent ideas for practicing consultants seems to be the necessity for the human service professional to determine at the outset of the helping relationship whether consultation or collaboration is in order. This determination can be made by assessing the skill level of the consultee: if high, then perhaps consultation is in order; if not, then the consultee can either be trained to manage the case and then consulted with, or the human service professional can suggest a collaborative relationship and take part in the treatment. On the other hand, the counselor or psychologist may want to consider collaborating in all cases and programs by the very fact of being an in-house professional.

Mental health collaboration can be particularly suitable for school-based human service professionals (Caplan et al., 1994). Caplan and Caplan (1993) use the terms *collaborating professional* and *collaborating specialist* to describe the counselor or psychologist in a school providing collaboration. For example, a school-based mental health professional might consult with a teacher about classroom management procedures for an acting out student while collaborating with the teacher by providing counseling services to the student to help reduce the behavior. As this example demonstrates, there is no inherent conflict between collaboration and consultation. In addition, as this example suggests, the mental health professional is responsible for certain aspects (helping the student adjust to the situation behaviorally) of the case, as is the teacher (making sure appropriate learning occurs). Caplan's (1993) recent writings strongly suggest that mental health collaboration should replace consultation as the method of choice by mental health workers who are staff members of an organization. At the same time, Caplan cautions about ignoring the differences between human service and for-profit organizations when considering mental health collaboration. Table 10.2 summarizes the differences between mental health consultation and mental health collaboration.

TABLE 10.2   **Mental Health Consultation and Mental Health Collaboration Contrasted on Key Dimensions**

DIMENSION	MENTAL HEALTH CONSULTATION	MENTAL HEALTH COLLABORATION
Location of consultant's home base	External to the organization	Internal to the organization
Type of psychological service	Generally indirect, with little or no client contact	Combines indirect and direct services, and includes client contact
Consultant-consultee relationship	Assumes a coordinate and non-hierarchical relationship	Acknowledges status and role differences within the organization and thus the likelihood of a hierarchical relationship
Consultee participation	Assumes voluntary participation	Assumes voluntary participation, but acknowledges the possibility of forced participation
Interpersonal working arrangement	Often dyadic, involving consultant and consultee	Generally team based, involving several collaborators
Confidentiality of communications within relationship	Assumes confidentiality to exist, with limits of confidentiality (if any) specified during initial contracting	Does not automatically assume confidentiality, given organization realities and pragmatic need to share relevant information among team members
Consultee freedom to accept or reject consultant advice	Yes	Not assumed to be true, as a collaborator's expertise in his or her specialty area is generally deferred to by team
Consultant responsibility for case/program outcome	No	Shares equal responsibility for overall outcome, and primary responsibility for mental health aspects of case or program

From: Caplan, G.R., Caplan, R.B., and Erchul, W.P. (1994). Caplanian mental health consultation: Historical background and current status. *Consulting Psychology Journal, 46*, p.7. By permission of publisher.

SUMMARY, TRENDS, AND CONCLUSIONS

Summary

In mental health consultation, a mental health expert (consultant) helps a human service worker or administrator (consultee) with a work-related problem. The approach is historically identified with Gerald Caplan (1970, 1974, 1977; also Caplan & Caplan, 1993) and has its origins in the psychodynamic school of psychotherapy. This model stresses the importance of the consultant-consultee relationship and emphasizes enabling consultees to apply what they learned in consultation to similar situations in the future.

The combination of two levels of mental health consultation (case and administrative) with two possible targets (the client or program and the consultee) produces the four types of mental health consultation: client-centered case, consultee-centered case, program-centered administrative, and consultee-centered administrative.

Consultees can have work-related concerns due a to lack of knowledge, skill, confidence, or objectivity. Depending on the type of consultation and the nature of the consultee's

CASE 10.1   Mental Health Consultation for School Consultants

Micheline is a school counselor assigned to a large urban junior high school. The school has been experiencing an increase in gang behavior along with an alarming increase in the number of students bringing weapons onto campus. Micheline was asked by representatives from a group of language arts teachers to consult with them on stress management.

In a meeting with the teachers, it was apparent to Micheline that they were experiencing a great deal of stress over possible violence in the classroom. Teachers noted that the increase in stress had begun to affect the quality of the group's communication adversely, had increased the number of teacher leave days, and had led many of the teachers to leave school at the earliest possible moment after student dismissal. The teachers related their concerns that the school administration had neither taken a strong enough stand with the gangs nor implemented adequate security procedures to prevent weapons on campus. Having discussed the matter with the principal and been told that the procedures for making the school secure were appropriate, adequate, and approved by the local superintendent's office, the teachers concluded that their only recourse was to create a self-help group to cope with the ongoing stress.

Micheline agreed to meet with the group for one hour after school once every two weeks with the focus being to form a peer support group and to train the teachers in stress management strategies. The first two meetings dealt with the nature of peer support groups among teachers and subsequent meetings were divided between stress management training and dealing with issues individual teachers raised.

Micheline began to feel that the teachers tended to look at her as the ultimate authority in the group instead of focusing on how to help one another, perhaps because she was training the group. In bringing up her concern, she was very surprised at the reaction: several of the teachers felt that although they were in a support group, Micheline would be the one who would be the leader and the expert, while others wondered why Micheline kept the group focused on work issues even when some members brought up very personal issues.

On hearing this feedback, Micheline suggested that she and the group renegotiate her role and had each member write down and then read what he or she expected from the group and from Micheline. As it turned out, most members wanted Micheline to be more active and directive. There was also a trend among the members to discuss how to make their classrooms more secure from gang activity and weapons.

Micheline agreed to the group's request, moving away from stress management training and toward teachers' concerns about particular students with regard to gang behavior or potential violence. She acted as a resource on gang behavior and ways of minimizing violence in the classroom. The group's evaluation of the consultation experience reflected a very positive attitude toward Micheline's role as a resource person. The evaluation also indicated that the teachers felt very supportive of one another even though the concept of a direct support group had been abandoned.

Commentary

Regardless of the initial contract and expectations of the parties involved in consultation, things change. Micheline showed both flexibility and resiliency in her work with the group as indicated by her willingness to renegotiate the nature of role with the group members. This case also brings out another very important point about mental health consultation: even though the consultant can make group-focused interventions such as stress management training, it is typical for individual consultees to want assistance with their own agendas, in this case, strategies for dealing with particular students.

CASE 10.2   Mental Health Consultation for Community Consultants

The consultee, Clover, is a family resource coordinator for a New Start program for low-income single mothers. The program provides support in such areas as finding work, raising children, developing budgets, personal, career, and family counseling, and advocacy. The program helps women set and meet goals that lead to self-sufficiency. Clover is a support person for the women and maintains contact with them over a two-year period. She was having some difficulties in helping one client meet her program goals and had asked Della, a community counselor with a local mental health center, to consult. Clover had made several home visits with the client, who avoided any significant discussion of her problems and had difficulty being assertive—this was a trait Clover wanted the woman to deal with. The woman also had difficulty with minor bouts of depression and exhibited self-esteem issues. Clover had asked Della for assistance in building stronger rapport with the client and for methods to motivate her to work on her goals.

Della took time during the first session to build rapport with Clover, and then asked how she had proceeded with the case so far—in particular what interventions had already been implemented to resolve the problems. In looking for any lack of skill, confidence, or objectivity in

Clover, Della determined that client-centered case consultation was appropriate. Clover admitted that she had resorted to persuasion and a few gentle confrontations. In looking over the client's written goals and history, Della wanted more data so she could further determine Clover's strengths and limitations in managing the case and better assess the client's difficulties. She asked Clover to contact the client for a home visit and for permission to go along.

During the home visit Della took a low profile, observing Clover and the client as Clover again went over the client's goals and the lack of progress being made toward them. As Della drove back with Clover to her office, they discussed what happened during the home visit. Della questioned Clover about alternative approaches to focusing directly on the client's goals. Della mentioned that she saw the client as reluctant rather than resistant. Perhaps taking the first step toward accomplishing her goals was just too much for the client.

Della then wrote a detailed report that contained recommendations on how Clover might manage the case, a brief analysis of the client including her lack of any type of social support system, and the conclusion that such a support system should be the primary goal for Clover to help the client develop. Della listed several

interventions that she knew Clover was familiar with or could obtain resources for, among which were peer counseling, a singles support group, strength bombardment, and goal attainment scaling.

Della met with Clover one more time to go over the report and encouraged her to follow through. They agreed to meet in a month to discuss Clover's progress with her client, and Della encouraged her to call if any glitches showed up in the plan.

Commentary

This case illustrates the skill of determining which type of mental health consultation to employ. Notice that this decisions, although not irrevocable, did guide Della in her work with Clover. If Della had determined that consultee-centered case consultation was in order, she would have proceeded in a very different manner. Notice that Della was not reluctant to share her expertise with Clover and that she based her recommendations on direct observation of the client. Such observations are time consuming and raise the issue of whether alternative ways of observing through audio or videotapes are as legitimate as direct observation. This case also highlights the importance of assessing the consultee's skills to ensure that the consultant's recommendations are doable.

difficulty, consultants have at their disposal a broad array of techniques, including the most innovative and controversial of these techniques—theme interference reduction. All of these approaches to mental health consultation share the common goals of helping the consultee be more effective in the present and the future and benefiting the client or program.

Trends

Several trends have occurred in mental health consultation since Caplan published his inaugural work on consultation in 1970. It is to his credit that many of these trends involve adaptations of his model, such as reconsideration of who may qualify as a consultee, and innovations in methods of working with consultees.

One trend, described earlier in this chapter, is the move toward using collaboration when internal consultants need to take some direct responsibility for part of the plan to help the client system. This is a rather dramatic move away from traditional consultation, in which the consultee maintains responsibility for the outcome of the plan. The concept of reciprocal consultation, which is implicit in collaboration, is not well developed in Caplan's writings. Rather than focusing on how professionals working with the same client system can consult with one another about the client system, Caplan's writings emphasize each professional implementing a part of a mutually agreed-upon plan.

Another trend in mental health consultation is the inclusion of nonprofessionals as consultees (Altrocchi, 1972). Parents, volunteers (such as hospice workers), and paraprofessionals (such as mental health technicians) all work with people in ways that can loosely be described as providing human services. Con-

sultants can help these workers deal more effectively with the people they serve by using essentially the same methods used with professionals. However, Caplan's consultee-centered model does not apply to parents because it is unlikely that they can be objective about their children. Some experts in the field of mental health consultation (Heller & Monahan, 1983; Hodges & Cooper, 1983; Kuehnel & Kuehnel, 1983b; Osterweil, 1988; Parsons & Meyers, 1984; Schmuck, 1983) have modified Caplan's original formulations.

The issue of whether or not the consultant should directly confront consultee defenses has received some attention. Some authors (Dougherty et al., 1996; Parsons, 1996) take a positive view of such confrontation. These authors disagree with Caplan's contention that direct confrontation takes away a consultee's defenses and that the time available in consultation for providing defensive coping strategies is too short. Proponents of direct confrontation argue that it is time effective, much less dangerous than Caplan implies, and does not diminish self-esteem (Meyers, 1981).

Theme interference reduction has also been modified. Heller and Monahan (1983) reconceived theme interference as being due to stereotypes and produced a method for alleviating these stereotypes without having to focus on manipulating the consultee or on the psychodynamic influence that originated the theme interference reduction methods.

Group consultation has received positive attention because of its cost-effectiveness and the realization that it may be as effective as individual consultation, particularly in promoting innovation (Caplan, 1974, 1977; Davis & Hartsough, 1992; Caplan & Caplan, 1993; Counselman & Weber, 1994). For example, school-based and external consultants are involved in teacher retention through the use of support groups using a consultee-centered model to group consultation (Babinsky & Rogers, 1998).

Gibson (1988) notes that there is an increasing demand for advocacy consultation in the mental health movement. Mental health consultants are involved in the development of buffer programs that help individuals such as AIDS patients from being excluded from the community or address the outreach needs of gerontological populations (Gibson, 1988). Drum and Valdese (1988) have developed a system for determining levels of client system needs and the degree to which advocacy is appropriate for each level. Advocacy consultation can also be linked to network-building consultation in which human service consultants work with community groups and/or agencies for the purposes of sharing information, promoting linkages, and developing a unified response to mental health issues that arise (Williams, 1982). For example, a mental health professional might proactively assist a small rural community in developing a network for assisting the community's AIDS patients. Advocacy can also be involved in grass-roots consultation (Williams, 1982), in which mental health consultants assist groups and/or agencies in dealing with issues that have mental health implications for them or their community. For example, a mental health worker might help neighborhood groups develop strategies for keeping drug pushers out of their neighborhood.

There is some evidence that groups of consultees may move from discussing client-centered issues to discussing their own functioning in their work setting (Steinberg & Hughes, 1987). Hence, there may well be a trend developing for mental health consultants to also function as process organizational consultants.

Mental health consultants are getting more involved in staff development (Dorn, 1986). McCollum (1981) has developed a model to guide mental health consultants teaching cognitive, emotional, and behavioral approaches to dealing with the normal stressors of groups like parents and teachers.

Mental health consultants are also increasingly working with different types of support groups for families with special needs, parents, teachers, and other workers. For example, consultants assist support groups for families of the mentally ill, families being served by hospice, teachers under stress, and workers considering career changes. This trend capitalizes on the increasing popularity of the mutual help movement (Gottlieb, 1983; Wintersteen & Young, 1988). In addition, there is a demand for mental health consultants to increase their skills in helping groups organize, recruit members, and make themselves known to the larger community (Werner & Tyler, 1993; Wintersteen & Young, 1988).

Another trend is the increasing amount of mental health consultation performed in medical settings (Pace et al., 1995; Rusnack, 1989). For example, a mental health consultant may be asked to assist a physician concerning a patient's unwillingness to take medication. In another example, administrators of nursing homes often rely on mental health consultants to assist with issues residents present such as depression, combative behavior, and confusion (Crose & Kixmiller, 1994). Mental health consultants are increasingly being asked to conduct organizational consultation in medical settings (Drotar, 1987), for example, in the areas of program development or communication between hospital departments.

Also on the increase is the technical assistance mental health consultants provide agencies (Sullivan, 1991). Such assistance frequently takes the form of outreach consultation and involves the direct dissemination of knowledge and skills to human service agencies (Sullivan & Rapp, 1991). For example, mental health consultants are increasingly being called on to assist in programs that lead to independent living, are designed to decrease psychiatric hospitalization, and whose objectives are to increase the number of clients served by human service agencies (Sullivan, 1991). In another example, consultants engage in psychoeducational group intervention that addresses the needs of adults caring for aging parents (Schwiebert & Myers, 1994). Finally, in yet another example, mental health consultants may serve as key members of the multidisciplinary team with hospice organizations (Lindberg, 1996).

The onset of managed care has also impacted mental health consultation. Having to "do more with less" has created opportunities, particularly for psychologists, in providing consultation such as that based on personality assessment to other therapists and clients' families (Quirk et al., 1995). Increasingly, psychologists are marketing themselves and the clinical utility of their assessment skills with organizations such as HMOs. Even mental health centers themselves are increasingly seeking organizational consultation from mental health providers (Backer, 1993). Caplan's administrative consultation models can be particularly appropriate for mental health centers because the models are user friendly for practitioners and can be adapted to deal with the impact of managed care yet still remain innovative. "The adaptation of organization development concepts in mental health organizations has made those organizations amenable to consultation in their attempts to manage the change that is

happening anyway" (Backer, 1993, p. 157). Increasingly, organizational constructs such as culture are being used to assist consultants in helping human services agencies cope with change.

There has been an increase in the involvement of personnel from counseling and psychological services centers in post-secondary education settings to participate in consultation with other units in the educational institution (Lamb, 1992; Silverman, 1993). Consultants provide guidance on retention efforts, students in academic difficulty, relationships between culturally different groups, and issues surrounding fraternities and sororities. Particular attention is being paid to working with faculty and administrators concerning disruptive students (Amada, 1993) and student-athletes (Gabbard & Halischak, 1993).

There has been a move toward increased use of mental health consultants in business and industry settings, particularly through EAPs (Shosh, 1996) and organization development initiatives (Levinson, 1993). One of the most common tasks for consultants is in helping employees adjust to major changes in companies, such as changes from line production to team production.

Finally, there is a trend for consultation to look beyond the problem-solving paradigm, as well as increasing support for the concept of empowering consultees, with the consultant taking on the role of resource person. For example, a consultant may act as a resource person for assisting the administrators of a domestic-violence program and the administrators of a substance-abuse program communicate more effectively. In all actuality, this is what consultants who take on a collaborative mode do when they are with a very skillful consultee. There is a corresponding move away from the problem-solving approach, which places the consultant in the expert mode.

Conclusions

Mental health consultation has contributed significantly to the psychological well-being of our society. First, it has made possible increased and better delivery of human services to client systems through the use of a pyramid structure in which consultants assist consultees working with clients or programs. Thus, a relatively large segment of the population can be served by a relatively small number of professionals. Second, it has promoted mental health and has helped to create positive public attitudes concerning the delivery of human services. A significant portion of our society now views mental health as everyone's business. Third, it has allowed untold thousands of human service professionals to improve and refine their skills, which has benefited the clients with whom they work. Fourth, mental health consultation has taught us a hard lesson in regard to our fast-paced society: namely, unhurried and systematic reflection increases the consultee's awareness of the range of options available, counteracts premature and emotionally based closure, and reestablishes a state of equilibrium (Caplan et al., 1994, p. 4). This position has tempered the tendency on the part of consultants to give in to the time constraints placed on them and their consultees' efforts in organizations such as schools where a quick fix is often considered better than nothing. Finally, it has reemphasized the notion that personal issues can affect our work lives for better or worse. Indeed, human service professionals may bear the following dictum in mind throughout their careers: Physician heal thyself.

Even though there is no doubt that mental health consultation has had a broad and positive impact, it is not without criticism. One basic criticism is that even though mental health consultation has been defined, it has been done so more in terms of what consultants do, than in terms of what the concept itself means. This has led to some controversy over the boundaries of consultation (Mazade, 1983). Mazade (1983) contends that the boundaries of mental health consultation are too broad: until there is a better definition of mental health consultation and a more consistent set of expectations concerning what mental health consultants do, research and attempts to define relevant and irrelevant delivery of services to consultees will suffer.

Bloom (1984) related several criticisms of mental health consultation made by Gottlieb (1974). First, because mental health consultation focuses on clients and their issues, consultees seek new cases rather than perform preventative measures. Hence, mental health case consultation may work at cross-purposes with primary prevention. Second, the value of consultation is limited when the individual consultee (instead of the consultee institution) is the target for change. Third, mental health consultation can erroneously assume that consultees are not functioning effectively with their cases and programs when in fact they are (Gottlieb, 1974). Caplan and Caplan (1993) have also recently made this criticism.

Most of the criticisms of mental health consultation have been directed at Caplan's (1970) model. For example, Beisser and Green (1972) criticize Caplan for creating a model that only works in an ideal situation that is rarely, if ever, obtained. Caplan's model has also been described as elitist (Beisser & Green, 1972), a vestige of a time when consultees had limited training in their field and few well-trained consultants were available to assist them. A more preventative perspective would characterize consultee-centered case consultation, for example, as the development of knowledge, skill, confidence or objectivity in the consultee (Meyers et al., 1993). As it stands, the model has a deficit perspective in that it assumes there is something wrong with the consultee. Hence, the model focuses on problem solving rather than prevention and has thus not developed a larger plan to assist communities in creating structures that prevent mental illness (Trickett, 1993). Although Caplan views his model as preventative, there is little about prevention in his writing regarding consultation (Meyers et al., 1993).

Caplan also underestimates the amount of time needed to build relationships with individual consultees, particularly in consultee-centered approaches to consultation (Gallessich, 1982). Even the psychodynamic assumptions underlying theme interference reduction have been questioned, and theme reduction techniques have been criticized as being manipulative (Heller & Monahan, 1983; Zusman, 1972) and unsupported by research (Gresham & Kendall, 1987). Henning-Stout (1993) and even Caplan (1993) himself have suggested that Caplan was perhaps too preoccupied with theme interference reduction when he developed his model.

Further, consultants who are also therapists may have much more difficulty than Caplan suggests in avoiding direct therapeutic interventions to consultees who are too emotionally involved in their cases (Gallessich, 1982). The transfer of effect, discussed earlier as a key concept, has been increasingly questioned; only minimal research supports this concept's existence (Gallessich, 1982). Finally, Caplan's view

of a coordinate, nonhierarchical relationship is criticized because consultants, particularly in consultee-centered case consultation, do not always act as if the relationship were equal.

SUGGESTIONS FOR EFFECTIVE PRACTICE

- Listen to how the consultees describe the situation for which they requested assistance as a guide to determine whether to use client-centered or consultee-centered consultation.

- Avoid using techniques like theme interference reduction unless you have been trained and directly supervised in their use.

- Consider the importance of administrative consultation even though the primary work you will do will be case consultation.

- Don't do for consultees and fellow collaborators what they can do for themselves.

QUESTIONS FOR REFLECTION

1. How did the psychodynamic perspective influence Caplan?

2. Do you believe that the transfer of effect really takes place in mental health consultation? On what do you base your belief?

3. What does Caplan mean when he describes the consultation relationship as coordinate and nonhierarchical?

4. What are three basic differences between program-centered administrative consultation and consultee-centered administrative consultation?

5. To what extent do you agree that mental health collaboration is the service of choice for in-house mental health practitioners?

6. What ethical issues are raised by the use of techniques for reducing theme interference?

7. Is manipulation ever a legitimate consultant intervention? Why or why not?

8. Which of Caplan's four types of consultation would you feel most comfortable using? Why?

9. Do you feel that the consultee-centered case type demands too much skill on the part of the consultant to be used effectively by the majority of mental health consultants? Justify your position.

10. What does the ecological perspective add to mental health consultation?

SUGGESTED SUPPLEMENTARY READINGS

If you are interested in more detail and depth about mental health consultation, the following selected readings are recommended:

Caplan, G. (1970). *The theory and practice of mental health consultation.* New York: Basic Books. This classic on mental health consultation was the primary source for this chapter and presents a nice blend of theoretical and practical aspects. Of particular interest is Caplan's discussion of consultee-centered case consultation. Many of today's mental health professionals have used Caplan's ideas as a basis for developing their own particular style and approach to consultation.

Caplan, G., and Caplan, R. B. (1993). *Mental health consultation and collaboration.* San Francisco: Jossey-Bass. The first part of this text is a reprint of the majority of Caplan's 1970 text. The latter part is filled with Caplan and Caplan's ideas on mental health collaboration and methodological and technical issues. New material includes discussion of the significance of manipulation, when to use consultation, and key modifications in Caplan's theory since 1970. The ideas and case studies on collaboration are quite informative.

Kelly, J. G. (1987). An ecological paradigm: Defining mental health consultation as preventative service. *Prevention in Human Services, 4(3–4),* 1–36. This article provides a scholarly treatment of the ecological perspective. Kelly presents a conceptual framework, perspective, and three premises that underlie preventative consultation, and then goes on to discuss 10 principles of the ecological perspective. The reading is somewhat challenging but a must for those who want to deepen their understanding of the ecological perspective.

11

Behavioral Consultation

Behavioral consultation evolved from the behavioral paradigm based on positivism (Henning-Stout, 1993). It is a popular approach to consultation that applies behavioral technology to the consultation process (Elliot & Busse, 1993). The expanding application of behavioral technology to mental health and educational concerns has led to behavioral consultation's immense popularity (Noell, 1996). While behavioral consultants specialize in this approach, all consultants make occasional use of behavioral approaches to consultation (Gallessich, 1982). A consultant functioning within this framework needs to be skilled in behavioral theory and practice (Feld, Bergan, & Stone, 1987; Kratochwill & Bergan, 1990) and should become familiar with the work of such leaders in behavioral psychology as B. F. Skinner and Albert Bandura.

This chapter presents three models of behavioral consultation suggested by Vernberg and Reppucci (1986). *Behavioral technology training* teaches specific behavioral technology skills to consultees (Vernberg & Reppucci, 1986). *Behavioral system consultation* analyzes and modifies an organization's processes and structures using behavioral technology principles (Vernberg & Reppucci, 1986). In *behavioral case consultation* the consultant helps as consultees apply behavioral principles to a case.

As you read this chapter, consider the following questions:

1. What makes behavioral consultation "behavioral"?

2. What unique ethical issues, if any, might arise from the use of behavioral consultation?

3. Is this model's emphasis on measurement an asset or a liability?

4. What are the basic differences among the three approaches to behavioral consultation described in this chapter?

5. What special skills does a behavioral consultant need?

INTRODUCTION

The following is an example of behavioral consultation:

Case Example

You are a schoolteacher who asks a school counselor to consult with you concerning one of your students who causes disturbances by talking at inappropriate times throughout the school day. The counselor asks you to describe exactly those behaviors you consider to be "inappropriate" as well as your and the child's behaviors immediately before and after the undesirable behavior occurs. Based on your description and direct observations of the child, the school counselor leads you through a problem-solving process to eliminate the child's inappropriate behavior. Strategies that you can implement and appropriate rewards and punishments are discussed. You agree to implement the program, and the school counselor agrees to help you measure the subsequent frequency of the child's inappropriate behavior.

Chances are excellent that the school counselor in this example was using a model of behavioral consultation. Behavioral consultation is based on behavioral psychology, which has had a tremendous influence on all areas of human services. Behavioral psychology applies theory and research findings to behavior change techniques in systematic, problem-solving procedures (Martens, 1993; Gmeinder & Kratochwill,

1998). It stresses the principles of learning in understanding how behavior is acquired and changed. Behavioral models of consultation are based on the idea that because most behavior is learned, it can be unlearned and new behavior can take its place. The result of consultation is some change in behavior in the consultee and/or the client system. Therefore, the principles of behavior change are combined with indirect service by the consultant to form the basis for consultation (Gutkin & Curtis, 1982).

When the behavioral consultant uses principles of learning to help consultees bring about desired changes in themselves or their clients, these principles are translated into empirically validated behavioral techniques (Tombari & Davis, 1979). Two key aspects of this type of consultation are a focus on *behavior change* and an extensive use of the *scientific method*.

Behavioral consultation can be used in a variety of settings, including mental health centers, schools, and other human service organizations. In addition to its wide applicability, behavioral consultation is one of the most frequently practiced forms of consultation (Gutkin & Curtis, 1982); it is, for example, the most frequently reported method for working with other professionals in school classroom management (Meyers, Parsons, & Martin, 1979, Schottle & Peltier, 1996).

Historical Background

Behavioral consultation has its roots in behavior therapy: it developed out of experimental psychology, which encompasses not only operant and classical conditioning but also social, developmental, and cognitive psychology (Keller, 1981).

In the early 1900s, John Watson founded the behavioral school of psychology, which shunned covert events such as cognitions and restricted the parameters of psychology to observable behaviors only. As behaviorism became a strong force in experimental psychology, it was applied to the study of people's personal problems (Lutzker & Martin, 1981). Behaviorism strongly influenced operant conditioning, classical conditioning, modeling, behavioral ecology, and cognitive-behavior modification.

In the 1940s behaviorism became the dominating force in psychology under the guidance of Harvard psychologist B. F. Skinner. In developing the concept of operant conditioning, Skinner researched such principles of behavior change as reinforcement, punishment, and shaping, as well as their applications to humans (Skinner, 1953). From the 1950s through today, many behaviorists have applied learning theory in developing treatment techniques for a variety of personal problems.

Psychotherapists such as Wolpe, Lazarus, and Eysenck were pioneers in applying the Pavlovian model of classical conditioning to the treatment of human psychological disorders (Lutzker & Martin, 1981). Their behavioral therapies were characterized by specific techniques validated by case histories (Rimm & Cunningham, 1985).

Until the 1960s, behavior therapy was based primarily on the learning principles known as operant and classical conditioning. In the late 1960s Albert Bandura popularized modeling, a powerful social learning theory based on observation and imitation of certain behaviors under conditions of reinforcement (Bandura, 1977; Matson, 1985; Perry & Furukawa, 1986).

In the 1970s behavioral ecology (Willems, 1974) and systems theory (Morasky, 1982) began to receive attention. In behavioral ecology, people are considered a part of a multilayered ecological environment. The settings in

which people behave are interactive, and a change in behavior for one setting could affect behavior in another setting. For example, the assertiveness behaviors a client learns in the workplace may produce different results when used in the home.

In the mid-1970s the cognitive-behavioral therapy movement became popular. This movement asserts that what we think or say to ourselves can affect our behavior for better or worse and that there is a connection between what a human thinks and whether or not a personal problem is likely to develop. Donald Meichenbaum (1977, 1985), a leader in this field, has shown that changing self-statements in an appropriate way can lead to desirable behavior change. For example, people who instruct themselves to cope with perceived stress are more likely to be able to manage it effectively than are people who engage in self-talk that expresses doubt in their ability to deal with stress.

Today, the behavior therapy movement has grown to include nationwide societies such as the Association for the Advancement of Behavior Therapy (Lutzker & Martin, 1981). At the same time, this growth and expansion have produced such diversity that it is more accurate to speak of multiple behavior therapies rather than one (Corey, 1996), and consequently behavior therapy has become a difficult concept to define (Patterson, 1986; Rimm & Cunningham, 1985). The unifying factor underlying behavioral therapies is their derivation from experimentally established principles and procedures (Keller, 1981) and the focus on the importance of learning and the careful assessment of behavior (Kazdin, 1995).

As the effectiveness of behavioral therapy became increasingly apparent, there occurred a parallel increase in requests from human service providers for assistance in the design and implementation of behavior change programs (Russell, 1978). Hence, the role of the behavioral therapist or counselor was expanded to include that of behavioral consultant. Behavioral consultation was first practiced in organizations that require high levels of client control, such as state mental hospitals (Gallessich, 1985). As behavior therapy came to be used in a variety of settings, behavioral consultation was increasingly used in mental health centers, schools, and other human service organizations. Most of the consultation provided by behavioral consultants consisted of casework; that is, the consultant helped a consultee apply behavioral principles to a specific problem so as to help a client or group of clients. Bergan's (1977) text was the first definitive expression of behavioral case consultation. Although this model tended to focus on interventions that relied on behavior modification, it has expanded to include interventions from diverse theoretical origins (Kratochwill, Elliot, & Carrington Rotto, 1995). The influence of behavioral ecology and behavioral training models in the 1970s broadened the role of today's behavioral consultant to include behavioral system consultation and training in behavioral technology. Proponents of behavioral consultation tend to lead the way in designing and conducting research related to consultation with most of the focus being on school-based consultation.

BEHAVIORAL

CONSULTATION DEFINED

Behavioral consultation "encompasses a wide variety of activities conducted in a broad range of settings with diverse populations" (Vernberg & Reppucci, 1986, p. 65). Because the conceptual framework that underlies behavioral consultation (behavior therapy) has become diffuse, behavioral consultation does not possess a central theory of consultation (Gallessich, 1985). According to Keller (1981), "behavioral consultation is based upon a theory of change that is derived from a broad-based social learning model encompassing diverse streams of psychological and social science research and theory" (p. 64). When all these factors are taken into consideration, defining behavioral consultation clearly becomes a difficult task.

In its broadest sense behavioral consultation is "a problem-solving endeavor that occurs within a behavioral framework" (Feld et al., 1987, p. 185). According to Keller (1981), behavioral consultation involves a "relationship whereby services consistent with a behavioral orientation are provided to a client through the mediation of important others in that client's environment, that is, indirect service" (p. 65). Note that this actually defines behavioral case consultation because its major emphasis is on helping a consultee help a client. Keller's (1981) definition reflects a traditional classification scheme: mental health consultation focuses on the consultee so that the client will be helped; behavioral consultation focuses on the client so that the client can be helped; and organizational consultation focuses on helping the system so that the client system can function better (Hawryluk & Smallwood, 1986).

Four characteristics typify behavioral consultation of any form (Vernberg & Reppucci, 1986, p. 50; Kratochowill, Elliot, & Carrington Rotto, 1995):

- the use of indirect service delivery models
- a reliance on behavioral technology principles to design, implement, and assess consultative interventions

- a diversity of intervention goals ranging from solving problematic situations to enhancing competence to empowering

- changes aimed at various targets (for example, individuals, groups, organizations, and communities) in different settings (that is, from single settings to multiple settings)

In effect, these characteristics broaden behavioral consultation from a case-oriented concept to one that includes the training and system forms of consultation.

Combining Keller's (1981) definition with ideas suggested by Vernberg and Reppucci (1986) produces the following definition of behavioral consultation: a relationship whereby services consistent with a behavioral orientation are provided either indirectly to a client or a system (through the mediation of important others in the client's environment or of those charged with the system's well-being) or directly by training consultees to enhance their skills with clients or systems.

Such a definition is consistent with nine characteristics or assumptions that typify behavioral consultation and account for its uniqueness (Henning-Stout, 1993, pp. 25–26):

- All behaviors are learned.

- The establishment, maintenance, and change of social behavior can be explained through observation of functional interactions of the individual, his or her behavior, and the environment.

- Assessment, intervention, and evaluation of the intervention's effectiveness are directly linked.

- Behaviors of focus must be observable, measurable, and quantifiable.

- Environmental antecedents provide powerful points for initiating change.

- Because learning histories vary, intervention is necessarily idiosyncratic.

- Understanding and intervening with any behavior are guided and modified according to systematically collected data reflecting the frequency, intensity, or duration of that behavior.

- For one person's behavior to be changed, behaviors in other individuals interacting within the environment of focus must also be modified.

Recent additional characteristics include a problem-solving orientation, emphasis on a collegial relationship, and a focus on a structured interview process (Bergan & Kratochwill, 1990; Sheridan, Kratochwill, & Bergan, 1996). For example, emphasis on the collegial relationship focuses on the idea that the behavioral consultant is a content expert and the consultee is an expert on the situation at hand. Whereas some models such as organizational consultation demand only process expertise (e.g., process consultation), behavioral consultation demands both process and content expertise.

These characteristics and assumptions reflect behavioral consultation's emphasis on quantification and measurement, as well as its perspective regarding how behavior is learned and changed.

All three forms of behavioral consultation tend to follow a set problem-solving sequence (Lutzker & Martin, 1981; Zifferblatt & Hendricks, 1974):

1. description of the problem in behavioral terms

2. a functional analysis of the problem's antecedents and consequences

3. selection of a target behavior

4. generation of behavioral objectives

5. design and implementation of a behavior change program

6. evaluation of the behavior change program

It might occur to some that the behavioral technology training form of consultation does not fit this sequence perfectly. In this form of consultation the implementation step of the sequence consists of the training sessions. (Steps One through Four will already have been accomplished prior to the training.) Further, Lutzker and Martin (1981) note that the logic concerning behavior change principles that is used in training is the same as that used in any other application of behavior change.

KEY CONCEPTS OF BEHAVIORAL CONSULTATION

Next we'll discuss the following key concepts of behavioral consultation: its scientific view of behavior, its emphasis on current influences on behavior, and the principles of behavior change. An understanding of these key concepts will help clarify why behavioral consultation proceeds as it does.

Scientific View of Behavior

Behavioral consultation, like the behavior therapy that spawned it, is grounded in a scientific view of human behavior, which implies the use of a systematic and structured approach to the delivery of human services such as consultation. Because knowledge obtained from empirical research is valued so highly by behavioral consultants, such research is subjected to scientific validation, or in other words is put to the scientific test. Such evaluation and subsequent validation are essential to the advancement of behavioral consultation beyond its current state of practice

(Vernberg & Reppucci, 1986). This empirical testing process frequently involves controlled experiments (Rimm & Cunningham, 1985), a discussion of which is beyond the scope of this text. Interested readers can consult Lutzker and Martin (1981) for a concise discussion of experimental designs for behavior change strategies. The emphasis on scientific investigation also leads behavioral consultants to use empirically validated consultation interventions because they believe that such a method of operation increases the likelihood that consultation will be successful (Bergan & Kratochwill, 1990).

Emphasis on Current Influences on Behavior

Behavioral consultation focuses on current behavior as well (Kazdin, 1995). For the most part, behavioral consultation takes the position that because certain current behaviors constitute the problem in a particular situation (Patterson, 1986), behavioral consultation should focus on those behaviors. Behavioral consultation, as Bergan (1977) notes, "defines problems presented in consultation as being outside the skin of the client" (p. 26). It is the description of behavior, not the description of a person, that is essential. Thus, by the standards of behavioral consultation it is better to describe a client's hitting behavior in terms of its environmental antecedents and consequences than to describe the client as aggressive.

By focusing on current behaviors, behavioral consultation is better able to discriminate between existing and desired behavior (Bergan & Kratochwill, 1990). Such discrimination allows for defining the goals of consultation in behavioral terms. The consultant and consultee can mutually determine what behaviors currently exist and what alternative behaviors are desired; they then set behavioral goals, which create the conditions for more rigorous evaluation of the effects of consultation. Past behavior is viewed as important only to the degree that it assists in present interventions (Rimm & Cunningham, 1985). As a result, behavioral consultants do little to help consultees or the consultees' clients gain insight into their problems or concerns. Rather, they concentrate on directive and active treatment of current behavior (Kazdin, 1995).

Principles of Behavior Change

Behavioral consultation assumes that behavior is lawful (that is, orderly, following a set of rules) and that changing the consequences of behavior by using the principles of learning produces a change in behavior (Karoly & Harris, 1986; Kazdin, 1995). The consultant helps the consultee select these principles for use in the problem-solving process (Bergan & Kratochwill, 1990).

Behavior consultants use such principles as reinforcement, punishment, extinction, shaping, and modeling in the behavior change process. The consultant uses these principles to examine and understand the client's behavior, to examine the consultee's behavior, and to determine how to proceed with the course of consultation (Russell, 1978). These principles can also be used by consultees in their own work with clients.

There has been a trend to use *social learning theory* to integrate different learning paradigms. Social learning theory uses various learning models to explain behavior while emphasizing the context of events, human social development, and internal perceptions of events. Social learning theory's major contribution is its recognition of multiple influences (such as cognitions and the environment) on behavior

while at the same time offering a framework for explaining behavior (Kazdin, 1995).

For an excellent, detailed introduction to the principles of behavior, consult Kanfer and Goldstein's *Helping People Change* (1991) or Kazdin's *Behavior Modification in Applied Settings* (1995). A valuable resource for locating techniques based on behavioral principles is Bellack and Hersen's *Dictionary of Behavior Therapy Techniques* (1985).

THE CONSULTATION PROCESS

Behavioral consultation can take three forms: behavioral technology training, behavioral system consultation, and behavioral case consultation (Vernberg & Reppucci, 1986). All three forms have the following characteristics: indirect service to the client system, use of behavioral technology principles throughout the consultation process, a problem-solving orientation, and empirical validation of interventions (Vernberg & Reppucci, 1986).

Next we'll examine each of the three forms of behavioral consultation in terms of goals, the consultant's function and role, the consultee's experience in consultation, and the use of consultation techniques and procedures.

Behavioral Technology Training

This approach to behavioral consultation is used when consultees seek to increase general usage of behavioral technology principles when working with clients. Consultees tend to be professionals such as teachers (Allen & Forman, 1984), caretakers such as paraprofessionals (Jeger & McClure, 1982; Liberman, Kuehnel, Kuehnel, Eckman, & Rosenstein, 1982), or parents (Gresham & Lemanek, 1987; Kramer, 1990).

Consultants train consultees in general behavioral principles or specific behavioral technology skills (Bergan & Kratochwill, 1990; Watson & Robinson, 1996) or both (Vernberg & Reppucci, 1986; Elliot & Busse, 1993). Behavioral technology training can be formal or informal and be given to individuals (for example, in training a therapist to perform systematic desensitization) or groups (for example, in training special education teachers in token economy procedures). The education/training model of consultation discussed in Chapter 9 is similar to the process involved in behavioral technology training.

Behavioral technology training has several justifications for its existence (Vernberg & Reppucci, 1986). Consultees who use behavioral technology are frequently successful. An understanding of behavioral technology increases the likelihood that behavioral programs will be implemented appropriately. Consultees who understand behavioral technology are likely to generalize it to new situations and thus enhance all aspects of their lives. Behavioral technology is cost effective and efficient.

The goal of behavioral technology training is increased consultee competence in the use of general and/or specific behavioral technology procedures. The consultant functions as a resource person and trainer. The consultee is a trainee expected to apply learned procedures with appropriate work-related concerns. As is the case in most types of education/training consultation, the steps involved are conducting a needs assessment, planning the training, performing it, and evaluation.

Behavioral technology training usually consists of behavior modification procedures and, more recently, cognitive-behavioral approaches (Forman, 1984). It has been provided to a variety of human service professions, especially schoolteachers. It has also been used with a variety of nonprofessional caretaking roles such as parenting and paraprofessional services in human service settings. There is strong empirical evidence that behavioral technology training of consultees leads to improved client behavior (Vernberg & Reppucci, 1986).

Problems encountered in evaluation of behavioral technology training revolve around whether it is generalized to settings beyond the training and whether consultees continue to use the results of training in intended environments (Elliot & Busse, 1993). Consultants who use behavioral technology training must decide what form of this training is best for which type of consultee and under what conditions (Vernberg & Reppucci, 1986).

Behavioral technology training can be a particularly important intervention in the schools, though some authors (for example, Rosenfield, 1985) suggest that teachers tend not to use its interventions in the classroom, or, if they do, they give up on them early before the desired outcomes have developed. This happens because (1) teachers using behavioral technology are responsible for solutions to the problem, though not for the child's problem, (2) teachers' working knowledge of behavioral technology is limited, and (3) the underlying assumptions of behavioral technology may be at odds with teachers' explanations of human conduct. Rosenfield (1985) cites an example in which an elementary school teacher gave up on a successful classroom management project agreed to in consultation because her aide didn't like it.

Implications for Consultants Rosenfield (1985) has made some suggestions for consultants regarding behavioral technology training. They should be seen as resources for classroom practice and need to encourage teachers to be resource persons among themselves. Teachers should be encouraged to use techniques that allow them to put some of themselves into the implementation. It is very important that they understand the underlying assumptions of behavioral technology since they frequently modify the consultant's suggestions and must do so constructively. Consultants need to be available to teachers since some research suggests that teachers turn to resources that are convenient.

Because the language of behavior modification can cause a clash of values, consultants need to choose meaningful and acceptable words in behavioral technology training. Time should be provided at the outset of training for discussion and experiential learning related to values regarding behavioral technology. Teachers need to be in control of the use of behavioral technology and see interventions as congruent with their values. Consultants need to actively promote their suggestions rather than thinking teachers will use them because they think they will work. Behavioral consultants are advised to develop behavioral technology training with the consultee's frame of reference in mind. When working with teachers, the consultant should plan the training with their daily routine and classroom life in mind.

For interesting descriptions of behavioral technology training, consult McDougall, Reschly, and Corkery (1988); Tunnecliffe, Leach, and Tunnecliffe (1986); and Flanagan, Cray, and Meter (1983). Watson and Robinson (1996) present an interesting approach in which they incorporate behavioral technology training (via direct instructional methods) into traditional behavioral consultation.

An Example of Behavioral Technology Training A school counselor acting as a consultant conducts a three-session workshop for teachers on "Catching Students Being Good." The workshop focuses on effectively using the principles of extinction and positive reinforcement and covers an overview of the concepts and what to expect in using them, situations from the classroom that illustrate how the principles can be used effectively, and general rules for using these kinds of reinforcement. The teachers then practice using the principles in comparable classroom situations and receive feedback on their performances as well as hints for remembering to use the principles in the classroom. Finally, the consultant agrees to observe each teacher applying the principles in the classroom and to provide feedback.

Behavioral System Consultation

In behavioral system consultation, behavioral technology principles are applied to a social system (Vernberg & Reppucci, 1986). Consultants use behavioral technology principles to analyze and change interactions among the various subsystems of a larger social system, such as a school or mental health center or between two or more interactive systems. For example, a behavioral consultant might interact with the staff at a substance-abuse clinic and the staff at a halfway house for substance abusers to assure proper coordination of treatment efforts. The goal of behavioral system consultation is to enhance the efficiency and effectiveness of a system in terms of its stated functions (Vernberg & Reppucci, 1986) and to focus on the process and structure of the system itself (Vernberg & Reppucci, 1986), whereas behavioral case consultation focuses on an individual client within a system.

Behavioral system consultation is influenced by the research and theory of behavioral ecology and systems theory. Behavioral ecology, which states that humans are part of a multilevel system called an ecological environment (Willems, 1974), is a mix of individual approaches derived from traditional behavior modification and ecological approaches that study environments and social systems (Jeger & Slotnick, 1982).

The settings in which individuals operate are interdependent. For example, what happens to people in their work can affect their home life. Behavioral ecology focuses on the interactions between individuals and their environments (Jeger & Slotnick, 1982). The interaction is seen as a series of units, and a change in one unit effects change in the other units. The environment is seen as putting demands on individuals who have a variety of resources available to meet these demands. The "goodness of fit" between the demands and the resources (Jeger & Slotnick, 1982, p. 10) determines whether or not there is a problem.

When a problem is perceived, consultants are one solution. Consultative interventions in the behavioral-ecological approach are typically adaptive in nature and systems centered rather than individual centered (Jeger & Slotnick, 1982). Interventions strengthen a person's ability to adapt by increasing access to information and autonomy and by improving internal organization. In addition, such interventions take both long-term and short-term perspectives. The goal of behavioral-ecological interventions is to match the demands of the system to the resources of the persons in that environment (Jeger & Slotnick, 1982).

Because of its comprehensiveness, Maher's (1981) model of system consultation will be summarized here. Despite this model's development for use by school psychologists, its applicability is easily extended for use by other human service professionals in a variety of settings, including business and industry (Maher, 1993). Additional information on behavioral systems consultation has been incorporated from the work of Pace et al. (1995) who note that "this approach incorporates contemporary systems theory, empirically derived behavior change strategies with a focus on measurable outcomes, multiple-level intervention, and the benefits of interdisciplinary and transdiciplinary approaches" (Pace et al., 1995, p. 128). In my opinion, the work of Pace et al. (1995) might better be described as a form of behavioral systems collaboration. Readers might benefit from a review of systems theory (Chapter 8) before they read the sections that follow.

Consultation Goals   The primary goal of behavioral system consultation or collaboration is to help a social system function more effectively in terms of its stated mission. This goal is accomplished through a combination of individual, group, and system-wide interventions, the last of these being the most prevalent. The system itself is the client and the people with whom the consultant works are the consultees. For example, in a school setting, the classroom is the client system, not an individual student. Consultees' increased future functioning relative to their job duties within the system can be a secondary goal. In behavioral system collaboration, the human services professional on the team is responsible for the psychological aspects of the case. For example, a psychologist may work on a team involving a primary care physician and other caregivers.

Consultant Function and Roles As in the other types of behavioral consultation, the consultant acts as an expert, but in behavior system consultation the consultant must specifically be expert in systems theory and behavioral ecology. The consultant guides the consultee (referred to by Maher [1981] as the "referral agent") through a systematic problem-solving process and ensures that the steps of system definition, assessment, intervention, and evaluation are accomplished.

Even though the consultant is an expert in behavioral technology, systems, and behavioral ecology, the nature of the consultation relationship is collaborative; consultees participate to the degree their skills and knowledge permit. Hence, Maher's model is quite compatible with the model described by Pace et al. (1995). Although Maher (1981) is vague about whether the consultant actually participates directly in implementing the intervention, the consultee remains the primary instrument of change in the system and the consultant provides the consultee with whatever assistance is deemed necessary. As in any other form of consultation, the consultant allows the consultee complete freedom of choice. In the model proposed by Pace et al. (1995), there is the strong implication that the human services professional participates in the intervention as part of the team.

The consultant provides the consultee with whatever knowledge about the behavioral technology, systems, and behavioral ecology that is needed for successful consultation. Although Maher (1981) does not directly mention training of consultees, it can be assumed, as in Bergan's (1977) model, that some training of consultees may take place in topics crucial to the successful accomplishment of each stage of the consultation. Pace et al. (1995) note that

training by the human service worker is most likely essential.

Consultee Experience in Consultation Although Maher (1981) makes no specific statement regarding the consultee's behavior (except in reference to collaboration in the consultation process), certain assumptions can be made. Perhaps the consultee's most important function is that of decision-maker. Although the consultee and consultant are peers, in the end it is the consultee who decides how consultation is to proceed. The consultee is charged with providing the consultant with fully accurate information, which can include descriptions of the problem or of the system's parameters, suggestions for gathering data, or feedback on the feasibility of possible interventions. Further, the consultee is responsible for carrying out the implementation. (As in behavioral case consultation, the consultee may designate another party to carry out the implementation.)

Behavioral systems collaboration is similar except that there is opportunity for mutual influencing among team members and that a variety of parties can carry out different functions related to helping the patient or program.

Application: Consultation Techniques and Procedures Behavioral system consultation assumes that all or part of a system is experiencing some functional difficulty; it consists of the stages of system definition, assessment, intervention, and evaluation (Maher, 1981).

System Definition For consultation or collaboration to be successful, information must be gathered about the behavior of members of the system relative to the system's goals and structures. Thus, there are the two steps of defining the system structure and defining the system process.

In determining the *structure* of a system, the consultant and consultee or the collaborators define the system's parameters with regard to time and space, including such variables as physical setting and boundaries (for example, where the system is located), environmental design (for example, the system's physical plant), number of system members (that is, demographic data), and policies and procedures (for example, rules and regulations).

In determining the *process* of a system, the consultant and consultee or the collaborators define the system's parameters in terms of the behavior of the system's members, including such variables as assessment functions (that is, how behavior of various systems' groups will be measured), intervention functions (that is, how the system tries to change on its own), evaluation functions (that is, how the quality of the system's functions is determined), and communications functions (that is, who talks to whom, in what manner, and how often).

In defining both the structure and process of a system, the parties involved rely on observations of the system's everyday functions, written records, and interviews of key members in the system.

System Assessment Once the system's structural and process factors are known, it is time to assess the system in terms of those factors. Assessment is a joint effort of the consultant and consultee or the collaborators to gather appropriate information concerning the interrelationships among identified structures and processes using direct observation, interviews, and appropriate standardized instruments.

Assessment of the structure includes gathering data about environmental restrictions and determining the degree to which the system's operating procedures are known and followed by its members. Assessment of the system's process involves gathering information about specific behaviors of the members. The most and least productive members are determined, as are those who either facilitate or block productive behavior. Based on the system's structural and process limitations, the parties involved can then decide which parts of the system are operating adequately and which are "dysfunctional" (Maher, 1981, p. 502). The presence of dysfunctional parts of the system can point to problems that consultation/collaboration might address.

System Intervention The consultant and consultee or collaborators use three steps in system intervention to eliminate structural and process limitations: they prioritize system needs, specify behavioral outcomes goals, and design and implement intervention programs.

The parties involved first decide which needs should be addressed first. Second, they specify goals, stated in behavioral terms, that are concrete and measurable. Such goals set the direction of subsequent interventions and allow for rigorous evaluation of consultation efforts. Third, they design and implement a program to meet those goals. An array of programs is generated, and the advantages and disadvantages as well as the human, technological, informational, and financial resources required for each are determined and evaluated. Based on the outcome, the consultant and consultee or collaborators choose and implement the most appropriate plan, which may target all or part of the organization/system.

System Evaluation This stage evaluates the intervention program operations and system change.

In evaluating the operations of the intervention program, the parties involved determine whether the program was implemented in the way intended and with the results expected. This in turn helps to determine which activities were responsible for the outcome and to modify the program for future use. Information is sought on the utilization of human resources involved in the program, the extent to which data has been collected according to plan, and the presence of positive and/or negative side effects. One method of evaluation is retrospective reporting, in which those involved in the program are interviewed for their views of how things went. A second method is the observation of participants while they are engaged in the program.

In evaluating system change, the participants determine what structural and process changes occurred and how these changes influenced the system's operation relative to the set goal. They also determine the degree to which observed changes were due to the intervention, not extraneous factors. If behavior in the system changes in the desired direction, the change is attributed to the program. For example, Cooper and Newbold (1994) report an effective use of behavioral systems consultation in which a small and large group feedback was employed to help employees develop more safety with regard to lifting, equipment use, and hand/body positioning.

An Example of Behavioral System Consultation A human service professor from a university is consulting with a human service agency about enhancing its effectiveness. The consultant and the designated consultee first define the system in terms of its structure and process. While the first of these is easy, it takes them quite a bit longer to define the system's process. They examine each of the agency's subsystems (for example, the technological subsystem, which consists of the case workers) in terms of how communication takes place, how the behavior of the subsystem is measured and evaluated, and how the subsystem attempts to solve its own problems.

After defining the system, the consultant guides the consultee in assessing the interaction between the identified structural and process factors. They determine that part of the system's limitations is due to poor "top-down" communication and lack of adequate autonomy for the agency's case workers.

In intervening to rectify the matter, they identify poor "top-down" communication as the most important problem. They set the objective of having a regular weekly staff meeting in which all participants are allowed to submit agenda items and all important information is discussed. In addition, the final 10 minutes of each meeting is allocated for discussion of any topic that an individual wants to bring up.

The consultant and consultee generate three possible programs, weigh their advantages and disadvantages, and decide that the consultant will be a participant/observer at the first meeting and will provide feedback to the group. Based on this feedback, the group will decide how to modify procedures for conducting subsequent staff meetings. Following this intervention, the consultee agrees to monitor staff meetings on a regular basis to make sure the desired changes in "top-down" communication indeed occur. The changes in the system are evaluated six months later by surveying the staff.

Behavioral Case Consultation

In *behavioral case consultation* a consultant provides direct, behavior-based service to a consultee concerning the management of a client or group of clients assigned to the consultee.

Until recently the term *behavioral consultation* was identified with behavioral case consultation. Most case approaches to behavioral consultation (for example, Bergan & Kratochwill, 1990; Gutkin & Curtis, 1982; Keller, 1981; Kuehnel & Kuehnel, 1983a, 1983b; Russell, 1978) still rely heavily on operant conditioning. However, more recent models use a variety of models such as the social learning theory developed by Bandura (1977). By far the most comprehensive approach to behavioral case consultation is that of Bergan and Kratochwill (1990); indeed, most other models are basic variations of Bergan's (1977) original model. Behavioral case consultation consists of a series of stages that provide form and focus to the problem solving engaged in by the consultant and consultee (Kratochwill et al., 1995). The challenge of behavioral consultation is to "select treatment strategies from a pool of potentially effective strategies that can be . . . managed by people who have not had specific training in behavioral change methods" (Elliot & Busse, 1993, p. 180).

Consultation Goals In behavioral case consultation, the consultee presents a work-related concern with a client to the consultant, who uses expertise in the principles of learning to "manage the consultee's management of the case," that is, to help the consultee make positive changes in the client's environment (Feld et al., 1987) and therefore in the client's behavior (Tombari & Davis, 1979). Recently, some authorities on behavioral consultation (for example, Hawryluk & Smallwood, 1986; Bergan & Kratochwill, 1990) have suggested that a second, complementary goal is to effect change in the consultee. This goal is necessary when factors related to both the consultee and the client affect the problem (Hawryluk & Smallwood,

1986; Russell, 1978). Keller (1981) even suggests that behavioral case consultation can be consultee centered, enhancing the consultee's professional functioning.

Consultant Function and Roles Behavioral consultants use a systematic problem-solving process to assist consultees with their clients (Bergan & Kratochwill, 1990). Behavioral consultants frequently act as experts to ensure that the stages of problem identification, problem analysis, plan implementation, and problem evaluation occur and are adequately accomplished.

Although the consultant is called on to provide expertise, most behavioral consultants take a collaborative approach to the consultation relationship. Even though the content and process of consultation are under the consultant's control, the consultee is encouraged to become involved in content- and process-related decision making to the degree his or her knowledge and skill in the behavioral approach permit. The consultant helps the consultee determine the best course of action in the case and suggests an array of choices from which he or she can choose (Tombari & Davis, 1979). Because the consultee is the primary instrument of change in the client, the consultant avoids giving direct advice or dictating the consultee's behavior (Tombari & Davis, 1979).

The consultant provides knowledge concerning those principles of learning pertinent to the case and whatever knowledge is needed to help the consultee accomplish each of the consultation stages. In some cases, the consultant must train the consultee in the use of strategies based on principles of learning. However, Bergan's model does not emphasize consultee training to a great degree.

To ensure that the stages of consultation occur and are successfully accomplished, the

TABLE 11.1   Classification of Verbal Interchanges

MESSAGE SOURCE	MESSAGE CONTENT	MESSAGE PROCESS	MESSAGE CONTROL
Consultant	Background/environment	Specification	Elicitor
Consultee	Behavior-setting	Evaluation	Emitter
	Behavior	Inference	
	Individual characteristics	Summarization	
	Observation	Validation	
	Plan		
	Other		

consultant guides the consultee's behavior through the use of selected types of verbalizations. Thus, the consultant makes sure that problem identification occurs, but the consultee controls the process whereby identification of the problem occurs. The consultant must inform the consultee about the use of this form of management at the outset of consultation and be satisfied that he or she is seeking services voluntarily. Management of the consultation process by using verbal skills in structuring the consultant-consultee interaction is, then, the major task of the consultant.

Verbal Interaction Techniques Because consultation can be reduced to a series of verbal interactions between the consultant and the consultee, these interactions must not be left to chance (Bergan & Kratochwill, 1990). The consultant controls not only his or her own verbalizations, but also those of the consultee. There is some empirical support that the content of the consultee's responses tends to match that of the consultant's questions, thus providing the consultant with a tremendous amount of influence in controlling all aspects of the consultation process (Turco & Skinner, 1991). There is also some evidence to suggest that consultants with high dominance scores on personality inventories are perceived as more

effective by consultees (Erchul, 1987). The consultant does not attempt to control the specific content of the consultee's verbalizations during consultation, but rather attempts to encourage him or her to produce the various type of verbalizations needed to achieve the task at hand in the consultation process.

Bergan produced a classification system to assist consultants in controlling the verbalizations in consultation (see Table 11.1). Verbal interchanges can be classified in terms of message source, content, process, and control. Judicious use of this classification system can enable the consultant to successfully guide the consultee through the consultation process.

Message Source The message source simply indicates whether the verbalization comes from the consultant or the consultee.

Message Content Message content refers to what is discussed by the consultant and the consultee. The consultant usually controls the content of verbalizations in consultation, which includes seven subcategories: background/ environment, behavior setting, behavior, individual characteristics, observation, plan, and other. The verbalizations that occur in behavioral case consultation are to be controlled by the consultant because what is talked about in consultation directly relates to the course and degree of success of the consultation. By determining what to discuss and when, the consultant can help the consultee work with the client more efficiently and effectively.

Message Process Consultants control not only the things that are talked about but also the way in which they are discussed—the message process. Consultant-consultee verbal exchanges can be categorized by type of verbal process. As noted by Bergan (1977), "the message-process category classifies verbal messages in accordance with the kinds of speaker actions they describe vis-a-vis the content of conversation" (p. 38). Process, then, refers to the type of verbal action conveyed in a message. The five message-process subcategories are specification, evaluation, inference, summarization, and validation. Each of these processes can describe what is occurring in each of the content subcategories. Consider the content subcategory "plan." By using each of the processes, the plan could be specified, evaluated, inferred about, summarized, or validated. The consultant, then, should know not only what to talk about, but the way in which it should be talked about.

Message Control The consultant is charged with guiding the consultee through a successful consultation experience and must control the consultee's verbal behavior to do so. To this end, the consultant must determine, not only what (content) and how things are to be discussed (process), but also who is going to talk about them (control). In effect, the consultant uses message control to either give input or to get input from the consultee. (The consultee can also use message control for the same purpose.)

In message control behavior, the speaker's verbiage is classified in terms of whether or not it will have a direct effect on the receiver's re-

sponse. If a direct verbal response is intended (and is thus considered controlling), the message is called an *elicitor*. If the message is not intended to obtain a direct response (and thus does not control the receiver's response), it is termed an *emitter*.

Elicitors usually take the form of either direct or indirect questions that ask the consultee to engage in specification, evaluation, inference, summarization, or validation in one of the message content subcategories. The consultant could ask the consultee to use a verbal process about the conditions affecting the client's behavior, the behavior itself, related observations, or pertinent plans. There is some evidence that being specific when questioning consultees is related to the effectiveness of consultation (Anderson, Kratochwill, & Bergan, 1986).

An emitter does not call for a reaction from the listener. When consultants use emitters, they provide both content and process information to consultees without attempting to control the consultee's response. Emitters usually take the form of declarative statements.

Consultee Experience in Consultation
The consultee is expected to work with the consultant toward the successful completion of the consultation process and to be actively involved in the problem-solving process (Martens, 1993). As in other forms of case consultation, such as Caplan's (1970) client-centered case consultation, the consultee is a link between the consultant and the client and functions as a professional collaborator. The consultee's four primary duties in the consultation process are to specify or describe, to evaluate or decide, to provide direct services to the client, and to supervise the client's actions.

The consultee should describe as specifically as possible the details of the case and the nature of the work-related problem. The consultee should respond to the consultant's prompts and probes as accurately as possible and provide him or her with the most comprehensive, detailed picture of the work-related concern possible.

The consultee's role as evaluator or decision maker reflects the peer nature of all consultation: the consultant may make a recommendation concerning a case, but it is the consultee's task to determine what to do with that recommendation. Bergan (1977) relates an example of this consultee role in noting that the consultant might help the consultee select a method for measuring client behavior, but the consultee would have to evaluate that measurement's effectiveness in achieving desired outcomes.

Of course, a primary role of the consultee is to continue to work with the client. Such work can include performing a particular caregiving role relative to the client (for example, teacher to student or counselor to client) and collecting data regarding the client's behavior. Frequently, the consultee's work with the client will be adaptations of the consultant's recommendations. A critical part of the consultee's work with the client involves the client in the selection of the goals and processes of consultation; this is frequently accomplished by having the consultee discuss with the client what the consultant and consultee are thinking about doing concerning the client.

A final (and relatively rare) consultee role is that of supervisor, as when a consultee is a teacher and the client is a student under that teacher's responsibility. However, the consultee may also supervise the involvement of other people working on the client's treatment. For example, a teacher who is a consultee may supervise a teacher's aide who is collecting baseline data on a student's (the client's) behavior.

Application: Consultant Techniques and Procedures Both types of behavioral case consultation—developmental and problem-centered—concern changes in client behavior (Bergan, 1977). Developmental consultation deals with more or less long-term behavior change, whereas problem-centered consultation deals with problems that call for immediate attention (for example, crises). Most of the literature on behavioral case consultation refers to developmental consultation because it is by far the more extensively used, and thus our discussion of behavioral case consultation will be limited to developmental consultation.

According to Bergan and Kratochwill (1990), there are four stages to the behavioral consultation process. The first stage consists of the *Problem Identification Interview* (PII) during which the consultant focuses on "the specification of a problem by emphasizing the selection and definition of a target behavior and by the determination of baseline data collection procedures" (Krathochwill, Elliot, & Busse, 1995, p. 87). Problem analysis and plan implementation are dealt with through the *Problem Analysis Interview* (PAI). The objectives of this interview "are to validate the problem through examination of baseline data, analyze the problem and related variable, . . . and develop an intervention plan" (Kratochwill, Elliot, & Busse, 1995, p. 88). During the third stage, plan implementation, the consultant is "on call" as the consultee implements the plan. The fourth stage of consultation is accomplished through the *Treatment Evaluation Interview* (TEI) during which the consultant and consultee assess the degree of success in meeting the plan's goals. There are typically three to four sessions between the consultant and the consultee in this model.

Problem Identification Stage This stage provides the momentum for the entire consultation process (Tombari & Davis, 1979; Kratochwill, Elliot, & Busse, 1995). The term *problem identification* sounds quite simple, but from a behavioral perspective defining the problem can be a complex and difficult matter. This stage is crucial because what occurs in it will determine the direction that consultation takes (Tombari & Davis, 1979; Witt & Elliot, 1983) and affects whether or not consultation will be successful (Feld et al., 1987). In fact, this stage is considered the most critical because its outcome is the formulation and implementation of a plan (Kratochowill et al., 1995). Bergan and Tombari (1976) found that if the problem identification stage was not successfully completed, the entire consultation process might be irreversibly damaged. How well consultees define problems has received some attention in consultation research (see Conoley & Conoley, 1992).

During the problem identification process, the consultant helps the consultee accomplish the following steps:

1. Designate the general and specific client performance goals to be achieved in consultation.

2. Determine how to measure the designated goals.

3. Assess current client performance in terms of the designated goals.

4. Examine the results of the assessment.

5. Discern the discrepancy between current and desired client performance.

These steps are accomplished by two consultant-led interviews, the first a problem identification interview in which Steps One and Two are accomplished. Step Three is accomplished by the consultee. The second is a follow-up interview in which Steps Four and Five are accomplished. The problem identification stage ends once the discrepancy between current and desired client behavior has been specified (Feld et al., 1987).

In the problem identification stage, the consultant uses more elicitors than emitters—more specifications, validations, and summarizations than inferences and evaluations—and more verbalizations in the behavior, behavior-setting, and observation categories than in other content categories.

When successfully accomplished, the problem identification stage results in a well-specified problem defined by the discrepancy between current performance (as measured by collected data) and desired performance (as indicated by stated goals) (Feld et al., 1987). Successful problem identification sets the stage for problem analysis.

Problem Analysis Stage In this stage the consultant determines the conditions maintaining the client's problem behavior and formulates a plan to alleviate that behavior. The consultant jointly pursues these two tasks with the consultee. This stage can thus be divided into two phases that contain a total of five steps:

Phase 1: Problem Analysis

1. Choose a procedure for analyzing the problem.

2. Conduct a conditions and/or skills analysis.

Phase 2: Plan Formulation

3. Develop plan strategies.

4. Develop plan tactics.

5. Establish procedures for assessing the plan's effectiveness.

These steps are accomplished by means of one or more interviews, during which the client's problem behavior is examined from one of two perspectives: internal and external conditions related to the behavior, or a skills deficit in the client. The consultant and consul-tee must first decide whether to conduct an analysis of the conditions surrounding the be-havior, the skills of the client, or both. Bergan and Kratochwill (1990) suggest that a condi-tions analysis be performed if the problem be-havior tends to be variable over conditions; if the problem behavior remains constant over conditions, then a skills analysis is recom-mended, as is the case when increased self-direction on the part of the client is desired. Once the consultant and consultee decide on which type of analysis to perform, Step One is accomplished.

In Step Two, conducting an analysis of the problem, the consultant and consultee work together to determine what conditions and/or skills need to be changed to resolve the client's problem successfully.

Consultation next enters Step Three, devel-oping plan strategies, during which a system-atic course of action to use with the client is developed. The consultant usually starts out by suggesting a broad strategy that seems promis-ing based on the conditions or skills analysis performed earlier. In general, the consultant and consultee determine which principles of learning should be used and convert them into strategies to help the client. For example, a consultant might suggest using positive rein-forcement as a strategy to change the client's behavior but allow the consultee flexibility in its use.

In Step Four, the consultant and consultee consider the tactics involved in implementing the strategy, and in Step Five they establish pro-cedures for determining the plan's effectiveness. If a conditions analysis was performed, then those same techniques are used for assessment purposes. If a skills analysis was performed, then methods for measuring skill acquisition need to

be used. Bergan and Kratochwill (1990) suggest that items used in the skills analysis be adapted to measure skill acquisition. Once assessment procedures have been established, consultation moves to the plan implementation stage. The bottom line is that the consultant and consultee develop a plan that is acceptable both objec-tively (i.e., empirically sound) and subjectively (i.e., mutually acceptable) (Sheridan, Kratoch-will, & Bergan, 1996).

In the problem analysis stage, as in the ear-lier problem identification stage, the consul-tant uses more elicitors than emitters and more specifications, validations, and summa-rizations than inferences and evaluations. Whereas the problem identification stage had a balance of verbalizations in the behavior, behavior-setting, and observation subcate-gories, the problem analysis stage has a balance of verbalizations in the behavior, behavior-setting, and plan subcategories. The problem analysis stage builds naturally on the problem identification stage (Kratochwill, Elliot, & Busse, 1995).

Plan Implementation Stage The result of suc-cessful problem analysis is a plan designed to assist the client system. In this stage, what was planned during the problem analysis stage is put into effect. Good planning does not neces-sarily lead to good implementation, and thus the consultant's task is to ensure adequate implementation. To this end, the consultant guides the consultee in accomplishing two steps of this stage: preparing for and carrying out the implementation. This stage is different from the previous two stages in that there is no formal interview between the consultant and the consultee.

In preparing for plan implementation, roles related to the implementation are assigned, required materials are gathered, and skills necessary for implementation are affirmed. The consultee generally takes the roles of the plan implementation director, plan executor, and observer of client behavior. The consultant is responsible for determining the need for and providing any training of the consultee (or a designee of the consultee) to adequately perform these roles. Training can be very time consuming, so any plans should take the strengths of consultees into consideration (Tombari & Davis, 1979; Kratochwill, Elliot, & Busse, 1995). Once the appropriate roles have been assigned and arrangements for use of materials made, the consultant and consultee implement the plan, during which the consultee attempts to help the client with the consultant's guidance. Plans should be time efficient, least restrictive, and of low risk to the client system (Kratochwill, Elliot, & Busse, 1995). The consultant is available to assist with any revisions to the plan that become necessary as the implementation proceeds.

Treatment Evaluation Stage Behavioral case consultation stresses evaluation of consultation more than any other model of consultation (Tombari & Davis, 1979). Considerable time is spent evaluating the goals of consultation and the effectiveness of the plan, which determine what happens next in the consultation process. The problem evaluation stage has three steps: evaluating goal attainment, evaluating plan effectiveness, and postimplementation planning (Bergan, 1977). In reality, plan evaluation is often not as rigorous as that used in research, but nonetheless there needs to be adequate support to verify outcomes. For example, outcome criteria should involve measures of the degree to which desired behaviors were demonstrated over time (Kratochwill, Elliot, & Busse, 1995).

Goal attainment is assessed by determining whether the client's behavior change adequately met previously set standards. Recall that the problem was defined in terms of a discrepancy between current and desired levels of behavior. In evaluation, the degree to which desired and observed behaviors coincide is judged to determine whether the goals of consultation have been met. There is some evidence to suggest that multiple measures should be used in behavioral consultation (see, for example, Fuchs & Fuchs, 1989).

There are three possibilities in terms of goal attainment: no progress, some progress, and accomplishment. If there has been no progress, the consultant typically suggests a return to the problem analysis stage, or perhaps to the goal identification step within the problem identification stage. In some situations, consultation may be terminated and replaced by another type of service. If there is some progress in goal attainment, the consultant usually suggests a return to the problem analysis stage. On occasion, the consultant might suggest a return to the problem identification stage to reexamine goals; on rare occasions, he or she might recommend termination. If the goals have been accomplished, the consultant and consultee proceed to evaluate the plan's effectiveness.

Behavioral consultants believe that even though the goals of consultation have been achieved, an appropriate design must be used in evaluating the plan so as to demonstrate that the plan was indeed responsible for the success of consultation (Feld et al., 1987). Plan evaluation has no direct bearing on the case, but it can be used in solving similar concerns in the future. Plan effectiveness is determined by applying an appropriate evaluation design that states when client behaviors are to be measured and when plan implementations are made relative to those measurements. Interested readers should consult Bergan and Kratochwill (1990) for a discussion on evaluation design, for such a detailed discussion is beyond the scope of this book.

Step Three in problem evaluation is postimplementation planning. The consultant and consultee design a plan for use after consultation has formally been terminated. Such a plan prevents the problem from recurring and provides a way for the consultee to reestablish contact should the problem behavior return to undesirable levels. Sometimes this plan is left intact and maintained, especially when it is relatively easy to implement and when there is some likelihood that the client's behavior would return were the plan eliminated. A new plan is often implemented when it is determined that it is as effective but more convenient than the first plan. Moving from tangible to nontangible reinforcers is a common example of this type of strategy. Finally, a program can be removed once it has been determined that it is no longer needed to maintain the performance levels desired of the client. Whatever the postimplementation plan, behavioral consultants suggest that consultees continue to monitor client behavior for some period of time.

When the goals of consultation and the implementation plan have been evaluated and postimplementation plans made, consultation is terminated. During this stage, the consultant uses a balance of elicitors and emitters; more specifications, summarizations, validations, and inferences than evaluations; and more verbalizations in the behavior, plan, and observation subcategories.

On occasion, the consultant may want to formally communicate the results of an intervention program to a consultee. Figure 11.1 illustrates the format for such a report.

An Example of Behavioral Case Consultation. A counselor working as a mental health consultant is assisting a family therapist with a family. The consultant has expertise concerning runaway youths. Two of the family's three teenagers have run away. The family therapist wants to consult with the counselor before using certain interventions with the family.

Together, the consultant and consultee define what is meant by "running away" behavior. They functionally analyze the behavior in terms of what occurs before and after its occurrence and devise a plan based on rewarding responsible behavior that has the goal of decreasing the target behavior. The consultee then implements the strategy with the family and evaluates it at its conclusion.

CONJOINT BEHAVIORAL CONSULTATION

There is a trend in behavioral consultation in schools to use parents and teachers as conjoint consultees (Colton & Sheridan, 1998; Sheridan, 1997; Sheridan & Kratochwill, 1992; Sheridan, Kratochwill, & Bergan, 1996; Sheridan, Kratochwill, & Elliot, 1990). This method consists of involvement of teacher-parent pairs who together serve as consultees (Sheridan, Kratochwill, & Bergan, 1996). Designed to bridge the gap between the school and the home and maximize the spread of effects from one setting to another, conjoint behavioral consultation emphasizes continuous data collection and programming between the school, home, and community. This approach has been a logical step in attempting to link the significant settings in a student's life such

I. Background Information

    A. Demographic Information on the Child

    B. Ecological Context of the Problem

II. Problem Definition.

    A. Referral Problem

    B. Target Behavior

    C. Desired Outcome Behaviors

    D. Critical Setting/Situations for Change

    E. Preliminary Functional Analysis

III. Problem Analysis

    A. Description of Assessment or Data Recording Procedures

    B. Rationale for Use of Data Collection Procedures

    C. Presentation and Discussion of Data

IV. Intervention Plan

    A. Basic Design

    B. Contingencies

    C. Criterion for Contingencies

    D. Acceptability of Interventions to Teacher/Parent and Child

    E. Personnel Involved in Intervention Implementation

    F. Setting and Time

    G. Resources

    H. Procedures for Promoting New Behaviors

    I. Procedures for Increasing Existing Behaviors

    J. Procedures for Reducing Interfering Problem Behaviors

    K. Procedures for Facilitating Generalizations

    L. Treatment Integrity Checks

V. Plan Evaluation

    A. Change in Behavior via Direct Observation

    B. Change in Teacher/Parent Performance Ratings

    C. Mainstreamed Peer Comparison

    D. Outcome Interview with Significant Adults

    E. Intervention Side Effects

VI. Summary and Recommendations

    A. Summary and Results Obtained

    B. Discussion of Effectiveness

    C. Suggestions for Increasing Program Effectiveness

    D. Suggestions for Future Follow-Up

SOURCE: From Kratochwill, T. R., Elliot, S. N., and P. Carrington Rotto (1995). In A. Thomas and J. Grimes (Eds.), *Best practices in school psychology* (3rd ed., pp. 519–537). Washington, DC: National Association of School Psychologists. By permission of the publisher.

FIGURE 11.1   Outline for Writing a Behavioral Consultation Case Report

as home, school, and primary community arenas (Kratochwill, Elliot, & Carrington Rotto, 1995). Conjoint behavioral consultation is defined as "a structured, indirect form of service-delivery, in which parents and others are joined to work together to address the academic, social, or behavioral needs of an individual for whom both parties bear some responsibility" (Sheridan & Kratochwill, 1992, p. 122). Although the addition of more consultees complicates this approach, the benefits can be more than worth the costs. For example, this approach can expedite change across the home and school settings.

Although this approach has some empirical validity, it is in its infancy. This consultation approach serves the two goals of bridging the gap between the home and the school and maximizing the potential of treatment effects in both places. Due to the increased attention this model is receiving, I include a summary of it here. Bear in mind that this model builds directly upon that of Bergan and Kratochwill (1990).

COLLABORATION FROM A BEHAVIORAL PERSPECTIVE

Very little has been written about behavioral collaboration as distinct from behavioral consultation. This is most likely due to the fact that much of behavioral consultation is practiced in the schools and many of the professionals in the typical school are not familiar with the intricacies of implementing behavioral interventions to the degree that treatment integrity can be ensured. As a result, the human service professional often has no choice but to take on an expert mode of consultation. The use of behavioral collaboration can be increased by individ-

ual organizations making effective use of behavioral technology training. To the degree that other professionals can become skilled in behavioral interventions, behavioral collaboration can become a frequently used service. Another way to increase the use of behavioral collaboration is for the human service professionals to provide direct service to the client system while providing consultation to the consultee. In that way, the professional is taking some specific as well as general responsibility for the outcome of the case.

SUMMARY, TRENDS, AND CONCLUSIONS

Summary

Behavioral consultation is a process in which a consultant uses the principles of learning to assist one or more consultees having a work-related problem with a client or client system. Behavioral consultation owes its heritage primarily to behavior therapy and behavioral psychology. The boundaries of behavioral consultation tend to expand in direct relationship to advances in these two areas.

The result of all behavioral consultation is a change in behavior in the client, the consultee, or both that is accomplished through a systematic problem-solving process. The consultant-consultee relationship is a collaborative one in which the consultant is an expert who guides the consultee through the consultation process using the principles of learning.

Behavioral consultation can be performed in case, system, or training approaches. In the case approach, by far the most common, the consultant helps the consultee manage a client's case. It has changed little since it was formulated

---

CASE 11.1   Behavioral Collaboration for School Consultants

Monica is a school-based consultant in an inner-city elementary school. She has received extensive training in behavioral case consultation and cognitive behavioral interventions. Her consultee is Jose, a fifth-grade math/science teacher. Jose has participated in some behavioral technology training sessions in the recent past.

In their first two meetings, Monica and Jose engaged in problem identification and analysis. Jose reported that he was having difficulties with four aggressive boys in one of his classes. Jose was concerned that the children in his class were not learning enough because of the time he had to spend "keeping his thumbs on" the boys, who exhibited verbal and physical forms of aggression to their classmates and each other. Jose was worried about the harm they were causing. He felt that they were well on their way to dropping out, and he wanted to do everything he could to keep them in school.

For one week Monica had Jose write down his descriptions of exactly what the boys did when they were "verbally and physically aggressive." In the meantime, she observed the boys in Jose's classroom on three different days and did the same thing. Based on a comparison of their notes, they came to a consensus on operationalizing the behaviors that were problematic. In

their analysis they examined the boys' behavior, the classroom conditions, and Jose's behavior at the time the undesirable behaviors were emitted. It was found that Jose used proximity control and appropriate verbal responses to the boys when they were acting out, as well as the "assertive discipline" techniques that were prescribed schoolwide. In analyzing the boys' behavior, they came to the conclusion that their verbal and physical aggression was due to poor anger-coping techniques. The boys came to math class right after a physical education class, whose focus was competitive sports. The boys seemed to be angry when they or their teammates didn't do particularly well in competition.

The physical education teacher wanted nothing to do with the attempt to help the boys and said, "If they can't cut it now, they never will." So Monica and Jose determined that the boys needed training in anger-coping skills but also, and most importantly, the ability to demonstrate the newly learned skills in Jose's classroom. So Monica agreed to counsel the boys using a cognitive behavioral and coping skills approach to anger control. As far as the consultation process with Jose went, he agreed to monitor the boys' behavior in the classroom and cue them when necessary to implement

their newly learned skills. When they effectively used their coping skills, Jose would reward the boys with tokens that could be used to "buy" a variety of items Jose had for rewarding good conduct and academic achievement.

Jose implemented his monitoring program at the same time Monica began the coping skills training. Jose's charts showed slow but steady decreases in the boys' verbal and physical aggression. He contacted Monica on a couple of occasions to make sure that he was accurately identifying the boys' attempts to use their coping skills. After Monica had finished the training group, she met with Jose one more time to plan how he was going to fade the cueing and reward system over the semester.

Commentary

Notice how this case nicely illustrates collaboration using a behavioral model. Both Monica and Jose own a piece of the helping "pie." At the same time Monica uses her expertise to assist Jose in developing a token economy program for the boys. She also follows up with him periodically to help him with the details of the program. This case shows how consultants, through collaboration, can serve the client system directly while assisting a fellow collaborator to work more effectively with that same client system.

---

by Bergan in 1977 (Noell & Witt, 1996). In the system approach, a system or some part of it is modified through use of behavioral principles. Behavioral technology training consultation involves training the consultee in the use of general and/or specific behavioral principles for future use with clients and client systems.

The basic assumptions of behavioral consultation are that behavior can be viewed scientifically, overt and current behavior is the focus of change, and behavior is lawful and subject to systematic change. Among the procedures advocated by behavioral consultants are use of direct assessment, operationalization of goals, objective

CASE 11.2   Behavioral Consultation for Community Consultants

The consultee is a qualified mental retardation specialist with Washington County Citizens for the Handicapped, an organization that operates a six-resident intermediate care facility for the mentally retarded (ICF-MR). As a qualified professional, the consultee is responsible for ensuring that "active treatment" is provided for each resident in accordance with state and federal regulations governing ICF-MR group homes. The consultant was asked to help the consultee develop an appropriate program for each demonstrated need.

The 30-year-old client, Ms. Jones, has been demonstrating aggressive behaviors: striking other home members and some of the staff, particularly a female staff member. The consultee wanted assistance in developing a behavior program to increase Ms. Jones's positive social behavior and reduce her unacceptable behaviors in a nonrestrictive manner that would not violate her client rights.

The consultant built rapport with the consultee during the first session as they discussed Ms. Jones. They defined *striking* as hitting out at another and *socially appropriate behavior* as smiling at others, being next to others without striking, talking to others about routine matters, and engaging in social activities while following any rules.

The consultant then observed the client for five consecutive days at 15-minute intervals for one hour each in the morning and the evening during social activities. A graph of the incidence of striking behavior showed that Ms. Jones tended to strike out at others in the evening during social activities. Her socially appropriate behavior index was fairly average during other times. The consultant and the consultee agreed that it would be important to create a reinforcement program for Ms. Jones so as to increase the number of socially appropriate behaviors during the evening hours.

During the next session they discussed Ms. Jones's strengths and skills as well as environmental conditions that might be influencing her striking out behavior. By applying their mutual knowledge bases to the problem, they agreed that Ms. Jones tended to sit by Mr. Smith. Whenever she was not sitting by Mr. Smith in the evenings, she tended to strike at another group member, typically another female. She did not have a history of striking at Mr. Smith.

Based on this and other observations, the consultant and consultee developed a program that involved a type of "time out" procedure in which Ms. Jones would be escorted to her room any time she attempted to strike anyone. She would then be free to leave her room and join in social activities after a 10-minute period. Ms. Jones was also rewarded with additional activity therapy time when she fulfilled the token economy procedures indicated in her treatment plan. The program called for a 90 percent decrease in the striking behavior and a 30 percent increase in socially acceptable behaviors.

The program was approved by the Human Rights Committee and was signed by the client's guardian. The consultee implemented the program with the consultant being "on call" for any monitoring that was needed. It was obvious that within one month of implementing the plan, Ms. Jones had almost totally stopped her striking-out behavior and had significantly increased the frequency of her socially acceptable behaviors.

Further data and information were gathered and analyzed. Every indication was that the plan was a success. In a final interview the consultant and consultee reviewed the case. Both were pleased with Ms. Jones's success, but they still wondered what part Mr. Smith had played in influencing her behavior.

Commentary

This case nicely illustrates the use of behavioral consultation in a somewhat delicate situation. The case also demonstrates one of the premises of behavioral consultation, namely, that the cause of a behavior does not necessarily have to be understood to effectively change that behavior. Notice how the consultant and consultee worked together in reinforcing the appropriate target behaviors exhibited by Ms. Jones while at the same time enforcing consequences for inappropriate behavior. Clearly, behavioral consultation focuses on assessing and operationalizing behavior prior to intervening. This strength of behavior consultation suggests to consultants the critical nature of knowing what it is that is to be changed through an intervention.

measurement of target behaviors, and assessment of both the goals of consultation and the consultation plan. Behavior consultation has been successfully applied in a variety of settings but is most frequently used when there are high levels of client or system control.

Trends

The major trends in behavioral consultation are linked to developments in behavior therapy and behavioral psychology; findings in these areas are quickly incorporated into the practices of behavioral consultants.

A major trend in the field is the expansion of behavioral consultation to include behavioral system and behavioral technology training approaches, which has allowed the field to move beyond traditional case consultation. An example of this trend is the work of Martens and Witt (1988), who discuss the utility of a systems approach to classroom behavior change. The focus of treatment is not on solving an immediate problem, but rather on improving the overall ability of the classroom to "function as an interactive system capable of self-regulation" (Martens & Witt, 1988, p. 272).

Instead of relying solely on the current abilities of the consultee, consultants now are taking increasing responsibility for assessment and are teaching intervention procedures to consultees (Noell, 1996). Direct behavioral consultation (Watson & Robinson, 1996) has been receiving increasing attention. This model differs from traditional behavioral case consultation in that the consultant avoids didactic instruction in teaching consultees the skills necessary to effectively implement interventions. For example, instructional methods include role playing, modeling, and coaching.

Another trend in behavioral consultation is an increased tendency to include other forms of behavioral technology in addition to those based on operant conditioning, classical conditioning, and observational learning. The cognitive-behavioral and behavioral ecology movements have made strong headway and now have a place in all behavioral consultation approaches (Vernberg & Reppucci, 1986). Cognitive behavioral theory has greatly expanded the number of potential interventions available to consultants and permits more flexibility in developing plans (Lochman, Lampron, Gemmer, Harris, & Wyckoff, 1990; Meyers & Yelich, 1989).

Behavioral consultants are becoming increasingly aware that the success of any approach to behavioral consultation is in part determined by the environment in which consultation occurs (Dickinson & Bradshaw, 1992). Behavioral consultants now tend to more fully consider organizational issues such as the consultee institution's history and structure (Forman, 1984; Hughes, 1980; Reppucci, 1977; Reppucci & Saunders, 1983). In educational settings, behavioral consultants tend to work more closely with teachers in helping them enhance their instructional and behavioral management of classrooms (Feld et al., 1987).

In terms of the consultant-consultee relationship, behavioral consultants are devoting more attention to the development of relationships based on rapport with their consultees and the consultee variables that may affect the success of consultation (Hawryluk & Smallwood, 1986). As Rosenfield (1991) notes: "Behavioral consultants need to attend to factors such as communication strategies that facilitate shared responsibility as well as to understand consultees' explanations for their problems and their treatment expectations" (p. 329).

Behavioral consultation methods, traditionally used in school and hospital settings, are increasingly being used in business and industry settings. For example, behavioral systems approaches have been used to increase the frequency of occurrence of safe lifting behaviors among workers (Cooper & Newbold, 1994).

Conclusions

The major contribution of behavioral consultation has been its emphasis on approaching consultation in a systematic way. Consultants can be taught to perform behavioral consultation in a straightforward, step-by-step manner, which has reinforced the view that consultation is a sequential process made up of identifiable stages. There is considerable evidence that behavioral consultation is effective (Erchul & Schulte, 1996).

A second major contribution of behavioral consultation, its emphasis on specifics, has contributed to more effective methods in setting the goals of consultation, gathering data on the perceived problem, and most importantly, in evaluating the effects of consultation. Behavioral consultation's emphasis on specifics and measurement has encouraged consultants to be more accountable for their consultation efforts. Further, behavioral consultation's emphasis on specifics has allowed it to have the most research activity and empirical support among consultation models (Sheridan, Kratochwill, & Bergan, 1996).

Behavioral consultation has also emphasized treatment acceptability, treatment integrity, and treatment evaluation. More than any other model, behavioral consultation has focused on ensuring that consultees implement plans that they believe are satisfactory, that they

are skilled to accomplish and that they, along with the consultant, agree need to be rigorously evaluated.

Another contribution of behavioral consultation is the training of consultants in techniques from behavioral and cognitive-behavioral approaches to counseling and psychotherapy. Hence, schoolteachers are frequently able to use behavior modification procedures, and many counselors can use stress inoculation training.

Behavioral consultation is not without its limitations and criticisms. Limitations include lack of standardization of consultation procedures, little or no consultee training, and problems surrounding problem identification (Kratochwill & Van Someren, 1995).

One major criticism surrounds the inappropriate control of client (and sometimes consultee) behavior. Vernberg and Reppucci (1986) note that behavioral consultants may be used inadvertently to control rather than treat consultees' clients and client systems. Behavioral consultation needs to better link program implementation with safeguards of client and client system rights.

A second criticism is that behavioral consultation does not adequately take into account consultees' thoughts and feelings regarding the use of behavioral principles with clients (Kratochwill & Van Someren, 1985). Many times consultees have reservations about using behavioral interventions with clients because of perceived technical problems or manipulative behavioral procedures and because of concerns about their ability to implement the required procedures. Researchers have begun to address this issue by exploring consultee reactions to consultant language (such as the use of jargon) and consultee involvement in selecting interventions as they relate to consultee acceptability of suggested interventions (Rhoades & Kratochwill, 1992; Sheridan, 1992). There have also been writings aimed specifically at the use of relational variables in the context of behavioral consultation (Rosenfield, 1991; Kratochwill, Elliot, & Carrington Rotto, 1995). As Kratochwill, Elliot, and Carrington Rotto (1995) point out: "the interpersonal or therapeutic relationship skills . . . are as important to the delivery of behavioral consultation as knowledge of assessment and intervention methods" (p. 522).

Behavioral consultation is often criticized for the difficulties involved in applying behavioral procedures in real life or in natural environments (Kazdin, 1995; Witt, Gresham, & Noell, 1996a). For example, it is one thing to help a teacher make a plan to control the behavior of a seventh-grade boy but quite another to implement the program in a classroom with 36 students.

Some consultants' neglect of a collaborative approach to consultation is frequently cited as a criticism of behavioral consultation (Conoley & Conoley, 1982). Because some work-related problems can be addressed simply by using behavioral interventions, some behavioral consultants adopt the role of expert and perform most of the consultation tasks except the intervention. The long-term positive effects on the consultee's future performance are likely to be negligible as a result. A closely related criticism is that some behavioral consultants rely too much on pet interventions (for example, on tangible reinforcers) when designing intervention programs with their consultees (Tombari & Davis, 1979).

Behavioral consultation is also criticized for not maintaining the "integrity of the treatment" (Vernberg & Reppucci, 1986; Elliot & Busse, 1993). Frequently the agreed-upon treatment plan is not implemented as planned due to a lack of adequate financial and/or human resources. Therefore, behavioral consultation does not always practice what it preaches—adequate monitoring of program implementation.

Behavioral consultation has been criticized for creating a degree of orthodoxy that has led to a somewhat rigid model rather than an evolving model subject to change (Noell & Witt, 1996). Some authors challenge some of the fundamental assumptions of behavioral consultation, such as that talking to consultees is adequate to get them to change their behavior and empower them to generalize the problem-solving skills learned in consultation to similar situations in the future (Witt et al., 1996a; Witt, Gresham, & Noell, 1996b).

With one exception, each of these criticisms suggests that the shortcomings of behavioral consultation result from inadequacies of practicing behavioral consultants rather than from the failings of consultation approach. As with the other models of consultation covered in this text, the remedy to this situation may well be better training and a refinement of approaches to behavioral consultation.

SUGGESTIONS FOR EFFECTIVE PRACTICE

- Avoid behavioral jargon at all times.
- Note the importance of relational issues.
- Consider training prospective consultees in behavioral interventions as part of their staff development training.
- Make the goals of consultation and collaboration as concrete and specific as possible.
- Recall the importance of evaluation of the plan and the consultation process.

QUESTIONS FOR REFLECTION

1. Could any individual behavioral consultant incorporate the findings from operant conditioning, classical conditioning, observational learning, the cognitive-behavioral movement, and behavioral ecology into the practice of consultation? Justify your answer.

2. What are the essential characteristics of any approach to behavioral consultation?

3. To what degree are the underlying assumptions of each of the influences on behavioral consultation compatible with each other?

4. When would you, as a behavioral consultant, incorporate punishment into a treatment plan? Justify your answer.

5. How can a consultant using the behavioral case consultation approach avoid manipulating and excessively controlling the consultee's verbal behavior?

6. Which of the three subcategories of verbalizations would an organizational process consultant employ most frequently? How would this compare with a consultant employing behavioral case consultation?

7. Which of the three subcategories of verbalizations would a mental health consultant using consultee-centered case consultation employ most frequently? How would this compare with a consultant using behavioral case consultation?

8. What strengths does behavioral ecology add to behavioral system consultation?

9. Why does a consultant using behavioral technology training need to be a "good teacher"?

10. When you consider both the contributions and criticisms of behavioral consultation, what conclusions do you draw?

SUGGESTED SUPPLEMENTARY READINGS

Those further interested in behavioral consultation should consult the following suggested readings:

Bergan, J. R., and Kratochwill, T. R. (1990). *Behavioral consultation and therapy.* New York: Plenum. This text is, in effect, a second edition of Bergan's (1977) classic text *Behavioral Consultation.* This is "the book" on behavioral case consultation. Although the authors assume consultants will be working in a school setting, readers can easily apply the ideas in the text to any human service setting. The authors devote at least a full chapter to each of the four stages of behavioral consultation, and extensive treatment of verbal interaction techniques is also provided. A case study section is provided to demonstrate precisely how a behavioral consultant would proceed. The major difference in this text from Bergan's (1977) text is the addition of a chapter on methodological and conceptual issues in behavioral consultation outcome research. Be advised that this book is laborious reading but well worth the effort.

Kratochwill, T. R., and Bergan, J. R. (1990). *Behavioral consultation in applied settings: An individual guide.* New York: Plenum. This guide is a fine resource for those who want to better understand the basics of behavioral case consultation but who do not desire the in-depth discussion presented in the Bergan and Kratochwill text just described. It provides summaries of each of the stages of the behavioral case consultation model as developed by Kratochwill and Bergan, as well as exercises at the end of each chapter to help readers assess their understanding of the material.

Sheridan, S. M., Kratochwill, T. R., and Bergan, J. R. (1996). *Conjoint behavioral consultation: A procedural manual.* New York: Plenum. This model involves an expansion of traditional behavioral consultation to include conjoint consultation with parents and teachers. Of particular interest is Chapter 2 that discusses various approaches to working with parents such as parent education. Chapter 3 does an excellent job of discussing the conceptual bases of conjoint behavioral consultation and differentiates it from traditional behavioral consultation. This is an excellent resource for those interested in consulting with both parents and teachers from a behavioral perspective.

12

School-Based Consultation
and Collaboration

A great deal of what we know as consultation and collaboration occurs in schools. Because schools represent a microcosm of community life, they are excellent settings for consultation (Hansen et al., 1990) and collaboration. Human service professionals at all levels of public education are increasingly being called upon to provide consultation and collaboration services to teachers, administrators, and parents (Caplan & Caplan, 1993; Keys et al., 1998; Zins, Kratochwill, & Elliot, 1993; Ponti & Flower, 1993). When human service professionals are involved with staff development, parent groups, intervention teams, and program development and when they are being resources on a variety of topics, they are engaging in these services.

Today's educators are faced with a large number of difficult problems in schools. Social and demographic changes put students at risk academically, behaviorally, and emotionally (Conoley & Conoley, 1990). In addition, because administrators, parents, and other school support personnel affect the learning climate of the school, they should be considered appropriate targets for assistance (Hall & Mei-Ju, 1994). There is some evidence, however, that school-based professionals need to more effectively market their consultation and collaboration services (Pohlman, Hoffman, Dodds, & Pryzwansky, 1998).

Schools are different than other organizations such as mental health centers or business and industry settings. Because the context in which consultation occurs is important (Zins & Erchul, 1995), I dedicate an entire chapter to these services in a school context. Even though you may not work in a school, it is highly likely that you will collaborate or consult with school personnel. Awareness of consultation and collaboration in the context of a school is essential for all human service professionals.

As a means by which psychological services are delivered in a school, consultation is an indirect service to students and attempts to help others work more effectively with students. Collaboration combines indirect and direct services to students. Thus, students are the ultimate beneficiaries of the consultant's services, and both the direct and ultimate beneficiaries of collaboration. There are far more students who need assistance with personal and educational concerns than can be managed by in-school human service professionals (Gutkin & Curtis, 1990). The overwhelming number of children needing mental health services continues to be a problem in our schools, making consultation an increasing important professional service (Meyers et al., 1993).

Consultation and collaboration services have been a large part of the work of school professionals since the passing of federal legislation and state regulations governing the education of handicapped students and the increasing emphasis being placed on primary prevention (Zins & Curtis, 1984). As mental health and instructional needs of students have become of increasing concern, interest in these services has increased commensurately.

This chapter surveys the scope of school consultation and collaboration. We will briefly discuss their history and examine the nature of consulting with administrators, including how school consultants can use organization development consultation with their administrators. In addition, we will survey methods of consulting and collaborating with teachers. Adlerian and instructional consultation are included in this discussion. From there we will discuss consulting and collaborating with par-

ents, including parent case consultation and parent education. After a discussion of interagency collaboration, we will examine some pragmatic issues. Finally, we will reflect upon school consultation and collaboration at the beginning of the new millenium.

Here are some questions to consider as you read this chapter:

1. In what ways is consultation in the school different from consulting in the community?

2. What is unique about consulting and collaborating with teachers?

3. What special factors does a consultant have to take into consideration when consulting or collaborating with parents?

4. What special ethical issues does interagency collaboration in the schools raise?

5. How can collaboration be viewed as the service of choice over consultation for school-based human service professionals to provide?

INTRODUCTION

School-based interventions can be conceptualized as involving indirect service, direct service, or both. School psychologists, school counselors, and school social workers are the primary providers of consultation services. The primary goals of school-based consultation are to change students' behavior or the behavior of the adults involved with students (Lochman, Dunn, & Klimes-Dougan, 1993; Allen & Graden, 1995). In addition, counselors and psychologists based in schools are increasingly being called upon to assist in collaboration related to the organization change necessitated by several factors including school reform initiatives that have led to increased oversight, accountability, and standards (Knoff & Curtis, 1996). By consulting and collaborating with the significant others of students, school psychologists and counselors can help resolve concerns, prevent future problems, and provide developmental strategies (Gerler, 1992). In addition, by providing these services, counselors and psychologists can broaden the scope of their influence in the school (Dougherty, 1992b).

Increasing attention has been given to providing primary prevention services to those who have basic responsibility for students (teachers, administrators, and parents) that can positively affect school and home climates. This attention is due to federal legislation regarding children eligible for special services as well as to the school reform movement, which has spawned things such as year-round schooling. These interventions typically involve in-service training for teachers and parent education groups (Baker & Shaw, 1987).

Further, changes in school organization, combined with the school reform movement and its focus on empowerment, have led to an increased interest in collaboration as a method of enhancing the education of students and the effectiveness of the school as an organization (Curtis & Stollar, 1996). School counselors and school psychologists are being called upon to provide consultation and collaboration services to improve schools: teachers and administrators are learning powerful methods of helping students meet challenging academic standards; parents are involved in their children's school life; and students are motivated, industrious, and achievement oriented (Riley, 1996). To this end, school-based psychologists, counselors, and community mental health providers will be asked to provide consultation and collaboration to improve their own in-

dividual schools in these specific areas (Riley, 1996, p. 478):

- teaching, learning, and related standards
- use of technology
- governance, management, and accountability
- parent and community support and involvement
- making improvements systemwide
- promoting grassroots efforts
- dropout prevention strategies
- coordination with school-to-work programs
- milestones and timelines

Needless to say, to be effective, school-based psychologists and counselors should be aware of the educational, social, and emotional needs of children. They must understand how to communicate with teachers, administrators, and parents; and they must be aware of the forces operating in the local building, at the school system level, and in the community at large (Salmon, 1993). For example, consultation should be explained to adults in the school in such a way that they are not threatened by another adult helping them with the difficulties they are experiencing (Conoley & Wright, 1993).

The actual way in which consultation and collaboration occur varies according to the model of consultation being employed. Keys et al. (1998) make some important clarifications regarding the distinction between consultation and collaboration. The problem-solving process in collaboration and consultation are essentially the same.

What varies is that, in collaboration, there is an emphasis on shared expertise throughout the entire process (Keys et al., 1998). The "triadic–dependent relationship" style of consultation is known as the "expert" mode of consultation. In the "collaborative dependent" style, the consultant functions, not only as an expert, but also as a facilitator and educator. The consultee, however, still depends on the expertise of the consultant. The consultant educates the consultee about the problem-solving process and together they collaborate to identify and solve a problem. In other words, even though the consultant is collaborative she or he is still "in charge" of the process. This style of consultation is often what consultants are referring to when they say they are collaborating with their consultees. Some authors (e.g., Keys et al., 1998) believe traditional models are effective for dealing with normal, developmental problems, but that true collaboration is called for when dealing with more complex issues. Complex issues require true collaborative, interdependent approaches to dealing with problems.

School-based consultants need to move beyond being experts who make recommendations or experts with good process skills. Community and school mental health professionals are well positioned to lead their respective institutions into collaboration as a preferred mode of delivery that shares leadership, allows for multiple experts, and facilitates combined ownership of the problem and its solution. In collaboration, there is no assumption that any one person has enough expertise to diagnose and solve a problem.

Consider this example:

Case Example of School-Based Consultation

You are a school counselor who is asked by a teacher to help him "increase the motivation to learn" of an academically gifted junior who is failing the teacher's chemistry class. You and the teacher discuss in detail his concern. You develop a plan in which you will interview the student about his lack of achievement and report back to the teacher. The teacher agrees to observe the student's behavior in the classroom and search for any possible clues. You both agree to meet during the teacher's planning period to share your experiences and develop the next steps.

This example is just one of a variety of ways in which school-based human service professionals consult. It is important to remember that all you have read about in this text so far is applicable to school consultation. For example, the information about organizations discussed in Chapter 8 applies to schools.

The underlying premise for school consultation is that, by helping the significant others of students such as teachers and parents make appropriate changes, consultants can contribute to substantive, positive outcomes for students (Gutkin & Curtis, 1990). Through consultation, the consultant has the potential to positively affect more students than would be the case working with individual students (Bundy & Poppen, 1986; Meyers, Gaughan, & Pitt, 1990). Thus, consultants have the ability to significantly impact the mental health and development of children by improving the skills and knowledge of parents and those professionals who work with children at school.

There have been increased demands for consultation services for a variety of reasons (Sheridan, 1992). Consultation is viewed as an alternative method of service delivery for children requiring alternative assistance. There are some concerns related to the use of consultation in the schools. For example, effective consultation takes time, yet the time constraints in schools are myriad. Further, school administrators do not always view consultation as an important function in the school, and even when they do, other services such as testing and counseling compete for the time of counselors and psychologists.

Now consider this example:

Case Example of School-Based Collaboration

You are a school counselor who asks a teacher to collaborate in order to "increase the motivation to learn" of an academically gifted junior who is failing the teacher's chemistry class. You and the teacher discuss in detail his concern. Together, you develop a plan in which you will interview the student about his lack of achievement and report back to the teacher. The teacher agrees to observe the student's behavior in the classroom and search for any possible clues. You both agree to meet during the teacher's planning period to share your experiences and develop the next steps. After you both engage in these tasks, you develop a plan that allows both of you to take responsibility for some aspect of the case.

This example provides a description of the basic rudiments of school-based collaboration. Notice how it differs from the example of school-based consultation in which the teacher took all of the responsibility for the implementation of the plan. School-based collaboration allows for individual expertise to be used in a team situation. It builds relationships for other problem-solving activities such as consultation, maximizes productivity, and requires shared accountability (Cramer, 1998; Friend & Cook, 1996, 1997; Safran & Safran, 1998). Consultation and collaboration activities are typified by a cooperative relationship. The activities are

cooperative in that the relationship is one among equals, given possible differences in expertise and need, with each partner having different contributions to make. The activities are accomplished through a partnership in that the distribution of labor involved is specified and agreed upon. When consulting and collaborating with teachers and parents, it is important to consider training them in the skills of collaboration rather than to assume they have those skills (Ikeda, Tilly, Stumme, Volmer, & Allison, 1996).

Collaboration is particularly appropriate for multidisciplinary team conferences. At these meetings, professionals and sometimes parents attempt to develop an appropriate educational and/or behavioral plan for a student. As early as 1984, Zins and Curtis suggested the importance of having all parties at such meetings skilled in consultation to overcome the shortcomings at these types of meetings (Zins & Curtis, 1984).

The use of collaboration has actually been given momentum by federal and state legislation related to special education services and school reform (Shaw & Swerdick, 1995; Welch, 1998)—for example, the *Individuals with Disabilities Education Counselors Act* (IDEA) (Public Law [PL] 105-17). Counselors and psychologists who consult in schools will need to work on interdisciplinary and child study teams to help design the best program of intervention for a given child. School-based counselors and psychologists may well want to consider using collaboration whenever possible (Caplan & Caplan, 1993).

Although counselors and psychologists based in schools have become involved in collaboration for these reasons, they now have extended collaboration services to a variety of areas including program development and working with other professionals and parents to help students at risk. Collaboration, like an effective team, works best when the leadership of the process is shared over time (Shaw & Swerdick, 1995).

There are some schools that use collaboration extensively to "invent and reinvent" meaningful educational experiences for students (Thousand et al., 1996). For example some schools rely extensively on ad hoc problem-solving teams. When this occurs, there is less of the "shut the door of my classroom" attitude and more of a "let's look at the bigger picture" attitude. Collaboration emphasizes shared accountability for outcomes and a shared responsibility for participation and decision making (Friend & Cook, 1996).

Historical Background

The history of what we now call school-based consultation dates back to the 1920s. As early as 1925, there was mentioned in the role of school psychologists functions that would today be considered closely allied to consultation (Bramlett & Murphy, 1998). These included contributing to the study of children with learning problems and developing a mental hygiene program in the school (French, 1990).

But it was during the 1950s that the term *consultation* began to be used regularly as part of the consultant's functioning. The 1954 Thayer Conference all but made consultation a part of the school psychologist's role. Cottingham (1956) was among the first to recognize the need for special assistance for teachers by school-based counselors, which provided the basis for the consultation role in the elementary school. The rationale was that by acting as

consultants, school-based human service professionals could assist the school in developing a climate conducive to student growth and development, hence creating an avenue by which all students could be affected. When school-based human service workers delivered only direct services such as individual and group counseling, their impact on the school climate was limited since it was virtually impossible to reach all children in the school (Dinkmeyer & Carlson, 1973).

Impetus for consulting with parents came from the work of Faust (1968), who noted that students' relationships with their parents could affect their learning ability at school. Therefore, Faust (1968) strongly advocated consulting with parents but cautioned school personnel against using the "brush fire" (p. 86) approach in dealing with crises that teachers and administrators have with parents. He advocated the idea of parent training groups as well as consulting with parents about their individual children.

Faust (1968), however, gave priority to consulting with school personnel such as teachers and administrators over consulting with parents. Because of efficiency, he suggested that the most important form of consulting was with groups of teachers, not only with regard to student behavior but also concerning curriculum development and classroom activities. Faust was also one of the first to call for counselors to engage in in-service programs for school personnel.

In 1966, a report by the joint Committee on the Elementary School Counselor (ACES-ASCA, 1966) made consulting an official role for school counselors along with counseling and coordination. The literature on consultation for school counselors was very limited at this time. Kahnweiler (1979) reported locating 12 articles on consultation in counseling journals written between 1964 and 1968. By 1972, however, there had been articles published for counselors on topics such as Adlerian consultation, behavioral consultation, in-service programs for teachers, and parent consultation.

Fullmer and Bernard (1972) also advocated the role of school consultant as one who could provide in-service education to teachers on open communication and the wise use of tests, as well as on assisting work groups. Fullmer and Bernard were among the first to note that when consultation is successful, the consultant is made obsolete while at the same time increasing the long-term possibilities of the enhancement of the consultation role. These authors strongly advocated the use of group consultation.

Dinkmeyer and Carlson's (1973) text *Consulting: Facilitating Human Potential and Change Processes* advocated that school consultants be active change agents for improving the organizational climate of the school, thus expanding the concept of school consultant to include organizational consultation.

In 1975, the passage of Public Law 94-142 supported the use of consultation by school-based consultants regarding students with special needs. Subsequent federal and state legislation supported the use of consultation and collaboration as a viable method of indirect service in the schools. Today, there is increasing recognition of the importance of consultation by school-based consultants. As our society becomes even more culturally diverse and social and economic problems continue to grow. the demand for consultation services in the school is also growing.

The future of consultation in the schools is contingent upon not only assisting those who work with students at risk but also upon developing programs that enhance the psychological well-being of students, parents, and teachers (Conoley & Wright, 1993).

CONSULTING AND COLLABORATING WITH SCHOOL ADMINISTRATORS

The school's leadership is a powerful force in determining the extent to which consultation and collaboration are considered acceptable services (Bramlett & Murphy, 1998). Therefore, it is important that school psychologists and counselors not only inform administrators about these services, but that they actually engage administrators in these services (Bramlett & Murphy, 1998).

School-based consultants can consult with school administrators in a variety of ways. They frequently meet with principals to discuss particular children that have come to principals' attention. For example, a consultant may use a client-centered case approach with a principal who is trying to decide whether or not to expel a student from school. In addition, principals often request consultation regarding programs that operate in the school (Illback et al., 1990; Schmidt, 1993). For example, school consultants may be asked to evaluate their own in-school consultation programs (Dickinson & Adcox, 1984) or programs that involve cultural diversity (Pena, 1996) or institutionalize classroom-based group interventions (Robinson & Elias, 1993).

Principals frequently request school consultants to coconsult with external consultants when human services are the focus of the external consultants' assistance. Such collaboration can enhance the effectiveness of the external consultants' services (Curtis & Metz, 1986; Johnston & Gilliland, 1987). As in other contexts, when human service professionals collaborate with administrators, they take on responsibility for some of the outcome.

There is a move toward increased organization development consultation on the part of school-based consultants (Dougherty & Dougherty, 1991; Dustin & Ehly, 1992; Curtis & Stollar, 1995) because school administrators increasingly want assistance with goals that involve the entire school (Hansen et al., 1990; Ehly, 1993). For example, Total Quality Management (TQM) strategies are beginning to be used by school-based consultants (Smaby, Harrison, & Nelson, 1995). The TQM approach is usually implemented through the total quality group (TQG). School counselor and school psychologists can use TQG as a way of helping site-based management teams be most effective by focusing on group roles, social influence, and group stages either in providing staff development training in TQG or consulting with an existing TQG. Since case consultation and program consultation are covered elsewhere in this text, I will focus here on organization development consultation.

School Consultation and Organization Development Change

There is increased focus on organizational consultation in schools including groups of consultees, entire schools, and even school districts (Zins & Erchul, 1995). School counselors and school psychologists are being called upon to assist in implementing system–wide programs related to school reform that are driven by their central offices (Ikeda et al., 1996). These initiatives can include developing a collabora-tion program in each school, building assistance teams, determining the necessary processes for systems monitoring, and providing ongoing staff development.

The impetus for organizational consultation in the school has come from the school reform movement (Curtis & Stollar, 1996) as well as the realization that often what appears to be a child-focused problem is merely a symptom of a building or systems problem (Knoff, 1995). This approach appreciates and uses the unique characteristics of the school in the change process. In spite of the recent attention organization development has been receiving, its application to schools is not new (see, as examples, Illback & Zins, 1993, and Maher & Illback, 1983). Organization development consultation usually starts with the administrator of the school who involves the school-based consultant and other professionals in the change process (Curtis & Stollar, 1996). Such consultation is a way of making carefully planned, predictable changes in the school (Schmuck & Runkel, 1985; Elliot & Busse, 1993). Its goal is to enhance the school's effectiveness by helping school personnel understand and effectively act on problems and move toward self-renewal. This type of consultation can be long-term, lasting for several years (Knoff, 1995). One of the first steps in using organization development consultation is to train the stakeholders and gatekeepers in problem solving (Knoff, 1995). Examples include developing a team to enhance a school's climate, creating a task force to increase the number of parent volunteers in a school, assisting a faculty to move from a self-contained classroom to team teaching, and helping a planning team conduct a survey (Schmuck & Runkel, 1985).

When school-based consultants use organization development consultation, they generally adopt the systems approach described in

Chapter 8, which allows them to observe and intervene in the school's subsystems (Schmuck, 1990, 1995). For example, there may be a rift between teachers (the technological subsystem) and counselors (the supportive subsystem) concerning "pulling out" students for counseling services during class time. Organization development consultation would attempt to help these subsystems function more smoothly together. This view keeps in mind the school's ability to manage change (Schmuck & Runkel, 1985). For example, if the cultural diversity of a school's student body is increasing, the school-based consultant may be placed in charge of a school-wide program to accommodate this change. Finally, organization development consultation looks to the satisfaction of school personnel, since satisfied workers are productive workers. The school-based consultant operating from an organization consultation perspective might well monitor the school's morale as one indicator of whether change is necessary.

Organization development consultation follows the steps presented in the generic model in Chapters 3 through 6, and its primary interventions include process observation and feedback, training, and survey feedback. The typical targets of organization development consultation are the school's structure (for example, policies), processes (for example, ways of planning), and behavior (for example, roles of personnel) (Illback et al., 1990). When human service professionals collaborate from an organizational development framework, they take on responsibility for some aspect of the outcome.

A Brief Example of Organization Development Consultation Wes is a school-based consultant with training in organization development. His school is rapidly undergoing changes in the cultural diversity of its student body, for which his principal has asked for assistance in developing a plan to help the school adjust. Wes begins by assessing the degree to which the school is adjusting to the change and compares his findings with the desired state of affairs. He surveys the staff and conducts structured interviews with randomly selected teachers and support personnel.

Wes draws two conclusions as a result: The entire school staff is not well trained in multicultural education and has unrealistic fears of increased violence and vandalism at the school. Wes creates and submits to the principal a plan involving an in-service program on multicultural education, visitations by staff to schools experiencing cultural diversity, and the development of a special committee to develop ongoing plans for adjustment and monitoring progress.

CONSULTING AND COLLABORATING WITH TEACHERS

Traditionally, school counselors and psychologists have worked with teachers to establish interventions in the regular classroom as a way to reduce special education placements (Kratochwill, Elliot, & Carrington Rotto, 1995). These efforts have led to increased consultation activities with personnel such as special education teachers, teachers of children with behavioral disorders, and teachers in charge of programs for preschool children. School-based consultants have assisted teachers with both academically and behavioral challenged children as well as those with less severe concerns. More recently, school psychologists and counselors have engaged in collaboration as a method of providing service to students and their families.

School consultation and collaboration can be effective and efficient ways to help teachers enhance their professional skills and to generalize the effects of psychoeducational interventions (Meyers, 1985; Caplan & Caplan, 1993). There is some evidence that teachers perceive part of the human service professional's role as that of consultant (Ginter, Scalise, & Presse, 1990; Hughes, Grossman, & Barker, 1990).

Many articles document teachers being helped with a variety of topics, such as conducting effective parent conferences (Johns, 1992), enhancing the self-concept of students (Braucht & Weime, 1992; Leonard & Gottsdanker-Willekens, 1987), choosing instructional methodologies (Margolis, 1990), engaging in conflict resolution (McFarland, 1992), and dealing with other common problems (Stenho, 1995). The nature of the consultation relationship and its influence on the teacher determine whether or not the teacher is going to follow through with the consultant's recommendations and implement the interventions (O'Keefe & Medway, 1997). There is some evidence that the number of teachers who are willing to engage is increased by: the consultant being based in the school; consultation services being offered rather than waiting for requests; the teachers perceiving that the consultant has excellent problem-solving skills; and the teachers perceiving that they themselves have good problem-solving skills (Stenger, Tollefson, & Fine, 1992).

One way to conceptualize school-based interventions is through a matrix of change agents and intervention categories (Lentz et al., 1996). Change agents include students themselves, peers, the home, the teacher, and other school adults. The general category of intervention includes contingency-based (for example, praise after task completion); antecedent-based (for example, changing prompts); teaching academic skills; teaching learning strategies; teaching appropriate social behaviors; and teaching

coping or problem-solving strategies (for example, personal problem-solving strategies).

On the other hand, in collaboration, in which most parties are providing direct service and have responsibility for part of the outcome, the issue becomes getting everyone "on board" with what needs to happen.

There are a variety of models from which school consultants and their consultees can choose. Popular models such as education/training consultation (Shapiro, Dupaul, Bradley, & Bailey, 1996), behavioral consultation, and mental health consultation have already been discussed elsewhere in this text. I have chosen two other models that are popular in school consultation to discuss in this chapter: Adlerian consultation (Dinkmeyer & Carlson, 1973; Dinkmeyer, Pew, & Dinkmeyer, 1979) and instructional consultation (Rosenfield, 1987).

Adlerian Consultation

Adlerian consultation with teachers is based on the works of Alfred Adler's individual psychology. The major proponents of Adlerian consultation in schools have been Don Dinkmeyer, Jon Carlson, and their colleagues. This discussion is based on writings by Dinkmeyer et al. (1979), Dinkmeyer and Carlson (1973), and Kottman (1995). Adlerian school consultation is based on four assumptions (Dinkmeyer et al., 1979, pp. 190–191):

- Teachers cannot take responsibility for student behavior.

- Teachers should be more involved with encouragement than with praise.

- Teachers cannot always prevent failure on the part of students.

- Teachers need to try to meet the affective as well as the cognitive needs of students more effectively.

Case Consultation How consultation proceeds with an individual teacher depends on his or her perceived needs, but usually a collaborative mode is employed. In case consultation, Adlerian consultants frequently use a detailed referral form, which the teacher fills out prior to the first consultation session and which provides the consultation a beginning point. In addition to using the referral form, the consultant asks the teacher to tell his or her story in such a way that the dynamics of the teacher-student relationship are evident (Kottman, 1995). As the teacher relates his or her beliefs about the child's behavior, the consultant tunes into the teacher's feelings so as to further understand the possible goal of the student's behavior. The consultant may also observe the child in the teacher's classroom. The consultant and teacher then make a tentative hypothesis about the goal of the child's behavior and discuss possible alternatives from which the teacher may choose. The alternatives are based on the realization that to change the student's behavior, the teacher must change his or her own behavior first.

A Brief Example of Adlerian Case Consultation Alfred, a school-based consultant, is working with Howard, a middle school teacher who has voluntarily sought out consultation regarding a seventh-grader who seems to be rapidly becoming the class clown. Howard has completed and submitted the referral form. Alfred establishes rapport with Howard and together they get specific examples of the student's behavior and then determine Howard's feelings and reactions to the behavior. Howard reports that he is mostly annoyed because constantly reprimanding the boy gets in the way of his teaching the class. The consultant observes the student in class and conducts a diagnostic interview with him. In the meantime, Howard is keeping a record of the boy's acting out behavior. Alfred and Howard then hold a planning session and determine that the boy's primary goal is attention. They develop a plan in which Howard changes how he responds to the student. Alfred agrees to follow up with Howard within a week.

C-Group The C-group is a group Adlerian consultation method so named because all of the forces operant in the group begin with the letter *C*. These forces include consultation, collaboration, clarification, confrontation, cohesion, commitment, change, concern, caring, confidentiality, and communication. The C-group is an alternative to traditional staff development training in which ideas about behavior are disseminated. As Dinkmeyer and Carlson (1973) have noted, "unless there is personal involvement and opportunity to test out ideas, match them to one's style of life, internalize the new concepts, and then exchange results with other professionals, little change will occur" (p. 223).

The typical group consists of four to six teachers and the consultant. It meets once a week for about an hour and has a life of about six to eight sessions. It is based on the rationale that most problems are interpersonal in nature, classroom and otherwise, and that these problems are best solved in an open, safe group setting. Teachers present problems they are having with individual students and the group discusses them.

The purposes of the consultation group are to help teachers understand patterns of student behaviors and ways to improve those patterns, as well as to provide teachers with an arena in which they can openly communicate, understand the practical application of Adlerian ideas

about human behavior, and experience the rewards of group learning.

Outcomes for teachers include the satisfaction of sharing similar concerns, acquiring more
effective ways of dealing with student misbehavior, understanding their interpersonal relations
better, and learning about how to lead classroom
discussions concerning affective topics.

A Brief Example of a C-Group Loretta is
a school consultant leading a C-group for a
group of six elementary school teachers. The
first meeting has all of the teachers sharing
something about themselves with Loretta
pointing out similarities in their concerns and
building rapport among the teachers. In subsequent meetings, Loretta shares Adler's ideas
on the purposive nature of human behavior,
which gives the group a common ground for
approaching their concerns. She also encourages the members to share anecdotes and helps
them identify and share their feelings as they
relate to such anecdotes. The concept of discouragement is discussed as well as practical
methods of working with misbehavior. Loretta
maintains control over the group's process by
keeping it focused and encourages the teachers
to help one another with their concerns about
students. During the group meeting Loretta
passes out a variety of handouts on Adler's ideas
on children. The group then applies this information to the children they are seeking to help.

Instructional Consultation

Instructional consultation (Rosenfield, 1987,
1992) is a relatively new model for helping
teachers modify their instructional behavior
and more effectively create a learning environment for students. The success of this consultation is dependent on the quality of the

consultant-consultee relationship and the degree to which suggested interventions are carried out and followed up.

Instructional consultation is a collaborative
process in which a problem is identified and
interventions are selected and made. Since the
planned interventions typically require that the
consultee change his or her instructional style,
a strong consultant-consultee relationship
based on trust and mutual sharing is essential.

The most common roles of the instructional consultant appear to be those of collaborator and educational trainer but may also
include being an advocate for a particular instructional technique or service for a given student. The consultant often functions as a fact
finder and observes and collects data to define
the problem more clearly. The consultant may
assess the student's learning, the teacher's instructional style, and the teaching-learning
process. The consultant attempts to collaborate
whenever possible but is obviously an expert as
far as instructional improvement goes.

Prior to accepting consultees, the consultant suggests a referral process within the
school. With the process in place, teachers will
be informed of the nature of consultation and
its collaborative intent and nonsupervisory nature. They will also understand that they are in
control of how the problems presented will be
solved and that the consultant will function as
a resource person.

The consultant clearly informs the consultee about the consultation process and its potential benefits. The consultee needs to enter
the consultation relationship with an expectation of success, a nondefensive attitude, the motivation to discuss the problem situation openly,
and a willingness to make changes. It is helpful
if the consultee is knowledgeable about or willing to be trained in problem-solving strategies.

The consultation procedure includes the following steps: establishing a collaborative relationship, identifying the problem, observing the classroom, assessing curriculum-based learning, planning instructional interventions, and terminating.

The problem is identified in terms of the student behaviors that concern the teacher and the learning environment in which the student resides. Clarifying the problem at this stage requires strong communication skills from consultant and consultee.

The consultant often learns the teacher's instructional goals and plans prior to making objective and systematic observations of the student and the learning environment as a step in problem identification. The consultant's findings are discussed soon after the observation.

As the assessment of the problem is curriculum based, the consultant must understand the scope and sequence of the material as well as the teacher's attitudes about the curriculum. For example, is the teacher being driven to complete the coverage of certain material at the expense of mastery by the student? This assessment provides a basis for planning intervention strategies.

The consultant and teacher refine the problem, discuss alternatives, and brainstorm possible interventions that will improve the management of the student (for example, time on task) and the management of learning (for example, instructional style). From the list of available strategies, the teacher selects ones that are feasible from the point of view of time, resources, and classroom structure.

As these strategies are put into place, the consultant monitors the process on a regular basis and helps make modifications as necessary. Based on the results, the consultant and consultee will then terminate the relationship. The consultant typically makes and submits a complete write-up of the consultation experience.

Recent developments in this model include the concept of instructional consultation teams (Rosenfield, 1992). These teams can have the impact of changing the school culture to be more accepting of a collaborative, problem-solving focus and can create a shift to arranging systemic variables from a traditional view which looks for deficits in a given student.

In conclusion, there is some question in this author's mind as to whether most school-based human service consultants have an adequate background in the teaching-learning process to be effective in this type of consultation. It is one thing to assist in classroom management; it is quite another to analyze learning problems. This model has received attention, however, particularly in school psychology circles.

A Brief Example of Instructional Consultations[1] Wilma is a fourth-grade teacher, who has recently had a new child, Maria, enter her room from another school district. School records indicated that her attendance over the past three years had been erratic. Wilma had placed Maria in the slower reading group. Maria is a quiet, unassuming child who appears to listen to directions in class but has not been able to complete classroom work assigned to her, especially in reading. She stays at her seat for about five minutes during independent work time and then begins to move around the room. Because Wilma has had such a small amount of written work from Maria, she has little information to help her discover Maria's reading level, and there are no test scores in her school records to indicate past in-

---

[1]The author would like to thank Carole Williford for this case study.

structional evaluations. Wilma feels this child would be better served by more individual attention and that she should be removed from her classroom for at least a part of the day for special services. Wilma has no assistant and states that she cannot slow the progress of the class for this one student.

Wilma came to the first meeting with the consultant convinced that moving the child from the classroom was the best option. After listening carefully to Wilma's explanation of the problem, the consultant presented the advantages of working together to identify specific areas of concern in Maria's academic performance. While Wilma was still unsure she could comfortably commit the extra time needed to help Maria, she was willing to work with the consultant to define Maria's reading problem more fully. Wilma and the consultant agreed to two classroom visits for the consultant and a follow-up meeting. The observations were planned to systematically assess Maria's reading performance level as well as her interactive patterns with the teacher, other students, and the classroom environment as a whole. The consultant and teacher discussed the instruction that would be taking place on observation days and the objectives Wilma planned to achieve. The consultant planned to review the scope and sequence expectations of fourth-grade reading materials so that she could more adequately determine Maria's instructional level.

After the classroom observations, the consultant and Wilma discussed what the consultant had learned from observing Maria, the classroom environment, Wilma's relationship with Maria, and the performance of the other children with respect to Maria. From this information they refined the instructional problem to be addressed. The consultant agreed to assess Maria's current reading instructional level

formally, and permission forms for this were sent to Maria's parents.

Once these data were collected, Wilma and the consultant met once more to determine how best to meet Maria's reading needs. They brainstormed potential approaches—from peer teaching to classroom volunteer parents—and Wilma chose the best alternative. They plan step-by-step intervention strategies and agree to talk by phone weekly to make any needed modifications in the interventions. Once Wilma is satisfied with Maria's progress, they will agree to terminate. The consultant will document the consultation through a written report to the teacher and the school and consultation will end.

A Final Note on Consultation with Teachers   There is, in my opinion, a bottom line for effectively consulting with teachers. When consultants work with teachers, it is very important that teachers do *not* view consultation as a process with the following underlying message: How can I (the consultant) help you do your job better without my having to do anything myself? For consultation with teachers to be effective, teachers need to perceive the consultation process as an enterprise with an equitable workload distribution that requires minimal time, all the while being optimally helpful. As you might guess, collaboration may well be the service of choice for work with teachers.

CONSULTING AND COLLABORATING WITH PARENTS

Schools are consciously attempting to assist children and increase parental involvement in the school (Good et al., 1997). The benefits of partnerships between parents and schools have been demonstrated time and again (Colton & Sheridan, 1998). Among other things, this initiative is due to the increasing social problems that our country is experiencing along with their impact on the schools. Additionally, family involvement in the school can positively impact academic achievement (Christenson, 1995). The 1980s brought a resurgence of emphasis on the school–home relationship (Ritchie & Partin, 1994). In spite of the need, parents often have low levels of involvement in the schools (Sheridan & Kratochwill, 1992). The need for parental involvement is well stated by Riley (1996): "Thirty years of research make it clear: Parents and families are pivotal to children's learning" (p. 480).

School-based consultation and collaboration can be keys to parent involvement on a broader scale. There are great numbers of parents who are confused about their roles and relationships with their children (Kottman & Wilborn, 1992; Kottman, 1995). Changes in our society have increased the stress levels of parenting significantly. The family and school are both very powerful forces in influencing the learning and development of children (Strother & Jacobs, 1986). This implies that human service professionals in the schools are expected to have significant contact with parents, largely through consultation and collaboration.

Parent consultation usually takes the form of either direct case consultation about a given child, parent education, or parent training; hence the increasing popularity of the term "parent involvement" (Sheridan, Kratochwill, & Bergan, 1996). These approaches to working with parents are often used interchangeably. However, as Sheridan (1993b) points out, there are several differences. These approaches vary in terms of the breadth of information provided (with parent education being highest), the depth of skill development (with parent consultation being the highest), the specificity of skill/knowledge imparted (with parent consultation being the highest), and individuality of focus (with parent consultation being the highest). Some authors (e.g., Weiss, 1996) suggest that it is best for human services professionals to assume that all parents are interested in their child's welfare and try to involve even those who consistently reject invitations for involvement.

Due to collaboration's emphasis on mutual accountability for outcomes, parents may more likely become involved when they are offered this service. In this manner, parents become instigators of change rather than the target of change. School-based professionals demonstrate their commitment to the child by delivering direct services to the child. Even if human services professionals are gearing their efforts toward the psychological well-being of the child it is best to link these efforts to the academic achievement of the child as the academic success of their children is a top priority of parents.

Through consultation and collaboration, human service professionals can help parents to assist their children in the successful accomplishment of developmental tasks and prevent early school problems from impacting normal child development (Conroy & Mayer, 1994). Through collaboration, parents are not on their own, but have the assistance of a trained professional who is willing to assist in providing some assistance to their child. Consultants will want to make sure that they create strong relationships with parents in order to help them follow through on the consultant's recommendations (Maital, 1996).

Parent consultation and collaboration create the opportunity for the school and parents to work as a team for the benefit of the school and family (Downing & Harrison, 1991). Many times, consultants provide a variety of services to parents simultaneously. Knoff and Batsche (1993) report a program that combines parent training, tutoring, and support. These activities involve training parents in tutoring, in their children's academic curriculum, and in behavior management; supervision of parent's tutoring with their and others' children; consultation with parents as they initiate tutoring in their home; and the creation of parent drop-in centers designed to encourage parental participation in the schools (p. 137).

Finally, school-based consultants will want to make sure that all parents are aware of consultation and collaboration services and feel welcome to use them (Cole, Thomas, & Lee, 1988). At the same time, school-based consultants may want to redefine their job roles to include more parent consultation. There is some research (see Ritchie & Partin, 1994) suggesting that while school-based consultants are aware of the benefits of parent consultation, they do not engage in this function frequently enough.

Parent Case Consultation

Parents may seek out consultation for a variety of reasons ranging from concern over their child's moving into or out of the school to worries about their child's academic, emotional, or social behavior (Kottman, 1995; Ritchie, 1982; Ritchie & Partin, 1994). There are many approaches to parent case consultation, among the more popular of which are the Adlerian, behavioral (Kratochwill, Elliot, & Carrington Rotto, 1995), and mental health approaches. There has been some application of family therapy models to parent consultation (Nicoll, 1992). Regardless of the model used, a

positive consultation experience can promote increased positive involvement by parents in the school life of their child and improve family relationships (Kottman, 1995; Sheridan, 1993b; Strother & Jacobs, 1986). You should note that there is very little empirical research that supports the efficacy of parent consultation (Sheridan, Kratochwill, & Bergan, 1996).

A Brief Example of Parent Case Consultation Using a Generic Model Sunny is a school consultant who has been approached by a parent named Mardy. Recently tested for the academically gifted program at her school, Mardy's daughter had failed to meet the program's criteria and was concerned that she would lose her friends, many of whom were already in the program. Mardy was worried about how she had taken the news.

Sunny quickly established with Mardy that they would be collaborating. Sunny assessed the parent's feelings about her daughter not being included in the program. Mardy noted that she just didn't meet the program's criteria and that that was okay. Mardy was not disappointed in her child or the school but wanted advice on how to help her daughter deal with this "defeat." Sunny provided Mardy with some information on how children take such setbacks and discussed the family dynamics that had occurred since the child had not made the program.

Mardy confessed that so far her strategy for helping had amounted to reassurance. Sunny and Mardy agreed that Mardy would use active listening with her daughter about the situation. In addition, Mardy would increase the time spent with her daughter doing special things, like going horseback riding, and would have her daughter invite some of her girlfriends to their house for a stayover. Sunny helped

Mardy put all of these activities into a plan and followed up by phone two weeks later to assist her with any loose ends.

Parent Education

Parent education is a variation of the education/training consultation model discussed in Chapter 9. Parent education tends to be high on breadth of information provided, low on skill development, low on specificity of information, and low on focusing on the concerns of individual parents (Sheridan, Welch, & Orme, 1996). Parent education groups have a variety of different possible goals such as improving communication, developing effective parenting skills, and increasing knowledge of child development (Kramer, 1990; Gmeinder & Kratochwill, 1998). Parent education is one way of promoting parent involvement in the schools (Conroy & Mayer, 1994). Parent education often subsumes parent training, with the basic difference being that parent training includes the acquisition of specific parenting skills (Sheridan, Welch, & Orme, 1996). For example, school psychologists and counselors can provide workshops for parents on helping children cope with divorce due to the fact that many parents lack the skill to help children cope effectively with the changes brought on by divorce (Parker, 1994).

Parent training groups are frequently based on the premise that parents can learn to help their children when they are taught by methods that go beyond didactic instruction, like modeling (Watson & Robinson, 1996).

There are three popular types of parent education groups (Kramer, 1990): parent effectiveness training (Gordon, 1970) based on the work of Carl Rogers, Adlerian approaches (Dinkmeyer & McKay, 1976; Kottman, 1995), and behavioral approaches based on social learning theory (Becker, 1971). These approaches or individual aspects of them can be provided to parents through multiweek parent programs, monthly parent nights, or through faculties such as a parent resource library (Conroy & Mayer, 1994). The empirical research on parent education is limited in scope and quality; practicing consultants should be cautious in estimating parent education's benefits (Kramer, 1990). One of the biggest challenges faced by consultants is getting parents who need parent education to attend; those who resist may need special consideration (Downing & Downing, 1991). Finally, there is some evidence that consultants can train parents to conduct parent groups effectively, thus freeing up the consultant for other activities (Kottman & Wilborn, 1992).

A Brief Example of Parent Education from an Adlerian Perspective Sylvia is a school consultant conducting a group of seven parents that meets once a week for eight weeks. To teach the Adlerian theory of human behavior as it relates to child-rearing and family life—one of her major goals—Sylvia provides each parent with the book *Raising a Responsible Child* (Dinkmeyer & McKay, 1973), the content of which forms the basis of the group's discussions.

During each session, the group discusses the activities and homework assignments from the previous session, as well as the current reading. Sylvia then leads the group in an exercise related to the reading, which the group likewise discusses, and assigns a new reading and homework assignment.

Sylvia attempts to get the group members to practice in their homes what they are learning in the group and provides motivational support to the parents as they implement what they have been learning.

Here are some bottom line suggestions for working with parents:

- Be multiculturally sensitive.

- Remember that most children do not come from a traditional, intact family.

- Avoid judgmental comments about the child or the parent/custodian.

- Make the parents active partners in the attempts to change their and their children's behavior.

- At all times give the honest impression of being competent, caring, and qualified.

- Use the existing strengths of the child and parents as the foundation for recommending strategies.

- Advocate for the child and the parents.

- Find an alternative to consultation if parents are unwilling to recognize a problem or are not willing or able to implement a problem-solving process.

Cross-Cultural Considerations

School counselors and psychologists will want to remember that, in our increasingly diverse society, they will encounter issues related to cultural diversity when working with parents. These issues can amplify the complexity of consultation (Brown, 1997; Soo-Hoo, 1998). For example, consultants will need to remember that some cultural groups view achievement in terms of the individual while others view it through group cooperation. This difference can impact the way a consultant works with parents about the school-related issues their child is facing.

School consultants will be asked to help address the developmental needs of an increasing number of students from culturally diverse backgrounds (Tarver Behring, & Ingraham, 1998). By the year 2020, it is estimated that the number of school-age children that will come from minority groups is over 50 percent. As Lee (1995) notes: "cultural pluralism . . . has become widely recognized as a major factor deserving increased understanding on the part of educators" (p. 4). There are six dimensions of racial/ethnic variability that consultants should be knowledgeable about: notions of kinship, roles and status, sex-role socialization, language, religion/spirituality, and ethnic identity (Lee, 1995). Lee points out that in their consultative function, school-based professionals can bridge potential gaps between the school and parents through "incorporation of the inherent strengths of families and communities into the educational process" (p. 13) and by promoting the use of cultural diversity as a way to enhance the soundness of the education of students.

Duncan (1995) suggests that awareness of racial identity can assist consultants in avoiding errors that might damage the consultation relationship. Duncan also points out that, when the client system is a culturally different student or group of students, consultants can be instrumental in pointing out to consultees the importance of taking sociocultural differences into account. This can be done in one-on-one consultation or through workshops and other types of organizational consultation. The interested reader is referred to articles on best practices in considering cultural factors in consultation by Nuttall, De Leon, and Valle (1990) and by Edens (1997).

Consultants will want to exercise caution in making any kind of generalizations regarding any characteristics of a given culture. For example, variables such as socioeconomic status and geographic location influence and shape a family's values (Flanagan & Miranda, 1995).

When consulting with parents in cross-cultural situations, consultants need to consider the impact of culture on children's academic achievement, children's behavior, modes of parental communication, and the family system itself (Moseley-Howard, 1995; Brown, 1997; Goldstein, 1998). The impact of culture on variables such as these can be accounted for by doing the following things when consulting (Moseley-Howard, 1995, pp. 343–344):

- Remain aware of the systemic impact upon the child.

- Evaluate the cultural milieu of the child and the degree of acculturation.

- Evaluate strengths of the culture of origin and its adaptive characteristics.

- Focus on development/readiness and all aspects of cognitive style.

- Be aware of characteristics influenced by culture that may have an impact on assessment and intervention results.

INTERAGENCY COLLABORATION

Agencies such as the school, social services, the local mental health center, the child evaluation center, family services organization, and often the family itself collaborate together to help selected children and their families. The rationale for interagency collaboration, in the case of students, is that the social and/or educational problems of a child affect all aspects of his or her life such as the home and school. The shared responsibility for the case shifts the focus from what the school can do to what the community

should do to provide services (Hobbs & Collison, 1995). The shared responsibility necessitates solid agreement on the roles and responsibilities of individual collaborators. You can imagine the complexity of this collaboration effort with different agencies with different mission statements and procedures for providing services. Further, the collaborating professionals will want to recognize that their team will have a distinct "personality" that will impact how the team will function (Garrett, 1998).

There has been an increased need for effective prevention programs serving at-risk youths and their families. As O'Callaghan (1993) notes, "many children are living in family, school, and community structures that are in crisis or simply not working" (p. 7). Counselors in school and community settings can be instrumental in developing and maintaining mental health programs for today's youth. Because school counselors and school psychologists have a primary responsibility for addressing the social and personal needs of students, they are thereby involved in school-community collaboration (Hobbs & Collison, 1995; Geroski, Rodgers, & Breen, 1997). They will work on interagency teams to plan, coordinate, evaluate, and provide direct services to students and their families. School-based personnel can function within collaborative teams in capacities such as making interventions at school, monitoring overall progress at school and home, and making suggestions to community-based mental health professionals.

Whereas more traditional expert modes of consultation were adequate in the past, the complexity of the problems faced by today's youths and their parents suggest that a more collaborative approach may be in order. "School-linked and school-based programs, with services located either at the school or in the community, offer a promising model for service delivery, and collaborative planning between schools and community has become critical to the success of such efforts" (Keys et al., 1995, p. 123). Collaboration has become increasingly popular as school and community agencies have realized how fragmented services for at-risk youth are. Consultants must develop multifaceted programs for at-risk youth and their families because the problems faced by these groups are multicausal and must be solved by addressing a larger context: there is no single answer to such problems (Lerner, 1995; Keys et al., 1998).

Although school and community counselors provide case-related services on a regular basis, collaborative consultation efforts are relatively new. These efforts have come about as schools and agencies have realized that no one person or no one organization can solve the complex issues and problems that need to be dealt with; hence service integration has been introduced among schools and agencies. In collaboration there are multiple experts who come together to "jointly identify problems to be addressed . . . to determine strategies and the role each person plays in implementing these strategies to carry out their roles interdependently, and to monitor progress (Keys et al., 1998, p. 124). Both school and community consultants, in order to use collaboration effectively, must see themselves as connected to a broader community (Keys et al., 1998).

By ensuring that collaboration services are delivered in a timely, efficient, and integrated manner, the consultant encourages collaboration efforts that focus on the healthy development of the child and his or her family. To deliver services of this level of quality the collaborating team needs to clarify and agree upon goals, determine the roles each collaborating professional will assume in meeting the defined goals, develop a plan in which the goals are adequately met, and design an evaluation plan that demonstrates the effectiveness of the plan.

In order to maximize the probability that an effective plan will be designed and implemented, the collaborating professionals will want to meet soon after the child and his or her family have been identified as needing services. By having several professionals as well as the family itself involved in planning and implementing the interventions that are part of the plan, a broad knowledge base is applied to the plan. On the other hand, it is essential that each collaborating professional recognizes the philosophical orientation, service limitations, and mission of the other agencies involved as part of the collaborating team. By being aware of boundary issues, collaborating professionals can be prepared to implement their "piece of the pie" without doing anything counterproductive to the efforts of other collaborating professionals. These issues highlight the importance of developing interagency policies that provide for a broad-based and comprehensive delivery system (Quinn & Cumblad, 1994).

The collaborating professionals will usually select a team facilitator, frequently a school counselor or school psychologist who will convene meetings, ensure documentation of meeting discussions, and make sure that progress on the individual collaborator's work with the family is discussed during meetings. The team facilitator will make sure that the plan is made and carried out with adjustments made as necessary. Further, the team facilitator has the responsibility to make sure an evaluation of the plan is made and shared. The facilitator has the collaborating professionals develop some kind of form that will enable the team to monitor the plan. For example, the plan will have the following sections: the problem identified along with the date of identification, a description of the goal developed to deal with the problem, a description of the intervention used to meet the goal along with a notation of which collaborating professionals were to do what and by when, followed by a section describing the outcome of the intervention.

When working with families, it is important to empower the family so that there is not a hierarchical difference between the family and the school. When collaborating with parents every attempt should be made to provide them with maximum input into meaningful participation in the collaboration team's work with them and their child (Friend & Cook, 1996). This type of group consensus seeking on how to proceed and follow up can increase the chances of success. Consistent use of language among various agencies, even to the point of developing a common brochure describing services, can minimize misunderstanding by parents as well as some school personnel (Ikeda et al., 1996).

Interagency collaboration can take time in terms of being out of the school building and the amount of paperwork necessary. Ways to minimize the constraints of time include rotating team meeting sites and using technology to store, retrieve, and communicate information (Hobbs & Collison, 1995). Collaboration involves trade-offs. School personnel have to give up some power in order to get the benefits of community responsibility.

Due to managed care, a trend in interagency collaboration includes increased involvement of health care service agencies with school and community integrated planing and service provision (Knoff, 1996). When professionals in these settings look across their settings and circumstances they will be able to define concerns and generate solutions in a joint

manner (Hellkamp, 1996), often using strategic planning (Knoff, 1996). Such strategic planning emphasis will determine who will provide services, how they will be provided, and whether health care reform will determine the provision of services (e.g., a certain limit on the number of sessions a family may have that insurance will pay for).

One caveat about interagency collaboration: School-based professionals will want to remember that many of their fellow collaborators from other agencies will have been trained in medical or behavioral science fields. There is the distinct possibility that the professional from outside of the school will have minimal time to spend with the student due to extremely high caseloads and other professional obligations.

PRAGMATIC ISSUES

There are a variety of pragmatic issues that face school-based psychologists and counselors in their consultation and collaboration activities due to the school setting. The areas around which these issues revolve are addressed next.

Ethical Issues All of the ethical issues discussed in Chapter 7 apply to school-based situations, though two of them take on particular significance in a school setting: confidentiality and informed consent (Dougherty, 1992a). As every practicing human service professional knows, maintaining confidentiality in a school is difficult, because there is a tendency in many schools for personnel to share information about students in inappropriate ways. It is easy to imagine how breaking teacher confidentiality unnecessarily could have disastrous effects. School-based counselors and psychologists must ensure that the limits to confidentiality are clearly defined and mutually agreed upon for each consultation and collaboration relationship.

Many school professionals are just becoming familiar with their own roles as consultants and collaborators, and the persons with whom they work such as teachers, administrators, and parents are often not familiar with exactly what constitutes consultation and collaboration including how the two differ (Hughes, Barker, Kernenoff, & Hart, 1993). Therefore, counselors and psychologists need to educate the persons to whom they are providing these services as to their nature whenever necessary.

School-based counselors and psychologists and external consultants may have to deal with the ethical issue of deciding whether to end a consultation or collaboration relationship and engage in more advocating roles to ensure that children in schools receive the services to which they are entitled (McMahon & Pruett, 1998). Counselors and psychologists can be placed in the predicament of trying to help a system that truly does not want assistance and, as a result, the students in the system suffer. In this case, the professional faces the dilemma of trying to change events through consultation or collaboration, or disengaging and taking a proactive, advocating role for the students in the system.

Training Issues For years, consultation was considered as "everything else" a school-based human service professional did. Collaboration was viewed as a mysterious term that meant something like consultation only that the person providing services was going to help the client system also. Even today, many counselors and psychologists have had little, if any, formal training and supervision in consultation and collaboration. In particular, school-based counselors and psychologists should have additional training in dealing with resistance, multicultural issues, and role conflict as they relate to consultation and collaboration (Deck, 1992; Hansen et al., 1990). Minimally trained school counselors and psychologists who want to practice these services are obligated to seek additional training. For example, inexperienced school counselors should be aware that, when consulting or collaborating, they may be less likely than experienced counselors to account for the negative aspects of the school's environment when planning interventions (Ross & Regan, 1990) and may use fewer variables when conducting these services (Salmon & Lehrer, 1989).

The global areas in which training in consultation and collaboration is needed include personal traits, expertise, knowledge and skills, and ethics (Campbell, 1992). Campbell (1992) suggests alternatives for school counselors who are seeking professional development; they can contact university or school district experts who offer in-service training and can participate in the increasing number of programs on consultation/collaboration at state and national conventions. Further, psychologists and counselors who work in the schools may learn a great deal about the dynamics of collaboration from their special education colleagues who have been attempting to put this service into place for over two decades. Finally, there are a variety of texts available that discuss consultation and collaboration. Some authors (e.g., Rosenfield, 1992) suggest that adequate training will take away some of the "self-imposed" time constraints regarding time to conduct consultation and collaboration.

Working with Other School–Based Professionals Because there may be several professionals in a school working to assist the same child, family, or program, there is the potential for both collaboration and conflict (Friend & Cook, 1996; Idol & Baran, 1992). I am of the opinion that collaboration is the most desirable way to proceed in such cases. Idol and Baran (1992) suggest some practical ways for collaboration to be enhanced and conflict minimized: Consultants should clearly define their roles and responsibilities with one another on an ongoing basis, adopt a model of consultation that all are comfortable with as a common ground for working together, attempt to obtain minimum competency in the skills necessary for implementing the adopted model of consultation, and adopt a framework consisting of problem-solving stages (like those discussed in Chapters 3–6 in this text) to guide the implementation of their model.

There are many examples of school psychologists and counselors collaborating with school-based management teams, teacher assistance teams, and department- and grade-level teams (West & Idol, 1993). Teams sometimes use catchy names to enhance cohesiveness and identity, for example, "PIT Crew" for a peer intervention team (Saver & Downes, 1991).

Unique School-Based Interventions There are several interventions unique to school settings (Mathias, 1992). One is consulting with the school's media person to develop a bibliotherapy section for children and a self-help section for teachers and parents in the school library. Another is the child study team in which several staff members pool their expertise to discuss how best to meet a child's educational needs. The school consultant often facilitates such teams. An alternative to the C-group discussed earlier is the "Teachers Need Teachers" (TNT) group, in which a group of teachers meets periodically to discuss students, their teaching, and how to support one another.

Organizational consultation interventions are designed to enhance the school climate

(Mathias, 1992), for example, a series of schoolwide activities such as "Buddies Week," "Warm Fuzzy Week," and a "How to get 'debugged' when someone bugs you" project. Many school consultants engage in such activities as well as the more generic and traditional types of consultation. Irrespective of the type of activities, treatment integrity, that is, the appropriate implementation of the activity by the consultee, is a critical issue.

Systems View of the School In a systems view of consultation, the student is examined in the context of school and family units (Brown, 1987). These units and their interaction (for example, teacher attitudes, parent child-rearing practices, communication patterns between parents and the school) then become eligible for attention and modification. Chapter 8 provides an overview of systems theory. Individual change can be facilitated when the wider system that directly interrelates with the student is considered (Brown, 1987).

Systems theory assumes the school to be the target for consultation intervention; to consult with a teacher represents a linear view of the child being responsible for negative behavior, and the teacher for correcting it. This may reinforce in the teacher's mind that the child, not the system, has the problem.

One concern is that not all teachers are comfortable with systems approaches; some want more concrete ways of approaching perceived problems (Brown, 1987). In addition, many school consultants have not been trained in systems methods. Finally, the systems view typically dictates that the consultant examine the child in interaction with a variety of levels of the ecosystem such as home, school, and community thus complicating the nature of the consultation relationship (Sheridan, Welch, & Orme, 1996).

Developing a Framework for Prevention and Intervention School-based consultants will want to have a clear understanding of how the activities of outreach, advocacy, and consultation fit together (Kurpius & Rozecki, 1992). *Outreach* is extending services to those in need of help and is often focused on prevention and making available services known to target groups. *Advocacy* has been discussed in Chapter 2 as a consultant role. Consultation and collaboration are typically classified as outreach activities. School counselors and psychologists may occasionally use all three activities to be effective (Kurpius & Rozecki, 1992). For example, once school personnel agree on what a particular student is to achieve, it becomes a matter for the school counselor, for example, to provide the student with the best chance of success through advocacy and consultation/collaboration with other school personnel, the family, and representatives of the community (Johnson & Johnson, 1988).

It is important for school-based human service professionals to understand that these roles are multidimensional. In general terms, school psychologists and counselors "have expanded the use of outreach, advocacy, and consultation in order to assist those populations who are in danger of becoming victims of educational, social, environmental, or psychological need brought on by a wide variety of perceptions and assumptions" (Kurpius & Rozecki, 1992, p. 176). Depending on the situation, these activities can be used within a framework that allows the use of remediation or prevention.

Problem Solving versus Empowerment There is some criticism of the tendency of school-based counselors and psychologists to engage in case consultation with teachers. Since traditional case consultation has a problem-solving focus, there is an implicit assumption that there is a solution for each concern a teacher has and that the solution can be accomplished without taking instructional practices into consideration (Witt, 1990a; Witt & Martens, 1988). An "empowerment" approach, in which the teacher is helped to identify needs, finds the resources to meet those needs, and links with those resources (Witt & Martens, 1988), may be better. Nonetheless, most case consultation/collaboration in the schools remains a problem-solving venture (Zins, 1993). However, because they will want to consult with strong as well as weak teachers, counselors and psychologists will want to make sure that these services are not viewed as remedial activities (Hughes et al., 1990). Additionally, the school personnel's preferences will have an effect on which of the various approaches to consultation/collaboration will be used (Friend & Cook 1996).

Time Constraints As you might recall from Chapter 8, time constraints are a large and real issue for conducting effective consultation. A limitation of school consultation and collaboration is that both take time to do well. There is very little free time at school for the people who work there, so it can be difficult for counselors and psychologists to engage teachers and administrators in these services, let alone parents who must often take time off from work to come to the school for any reason. The school environment encourages engagement in short consultations and collaborative efforts. A caveat echoed decades ago (Faust, 1968) should be well taken by all school-based counselors and psychologists: "It can be said that the short, unplanned individual consultation has value. At the same time, the counselor is required to decide whether such consultation is indeed what is required, or whether more depth and breadth are needed" (p. 55). More recently Caplan and Caplan (1993) have stressed the importance of "orderly and unhurried reflection during consultation discussions" (p. 43). On the other hand, counselors and psychologists need to find strategies to effectively cope with the very real time constraints placed upon consultation and collaboration during the school day. Effective time management on the part of school professionals is one obvious help in creating time for consultation and collaboration. Three other strategies include: early release/late arrival of students, use of substitutes, and teaching strategies that free up personnel (Friend & Cook, 1996). Another option is to adjust the school culture so that consultation and collaboration are seen as systematic, organized activities through which the school psychologist or school counselor provides assistance (Fall, 1995).

Cultural Change Schools are increasingly recognizing that positive, effective change may well necessitate a change in their "organizational culture" (see Chapter 8), which school counselors and psychologists must be knowledgeable of since they are being called on to assist with such changes (Burrello & Reitzug, 1993; Harris, 1991; Rosenthal, 1993). School counselors and psychologists are asked to help identify factors both inside and outside the school that suggest the need for change (for example, the need for special programs and an integrated method of approaching students with special needs). They assist administrators in formulating questions about cultural change, in leading staff discussions concerning these questions, and in articulating a core set of nonnegotiable beliefs about the organization.

SCHOOL CONSULTATION
IN THE 21ST CENTURY

What trends will occur in school consultation in the first years of the new millenium? What areas of need will have school personnel and parents calling for assistance from school consultants? Below, I describe some of the ways you, if you become a school consultant, may be using your skills in consultation.

Schools are dramatically expanding their services to prekindergarten children. Public education is being offered to children at risk from birth onward and to all 3- and 4-year-olds (Hohenshil & Brown, 1991; Fine & Kontos, 1992). Therefore, school-based consultants will increasingly be asked to offer services to the significant others of prekindergarten children (Bacon & Dougherty, 1992; Mowder, Willis, & Widerstrom, 1986). One implication of this trend is that school consultants will have to establish skill and knowledge competencies related to this age group to effectively consult on such children (Gerler & Myrick, 1991).

There will be an increase in "tri-level" service delivery (Norris, Burke, & Speer, 1990), a school-based model in which consultants train and then support teachers who act as consultants to their colleagues. This allows school consultants to make a stronger impact on the school and creates time for other activities such as organizational consultation.

School-based consultants will help their schools create a positive climate with regard to the school reform movement's continuing impact on public education (Parr, 1993). As we have noted, school-based consultants have increasingly been called on to help schools deal with four major concerns related to school reform: children at risk, reintegration of special students, school-community integration of services, and restructuring of schools (Dustin & Ehly, 1992; Mayer et al., 1993; Beck, 1994; Curtis & Stollar, 1995). In addition to their typical consultation practice, school-based consultants will be involved in projects designed to promote collegiality in the school, develop programs for students at risk as academic standards are increased, develop study skills programs, and ensure that the socioaffective domain is included in any curriculum planning. Other areas in which consultation and collaboration will be needed include: quality assurance, parent involvement, supporting teacher competence, and building student-focused community networks (Dwyer & Gorin, 1996).

With the significant rate of turnover in school personnel, such as teachers and the "aging" of school faculties, school-based consultants will increasingly be called upon to facilitate teacher support groups through a variety of models including consultee-centered consultation (Babinsky & Rogers, 1998). These groups may range from mentoring groups and teacher support groups to burnout prevention and stress management groups (Jellinek, 1990).

School-based consultants will also be increasingly called on to act as organizational consultants during a national crisis (Costello, Phelps, & Wilczenski, 1994; Kaplan, Geoffroy, & Burgess, 1993) or a local one, such as violence in the school place. School-based consultants will help schools develop crisis plans by working with teachers, parents, and mental health colleagues concerning appropriate crisis guidance and engaging in postcrisis debriefing activities.

There is a strong possibility that referral agencies will place part-time staff in the schools and that school consultants will be offered summer work by agencies within the school (Dustin, 1993). This has the potential to vastly improve the quality of consulting with other professionals.

Peer consultation groups are increasing in popularity (Pryzwansky, 1996; Logan, 1997) and will no doubt grow more common. In peer consultation groups, school counselors and school psychologists consult with one another and provide technical and supportive feedback to one another. The types of outcomes for peer consultation include improvements due to case consultation, solution-focused problem solving, peer support, constructive feedback, and access to needed resources and materials (Logan, 1997).

One model, the Structured Peer Consultation Model for School Counselors (SPCM-SC), consists of a nine-session model in which counselors collaborate together in dyads in 90-minute meetings every other week (Benshoff & Paisley, 1996). This structured model keeps the dyad on task while allowing for flexibility to their unique needs. This model was developed so that counselors could consult with one another about the cases they were dealing with.

Finally, there is a trend in school consultation to develop supportive linkages between homes and schools. As a result, there has been an increase in the attention given to ecological interventions such as classroom- and home-level management strategies as ways to change the behavior of individual students (Conoley & Wright, 1993).

SUGGESTIONS FOR EFFECTIVE PRACTICE

- As you plan in your practice, deliberately take into consideration the very real time constraints that school personnel face.

- Remember that many, if not most, of the students you will serve will not come from intact families.

- Bear in mind the importance of cultural diversity in your practice of school consultation and collaboration.

- Remember that schools are among the slowest of organizations to change.

QUESTIONS FOR REFLECTION

1. What strikes you as most notable about the history of school-based consultation?

2. To what degree do you see organizational consultation as a viable option when consulting with school administrators?

3. Do you see any possible pitfalls in consulting with school administrators who may also be your immediate superiors?

4. To what degree can Adlerian case consultation be used effectively at the elementary, middle, and secondary school levels?

5. Why is the Adlerian C-group a good alternative to traditional in-service programs for teachers?

6. Do you think that most school-based consultants are adequately trained in the teaching-learning process to employ instructional consultation effectively? Why?

7. What are some special factors consultants need to take into account when consulting with parents?

8. Which of the pragmatic issues covered in this chapter has the most relevance to your practice as a consultant?

9. What changes are going to impact how school-based consultants deliver their services in the 21st century?

10. To what degree can the mental health and behavioral models discussed in earlier chapters be implemented in a school setting?

SUGGESTED SUPPLEMENTARY READINGS

Consultation (special issue). (1992). *Elementary school guidance and counseling, 26,* 162–251. This special issue provides eight articles on school-based consultation. Topics include special school consultation in the 1990s; a comparison of outreach, advocacy, and consultation; school-based interventions; counselors and special educators consulting together; ethical issues; training; an in-service program on self-esteem; and a tool for assessing your skill as a school consultant. These articles provide some of the latest thinking in school-based consultation.

Gutkin, T. B., and Curtis, M. J. (1990). School-based consultation: theory, techniques, and research. In T. B. Gutkin and C. R. Reynolds (Eds.), *The handbook of school psychology* (2nd ed.) (pp. 577–611). New York: Wiley. This chapter covers a variety of topics on school-based consultation, including its characteristics, rationale for services, major approaches, and contemporary and future issues. Broad in scope, consultants will find a wealth of information in this chapter.

Flanagan, D. P., and Miranda, A. H. (1995). Best practices in working with culturally different families. In A. Thomas and J. Grimes (Eds.), *Best practices in school psychology* (3rd ed.) (pp. 1049–1060). Washington, DC: National Association of School Psychologists. This is an excellent article that provides a wealth of information for consultants who work with culturally different populations. The authors apply their views on multicultural helping to families in a very practical way. As the authors note:

"The rewards of developing effective skills for working with families whose cultures differ from our own . . . far outweigh the feelings of unfamiliarity and uncertainty that may be associated with initial cross-cultural interaction" (p. 1054).

13

Case Study Illustrations of
Consultation and
Collaboration

The purpose of this chapter is to help you apply theory to practice and obtain a more realistic picture of what transpires in consultation. It is important to remember that there are many different ways to carry out these services.

Recall that some approaches deal with the entire organization as the client (for example, process consultation), whereas some work with consultees who are delivering direct services to clients (for example, client-centered case mental health consultation). Therefore, strict comparison among the various approaches to the three models of consultation and collaboration is not possible because the different approaches are used to accomplish different things.

The next section describes a human service organization, Acme Human Services Center, in terms of its environment, people, structure, and activities, and the data concern-

ing the organization that were gathered in various ways from various sources. To demonstrate the many approaches to consultation, we will assume this human service organization delivers direct services to clients. Assume that, for each approach, the consultant has all the data mentioned for Acme Human Services Center. Each approach to consultation is then applied within this human service organization. Assume also that the contact persons in the organization know what kind of consultation is needed. (In reality, this happens only occasionally; thus, the overall context in which each consultation model is illustrated is somewhat unrealistic. However, the given illustration of each consultation approach will be very realistic.)

Each approach to consultation is discussed in terms of its goals, the consultant's role and function, the consultee's experience in consultation, and the application of the approach. The final case study, a composite of various approaches, illustrates how the ideas, goals, concepts, and techniques from various approaches can be synthesized and applied by a consultant in a given setting.

After we finish the Acme case studies, we will compare school-based consultation and collaboration by using transcripts of two very similar cases. You will have to read these two transcripts very carefully to detect the more-or-less subtle differences in the processes involved in these services. I have deliberately chosen the situation for consultation and collaboration so that you can quickly develop an appreciation for similarities and differences through comparing and contrasting the same case.

As you read the chapter, I suggest you remember the following:

- There are several ways to go about expertly performing each approach to consultation and collaboration.

- Most of the approaches are highly flexible with regard to how consultation and collaboration might proceed.

Consider the following questions as you read through this chapter:

1. Are the various approaches to consultation and collaboration more alike than they are different?

2. Based on the case studies in this chapter, are there any skills consultants need that are common to all the approaches discussed?

3. How can you use this chapter to help you develop your own personal model of consultation and collaboration?

4. Which of the different models seem most attractive to you personally?

5. In what ways would you apply the approaches presented in this chapter differently than the author did?

INTRODUCTION

Assume that you are equally talented in each of the approaches to organizational, mental health, and behavioral consultation. Imagine further that you are called into a human service organization and asked to perform, in turn, each approach to consultation. You would be asked to perform the education/training, program, doctor-patient, and process approaches to organizational consultation. You would next be asked to perform the client-centered case, consultee-centered case, program-centered administrative, and consultee-centered administrative approaches to mental health consultation. You would then be asked to provide the behavioral technology training, behavioral system, and behavioral case approaches to behavioral consultation.

Finally, you would need to ask yourself several questions before proceeding with each approach:

- What assumptions do I need to make according to the approach I am about to use?

- What are the goals of the approach I am about to use?

- What consultant roles and functions will be demanded of me?

- What will my consultees experience during the consultation process?

- In specific terms, how will I go about applying this particular approach?

Illustrations of each approach to consultation or collaboration in more or less the same context can provide you several learning experiences, including:

- a real-life feel for how the approaches work

- a deeper understanding of how the approaches converge and diverge in theory and practice

- an opportunity to begin developing personal preferences for some approaches over others

In addition, the studies are a basis for forming your own personal model of consultation and collaboration, a lifelong process of development based on your professional and personal experiences. The keys to a useful personal model of these services are fourfold:

1. Know your own values about life in general and these services in particular.

2. Know your personal and professional strengths and limitations.

3. Know and be able to practice as many approaches to consultation and collaboration as possible.

4. Know what the organizations you are serving really need from you before you start.

THE CASE: ACME HUMAN SERVICES CENTER

A Description of the Organization

Acme Human Services Center is a private institution that provides a variety of counseling and psychological services in a wide portion of a rural southeastern state. The Center is located in a city with a population of 90,000 and provides services to many of the small surrounding communities. The population base is 70 percent white, 20 percent African American, and 10 percent other minorities, including Latinos and Asian Americans. Textiles, furniture manufacturing, automobile assembly, and agriculture are the main industries of the area, which has been labeled economically depressed. There is a high unemployment rate and a moderate crime rate. Referendums for civic improvements such as schools and recreation centers are continually voted down by the populace. A four-year university in the area provides a variety of cultural, recreational, and social events. The casual observer would note the presence of modern churches, parks, music and drama organizations, and library facilities.

In competition with the Center, which has been in operation for 10 years under the same director, are two other small private practice corporations, a small number of individuals in private practice, and a local community mental health center that has been in existence for 20 years. The Center has a professional staff of 15: one psychiatrist, one nurse, two doctoral-level psychologists, two doctoral-level counselors, two master's-level school psychologists, two master's-level counselors, two master's-level clinical psychologists, and three master's-level social workers. Two clerical staff members and one mental health technician also work there.

To provide community-based services, the Center offers a variety of outpatient programs. Its clients are referred by schools, physicians, juvenile and adult court systems, the social services department, and occasionally the local mental health center. The basic realm of services is divided into several categories, including adult mental health services, child and adolescent mental health services, substance-abuse services, community consultation services, and employee assistance program services. Plans for providing mental retardation services are being considered.

The Center has no written role and mission statement. Its founder, a psychiatrist, feels that its mission is to help citizens develop and maintain an adequate level of social and personal well-being and dignity. Dramatic growth over the past four years due to the addition of the substance abuse and employee assistance programs has led to a doubling of the organization's income and the hiring of five additional staff during that time.

The Organization's Problems

When the director of the organization last reviewed its progress, he listed problems that had emerged so that steps could be taken to solve them. He thought that such a procedure would help the organization maintain and perhaps enhance its financial position. As he reflected on the past four years, he listed the following problems:

1. an increase in referrals of cocaine-related substance abusers with no true "experts" on the staff to handle them

2. a lack of knowledge about how to evaluate the effectiveness of the employee assistance programs

3. increasing concern over the deteriorating relationship between the staffs of the child and adolescent program and the adult program

4. too much of the decision-making responsibility in the hands of one leader for an increasingly complex organization

5. insufficient time for program heads to consult on cases

6. a lack of definite direction in the substance-abuse program

7. an increase in the number of "acting out" adolescents as clients

8. an increase in requests from schools for assistance in classroom management techniques

9. the need for each program to clarify its own specific goals and objectives

10. a growing concern over staff morale in general

Although the agency director knew that he had a few staff people who could function as internal consultants, he felt that objectivity was at a premium and thus decided to seek outside consultation for each of the problem areas. The director, himself a well-known consultant in the area, was easily able to identify an effective type of consultation that would be likely to solve each problem.

Because the staff had no true experts in cocaine-related substance abuse, an education/training organizational consultation was selected. The inability to evaluate the employee assistance programs could be resolved through program evaluation consultation. Because the deterioration of the relationships between the two staffs was a mystery as far as the director was concerned, a doctor-patient type of organizational consultation was in order. The centralization of leadership in an increasingly complex organization called for a review of how decisions are made and what other possibilities existed, and thus a process form of organizational consultation seemed appropriate. Because program heads were increasingly taxed with other duties, they had little time to consult with the psychologists, counselors, and social workers who provided direct services to clients; client-centered and possibly consultee-centered case mental health consultation seemed correct for this problem. The lack of definite direction in the substance-abuse program called for either program-centered administrative or consultee-centered program mental health consultation. The increasing number of requests from schools for assistance in classroom management techniques required training the agency's staff, so behavioral technology training consultation was needed. Each program could formulate its own specific goals and objectives with the assistance of behavioral system consultation. Finally, the increasing number of "acting out" adolescents clearly required behavioral case consultation.

Existing Data on the Organization

The organization's internal environment is frantically paced: everyone seems so busy that there is little time for social interaction at work. Office doors remain closed during the day, even when clients are not being seen. Paperwork appears to be backlogged in spite of computer-assisted office support. A trained observer would label the environment as unstable and heterogeneous.

The organization's personnel are cordial with one another, yet relationships tend to be superficial. Efficiency and productivity are high but come at a price, for little discussion occurs relative to the direction the Center should take. Although personnel feel secure about their jobs, it is evident that morale and a sense of teamwork are declining. The competition between the child and adolescent program and the adult program has caused some intense (but suppressed) negative feelings between some program members.

The organization is bureaucratic: The Center director makes all decisions and only infrequently consults with program directors. Lines of communication follow a vertical chain of command, and thus the ideas of many of the therapists are not solicited. Employees were hired for specific purposes and are to work

only to achieve those purposes. The rules of the organization, although explicitly stated in a manual, are never discussed. The director keeps a complete but disorganized set of records.

Change occurs at the Center in a "top-down" fashion. Typically, members are informed of changes through memoranda, although the nature of changes is described without any rationale. Clearly there is the assumption that each change will be acceptable and willingly carried out without discussion.

The Center does not place adequate emphasis on the personal or professional growth of its staff. It assumes that talented people have been hired and that they will take care of their own professional and personal needs. No attempts are made to include employees in the emotional "ownership" of the Center. An environment that nurtures employee growth is lacking, and networking is not used as a supplement to the director's leadership.

As a whole, the organization is in trouble. Although it and the demand for diversified services are growing rapidly, it is run as if it were still a small operation with a simple mission. The organization is still doing what it does well, but the price it is paying has alerted the director to the need for consultation.

THE APPROACHES TO CONSULTATION AND COLLABORATION

In each of the approaches illustrated in this section, you can assume that the consultant engages in all the appropriate behaviors expected of a highly professional, competent consultant. Most approaches to consultation adhere to some version of the generic model previously discussed. You can also assume that the consultant proceeds in the same sequence as the generic model. Thus, a good working relationship is established, a problem defined, a contract agreed upon, and entry accomplished. For the sake of brevity, I do not describe these basics of effective consultation behavior in each illustration. Rather, I attempt to provide the essence of each approach so that you can make appropriate comparisons and contrasts.

Organizational Consultation

Education/Training Approach As I consult with Acme Human Services Center within the education/training framework, I attempt to enhance the overall effectiveness of the organization by improving the professional effectiveness of the members of the substance-abuse program with respect to cocaine-related substance-abuse counseling. I assume that a blend of didactic and experiential learning is the best approach. The members of the substance-abuse team would probably need information related to cocaine abuse and some skills in working with drug abusers.

As a consultant using this approach, I function as an expert technological advisor, teacher, and trainer. Because I realize that the staff of the substance-abuse program is small and consists of skilled professionals, I tailor my consultation to their specific needs and am quite specific in the education and training I provide them.

The role of the consultees is that of learners. They have all volunteered for the consultation and meet my expectations that they will be interested and cooperative learners and will invest themselves in the consultation process. They realize that they need some assistance in working with cocaine abusers and are highly involved in the entire consultation process.

My first step is to conduct a needs assessment of the consultees to make sure that they perceive a need for education and training in cocaine abuse. Further, I want to assess what they know and can already do related to working with cocaine abusers and to determine what they must learn in order to work more effectively with cocaine abusers. I construct a questionnaire to acquire this information and hold a brief meeting with each consultee. I then hold one meeting with the entire group to determine whether the information I received from them accurately reflects their perceptions of their needs.

I plan the education/training based on the results of the needs assessment, which indicate that the staff requires information and training in diagnosing cocaine abuse, particularly in determining patterns of pathological use, impairments of social and occupational functioning related to its use, duration of the disturbance, and the probability of relapse into abuse. Utilizing the principles of adult learning, I assume that the participants are self-directing, can discuss many of their own experiences pertinent to the topic, and are ready to learn. For the primary tools of consultation, I plan a series of activities around the expressed needs of the consultees: lectures with audiovisual aids, several small group discussions, modeling and practice of diagnostic skills related to cocaine abuse, and feedback. I determine that four, two-hour sessions are needed to accomplish the goals of consultation.

As I implement the education/training consultation, I create a climate of mutual respect and am particularly careful not to "speak down" to the consultees or flaunt my knowledge of cocaine abuse. I am very open about what I know and don't know about the topic and about my experiences in working with cocaine abusers.

During the course of consultation I include some of my own successes and failures with cocaine abusers. I remain flexible, keep a professional yet light atmosphere, and use humor when appropriate. I provide a great deal of time for practice of the skills required by the consultees, particularly during the last two sessions.

In evaluating the education/training, I use pre- and postintervention questionnaires on the consultees' knowledge of cocaine abuse and behavioral checklists to determine their levels of functioning in applying their newly acquired skills. I have them evaluate the consultation in terms of its effect, adequacy, and value. Finally, I arrange for a follow-up meeting in 60 days to assess the impact of the training and for ironing out any anticipated problems.

Program Approach As a consultant with a program orientation, I am very much interested in working with the Acme Human Services Center in evaluating the relative success of its employee assistance programs. The goal of a program evaluation consultation is to improve current decision making about how a program should function. I have been hired to answer the question To what degree are the goals of the employee assistance program being met? In addition, I have been retained to assist the Center director and the program heads to be more effective program evaluators in their own rights.

My role is that of technological expert in program evaluation. I attempt to provide accurate, timely, and useful information to the director and program heads. I use as much of a collaborative approach as the skills of the consultees permit. I meet with the consultees to review the goals of the employee assistance program, develop a possible program evaluation design, and present it to the consultees for their feedback. I

obtain their feedback and redesign the evaluation accordingly. Much of my time is spent in preparing and planning the evaluation design.

The consultees provide me with as much information as possible about the program, for such information is needed when I design the evaluation. I spend a lot of time with the consultees to become very familiar with the program and ask the director to give the head of the employee assistance program a great deal of time so that she will feel free to cooperate, and I also discuss with the director what he intends to do with the results of the program evaluation. His reply indicates that my evaluation will be used for modifying the programs (if necessary) and for running the program on a day-to-day basis.

After preparing the program evaluation design, I collect some of the data and have consultees collect the rest of it. To evaluate the goals of the employee assistance program, data is collected on how many clients are served, the effects of the services for them, attitudes of clients and providers toward the program, and attitudes of members of the organizations in which employee assistance programs are provided (including those who did not partake of the services). We collected this data by using questionnaires and surveys, by observing the programs (but not the direct delivery of services to clients), by conducting interviews of a few randomly selected volunteer service providers and clients, and by examining the program's records on the number of clients for the various services offered and the duration of those services.

After collecting the data, I analyze it, bearing in mind the four standards of proper evaluation: accuracy, utility, feasibility, and propriety. I keep all the appropriate parties involved and apprised of my findings as they emerge.

My findings indicate that only 3 percent of the employees use the employee assistance program for an average of three contacts. Reasons for this scant participation are the stigma of being seen going to a counselor at work and fear that confidentiality will somehow be broken. Attitudes of clients and service providers are quite positive in terms of the perceived effectiveness of the services provided. Nonusers of the program indicate that they would be more likely to participate if services were provided at the Center, not at the work site, and if the program did not have a reputation for serving only substance abusers. Intervention measures that counselors took with their clients resulted in positive gains by the clients.

My final task is to present this data to the director and program head. I suggest that all personnel involved in the program be present at a "feedback meeting" in which I outline the results of the evaluation and facilitate a planning session based on the evaluation. At that meeting, I use graphics to explain the evaluation and what the data represent and mean. I avoid jargon but take care not to appear condescending. I then facilitate a planning session in which plans are made to publicize the program more thoroughly and promote it as a positive growth experience for the participants. Plans are also made to permit the employees the option of coming to the Center for services. I then summarize the evaluation, describe the next steps in which the consultees engage, and make arrangements for a follow-up visit.

Doctor-Patient Approach The director had no idea why there was friction between the child and adolescent program and the adult program. When an organization knows that something is wrong but doesn't know the reason, the doctor-patient model of consultation can be very helpful.

As a consultant using this approach, my job is to find out what is wrong and prescribe a solution. The organization is purchasing my expertise in diagnosis and prescription concerning the conflict between the two programs. I realize that my very presence is an intervention that affects how the problem will be diagnosed. Because of this, I spend time building effective relationships with the parties involved in and affected by the consultation to increase the probability that the information obtained from the parties involved will be straightforward and honest.

My primary goal is to define the problem that is causing friction between the two programs and recommend a viable solution. I assume that the friction is merely a symptom of some broader problem. At this time I am not concerned about helping the organization enhance its diagnostic and prescriptive abilities.

In the doctor-patient approach, I function as an expert. I create relationships with the appropriate parties, collect and analyze information, make a diagnosis, and prescribe a solution. I must be able to "read" the organization and determine what data to obtain and how to obtain it.

The consultees are the "patients"; and I need them to describe the symptoms of the problem as they see them. I attempt to create conditions in which they can provide truthful, complete information, and so I ensure that they understand and are willing to implement my solution. I gather data about the organization's purpose, structure, internal relationships, leadership, and program for rewards. I gather this data by interviewing each member of each program about their program and their perceptions of the other program. Confidentiality is assured to all involved.

From these interviews the child and adolescent program emerges as one that perceives itself to be out of favor with the director; the members see themselves as "second-class citizens" in his eyes and they question how they fit into his future plans. Some members even think that the entire program might be scrapped so that the organization could become involved to a greater degree in the more profitable adult service area. In addition, the head of the adult program is seen as a favorite of the director who has undue influence in the day-to-day operation of the entire agency. These factors have caused the strain between the two programs.

Based on this analysis, I formulate some solutions that are tailored to the organization and its capability for solving its own problems. First, I recommend a series of group meetings between the members of the two programs using third-party conflict resolution. Second, I recommend that the director make a written statement concerning the short- and long-term future of each program.

Third, I recommend that he appoint all program heads to an advisory committee that he will chair. Finally, I encourage him to implement these changes.

Process Approach The Center's director knows that the leadership style of the organization must change. He used to believe that an effective leader needed to control all the factors related to running an organization: employees' work-related behavior, record keeping, and decision making. This procedure worked relatively effectively until the Center started to grow in size and complexity. The director then continually found himself in a reactive posture he described in this way: "I feel like I am running from one brush fire to another. I am putting in 16-hour days. All the stress is affecting how I relate to clients and my employees. I think I need my own personal employee assistance program!"

As a process consultant, I realize that leadership is a process variable in managing any organization. The director already knows that leadership style changes are imperative, so I am confident that some substantial progress can be made in changing how the organization is managed. He has asked me to observe him in action for one week to get a feel for how he manages, and he also asked me to observe each of the program heads for two days. These observations give me some ideas about their decision-making styles and underlying assumptions about the nature of human beings that inevitably influence leadership style.

My goals as a process consultant are to help the director and the program heads become aware of their everyday leadership and decision-making behaviors and to help them identify and modify them in ways that are consistent with their goals. I accomplish these outcomes by being a facilitator of self-discovery for each consultee. I assist in gathering data to shed light on leadership and decision-making procedures as they relate to the current state of affairs within the organization. In addition, I help the consultees diagnose what is being done and what yet needs to be done.

The director's goal is to delegate more authority, decision-making responsibility, and administrative tasks to the program heads. The program heads' goal is to develop leadership and decision-making skills that are necessary for their new responsibilities. Their roles are those of active collaborators; they must translate their vague perceptions into specific insights and then act on those insights.

I provide minimum structure in carrying out my assignment and use clarifying questions and probes to stimulate the consultees' thoughts on their own current behavior. As human service professionals with administrative experience, the consultees have decision-making and problem-solving skills on which I can capitalize. They also suggest interventions they think would be helpful. In this case, they ask for feedback on their leadership and decision-making skills.

I proceed by helping the consultees set goals and by observing them as they attempt to accomplish them. I help the consultees gather data concerning employees' perceptions of the leadership styles and decision-making procedures within the organization. Based on all this data, I help the consultees diagnose their problem—the need for practice in leadership and decision-making skills that involve input from all levels of the organization. I act as "director" and set up several role-playing situations in which the consultees practice the new skills. The director, for example, practices setting agendas for meetings, delegating authority, soliciting input from subordinates, and creating a strategic planning committee. The heads practice confrontation meetings, assertive behavior, and conflict resolution skills. After each role-playing segment, I coach the consultees in how they can increase their leadership and decision-making skills in an interpersonally effective manner. In addition, I make a few structural recommendations concerning how lines of authority can be set up within a small organization like the Center. I then help them develop ways to monitor their own progress in these areas.

Mental Health Consultation

Client-Centered Case Approach Client-centered case consultation does not deal with issues residing within the consultee. Rather, the contract specifies that I, as a mental health consultant, examine the consultee's client concern-

ing some professional matter and write a report that includes recommendations. I operate in a fashion analogous to the doctor-patient approach to organizational consultation except that the diagnosis and prescription are based on data concerning a client, not some aspect of the organization.

My focus is on the client, and my aim is to advise the consultee on how to "fix" some problem concerning the client under consideration. I examine the client, make some form of assessment and diagnosis, and provide the consultee with a report containing suggestions and recommendations to help the client. I spend very little time with the consultee.

A counselor from the Center seeks my help in determining how to go about getting a mother and teenage daughter to communicate openly during their counseling sessions. I function as an expert in parent-child interactions and use my expertise in diagnosing the causes of toxic relationships and in prescribing remedies for improving them.

The counselor is to provide me with as much pertinent information as possible regarding the difficulties the clients are having in communicating with each other in general and in the counseling sessions in particular. She gathers additional information on the client's family and relates it to me and is responsible for reading my report and determining whether to implement the recommendations I make.

I meet with the counselor for one session at the Center, during which I build a relationship with her and get a feel for her perceptions of the particulars of the work-related problem. I assess her general abilities as she discusses the case and consider the strengths and weaknesses of the Center. As I do this, I come to the realization that my consultee is likely to get very little individual or group supervision on this case because of the very busy state of affairs at the Center. I realize that I need to devise a plan that is short term and well within the counselor's level of expertise. My assessment is that she is a talented professional but has had relatively little experience in helping parents and children work through communication difficulties during the counseling process.

Next I interview the mother and daughter, first together and then separately. My talk with the mother reveals that she had found out about and told her husband about a sexual experience of their daughter. I pursue this topic in terms of the current state of affairs in the mother-daughter relationship.

Based on all the information I have gathered, I write up a report for the counselor and discuss it with her at our final meeting. After telling her that she is under no obligation to follow through on my recommendations, I proceed to share them with her. I suggest that she see the mother and daughter on an individual basis for two or three sessions to get to know each of them better and to develop a more trusting relationship with each. This would create the conditions that enable the mother and daughter to communicate more effectively in subsequent sessions together. I also suggest that she utilize a nondirective counseling style for the purpose of enhancing the relationship between the mother and daughter. These recommendations are well within the professional competencies of the counselor and have a high probability of being successful. No special training is necessary, nor were there any increased demands for supervision. As a final step, I arrange for a follow-up session in about six weeks.

Consultee-Centered Case Approach In applying consultee-centered case consultation, my primary goal is to improve the ability of my consultee to work more effectively with the

current client and with similar clients in the future. I am retained as a consultant because no one at the Center has sufficient time for routine consultation. I am available to all staff. The case at hand involves a psychologist with a female client who, in the words of the psychologist, "has a lot of anger inside of her that she needs to express." As I listen, I develop a strong hunch that some of the unresolved needs of the consultee are blocking his effectiveness in the case.

I play the roles of detective, expert, and educator in this approach to mental health consultation. I determine what emotional and cognitive factors within the consultee are blocking progress in the case and give the consultee specific information he can use to help the client. While discussing the case, the consultee mentions how much anger the client has and how important it is for the client to deal with that anger. He discusses the case with some emotion, even a sense of desperation. He knows that I am going to make some recommendation to him, but he seems driven to convince me that I should recommend that anger be the central focus of the therapy.

As a matter of procedure, I do not interview or examine the client, but proceed by listening to my consultee's subjective view of the case. I determine that he is suffering from a lack of professional objectivity and that there is little available supervisory assistance from members of the Center. In deciding to make some interventions designed to help the consultee regain more professional objectivity, I ask him specific, detailed questions about the client's anger and the therapy interventions that have been used thus far, since I'm more interested in his version of the case than I am in the actual facts of the case. I'm hoping that by discussing the client's need to express anger, the consultee will develop a broader, more objective perspective on the case.

I determine that theme interference is causing the lack of objectivity. It is as if the consultee is saying, "Unless she deals with the repressed anger in our therapy sessions, we will never make progress in therapy." He cannot see that there are several ways to help the client besides helping her get in touch with and express her anger.

I attempt to use theme interference reduction through a combination of techniques. First, I keep the discussion on the client and remain calm in discussing the case. In addition, I remain very calm and objective about my relationship with the consultee. Finally, I tell him a parable about a former client of mine who was similar to his. The client in my story never dealt with her repressed anger but still benefited tremendously from therapy. As I discuss the story, I notice a sense of reduced tension in the consultee about the case. He seems more objective and hopeful, and I close the session by calmly scheduling a follow-up meeting. I express continued hopefulness and interest in the progress of the case.

Program-Centered Administrative Approach   When applying program-centered administrative consultation, I work with the Center's director and the head of the substance-abuse program, both of whom want to develop a sense of direction for the program. My specific goal is to help them develop that sense of direction and therefore fix the program. My general goals are to enhance the overall functioning of the program and increase the program development skills of the director and the program head.

My role is that of an expert familiar with substance-abuse programs and how they operate. I collect information on the program and how it works, analyze that information, and recommend some solutions. I use my expertise in organizational theory to determine how to collect the information I need.

My consultees discuss with me why they hired me in the first place and what they think they want from consultation. They point out some of the organization's idiosyncrasies and make suggestions about which staff I should contact in gathering information on the program. The administrators help me develop a timetable for consultation and the methods by which they will sanction my work throughout the Center. They provide me with as much information about the organization as possible, respond openly to my questions, and then develop a list of their reasons why the substance-abuse program has a lack of direction. Finally, they wish me good luck and let me know that they are available any time I have questions or need anything. They realize that they will have limited contact with me.

The program concerns treatment, not prevention. In concentrating on management and giving some attention to program accomplishments, I examine agency records on unemployment rates, arrests for drug use and possession, and substance-use driving offenses. I interview key staff and administrators and find out that no one uses the information. Further, there are no records on the types of substances clients are abusing. No outcomes are recorded as a part of the program's objectives. Counselors and therapists in the program see clients as part of their caseloads but have little input into the overall workings of the program.

I proceed through the stages of formulating a simplistic solution, first becoming very confused about the entire situation and then getting a firm grasp of the consultation problem. Based on this information, I develop a set of tentative recommendations, which I feed back to all parties involved irrespective of their ranks within the organization. Based on the reactions I get, I modify those recommendations. The final list of recommendations looks something like this:

- Use available data to determine community needs relative to substance abuse and, based on current staff, modify the program.
- Set objectives and develop a philosophy for the program.
- Point out that alcohol and cocaine abuse are on the rise in the community and that treatment of these illnesses could become the central focus of the program.
- Keep detailed records of the contacts personnel have with substance-abuse cases.

These recommendations and the report that contains them are distributed to the appropriate people at the Center. It is up to the director to determine if and how my recommendations are to be implemented. I then set up a follow-up session to occur six months from the date of the report's distribution.

Consultee-Centered Administrative Approach As a consultant applying consultee-centered administrative consultation, I am involved in the most complex and demanding type of mental health consultation. I am asked to work with the director and the head of the substance-abuse program regarding the program's lack of direction. The difference between this consultation and the example just described under program-centered mental health consultation is that its main goal is to enhance the consultee's program development and maintenance skills, and its secondary goal is to improve specific programs.

My role is that of both expert and facilitator. I expect consultation to take a long time because I involve the consultees in every step along the way to help them improve their skills in developing plans and strategies related to the successful running of the substance-abuse program. I need the skills of knowing about organizations, how they are best managed, and how they change for the better. I also need the skill of "reading" an organization to pinpoint possible problem areas. I move about the Center as if I were a member and try to understand it from the employees' perspective. Because my role is complex, I need to make sure that the administrator lets everyone involved know precisely what my role is to be.

The director and program head are involved with me as much as possible in this collaborative effort. They lay the groundwork for my presence within the organization and provide the necessary sanctions. They arrange times for me to meet with everyone involved in the substance-abuse program so that I can present my findings.

As I begin to "float" through the Center, I make sure that no one regards me as a "spy" for the director. I want everyone in the program to see me as a helper, not a threat to their security. I am careful to build trusting relationships not only with the director and program head but with all members of the program. The consultees know that their skills will be enhanced by gathering and discussing the data; I therefore get them to uncover what is needed to give the program a sense of direction. I help them use group meetings, interviews, and questionnaires as data collection devices and then help them discuss the data in meetings involving the entire program staff. As the consultees discuss the information, I notice that they incorrectly think they know what is happening in the program and where it is going. In helping them be more objective in analyzing the data, I point out some key factors: there is no philosophy surrounding the program; there are no written objectives and goals for the program. This increases their objectivity. In being very patient and in trying not to force my ideas on them, I take a relatively nondirective stance and ask them what they think various kinds of data mean.

Through my efforts the director and program head realize that if the substance-abuse program had a well-defined sense of direction—complete with philosophy, goals, objectives, and a strategic plan for the next five years—then a great deal of stress would be alleviated for all the parties involved. The director then appoints the head of the substance-abuse program to head a committee charged with developing such direction. It consists entirely of substance-abuse program employees, who are paid an honorarium beyond their normal salaries for their work. I agree to help the program head run this committee and to help him try out new leadership styles and techniques as the committee attempts to fulfill its charge.

Ecological Perspective   In using the ecological perspective to mental health consultation, I employ a preventative approach. My "client" is Acme itself—a unique institution and not "just another human service center." Therefore, my first task is to become very familiar with the internal environment at Acme and with the community it exists in. I examine the history of Acme's development in the community and review its orientation procedures for new staff and how people are acknowledged on an everyday basis.

My interventions are aimed at helping the organization develop long-term adaptive processes so it can continue to flourish as its external and internal environments change. I empower the staff to help one another and scan the entire organization for the resources (that is, people, events, and places) that are over- and underused. I believe that the power for change resides in the consultees, so, as I build strong collaborative relationships with all the staff, I try to develop strong relationships with the consultees and make special note of their strengths.

Though the staff feel well paid and professionally appreciated, the interviews with selected staff members reveal a conflict between two teams and a general concern over having any voice in how the Center should be run. I help the members set up a network of effective communication in which they can support and act as resources for each other. I also suggest that the director establish work groups to enhance staff "ownership" of what goes on in the Center. I encourage the staff to develop special events at work that are not work related, such as "birthday breaks" and fun "bull sessions." Finally, I help develop a procedure for a community advisory group and an internal professional development group. My written report to the director (with a copy to each staff member) summarizes the elements and findings of the consultation and schedules two follow-up sessions three and six months later.

Behavioral Consultation

Behavioral Technology Training Approach   When I consult from a behavioral technology training approach, I focus on enhancing my consultees' general and/or specific skills in this area. The Center, particularly the child and adolescent program, was receiving more and more requests for classroom management strategies in the classrooms' procedures from the local school system. None of the staff had professional experience with schools but most had good general behavioral technology skills. Because of my expertise in behavioral technology and my many years of working with school systems in such training, I was retained to train the entire staff of the child and adolescent program in behavioral classroom management skills.

My goal is to increase the consultees' skills in classroom management techniques so that they in turn can use behavior technology with schoolteachers concerned with classroom management. I make sure that the consultees have enough accurate information concerning classroom management behavioral technology, have developed related competencies, and have a positive attitude toward the use of these skills. The consultees should learn as best they can, integrate their knowledge about behavioral technology approaches to classroom management into their consultation skills, and attempt to create a positive attitude toward the use of behavioral technology in the classroom.

Based on input from all the parties involved, including school personnel, I develop and implement a training plan using lectures, modeling, behavioral rehearsal, feedback, and reinforcement as my primary tools. Modeling followed by rehearsal and practice with feedback are stressed so that the consultee is able to perform the required skills well. I go to great lengths to demythologize behavior modification in the classroom and provide rules of thumb for proceeding with classroom management procedures, such as conducting observations and establishing token economies and "time-out" procedures. I have the Center's director announce specifically why this training is important to the consultees and the Center; he also comments on the types of rewards the consultees can expect from participation in the training.

I evaluate the training in several ways, first with a questionnaire that reveals attitudes toward the training itself and then with a test that has the consultees state specifically what they have learned and their attitudes toward their newly acquired knowledge and skills. A very important part of the evaluation comes six months later, when I observe the staff consult with teachers on classroom management procedures derived from behavioral technology. At that time, I assess the degree to which they have transferred their knowledge and skills to actual school settings and how effectively they use those skills.

Behavioral System Approach My goal in this approach is to enhance the efficiency and effectiveness of the Center in terms of its stated function. The director invites me to "take a look at the Center" and then make some recommendations. He notes that the Center is growing very rapidly and that its affairs are in a constant state of disarray.

As an expert in behavioral technology and systems theory, I accomplish my goals by collaboratively guiding the director and program heads through defining and assessing the system, making selected interventions, and evaluating the effects. I use behavioral technology to help the organization function more efficiently.

As joint collaborators, the consultees determine what is to be done in consultation and how the results of consultation will be used. To accomplish this, they provide me with as much accurate information as they can. As the change agents within the Center, they have both the power and perspective to accomplish the goals of consultation.

I proceed by helping the consultees define the Center in terms of its structure and activities. We observe what goes on in the everyday routine for a week, share our perceptions, and come to a consensus. Once we have characterized the Center adequately, we are ready to assess it. We design questionnaires and arrange to observe the various subsystems to evaluate the overall system. We try to answer the question, What are the effects of the Center's structure and activities on the behavior of its members?

The major answer we obtain is that there is lack of direction among the members because there are no defined goals and objectives for the various programs the Center offers. The consultees and I determine that the highest priority must be given to having each program develop, spell out, and adhere to a set of behavioral goals and objectives. We next set behavioral outcome goals that include what is to be accomplished, when, by whom, and under what conditions.

Criteria are set up to assess the quality of these goals, which are then evaluated. I suggest that the various programs modify their activities and structure to coincide with their newly written behavioral goals and objectives. The consultees agree. We then develop an evaluation to determine how well each program behaves according to its specific goals and objectives. I arrange for a follow-up in six months to help the consultees discuss these evaluations and make appropriate adjustments.

Case Approach As in client-centered case mental health consultation, my main objective in behavioral case consultation is to assist the consultee with a work-related problem in a given case. The difference between the two approaches is that in behavioral case consultation my work is within a behavioral framework. I work as a consultant in the Center and am available one day a week.

My consultee is a master's-level social worker at the Center whose client is a schoolteacher who wants to overcome his fear of flying in airplanes. I am an expert in behavioral technology and its application to counseling/therapy. I keep that role of expert throughout the consultation process, although I collaborate whenever possible with the consultee. Though I control the process of consultation, the consultee determines the best course of action to take in regard to the case. I provide knowledge concerning the learning principles related to phobias about flying and make sure that all the stages of the consultation process are successfully accomplished.

As my link to the client, the consultee provides me with as much specific information as possible concerning the case. I lead her through the stages of problem identification, problem analysis, plan implementation, and problem evaluation. We verify that a phobia about flying in airplanes exists and determine that he does not possess "free floating" anxiety, but only a few situation-specific anxieties. Our goal is to have the client actually ride in an airplane with minimal anxiety, and we determine that this can be easily measured by having the client use a checklist during the flight and by intermittently taking a pulse rate.

I illustrate how the process of classical conditioning has probably occurred and created the client's phobia. The consultee and I then examine how this conditioning maintains the client's phobia. Next, we plan how the consultee will use systematic desensitization with the client.

Because the consultee does not know the procedure, I train her and monitor her handling of the case. I show her how to apply the general technique to the specific needs of the client by helping her develop a personalized strategy. I give her some books and videotapes so that she can do some independent studying. I role-play systematic desensitization procedures with her, taking the role of her client. We design an evaluation that includes not only the successful completion of the desensitization strategy, but also whether or not the client actually flies in an airplane with acceptable levels of anxiety. We then arrange for a follow-up session in three months. When she feels ready, the consultee prepares to follow through on what she has learned.

SCHOOL-BASED CONSULTATION EXAMPLE

Background

Ms. Gentry, a fifth grade teacher, has requested the assistance of Ms. Hall, a school psychologist, in dealing with a student who has difficulty with self-control. Ms. Gentry and Ms. Hall have met before to discuss other students. They have a good rapport with one another and share a strong respect for each other's professional abilities.

C1 (Consultant): Ms. Gentry, hi, it's good to see you. How's it going?

T1 (Teacher): Oh, better I guess. You know I really appreciate your meeting with me. I'm so frustrated. This kid is really disrupting the whole class, and I don't know what to do about it.

C2: This is Tommy. He's the ten-year-old you mentioned the other day . . .

T2: Yes. You know he's a bright kid, but I just can't get him to stay focused. He's always out of his seat with a thousand excuses . . . the bathroom, the water fountain, the trash can. And, of course this interferes with the work of the other students. As you know, we tested him but he doesn't qualify for any special services.

He's of normal intelligence, and there's no LD or ADHD indications.

C3: Hmm. Okay, let me see . . . no special needs, normal IQ, but he consistently gets out of his seat, and when he's up he's not only not working himself, but he also gets others off task. Anything else?

T3: No that's about it. You know, he's not a bad child. He doesn't mean to cause problems. He's just very social and very active.

C4: Okay, so there don't seem to be emotional problems either. He's just out of control and doesn't seem able to follow the class rules.

T4: Right. He just acts without thinking. He's not manipulative or mean. He needs to learn to control himself. I don't know what to do! I've got to do something. Tommy's not learning a thing, and he's keeping the rest of the class from learning too. My test scores this year are going to stink. Can you help?

C5: Yes, we can work together on this. We could use the problem-solving formula we've used in the past. We'll get some more details on what's going on with Tommy. Goals will probably help once I get a more precise picture of what's going on. We'll establish some realistic goals and then design a plan. If it's okay with you, we'll use this little form I've developed to help us save time. (See Figure 13.1).

T5: Thanks. I appreciate your listening and your help. Maybe we could use a plan like the one we used for Jimmy. You know, it's nice to have a counselor like you. Your plans are sensible and easily implemented.

Consultant and Teacher Reflections

Consultant: *At times it may be easier to utilize a ready-made form. This form can either be completed independently or during an interview with the*

Global Goals

1. *Tommy learns to potential.*

2. *More effective learning environment for the whole class.*

Specific Goals

Tommy remains in seat during seatwork and discussion.

Plan:

Noted Obstacles:

Baseline Data:

Monitoring Data:

Conclusions:

Tommy develops insight as to how his behavior affects others.

Plan:

Noted Obstacles:

Baseline Data:

Monitoring Data:

Conclusions:

Tommy participates in discussion.

Plan:

Noted Obstacles:

Baseline Data:

Monitoring Data:

Conclusions:

Tommy follows directions.

Plan:

Noted Obstacles:

Baseline Data:

Monitoring Data:

Conclusions:

FIGURE 13.1 Consultation Summary Sheet

teacher. With some teachers, this may lower the initial resistance to the consultative process. Some teachers become quite protective of their planning time. They may get as little as 45 minutes a day for planning and grading. These behaviors seem to call for a behavioral management situation. Does Ms. Gentry have the time and skills to apply the consistency required to implement a behavior management program?

Teacher: *I wonder what is going on with this child. There's something wrong because he is not doing the work. Could it be my teaching style or approach to him? How am I gong to explain his behavior if the principal walks in to observe the class? Worse yet, what if the entire class gets off task while the principal is there in my room? Well, at least this consultant is listening to me and seems to* *understand. I really need that. I wonder if the consultant is going to get the impression that I can't motivate or control the class? I wonder if the consultant will think I complain too much.*

C6: Well, thanks. Let's hope we can make some changes for the better. Okay, you basically said, "Good kid, good intentions, average IQ, no emotional or learning problems, just out of control." . . . Tell me more. How long has this been going on?

T6: Tommy's behavior has been a problem since the beginning of the year. I've tried different techniques in dealing with Tommy's behavior, but nothing seems to work. For example, after leaving his seat in the middle of a test, he knocked a little girl's paper off her desk. She became very upset and wasn't able to finish her test. This seemed to be the last straw so to speak. At this time I called for a parent-teacher conference with Tommy's mother and father. When I informed them of the problem, they seemed surprised and concerned. At this time I asked them about Tommy's behavior at home. His parents told me that they usually did not have problems with Tommy at home, except at bedtime. His parents don't sound very strict. I got the impression that their expectations of him are only that he eat with the family and be in bed on time. Tommy basically decides what he does with his time. His mother felt that Tommy's behavior could easily be controlled by explaining the rules to him. She didn't seem to understand that I had already made several attempts to control his behavior, including explaining the rules, but always failed.

C7: That's got to be frustrating to have tried different types of behavior control and gotten nowhere and then find that there are not many expectations at home. Maybe we can

design something new that gets better results. Is that your primary concern?

T7: That is definitely my primary concern because his behavior is not only disrupting *his* academic achievement but disrupting the concentration of the class as a whole.

C8: I think we have a pretty good idea about the nature of the problem. Now let's talk a little bit about goals. What would you like to see happen regarding Tommy's behavior?

Consultant and Teacher Reflections

Consultant: *Tommy's parents sound loose. I wonder what kind of messages Tommy's parents send him about how to respond to Ms. Gentry's expectations? I also wonder if Tommy's acting out behavior is a result of lack of control, attention getting, rebelliousness, or something else? A behavior management program may be effective with the first two causes, but, if he is motivated by rebelliousness, I wonder if such a program would work.*

Teacher: *Well maybe I am too strict. Who knows? You know I tried those things I mentioned to the consultant, but did I try hard enough and long enough and do them correctly? Why are these parents so lenient with this child?*

T8: Basically, I would like for Tommy to be able to perform up to his potential in the classroom. He needs to get some control over his behavior in order to concentrate. He needs to change his behaviors so he's not distracting to the other kids in the classroom.

C9: Those things really seem to go hand in hand. If he is able to gain some control over his behavior, he should be less likely to disturb the other children in the class. You would also like him to work more toward his academic potential. Those really seem like good global goals for Tommy. In order to help him most effectively we need to clarify two things: What do we mean by saying Tommy will be working to his academic potential? And regarding behavior—What would Tommy be doing if he did have more control over his actions? Do you agree that these are the two areas we should focus on?

T9: I believe that his behavior is affecting his academic performance and, if changed, will positively impact his performance in class. So, I believe his behavior should be the main focus of our intervention.

C10: Okay, do you mind if I jot this down as we go? Let's begin with Tommy's having more control over his behavior. Can you list five things that you would like to see Tommy doing that he's not doing now? Or five behaviors that you'd like to see him do less frequently? This will help us set some specific goals.

T10: First of all, I would like Tommy to be aware of other children and how his behavior affects them. I would like for him to remain in his seat more often. I would like for him to be able to listen and interact appropriately in class discussions. And I would like for him to be able to follow instructions better.

C11: Those four suggestions seem like very good ones for a start. Let me summarize our goals: We talked about the global goals of helping Tommy to learn and achieve up to his potential as well as to obtain some control over his behavior in order for you to have a more effective learning climate for the whole class. The more specific goals that you stated include giving him some insight into how his behavior affects others. You would also like him to remain in his seat more. You want him to participate in class discussions. And lastly, you would like him to follow instructions more consis-

tently. Are those some of the ideas that you had in mind?

T11: Yes. That about sums it up.

C12: Okay, now let's take each of these goals and see how we might measure progress in each area. For example, how would we know that Tommy better understands how his behavior affects other children in the classroom?

T12: I don't know, maybe through observations or his journaling. I would imagine if other goals are progressing that he would have a better understanding about how his behavior is affecting others.

C13: Sure, progress in other areas may give us some insight. That sounds really good. I did have one thought. What would happen if you had a 5- or 10-minute weekly meeting with Tommy to discuss some things that happened during that day or the week to create an awareness of other people's feelings? For example you could say, "I wonder how Mary felt when you went by and knocked down her paper?"

T13: 5 or 10 minutes . . . I could do that. I certainly spend more time on him than that now.

C14: We could use that then as one means of measuring progress toward our goal. Does that sound okay?

T14: Yes.

C15: Well, let's move on to the next goal of having Tommy stay in his seat more often. How do you think we might measure progress toward that goal?

T15: I suppose I could watch and observe over time. Perhaps take some data each day and note how the behavior decreases over time.

C16: Yes. One of the things we could do in this situation would be to take a baseline of

Tommy's behavior as well as determining the standard amount of times other kids get out of their seats in a day. Then, as you said, we can observe and collect data to measure progress over time. What about measuring progress with listening and interacting during lessons? How would you measure progress regarding this goal?

T16: I'm not sure, can we talk about that?

C17: I see what you mean. That is a difficult goal to identify. How about eye contact? It's an indicator of attentiveness. Maybe you might note how well Tommy is maintaining eye contact. If you take note of how often he is able to maintain eye contact throughout the day, these behaviors may be a good measure of attentiveness. Perhaps we could come up with more specifics about that, but for now that seems like a good general technique for obtaining information. Then interaction of course implies . . .

T17: Right, that he's participating in class discussions and answering questions.

C18: Again, we could take a baseline of frequency of behavior then compare it over time. You know, you've got enough to do. Why don't I determine this baseline data for you unless you think my presence will make Tommy act differently? We haven't discussed a plan yet, but I would be willing to come into the class at some point in the day and get this data for you so you would still be able to concentrate on the rest of the class.

T18: Okay, thanks.

C19: Let's move on to our goal of following instructions. How would you measure progress toward that goal?

T19: I would observe his behaviors, establish a baseline, and note progress over time in the form of following instructions during the day or week.

C20: So, we would actually measure progress by Tommy becoming more compliant. I do think that though we are focusing primarily on changing Tommy's behavior that we may have to change some of your techniques and classroom management behaviors. For example, you may have to give Tommy more attention at the beginning of the implementation relative to other children in the class. Is this all right with you?

T20: I can do that.

Consultant and Teacher Reflections

Consultant: *If Tommy realizes that other students resent his behavior, it may worsen the situation. We need to emphasize how his popularity will grow with more participation and compliant behavior. How can I get Ms. Gentry to realize the importance of emphasizing his growth in popularity rather than the negative side of his current behavior? Journaling is such a subjective measure to use for feedback. The negative impact Tommy's behavior has had on others may well be too sensitive for him to directly express in a journal or interview with Ms. Gentry. Is this an appropriate measure of any of our goals? Test scores are probably more important than Ms. Gentry is letting on. Perhaps they themselves should be the target of change here. The focus on improving test scores could keep Ms. Gentry fully focused and invested in the process while providing some concrete feedback for Tommy.*

Teacher: *Setting up goals and measuring progress. Is this going to work? What if I put all of this time and energy into Tommy and he doesn't change? Why does everything mean more work for me? At least the consultant seems to think that the things I will try will work and is willing to help out in the process. But give Tommy more attention? How can I possibly do that?*

C21: I believe we've come up with enough goals. Now I think we're ready to take a look at what techniques you've tried so far. This will probably give us some clues as to what directions we will take with any further plan and will also give us ideas about the best ways to work with Tommy. So, what have you tried so far, and what have you found to be helpful?

T21: When I first noticed Tommy's deviant behaviors, I would simply remind him to remain in his seat or to pay attention to the lesson, but he often would not comply. Then I moved his desk to the front of the class where I hoped he would better be able to concentrate, but this did not seem to help. I moved on to the removal of privileges such as time at recess as well as setting up a parent-teacher conference, which I mentioned previously. None of these things seemed to improve Tommy's behavior, though some worked better than others. The removal of privileges improved Tommy's behavior for a short period of time, but I don't enjoy using negative reinforcement with children. Especially since the effects seem to lessen after a few days. Tommy's mother suggested that I might reward him, but I have not implemented a plan using a reward system.

C22: You've really tried several good things. I'm a little concerned that none of them have been effective with Tommy. I understand your hesitance to use negative reinforcement, and since it has been only minimally effective, we won't include that in our plan. Do you feel that there is anything that you haven't tried that may be effective?

T22: No, I've tried all my usual tricks. I'm really frustrated with Tommy and his behavior. So, I don't really know where to go from here. I can usually get through to kids, but nothing seems to work with Tommy.

C23: Since his parents suggest that he enjoys rewards, perhaps we could design a system of positive reinforcement. Kids his age really respond to rewards. Do you have any ideas in this area?

T23: Mrs. Jones uses some sort of system of sticker reinforcement that I could use for the whole class.

C24: That's a good idea. Tommy wouldn't feel singled out, and maybe he could benefit from some peer modeling. You can even take this system a step further by creating really cool stickers with clip art to get the kids really enthusiastic. Does that sound like something you would have time for? I know how busy you are.

T24: Sure that sounds like a good idea. I believe you're right in the effectiveness of the entire class. As much as Tommy doesn't realize how his behavior affects others, he does seem to be influenced by his peers and their behaviors.

C25: Right, that really builds in the peer modeling idea. When he sees other kids performing in a certain way for a certain reward, Tommy may get the idea. Okay, it seems like we have a lot of good ideas. How about if we take the goals and create some rules and a reward system. To keep this manageable in terms of time, we'll only keep records on Tommy's behavior.

T25: Maybe this will work. Tommy will know what's expected and will respond to the positive reinforcement he's used to at home.

C26: Of course, the structure of your class will be slightly different as a result of record keeping. We also want the reinforcement to be consistent. Do you anticipate any problems or difficulties in this area?

T26: Listen, the way I feel today, I will try anything.

C27: I know students like Tommy can be a real challenge. The next step, then, is that we need to outline a plan of action. We have our basic goals. We know what we want to accomplish. I see the plan as using a peer-modeling program based on sticker reinforcement to facilitate appropriate behavior for Tommy. Let's try to put the logistical aspects of the plan into operation. What do you think would be the first step in putting this program into place?

T27: Well, I feel like I need to touch base with Tommy's parents again to let them know what we're doing. Then perhaps present the idea to Tommy himself.

C28: You're right. Tommy is a vital part of this plan, but perhaps presenting the program to the class as a whole rather than isolating Tommy would create less self-consciousness in Tommy about his behavior. To assure the effectiveness of this program for Tommy you could give him a little more attention—more eye contact and one-on-one time—in addition to making sure he's meeting his goals.

T28: Right.

C29: I told you I'd do the baselines, so I'll take care of that.

T29: Okay.

C30: So, we'll start by talking to his parents. Then the second step would be for me to come in and baseline some of his behaviors. Then thirdly, you should develop a procedure for presenting the reward system to the class.

T30: Okay.

C31: Now that we know what we're going to do and how we're going to do it, when do you think you would be ready to start?

T31: Anytime, as soon as possible. It should only take me a few days to set up a meeting with Tommy's parents. You can come in to the classroom whenever you have time within the next couple of weeks. Then we could proceed with the implementation of the reward system.

C32: Okay, I can come in about 9 A.M. on Wednesday. How does that sound?

T32: That would be fine.

C33: Look, I know you have very little free time, but I would like to give you a pamphlet on token economies that may act as a reference during the implementation of the plan. Then we need to figure out how our plan might be making progress.

T33: Well, we will be able to look at Tommy's baselines and then follow his progress. We could even plot the data we collect in class on a graph so that we have concrete evidence of change. Yeah, that works.

Consultant and Teacher Reflections

Consultant: *The negative reinforcement probably did not work because it is not used at home. I'm glad Ms. Gentry is not insisting on the use of negative reinforcement! I need to make sure that these techniques are clearly spelled out to Ms. Gentry and that they are implemented with integrity and for long enough to be effective. I'm not sure that what she has tried previously has been thoroughly implemented at a level consistent enough to be effective. I'm concerned about altering her class structure to assist record keeping. How can I minimize the level of intrusiveness this will make into her regular classroom routine?*

Teacher: *Okay, I am only investing 5–10 minutes a day on Tommy. That doesn't sound like much, but I seldom get time to breathe as it is. Is it fair that Tommy gets all of this extra attention when other better-behaved students get less? Am I taking* *too much time away from Tommy? Maybe some of the other teachers are correct. Maybe there is no point in all of this extra effort for one child who doesn't "deserve it." Yet the consultant seems to think there is hope. I wonder. Okay. Sticker program for the entire class . . . maybe Terry and Jackie's behavior can be addressed at the same time. What about the record keeping for all of this? That could be a lot. I wonder what system I could use that I'll feel comfortable with? All right. Nine Wednesday morning. That's math time. What kind of process do I need to use for the consultant to get a baseline on Tommy? I can't forget to call Tommy's parents. I wish the consultant had offered to do that. She knows more about this than I do.*

C34: Good. Okay, what have we left out?

T34: I don't know. I feel good about this plan. It will definitely be a step in a positive direction for my class and Tommy.

C35: Can we schedule a time to get back together for about 20 minutes, perhaps during your planning period on Monday? Then we can make sure everything is ready and you can let me know some specific things I should look for with Tommy on Wednesday.

T35: Okay.

C36: I feel really good about our plan of action. We've put together a lot of good ideas, and I think it has a good chance of being successful. Now, let me be sure I've got this straight . . .

T36: Okay. We've gone through a problem-solving process in which we identified the problem as being certain aspects of Tommy's behavior. We then developed a plan involving peer modeling and a sticker reward system, which we used to develop a system of implementation.

C37: Great. So you feel good about this?

T37: Sure.

C38: Well listen, I really appreciate working with you, and I hope we can do this again. Tommy is fortunate to have a teacher like you. The kids respond to you, and I can see why. With all you've got going on you're still concerned about helping, not blaming children like Tommy.

T38: Thanks. I try. And I guess if this doesn't work, we'll try something else.

Consultant and Teacher Reflections

Consultant: *Ms. Gentry seems to have bought into this process. I'm encouraged that she is approaching this from a broad-based perspective. I need to remember to reinforce her and to mention, in an appropriate way, her efforts to the principal. Hmm . . . I wonder if I should say anything to the principal. If I did, it could be misinterpreted by Ms. Gentry as well as others. Better not. This is the fourth case in which a token economy has been used this month. Maybe I should conduct some staff development training on the next workday. That would save a lot of us some time and perhaps plant some seeds for some future requests for consultation.*

Teacher: *Baseline, sticker reward system, monitoring—these are going to take time. I'll try them, but I'm not sure about all of this. Well, okay, I'll try it for a few weeks.*

SCHOOL-BASED COLLABORATION EXAMPLE

Background

Ms. Gentry, a fifth grade teacher, and Ms. Hall, a school counselor, decide to collaborate to assist a student who has difficulty with self-control. Ms. Gentry and Ms. Hall collaborated before to discuss other students. They have a good rapport with one another and share a strong respect for each other's professional abilities. As you read this case be sure to compare and contrast it with the preceding consultation case. In that way, you will notice both the similarities and differences between these two services. For example, in this case you note that the counselor takes much more responsibility for some of the outcome of the case than the psychologist in the preceding example did.

C1 (Collaborator): Ms. Gentry, hi, it's good to see you. How's it going?

T1 (Teacher): Oh, better I guess. You know I really appreciate your meeting with me. I'm so frustrated. This kid is really disrupting the whole class, and I don't know what to do about it.

C2: This is Tommy. He's the ten-year-old you mentioned the other day. I have noticed him in the hallway a lot recently.

T2: Yes. You know he's a bright kid, but I just can't get him to stay focused. He's always out of his seat with a thousand excuses . . . the bathroom, the water fountain, the trash can. And, of course this interferes with the work of the other students. As you know, we tested him but he doesn't qualify for any special services. He's of normal intelligence, and there's no LD or ADHD indications.

C3: Hmm. Okay, let me see . . . no special needs, normal IQ, but he consistently gets out of his seat, and when he's up he's not only not working himself, but he also gets others off task. I notice in the hall that he "gets in the faces" of other students a lot but in a playful manner. Anything else?

T3: No, that's about it. You know, he's not a bad child. He doesn't mean to cause problems. He's just very social and very active.

C4: Okay, so there don't seem to be emotional problems either. He's just out of control and doesn't seem able to follow the class rules. You know, that's exactly how he is in the hallway.

T4: Right. He just acts without thinking. He's not manipulative or mean. He needs to learn to control himself. I don't know what to do! I've got to do something. Tommy's not learning a thing, and he's keeping the rest of the class from learning too. My test scores this year are going to stink. I sure would like for us to try to work together to help him.

C5: Me too. We could use the problem-solving formula we've used in the past. We'll get some more details on what's going on with Tommy. Goals will probably help once we get a more precise picture of what's going on. We'll establish some realistic goals and then design a plan. You can be in charge of the classroom part of it and I will counsel with him and be responsible for that. I think he will be willing to work with me, and I'll work on changing the same behaviors you're trying to change in class. If it's okay with you we'll use that little form we developed last year to help us save time. (See Figure 13.1—The teacher and the collaborator would use the same form that was used in the consultation example with the exception that a "Responsible Party" column would be added to indicate who is responsible for each goal.) You know, I really enjoy working with you. Together, we have a better chance of helping Tommy than either one of us would have alone.

T5: Maybe we could use a plan like the one we used for Jimmy. You know, it's nice to have a counselor like you. Your plans are sensible and easily implemented.

Collaborator and Teacher Reflections

Collaborator: *At times it may be easier to utilize a ready-made form. This form can either be completed independently or during an interview with the teacher. Some teachers may prefer to use a different form or none at all. It is more important to create the conditions in which the teacher is willing to add his or her expertise to assist me in putting together and implementing my part of the plan. For example, I know she can help me determine the things that Tommy and I can work on in counseling. Some teachers become quite protective of their planning time. They may get as little as 45 minutes a day for planning and grading. By collaborating, I might help Ms. Gentry to be even more willing to spend the time it takes to help Tommy. These behaviors seem to call for a behavioral management situation. Does Ms. Gentry have the time and skills to apply the consistency required to implement a behavior management program?*

Teacher: *I wonder what is going on with this child. There's something wrong because he is not doing the work. Could it be my teaching style or approach to him? How am I going to explain his behavior if the principal walks in to observe the class? Worse yet, what if the entire class gets off task while the principal is there in my room? Well, at least Ms. Hall and I are going to work together. She listens to me and seems to understand. I really need that. I wonder if Ms. Hall is going to get the impression that I can't motivate or control the class? I wonder if she will think I complain too much. I'm glad she is going to work with Tommy in counseling. That way I am not responsible for everything about getting him changed. Perhaps by working together we can make good progress in a short amount of time.*

C6: Well, thanks. Let's hope by working together and each having "a piece of the pie" in helping Tommy that we can make some changes for the better. Okay, you basically said,

"Good kid, good intentions, average IQ, no emotional or learning problems, just out of control." That's my read on this too. Let's share some more about our perceptions of Tommy. For example, I am curious how long has this been going on.

T6: Tommy's behavior has been a problem since the beginning of the year. I've tried different techniques in dealing with Tommy's behavior, but nothing seems to work. For example, after leaving his seat in the middle of a test, he knocked a little girl's paper off her desk. She became very upset and wasn't able to finish her test. This seemed to be the last straw so to speak. At this time I called for a parent-teacher conference with Tommy's mother and father. When I informed them of the problem, they seemed surprised and concerned. At this time I asked them about Tommy's behavior at home. His parents told me that they usually did not have problems with Tommy at home, except at bedtime. His parents don't sound very strict. I got the impression that their expectations of him are only that he eat with the family and be in bed on time. Tommy basically decides what he does with his time. His mother felt that Tommy's behavior could easily be controlled by explaining the rules to him. She didn't seem to understand that I had already made several attempts to control his behavior, including explaining the rules, but always failed.

C7: That's got to be frustrating to have tried different types of behavior control and gotten nowhere and then find that there are not many expectations at home. Maybe we can design something new that gets better results. Is that your primary concern?

T7: That is definitely my primary concern because his behavior is not only disrupting *his*

academic achievement but disrupting the concentration of the class as a whole.

C8: I think we have a pretty good idea about the nature of the problem. Now let's talk a little bit about goals. What would we like to see happen regarding Tommy's behavior?

Collaborator and Teacher Reflections

Collaborator: *Tommy's parents sound loose. I wonder what kind of messages Tommy's parents send him about how to respond to Ms. Gentry's expectations? Maybe we need to involve them in our attempts to help Tommy. I also wonder if Tommy's acting out behavior is a result of lack of control, attention getting, rebelliousness or something else? A behavior management program may be effective with the first two causes, but if he is motivated by rebelliousness, I wonder if such a program would work. All of this makes me think that I should work with him in counseling.*

Teacher: *Well maybe I am too strict. Who knows? You know I tried those things I mentioned to Ms. Hall, but did I try hard enough and long enough and do them correctly? Why are these parents so lenient with this child? Maybe Ms. Hall and I should make a home visit part of the plan.*

T8: Well, for my part, I would like for Tommy to be able to perform up to his potential in the classroom. He needs to get some control over his behavior in order to concentrate. He needs to change his behaviors so he's not distracting to the other kids in the classroom.

C9: I agree. That's what I want to do. Those things really seem to go hand in hand. If he is able to gain some control over his behavior, he should be less likely to disturb the other children in the class. We would also want him to work more toward his academic poten-

tial. Those really seem like good global goals for Tommy. In order to help him most effectively we need to clarify two things: What do we mean by saying Tommy will be working to his academic potential? And regarding behavior—What would Tommy be doing if he did have more control over his actions? I think that these are the two areas we should focus on. Do you agree?

T9: I believe that his behavior is affecting his academic performance and, if changed, will positively impact his performance in class. So, I believe his behavior should be the main focus of our intervention. Okay, I will jot this down as we go along.

C10: Great. Let's begin with Tommy's having more control over his behavior. Let's list some things that we would like to see Tommy doing that he's not doing now. Or some behaviors that we'd like to see him do less frequently. This will help us set some specific goals. For example, I want him to walk down the hallway without disturbing others. I also want him to learn better social skills through the counseling I'll be providing him.

T10: For me, well let's see. First of all, I would like Tommy to be aware of other children and how his behavior affects them. I would like for him to remain in his seat more often. I would like for him to be able to listen and interact appropriately in class discussions. And I would like for him to be able to follow instructions better.

C11: Those four suggestions seem like very good ones for a start. Let's summarize our goals: We talked about the global goals of helping Tommy to learn and achieve up to his potential as well as to obtain some control over his behavior in order for you to have a more effective learning climate for the whole class. The more specific goals that we stated include giving him some insight into how his behavior affects others. We would also like him to remain in his seat more. We want him to participate in class discussions. And lastly, we would like him to follow instructions more consistently.

T11: We also want him to learn better social skills and behave properly in the hallway. I know one thing. He's not gong to be in the hallway much any more. At any rate we are going to have to figure out how we know what kind of progress is being made.

C12: Good point. Let's take each of these goals and see how we might measure progress in each area. For example, how would we know that Tommy better understands how his behavior affects other children in the classroom?

T12: I don't know, maybe through observations or his journaling. I would imagine if other goals are progressing that he would have a better understanding about how his behavior is affecting others.

C13: Sure, progress in other areas may give us some insight. That sounds really good. I did have one thought. What would happen if you had a 5- or 10-minute weekly meeting with Tommy to discuss some things that happened during that day or the week to create an awareness of other people's feelings? For example you could say, "I wonder how Mary felt when you went by and knocked down her paper?"

T13: 5 or 10 minutes . . . I could do that. I certainly spend more time on him than that now.

C14: We could use that then as one means of measuring progress toward our goal. Does that sound okay?

T14: Sounds okay to me. Well, let's move on to the next goal of having Tommy stay in his seat more often. How do you think we might measure progress toward that goal?

C15: What's your take on this?

T15: I suppose I could watch and observe over time. Perhaps take some data each day and note how the behavior decreases over time.

C16: Yes. One of the things we could do in this situation would be to take a baseline of Tommy's behavior as well as determining the standard amount of times other kids get out of their seats in a day. Then, as you said, we can observe and collect data to measure progress over time. What about measuring progress with listening and interacting during lessons? How would you measure progress regarding this goal?

T16: I'm not sure, can we talk about that?

C17: I see what you mean. That is a difficult goal to identify. How about eye contact? It's an indicator of attentiveness. Maybe you might note how well Tommy is maintaining eye contact. If you take note of how often he is able to maintain eye contact throughout the day, these behaviors may be a good measure of attentiveness. Perhaps we could come up with more specifics about that, but for now that seems like a good general technique for obtaining information. Then interaction of course implies . . .

T17: Right, that he's participating in class discussions and answering questions.

C18: Again, we could take a baseline of frequency of behavior then compare it over time. You know, you've got enough to do. Why don't I determine this baseline data for you unless you think my presence will make

Tommy act differently? We haven't discussed a plan yet, but I would be willing to come into the class at some point in the day and get this data for you so you would still be able to concentrate on the rest of the class. I'd like to share this information with you. Maybe you can give me some ideas for working with him in counseling after you look at it.

T18: Okay, thanks. Now let's talk about him following directions.

C19: Good idea. Our goal is for him to follow instructions better. How can we measure progress toward that goal?

T19: I would observe his behaviors, establish a baseline, and note progress over time in the form of following instructions during the day or week.

C20: So, we would actually measure progress by Tommy becoming more compliant. I do think that though we are focusing primarily on changing Tommy's behavior that we may have to change some of your techniques and classroom management behaviors. For example, you may have to give Tommy more attention at the beginning of the implementation relative to other children in the class. Is this all right with you?

T20: I can do that. In your counseling with him you can reinforce these behaviors. I wonder if he should be in a group rather than one-on-one with you. I guess I keep going back to the social skills and the fact that the group is a great place to practice them in vivo. We can talk about that later.

Collaborator and Teacher Reflections

Collaborator: *If Tommy realizes that other students resent his behavior, it may worsen the situation. We need to emphasize how his popularity will grow with more participation and compliant behavior. How can I get Ms. Gentry to realize the importance of emphasizing his growth in popularity rather than the negative side of his current behavior? Journaling is such a subjective measure to use for feedback. The negative impact Tommy's behavior has had on others may well be too sensitive for him to directly express in a journal or interview with Ms. Gentry. Is this an appropriate measure of any of our goals? Test scores are probably more important than Ms. Gentry is letting on. Perhaps they themselves should be the target of change here. The focus on improving test scores could keep Ms. Gentry fully focused and invested in the process while providing some concrete feedback for Tommy. I'm glad Ms. Gentry is willing to make some suggestions, like the group suggestion, to me. It shows that we are truly collaborating here. It's nice to have some external validation of my ideas, or even some new ones from an informed source.*

Teacher: *Setting up goals and measuring progress. Is this going to work? What if I put all of this time and energy into Tommy and he doesn't change? Why does everything mean more work for me? At least Ms. Hall seems to think that the things I will try will work and is willing to help out in the process. But give Tommy more attention? How can I possibly do that? I like how Ms. Hall was open to my idea about working with Tommy in a group. It is nice to see that I can help her some as she is helping me. Maybe we will get somewhere on all of this and I won't end up having to do all of the work.*

C21: I believe we've come up with enough goals. Now I think we're ready to take a look at what techniques we've tried so far. This will probably give us some clues as to what directions to take with Tommy. It will help us to develop a better plan and figure out some possible ways to work with Tommy. I don't have anything to report because I haven't had him in counseling before and haven't really done anything about his behavior in the classroom. What about you? What have you tried so far, and what have you found to be helpful with him in the classroom?

T21: When I first noticed Tommy's deviant behaviors, I would simply remind him to remain in his seat or to pay attention to the lesson, but he often would not comply. Then I moved his desk to the front of the class where I hoped he would better be able to concentrate, but this did not seem to help. I moved on to the removal of privileges such as time at recess as well as setting up a parent-teacher conference, which I mentioned previously. None of these things seemed to improve Tommy's behavior, though some worked better than others. The removal of privileges improved Tommy's behavior for a short period of time, but I don't enjoy using negative reinforcement with children. Especially since the effects seem to lessen after a few days. Tommy's mother suggested that I might reward him, but I have not implemented a plan using a reward system. By the way, we need to involve the parents in this one. I think they are a piece of what's wrong.

C22: I agree with involving the parents. I really think you've really tried several good things. I'm a little concerned that none of them have been effective with Tommy. I understand your hesitance to use negative reinforcement, and since it has been only minimally effective, we won't include that in our plan. Do you feel that there is anything that you haven't tried that may be effective?

T22: No, I've tried all my usual tricks. I'm really frustrated with Tommy and his behavior. So, I don't really know where to go from here. I can usually get through to kids, but nothing

seems to work with Tommy. Since his parents suggest that he enjoys rewards, perhaps we could design a system of positive reinforcement. Kids his age really respond to rewards. Do you have any ideas in this area?

C23: Well, sometimes sticker reinforcement works well with students like Tommy.

T23: Mrs. Jones uses some sort of system of sticker reinforcement that I could use for the whole class.

C24: That's a good idea. Tommy wouldn't feel singled out, and maybe he could benefit from some peer modeling. Does that sound like something you would have time for? I know how busy you are.

T24: Sure, that sounds like a good idea; I was on the same track as you when you started talking. I can even take this system a step further by creating really cool stickers with clip art to get the kids really enthusiastic. I believe we're right in the effectiveness of the entire class. As much as Tommy doesn't realize how his behavior affects others, he does seem to be influenced by his peers and their behaviors.

C25: Right, that really builds in the peer modeling idea. When he sees other kids performing in a certain way for a certain reward, Tommy may get the idea. Okay, it seems like we have a lot of good ideas. How about if we take the goals and create some rules and a reward system. We have to keep this thing manageable.

T25: To keep this manageable in terms of time, we'll only keep records on Tommy's behavior. Maybe this will work. Tommy will know what's expected and will respond to the positive reinforcement he's used to at home.

C26: Of course, the structure of your class will be slightly different as a result of record keeping. We also want the reinforcement to be consistent. Do you anticipate any problems or difficulties in this area?

T26: Listen, the way I feel today, I will try anything. I can do this.

C27: I know students like Tommy can be a real challenge. Part of me is wondering how I am going to convince him that counseling is in his best interest. Well, back to the reward system. The next step, then, is that we need to outline a plan of action. We have our basic goals. We know what we want to accomplish. I see the plan as using a peer-modeling program based on sticker reinforcement to facilitate appropriate behavior for Tommy. Let's try to put the logistical aspects of the plan into operation.

T27: Well, I think the first step in putting this program into place is to touch base with Tommy's parents again to let them know what we're doing. Then we could present the idea to Tommy himself.

C28: You're right. Maybe we should use your idea of a home visit to enlist their support and maybe their participation. Tommy is a vital part of this plan, but perhaps presenting the program to the class as a whole rather than isolating Tommy would create less self-consciousness in Tommy about his behavior. To assure the effectiveness of this program for Tommy you could give him a little more attention—more eye contact and one-on-one time—in addition to making sure he's meeting his goals.

T28: Right.

C29: I told you I'd do the baselines, so I'll take care of that.

T29: Okay. So, we'll start by talking to his parents. Then the second step would be for you to come in and baseline some of his behaviors. Then thirdly, I should develop a procedure for presenting the reward system to the class.

C30: That will work for me. I'll think about the visit to the home and how we should go about approaching the parents. I'll think of some questions for you about how I might proceed with Tommy in counseling, like what he sees as rewarding and so forth.

T30: Okay.

C31: Now that we know what we're going to do and how we're going to do it, when do you think you would be ready to start?

T31: Anytime, as soon as possible. It should only take you a few days to set up a meeting with Tommy's parents. You can come in to the classroom whenever you have time within the next couple of weeks. Then we could proceed with the implementation of the reward system. I will create a list of information on Tommy you can use in counseling. I am assuming you are still thinking about working with him in a group?

C32: Yes, I might have a couple of sessions one-on-one to gain a relationship and get him used to the process so he can be more ready for a group. About the baselining, I can come in about 9 A.M. on Wednesday. How does that sound?

T32: That would be fine.

C33: Look, I know you have very little free time, but I would like to give you a pamphlet on token economies that may act as a reference during the implementation of the plan. Then we need to figure out how our plan might be making progress.

T33: Well, we will be able to look at Tommy's baselines and then follow his progress.

We could even plot the data we collect in class on a graph so that we have concrete evidence of change. Yeah, that works. By the way, I have put together some of his work so you can get a feel for what he does academically.

Collaborator and Teacher Reflections

Collaborator: *The negative reinforcement probably did not work because it is not used at home. I'm glad Ms. Gentry is not insisting on the use of negative reinforcement! I need to make sure that these techniques are clearly spelled out to Ms. Gentry and that they are implemented with integrity and for long enough to be effective. I'm not sure that what she has tried previously has been thoroughly implemented at a level consistent enough to be effective. I'm concerned about altering her class structure to assist record keeping. How can I minimize the level of intrusiveness this will make into her regular classroom routine? I am concerned that the parents will play "No problem" with us and defend Tommy as being okay and imply that the problem is in the school. Ms. Gentry and I will need to make sure we are together on how we will approach the parents. I think Tommy can fit into a group. If his social skills are poor, the other kids may reject him pretty quickly. I guess individual counseling at the beginning will prevent some of that.*

Teacher: *Okay, I am only investing 5–10 minutes a day on Tommy. That doesn't sound like much, but I seldom get time to breathe as it is. Is it fair that Tommy gets all of this extra attention when other better-behaved students get less? Am I taking too much time away from Tommy? Maybe some of the other teachers are correct. Maybe there is no point in all of this extra effort for one child who doesn't "deserve it." Yet Ms. Hall seems to think there is hope. I wonder. Okay. Sticker program for the entire class . . . maybe Terry and Jackie's behav-ior can be addressed at the same time. What about the record keeping for all of this? That could be a lot. I wonder what system I could use that I'll feel comfortable with? All right. Nine Wednesday morning. That's math time. What kind of process do I need to use for Ms. Hall to get a baseline on Tommy? We can't forget to call Tommy's parents. We have to make sure we are on the same wavelength before we approach them. I don't like home visits, but this one may be worth it. Something has to change with Tommy. Ms. Hall knows more about this than I do, but I know Tommy better. I'm glad Ms. Hall is going to do group work with Tommy. I don't think that individual counseling as the only treatment would work that well with Tommy. I am glad that she was open to my advice.*

C34: Good. Okay, what have we left out?

T34: I don't know. I feel good about this plan. It will definitely be a step in a positive direction for my class and Tommy.

C35: Can we schedule a time to get back together for about 20 minutes, perhaps during your planning period on Monday? Then we can make sure everything is ready and you can let me know some specific things I should look for with Tommy on Wednesday.

T35: Okay.

C36: I feel really good about our plan of action. We've put together a lot of good ideas, and I think it has a good chance of being successful. Now, let me be sure I've got this straight . . .

T36: Okay. We've gone through a problem-solving process in which we identified the problem as being certain aspects of Tommy's behavior. We then developed a plan involving peer modeling and a sticker reward system, which we used to develop a system of implementation. Then we developed a plan whereby we would try to engage the parents in helping him by making a home visit. You are going to work with Tommy in counseling and I am going to get you some ideas on things I think might work for you when you counsel him.

C37: Great. I feel good about this.

T37: Me too. I think by working together on this that we can hopefully help Tommy.

C38: Well listen, I really appreciate working with you, and I hope we can do this again. Tommy is fortunate to have a teacher like you. The kids respond to you, and I can see why. With all you've got going on you're still concerned about helping, not blaming children like Tommy.

T38: Thanks. I try. And I guess if this doesn't work, we'll try something else. By the way, a lot of counselors would just come in and work out something for *me* to do. Then they would go off and work with someone else. It makes me feel real good to know that I have a partner in this. I have support and someone who is working toward the same ends. It's a nice feeling to know that we are in this together.

Collaborator and Teacher Reflections

Collaborator: *Ms. Gentry seems to have bought into this process. I'm encouraged that she is approaching this from a broad-based perspective. I need to remember to reinforce her and to mention, in an appropriate way, her efforts to the principal. Hmm . . . I wonder if I should say anything to the principal. If I did, Ms. Gentry as well as others could misinterpret it. Better not. Ms. Gentry's investment in this goes to show how sometimes collaboration is a better way to go than consultation. I think either service would work with her but I can think of many teachers who would want me to work with their students while they are working*

with the student also. This is the fourth case in which a token economy has been used this month. Maybe I should conduct some staff development training on the next workday. That would save a lot of us some time and perhaps plant some seeds for some future requests for collaboration. Better yet, I should ask for a few minutes at our next faculty meeting and discuss collaboration and consultation. It never hurts to keep these ideas in front of teachers and principals.

Teacher: *Baseline, sticker reward system, monitoring, and a home visit—these are going to take time. But so is Ms. Hall's counseling Tommy. I'll try my end of this for a few weeks. After all I won't be alone. It's not like we aren't going to help one another with each of our responsibilities in helping Tommy. All I can say is that I am relieved I'm not the only one responsible for helping Tommy change here.*

SUMMARY

This chapter encourages you to begin assessing your own personal model of consultation and collaboration. It has applied the various approaches to organizational, mental health, and behavioral consultation to some work-related problem within a particular organization. Table 13.1 summarizes the major focus of each approach.

In addition, we compared two transcripts of similar cases involving school-based consultation and collaboration to help you differentiate between these two services.

SUGGESTIONS FOR EFFECTIVE PRACTICE

- Remember to develop and follow your own personal model of consultation and collaboration.

Table 13.1   The Major Focus of Several Consultation and Collaboration Approaches

APPROACH	MAJOR FOCUS
Organizational	
Educational/Training	Training or educating consultees to be more effective in some area
Program	Assisting an organization with some aspect of a program, frequently evaluation
Doctor-Patient	Entering an organization, diagnosing a problem, and prescribing a solution
Process	Assisting consultees in becoming better decision makers and problem solvers in the future
Mental Health	
Client-Centered Case	Helping a consultee with a client (with minimal contact with the consultee)
Consultee-Centered Case	Considers work-related problem to reside in the consultee; helping consultee by focusing on case
Program-Centered Administrative	Helping an administrator fix a program-related problem
Consultee-Centered Administrative	Helping an administrator and other consultees develop their skills to improve the mental health aspects of the organization and its programs
Ecological	Changing the human-environment interface
Behavioral	
Training	Training consultees to improve their general and/or specific skill areas of behavioral technology
System	Assisting an organization in being more effective by using behavioral technology
Case	Helping a consultee apply behavioral technology to a case

- Read case studies and transcripts of consultation and collaboration cases often to maintain a sense of how others deal with the nuts and bolts of effective practice.

- Remember to do what you love, and love what you do!

QUESTIONS FOR REFLECTION

1. Which of the approaches just described in the Acme case most emphasize the quality of the consultation relationship?

2. Of the Acme cases just described, in which would consultation be the most difficult to evaluate adequately?

3. In the Acme case, do you see similarities among behavioral system consultation, doctor–patient consultation, and process consultation? Explain your answer.

4. Would you proceed in a manner different from mine if you were asked to perform process consultation with Acme? If so, how?

5. What similarities did you notice in the school–based consultation and collaboration transcripts?

6. What differences did you detect in the school–based consultation and collaboration transcripts?

7. Based on your reading of this chapter, which approach appeals to you the most? Why?

8. Of the cases discussed, in which one would you most like to have been the consultant or a collaborating professional? Why?

9. With which approach would you have the most difficulty in the role of consultant or collaborator? Why?

10. For which approaches would you actively seek out additional training?

SUGGESTED SUPPLEMENTARY READINGS

Alpert, J. L. (1982). *Psychological consultation in educational settings*. San Francisco: Jossey-Bass. This text may be two decades old, but it consists of a series of detailed reports about consultation. Using a type of case study format, each chapter emphasizes a different type of consultation in an educational setting. A final section of the book discusses issues such as the consultant's knowledge of the system, vested interests, and degree of accountability to the system. This book is limited in that it focuses only on consultation in educational settings; still, it provides the reader a wealth of anecdotes about consultation not found in journal articles or most texts. Read this book if you want to get a feel for the "hands-on" aspects of consultation.

Blake, R. R., and Mouton, J. S. (1983). *Consultation: A handbook for individual and organization development* (2nd ed.). Reading, MA: Addison-Wesley. Every chapter in this text is filled with brief examples of consultation interventions with individuals, groups, and organizations. Problem areas addressed range from morale to leadership, and examples are provided across a variety of settings. A reading of this lengthy text will provide a wealth of information about the great diversity of consultation interventions. Don't let the 1983 copyright deter you from reading the rich material related to interventions in this text.

Dougherty, A. M. (2000). Psychological consultation and collaboration: A casebook (3rd ed.). Belmont, CA: Wadsworth. This text provides several case studies of human services consultation and collaboration. The final chapter provides several practice cases. This case studies book is designed to accompany the present text. Its focus is to provide a nuts-and-bolts approach to understanding how to provide services in consultation and collaboration.

Epilogue

I hope you have enjoyed and benefited from this book. Providing consultation and collaboration can be among the most challenging and enjoyable professional activities in which you engage. As you reflect on what you have read and practiced, let me leave you with some concluding thoughts.

There is no "one-minute manager" type of consultation or collaboration. To be accomplished effectively, these services take time—a difficult prospect in the "quick fix" society we live in.

Appreciate the challenge of the complexity of these services. Take care not to be overwhelmed by all the variables that affect their processes. If you give your best effort when you consult and collaborate and trust the process, then anxiety and doubt will not overburden you.

To enhance your effectiveness as a consultant and as a collaborator, continue your professional and personal development. You will need to become familiar with the literature on consultation and collaboration, have some supervised field experience in performing them, gain a sense of the organizational context in which they occur, and possess some degree of knowledge of who you are as a person. Taken together these will provide a cognitive map to guide your practice.

When in doubt, collaborate. Collaboration minimizes the probability of a negative experience and at the same time maximizes the input into the problem-solving process. It is also empowering by nature. Consultation and collaboration are relationships among humans—they need to be performed with a personal touch. Each is more than a science, more than an art, more than a craft: each is all of these things along with commitment—to oneself as a helper, to the people with whom one is working, and to the ever-challenging task of trying to help others work more effectively.

Good luck and best wishes!

References

ACES-ASCA Joint Committee on the Elementary School Counselor. (1966). The elementary school counselor: Preliminary statement. *Personnel and Guidance Journal, 61,* 658–661.

Adams, J. D., & Spencer, S. (1986). Consulting with the strategic leadership perspective. *Consultation, 5,* 149–159.

Adelman, H. S., & Taylor, L. (1998). Toward a scale-up model for replicating new approaches to schooling. *Journal of Educational and Psychological Consultation, 8,* 197–230.

Adlerfer, C. P. (1990). Organizational consultation: The state of the field. *Journal of Applied Behavioral Science, 23,* 281–284.

Allen, C. T., & Forman, S. G. (1984). Efficacy of methods of training teachers in behavior modification. *School Psychology Review, 13(1),* 26–32.

Allen, J. M. (1994). School counselors collaborating for success. ERIC document #EDO-CG-94-27. Greensboro, NC: ERIC/CASS.

Allen, S. J., & Graden, S. J. (1995). Best practices in collaborative problem solving for intervention design. In A. Thomas & J. Grimes (Eds.), *Best practices in school psy-chology* (3rd ed., pp. 667–678). Washington, DC: National Association of School Psychologists.

Alpert, J. L. (Ed.). (1982). *Psychological consultation in educational settings.* San Francisco: Jossey-Bass.

Alpert, J., & Silverstein, J. (1985). Mental health consultation: Historical, present and future perspectives. In J. R. Bergan (Ed.), *School psychology in contemporary society* (pp. 121–138). Columbus, OH: Merrill.

Altrocchi, J. (1972). Mental health consultation. In S. E. Golarm & C. Eisdorfer (Eds.), *Handbook of community mental health* (pp. 477–508). New York: Appleton-Century-Crofts.

Amada, G. (1993). The role of the mental health consultant in dealing with disruptive college students. *Journal of College Student Psychotherapy, 8,* 121–127.

American Association for Counseling and Development. (1991). Multiculturalism as a fourth force in counseling. *Journal of Counseling and Development, 70(1).* Alexandria, VA: Author.

American Association for Counseling and Development. (1995). *Ethical standards* (rev. ed.). Alexandria, VA: Author.

American Counseling Association. (1995). *Code of ethics and standards of practice* (rev. ed.). Alexandria, VA: Author.

American Psychological Association. (1993). Guidelines for providers of psychological services to ethnic, linguistic, and culturally diverse populations. *American Psychologist, 48(1),* 45–48.

American Psychological Association. (1995). *Ethical principles of psychologists and code of conduct* (rev. ed.). Washington, DC: Author.

American Society for Training and Development. (1992). *1992 Who's who in training and development.* Alexandria, VA: Author.

Anderson, B. S. (1996). *The counselor and the law* (4th ed.). Alexandria, VA: American Counseling Association.

Anderson, D. (1992). A case for standards of counseling practice. *Journal of Counseling and Development, 71,* 22–26.

Anderson, T. K., Kratochwill, T. R., & Bergan, J. R. (1986). Training teachers in behavioral consultation and therapy: An analysis of verbal behaviors. *Journal of School Psychology, 24,* 229–241.

Anderson, W. R., Frieden, B. J., & Murphy, M. J. (Eds.). (1977). *Managing human services.* Washington, DC: International City Management Association.

Aplin, J. C. (1978). Structural change vs. behavioral change. *Personnel and Guidance Journal, 56(7),* 407–411.

Argyris, C. (1964). *Integrating the individual and the organization.* New York: Wiley.

Argyris, C. (1970). *Intervention theory and method: A behavioral science view.* Reading, MA: Addison-Wesley.

Argyris, C. (1976). Explorations in consulting-client relationships. In W. G. Bennis, K. D. Benne, R. Chin, & K. E. Corey (Eds.), *The planning of change* (3rd ed., pp. 331–352). New York: Holt, Rinehart & Winston.

Armenakis, A. A., & Burdg, H. B. (1988). Consultation research: Contributions to practice and directions for improvement. *Journal of Management, 14,* 339–365.

Armenakis, A. A., Burdg, H. B., & Metzger, R. O. (1989). Invited commentary: Current issues in consultant selection. *Consultation, 8,* 133–142.

Armstrong, I. R., & Wheatley, W. J. (1990). Diagnosing the needs of small business clients: A methodology for consultants. *Consultation, 8,* 25–40.

Arredondo, P., Toporek, R., Brown, S. P., Jones, J., Locke, D. C., Sanchez, J., & Stadler, H. (1996). Operationalization of the multicultural counseling competencies. *Journal of Multicultural Counseling and Development, 24(1),* 42–78.

Ary, D., Jacobs, L. C., & Razavieh, A. (1985). *Introduction to research in education* (3rd ed.). New York: Holt, Rinehart & Winston.

Ashford, S. J., & Cummings, L. L. (1983). Feedback as an individual resource: Personal strategies of creating information. *Organizational Behavior and Human Performance, 32,* 370–398.

Association for Specialists in Group Work. (1989). *Ethical guidelines for group counselors.* Alexandria, VA: Author.

Association for Specialists in Group Work. (1990). *Professional standards for the training of group workers.* Alexandria, VA: Author.

Axelson, J. A. (1993). *Counseling and development in a multicultural society* (2nd ed.). Pacific Grove, CA: Brooks/Cole.

Baard, P. P. (1994). A motivational model for consulting with not-for-profit organizations: A study of church growth and participation. *Consulting Psychology Journal: Practice & Research, 46,* 19–31.

Babcock, N. L., & Pryzwansky, W. B. (1983). Models of consultation: Preferences of educational professionals at five stages of service. *Journal of School Psychology, 21,* 359–366.

Babinski, L. M., & Rogers, D. L. (1998). Supporting new teachers through consultee-centered group consultation. *Journal of Educational and Psychological Consultation, 9,* 285–308.

Backer, T. E. (1985). The future of organizational consulting. *Consultation, 4(1),* 17–29.

Backer, T. E. (1988). Workplace drug abuse programs: Consultation issues and opportunities. *Consultation, 7,* 216–227.

Backer, T. E. (1993). Consulting on innovation and change with public mental health organizations: The Caplan approach. In W. P. Erchul (Ed.), *Consultation in community, school, and organizational practice* (pp. 149–162). Washington, DC: Taylor & Francis.

Bacon, E. H., & Dougherty, A. M. (1992). Consultation in preschool settings. *Elementary School Guidance and Counseling, 27,* 24–32.

Baker, S. B., & Shaw, M. C. (1987). *Improving counseling through primary prevention.* Columbus, OH: Merrill.

Bandura, A. (1977). *Social learning theory.* Englewood Cliffs, NJ: Prentice-Hall.

Barak, A. (1994). A cognitive-behavioral educational workshop to combat sexual harassment in the workplace. *Journal of Counseling & Development, 8,* 595–602.

Bardon, J. (1986). Psychology and schooling: The interrelationships among persons, processes, and products. In S. N. Elliot & J. C. Witt (Eds.), *The delivery of psychological services in schools: Concepts, processes, and issues* (pp. 53–80). Hillsdale, NJ: Erlbaum.

Barlow, D. H., Hayes, S. C., & Nelson, R. O. (1984). *The scientist practitioner*. New York: Pergamon Press.

Barlow, D. H., & Hersen, M. (1984). *Single case experimental designs* (2nd ed.). New York: Pergamon Press.

Barnett, D., & Lentz, F. E., Jr. (1993). Functional outcome analysis: A good heuristic that went a bridge too far. *School Psychology Quarterly, 8*, 231–237.

Beck, V. (1994). Opportunity plus: A school- and community-based tutorial program for elementary students. *Elementary School Guidance & Counseling, 29*, 156–160.

Becker, W. O. (1971). *Parents are teachers*. Champaign, IL: Research Press.

Beckhard, R. (1979). Organization changing through consulting and training. In D. P. Sinha (Ed.), *Consultants and consultant styles* (pp. 17–44). New Delhi, India: Vision Books.

Beer, M. (1980). *Organization change and development: A systems view*. Glenview, IL: Scott, Foresman.

Beer, M., & Spector, B. (1993). Organizational diagnosis: Its role in organizational learning. *Journal of Counseling and Development, 71*, 642–650.

Beer, M., & Walton, R. E. (1990). Developing the competitive organization: Interventions and strategies. *American Psychologist, 45(2)*, 154–161.

Beisser, A. R., & Green, R. (1972). *Mental health consultation and education*. Palo Alto, CA: National Press Books.

Bell, C. R., & Nadler, L. (Eds.). (1985). *Clients and consultants: Meeting and exceeding expectations* (2nd ed.). Houston: Gulf Publishing.

Bellack, A. S., & Hersen, M. (Eds.). (1985). *Dictionary of behavior therapy techniques*. New York: Pergamon Press.

Bellman, G. M. (1990). *The consultant's calling*. San Francisco: Jossey-Bass.

Bennis, W. G., Benne, K. D., Chin, R., & Corey, K. E. (Eds.). (1985). *The planning of change* (4th ed.). New York: Holt, Rinehart & Winston.

Benshoff, J. M., & Paisley, P. O. (1996). The structured peer consultation model for school counselors. *Journal for Counseling & Development, 74*, 314–318.

Bergan, J. R. (1977). *Behavioral consultation*. Columbus, OH: Merrill

Bergan, J. R., & Kratochwill, T. R. (1990). *Behavioral consultation and therapy*. New York: Plenum.

Bergan, J. R., & Tombari, M. L. (1976). Consultant skill and efficiency and the implementation and outcomes of consultation. *Journal of School Psychology, 14(1)*, 3–14.

Bersoff, D. N. (1996). The virtue of principle ethics. *The Counseling Psychologist, 24(1)*, 86–91.

Bianco-Mathis, V., & Veazey, N. (1996). Consultant dilemmas: Lessons from the trenches. *Training and Development Journal*, (July), 39–42.

Birnbrauer, H. (1987). Evaluation techniques that work. *Training and Development Journal, 41(7)*, 53–55.

Bittel, L. R. (1972). *The nine master keys of management*. New York: McGraw-Hill.

Blake, R. R., & Mouton, J. S. (1983). *Consultation: A handbook for individual and organization development* (2nd ed.). Reading, MA: Addison-Wesley.

Block, P. (1981). *Flawless consulting: A guide to getting your expertise used*. Austin, TX: Learning Concepts.

Bloom, B. L. (1984). *Community mental health: A general introduction* (2nd ed.). Pacific Grove, CA: Brooks/Cole.

Boss, R. W. (1985). The psychological contract: A key to effective organization development consultation. *Consultation, 4(4)*, 284–304.

Boss, R. W. (1993). The psychological contract. In R. T. Golembiewski (Ed.), *Handbook of organizational consultation* (pp. 65–74). New York: Marcel Dekker, Inc.

Brack, G., Jones, E. S., Smith, R. M., White, J., & Brack, C. J. (1993). A primer on consultation theory: Building a flexible world view. *Journal of Counseling and Development, 71*, 619–628.

Bradley, D. F. (1994). A framework for the acquisition of collaborative consultation skills. *Journal of Educational and Psychological Consultation, 5*, 51–68.

Bramlett, R. K., & Murphy, J. J. (1998). School psychology perspectives on consultation: Key contributions to the field. *Journal of Educational and Psychology Consultation, 9*, 29–55.

Braucht, S., & Weime, B. (1992). The school counselor as consultant on self-esteem: An example. *Elementary School Guidance and Counseling, 26*, 229–236.

Brehm, J. W. (1966). *A theory of psychological reactance*. New York: Academic Press.

Brett, J. M., Goldberg, S. B., & Ury, W. L. (1990). Designing systems for resolving disputes in organizations. *American Psychologist, 45(2)*, 162–170.

Brown, D. (1988). Empowerment through advocacy. In D. J. Kurpius & D. Brown (Eds.), *Handbook of consultation: An intervention for advocacy and outreach* (pp. 5–17). Alexandria, VA: American Association for Counseling and Development.

Brown, D. (1993). Defining human services consultation. In J. E. Zins, T. R. Kratochwill, & S. N. Elliot (Eds.). *Handbook of consultation for children*. San Francisco: Jossey-Bass.

Brown, D. (1997). Implications of cultural values for cross-cultural consultation with families. *Journal of Counseling and Development, 76,* 29–35.

Brown, D. T., & Kurpius, D. J. (1985). Guest editors' introduction. *The Counseling Psychologist, 13(3),* 333–335.

Brown D., Kurpius, D. J., & Morris, J. R. (1988). *Handbook of consultation with individuals and small groups.* Alexandria, VA: American Association for Counseling and Development.

Brown, D., Pryzwansky, W. B., & Schulte, A. C. (1991). *Psychological consultation: Introduction to theory and practice* (2nd ed.). Boston: Allyn & Bacon.

Brown, D., Pryzwansky, W. B., & Schulte, A. C. (1995). *Psychological consultation: Introduction to theory and practice* (3rd ed.). Boston: Allyn & Bacon.

Brown, J. E. (1987). A systemic view of psychological consultation in the schools. *Canadian Journal of Counseling, 21,* 114–124.

Brubaker, J. C. (1978). Futures consultation: Designing desirable futures. *Personnel and Guidance Journal, 56,* 428–431.

Bundy, M. L., & Poppen, W. A. (1986). School counselors' effectiveness as consultants: A research review. *Elementary School Guidance and Counseling, 20,* 215–222.

Burges, B. (1976). *Facts and figures: A layman's guide to conducting surveys.* Boston: Institute for Responsive Education.

Burke, W. W. (1980). Organization development and bureaucracy in the 1980's. *Journal of Applied Behavioral Science, 16(3),* 423–437.

Burke, W. W. (1993). The changing world of organizational change. *Consulting Psychology Journal, 45,* 9–17.

Burrello, L. C., & Reitzug, U. C. (1993). Transforming context and developing culture in schools. *Journal of Counseling and Development, 71,* 669–677.

Butler, W. M., Leitenberg, H., & Fuselier, G. D. (1993). The use of mental health professional consultants to police hostage negotiation teams. *Behavioral Sciences and the Law, 11,* 213–221.

Buysse, V., Schulte, A. C., Pierce, P. P., & Terry, D. (1994). Models and styles of consultation: Preferences of professionals in early intervention. *Journal of Early Intervention, 18,* 302–310.

Calfee, B. E. (1997). Lawsuit prevention techniques. In *The Hatherleigh guide to ethics in therapy* (pp. 109–125). New York: Hatherleigh Press.

Campbell, C. A. (1992). The school counselor as consultant: Assessing your aptitude. *Elementary School Guidance and Counseling, 26,* 237–250.

Campbell, C. A. (1993). Strategies for reducing parent resistance to consultation in the schools. *Elementary School Guidance and Counseling, 28,* 83–91.

Caplan, G. (1970). *The theory and practice of mental health consultation.* New York: Basic Books.

Caplan, G. (1974). *Support systems and community health: Lectures in concept development.* New York: Behavioral Publications.

Caplan, G. (1977). Mental health consultation: Retrospect and prospect. In S. C. Plog & P. I. Ahmed (Eds.), *Principles and techniques of mental health consultation* (pp. 9–21). New York: Plenum.

Caplan, G. (1993). Epilogue. In W. P. Erchul (Ed.), *Consultation in community, school, and organizational practice* (pp. 205–213). Washington, DC: Taylor & Francis.

Caplan, G. (1993). Mental health consultation, community mental health, and population-oriented psychiatry. In W. P. Erchul (Ed.), *Consultation in community, school, and organizational practice* (pp. 41–55). Washington, DC: Taylor & Francis.

Caplan, G., & Caplan, R. B. (1993). *Mental health consultation and collaboration.* San Francisco: Jossey-Bass.

Caplan, G., Caplan, R. B., & Erchul, W. P. (1994). Caplanian mental health consultation: Historical background and current status. *Consulting Psychology Journal: Practice & Research, 46,* 2–12.

Carlisle, H. (1982). *Management: Concepts, methods, and applications* (2nd ed.). Chicago: Science Research Associates.

Carner, L. A. (1982). Developing a consultative contract. In J. L. Alpert (Ed.), *Psychological consultation in educational settings* (pp. 8–32). San Francisco: Jossey-Bass.

Case, T. L., Vandenberg, R. J., & Meredith, P. H. (1990). Internal and external change agents. *Leadership & Organization Development Journal, 11(1),* 4–15.

Chalofsky, N., & Lincoln, C. I. (1983). *Up the HRD ladder: A guide for professional growth.* Reading, MA: Addison-Wesley.

Champion, D. P., Kiel, D. H., & McLendon, J. A. (1990). Choosing a consulting role. *Training and Development Journal,* (February), 66–69.

Chapiro, J. (1981). What kind of a system is an organization and with what metaphors do we describe it? In R. Lippitt & G. Lippitt (Eds.), *Systems thinking—a resource for organization diagnosis and intervention* (Vol. 3, pp. 35–42). Washington, DC: International Consultants Foundation Series.

Cherniss, C. (1976). Preentry issues in consultation. *American Journal of Community Psychology, 4(1),* 13–24.

Cherniss, C. (1993). Preentry issues revisited. In R. T. Golembiewski (Ed.), *Handbook of organizational consultation* (pp. 113–118). New York: Marcel Dekker, Inc.

Cherniss, C. (1998). Teacher empowerment, consultation, and the creation of new programs in schools. *Journal of Educational and Psychological Consultation, 8,* 135–152.

Chin, R., & Benne, K. D. (Eds.). (1985). *The planning of change* (4th ed.). New York: Holt, Rinehart & Winston.

Chowanec, G. D. (1993). TQM: Evaluating service quality. *Consulting Psychology Journal, 45,* 31–32.

Christenson, S. L. (1995). Families and schools: What is the role of the school psychologist? *School Psychology Quarterly, 10,* 118–132.

Clayton, S., & Bongar, B. (1994). The use of consultation in psychological practice: Ethical, legal and clinical considerations. *Ethics & Behavior, 4,* 43–57.

Cleven, C. A., & Gutkin, T. B. (1988). Cognitive modeling of consultation processes: A means for improving consultees' problem definition skills. *Journal of School Psychology, 26(4),* 379–389.

Cohen, E., & Osterweil, Z. (1986). An "Issue-focused" model of mental health consultation with groups of teachers. *Journal of School Psychology, 24(3),* 243–256.

Cole, S. M., Thomas, A. R., & Lee, C. C. (1988). School counselor and school psychologist: Partners in minority family outreach. *Journal of Multicultural Counseling and Development, 16,* 110–116.

Colton, D. L., & Sheridan, S. M. (1998). Conjoint behavioral consultation and social skills training: Enhancing the play behaviors of boys with attention deficit hyperactivity disorder. *Journal of Educational and Psychological Consultation, 9,* 3–28.

Conoley, J. C., & Conoley, C. W. (1982). The effects of two conditions of client-centered consultation on student-teacher problem descriptions and remedial plans. *Journal of School Psychology, 20,* 323–328.

Conoley, J. C., & Conoley, C. W. (1985). The school consultant as advocate: A perspective for trainers. *School Psychology International, 6(4),* 219–224.

Conoley, J. C., & Conoley, C. W. (1990). Staff consultative work in schools. In N. Jones & N. Frederickson (Eds.), *Refocusing educational psychology* (pp. 84–103). London: Falmer.

Conoley, J. C., & Conoley, C. W. (1992). *School consultation: Practice and training* (2nd ed.). Boston: Allyn & Bacon.

Conoley, C. W., Conoley, J. C., & Gumm, W. B., II. (1992). Effects of consultee problem presentation and consultant training on consultant problem definition. *Journal of Counseling and Development, 71,* 60–62.

Conoley, C. W., Conoley, J. C., Ivey, D. C., & Scheel, M. J. (1991). Enhancing consultation by matching the consultees' perspectives. *Journal of Counseling and Development, 69,* 546–549.

Conoley, J. C., & Gutkin, T. B. (1986). School psychology: A re-conceptualization of service delivery realities. In S. N. Elliott & J. C. Witt (Eds.), *The delivery of psychological services in schools* (pp. 393–424). Hillsdale, NJ: Erlbaum.

Conoley, J. C., & Haynes, G. (1992). Ecological perspectives. In R. D'Amato and B. Rothlisberg (Eds.), *Psychological perspectives on interaction* (pp. 177–189). White Plains, NY: Longman Publishing.

Conoley, J. C., & Wright, C. (1993). Caplan's ideas and the future of psychology in the schools. In W. P. Erchul (Ed.), *Consultation in community, school, and organizational practice* (pp. 177–192). Washington, DC: Taylor & Francis.

Conroy, E., & Mayer, S. (1994). Strategies for consulting with parents. *Elementary School Guidance & Counseling, 29,* 60–66.

Consultation I: Conceptual, structural, and operational dimensions (special issue). (1993a). *Journal of Counseling and Development, 71,* 596–709.

Consultation II: Prevention, preparation, and key issues. (special issue). (1993b). *Journal of Counseling and Development, 71,* 115–223.

Conyne, R. K., & O'Neil, J. M. (Eds.). (1992). *Organizational consultation: A casebook.* Newbury Park, CA: Sage.

Conyne, R. K., Rapin, L. S., & Rand, J. M. (1997). A model for leading task groups. In H. Forester-Miller and J. A. Kottler (Eds.), *Issues and challenges for group practitioners* (pp. 117–130). Denver: Love Publishing Company.

Cook, D. W. (1989). Systematic need assessment: A primer. *Journal of Counseling and Development, 67,* 462–464.

Cooke, R. A. (1979). Managing change in organizations. In G. Zaltman (Ed.), *Management principles for nonprofit agencies and organizations* (pp. 154–209). New York: AMACOM.

Cooper, S., & Hodges, W. F. (Eds.). (1983). *The mental health consultation field.* New York: Human Sciences Press.

Cooper, S. E., & Newbold, R. C. (1994). Combining external and internal behavioral system consultation to enhance plant safety. *Consulting Psychology Journal, 46,* 32–41.

Cooper, S. E., & O'Connor, R. M., Jr. (1993). Standards for organizational consultation assessment and evaluation instruments. *Journal of Counseling and Development, 71,* 651–660.

Corey, G. (1996). *Theory and practice of counseling and psychotherapy* (5th ed.). Pacific Grove, CA: Brooks/Cole.

Corey, G., Corey, M. S., & Callanan, P. (1998). *Issues and ethics in the helping professions* (5th ed.). Pacific Grove, CA: Brooks/Cole.

Correa, V. I., & Tulbert, B. (1993). Collaboration between school personnel in special education and Hispanic families. *Journal of Educational and Psychological Consultation, 4,* 253–265.

Cosier, R. A., & Dalton, D. R. (1993). Management consulting: Planning, entry, performance. *Journal of Counseling and Development, 72(2),* 191–198.

Costello, M., Phelps, L., & Wilczenski, F. (1994). Children and military conflict: Current issues and treatment implications. *School Counselor, 41,* 220–225.

Cottingham, H. E. (1956). *Guidance in the elementary schools: Principles and practice.* Bloomington, IL: McKnight & McKnight.

Counselman, E. F., & Weber, R. L. (1994). Leadership of mental health consultation groups: A model for group therapists. *International Journal of Group Psychotherapy, 44,* 349–360.

Covey, S. R. (1991). *Principle-centered leadership.* New York: Simon and Schuster.

Cramer, S. F. (1998). *Collaboration.* Boston: Allyn & Bacon.

Crego, C. A. (1985). Ethics: The need for improved consultation training. *Counseling Psychologist, 13(3),* 473–476.

Crose, R., & Kixmiller, J. S. (1994). Counseling psychologists as nursing home consultants: What do administrators want? *Counseling Psychologist, 22,* 104–114.

Cross, P. (1984). *Adults as learners.* San Francisco: Jossey-Bass.

Curtis, M. J., & Metz, L. W. (1986). System level intervention in a school for handicapped children. *School Psychology Review, 15,* 510–518.

Curtis, M. J., & Stollar, S. A. (1995). Best practices in system-level consultation and organizational change. In A. Thomas and J. Grimes (Eds.), *Best Practices in School Psychology* (3rd ed., pp. 51–58). Washington, DC: National Association of School Psychologists.

Curtis, M. J., & Stollar, S. A. (1996). Applying principles and practices of organizational change to school reform. *School Psychology Review, 25,* 409–417.

Daniels, T. D., & Dewine, S. (1990). Communication process as target and tool for consultancy intervention: Rethinking a hackneyed theme. *Journal of Educational and Psychological Consultation, 2,* 303–322.

Das, A. K. (1995). Rethinking multicultural counseling: Implications for counselor education. *Journal of Counseling and Development, 74(1),* 45–52.

Davis, J. M., & Hartsough, C. S. (1992). Assessing psychosocial environment in mental health consultation groups. *Psychology in the Schools, 29,* 224–228.

Deck, M. D. (1992). Training school counselors to be consultants. *Elementary School Guidance and Counseling, 26,* 221–228.

Deitz, P. E., & Reese, J. T. (1986). The perils of police psychology: 10 strategies for minimizing role conflicts when providing mental health services and consultation to law enforcement agencies. *Behavioral Sciences and the Law, 4,* 385–400.

Dekom, A. K. (1969). *The internal consultant.* New York: American Management Association.

Delbecq, A. L., Van De Ven, A. H., & Gustafson, D. H. (1975). *Group techniques for program planning: A guide to nominal group and delphi processes.* Glenview, IL: Scott, Foresman.

Dewar, A. L. (1980). *The quality circle guide to participation management.* Englewood Cliffs, NJ: Prentice-Hall.

Dickinson, D. J., & Adcox, S. (1984). Program evaluation of a school consultation program. *Psychology in the Schools, 21,* 336–342.

Dickinson, D. J., & Bradshaw, S. P. (1992). Multiplying effectiveness: Combining consultation with counseling. *School Counselor, 40,* 118–124.

Dinkmeyer, D., & Carlson, J. (1973). *Consulting: Facilitating human potential and change processes.* Columbus, OH: Merrill.

Dinkmeyer, D., & McKay, G. (1973). *Raising a responsible child.* New York: Simon & Schuster.

Dinkmeyer, D. C., & McKay, G. (1976). *Systematic training for effective parenting (STEP).* Circle Pines, MN: American Guidance Service.

Dinkmeyer, D. C., Pew, W. L., & Dinkmeyer, D. C., Jr. (1979). *Adlerian counseling and psychotherapy.* Monterey, CA: Brooks/Cole.

Dixon, D. N., & Dixon, D. E. (1993). Research in consultation: Toward better analogues and outcome measures. *Journal of Counseling and Development, 71,* 700–702.

Dodson-Chaneske, D. (1988). Mental health consultation to a police department. *Journal of Human Behavior and Learning, 5,* 35–38.

Dodson, W. W., & Vaccaro, B. (1988). Mental health consultation in campus discipline: A program of primary prevention. *Journal of American College Health, 37(2),* 85–88.

Dorn, F. J. (1986). The road to workshop consultation: Some directions for the new traveler. *American Mental Health Counselors Journal, 8(2),* 53–59.

Douce, L. A. (1993). AIDS and HIV: Hopes and challenges for the 1990's. *Journal for Counseling and Development, 71,* 259–260.

Dougherty, A. M. (1992a). Ethical issues in consultation. *Elementary School Guidance and Counseling, 26,* 214–220.

Dougherty, A. M. (1992b). School consultation in the 1990s. *Elementary School Guidance and Counseling, 26,* 163–164.

Dougherty, A. M. (1996–97, Fall/Winter). The importance of effective communication in consultation. *The Consulting Edge, 4,* 1–2, 4–7.

Dougherty, A. M. (1997a). The school counselor's role. In B. Herlihy and G. Corey, *Boundary issues in counseling* (pp. 147–150). Alexandria, VA: American Counseling Association.

Dougherty, A. M. (1997b). Consultation issues. In B. Herlihy and G. Corey, *Boundary issues in counseling* (pp. 80–82). Alexandria, VA: American Counseling Association.

Dougherty, A. M. (2000). *Psychological consultation and collaboration: A casebook* (3rd ed.). Belmont, CA: Wadsworth.

Dougherty, A. M., & Dougherty, L. P. (1991). Using your school counselor as an organizational consultant. *American Middle School Education, 12(2),* 37–44.

Dougherty, A. M., Dougherty, L. P., & Purcell, D. (1991). The sources and management of resistance to consultation. *School Counselor, 38,* 178–186.

Dougherty, A. M., Henderson, B. B., & Lindsey, B. (1997). The effectiveness of direct versus indirect confrontation as a function of stage of consultation: Results of an exploratory investigation. *Journal of Educational and Psychological Consultation, 8,* 361–372.

Dougherty, A. M., Henderson, B. B., Tack, F. E., Deck, M. D, Worley, V., & Page, J. R. (1997). The relation of facilitative conditions, consultant experience, and stage of consultation to consultees' perceptions of the use of direct confrontation. *Journal of Educational and Psychological Consultation, 8,* 21–40.

Dougherty, A. M., Tack, F. E., Fullam, C. B., & Hammer, L. A. (1996). Disengagement: A neglected aspect of the consultation process. *Journal of Educational and Psychological Consultation, 7,* 259–274.

Dougherty, A. M., & Taylor, B. L. B. (1983). Evaluation of peer helper programs. *Elementary School Guidance and Counseling, 18(2),* 130–136.

Downing, J., & Downing, S. (1991). Consultation with resistant parents. *Elementary School Guidance and Counseling, 25,* 296–301.

Downing, J., & Harrison, T. (1991). Parents' tough beat. *The School Counselor, 39,* 91–97.

Drotar, D. (1987). Psychological consultation in medical settings: Challenges and constraints. In J. R. McNamara and M. A. Appel (Eds.), *Critical issues, development, and trends in professional psychology* (Vol. 3, pp. 80–111). New York: Praeger.

Drum, D. J., & Valdese, L. E (1988). Advocacy and outreach: Applications to college/university settings. In D. J. Kurpius & D. Brown (Eds.), *Handbook of consultation: An intervention for advocacy and outreach* (pp. 38–60). Alexandria, VA: American Association for Counseling and Development.

Duncan, C. F. (1995). Cross-cultural school consultation. In C. C. Lee (Ed.), *Counseling for diversity: A guide for school counselors and related professionals* (pp. 128–141). Boston: Allyn & Bacon.

Duncan, C. F., & Pryzwansky, W. B. (1988). Consultation research: Trends in doctoral dissertations 1978–1985. *Journal of School Psychology, 26,* 107–119.

Duncan, C., & Pryzwansky, W. B. (1993). Effects of race, racial identity development, and orientation style on perceived consultant effectiveness. *Journal of Multicultural Counseling and Development, 21,* 88–96.

Dunson R. M., III, Hughes, J. N., & Jackson, T. W. (1994). Effect of behavioral consultation on student and teacher behavior. *Journal of School Psychology, 32,* 247–266.

Dustin, D. (1993). School consultation in the nineties. Paper presented at the annual convention of the American Counseling Association, Atlanta, GA.

Dustin, D., & Ehly, S. (1984). Skills for effective consultation. *School Counselor, 32,* 23–29.

Dustin, D., & Ehly, S. (1992). School consultation in the 1990s. *Elementary School Guidance and Counseling, 26,* 165–175.

Dworkin, A. L., & Dworkin, E. P. (1975). A conceptual overview of selected consultation models. *American Journal of Community Psychology, 3(2),* 151–159.

Dwyer, K. P., & Gorin, S. (1996). A national perspective of school psychology in the context of school reform. *School Psychology Review, 25,* 507–511.

Eden, D. (1990). Consultant as messiah: Applying expectation effects in managerial consultation. *Consultation, 9,* 37–50.

Edens, J. F. (1997). Home visitation programs with ethnic minority families: Cultural issues in parent consultation. *Journal of Educational and Psychological Consultation, 8*, 373–383.

Egan, G. (1985). *Change agent skills in helping and human service settings.* Pacific Grove, CA: Brooks/Cole.

Egan, G. (1990). *The skilled helper* (4th ed.). Pacific Grove, CA: Brooks/Cole.

Egan, G. (1994). *The skilled helper* (5th ed.). Pacific Grove, CA: Brooks/Cole.

Egan, G. (1998). *The skilled helper* (6th ed.). Pacific Grove, CA: Brooks/Cole.

Egan, G., & Cowan, M. A. (1979). *People in systems: A model for development in the human-service professions and education.* Pacific Grove, CA: Brooks/Cole.

Ehly, S. (1993). Overview of group interventions for special service providers. *Special Services in the Schools, 18*, 9–38.

Elliot, S. N., & Busse, R. T. (1993). Effective treatments with behavioral consultation. In J. E. Zins, T. R. Kratochwill, & S. N. Elliot (Eds.), *Handbook of consultation services for children* (pp. 179–203). San Francisco: Jossey-Bass.

Erchul, W. P. (1987). A relational communication analysis of control in school consultation. *Professional School Psychology, 2(2)*, 113–124.

Erchul, W. P. (1993a). Reflections on mental health consultation: An interview with Gerald Caplan. In W. P. Erchul (Ed.), *Consultation in community, school, and organizational practice* (pp. 57–72). Washington, DC: Taylor & Francis.

Erchul, W. P. (1993b). Selected interpersonal perspectives in consultation research. *School Psychology Quarterly, 8*, 38–49.

Erchul, W. P., & Chewning, T. G. (1990). Behavioral consultation from a request-centered relational communication perspective. *Professional School Psychology, 5*, 1–20.

Erchul, W. P., & Conoley, C. W. (1991). Helpful theories to guide counselors' practice of school-based consultation. *Elementary School Guidance and Counseling, 25*, 204–211.

Erchul, W. P., & Martens, B. K. (1997). *School consultation: Conceptual and empirical bases of practice.* New York: Plenum.

Erchul, W. P., & Raven, B. H. (1997). Social power in school consultation: A contemporary view of French and Raven's bases of power model. *Journal of School Psychology, 35*, 137–171.

Erchul, W. P., & Schulte, A. C. (1993). Gerald Caplan's contributions to professional psychology: Conceptual underpinnings. In W. P. Erchul (Ed.), *Consultation in community, school, and organizational practice* (pp. 3–39). Washington, DC: Taylor & Francis.

Erchul, W. P., & Schulte, A. C. (1996). Behavioral consultation as a work in progress. *Journal of Educational and Psychological Consultation, 7*, 345–354.

Erhardt, K. E., Barnett, D. W., Lentz, F. E., Jr., Stollar, S. A., & Reifin, L. H. (1996). Innovative methodology in ecological consultation: Use of scripts to promote treatment acceptability and integrity. *School Psychology Quarterly, 11*, 149–168.

Fagan, T. K. (1995). Trends in the history of school psychology in the United States. In A. Thomas and J. Grimes (Eds.), *Best practices in school psychology* (3rd ed., pp. 59–67). Washington, DC: National Association of School Psychologists.

Fall, M. (1995). Planning for consultation: An aid for the elementary school counselor. *The School Counselor, 43*, 151–156.

Fanibanda, D. K. (1976). Ethical issues of mental health consultation. *Professional Psychology, 7*, 547–552.

Faust, V. (1968). *The counselor-consultant in the elementary school.* Boston: Houghton Mifflin.

Feld, J. K., Bergan, J. R., & Stone, C. A. (1987). Behavioral consultation. In C. A. Maher & S. G. Forman (Eds.), *A behavioral approach to education of children and youth* (pp. 183–219). Hillsdale, NJ: Erlbaum.

Fine, N., & Kontos, S. (1992). Indirect service delivery through consultation: Review and implications for early intervention. *Journal of Early Intervention, 16*, 221–233.

Fisher, R., & Brown, S. (1988). *Getting together.* New York: Penguin.

Fisher, R., & Ury, W. (1981). *Getting to yes: Negotiating without giving in.* New York: Penguin.

Flanagan, D. P., & Miranda, A. H. (1995). Best practices in working with culturally different families. In A. Thomas and J. Grimes (Eds.), *Best practices in school psychology* (3rd ed., pp. 1049–1060). Washington, DC: National Association of School Psychologists.

Flanagan, S. G., Cray, M. E., & Meter, D. V. (1983). A facility-wide consultation and training team as a catalyst in promoting institutional change. *Analysis and Intervention in Developmental Disabilities, 3*, 151–169.

Ford, C. H. (1979). Developing a successful client-consultant relationship. In C. R. Bell & L. Nadler (Eds.), *The client-consultant handbook* (pp. 8–21). Houston: Gulf Publishing.

Fordyce, J. K., & Weil, R. (1971). *Managing with people.* Reading, MA: Addison-Wesley.

Fordyce, J. K., & Weil, R. (1978). Methods for finding out what is going on. In W. L. French, C. H. Bell, Jr., & R. A. Zawacki (Eds.), *Organization development: Theory, practice, and research* (pp. 121–129). Dallas: Business Publications.

Forman, S. G. (1984). Behavioral and cognitive-behavioral approaches to staff development. In C. A. Maher, R. J. Illback, and J. E. Zins (Eds.), *Organizational psychology in the schools: A handbook for professionals* (pp. 302–322). Springfield, IL: Charles C. Thomas.

Forman, S. G. (1995). Organizational factors and consultation outcome. *Journal of Educational and Psychological Consultation, 6,* 191–195.

French, J. L. (1990). History of school psychology. In T. B. Gutkin and C. R. Reynolds (Eds.), *The handbook of school psychology* (2nd ed., pp. 3–20). New York: Wiley.

French, J. R. P., Jr., & Raven, B. H. (1959). The bases of social power. In D. Cartwright (Ed.), *Studies in social power* (pp. 150–167). Ann Arbor, MI: Institute for Social Research.

French, W. L. (1972). Organizational development: Objectives, assumptions and strategies. In N. Margulies & A. P. Raia (Eds.), *Organizational development values, process, and technology* (pp. 31–49). New York: McGraw-Hill.

French, W. L., & Bell, C. H., Jr. (1990). *Organization development: Behavioral science interventions for organization improvement* (4th ed.). Englewood Cliffs, NJ: Prentice-Hall.

French, W. L., Bell, C. H., Jr., & Zawacki, R. A. (Eds.). (1978). *Organization development: Theory, practice, and research.* Dallas: Business Publications.

Friedlander, E., & Brown, L. D. (1974). Organization development. In M. R. Rosenzweig & L. W. Porter (Eds.), *Annual Review of Psychology, 25* (pp. 219–340). Palo Alto, CA: Annual Reviews.

Friend, M., & Cook, L. (1996). *Interactions: Collaboration skills for school professionals* (2nd ed.). New York: Longmans.

Friend, M., & Cook, L. (1997). Student-centered teams in schools: Still in search of an identity. *Journal of Educational and Psychological Consultation, 8,* 3–20.

Froehle, T. C., & Rominger, R. L., III. (1993). Directions in consultation research: Bridging the gap between science and practice. *Journal of Counseling and Development, 71,* 693–699.

Frohman, M. A., Sashkin, M., & Kavanagh, M. J. (1978). Action-research as applied to organization development. In W. L. French, C. H. Bell, Jr., & R. A. Zawacki (Eds.), *Organization development: Theory, practice, and research.* Dallas: Business Publications.

Fuchs, D., & Fuchs, L. S. (1989). Exploring effective and efficient prereferral interventions: A component analysis of behavioral consultation. *School Psychology Review, 8(2),* 260–283.

Fuchs, D., Fuchs, L. S., Dulan, J., Roberts, H., & Fernstrom, P. (1992). Where is the research on consultation effectiveness? *Journal of Educational and Psychological Consultation, 3,* 151–174.

Fullmer, D. W., & Bernard, H. W. (1972). *The school counselor consultant.* Boston: Houghton Mifflin.

Fuqua, D. R., & Kurpius, D. J. (1993). Conceptual models in organizational consultation. *Journal of Counseling and Development, 71,* 607–618.

Fuqua, D. R., & Newman, J. L. (1983). Models, principles, and methods of data utilization in organizational consultation. Paper presented at the American Personnel and Guidance Association Annual Convention, Washington, DC.

Fuqua, D. R., & Newman, J. L. (1985). Individual consultation. *Counseling Psychologist, 13(3),* 390–395.

Gabbard, C., & Halischak, K. (1993). Consulting opportunities: Working with student-athletes at a university. *Counseling Psychologist, 21,* 386–398.

Gallessich, J. (1982). *The profession and practice of consultation.* San Francisco: Jossey-Bass.

Gallessich, J. (1985). Toward a meta-theory of consultation. *Counseling Psychologist, 13(3),* 336–354.

Gallessich, J., Long, K. M., & Jennings, S. (1986). Training of mental health consultants. In F. V. Mannino, E. J. Trickett, M. E. Shore, M. G. Kidder, & G. Levin (Eds.), *Handbook of mental health consultation* (pp. 279–317). Rockville, MD: National Institute of Mental Health.

Garland, F. N. (1993). Combat stress control in the postwar theater: Mental health consultation during redeployment phase of Operation Desert Storm. *Military Medicine, 158,* 334–337.

Garmston, R. J., & Wellman, B. M. (1992). *How to make presentations that teach and transform.* Alexandria, VA: Association for Supervision and Curriculum Development.

Garrett, J. N. (1998). Local interagency coordinating council personality: A factor in consultation. *Journal of Educational and Psychological Consultation, 9,* 261–266.

Gemmill, G., & Costello, M. (1990). Group mirroring as a means for exploring the group shadow: A perspective for organizational consultation. *Consultation, 9,* 277–291.

Gemmill, G., & Wynkoop, C. (1990). The psychodynamics of the client-consultant nexus in organizational process consulting. *Consultation, 9,* 129–140.

Gerler, E. R., Jr. (1992). Consultation and school counseling. *Elementary School Guidance and Counseling, 26,* 162.

Gerler, E. R., Jr., & Myrick, R. D. (1991). The elementary school counselor's work with prekindergarten children: Implications for counselor education programs. *Elementary School Guidance and Counseling, 26,* 67–75.

Geroski, A. M., Rodgers, K. A., & Breen, D. T. (1997). Using the DSM-IV to enhance collaboration among school counselors, clinical counselors, and primary care physicians. *Journal of Counseling & Development, 75,* 231–239.

Gibbs, J. T. (1980). The interpersonal orientation in mental health consultation: Toward a model of ethnic variations in consultation. *Journal of Community Psychology, 8,* 195–207.

Gibson, G. (1988). Consultation as advocacy and outreach in community mental health settings: Theory to practice. In D. J. Kurpius & D. Brown (Eds.), *Handbook of consultation: An intervention for advocacy and outreach* (pp. 27–37). Alexandria, VA: American Association for Counseling and Development.

Gibson, G., & Chard, K. M. (1994). Quantifying the effects of community mental health consultation interventions. *Consulting Psychology Journal, 46,* 13–25.

Gilmore, T. N. (1993). Issues in ending consultancies. In R. T. Golembiewski (Ed.), *Handbook of organizational consultation* (pp. 253–261). New York: Marcel.

Ginter, E. J., Scalise, J. J., & Presse, N. (1990). The elementary school counselor's role: Perceptions of teachers. *School Counselor, 38,* 19–23.

Glaser, E. M. (1981). Ethical issues in consultation practice with organizations. *Consultation, 1(1),* 12–16.

Glidewell, J. C. (1959). The entry problem in consultation. *Journal of Social Issues, 15(2),* 51–59.

Gmeinder K. L., & Kratochwill, T. R. (1998). Short-term, home-based intervention for child noncompliance using behavioral consultation and a self-help manual. *Journal of Educational and Psychological Consultation, 9,* 91–117.

Goldstein, B. S. C. (1998). Creating a context for collaborative consultation: Working across bicultural communities. *Journal of Educational and Psychological Consultation, 9,* 367–374.

Goldstein, L., & Gilliam, P. (1990). Training system issues in the year 2000. *American Psychologist, 45(2),* 134–143.

Golembiewski, R. T. (1969). Organization development in public agencies: Perspectives in theory and practice. *Public Administration Review, 29,* 367–377.

Golembiewski, R. T. (1990). Personal perspectives on "Radical Dissent and Learning in Human Systems." *Consultation, 9,* 159–165.

Golembiewski, R. T. (1993a). Features of energizing data. In R. T. Golembiewski (Ed.), *Handbook of organizational consultation* (pp. 323–325). New York: Marcel Dekker, Inc.

Golembiewski, R. T. (1993b). Role analysis technique. In R. T. Golembiewski (Ed.), *Handbook of organizational consultation* (pp. 357–358). New York: Marcel Dekker, Inc.

Golembiewski, R. T. (1993c). Stakeholders in consultation. In R. T. Golembiewski (Ed.), *Handbook of organizational consultation* (pp. 367–371). New York: Marcel Dekker, Inc.

Golembiewski, R. T. (1993d). Third-party consultation. In R. T. Golembiewski (Ed.), *Handbook of organizational consultation* (pp. 393–398). New York: Marcel Dekker, Inc.

Golembiewski, R. T. (1993e). Toward a process orientation. In R. T. Golembiewski (Ed.), *Handbook of organizational consultation* (pp. 383–386). New York: Marcel Dekker, Inc.

Golembiewski, R. T., & Rauschenberg, F. (1993). Third-party consultation: Basic features and one misapplication. In R. T. Golembiewski (Ed.), *Handbook of organizational consultation* (pp. 393–398). New York: Marcel Dekker, Inc.

Golembiewski, R. T., & Sun, B. (1989). Consulting is definitely worth the cost: Success rates in OD and QWL Consultation. *Consultation, 8,* 203–208.

Good, T. L., Wiley, A. R., Thomas, R. E., Stewart, E., McCoy, J., Kloos, B., Hunt, G. D., Moore, T., & Rappaport, J. (1997). Bridging the gap between schools and community: Organizing for family involvement in a low-income neighborhood. *Journal of Educational and Psychological Consultation, 8,* 277–296.

Goode, W. J., & Hatt, P. K. (1972). The collection of data by questionnaire. In N. Margulies & A. P. Raia (Eds.), *Organizational development: Values, process, and technology* (pp. 163–185). New York: McGraw-Hill.

Goodstein, L. D. (1978). *Consulting with human service systems.* Reading, MA: Addison Wesley.

Goodstein, L. D. (1985). Through a glass darkly: A commentary on Backer's "The future of organizational consulting." *Consultation, 4(1),* 30–33.

Gordon, T. (1970). *Parent effectiveness training.* New York: Wyden.

Gottlieb, B. H. (1974). Re-examining the preventive potential of mental health consultation. *Canada's Mental Health, 22,* 4–6.

Gottlieb, B. H. (1983). Opportunities for collaboration with informal support systems. In S. Cooper and W. F. Hodges (Eds.), *The mental health consultation field* (pp. 181–203). New York: Human Sciences Press.

Graden, J. L. (1989). Reactions to school consultation: Some considerations from a problem-solving perspective. *Professional School Psychology, 4,* 29–35.

Granda, K. (1992). Consultant personal and working framework and its impact on member-authority relations in small groups. Unpublished doctoral dissertation, Northwestern University. *Dissertation Abstracts International, 53 (11),* May 1993.

Greiner, L. E. (1967). Patterns of organizational change. *Harvard Business Review,* (May/June), 119–130.

Greiner, L. (1988). The consultant as confidant. *Consultation, 7,* 38–40.

Greiner, L. E., & Metzger, R. O. (1983). *Consulting to management: Insights to building and managing a successful practice.* Englewood Cliffs, NJ: Prentice-Hall.

Gresham, E. M., & Kendall, G. K. (1987). School consultation research: Methodological critique and future research directions. *School Psychology Review, 16,* 303–316.

Gresham, E. M., & Lemanek, K. L. (1987). Parent education. In C. A. Maher and S. G. Forman (Eds.), *A behavioral approach to education of children and youth* (pp. 153–181). Hillsdale, NJ: Erlbaum.

Gresham, F. M., & Lopez, M. F. (1996). Social validation: A unifying concept for school-based consultation research and practice. *School Psychology Quarterly, 11,* 204–227.

Gresham, F. M., & Noell, G. H. (1993). Documenting the effectiveness of consultation outcomes. In J. E. Zins, T. R. Kratochwill, & S. N. Elliot (Eds.), *Handbook of consultation services for children* (pp. 249–273). San Francisco: Jossey-Bass.

Grigsby, R. K. (1992). Mental health consultation at a youth shelter: An ethnographic approach. *Child and Youth Care Forum 21,* 247–261.

Gutkin, T. (1993). Conducting consultation research. In J. E. Zins, T. R. Kratochwill, & S. N. Elliot (Eds.), *Handbook of consultation services for children* (pp. 227–248). San Francisco: Jossey-Bass.

Gutkin, T. B. (1996). Patterns of consultant and consultee verbalizations: Examining communication leadership during initial consultation interviews. *Journal of School Psychology, 34(3),* 199–219.

Gutkin, T. B. (1997). An introduction to the mini-series: The social psychology of interpersonal influence with adults. *Journal of School Psychology, 35,* 105–106.

Gutkin, T. B., & Curtis, M. J. (1982). School-based consultation: Theory and techniques. In C. Reynolds & T. B. Gutkin (Eds.), *The handbook of school psychology* (pp. 796–828). New York: Wiley.

Gutkin, T. B., & Curtis, M. J. (1990). School-based consultation: Theory, techniques, and research. In T. B. Gutkin and C. R. Reynolds (Eds.), *The handbook of school psychology* (2nd ed., pp. 577–611). New York: Wiley.

Hagedorn, H. J., Beck, K. J., Nuebert, S. F., & Werlin, S. H. (1976). Working manual of simple program evaluation techniques for community mental health centers. Rockville, MD: Arthur D. Little, for the National Institute of Mental Health.

Hall, A. S., & Mei-Ju, L. (1994). An integrative consultation framework: A practical tool for elementary school counselors. *Elementary School Guidance & Counseling, 29,* 16–27.

Hamiliton, E. E. (1988). The facilitation of organizational change: An empirical study of factors predicting change agents' effectiveness. *Journal of Applied Behavioral Science, 24,* 37–59.

Hanko, G. (1987). Group consultation with mainstream teachers. *Educational and Child Psychology, 4(3–4),* 123–130.

Hansen, J. C., Himes, B. S., & Meier, S. (1990). *Consultation: Concepts and practices.* Englewood Cliffs, NJ: Prentice-Hall.

Hardesty, P. H., & Dillard, J. M. (1994). The role of elementary school counselors compared with their middle and secondary school counterparts. *Elementary School Guidance & Counseling, 29,* 83–91.

Harris, K. C. (1991). An expanded view on consultation competencies for educators serving culturally and linguistically diverse exceptional students. *Teacher Education and Special Education, 14(1),* 25–29.

Hawryluk, M. K., & Smallwood, D. L. (1986). Assessing and addressing consultee variables in school-based behavioral consultation. *School Psychology Review, 15(4),* 519–528.

Hayes, J., & Prakasam, R. (1989). Culture: The efficacy of different modes of consultation. *Leadership and Organization Development Journal, 10(1),* 24–32.

Hays, P. A. (1996). Addressing the complexities of culture and gender in counseling. *Journal of Counseling and Development, 74,* 332–338.

Heller, K., & Monahan, J. (1983). Individual-process consultation. In S. Cooper and W. F. Hodges (Eds.), *The mental health consultation field* (pp. 19–25). New York: Human Sciences Press.

Hellkamp, D. T. (1996). A multidisciplinary collaborative management and consulting model: The inner workings and future challenges. *Journal of Educational and Psychological Consultation, 7,* 79–85.

Henning-Stout, M. (1993). Theoretical and empirical bases of consultation. In J. E. Zins, T. R. Kratochwill, and S. N. Elliot (Eds.), *Handbook of consultation services for children* (pp. 15–45). San Francisco: Jossey-Bass.

Henning-Stout, M. (1994). Consultation and connected knowing: What we know is determined by the questions we ask. *Journal of Educational and Psychological Consultation, 5,* 5–21.

Henning-Stout, M., & Conoley, J. C. (1987). Consultation and counseling as procedurally divergent: Analysis of verbal behavior. *Professional Psychology: Research and Practice, 18,* 124–127

Heppner, P. P., Kivlighan, D. M., Jr., & Wampold, B. E. (1992). *Research design in counseling.* Pacific Grove, CA: Brooks/Cole.

Herlihy, B., & Corey, G. (1997). *Boundary issues in counseling.* Alexandria, VA: American Counseling Association.

Hershenson, D. B., & Power, P. W. (1987). *Mental health counseling: Theory and practice.* New York: Pergarnon Press.

Heyel, C. (Ed.). (1973). *Encyclopedia of management* (2nd ed.). New York: Van Nostrand Reinhold.

Hobbs, B. B., & Collison, B. B. (1995). School-community agency collaboration: Implications for the school counselor. *The School Counselor, 43,* 58–65.

Hodges, W. F., & Cooper, S. (1983). General introduction. In S. Cooper & W. E Hodges (Eds.), *The mental health consultation field* (pp. 19–25). New York: Human Sciences Press.

Hohenshil, T. H. (1996). Editorial: Role of assessment and diagnosis in counseling. *Journal of Counseling and Development, 75,* 64–67.

Hohenshil, T. H., & Brown, M. B. (1991). Public school counseling services for prekindergarten children. *Elementary School Guidance and Counseling, 26,* 4–11.

Hosie, T. W. (1994). Program evaluation: A potential area of expertise for counselors. *Counselor Education and Supervision, 33,* 349–362.

Houk, J. L., & Lewandowski, L. J. (1996). Consultant verbal control and consultee perceptions. *Journal of Educational and Psychological Consultation, 7,* 107–118.

House, R. M., & Walker, C. M. (1993). Preventing AIDS through education. *Journal of Counseling and Development, 71,* 282–289.

Hughes, J. (1980). Organizational issues consultants need to bear in mind. *School Psychology Review, 9,* 103–107.

Hughes, J. (1983). The application of cognitive dissonance theory to consultation. *Journal of School Psychology, 21,* 349–357

Hughes, J. N. (1986). Ethical issues in school consultation. *School Psychology Review, 15(4),* 489–499.

Hughes, J. N., Barker, D., Kemenoff, S., & Hart, M. (1993). Problem ownership, casual attributions, and self-efficacy as predictors of teachers' referral decisions. *Journal of Educational and Psychological Consultation, 4(4),* 369–384.

Hughes, J. N., & Deforest, P. A. (1993). Consultant directiveness and support as predictors of consultation outcomes. *Journal of School Psychology, 31,* 355–373.

Hughes, J. N., & Falk, R. S. (1981). Resistance, reactance, and consultation. *Journal of School Psychology, 19,* 134–141.

Hughes, J. N., Grossman, P., & Barker, D. (1990). Teachers' expectancies, participation in consultation, and perceptions of consultant helpfulness. *School Psychology Quarterly, 5,* 167–179.

Huse, E. E. (1978). Organization development. *Personnel and Guidance Journal, 56(7),* 403–406.

Huse, E. R. (1975). *Organization development and change.* St. Paul, MN: West.

Hyatt, S. P., & Tingstrom, D. H. (1993). Consultant's use of jargon during intervention presentation: An evaluation of presentation modality and type of intervention. *School Psychology Quarterly, 8,* 99–109.

Hyman, A. (1993). A model for psychological consultation with retarded adults living in community residences. *Journal of Developmental and Physical Disabilities, 5,* 369–376.

Idol, L. (1998). Collaboration in the schools: A master plan for staff development. *Journal of Educational and Psychological Consultation, 9,* 155–163.

Idol, L., & Baran, S. (1992). Elementary school counselors and special educators consulting together: Perilous pitfalls or opportunities to collaborate? *Elementary School Guidance and Counseling, 26,* 202–213.

Ikeda, M. J., Tilly, W. D., Stumme, J., Volmer, L., & Allison, R. (1996). Agency-wide implementation of problem solving consultation: Foundations, current implementation, and future directions. *School Psychology Quarterly, 11,* 228–243.

Illback, R. J., & Zins, J. E. (1993). Organizational perspectives in child consultation. In J. E. Zins, T. R. Kratochwill, & S. N. Elliot (Eds.), *Handbook of consultation services for children* (pp. 87–109). San Francisco: Jossey-Bass.

Illback, R. J., Zins, J. E., Maher, C. A., & Greenberg, R. (1990). An overview of principles and procedures of program planning and evaluation. In T. B. Gutkin and C. R. Reynolds (Eds.), *The handbook of school psychology* (2nd ed., pp. 799–820). New York: Wiley.

Iscoe, I. (1993). Gerald Caplan's conceptual and qualitative contributions to community psychology: Views from an old timer. In W. P. Erchul (Ed.), *Consultation in community, school, and organizational practice* (pp. 87–98). Washington, DC: Taylor & Francis.

Isgar, T., & Isgar, S. (1993). High-performing teams. In R. T. Golembiewski (Ed.), *Handbook of organizational consultation* (pp. 417–418). New York: Marcel Dekker.

Ivancevich, J. M., Matteson, M. T., Freedman, S. M., & Phillips, J. S. (1990). Worksite stress management interventions. *American Psychologist, 45(2)*, 252–261.

Ivancevich, A. L., Szilagyi, D., Jr., & Wallace, M. C., Jr. (1977). *Organizational behavior and performance.* Santa Monica, CA: Scott, Foresman.

Ivey, A. E., Ivey, M. B., & Simek-Morgan, L. (1993). *Counseling and psychotherapy: A multicultural perspective* (3rd ed.). Boston: Allyn & Bacon.

Jackson, D. N., & Hayes, D. H. (1993). Multicultural issues in consultation. *Journal of Counseling and Development, 72(2)*, 144–147.

James, R. K., & Dougherty, A. M. (1985). Doing your own dog and pony show: A guide for the perplexed school counselor. *School Counselor, 20*, 11–18.

Janis, I. L., & Mann, L. (1977). *Decision making: A psychological analysis of conflict, choice, and commitment.* New York: Free Press.

Jarvis, P. E., & Nelson, S. (1967). Familiarization: A vital step in mental health consultation. *Community Mental Health Journal, 7(3)*, 343–348.

Jeger, A. M., & McClure, G. (1982). An experiential evaluation and process analysis of a behavioral consultation program. In A. M. Jeger and R. S. Slotnick (Eds.), *Community mental health and behavioral-ecology: A handbook of theory, research, and practice* (pp. 389–401). New York: Plenum.

Jeger, A. M., & Slotnick, R. S. (Eds.). (1982). *Community mental health and behavioral ecology: A handbook of theory, research, and practice.* New York: Plenum.

Jellinek, M. S. (1990). School consultation: Evolving issues. *Journal of American Academy of Child and Adolescent Psychiatry, 29,* 311–314.

Jennings, K. R. (1988). Testing a model of quality circle processes: Implications for practice and consultation, *Consultation, 7(1)*, 19–28.

Jenster, P.V., & Bigler, W. R. (1989). Analyzing the strategy-culture linkage: A procedural guide for consultants. *Consultation, 8*, 25–40.

Jerrell, J. M., & Jerrell, S. L. (1981). Organizational consultation in school systems. In J. C. Conoley (Ed.), *Consultation in schools* (pp. 133–156). New York: Academic Press.

Johns, K. M. (1992). Lowering beginning teacher anxiety about parent-teacher conferences through role-playing. *School Counselor, 40*, 146–152.

Johnson, C. D., & Johnson, S. K. (1988). Advocacy and outreach through consultation: Applications to educational settings. In D. J. Kurpius & D. Brown (Eds.), *Handbook of consultation: An intervention for advocacy and outreach* (pp. 61–76). Alexandria, VA: American Association for Counseling and Development.

Johnson, J. J., & Pugach, M. C. (1996). The emerging third wave of collaboration: Beyond problem solving. In W. Stainbach and S. Stainback (Eds.), *Controversial issues confronting special education* (2nd ed., pp. 196–204). Boston: Allyn & Bacon.

Johnston, R., & Gilliland, B. E. (1987). A program for effective interaction between school systems and consultants. *School Counselor, 35*, 110–119.

Jones, S. (1986). Addressing internal politics: A role for modeling in consultant-client interaction. *Small Group Behavior, 17*, 67–81.

Jordan, A. E., & Meara, N. M. (1990). Ethics and the professional practice of psychologists: The role of virtue and principles. *Professional Psychology: Research and Practice, 21*, 107–114.

Juras, J. L., Mackin, J. R., Curtis, S. E., & Foster-Fishman, P. G. (1998). Key concepts of community psychology: Implications for consulting in educational and human service settings. *Journal of Educational and Psychological Consultation, 8*, 111–133.

Kahnweiler, W. M. (1979). The school counselor as consultant: A historical review. *Personnel and Guidance Journal, 57*, 374–379.

Kanfer, F. H., & Goldstein, A. P. (Eds.). (1991). *Helping people change* (4th ed.). New York: Pergamon Press.

Kaplan, L. S., Geoffroy, K. E., & Burgess, D. G. (1993). Counselors as consultants during a national crisis. *School Counselor, 41*, 60–64.

Karoly, P., & Harris, A. (1986). Operant methods. In F. H. Kanfer & A. P. Goldstein (Eds.), *Helping people change* (pp. 111–144). New York: Pergamon Press.

Katz, D., & Kahn, R. L. (1978). *The social psychology of organizations* (2nd ed.). New York: Wiley.

Katz, D., & Kahn, R. L. (1990). *The social psychology of organizations* (4th ed.). New York: Wiley.

Katzell, R., & Thompson, D. (1990). Work motivation: Theory and practice. *American Psychologist, 45(2)*, 144–153.

Kazdin, A. E. (1995). *Behavior modification in applied settings* (5th ed.). Pacific Grove, CA: Brooks/Cole.

Keller, H. R. (1981). Behavioral consultation. In J. C. Conoley (Ed.), *Consultation in schools: Theory, research, and procedures* (pp. 59–99). New York: Academic Press.

Kelley, R. E. (1981). *Consulting: The complete guide to a profitable career.* New York: Scribner's.

Kelly, J. G. (1983). Consultation as a process of creating power: An ecological view. In S. Cooper & W. F. Hodges (Eds.), *The mental health consultation field* (pp. 153–171). New York: Human Sciences Press.

Kelly, J. G. (1987). An ecological paradigm: Defining mental health consultation as a preventative service. *Prevention in Human Services, 4(3–4)*, 1–36.

Kelly, J. G. (1993). Gerald Caplan's paradigm: Bridging psychotherapy and public health practice. In W. P. Erchul (Ed.), *Consultation in community, school, and organizational practice* (pp. 75–85). Washington, DC: Taylor & Francis.

Kets De Vries, M. F. R., & Associates (Eds.). (1991). *Organizations on the couch.* San Francisco: Jossey-Bass.

Keys, S. G., Bemak, F., Carpenter, S. L., & King-Sear, M. E. (1998). Collaborative consultant: A new role for counselors serving at-risk youths. *Journal of Counseling & Development, 7*, 123–133.

Khandwalla, P. N. (1977). *The design of organizations.* New York: Harcourt Brace Jovanovich.

Kirby, J. H. (1985). *Consultation: Practice and practitioner.* Muncie, IN: Accelerated Development.

Kirkpatrick, D. L. (1975). *Evaluating training programs.* Madison, WI: American Society for Training and Development.

Kitchener, K. S., & Harding, S. S. (1990). Dual role relationships. In B. Herlihy and L. B. Golden (Eds.), *American Association for Counseling and Development ethical standards casebook* (4th ed., pp. 146–154). Alexandria, VA: American Association for Counseling and Development.

Klein, D. (1969). Some notes on the dynamics of resistance to change: The defender role. In W. G. Bennis, K. D. Benne, & R. Chin (Eds.), *The planning of change* (2nd ed., pp. 498–507). New York: Holt, Rinehart & Winston.

Klein, D. C. (1983). Future directions for consultation by mental health systems. In S. Cooper & W. F. Hodges (Eds.), *The mental health consultation field* (pp. 221–229). New York: Human Sciences Press.

Kloos, B., McCoy, J., Stewart, E., Thomas, R. E., Wiley, A., Good, T. L., Hunt, G. D., Moore, T., & Rappaport, J. (1998). Bridging the gap: A community-based, open systems approach to school and neighborhood con-sultation. *Journal of Educational and Psychological Consultation, 8*, 175–196.

Knoff, H. M. (1988). Clinical supervision, consultation, and counseling: A comparative analysis for supervisors and other educational leaders. *Journal of Curriculum and Supervision, 3*, 240–252.

Knoff, H. M. (1995). Best practices in facilitating school-based organizational change and strategic planning. In A. Thomas and J. Grimes (Eds.), *Best practices in school psychology* (3rd ed., pp. 239–252). Washington, DC: National Association of School Psychologists.

Knoff, H. M. (1996). The interface of school, community, and health care reform: Organizational directions toward effective services for children and youth. *School Psychology Review, 25*, 446–464.

Knoff, H. M., & Batsche, G. M. (1993). A school reform process for at-risk students: Applying Caplan's organizational consultation principles to guide prevention, intervention, and home-school cooperation. In W. P. Erchul (Ed.), *Consultation in community, school, and organizational practice* (pp. 123–147). Washington, DC: Taylor & Francis.

Knoff, H. M., Kottman, T., & Wilborn, B. L. (1992). Parents helping parents: Multiplying the counselor's effectiveness. *School Counselor, 40*, 10–14.

Knoff, H. M., & Curtis, M. J. (1996). Organizational change and school reform: School psychology at a professional crossroad: Introduction to the miniseries. *School Psychology Review, 25*, 406–408.

Knoff, H. M., McKenna, A. E, & Riser, K. (1991). Toward a consultant effectiveness scale: Investigating the characteristics of effective consultants. *School Psychology Review, 20*, 81–96.

Knoff, H. M., Sullivan P., & Liu, D. (1995). Teachers' ratings of effective school psychology consultants: An exploratory factor analysis study. *Journal of School Psychology, 33*, 39–57.

Knowles, M. S., & Associates. (1984). *Andragogy in action.* San Francisco: Jossey Bass.

Knox, A. B. (1977). *Adult development and learning: A handbook on individual growth and competence in the adult years.* San Francisco: Jossey-Bass.

Knox, A. B. (1986). *Helping adults learn.* San Francisco: Jossey-Bass.

Kolb, D. A., & Frohman, A. L. (1970). An organization development approach to consulting. *Sloan Management Review, 12(1)*, 51–65.

Kormanski, C., & Eschbach, L. (1997). From group leader to process consultant. In H. Forester-Miller and J. A. Kottler (Eds.), *Issues and challenges for group practitioners* (pp. 133–164). Denver: Love Publishing Company.

Kottman, T. (1995). *Partners in play.* Alexandria, VA: American Counseling Association.

Kottman, T., & Wilborn, B. L. (1992). Parents helping parents: Multiplying the counselor's effectiveness. *School Counselor, 40*, 10–14.

Kovach, B. E. (1998). Pyramids, circles, and teams: Confronting leadership issues. *Consulting Psychology Journal, 50*, 164–172.

Kramer, J. J. (1990). Training parents as behavior change agents: Successes, failures, and suggestions for school psychologists. In T. B. Gutkin and C. R. Reynolds (Eds.), *The handbook of school psychology* (2nd ed., pp. 683–702). New York: Wiley.

Kratochwill, T. R., & Bergan, J. R. (1990). *Behavioral consultation in applied settings: An individual guide.* New York: Plenum.

Kratochwill, T. R., Elliot, S. N., & Busse, R. T. (1995). Behavioral consultation: A five-year evaluation of consultant and client outcomes. *School Psychology Quarterly, 10,* 87–110.

Kratochwill, T. R., Elliot, S. N., & Carrington Rotto, P. (1995). Best practices in school-based behavioral consultation. In A. Thomas and J. Grimes (Eds.), *Best practices in school psychology* (3rd ed., pp. 519–537). Washington, DC: National Association of School Psychologists.

Kratochwill, T. R., Mace, F. C., & Bissel, M. S. (1987). Program evaluation and research. In C. A. Maher & S. G. Foreman (Eds.), *A behavioral approach to education of children and youth* (pp. 253–288). Hillsdale, NJ: Erlbaum.

Kratochwill, T. R., & Van Someren, K. R. (1985). Barriers to treatment success in behavioral consultation: Current limitations and future directions. *Journal of School Psychology, 23,* 225–239.

Kratochwill, T. R., & Van Someren, K. R. (1995). Barriers to treatment success in behavioral consultation: Current limitations and future directions. *Journal of Educational and Psychological Consultation, 6,* 125–143.

Kress, J. S., Cimring, B. R., & Elias, M. J. (1998). Community psychology consultation and the transition to institutional ownership and operation of intervention. *Journal of Educational and Psychological Consultation, 8,* 231–253.

Kressel, K., Bailey, J. R., & Forman, S. F. (1999). Psychological consultation in higher education: Lessons from a university faculty development center. *Journal of Educational and Psychological Consultation, 10,* 51–82.

Kruger, L. J., & Struzziero, J. (1998). Computer-mediated peer support of consultation: Case description and evaluation. *Journal of Educational and Psychological Consultation, 8,* 75–90.

Kuehnel, T. G., & Kuehnel, J. M. (1983a). Consultation training from a behavioral perspective. In J. L. Alpert and J. Meyers (Eds.), *Training in consultation* (pp. 85–103). Springfield, IL: Charles C. Thomas.

Kuehnel, T. G., & Kuehnel, J. M. (1983b). Mental health consultation. In S. Cooper & W. E. Hodges (Eds.), *The mental health consultation field* (pp. 39–56). New York: Human Sciences Press.

Kuh, G. D. (1993). Appraising the character of a college. *Journal of Counseling and Development, 71,* 661–668.

Kurpius, D. J. (1978). Consultation theory and process: An integrated model. *Personnel and Guidance Journal, 56(6),* 335–338.

Kurpius, D. J. (1985). Consultation interventions: Successes, failures, and proposals. *Journal of Counseling Psychology, 13(3),* 368–389.

Kurpius, D. J. (1986). Consultation: An important human and organizational intervention. *Journal of Counseling and Human Service Professions, 1(1),* 58–66.

Kurpius, D. J. (1987). Response to "Consultation in special education." *Journal of Learning Disabilities, 20(8),* 495.

Kurpius, D. J., Brack, G., Brack, C. J., & Dunn, L. B. (1993). Maturation of systems consultation: Subtle issues inherent in the model. *Journal of Mental Health Consultation, 15,* 414–429.

Kurpius, D. J., & Fuqua, D. R. (1993a). Introduction to the special issues. *Journal of Counseling and Development, 71,* 596–597.

Kurpius, D. J., & Fuqua, D. R. (1993b). Fundamental issues in defining consultation. *Journal of Counseling and Development, 71,* 598–600.

Kurpius, D. J., Fuqua, D. R., & Rozecki, T. (1993). The consulting process: A multidimensional approach. *Journal of Counseling and Development, 71,* 601–606.

Kurpius, D. J., & Lewis, J. E. (1988). Introduction to consultation: An intervention for advocacy and outreach. In D. J. Kurpius & D. Brown (Eds.), *Handbook of consultation: An intervention for advocacy and outreach* (pp. 1–4). Alexandria, VA: American Association for Counseling and Development.

Kurpius, D. J., & Robinson, S. E. (1978). An overview of consultation. *Personnel and Guidance Journal, 56(6),* 321–323.

Kurpius, D. J., & Rozecki, T. (1992). Outreach, advocacy, and consultation: A framework for prevention and intervention. *Elementary School Guidance and Counseling, 26,* 176–189.

Kurpius, D. J., & Rozecki, T. G. (1993). Strategies for improving interpersonal communication. In J. E. Zins, Kratochwill, T. R., and S. N. Elliot (Eds.), *Handbook of consultation services for children.* (pp. 137–158). San Francisco: Jossey-Bass.

Lamb, C. S. (1992). Managing disruptive students: The mental health practitioner as a consultant for faculty and staff. *Journal of College Student Psychotherapy, 7,* 23–39.

Lange, A., & Grieger, R. (1993). Integrating RET into management consulting and training. *Journal of Rational-Emotive & Cognitive-Behavior Therapy, 11,* 51–57.

Latham, G. P., & Lee, T. W. (1986). Goal setting. In E. A. Locke (Ed.), *Generalizing from laboratory to field settings* (pp. 101–117). Lexington, MA: Lexington Books.

Lawson, H. A. (1998). Academically based community scholarship, consultation as collaborative problem-solving, and a collective-responsibility model for the helping fields. *Journal of Psychological and Educational Consultation, 9,* 195–232.

Ledford, G. E., Jr. (1990). Smart clients, foolish questions: On dumb questions and the clients who love them. *Consultation, 9,* 323–328.

Lee, C. C. (1995). School counseling and cultural diversity: A framework for effective practice. In C. C. Lee (Ed.), *Counseling for diversity: A guide for school counselors and related professionals* (pp. 3–17). Boston, MA: Allyn & Bacon.

Lee, C. C., & Richardson, B. L. (1991). *Multicultural issues in counseling: New approaches to diversity.* Alexandria, VA: American Counseling Association.

Lee, R. J. (1993). Getting things done in changing organizations. In R. T. Golembiewski (Ed.), *Handbook of organizational consultation* (pp. 495–499). New York: Marcel Dekker.

Lentz, F. E., Allen, S., J., & Erhardt, K. E. (1996). The conceptual elements of strong interventions in school settings. *School Psychology Quarterly, 11(2),* 118–136.

Leonard, P. Y., & Gottsdanker-Willekens, A. E. (1987). The elementary school counselor as consultant for self-concept enhancement. *School Counselor, 34,* 245–255.

Lerner, R. M. (1995). *America's youth in crisis: Challenges and opportunities for programs and policies.* Thousand Oaks, CA: Sage.

Levine, H. Z. (1985). Consensus on employee assistance programs. *Personnel, 62(4),* 14–19.

Levinson, H. (1985). Invited commentary: Consultation by cliche. *Consultation, 4(2),* 165–170.

Levinson, H. (1993). Looking ahead: Caplan's ideas and the future of organizational consultation. In W. P. Er-

chul (Ed.), *Consultation in community, school, and organizational practice* (pp. 193–204). Washington, DC: Taylor & Francis.

Lewin, K. (1945). Research center for group dynamics. *Sociometry, 8(2),* 9.

Lewin, K. (1951). *Field theory in social sciences.* New York: Harper & Row.

Lewis, J. A., & Lewis, M. D. (1986). *Counseling programs for employees in the workplace.* Pacific Grove, CA: Brooks/Cole.

Lewis, J. A., Lewis, M. D., & Souflee, S., Jr. (1991). *Management of human service programs* (2nd ed.). Pacific Grove, CA: Brooks/Cole.

Liberman, R. P., Kuehnel, T. G., Kuehnel, J. M., Eckman, T., & Rosenstein, J. (1982). The behavioral analysis and modification project for community mental health. In A. M. Jeger and R. S. Slotnick (Eds.), *Community mental health and behavioral ecology: A handbook of theory, research, and practice* (pp. 95–112). New York: Plenum.

Lindberg, S. P. (1996) The mental health counselor and hospice. In W. J. Weikel and A. J. Palmo (Eds.), *Foundations of mental health counseling* (2nd ed., pp. 229–231). Springfield, IL: Thomas Books.

Lippitt, G. (1969). *Organizational renewal: Achieving viability in a changing world.* New York: Dutton.

Lippitt, G. L. (1982a). *Organizational renewal: A holistic approach to organization development* (2nd ed.). Englewood Cliffs, NJ: Prentice-Hall.

Lippitt, G. L. (1982b). Managing conflict in today's organizations. *Training and Development Journal* (July), 1–5.

Lippitt, G. L. (1993). Models of organizational change. In R. T. Golembiewski (Ed.), *Handbook of organizational consultation* (pp. 501–508). New York: Marcel Dekker.

Lippitt, G. L., Langseth, P., & Mossop, J. (1985). *Implementing organizational change.* San Francisco: Jossey-Bass.

Lippitt, G., & Lippitt, R. (1986). *The consulting process in action.* (2nd ed.) La Jolla, CA: University Associates.

Lippitt, G. L., & Nadler, L. (1979). Emerging roles of the training director. In C. R. Bell & L. Nadler (Eds.), *The client-consultant handbook* (pp. 44–49). Houston: Gulf Publishing.

Lippitt, R. (1983). Ethical issues and criteria in intervention decisions. In S. Cooper and W. F. Hodges (Eds.), *The mental health consultation field* (pp. 139–151). New York: Human Sciences Press.

Lochman, J. E., Dunn, S. E., & Klimes-Dugan, B. K. (1993). An intervention and consultation model from a social cognitive perspective: A description of the anger coping program. *School Psychology Review, 22,* 458–471.

Lochman, J. E., Lampron, L. B., Gemmer, T. C., Harris, S. R., & Wyckoff, G. M. (1989). Teacher consultation and cognitive-behavioral interventions with aggressive boys. *Psychology in the Schools, 26,* 179–188.

Locke, E. A., & Latham, G. P. (1984). *Goal setting: A motivational technique that works.* Englewood Cliffs, NJ: Prentice-Hall.

Logan, W. L. (1997). Peer consultation group: Doing what works for counselors. *Professional School Counseling, 1,* 4–6.

Lorsch, J. W., & Lawrence, P. (1972). The diagnosis of organizational problems. In N. Margulies & A. P. Raia (Eds.), *Organizational development: Values, process, and technology* (pp. 218–228). New York: McGraw-Hill.

Lowman, R. L. (1985). Ethical practice of psychological consultation: Not an impossible dream. *Counseling Psychologist, 13(3),* 466–472.

Luke, R. A., Jr. (1993). Workplace issues in the '90s. In R. T. Golembiewski (Ed.), *Handbook of organizational consultation* (pp. 525–534). New York: Marcel Dekker.

Lundberg, C. C. (1985). Consultant feedback: A metaphor technique. *Consultation, 4(2),* 145–151.

Lundberg, C. C. (1988). The consultant as cultural spokesperson. *Consultation, 7,* 41–44.

Lundberg, C. C. (1993). Knowing and surfacing organizational culture. In R. T. Golembiewski (Ed.), *Handbook of organizational consultation* (pp. 535–547). New York: Marcel Dekker.

Lutzker, J. R., & Martin, J. A. (1981). *Behavior change.* Pacific Grove, CA: Brooks/Cole.

Maas, K., & Mann-Feder, V. (1994). Successful consultation in youth care: The role of initial contracting. *Journal of Child & Youth Care, 9(3),* 59–65.

MacLennan, B. W. (1986). The organization and delivery of mental health consultation in changing times. In F. V. Mannino, E. J. Trickett, M. F. Shore, M. G. Kidder, & G. Levine (Eds.), *Handbook of mental health consultation* (pp. 319–345). Rockville, MD: National Institute of Mental Health.

MacLennan, B. W., Quinn, R. D., & Schroeder, D. (1975). The scope of community mental health consultation. In E. V. Mannino, B. W. MacLennan, & M. E. Shore (Eds.), *The practice of mental health consultation* (pp. 3–24). Rockville, MD: National Institute of Mental Health.

MacMann, G. M., Barnett, D. W., Allen, S. J., Bramlett, R. K., Hall, J. D., & Ehrhardt, K. E. (1996). Problem solving and intervention design: Guidelines for the evaluation of technical adequacy. *School Psychology Quarterly, 11,* 137–148.

Maher, C. A. (1981). Interventions with school social systems: A behavioral-systems approach. *School Psychology Review, 10(4),* 499–510.

Maher, C. A. (1993). Providing consultation services in business settings. In J. E. Zins, T. R. Kratochwill, & S. N. Elliot (Eds.), *Handbook of consultation services for children* (pp. 317–328). San Francisco: Jossey-Bass.

Maher, C. A., Cook, S. A., & Kruger, L. J. (1987). Human resource development. In C. A. Maher & S. G. Forman (Eds.), *A behavioral approach to education of children and youth* (pp. 221–252). Hillsdale, NJ: Erlbaum.

Maher, C. A., & Illback, R. J. (1983). Planning for organizational change in schools: Alternative approaches and procedures. *School Psychology Review, 12,* 460–466.

Maital, S. L. (1996). Integration of behavioral and mental health consultation as a means of overcoming resistance. *Journal of Educational and Psychological Consultation, 7,* 291–303.

Malony, H. N. (1991). Congregational consultation. *Prevention in Human Services, 1(3),* 289–315.

Mann, P. A. (1978). Mental health consultation in school settings. *Personnel and Guidance Journal, 56(6),* 369–373.

Mann, P. A. (1983). Transition points in consultation entry, transfer, and termination. In S. Cooper & W. E. Hodges (Eds.), *The mental health consultation field* (pp. 99–105). New York: Human Sciences Press.

Mannino, F. V., MacLennan, B. W., & Shore, M. E. (Eds.). (1975). *The practice of mental health consultation.* New York: Gardner.

Mannino, F. V., & Shore, M. E. (1986). Understanding consultation: Some orienting dimensions. *Counseling Psychologist, 13(3),* 363–367

Margolis, H. (1990). Helping implement co-operative learning. *School Psychology International, 11,* 309–318.

Margulies, N. (1988). The consultant as political strategist. *Consultation, 7,* 31–33.

Margulies, N., & Raia, A. P. (1972). Emerging issues in organization development. In N. Margulies and A. P. Raia (Eds.), *Organizational development: Values, process, and technology* (pp. 475–478). New York: McGraw-Hill.

Marks. E. S. (1995). *Entry strategies for school consultation.* New York: Guilford.

Maris, T. L. (1985). Characteristics of successful management consultants. *Consultation, 4(3),* 258–263.

Marshall, C., & Rossman, G. B. (1995). *Designing qualitative research* (2nd ed.). Thousand Oaks, CA: Sage Publications.

Martens, B. K. (1993). A behavioral approach to consultation. In J. E. Zins, T. R. Kratochwill, and S. N. Elliot (Eds.), *Handbook of consultation services for children* (pp. 65–86). San Francisco: Jossey-Bass.

Martens, B. K., Kelly, S. Q., & Diskin, M. T. (1996). The effects of two sequential-request strategies on teachers' acceptability and use of a classroom intervention. *Journal of Educational and Psychological Consultation, 7,* 211–221.

Martens, B. K., Lewandowski, L. J., & Houk, J. L. (1989). The effects of entry information on the consultation process. *School Psychology Review, 18,* 225–234.

Martens, B. K., & Witt, J. C. (1988). Expanding the scope of behavioral consultation: A systems approach to classroom behavior change. *Professional School Psychology, 3(4),* 271–281.

Martin, R. P. (1983). Consultant, consultee, and client explanations of each others' behavior in consultation. *School Psychology Review, 12,* 35–41.

Mason, E. J., Demers, S. T., & Middleton, E. J. (1984). Integrating consultation and program evaluation in school psychology. *Journal of School Psychology, 22,* 273–283.

Mathias, C. E. (1992). Touching the lives of children: Consultative interventions that work. *Elementary School Guidance and Counseling, 26,* 190–201.

Matson, J. (1985). Modeling. In A. S. Bellack & M. Hersen (Eds.), *Dictionary of behavior therapy techniques* (pp. 150–151). New York: Pergamon Press.

Matthews, J. (1983). *The effective use of management consultants in higher education.* Boulder, CO: National Center for Higher Education Management Services.

Matuszek, P. A. (1981). Program evaluation as consultation. In J. C. Conoley (Ed.), *Consultation in schools* (pp. 179–200). New York: Academic Press.

Mayer, G. R., Mitchell, L. K., Clementi, T., Clemet-Robinson, E., Myatt, R., & Bullara, D. T. (1993). A dropout prevention program for at-risk high school students: Emphasizing consulting to promote positive classroom climates. *Education and Treatment of Children, 16,* 135–146.

Mazade, N. A. (1983). In conclusion the past, present, and future in consultation. In S. Cooper & W. E. Hodges (Eds.), *The mental health consultation field* (pp. 233–242). New York: Human Sciences Press.

Mazade, N. A. (1985). Issues in consultation. *Consultation, 4(1),* 7–16.

McAuliffe, G. (1993). Career as an imaginative quest. *American Counselor, 2(1),* 13–16, 36.

McCarthy, M. M., & Sorenson, G. P. (1993). School counselors: Legal duties and liabilities. *Journal of Counseling and Development, 72(2),* 159–167.

McCollum, M. G. (1981). Recasting a role for mental health educators. *American Mental Health Counselors Journal, 3(1),* 37–47.

McDougall, L. M., Reschly, D. J., & Corkery, J. M. (1988). Changes in referral interviews with teachers after behavioral consultation training. *Journal of School Psychology, 26,* 225–232.

McFarland, W. P. (1992). Counselors teaching peaceful conflict resolution. *Journal of Counseling and Development, 71,* 18–21.

McGowan, S. (1993). Employees, managers work it out after layoffs. *Guidepost, 35(10),* 1–10.

McKeachie, W. J. (1986). *Teaching tips: A guidebook for the beginning teacher* (8th ed.). Boston: Heath.

McMahon, T. J., & Pruett, M. K. (1998). On the proverbial horns of an ethical dilemma: School consultation, child advocacy, and adversarial intervention. *Journal of Educational and Psychological Consultation, 9,* 75–85.

Meade, C. J., Hamilton, M. K., & Yuen, R. K-W. (1982). Consultation research: The time has come the walrus said. *Counseling Psychologist, 4,* 39–51.

Medway, F. J. (1989). Further considerations on a cognitive problem-solving perspective on school consultation. *Professional School Psychology, 4,* 21–27.

Meeks, S. (1996). Psychological consultation to nursing homes: Description of a six-year practice. *Psychotherapy, 33,* 19–29.

Meichenbaum, D. (1977). *Cognitive-behavior modification: An integrative approach.* New York: Plenum.

Meichenbaum, D. (1985). *Stress inoculation training.* New York: Pergamon Press.

Mendoza, D. W. (1993). A review of Gerald Caplan's *Theory and practice of mental health consultation. Journal of Counseling and Development, 71,* 629–635.

Merron, K. (1993). Let's bury the term "resistance." *Organization Development Journal, 11(4),* 77–86.

Meyers, J. (1981). Mental health consultation. In J. C. Conoley (Ed.), *Consultation in schools: Theory, research, and procedures* (pp. 35–58). New York: Academic Press.

Meyers, J. (1985). Consultation as a basis for delivery of school psychological services. *Programs in School Psychology, 40(1),* 3–4.

Meyers, J., Brent, D., Faherty, E., & Modafferi, C. (1993). Caplan's contributions to the practice of psychology in schools. In W. P. Erchul (Ed.), *Consultation in community, school, and organizational practice* (pp. 99–122). Washington, DC: Taylor & Francis.

Meyers, J., Gaughan, E., & Pitt, N. (1990). Contributions of community psychology to school psychology. In T. B. Gutkin & C. R. Reynolds (Eds.), *The handbook of school psychology* (2nd ed., pp. 198–217). New York: Wiley.

Meyers, J., Parsons, R. D., & Martin, R. (1979). *Mental health consultation in the schools.* San Francisco: Jossey-Bass.

Meyers, J., & Yelich, G. (1989). Cognitive-behavioral approaches in psychoeducational consultation. In J. N. Hughes and R. J. Hall (Eds.), *Cognitive-behavioral psychology in the schools* (pp. 501–535). New York: Guilford.

Miranda, A. H. (1993). Consultation with culturally diverse families. *Journal of Educational and Psychological Consultation, 4,* 89–93.

Mitchell, T. R. (1978). *People in organizations: Understanding their behavior.* New York: McGraw-Hill.

Morasky, R. L. (1982). *Behavioral systems.* New York: Praeger.

Moseley-Howard, G. S. (1995). Best practices in considering the role of culture. In A. Thomas and J. Grimes (Eds.), *Best practices in school psychology* (3rd ed., pp. 337–345). Washington, DC: National Association of School Psychologists.

Mowder, B. A., Willis, W. G., & Widerstrom, A. H. (1986). Consultation and handicapped preschoolers: Priorities, goals, and models. *Psychology in the Schools, 23,* 373–379.

Murrell, K. L. (1993). Process consulting. In R. T. Golembiewski (Ed.), *Handbook of organizational consultation* (pp. 579–582). New York: Marcel Dekker, Inc.

Myers, D. W. (1988). Preparation for EAP consulting work. *Consultation, 7,* 204–215.

Nadler, D. A. (1977). *Feedback and organization development: Using data-based methods.* Reading, MA: Addison-Wesley.

Nadler, L. (1980). *Corporate human resources development: A managerial tool.* New York: Van Nostrand Reinhold.

National Association of Social Workers. (1996). *Code of ethics* (rev. ed.). Silver Springs, MD: Author.

National Board for Certified Counselors. (1997). *National board for certified counselors code of ethics.* Alexandria, VA: Author.

National Board for Certified Counselors. (1998). *Standards for the ethical practice of webcounseling.* Alexandria, VA: Author.

National Organization for Human Service Education. (1995). *Ethical standards of the national organization for human service organizations.* Author.

Naumann, W. C., Gutkin, T. B., & Sandoval, S. R. (1996). The impact of consultant race and student race on perceptions of consultant effectiveness and intervention acceptability. *Journal of Educational and Psychological Consultation, 7,* 151–160.

Neilsen, E. H. (1984). *Becoming an OD practitioner.* Englewood Cliffs, NJ: Prentice-Hall.

Nevis, E. (1987). *Organizational counsulting.* Cleveland, OH: Gestalt Institute of Cleveland Press.

Newman, J. L. (1993). Ethical issues in consultation. *Journal of Counseling and Development, 72(2),* 148–156.

Newman, J. L., & Fuqua, D. R. (1984). Data-based consultation in student affairs. *Journal of College Student Personnel, 25,* 206–212.

Newman, J. L., Gray, E. A., & Fuqua, D. R. (1996). Beyond ethical decision making. *Consulting Psychology Journal, 48,* 230–236.

Nicoll, W. G. (1992). A family counseling and consultation model for school counselors. *School Counselor, 39,* 351–361.

Noble, B., & Dickinson, D. J. (1988). Utility of school psychologists' recommendations: Perception of elementary teachers. *Psychology in the Schools, 25,* 412–418.

Noell, G. H. (1996). New directions in behavioral consultation. *School Psychology Quarterly, 11,* 187–188.

Noell, G. H., & Gresham, F. M. (1993). Functional outcome analysis: Do the benefits of consultation and prereferral intervention justify the costs? *School Psychology Quarterly, 8,* 200–226.

Noell, G. H., & Witt, J. C. (1996). A critical re-evaluation of five fundamental assumptions underlying behavioral consultation. *School Psychology Quarterly, 11,* 189–203.

Norris, D. A., Burke, J. P., & Speer, A. L. (1990). Tri-level delivery: An alternative consultation model. *School Psychology Quarterly, 5,* 89–110.

Nuttall, E. V., De Leon, B., & Valle, M. (1990). Best practices in considering cultural factors. In A. Thomas and J. Grimes (Eds.). *Best practices in school psychology* (2nd ed., pp. 219–233). Washington, DC: NASP.

O'Callaghan, J. B. (1993). *School-based collaboration with families.* San Francisco: Jossey-Bass.

O'Connell, J. J. (1990). Process consulting in a content field: Socrates in strategy. *Consultation, 9,* 199–208.

O'Conner, W. A., & Lubin, B. (1984). *Ecological approaches to clinical and community psychology.* New York: Wiley.

O'Driscoll, M. P., & Eubanks, J. L. (1992). Consultant and client perceptions of consultant competencies: Implications for OD consulting. *Organization Development Journal, 10(4),* 53–59.

Offermann, L. R., & Gowing, M. K. (1990). Organizations of the future. *American Psychologist, 45(2),* 95–108.

Oher, J. M. (1993). Survey research to measure EAP customer satisfaction: A quality improvement tool. *Employee Assistance Quarterly, 8(4),* 41–75.

O'Keefe, D. J., & Medway, F. J. (1997). The application of persuasion research to consultation in school psychology. *Journal of School Psychology, 35,* 173–193.

O'Neill, P., & Trickett, E. J. (1982). *Community consultation.* San Francisco: Jossey-Bass.

Osterweil, Z. O. (1987). A structured process of problem definition in school consultation. *School Counselor, 34(5),* 345–352.

Osterweil, Z. O. (1988). A structured integrative model of mental health consultation in schools. *International Journal for the Advancement of Counselling, 11,* 37–49.

Osterweil, Z., & Plotnik, R. (1989). Mental health consultation: An evaluation of the issue-focused model. *School Psychology International, 10,* 293–299.

Otani, A. (1989). Client resistance in counseling: Its theoretical rationale and taxonomic classification. *Journal of Counseling and Development, 67,* 458–461.

Pace, T. M., Mullins, L. L., Chaney, J. M., & Olson, R. A. (1995). Psychological consultation with primary care physicians: Obstacles and opportunities in the medical setting. *Professional Psychology: Research and Practice, 26,* 123–131.

Parker, R. J. (1994). Helping children cope with divorce: A workshop for parents. *Elementary School Guidance & Counseling, 29,* 137–148.

Parr, G. (1993). Educational reforms in Texas and their implications for school counselors. *School Counselor, 41,* 44–47

Parsons, R. D. (1996). *The skilled consultant.* Boston: Allyn & Bacon.

Parsons, R. D., & Meyers, J. (1984). *Developing consultation skills.* San Francisco: Jossey-Bass.

Partin, R. L. (1993). School counselors' time: Where does it go? *School Counselor, 40,* 274–281.

Patterson, C. H. (1986). *Theories of counseling and psychotherapy* (4th ed.). New York: Harper & Row.

Patton, M. Q. (1986). *Utilization-focused evaluation.* Beverly Hills, CA: Sage.

Pearson, B., & Piazza, N. (1997). Classification of dual relationships in the helping professions. *Counselor Education and Supervision, 37,* 89–99.

Pedersen, P. B. (1997). The cultural context of the American Counseling Association code of ethics. *Journal of Counseling and Development, 76,* 23–28.

Pena, R. A. (1996). Multiculturalism and educational leadership: Keys to effective consultation. *Journal of Educational and Psychological Consultation, 7,* 315–325.

Perry, M. A., & Furukawa, M. J. (1986). Modeling methods. In E. H. Kanfer & A. P. Goldstein (Eds.), *Helping people change* (pp. 66–110). New York: Pergamon Press.

Peters, T. (1988). *Thriving on chaos.* New York: Harper-Collins.

Petti, T. A., Cornely, P. J., & McIntyre, A. (1993). A consultative study as a catalyst for improving mental health services for rural children and adolescents. *Hospital and Community Psychiatry, 44,* 262–265.

Petty, R. E., Heesacker M., & Hughes, J. N. (1997). The elaboration likelihood model: Implications for the practice of school psychology. *Journal of School Psychology, 35,* 107–136

Pfeiffer, J. W., & Jones, J. E. (Eds.). (1974). *A handbook of structured experiences for human relations training* (Vol. 3). La Jolla, CA: University Associates.

Pfeiffer, J. W., & Jones, J. E. (Eds.). (1977). Ethical considerations in consulting. In J. E. Jones and J. W. Pfeiffer (Eds.), *The 1977 annual handbook for group facilitators* (pp. 217–224). La Jolla, CA: University Associates.

Piersel, W. C., & Gutkin, T. B. (1983). Resistance to school-based consultation: A behavioral analysis of the problem. *Psychology in the Schools, 20,* 311–320.

Pipes, R. B. (1981). Consulting in organizations: The entry problem. In J. C. Conoley (Ed.), *Consultation in schools—theory, research, procedures* (pp. 11–33). New York: Academic Press.

Plummer, D. L. (1998). Approaching diversity training in the year 2000. *Consulting Psychology Journal, 50,* 181–189.

Pohlman, C., Hofffman, L. B., Dodds, A. H., & Pryzwansky, W. B. (1998). Utilization of school-based professional services: An exploratory analysis of perceptions of mentor teachers and student teachers. *Journal of Educational and Psychological Consultation, 9,* 347–365.

Ponti, C. R., & Flower, J. C. (1993). Consulting in elementary and secondary schools. In J. E. Zins, T. R. Kratochwill, & S. N. Elliot (Eds.), *Handbook of consultation services for children* (pp. 277–290). San Francisco: Jossey-Bass.

Prein, H. (1987). Strategies for third-party interventions. *Human Relations, 40,* 699–720.

Prilleltensky, I., Peirson, L., & Nelson, G. (1998). The application of community psychology values and guiding concepts to school consultation. *Journal of Educational and Psychological Consultation, 8,* 153–173.

Pruett, M. K. (1998). Statement of purpose for legal and ethical issues in consultation. *Journal of Educational and Psychological Consultation, 9,* 73–74.

Pryzwansky, W. B. (1989). Some further thoughts about the problem-finding challenge of consultation. *Professional School Psychology, 4,* 37–40.

Pryzwansky, W. B. (1993). Ethical consultation practice. In J. E. Zins, T. R. Kratochwill, & S. N. Elliot (Eds.),

Handbook of consultation services for children (pp. 329–348). San Francisco: Jossey-Bass.

Pryzwansky, W. B. (1996). Professionals' peer-mediated learning experiences: Another idea whose time has come. *Journal of Educational and Psychological Consultation, 7,* 71–78.

Pryzwansky, W. B., & Noblit. G. W. (1990). Understanding and improving consultation practice: The qualitative case study approach. *Journal of Educational and Psychological Consultation, 1,* 293–307.

Public Law 105-17, *Individuals with Disabilities Education Act,* 1997.

Pugh, D. S. (1966). Modern organizational theory: A psychological and sociological study. *Psychological Bulletin, 66(4),* 235–251.

Quinn, K., & Cumblad, C. (1994). Service providers' perceptions of interagency collaboration in their communites. *Journal of Emotional and Behavioral Disorders, 2,* 109–116.

Quirk, M. P., Strosahl, K., Kreilkamp, T., & Erdberg, P. (1995). Personality feedback consultation to families in a managed mental health care practice. *Professional Psychology Research and Practice, 26,* 27–32.

Raia, A. P. (1988). The consultant as conceptual therapist. *Consultation, 7,* 34–37.

Randolph, D. L., & D'Ilio, V. R. (1990). Factors influencing perceptions of consultant effectiveness. *Psychology: A Journal of Human Behavior, 27(13),* 12–19.

Randolph, D. L., & Graun, K. (1988). Resistance to consultation: A synthesis for counselor-consultants. *Journal of Counseling and Development, 67,* 182–184.

Redmon, W. K., Cullari, S., & Farris, H. E. (1985). An analysis of some important tasks and phases in consultation. *Journal of Community Psychology, 13,* 375–386.

Reed, C., Greer, A., McKay, C., & Knight, C. (1990). Process issues in consultancy. *Journal of Adolescence, 13(4),* 387–400.

Remley, T. P., Jr. (1988). Consultative advocacy differentiated from legal advocacy. In D. J. Kurpius & D. Brown (Eds.), *Handbook of consultation: An intervention for advocacy and outreach* (pp. 18–26). Alexandria, VA: American Association for Counseling and Development.

Remley, T. P., Jr. (1993). Consultation contracts. *Journal of Counseling and Development, 72,* 157–158.

Remley, T. P. (1996). The relationship between law and ethics. In B. Herlihy and G. Corey (Eds.), *American Counseling Association ethical standards casebook* (5th ed., pp. 285–292). Alexandria, VA: American Counseling Association.

Reppucci, N. D. (1977). Implementation issues for the behavior modifier as institutional change agent. *Behavior Therapy, 8,* 594–605.

Reppucci, N. D., & Saunders, J. (1983). Focal issues for institutional change. *Professional Psychology: Research and Practice, 14,* 514–528.

Reschly, D. J., & Wilson, M. (1995). School psychology practitioners and faculty: 1986 to 1991–trends in demographics, roles, satisfaction, and system reform. *School Psychology Review, 24,* 62–80.

Resnick, H., & King, J. (1985). Shadow consultation: Intervention in industry. *Social Work, 30,* 447–450.

Rhoades, M. M., & Kratochwill, T. R. (1992). Teacher reactions to behavioral consultation: An analysis of language and involvement. *School Psychology Quarterly, 7,* 47–59.

Rice, A. K. (1969). Individual, group, and intergroup process. *Human Relations, 22,* 565–584.

Ridley, C. R., & Mendoza, D. W. (1993). Operationalizing organizational effectiveness: The preeminent consultation task. *Journal of Counseling and Development, 72(2),* 168–177.

Riley, R. W. (1996). Improving America's schools. *School Psychology Review, 25,* 477–484.

Rimm, D. C., & Cunningham, H. M. (1985). Behavior therapies. In S. J. Lynn & J. P. Garske (Eds.), *Contemporary psychotherapies models and methods* (pp. 221–259). Columbus, OH: Merrill.

Ritchie, M. H. (1982). Parental consultation: Practical considerations. *School Counselor, 29,* 402–410.

Ritchie, M. H., & Partin, R. L. (1994). Parent education and consultation activities of school counselors. *School Counselor, 41,* 165–170.

Roberts, A. H., & Rust, J. O. (1994). Role and function of school psychologists, 1992–93: A comparative study. *Psychology in the Schools, 31,* 113–119.

Robinson, B. A., & Elias, M. J. (1993). Stabilizing classroom-based group interventions: Guidelines for special services providers and consultants. *Special Services in the Schools, 8,* 159–177.

Robinson, D., & Robinson, J. C. (1995). *Performance consulting.* San Francisco: Berrett-Kohler.

Robinson, S. E., & Gross, D. R. (1985). Ethics of consultation: The Canterville ghost. *Counseling Psychologist, 13(3),* 444–465.

Rockwood, G. R. (1993). Edgar Schein's process versus content consultation models. *Journal of Counseling and Development, 71,* 636–638.

Rogawski, A. S. (1978). The Caplanian model. *Personnel and Guidance Journal, 56,* 324–327

Rogers, C. R. (1961). *On becoming a person.* Boston: Houghton Mifflin.

Rosenfield, S. (1985). Teacher acceptance of behavioral principles. *Teacher Education and Special Education, 8(3),* 153–158.

Rosenfield, S. A. (1987). *Instructional consultation.* Hillsdale, NJ: Erlbaum.

Rosenfield, S. (1991). The relationship variable in behavioral consultation, *Journal of Behavioral Consultation, 1,* 329–336.

Rosenfield, S. A. (1992). Developing school-based consultation teams: A design for organizational change. *School Psychology Quarterly, 7,* 27–46.

Rosenthal, S. L. (1993). Educational consultation in the context of a medical setting. *Journal of Educational and Psychological Consultation, 4(4),* 391–394.

Ross, G. J. (1993). Peter Block's flawless consulting and the homunculus theory: Within each person is a perfect consultant. *Journal of Counseling and Development, 71,* 639–641.

Ross, J. A., & Regan, E. M. (1990). Strategies of experienced and inexperienced consultants. *Alberta Journal of Educational Research, 36(2),* 157–180.

Rudestam, K. E. (1982). *Experiential groups in theory and practice.* Pacific Grove, CA: Brooks/Cole.

Rusnack, B. L. (1989). The consultant's role. In M. L. Henk (Ed.), *Social work in primary care* (pp. 98–112). Newbury Park, CA: Sage.

Russell, M. L. (1978). Behavioral consultation: Theory and process. *Personnel and Guidance Journal, 56(6),* 346–350.

Russell-Chapin, L. A., & Stoner, C. R. (1995). Mental health counselors as consultants for diversity training. *Journal of Mental Health Counseling, 17,* 146–156.

Safran, S. P. (1991). The communication process and school-based consultation: What does the research say? *Journal of Educational and Psychological Consultation, 2,* 343–370.

Safran, S. P., & Safran, J.S. (1998). Prereferral consultation and intervention assistance teams revisited: Some new food for thought. *Journal of Educational and Psychological Consultation, 8,* 93–100.

Salmon, D. (1993). Anticipating the school consultant role: Changes in personal constructs following training. *School Psychology Quarterly, 8,* 301–317.

Salmon, D., & Lehrer, R. (1989). School consultant's implicit theories of action. *Professional School Psychology, 4,* 173–187.

Sampson J.P., Jr., Kolodinsky, R. W., & Greeno, B. P. (1997). Counseling on the information highway: Future possibilities and potential problems. *Journal of Counseling and Development, 75,* 203–212.

Sandland, K., & Dougherty, A. M. (1985). Using the nominal group technique with incarcerates. *Journal of Offender Counseling, 6,* 25–30.

Sandoval, J. (1996). Constructivism, consultee-centered consultation, and conceptual change. *Journal of Educational and Psychological Consultation, 7,* 89–97.

Saver, K., & Downes, B. (1991). PIT crew: A model for teacher collaboration in an elementary school. *Intervention in School and Clinic, 27(2),* 116–120.

Schein, E. H. (1969). *Process consultation: Its role in organization development* (1st ed.). Reading, MA: Addison-Wesley.

Schein, E. H. (1978). The role of the consultant: Content expert or process facilitator? *Personnel and Guidance Journal, 56(6),* 339–343.

Schein, E. H. (1987). *Process consultation: Lessons for managers and consultants* (Vol. 2). Reading, MA: Addison-Wesley.

Schein, E. H. (1988). *Process consultation: Its role in organization development* (Vol. 1, 2nd ed.). Reading, MA: Addison-Wesley.

Schein, E. H. (1990a). Back to the future: Recapturing the OD vision. In E. Massarick (Ed.), *Advances in Organization Development* (Vol. 1, pp. 13–26). Norwood, NJ: Ablex.

Schein, E. H. (1990b). Organizational culture. *American Psychologist, 45(2),* 109–119.

Schein, E. H. (1990c). Models of consultation: What do organizations of the 1990s need? *Consultation, 9,* 261–275.

Schein, E. H. (1993). Legitimating clinical research in the study of organizational culture. *Journal of Counseling and Development, 71,* 703–708.

Schein, E. H., & Greiner, L. E. (1977). Can organization development be fine tuned to bureaucracies? *Organization Dynamics, 5(3),* 48–61.

Schindler-Rainman, E. (1985). Invited commentary: The modern consultants renaissance person. *Consultation, 4(3),* 264–267

Schmidt, J. J. (1993). *Counseling in schools.* Needham Heights, MA: Allyn & Bacon.

Schmidt, J. J., & Osborne, W. L. (1981). Counseling and consulting: Separate processes or the same? *Personnel and Guidance Journal, 59,* 168–171.

Schmuck, R. A. (1976). Process consultation and organization development. *Professional Psychology, 7,* 626–635.

Schmuck, R. A. (1983). System-process mental health models. In S. Cooper & W. R. Hodges (Eds.), *The mental health consultation field* (pp. 71–90). New York: Human Sciences Press.

Schmuck, R. A. (1990). Organization development in schools: Contemporary concepts and practices. In T. B. Gutkin & C. R. Reynolds (Eds.), *The handbook of school psychology* (2nd ed., pp. 899–919). New York: Wiley.

Schmuck, R. A. (1995). Process consultation and organization development. *Journal of Educational and Psychological Consultation, 6,* 199–206.

Schmuck, R. A., & Runkel, P. J. (1985). Organization development in schools. *Consultation, 4,* 236–259.

Schottle, D. A., & Peltier, G. L. (1996). Should schools employ behavior management consultants? *Journal of Instructional Psychology, 23(2),* 128–130.

Schwiebert, V., & Myers, J. E. (1994). Midlife care givers: Effectiveness of a psychoeducational intervention for midlife adults with parent-care responsibilities. *Journal of Counseling and Development, 72,* 627–632.

Scriven, M. (1967). The methodology of evaluation. In R. Tyler, R. Gagne, & M. Scriven (Eds.), *Perspectives on curriculum evaluation* (AERA Monograph Series on Curriculum Evaluation). Chicago: Rand McNally.

Shapiro, E. S., DuPaul, G. J., Bradley, K. L., & Bailey, L. T. (1996). A school-based consultation program for service delivery to middle school students with attention-deficit/hyperactivity disorder. *Journal of Emotional & Behavioral Disorders, 4,* 73–81

Shaw, S. R., & Swerdik, M. E. (1995). Best practices in facilitating team functioning. In A. Thomas and J. Grimes (Eds.), *Best practices in school psychology* (3rd ed., pp. 153–159). Washington, DC: National Association of School Psychologists.

Sheeley, V. L., & Herlihy, B. (1986). The ethics of confidentiality and privileged communication. *Journal of Counseling and Human Service Professions, 1(1),* 141–148.

Sheridan, S. M. (1992). Consultant and client outcomes of competency-based behavioral consultation training. *School Psychology Quarterly, 7,* 245–270.

Sheridan, S. M. (1993a). Functional outcome analysis: Do the costs outweigh the benefits? *School Psychology Quarterly, 8,* 227–230.

Sheridan, S. M. (1993b). Models for working with parents. In J. E. Zins, T. R. Kratochwill, & S. N. Elliot (Eds.), *Handbook of consultation services for children* (pp. 110–133). San Francisco: Jossey-Bass.

Sheridan, S. M. (1997). Conceptual and empirical bases of conjoint behavioral consultation. *School Psychology Quarterly, 12,* 119–133.

Sheridan, S. M., & Kratochwill, T. R. (1992). Behavioral parent-teacher consultation: Conceptual and research considerations. *Journal of School Psychology, 30,* 117–139.

Sheridan, S. M., Kratochwill, T. R., & Bergan, J. R. (1996). *Conjoint behavioral consultation.* New York: Plenum Press.

Sheridan, S. M., Kratochwill, I. R., & Elliot, S. N. (1990). Behavioral consultation with parents and teachers: Delivering treatment for socially withdrawn children at home and at school. *School Psychology Review, 19,* 33–52.

Sheridan, S. M., Welch, M., & Orme, S. F. (1996). Is consultation effective? A review of outcome research. *Remedial and Special Education, 17,* 341–354.

Sherwood, J. J. (1993). Essential differences between traditional approaches to consulting and a collaborative approach. In R. T. Golembiewski (Ed.), *Handbook of organizational consultation* (pp. 687–691). New York: Marcel Dekker.

Shertzer, B., & Linden, J. D. (1979). *Fundamentals of individual appraisal.* Boston: Houghton Mifflin.

Short, R. J., Moore, S., & Williams, C. (1991). Social influence in consultation: Effect of degree and experience on consultees' perceptions. *Psychological Reports, 68,* 131–137.

Shosh, M. (1996). Counseling in business and industry. In W. J. Weikel and A. J. Palmo (Eds.), *Foundations of mental health counseling* (2nd ed., pp. 232–241). Springfield, IL: Thomas Books.

Shultz, J. (1984). Historical overview of OD counseling. In R. J. Lee & A. M. Freedman (Eds.), *Consultation skills reading* (pp. 1–3). Arlington, VA: National Training Labor Institute.

Silverman, M. M. (1993). Commentary: Consultation in a campus context: Collaboration, cooperation, and coordination. *Journal of College Student Psychotherapy, 7(3),* 49–55.

Sinha, D. P. (Ed.). (1979). *Consultants and consultant styles.* New Delhi, India: Vision Books.

Skinner, B. F. (1953). *Science and human behavior.* New York: Macmillan.

Smaby, M. H., Harrison, T. C., & Nelson, M. (1995). Elementary school counselors as total quality management consultants. *Elementary School Guidance & Counseling, 29,* 310–319.

Smart, D. W., & Smart, J. F. (1997). DSM-IV and culturally sensitive diagnosis: Some observations for counselors. *Journal of Counseling and Development, 75,* 392–398.

Smith, E. P., Connell, C. M., Wright, G., Sizer, M., Norman, J. M., Hurley, A., & Walker, S. N. (1997). An ecological model of home, school, and community partnerships: Implications for research and practice. *Journal of Educational and Psychological Consultation, 8,* 339–360.

Snow, D. L., & Gersick, K. E. (1986). Ethical and professional issues in mental health consultation. In R.V. Mannino, E. J. Trickett, M. Shore, M. G. Kidder, & G. Levin (Eds.), *Handbook of mental health consultation* (pp. 393–431). Rockville, MD: National Institute of Mental Health.

Soo-Hoo, T. (1998). Applying frame of reference and reframing techniques to improve school consultation in multicultural settings. *Journal of Educational and Psychological Consultation, 9,* 325–345.

Sperry, L. (1996). *Corporate therapy and consulting.* New York: Brunner/Mazel, Inc.

Stayer, E. M., & Dillard, J. W. (1986). A factor analysis approach to selecting a consultation style. *Psychology: A Quarterly Journal of Human Behavior, 23(4),* 1–8.

Steele, E. (1975). *Consulting for organizational change.* Amherst: University of Massachusetts Press.

Stein, R. H. (1990). *Ethical issues in counseling.* Buffalo, NY: Prometheus Books.

Steinberg, D., & Hughes, L. (1987). Work-centered issues in consultative work. *Journal of Adolescence, 10(3),* 309–316.

Stenger, M. K., Tollefson, N., & Fine, M. J. (1992). Variables that distinguish elementary teachers who participate in school-based consultation from those who do not. *School Psychology Quarterly, 7,* 271–284.

Stenho, J. J. (1995). Classroom consulting with reality therapy. *Journal of Reality Therapy, 15,* 81–86.

Steward. R. J. (1996). Training consulting psychologists to be sensitive to multicultural issues in organizational consultation. *Consulting Psychology Journal, 8,* 180–189.

Strong, S. R. (1968). Counseling: An interpersonal influence process. *Journal of Counseling Psychology, 15,* 215–224.

Strother, J., & Jacobs, E. (1986). Parent consultation: A practical approach. *School Counselor, 33,* 292–296.

Stum, D. L. (1982). DIRECT: A consultation skills training model. *Personnel and Guidance Journal, 60,* 296–301.

Sullivan, W. P. (1991). Community mental health: A model for social work consultants. *Research on Social Work Practice, 1,* 289–315.

Sullivan, W. P., & Rapp, C. A. (1991). Improving client outcomes: The Kansas technical assistance project. *Community Mental Health Journal, 27,* 327–336.

Summers, I., & White, D. E. (1980). Creativity techniques: Toward improvement of the decision process. In S. Ferguson and S. Ferguson (Eds.), *Intercommunication: Readings in organizational communication* (pp. 338–348). Rochelle Park, NJ: Hayden.

Sundstrom, E., DeMeuse, K. P., & Futrell, D. (1990). Work teams. *American Psychologist, 45(2),* 120–133.

Swartz, D., & Lippitt, G. (1975). Evaluating the consulting process. *Journal of European Training, 4,* 309–326.

Swenson, L. C. (1997). *Psychology and law* (2nd ed.). Pacific Grove, CA: Brooks/Cole.

Talbott, J. A. (1988). The elements of community consultation. *New Directions for Mental Health Services, 37,* 69–84.

Tannenbaum, S., Greene, V., & Glickman, A. (1989). The ethical reasoning process in an organizational consulting situation. *Professional Psychology: Research and Practice, 2,* 229–235.

Tarver Behring, R. K., & Ingraham, C. L. (1998). Culture as a central component of consultation: A call to the field. *Journal of Educational and Psychological Consultation, 9,* 57–72.

Taylor, L., & Adelman, H. S. (1998). Confidentiality: Competing principles, inevitable dilemmas. *Journal of Educational and Psychological Consultation, 9,* 267–275.

Thomas, C. C., Correa, V. L., & Morsink, C. V. (1995). *Interactive teaming.* Englewood Cliffs, NJ: Prentice-Hall.

Thomas, K. G. F., Gatz, M., & Luczak, S. E. (1997). A tale of two school districts: Lessons to be learned about the impact of relationship building and ecology on consultation. *Journal of Educational and Psychological Consultation, 8,* 297–320.

Thousand, J. S., Villa, R. A., Paolucci-Whitcomb, P., & Nevin, A. (1996). A rationale and vision for collaborative consultation. In W. Stainback and S. Stainback (Eds.), *Controversial issues confronting special education* (2nd ed., pp. 205–218). Boston: Allyn & Bacon.

Tichy, N. M. (1983). *Managing strategic change: Technical, political, and cultural dynamics.* New York: Wiley.

Tindal, G., Shinn, M. R., & Rodden-Nord, K. (1990). Contextually based school consultation: Influential variables. *Exceptional Children, 56,* 324–336.

Tingstrom, D. H., Little, S. G., & Stewart, K. J. (1990). School consultation from a social psychological perspective: A review. *School Consultation and Social Psychology, 27,* 41–50.

Tobias, L. L. (1990). *Psychological consulting to management.* New York: Brunner/Mazel.

Tobias, R. (1993). Underlying cultural issues that effect sound consultant/school collaboratives in developing multicultural programs. *Journal of Educational and Psychological Consultation, 4,* 237–251.

Tombari, M., & Davis, R. A. (1979). Behavioral consultation. In G. D. Phye & D. J. Reschly (Eds.), *School psychology perspectives and issues* (pp. 281–307). New York: Academic Press.

Trickett, E. J. (1986). Consultation as a preventative intervention: Comments on ecologically based case studies. *Prevention in Human Services, 4,* 187–204.

Trickett, E. J. (1992). Prevention ethics: Explicating the context of prevention activities. *Ethics & Behavior, 2,* 91–100.

Trickett, E. J. (1993). Gerald Caplan and the unfinished business of community psychology: A comment. In W. P. Erchul (Ed.), *Consultation in community, school, and organizational practice* (pp. 163–176). Washington, DC: Taylor & Francis.

Trickett, E. J., Kelly, J. G., & Vincent, T. A. (1984). The spirit of ecological inquiry in community research. In E. Susskind & D. C. Klein (Eds.), *Community research.* New York: Praeger.

Tunnecliffe, M. R., Leach, D. J., & Tunnecliffe, L. P. (1986). Relative efficacy of using behavioral consultation as an approach to teacher stress management. *Journal of School Psychology, 24,* 123–131.

Turco, T. L., & Skinner, C. H. (1991). An analysis of consultee verbal responses to structured consultant questions. *TACD Journal, 19(1),* 23–32.

Turnage, J. J. (1990). The challenge of new work place technology for psychology. *American Psychologist, 45(2),* 171–178.

Uhlemann, M. R., Lee, D.Y., & Martin, J. (1994). Client cognitive responses as a function of quality of counselor verbal responses. *Journal of Counseling and Development, 73,* 198–203.

Vernberg, E. M., & Reppucci, N. D. (1986). Behavioral consultation. In E V. Mannino, E. J. Trickett, M. F. Shore, M. G. Kidder, and G. Levin (Eds.), *Handbook of mental health consultation* (pp. 49–80). Rockville, MD: National Institute of Mental Health.

Vogt, J. F. (1989). A temporary team framework for enhancing client-consultant relationships. *Organization Development, 7(4),* 58–66.

Wallace, W. A., & Hall, D. L. (1996). *Psychological consultation.* Pacific Grove, CA: Brooks/Cole.

Waltman, G. H. (1989). Social work consultation services in rural areas. *Human Services in the Rural Environment, 12(3),* 17–21.

Watson, T. S., & Robinson, S. L. (1996). Direct behavioral consultation: An alternative to traditional behavioral consultation. *School Psychology Quarterly, 11,* 267–278.

Weinrach, S. G., & Thomas, K. R. (1998). Diversity-sensitive counseling today: A postmodern clash of values. *Journal of Counseling and Development, 76,* 115–122.

Weisbord, M. R. (1976). Organizational diagnosis: Six places to look for trouble with or without a theory. *Group and Organizational Studies, 1,* 430–447.

Weisbord, M. R. (1984). Client contact: Entry and contract. In R. J. Lee & A. M. Freedman (Eds.), *Consultation skills readings* (pp. 63–66). Bethel, ME: National Training Laboratories Institute.

Weisbord, M. R. (1985). The organization development contract revisited. *Consultation, 4(4),* 305–315.

Weiss, H. (1996). Family-school collaboration: Consultation to achieve organizational and community change. *Human Systems, 7,* 211–235.

Weissenburger, J. W., Fine, M. J., & Poggio, J. P. (1982). The relationship of selected consultant/teacher characteristics to consultation outcomes. *Journal of School Psychology, 20,* 263–270.

Welch, M. (1998). The IDEA of collaboration in special education: An introspective examination of paradigms and promise. *Journal of Educational and Psychological Consultation, 9,* 119–142.

Werner, J. L., & Tyler, J. M. (1993). Community-based interventions: A return to community mental health center's origins. *Journal of Counseling and Development, 71,* 689–692.

West, J. F., & Idol, L. (1987). School consultation (Part 1): An interdisciplinary perspective on theory, models, and research. *Journal of Learning Disabilities, 20(7),* 388–408.

West, J. F., & Idol, L. (1993). The counselor as consultant in the collaborative school. *Journal of Counseling and Development, 71,* 678–683.

Wheeler, D. D., & Janis, I. J. (1980). *A practical guide for making decisions.* New York: Free Press.

White, L. J., & Loos, V. E. (1996). The hidden client in school consultation. *Journal of Educational and Psychological Consultation, 7,* 161–177.

Wickstrom, K. F., & Witt, J. C. (1993). Resistance within school-based consultation. In J. E. Zins, T. R. Kratochwill, and S. N. Elliot (Eds.), *Handbook of consultation services for children* (pp. 159–178). San Francisco: Jossey-Bass.

Wigtil, J.V., & Kelsey, R. C. (1978). Team building as a consulting intervention for influencing learning environments. *Personnel and Guidance Journal, 56(7),* 412–416.

Wilcoxon, S. A. (1990). Developing consultation contracts: Applying foundational principles to critical issues. *Journal of Independent Social Work, 4(3),* 17–28.

Willems, E. P. (1974). Behavioral technology and behavioral ecology. *Journal of Applied Behavioral Analysis, 7,* 151–156.

Williams, R. T. (1982). An overview of consultation and education in the rural community. In P. A. Keler & J. D. Murray (Eds.), *Handbook of rural community mental health* (pp. 122–134). New York: Human Sciences Press.

Wintersteen, R. T., & Young, L. (1988). Effective professional collaboration with family support groups. *Psychosocial Rehabilitation Journal, 12,* 19–31.

Witt, J. C. (1990a). Face-to-face verbal interaction in school-based consultation: A review of the literature. *School Psychology Quarterly, 5,* 199–210.

Witt, J. C. (1990b). Complaining, precopernian thought and the univariate linear mind: Questions for school-based behavioral consultation research. *School Psychology Review, 19,* 367–377.

Witt, J. C., & Elliott, S. N. (1983). Assessment in behavioral consultation: The initial interview. *School Psychology Review, 12,* 42–49.

Witt, J. C., Gresham, F. M., & Noel, G. H. (1996a). What's behavioral about behavioral consultation? *Journal of Educational and Psychological Consultation, 7,* 327–344.

Witt, J. C., Gresham, F. M., & Noel, G. H. (1996b). The effectiveness and efficiency of behavioral consultation: Differing perspectives about epistemology and what we know. *Journal of Educational and Psychological Consultation, 7,* 355–360.

Witt, J. C., & Martens, B. K. (1988). Problems with problem-solving consultation: A re-analysis of assumptions, methods, and goals. *School Psychology Review, 17,* 211–226.

Wolf, R. S., & Pillemer, K. (1994). What's new in elder abuse programming? *The Gerontologist, 34,* 126–129.

Woody, R. H. (1989). Public policy, ethics government, and the law. *Professional School Psychology, 4,* 75–83.

Woody, R. H., & Associates. (1984). *The law and the practice of human services.* San Francisco: Jossey-Bass.

Wubbolding, R. (1990). Professional issues: Consultation and ethics, Part I. *Journal of Reality Therapy, 9(2),* 71–74.

Wubbolding, R. (1991a). Professional issues: Consultation and ethics, Part II. *Journal of Reality Therapy, 10(2),* 55–59.

Wubbolding, R. E. (1991b). Professional issues: Consultation: III. *Journal of Reality Therapy, 11(1),* 76–80.

Yolles, S. F. (1970). Foreword. In G. Caplan, *The theory and practice of mental health consultation.* New York: Basic Books.

Zand, D. E. (1978). Collateral organization: A new change strategy. In W. L. French, C. H. Bell, Jr., & R. A. Zawacki (Eds.), *Organization development: Theory, practice, and research* (pp. 293–307). Dallas: Business Publications.

Zifferblatt, S. M., & Hendricks, C. G. (1974). Applied behavioral analysis of societal problems: Population change, a case in point. *American Psychologist, 29,* 750–761.

Zins, J. E. (1993). Enhancing consultee problem-solving skills in consultation. *Journal of Counseling and Development, 72(2),* 185–190.

Zins, J. E. (1998). Expanding the conceptual foundations of consultation: Contributions of community psychology. *Journal of Educational and Psychological Consultation, 8,* 107–110.

Zins, J. E., & Curtis, M. J. (1984). Building consultation into the educational service delivery system. In C. A. Maher, R. J. Illback, & J. E. Zins (Eds.), *Organizational psychology in the schools: A handbook for professionals* (pp. 213–242). Springfield, IL: Thomas.

Zins, J. E., & Erchul, W. P. (1995). Best practices in school consultation. In A. Thomas and J. Grimes (Eds.), *Best practices in school psychology* (3rd ed., pp. 609–623). Washington, DC: National Association of School Psychologists.

Zins, J. E., Kratochwill, T. R., & Elliot, S. N. (1993). Current status of the field. In J. E. Zins, T. R. Kratochwill, and S. N. Elliot (Eds.), *Handbook of consultation services for children* (pp. 1–12). San Francisco: Jossey-Bass.

Zusman, J. (1972). Mental health consultation: Some theory and practice. In J. Zusman & D. L. Davidson (Eds.), *Practical aspects of mental health consultation.* Springfield, IL: Charles C. Thomas.

Name Index

Subject Index

Credits

Chapter 1: **11**, quotations from *The Profession and Practice of Consultation* by June Gallessich. Copyright © 1982 by Jossey-Bass, Inc. Publishers. This and all other quotes from the same source are adaptations by permission of the publisher and the author.

Chapter 3: **56–57**, quote from *School Consultation: A Guide to Practice and Training*, by J. C. Conoley and C. W. Conoley. This and all other quotes from the same source are reprinted with permission of Pergamon Journals Ltd. **58**, quote from *Clients & Consultants* by Chip R. Bell and Leonard Nadler, Editors. Copyright © 1985 by Gulf Publishing Company, Houston, TX. This and all other quotes from the same source are used with permission. All rights reserved. **58**, quote adapted from *The Consulting Process in Action* (2nd ed.), by G. Lippitt and R. Lippitt. Copyright © 1986 by Pfeiffer & Company, San Diego, CA. This and all other quotes from the same source are used with permission. **59**, quotes from "Developing a successful Client-Consultant Relationship," by C. R. Bell and L. Nadler. In *The Client-Consultant Handbook*, by Charles H. Ford. Copyright © 1979 by John Wiley & Sons, Inc. Reprinted by permission. **60**, quotes from S. Cooper and W. F. Hodges (Eds.), *The Mental Health Consultation Field*. Copyright © 1983 by Human Sciences Press. Reprinted by permission. **61**, paraphrased quote from "The Psychological Contract: A Key to Effective Organizational Development Consultation," by R. W. Boss. In *Consultation, 4(4)*, 1985. Copyright © 1985 by Human Sciences Press. Used by permission. **62**, **74**, from *Consulting: The Complete Guide to a Profitable Career* (rev. ed.), by Robert E. Kelley. Copyright © 1981, 1986 Robert E. Kelley. Reprinted with permission of Charles Scribner's Sons, an imprint of Macmillan Publishing. **75**, paraphrased ideas from A. A. Armenakis and H. B. Burdg, "Consultation research: Contributions to practice and directions for improvement." *Journal of Management, 14,* 1984, 339–365. This and all other material from same source used with permission. Copyright © 1988 JAI Press Inc.

Chapter 4: **78**, Figure 4.1 adapted from "Organization Development: Objectives, Assumptions and Strategies," by W. French. In Margulies and Raia (Eds.), *Organizational Development: Values, Process and Technology.* Copyright © 1972 by McGraw-Hill Book Company. Adapted by permission. **83**, paraphrased material from David A. Nadler, *Feedback and Organization Development* (pp. 133–135), Copyright © 1977 by Addison-Wesley Publishing Company, Inc. This and all other material from this source reprinted by permission of the publisher.